Lecture Notes in Computer Science 11191

Commenced Publication in 1973
Founding and Former Series Editors:
Gerhard Goos, Juris Hartmanis, and Jan van Leeuwen

More information about this series at http://www.springer.com/series/7409

Wouter Duivesteijn · Arno Siebes
Antti Ukkonen (Eds.)

Advances in Intelligent Data Analysis XVII

17th International Symposium, IDA 2018
's-Hertogenbosch, The Netherlands, October 24–26, 2018
Proceedings

Springer

Editors
Wouter Duivesteijn
Eindhoven University of Technology
Eindhoven
The Netherlands

Antti Ukkonen ⓘ
University of Helsinki
Helsinki
Finland

Arno Siebes
Department of Information
  and Computing Sciences
University Utrecht
Utrecht
The Netherlands

ISSN 0302-9743   ISSN 1611-3349 (electronic)
Lecture Notes in Computer Science
ISBN 978-3-030-01767-5   ISBN 978-3-030-01768-2   (eBook)
https://doi.org/10.1007/978-3-030-01768-2

Library of Congress Control Number: 2018956595

LNCS Sublibrary: SL3 – Information Systems and Applications, incl. Internet/Web, and HCI

This Springer imprint is published by the registered company Springer Nature Switzerland AG
The registered company address is: Gewerbestrasse 11, 6330 Cham, Switzerland

Preface

We are proud to present the proceedings of the 17th International Symposium on Intelligent Data Analysis (IDA 2018), which was held during October 24–28, 2018, in 's-Hertogenbosch, The Netherlands. The series started in 1995 and was held biannually until 2009. In 2010 the symposium refocused to support papers that go beyond established technology and offer genuinely novel and potentially game-changing ideas in the field of data analysis. The call for papers for this 2018 conference was formulated as follows:

"Complementary to other mainstream conferences in data science, IDA's mission is to promote ideas over performance: A solid motivation can be as convincing as exhaustive empirical evaluation. To this end, IDA creates an open atmosphere that encourages discussion and promotes innovative ideas in data analysis novel and game-changing ideas."

But, clearly, not all novel ideas are good ideas. To ensure the quality of all accepted papers, standard rigorous, single-blind peer evaluation of all papers was performed by the Program Committee (PC) consisting of established researchers in the field who evaluated the papers against the requirements set out in the call for papers. As in previous editions, this process was complemented by the PC advisors, a select set of senior researchers with a multi-year involvement in the IDA conference series. Whenever a PC advisor flagged a paper as both good and presenting an interesting, novel, idea with an informed, thoughtful, positive review, the paper was accepted irrespective of the other reviews.

As in previous installments, this somewhat special focus of IDA has resulted in the submission and acceptance of a number of highly innovative papers that would have had a hard time in the mainstream conferences. In fact, we are pleased and proud to have put together a very strong program. We received 65 paper submissions out of which 29 could be accepted. Every submission was reviewed by at least two PC members, and the majority of submissions had at least three reviews. Each accepted paper was offered a slot for oral presentation and, new this year, also offered a poster at a specially organized poster session to foster deeper discussions than the brief Q&A minutes often offered right after the presentation.

We were honored that the regular program was complemented by three distinguished invited speakers who fulfilled IDA's quest for novel, game-changing ideas:

- Tuuli Toivonen (University of Helsinki) talked about how modern data science and machine learning methods can be used for analyzing and understanding human accessibility and mobility in urban and natural environments.
- Luc de Raedt (KU Leuven) talked about his ERC project to automate data science. More specifically, he discussed how automated data wrangling approaches can be used for pre-processing and how both predictive and descriptive models can in principle be combined to automatically complete spreadsheets and relational databases.

– Johannes Fürnkranz (TU Darmstadt) talked about the need for interpretability biases. Ever since the start of the field, interpretability has been one of the holy grails. Usually this notion is operationalized as simplicity. In this talk, he questioned this assumption, in particular with respect to commonly used rule learning heuristics that aim at learning rules that are as simple as possible.

We also invited all keynote speakers to submit a paper on the topic of their presentation. Professors de Raedt and Fürnkranz decided to take this opportunity. These invited papers appear in a separate Invited Papers section in the beginning of the proceedings. Also, the first selected contribution is a slightly shorter position paper by Leo Lahti about the importance of tools to facilitate open data science.

Finally, the program was completed by the traditional IDA PhD poster session in which PhD students get the opportunity to promote their work.

The conference was held in the former chapel of the Jheronimus Academy of Data Science, and we are grateful for their willingness to host the conference. We wish to express our gratitude to all authors of all submitted papers, for their intellectual contributions; to the PC members and additional reviewers for their efforts in reviewing, discussing, and commenting on all submitted papers; to the program chair advisors for their active involvement; and to the IDA council for their ongoing guidance and support, in particular Elizabeth Bradley, Jaakko Hollmén, and Matthijs van Leeuwen. Also, the program chairs wish to thank the general chair of IDA 2017, David Weston, for his help with practical matters related to preparing the conference proceedings. Finally, we are grateful to our sponsors and supporters: KNIME, which funded the IDA Frontier Prize for the most visionary contribution, as well as The Netherlands Research School for Information and Knowledge Systems (SIKS), the *Artificial Intelligence* journal, and Springer.

August 2018   Wouter Duivesteijn
                                                                                    Arno Siebes
                                                                                    Antti Ukkonen

Organization

General Chair

Wouter Duivesteijn — Eindhoven University of Technology, The Netherlands

Program Chairs

Arno Siebes — Utrecht University, The Netherlands
Antti Ukkonen — University of Helsinki, Finland

Local Chair

Arjan Haring — Jheronimus Academy of Data Science, The Netherlands

Frontier Prize Chair

Michael Berthold — University of Konstanz, Germany

Advisory Chairs

Allan Tucker — Brunel University London, UK
Jaakko Hollmén — Aalto University, Finland
Matthijs van Leeuwen — Leiden University, The Netherlands

Organizing Committee

Arjan van den Born — Jheronimus Academy of Data Science, The Netherlands
Arjan Haring — Jheronimus Academy of Data Science, The Netherlands
Laura Niemeijer — Jheronimus Academy of Data Science, The Netherlands

Web and Social Media Chair

Simon van der Zon — Eindhoven University of Technology, The Netherlands

Program Committee Advisors

Michael Berthold — University of Konstanz, Germany
Hendrik Blockeel — Katholieke Universiteit Leuven, Belgium
Elizabeth Bradley — University of Colorado, USA
Tijl De Bie — Ghent University, Data Science Lab, Belgium
Elisa Fromont — Université de Rennes 1, France
Jaakko Hollmén — Aalto University, Finland

Frank Klawonn	Ostfalia University of Applied Sciences, Germany
Nada Lavrač	Jozef Stefan Institute, Slovenia
Matthijs van Leeuwen	Leiden University, The Netherlands
Panagiotis Papapetrou	Stockholm University, Sweden
Stephen Swift	Brunel University London, UK
Hannu Toivonen	University of Helsinki, Finland
Allan Tucker	Brunel University London, UK

Program Committee

Ana Aguiar	University of Porto, Portugal
Fabrizio Angiulli	DEIS, University of Calabria, Italy
Mahir Arzoky	Brunel University London, UK
Martin Atzmueller	Tilburg University, The Netherlands
José Luis Balcázar	Universitat Politècnica de Catalunya, Spain
Gustavo Batista	University of São Paulo, Brazil
Maria Bielikova	Slovak University of Technology in Bratislava, Slovakia
Christian Borgelt	Otto von Guericke University Magdeburg, Germany
Ulf Brefeld	Leuphana Universität Lüneburg, Germany
Paula Brito	University of Porto, Portugal
Ricardo Cachucho	Leiden University, The Netherlands
Loïc Cerf	Universidade Federal de Minas Gerais, Brazil
Edward Cohen	Imperial College London, UK
Paulo Cortez	University of Minho, Portugal
Bruno Cremilleux	Université de Caen, France
Andre de Carvalho	University of São Paulo, Brazil
José Del Campo-Ávila	Universidad de Málaga, Spain
Anton Dries	Katholieke Universiteit Leuven, Belgium
Brett Drury	SciCrop, Brazil
Nuno Escudeiro	Instituto Superior de Engenharia do Porto, Portugal
Ad Feelders	Utrecht University, The Netherlands
Peter Flach	University of Bristol, UK
Johannes Fürnkranz	TU Darmstadt, Germany
Tias Guns	Vrije Universiteit Brussel, Belgium
Andreas Henelius	Aalto University, Finland
Pedro Henriques Abreu	FCTUC-DEI/CISUC, Portugal
Frank Höppner	Ostfalia University of Applied Sciences, Germany
Ulf Johansson	Jönköping University, Sweden
Alipio M. Jorge	University of Porto, Portugal
Arno Knobbe	Leiden University, The Netherlands
Irena Koprinska	University of Sydney, Australia
Petra Kralj Novak	Jozef Stefan Institute, Slovenia
Rudolf Kruse	University of Magdeburg, Germany
Niklas Lavesson	Jönköping University, Sweden
Jose A. Lozano	University of the Basque Country, Spain
Ling Luo	CSIRO, Australia

George Magoulas	Birkbeck College, Knowledge Lab, University of London, UK
Vera Migueis	University of Porto, Portugal
Mohamed Nadif	Paris Descartes University, France
Andreas Nuernberger	Otto von Guericke University Magdeburg, Germany
Kaustubh Raosaheb Patil	Massachusetts Institute of Technology, USA
Mykola Pechenizkiy	Eindhoven University of Technology, The Netherlands
Ruggero G. Pensa	University of Torino, Italy
Marc Plantevit	LIRIS - Université Claude Bernard Lyon 1, France
Lubos Popelinsky	Masaryk University, Czech Republic
Alexandra Poulovassilis	Birkbeck College, University of London, UK
Miguel A. Prada	Universidad de Leon, France
Ronaldo Prati	Universidade Federal do ABC - UFABC, Brazil
Antonio Salmeron	University of Almería, Spain
Vítor Santos Costa	University of Porto, Portugal
Roberta Siciliano	University of Naples Federico II, Italy
Myra Spiliopoulou	Otto von Guericke University Magdeburg, Germany
Frank Takes	University of Amsterdam and Leiden University, The Netherlands
Melissa Turcotte	Los Alamos National Laboratory, USA
Peter van der Putten	Leiden University and Pegasystems, The Netherlands
Jan N. van Rijn	Leiden University, The Netherlands
Veronica Vinciotti	Brunel University London, UK
Jilles Vreeken	Max Planck Institute for Informatics and Saarland University, Germany
Leishi Zhang	Middlesex University, UK
Albrecht Zimmermann	Université Caen Normandie, France
Indre Zliobaite	University of Helsinki, Finland

Contents

Invited Papers

Elements of an Automatic Data Scientist

Luc De Raedt[(⊠)], Hendrik Blockeel, Samuel Kolb, Stefano Teso,
and Gust Verbruggen

Department of Computer Science, KU Leuven, Leuven, Belgium
{luc.deraedt,hendrik.blockeel,samuel.kolb,stefano.teso,
gust.verbruggen}@cs.kuleuven.be

Abstract. A simple but non-trivial setting for automating data science is introduced. Given are a set of worksheets in a spreadsheet and the goal is to automatically complete some values. We also outline elements of the SYNTH framework that tackles this task: SYNTH-A-SIZER, an automated data wrangling system for automatically transforming the problem into attribute-value format; TACLE, an inductive constraint learning system for inducing formulas in spreadsheets; MERCS, a versatile predictive learning system; as well as the autocompletion component that integrates these systems.

Keywords: Automated data science · Autocompletion
Data wrangling · Learning constraints · Versatile models

1 Introduction

The field of artificial intelligence (AI) can be viewed as the endeavor to automate all tasks that require intelligence when performed by humans [16,18]. As scientific activities do require intelligence, artificial intelligence researchers [14] have been developing robot scientists. While robot scientists typically target the natural sciences, this paper focuses on the automation of data science. Given the abundance of data, the needs to analyse data and the challenges in hiring data scientists, even partial automation of data science would make a radical impact on business. Indeed, automated data analysts are viewed as potentially the second most impactful AI-powered technology by business executives [1].

Automated data science is not really new as there have been many approaches to automating different aspects of data science, machine learning and data mining. However, these approaches are typically embedded in existing tools and workbenches that offer a multitude of operations, learning algorithms and parameter settings as well as graphical user interfaces visualizing particular workflows [20]. When the user specifies the task of interest (e.g., predicting a particular field), the intelligent data analysis assistant will then suggest a particular workflow (or sequence of algorithms) to use on the basis of built-in expert knowledge, past cases, meta-learning or using ontological knowledge for planning purposes. Work in the AutoML community [12] has focused on automatically selecting

© Springer Nature Switzerland AG 2018
W. Duivesteijn et al. (Eds.): IDA 2018, LNCS 11191, pp. 3–14, 2018.
https://doi.org/10.1007/978-3-030-01768-2_1

an adequate learning algorithm and setting appropriate hyperparameters for learning a given task. AutoML is based on the Programming by Optimisation paradigm [11], which employs algorithm selection and portfolio optimisation. Another fascinating approach is provided by the automated statistician [22], which starts from a data set, automatically fits a statistical model and then generates an explanation of the model in a paper written in natural language.

Characteristic for the existing approaches is that they assume that (1) the learning task is given, and (2) the data is already in the right format for the analysis. However, this is assuming that the most important problem has already been solved. Indeed, since the inception of the field of data mining, people like Usama Fayyad have argued that pre-processing (including the identification of the right targets for predictive modeling) typically takes 80 per cent of the effort in knowledge discovery and the actual data mining step (that is, finding the right model with a system) only requires 20 per cent. The SYNTH[1] approach advocated in the present paper aims at supporting all steps of the data analysis problem, including pre-processing and feature selection, identifying the learning task and synthesizing a model for the dataset. As this is clearly a (very) ambitious task, we identify a simple but highly non-trivial setting for studying automated data science in which one is given a set of tables (e.g., worksheets in a spreadsheet) and the task is to automatically complete some of the missing entries. Furthermore, we introduce some elements of an automated data scientist for tackling this task: automated data wrangling, flexible prediction, constraint learning and autocompletion.

2   Autocompletion in Spreadsheets

Let us introduce the problem studied in this paper using the example provided in Fig. 1. It is a typical (very simplified) business example of the use of a spreadsheet. It contains information about the sales of particular flavors of ice-cream in different countries and months, as well as information about the production time taken to produce one unit of ice-cream. Assuming that decisions need to be made about which flavors of ice-cream to retain in which countries, based on the total sales, costs and profitability. However, the left table is incomplete, as the values for August are not yet available, which would be problematic for the decision making process. However, human data analysts could produce reliable estimates for these missing values in order to facilitate the decision making process.

The question tackled in this paper is how to automatically complete such cells under the assumption, of course, that there are underlying regularities in the data and the data has been entered in the tables in a systematic manner.

Solving this problem requires a number of different steps: (1) discover the equation T stating that the column Total is equal to the sum of the columns June, July and August; (2) find a predictive model A for the column August

---

[1] SYNTH stands for Synthesising Inductive Data Models, and it is the topic of the ERC AdG project no. 694980; cf. https://synth.cs.kuleuven.be/.

using the available data; (3) find a predictive model P for the column Profit using the available data; (4) infer the missing values for August using A; (5) infer the missing values for Total using the equation T; and (6) infer the missing values for Profit using P.

Notice that this *autocompletion* setting is simple, yet challenging as in general it is not specified which steps need to be taken, that is, the different learning tasks are not given and the only assumption on the data format is that it is in a set of worksheets.

To address these different tasks, our Automic Data Scientist SYNTH uses a number of different components: SYNTH-A-SIZER [25] is an automatic data wrangling system that transforms a dataset into a traditional attribute-value learning format so that standard machine learning systems can be applied (cf. Sect. 3), MERCS [26] induces versatile predictive models (cf. Sect. 4), TACLE [15] induces constraints and formulas in spreadsheets (cf. Sect. 5), and the autocompletion component ties learning and inference together in a probabilistic framework. We now discuss each of these elements in turn.

Type	Country	June	July	August	Total	Profit
Vanilla	BE	610	190	670	1470	YES
Banana	BE	170	690	520	1380	YES
Chocolate	BE	560	320	140	1020	YES
Banana	DE	610	640	320	1570	NO
Speculaas	BE	300	270	290	860	NO
Chocolate	FR	430	350			
Banana	DE	250	650			
Chocolate	NL	210	280			

Type	ProdTime
Chocolate	60
Banana	40
Speculaas	70
Vanilla	40

Fig. 1. Two tables in a spreadsheet

3   Data Wrangling

The focus in the SYNTH setting is on working with spreadsheets while imposing as few assumptions on the user as possible. While it is assumed that the user is systematic, and that there exist regularities in the data that can be exploited by data analysis techniques, it not assumed that the user is able to put the spreadsheet in one of the formats required by standard data analysis and machine learning software. Rather the user should be able to work with the format of the spreadsheet that she created and the required data transformations should be hidden to the user.

That is where *automated data wrangling* steps in. Automated data wrangling integrates ideas from program synthesis with data science.

Our SYNTH-A-SIZER tackles the following task [25]. Given a dataset S and a machine learning algorithm M, find a transformed dataset $D = t(S)$ so that (1) D is in the format required by M, and (2) the unknown target model h can be learned (or approximated) by algorithm M on D. The transformation t is a program written in a domain specific language and consists of a sequence of simple data transformations. So far, we have made the assumption that the target format is in attribute-value form.

Automated data wrangling has received quite some attention recently. Some data wrangling tools focus on the layout of the data: Trifacta's WRANGLER system provides a graphical interface to transform spreadsheets without writing code and FLASHRELATE [2] allows for data extraction programs to be synthesised from input-output examples. Other tools focus on transforming the data itself to a standardised format [13,21]. Common to these approaches is the need for user-guidance, either in the form of examples or of intent. In return, they allow for a large variety of output formats. Within the SYNTH framework, however, it is clear that the transformed data will be used as input to a particular data analysis suite (so far assumed to be in attribute-value format). This imposes strong constraints on the format of transformed data and can be used to minimize the required user interaction. On the other hand, spreadsheets are notorious for being *semi-structured*. They exhibit some structure as all data is aligned in a grid, but there are no rules on how exactly the structure should be laid out. The same dataset has many representations in spreadsheet format and it is up to the data wrangler to discover and exploit the structure.

To illustrate the SYNTH-A-SIZER setting, consider Fig. 2a which contains a small car dealership interested in deciding when to offer discounts. There is also a separate table containing information about the employees pitching the sales. Running any machine learning algorithm on this data requires conversion into an appropriate format, such as attribute-value pairs. The following sequence of transformations (see [24,25] for details of the transformation) yields the desired representation in Fig. 2b: Split(*Sales*, 1), Fill(*Sales*, 1), Delete(*Sales*, 2), Join(*Sales*, *Employees*, 3, 1). Any attribute-value learning system can be applied on the resulting dataset, e.g., to learn a predictive model h for the last column. This model can then be applied to predict the target value of interest, which in our illustration is indicated by the question mark, and the resulting prediction can be mapped back to the spreadsheet in the original format to hide the details of the transformation and the learning from the end-user. Ideally, the only required input would be for the user to select the question mark. After marking the target value, the system has to figure out an appropriate target representation and synthesize an adequate program.

The main technique employed in our SYNTH-A-SIZER is *predictive synthesis*, meaning that we predict and evaluate the output of the synthesised program while searching for a solution. The search process is guided by heuristics that are based on two ideas. First, in an attribute-value format, the rows correspond to

Sales

Audi		
A1	Tim	no
A1	Megan	no
A4	Tim	yes
		2/3
BMW		
1	Megan	yes
1	Tim	?
		1/1

Employees

Tim	Junior
Megan	Senior

Tim	Junior	Audi	A1	no
Megan	Senior	Audi	A1	no
Tim	Junior	Audi	A4	yes
Megan	Senior	BMW	1	yes
Tim	Junior	BMW	1	?

(a) Car dealership data in a raw format

(b) The data from (a) as a single table and thus in attribute-value format

Fig. 2. Car dealership data.

the examples. Secondly, the attributes or the columns contain values belonging to the same domain. To exploit the first property, we allow the user to mark which cells belong together in the worksheets, that is, belong to the same example. The second property also provides a strong constraint on the target transformation, if the domains are given; [24] shows how this constraint can be exploited. In our more recent work [25], however, we heuristically evaluate the degree to which the values in a particular column belong to the same domain. Essentially, the cells in each column are checked for syntactic similarity against a reference cell selected by the user. The syntactic similarity is an edit distance metric on character level, meaning that replacing a digit by another digit is free. The combination of these two properties shows already promising results.

It should be mention that other types transformations could be used as well, for instance, after finding a suitable set of database dependencies, a set of tables could be mapped into a single table using standard database operations such as joins.

We are currently working on reducing the dependency on selecting a full example. By first discovering the domains in the data, syntactically as well as semantically, we can reduce this dependency of the heuristic on the user-input. In addition to changing the layout of the spreadsheets, automated wrangling approaches for data standardisation [21] are also to be incorporated. This step can be facilitated by domain detection [6] and will ultimately be performed without the need for examples—the output format will depend on the domains and on the machine learning algorithm targeted.

4   Versatile Models and Mercs

Autocompletion of tables requires the use of predictive models that are learned from data. Concerning the learning phase, an important difference with the standard setting of supervised learning is that, in the standard setting, the input space and output space are fixed in advance: whether one learns a random forest, a neural network, or any other predictive model, the learning algorithm needs to know which variables are the inputs, and which ones the outputs, before it starts learning.

In the SYNTH setting, the user may not know in advance which variables can most easily be predicted from which other variables. Ideally, a model is learned that in principle is able to predict any variable from any other variables; we call this type of predictive models *versatile* models. Once such a versatile model is available, it can be analyzed to determine which fields can be predicted from which other fields. This can be used by an intelligent or automatic user interface to reason about autocompletion of the data.

SYNTH will use a recently proposed approach to learning versatile models, called MERCS. MERCS stands for multidirectional ensembles of regression and classification trees. The basic idea behind it is simple. MERCS learns an ensemble of decision trees, where each tree may have a different set of target attributes (as opposed to classical ensembles, where a single target variable is given in advance and all trees try to predict that value); see Fig. 3 for an illustration. In its most basic version, MERCS could simply learn a classic ensemble for each variable separately. When there are k trees in an ensemble, and m variables in total, this requires learning mk trees. This number can go down by learning trees that predict multiple variables at the same time, so-called multi-target trees. If each tree in the multidirectional ensemble predicted v variables, then the number of trees required to have each variable predicted by k trees can be divided by v. Several authors [19,23] have shown that (ensembles of) multi-target trees often achieve accuracies comparable to that of their single-target counterparts, while being smaller, faster to learn, and faster at prediction time; they achieve state-of-the-art accuracy in a variety of domains.

Another type of models that could be used as versatile predictive models are probabilistic graphical models (PGMs), such as Bayesian networks, Markov networks, etc. The main difference between PGMs and MERCS is that PGMs model a joint probability distribution, whereas MERCS merely model a set of functions. While the latter is implicitly defined by the former, exact probabilistic inference using PGMs is NP-hard, and even approximate inference is NP-hard if guarantees are asked about the quality of the approximation [17].

In the SYNTH context, MERCS is supposed to predict the correct outcome, in those cases where it can be predicted. We do not necessarily want to know the probability of each possible value when there is uncertainty. This is an inherently simpler problem than probabilistic inference, and it may have simpler solutions. That this is indeed the case was shown by Van Wolputte et al. [26], who implemented and evaluated a first version of MERCS. In a comparison with a state-of-the-art Bayesian network learner, MERCS learned models with compa-

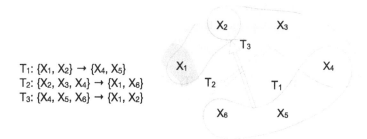

$T_1: \{X_1, X_2\} \rightarrow \{X_4, X_5\}$
$T_2: \{X_2, X_3, X_4\} \rightarrow \{X_1, X_6\}$
$T_3: \{X_4, X_5, X_6\} \rightarrow \{X_1, X_2\}$

Fig. 3. Schematic illustration of multidirectional ensembles. Each tree (T_1, T_2, T_3) takes a different set of input and output variables. In this example, each variable is predicted at least once; X_1 is predicted by two trees. Having trees simultaneously predict multiple outputs reduces the total number of trees needed to cover each potential target variable with a sufficient number of trees.

rable accuracy and training times, but with inference times that were orders of magnitude faster. In the context of SYNTH, this version of MERCS can be straightforwardly deployed for filling in values in a single table.

Apart from the automatic filling of tables, MERCS can also be used to detect errors. Indeed, any versatile model can be used for detecting anomalies by comparing predicted values with observed values; when both differ, this is an anomaly. Anomalies do not necessary indicate errors (there may be other reasons why a value is anomalous, apart from an entry error), but in many application contexts an entry error may indeed be the most likely cause of an anomaly.

When multiple tables are available, the spreadsheet is essentially a relational database, and predictions in one table may require information from different tables. That is, a relational learner may be required. To this aim, we are currently doing research on a relational version of MERCS, which will use first-order decision trees as learned by the relational learning system TILDE [5].

From a wider machine learning perspective, the MERCS approach leads to a variety of research questions, which are yet to be addressed. For instance:

- The variation in target sets introduces more variation among trees predicting one particular variable. Normally, variation is introduced through training set resampling and, in the case of random forests, randomness in the input attributes considered at each node. In MERCS, the co-targets of a given variable vary among trees, introducing additional variation that may, for instance, render resampling unnecessary.
- A given target variable's value is predicted by combining trees. Some of these trees may test attributes that are missing. In a standard ensemble, those attributes' value must be imputed, or the tree must deal with missing values in some other manner. In a MERCS model, the missing values can be predicted using other trees that have these attributes as targets. Different possible procedures are currently being explored regarding how this can be done. SYNTH's

autocompletion setting goes even further in that it wants to combine the pre-dictions made by versatile models with inference based on other types of theories, such as TACLE's constraint theories that are discussed next.

5   Learning Constraints and TacLe

The goal of TACLE [15] is to discover formulas and constraints in a spreadsheet. It is this component that could induce the equation T in the example for Fig. 1. An illustration of TACLE is given in Figs. 4 and 5, where the constraints shown in Fig. 5 are automatically induced from the three tables in Fig. 4.

To this end, TACLE has a set of *constraint templates* to specify which types of formulas it should look for. Every constraint template is made up of three parts: syntax, signature and definition. An example of a constraint template is column-wise sum, whose syntax is $B_2 = SUM_{col}(\mathbf{B}_1)$, where B_2 is a column and $\mathbf{B}_1$ a set of consecutive columns, i.e., a matrix. By filling in ranges of cell addresses for arguments $\mathbf{B}_1$ and B_2, we obtain an actual constraint that tells us that the i-th cell assigned to B_2 is equal to the sum of the i-th column of the cells assigned to $\mathbf{B}_1$. Discovering column-wise sum constraints is thus the task of finding assignments of cell ranges to constraint template arguments such that the assignment satisfies the constraint template. Checking whether an assignment satisfies a constraint template is done using the signature and definition of that template. The signature checks necessary conditions on the properties of the ranges, e.g., do they contain the right type of values (numeric for sum) and are the sizes of the ranges compatible, while the definition can be used to look up the actual values of the cells in those ranges, to compute their sums and to verify whether the results match.

The main challenges for learning constraints are dealing with the vast amount of possible assignments to every constraint template and avoiding the discovery of spurious constraints. To deal with these problems, TACLE includes a prepro-cessing step to convert spreadsheets to a more structured representation and subsequently tries to prune impossible sets of assignments from its search.

Internally, TACLE reasons over *tables* of equally-sized rows and/or columns, *blocks* which are continuous ranges of rows or columns with the same type (e.g., numeric or textual) and finally individual vectors (a row or a column) of type-consistent cells. Tables in a spreadsheet are detected either automatically or using a visual selection tool and can be automatically split into a minimal number of type-consistent blocks. Blocks group together neighboring vectors of the same type and vectors form the minimal level of granularity, i.e., constraints must always reason about entire vectors. For this initial step, there is clearly room for cross-fertilization between TACLE's pre-processing steps and SYNTH-A-SIZER's automatic transformation process.

TACLE employs a couple of strategies to prune impossible assignments.

First, when finding valid assignments for a constraint template, it considers two levels of granularity: reasoning over entire type-consistent blocks as detected in the previous phase (input blocks) and then reasoning over assignments of subsets of input blocks (subblocks and vectors). After precomputing the properties of every input block, it uses a constraint satisfaction solver to find assignments of input blocks to constraint template arguments that are *compatible* with the constraint template signature. Compatibility means that subsets of the input blocks could potentially satisfy the signature. This step eliminates whole sets of assignments that are incompatible. For every valid input block assignment TACLE generates all assignments of subblocks and tests if they fulfil the signature and definition.

Secondly, TACLE also considers dependencies between constraint templates. If a constraint template s_2 requires a constraint of type s_1 to hold on a subset A_d of its arguments A, then the search for valid assignments to s_2 is bootstrapped. Instead of generating all possible assignments to A, the values for A_d are prepopulated with valid assignments to s_2.

ID	Salesperson	Q1	Q2	Q3	Q4	Total	Rank		
1	James Smith	353	378	396	387	1514	2		
2	Maria Garcia	370	408	387	386	1551	1		
3	Micheal Jones	175	146	167	203	691	3		
4	Grace Hartman	93	98	96	105	392	4		
Block 1	*Block 2*				*Block 3*				
$T_1[:, 1]$	$T_1[:, 2]$				$T_1[:, 3:8]$				
							Customer	Contact	Contact Name
Total	991		1030	1046	1081	4148	Frank	1	James Smith
Average	247.75		257.5	261.5	270.25	1037	Sarah	3	Micheal Jones
Max	370		408	396	387	1551	George	3	Micheal Jones
Min	93		98	96	105	392	Mary	2	Maria Garcia
							Tim	4	Grace Hartman
			Block 4				*Block 5*	*Block 6*	*Block 7*
			$T_2[1:4, :]$				$T_3[:, 1]$	$T_3[:, 2]$	$T_3[:, 3]$

Fig. 4. Example spreadsheet. For illustration purposes (not present in the spreadsheet), gray coloring is used to show detected blocks (light gray for blocks with numeric data and darker gray for blocks with textual data) and block names and notations are provided in italic.

TACLE is one example of a system that learn constraints from examples. While constraints are ubiquitous in artificial intelligence, the learning of constraint theories has not received a lot of attention, but see [8] for an overview of the state-of-the-art and [3,4] for particular approaches coming from the field of constraint programming. TACLE and SYNTH-A-SIZER are also inspired on the program synthesis line of work originated in FLASHFILL [10].

$SERIES(T_1[:,1])$

$T_1[:,1] = RANK(T_1[:,5])$

$T_1[:,1] = RANK(T_1[:,6])$

$T_1[:,8] = RANK(T_1[:,7])$

$T_1[:,8] = RANK(T_1[:,3])$

$T_1[:,8] = RANK(T_1[:,4])$

$T_1[:,7] = SUM_{row}(T_1[:,3:6])$

$T_2[1,:] = SUM_{col}(T_1[:,3:7])$

$T_2[2,:] = AVERAGE_{col}(T_1[:,3:7])$

$T_2[3,:] = MAX_{col}(T_1[:,3:7])$

$T_2[4,:] = MIN_{col}(T_1[:,3:7])$

$T_3[:,2] = LOOKUP(T_3[:,3], T_1[:,2], T_1[:,1])$

$T_3[:,3] = LOOKUP(T_3[:,2], T_1[:,1], T_1[:,2])$

Fig. 5. Constraints extracted by *TaCLe* for the above tables.

6 Putting Everything Together

As mentioned in the introduction, we are given an (incomplete) dataset in the form of a set of tables or worksheets and the task is to automatically complete some of the missing entries. After pre-processing the dataset into an appropriate format and training predictive models and constraints on the latter, the remaining step is to aggregate the obtained predictions into a coherent, consistent completion of the data. Computing such an autocompletion, presenting it to the user of the system, and reacting to the user's actions are keystones of the SYNTH framework. We consider these tasks in turn.

The aggregation task is far from trivial. Indeed, a cell may hold arbitrary values (currencies, dates, names, phone numbers, etc.) and may depend on other cells (in the same or different tables) in complex ways, depending on the generative process behind it. For these reasons, different predictors, based on different cues and rationales, may output different and possibly inconsistent predictions for the cell's value. Choosing the "best" alternative requires one to take into consideration several factors, first and foremost the observed confidence in the predictors. In addition to the predictions themselves, the constraints (e.g., Excel formulas) output by the constraint learning must be taken into account as to avoid autocompleting the cell with infeasible values. Inferring the best autocompletion therefore involves *reasoning* over both confidences and constraints.

We introduce a new probabilistic reasoning layer—the SYNTH layer—that sits on top of the predictors and constraints and aggregates their outputs. The SYNTH layer independently estimates the confidence in the predictors, e.g., by cross-validation or by using historical performance information. Given this information, as well as the input predictions and constraints, the SYNTH layer solves the following inference problem: given an incomplete spreadsheet and a set of (possibly inconsistent) predictions for all the empty cells, find a completion of the spreadsheet that is both maximally likely and consistent. This can be cast as a probabilistic inference problem in a probabilistic programming language such as ProbLog [7,9].

The SYNTH layer is designed to integrate with and to complement existing spreadsheet software. The idea is to provide a real-time, mixed-initiative autocompletion interface whereby the user and the system collaborate to complete one or more spreadsheets. The autocompletion loop involves both a user, who is filling out one or more spreadsheets, and the SYNTH system, which continuously suggests potential values to be filled into the cells, rows, or columns that the user is currently working on. The suggestions are presented in a sidebar, so that the user can accept or reject them without being interrupted while working on the spreadsheet. The user can also select a range of cells and request to autocomplete them. Whenever the user updates the values of any cells or rejects a proposed values, the SYNTH system updates the relevant predictors and re-evaluates its confidence. The idea is that in this way SYNTH learns from the user feedback.

7 Conclusions

We have defined the SYNTH challenge for automated data science and described some elements of an initial attempts to tackle it. Essential for solving the auto-completion task is the ability to learn constraints and versatile predictive models, ways to deal with the data wrangling aspects, as well as techniques for deciding what to learn and how to perform inference with the resulting models.

Acknowledgments. This work has received funding from the European Research Council (ERC) under the European Union's Horizon 2020 research and innovation programme (grant agreement No [694980] SYNTH: Synthesising Inductive Data Models) and the Research Foundation, Flanders.

References

1. Bot.me: How artificial intelligence is pushing man and machine closer together. Technical Report, PwC (2017)
2. Barowy, D.W., Gulwani, S., Hart, T., Zorn, B.: Flashrelate: extracting relational data from semi-structured spreadsheets using examples. SIGPLAN Not. **50**(6), 218–228 (2015)
3. Beldiceanu, N., Simonis, H.: A model seeker: extracting global constraint models from positive examples. In: Proceedings 18th International Conference on Principles and Practice of Constraint Programming. Lecture Notes in Computer Science, vol. 7514, pp. 141–157 (2012)
4. Bessiere, C., Koriche, F., Lazaar, N., O'Sullivan, B.: Constraint acquisition. Artif. Intell. **244**, 315–342 (2017)
5. Blockeel, H., De Raedt, L.: Top-down induction of first-order logical decision trees. Artif. Intell. **101**(1–2), 285–297 (1998)
6. Contreras-Ochando, L., Martínez-Plumed, F., Ferri, C., Hernández-Orallo, J., Ramírez-Quintana, M.J., Katayama, S.: Domain specific induction for data wrangling automation (demo). AutoML @ ICML 2017 (2017)
7. De Raedt, L., Kimmig, A., Toivonen, H.: Problog: a probabilistic prolog and its application in link discovery. In: Proceedings 20th International Joint Conference on Artificial Intelligence (2007)
8. De Raedt, L., Passerini, A., Teso, S.: Learning constraints from examples. In: Proceedings 32nd AAAI Conference on Artificial Intelligence (2018)
9. Fierens, D., et al.: Inference and learning in probabilistic logic programs using weighted boolean formulas. Theory Pract. Log. Prog. **15**(3), 358–401 (2015)

10. Gulwani, S.: Automating string processing in spreadsheets using input-output examples. In: ACM SIGPLAN-SIGACT, POPL, pp. 317–330 (2011)
11. Hoos, H.H.: Programming by optimization. Commun. ACM **55**(2), 70–80 (2012)
12. Hutter, F., Kotthoff, L., Vanschoren, J. (eds.): AutoML: methods, systems, challenges (2018). Draft available from: https://www.ml4aad.org/book/
13. Jin, Z., Cafarella, M., Jagadish, H., Kandel, S., Minar, M.: Unifacta: profiling-driven string pattern standardization. arXiv preprint arXiv:1803.00701 (2018)
14. King, R.D., et al.: Functional genomic hypothesis generation and experimentation by a robot scientist. Nature **427**, 247–252 (2004)
15. Kolb, S., Paramonov, S., Guns, T., De Raedt, L.: Learning constraints in spreadsheets and tabular data. Mach. Learn. **106**(9–10), 1441–1468 (2017)
16. Kurzweil, R.: The Age of Intelligent Machines. MIT press, Cambridge (1990)
17. Kwisthout, J.: Approximate inference in bayesian networks: parameterized complexity results. Int. J. Approx. Reason. **93**, 119–131 (2018)
18. Russell, S., Norvig, P.: Artificial Intelligence: A Modern Approach, 3rd edn. Prentice Hall, Upper Saddle River (2010)
19. Schietgat, L., Vens, C., Struyf, J., Blockeel, H., Kocev, D., Dzeroski, S.: Predicting gene function using hierarchical multi-label decision tree ensembles. BMC Bioinform. 11(2) (2010)
20. Serban, F., Vanschoren, J., Kietz, J.U., Bernstein, A.: A survey of intelligent assistants for data analysis. ACM Comput. Surv. (CSUR) 45(3) (2013)
21. Singh, R., Gulwani, S.: Transforming spreadsheet data types using examples. SIGPLAN Not. **51**(1), 343–356 (2016)
22. Steinruecken, C., Smith, E., Janz, D., Lloyd, J., Ghahramani, Z.: The automated statistician (2018). Draft available from: https://www.ml4aad.org/book/
23. Vens, C., Struyf, J., Schietgat, L., Dzeroski, S., Blockeel, H.: Decision trees for hierarchical multi-label classification. Mach. Learn. **73**(2), 185–214 (2008)
24. Verbruggen, G., De Raedt, L.: Towards automated relational data wrangling. In: Proceedings of AutoML 2017@ ECML-PKDD: automatic selection, configuration and composition of machine learning algorithms, pp. 18–26 (2017)
25. Verbruggen, G., De Raedt, L.: Automatically wrangling spreadsheets into machine learning data formats. In: Duivesteijn, W., et al. (eds.) IDA 2018. LNCS, vol. 11191, pp. 367–379. Springer, Cham (2018)
26. Wolputte, E.V., Korneva, E., Blockeel, H.: MERCS: multi-directional ensembles of regression and classification trees. In: Proceedings 32nd AAAI Conference on Artificial Intelligence (2018)

The Need for Interpretability Biases

Johannes Fürnkranz[1](✉)(iD) and Tomáš Kliegr[2]

[1] Department of Computer Science, Knowledge Engineering Group,
TU Darmstadt, Darmstadt, Germany
`fuernkranz@ke.tu-darmstadt.de`
[2] Department of Information and Knowledge Engineering,
University of Economics, Prague, Czech Republic

Abstract. In his seminal paper, Mitchell has defined bias as "any basis for choosing one generalization over another, other than strict consistency with the observed training instances", such as the choice of the hypothesis language or any form of preference relation between its elements. The most commonly used form is a simplicity bias, which prefers simpler hypotheses over more complex ones, even in cases when the latter provide a better fit to the data. Such a bias not only helps to avoid overfitting, but is also commonly considered to foster interpretability. In this talk, we will question this assumption, in particular with respect to commonly used rule learning heuristics that aim at learning rules that are as simple as possible. We will, in contrary, argue that in many cases, short rules are not desirable from the point of view of interpretability, and present some evidence from crowdsourcing experiments that support this hypothesis. To understand interpretability, we must relate machine learning biases to cognitive biases, which let humans prefer certain explanations over others, even in cases when such a preference cannot be rationally justified. Only then can we develop suitable interpretability biases for machine learning.

1 Biases in Machine Learning

In his ground-breaking technical report "The need for biases in learning generalizations", Mitchell (1980) has established that generalization from examples is not possible without giving the learning algorithm some sort of direction in the form of a so-called *bias*. He defines bias as "any basis for choosing one generalization over another, other than strict consistency with the instances", and has later been generalized to include "any factor (including consistency with the instances) that influences the definition or selection of inductive hypotheses" (Gordon and desJardins, 1995). Bias-free learning can only lead to an enumeration of the version space of all possible models that are complete and consistent with the training data (Mitchell, 1977). This is in general infeasible, and would also be futile because, as Mitchell has argued, knowing the complete version

---

Much of the material in this paper is based on Fürnkranz et al. (2018).

© Springer Nature Switzerland AG 2018
W. Duivesteijn et al. (Eds.): IDA 2018, LNCS 11191, pp. 15–27, 2018.
https://doi.org/10.1007/978-3-030-01768-2_2

space does not allow any classification beyond a mere lookup of the seen training examples. For making an inductive leap, some of the theories within the version space must be preferred over others.

Mitchell (1980) listed several factors that may bias the learner, including constraints resulting from domain knowledge about possible valid theories, knowledge about the intended use of a theory such as misclassification costs, knowledge about the source of the data, or a preference for simple and more general theories. In particular the latter point is predominant in machine learning, where principles like Occam's Razor (Blumer et al., 1987) or Minimum Description Length (MDL) (Rissanen, 1978) are commonly used heuristics for model selection and pruning or regularization techniques are considered to be necessary ingredients for learning algorithms to fight the danger of overfitting (Schaffer, 1993). Maybe somewhat surprisingly, a preference for comprehensible or interpretable of models is not among the considered biases. Nevertheless, the need for learning comprehensible models also has been recognized early in machine learning and data mining.

2   Interpretability

Michalski (1983) formulated a *comprehensibility postulate*, which states that the "results of computer induction should be symbolic descriptions of given entities, semantically and structurally similar to those a human expert might produce observing the same entities. Components of these descriptions should be comprehensible as single chunks of information, directly interpretable in natural language". Muggleton et al. (2018) refer to Michie (1988) who discerns between weak learning, which focuses only on prediction, strong learning, which finds symbolic descriptions of the learned predictive theories, and ultra-strong learning, which is able to increase the performance of a human who has access to these theories. Kodratoff (1994) has observed that interpretability is an ill-defined concept, and has called upon several communities from both academia and industry to tackle this problem, to "find objective definitions of what comprehensibility is", and to open "the hunt for probably approximate comprehensible learning". For a good review of work on interpretability, we refer the reader to Freitas (2013) who surveys various aspects of interpretability, compares several classifier types with respect to their comprehensibility, and points out several drawbacks of model size as a single measure of interpretability.

3   Complexity Biases

Interpretability is often considered to correlate with model simplicity. It is conventional wisdom in machine learning and data mining that logical models such as rule sets are more interpretable than other models, and that among such rule-based models, simpler models are more interpretable than more complex ones. There are many plausible reasons why simpler models should be preferred over more complex models. Obviously, a shorter model can be interpreted with less effort than a more complex model of the same kind, in much the same way as reading one paragraph is quicker than reading one page. Nevertheless, a page of elaborate explanations may be more comprehensible than a single dense paragraph that provides the same information (as we all know from reading research papers). However, there have also been several results that throw doubt on this claim. In this section, we briefly discuss this issue in some depth, by first discussing the use of a simplicity bias in machine learning (Sect. 3.1), then taking the alternative point of view and recapitulating works where more complex theories are preferred (Sect. 3.2), and then summarizing the conflicting past evidence for either of the two views (Sect. 3.3).

3.1 The Bias for Simplicity

Michalski (1983) already states that inductive learning algorithms need to incorporate a preference criterion for selecting hypotheses to address the problem of the possibly unlimited number of hypotheses, and that this criterion is typically *simplicity*, referring to philosophical works on simplicity of scientific theories by Kemeny (1953) and Post (1960), which refine the initial postulate attributed to Ockham. Occam's Razor, *"Entia non sunt multiplicanda sine necessitate"*.[1] This statement, attributed to English philosopher and theologian William of Ockham (c. 1287–1347), has been put forward as support for a principle of parsimony in the philosophy of science (Hahn, 1930). In machine learning, this principle is generally interpreted as "given two explanations of the data, all other things being equal, the simpler explanation is preferable" (Blumer et al., 1987), or simply "choose the shortest explanation for the observed data" (Mitchell, 1997). While it is well-known that striving for simplicity often yields better predictive results—mostly because pruning or regularization techniques help to avoid overfitting—the exact formulation of the principle is still subject to debate (Domingos, 1999), and several cases have been observed where more complex theories perform better (Bensusan, 1998; Murphy and Pazzani, 1994; Webb, 1996).

Much of this debate focuses on the aspect of predictive accuracy. When it comes to understandability, the idea that simpler rules are more comprehensible is typically unchallenged. A nice counter example is due to Munroe (2013), who observed that route directions like "take every left that doesn't put you on a prime-numbered highway or street named for a president" could be most compressive but considerably less comprehensive. Although Domingos (1999) argues in his critical review that it is theoretically and empirically false to favor the simpler of two models with the same training-set error on the grounds that this would lead to lower generalization error, he concludes that Occam's Razor is nevertheless relevant for machine learning but should be interpreted as a preference for more *comprehensible* (rather than *simple*) model.

A particular implementation of Occam's razor in machine learning is the minimum description length (MDL; Rissanen 1978) or minimum message length (MML[2]; Wallace and Boulton 1968) principle, which is an information-theoretic

---

[1] Entities should not be multiplied beyond necessity.

[2] The differences between the two views are irrelevant for our argumentation.

formulation of the principle that smaller models should be preferred (Grünwald, 2007). The description length that should be minimized is the sum of the complexity of the model plus the complexity of the data encoded given the model. In this way, both the complexity and the accuracy of a model can be traded off: the description length of an empty model consists only of the data part, and it can be compared to the description length of a perfect model, which does not need additional information to encode the data. The theoretical foundation of this principle is based on the Kolmogorov complexity (Li and Vitányi, 1993), the essentially uncomputable length of the smallest model of the data. In practice, different coding schemes have been developed for encoding models and data and have, e.g., been used as pruning criterion (Cohen, 1995; Mehta et al., 1995; Quinlan, 1990) or for pattern evaluation (Vreeken et al., 2011). However, we are not aware of any work that relates MDL to interpretability.

3.2   The Bias for Complexity

Even though most systems have a bias toward simpler theories for the sake of overfitting avoidance and increased accuracy, some rule learning algorithms strive for more complex rules, and have good reasons for doing so. Already Michalski (1983) has noted that there are two different kinds of rules, discriminative and characteristic. *Discriminative rules* can quickly discriminate an object of one category from objects of other categories. A simple example is the rule

```
elephant :- trunk.
```

which states that an animal with a trunk is an elephant. This implication provides a simple but effective rule for recognizing elephants among all animals. However, it does not provide a very clear picture on properties of the elements of the target class. For example, from the above rule, we do not understand that elephants are also very large and heavy animals with a thick grey skin, tusks and big ears.

Characteristic rules, on the other hand, try to capture *all* properties that are common to the objects of the target class. A rule for characterizing elephants could be

```
heavy, large, grey, bigEars, tusks, trunk :- elephant.
```

Note that here the implication sign is reversed: we list all properties that are implied by the target class, i.e., by an animal being an elephant. From the point of understandability, characteristic rules are often preferable to discriminative rules. For example, in a customer profiling application, we might prefer to not only list a few characteristics that discriminate one customer group from the other, but are interested in all characteristics of each customer group.

Characteristic rules are very much related to *formal concept analysis* (Ganter and Wille, 1999; Wille, 1982). Informally, a concept is defined by its intent (the description of the concept, i.e., the conditions of its defining rule) and its extent (the instances that are covered by these conditions). A *formal concept* is then a

```
[2160|0]   p :- odor = foul.
[1152|0]   p :- gill-color = buff.
[ 256|0]   p :- odor = pungent.
```

(a) using the Laplace heuristic h_{Lap} for refinement

```
[2192|0]   p :- veil-color = white, gill-spacing = close, bruises? = no,
                ring-number = one, stalk-surface-above-ring = silky.
[ 864|0]   p :- veil-color = white, gill-spacing = close, gill-size = narrow,
                population = several, stalk-shape = tapering.
[ 336|0]   p :- stalk-color-below-ring = white, ring-type = pendant,
                stalk-color-above-ring = white, ring-number = one,
                cap-surface = smooth, stalk-root = bulbous, gill-spacing = close.
```

(b) using the inverted Laplace heuristic q_{Lap} for refinement

Fig. 1. Top three rules learned for the class poisonous in the *Mushroom* dataset.

concept where the extension and the intension are Pareto-maximal, i.e., a concept where no conditions can be added without reducing the number of covered examples. In Michalski's terminology, a formal concept is both discriminative and characteristic, i.e., a rule where the head is equivalent to the body.

It is well-known that formal concepts correspond to *closed itemsets* in association rule mining, i.e., to maximally specific itemsets (Stumme et al., 2002). Closed itemsets have been mined primarily because they are a unique and compact representative of equivalence classes of itemsets, which all cover the same instances (Zaki and Hsiao, 2002). However, while all itemsets in such an equivalence class are equivalent with respect to their support, they may not be equivalent with respect to their understandability or interestingness.

Consider, e.g., the infamous {diapers, beer} itemset that is commonly used as an example for a surprising finding in market based analysis. A possible explanation for this finding is that this rule captures the behavior of young family fathers who are sent to shop for their youngster and have to reward themselves with a six-pack. However, if we consider that a young family may not only need beer and diapers, the closed itemset of this particular combination may also include baby lotion, milk, porridge, bread, fruits, vegetables, cheese, sausages, soda, etc. In this extended context, diapers and beer appear to be considerably less surprising. Conversely, an association rule

$$beer :- diapers \qquad (1)$$

with an assumed confidence of 80%, which at first sight appears interesting because of the unexpectedly strong correlation between buying two seemingly unrelated items, becomes considerably less interesting if we learn that 80% of *all* customers buy beer, irrespective of whether they have bought diapers or not. In other words, the association rule 1 is considerably less plausible than the association rule

$$\begin{aligned} beer :- \, &diapers, \ baby \ lotion, \ milk, \ porridge, \ bread, \\ &fruits, \ vegetables, \ cheese, \ sausages, \ soda. \end{aligned} \qquad (2)$$

even if both rules may have very similar properties in terms of support and confidence.

Stecher et al. (2014) introduced so-called *inverted heuristics* for inductive rule learning. The key idea behind them is a rather technical observation based on a visualization of the behavior of rule learning heuristics in coverage space (Fürnkranz and Flach, 2005), namely that the evaluation of rule refinements is based on a bottom-up point of view, whereas the refinement process proceeds top-down, in a general-to-specific fashion. As a remedy, it was proposed to "invert" the point of view, resulting in heuristics that pay more attention to maintaining high coverage on the positive examples, whereas conventional heuristics focus more on quickly excluding negative examples. Somewhat unexpectedly, it turned out that this results in longer rules, which resemble characteristic rules instead of the conventionally learned discriminative rules. For example, Fig. 1 shows the two decision lists that have been found for the UCI *Mushroom* dataset[3] with the conventional Laplace heuristic h_{Lap} (top) and its inverted counterpart $\mathfrak{q}_{Lap}$ (bottom). Although fewer rules are learned with $\mathfrak{q}_{Lap}$, and thus the individual rules are more general on average, they are also considerably longer. Intuitively, these rules also look more convincing, because the first set of rules often only uses a single criterion (e.g., odor) to discriminate between edible and poisonous mushrooms. Stecher et al. (2016) and Valmarska et al. (2017) investigated the suitability of such rules for subgroup discovery, with somewhat inconclusive results.

3.3 Conflicting Evidence

There are many plausible reasons why simpler models should be preferred over more complex models. Obviously, a shorter model can be interpreted with less effort than a more complex model of the same kind, in much the same way as reading one paragraph is quicker than reading one page. Nevertheless, a page of elaborate explanations may be more comprehensible than a single dense paragraph that provides the same information (as we all know from reading research papers). Other reasons for preferring simpler models include that they are easier to falsify, that there are fewer simpler theories than complex theories, so the a priori chances that a simple theory fits the data are lower, or that simpler rules tend to be more general, cover more examples and their quality estimates are therefore statistically more reliable. However, even in cases where a simpler and a more complex rule covers the same number of examples, shorter rules are not necessarily more understandable. There are a few isolated empirical studies that add to this picture. However, the results on the relation between the size of representation and comprehensibility are limited and conflicting.

Larger Models are Less Comprehensible. Huysmans et al. (2011) were among the first that actually tried to empirically validate the often implicitly made claim that smaller models are more comprehensible. In particular, they related

---

[3] https://archive.ics.uci.edu/ml/datasets.html.

increased complexity to measurable events such as a decrease in answer accuracy, an increase in answer time, and a decrease in confidence. From this, they concluded that smaller models tend to be more comprehensible, proposing that there is a certain complexity threshold that limits the practical utility of a model. However, they also noted that in parts of their study, the correlation of model complexity with utility was less pronounced. The study also does not report on the domain knowledge the participants of their study had relating to the data used, so that it cannot be ruled out that the obtained result were caused by lack of domain knowledge. A similar study was later conducted by Piltaver et al. (2016), who found a clear relationship between model complexity and comprehensibility in decision trees.

Larger Models are More Comprehensible. A direct evaluation of the perceived understandability of classification models has been performed by Allahyari and Lavesson (2011). They elicited preferences on pairs of models which were generated from two UCI datasets: *Labor* and *Contact Lenses*. What is unique to this study is that the analysis took into account the estimated domain knowledge of the participants on each of the datasets. On *Labor*, participants were expected to have good domain knowledge but not so for *Contact Lenses*. The study was performed with 100 student subjects and involved several decision tree induction algorithms (J48, RIDOR, ID3) as well as rule learners (PRISM, Rep, JRip). It was found that *larger models* were considered as *more comprehensible* than smaller models on the *Labor* dataset whereas the users showed the opposite preference for *Contact Lenses*. Allahyari and Lavesson (2011) explain the discrepancy with the lack of prior knowledge for *Contact Lenses*, which makes it harder to understand complex models, whereas in the case of *Labor*, "... the larger or more complex classifiers did not diminish the understanding of the decision process, but may have even increased it through providing more steps and including more attributes for each decision step." In an earlier study, Kononenko (1993) found that medical experts rejected rules learned by a decision tree algorithm because they found them to be too short. Instead, they preferred explanations that were derived from a Naïve Bayes classifier, which essentially showed weights for all attributes, structured into confirming and rejecting attributes.

4   The Need for Interpretability Biases

A lot of work in interpretability has focused on the mere syntactic comprehensibility of a concept. For example, Muggleton et al. (2018) provide an operational definition of *comprehensibility*, which essentially captures how quickly a learned concept can be utilized in solving the problems from the same task domain, typically classifying new examples. In Fürnkranz et al. (2018), we have advocated the view that there is more to interpretability than the mere ability to syntactically parse and understand a given concept.

Consider, e.g., Fig. 2, which shows several possible explanations for why a city has a high quality of living, derived by the Explain-a-LOD system, which uses

```
QOL = High  :- Many events take place.
QOL = High  :- Host City of Olympic Summer Games.
QOL = Low   :- African Capital.
```

(a) rated highly by users

```
QOL = High :- # Records Made >= 1, # Companies/Organisations >= 22.
QOL = High :- # Bands >= 18, # Airlines founded in 2000 > 1.
QOL = Low  :- # Records Made = 0, Average January Temp <= 16.
```

(b) rated lowly by users

Fig. 2. Good discriminative rules for the quality of living of a city (Paulheim, 2012)

Linked Open Data as background knowledge for explaining statistics (Paulheim and Fürnkranz, 2012). Clearly, all rules are comprehensible, and can be easily applied in practice. Even though all of them are good discriminators on the provided data and can be equally well applied by an automated system, the first three appear to be more convincing to a human user. However, currently available rule learning systems would not be able to express a preference for the rules in Fig. 2(a) over those in Fig. 2(b). For doing so, one needs to capture not only the comprehensibility of a rule, but also its *plausibility*.

5   Cognitive Biases

In order to work towards interpretability biases for machine learning, it is useful to consider work in psychology on cognitive biases. Tversky and Kahneman (1974) defined a cognitive bias as a " systematic error in judgment and decision-making common to all human beings which can be due to cognitive limitations, motivational factors, and/or adaptations to natural environments. "

The presumably most famous example is the so-called *conjunctive fallacy*, exemplified by the *Linda problem* (cf. Fig. 3). In this problem, subjects are asked whether they consider it more plausible that a person Linda is more likely to be (a) a bank teller or (b) a feminist bank teller. Tversky and Kahneman (1983) report that based on the provided characteristics of Linda, 85% of the participants indicate (b) as the more probable option. This was essentially confirmed by various independent studies, even though the actual proportions may vary. However, of course, hypothesis (a) is more likely to be correct because a conjunction will never cover more cases than each of its constituents. For our purposes, this example reiterates the point that shorter explanations are not necessarily preferred by human subjects, and that a bias for interpretability should take other factors into account.

The conjunctive fallacy has received considerable attention in the psychological literature, and many possible explanations for this and related phenomena have been proposed (cf. Pohl 2017, for a survey). The results are predominantly attributed to the *representative heuristic* (Tversky and Kahneman, 1974),

Linda is 31 years old, single, outspoken, and very bright.
She majored in philosophy. As a student, she was deeply
concerned with issues of discrimination and social justice,
and also participated in anti-nuclear demonstrations.

Which is more probable?

(a) Linda is a bank teller.
(b) Linda is a bank teller and is active in the
    feminist movement.

Fig. 3. The Linda problem (Tversky and Kahneman, 1983).

according to which people tend to confuse probability with similarity, i.e., Linda
is more similar to our mental image of a feminist bank teller than to a generic
bank teller. Another potentially relevant explanation is given by Hertwig et al.
(2008), who hypothesizes that the humans tend to misunderstand conjunctions.
They discussed that "and" in natural language can express several relationships,
including temporal order, causal relationship, and most importantly, can also
indicate a union of sets instead of their intersection. For example, the sentence
"He invited friends and colleagues to the party" does not mean that all people
at the party were both colleagues and friends. Moreover, while the conjunctive
fallacy is possibly the best-documented result of the representativeness heuristic,
there is a number of other cognitive biases and heuristics that can be important
for interpretation of rule learning results. A survey of cognitive biases can be
found in (Pohl, 2017), and a discussion of their relevance for machine learning
in (Kliegr et al., 2018).

6   First Experimental Results

In previous work (Fürnkranz et al., 2018), we have evaluated a selection of cognitive biases in the very specific context of whether minimizing the complexity
or length of a rule will also lead to increased interpretability, which is often taken
for granted in machine learning research. More concretely, we reported on five
crowd-sourcing experiments conducted in order to gain first insights into differences in the plausibility of rule learning results. Users were confronted with pairs
of learned rules with approximately the same discriminative power (as measured
by conventional heuristics such as support and confidence), and were asked to
indicate which one seemed more plausible. The experiments were performed in
four domains, which were selected so that respondents can be expected to be
able to comprehend the given explanations (rules), but not to reliably judge their
validity without obtaining additional information. In this way, users were guided
to give an intuitive assessment of the plausibility of the provided explanation.

A first experiment explored the hypothesis whether the Occam's razor principle holds for the plausibility of rules, by investigating whether people consider shorter rules to be more plausible than longer rules. The results obtained for four different domains showed that this is not the case, in fact we observed statistically significant preference for longer rules on two datasets. In another experiment, we found support for the hypothesis that the elevated preference for longer rules is partly due to the misunderstanding of "and" that connects conditions in the presented rules: some people erroneously find rules with more conditions as more general. A third experiment show that when both confidence and support are explicitly stated, confidence positively affects plausibility and support is largely ignored. This confirms a prediction following from previous psychological research studying the *insensitivity to sample size* effect (Tversky and Kahneman, 1971). Other experiments investigated the relevance of attributes and literals used in the conditions of a rule. The results indicated that rule plausibility is affected already if a single condition is considered to be more relevant.[4] In order to investigate the effects of the recognition heuristic (Goldstein and Gigerenzer, 1999), we attempted to use PageRank computed from the Wikipedia knowledge graph as a proxy for how well a given condition is recognized. The results were inconclusive, on one of the datasets we observed plausibility being affected when all conditions in one rule were recognized comparatively more than in the alternative rule.

7   Conclusion

The main goal of this paper was to motivate that interpretability of rules is an important topic, which is more than a simple syntactic readability of the presented models. In particular, we believe that plausibility is an important aspect of interpretability, which, to our knowledge, has received too little attention in the literature. Learners can often find a large variety of rules with the same or similar discriminatory power as measured on hold-out data, but with large difference in their perceived credibility. Machine learning systems need interpretability biases in order to cope with such situations.

In our view, a research program that aims at a thorough investigation of interpretability in machine learning needs to resort to results in the psychological literature, in particular to cognitive biases and fallacies. We summarized some of these hypotheses, such as the conjunctive fallacy, and started to investigate to what extent these can serve as explanations for human preferences over different learned hypotheses. Moreover, it needs to be considered how cognitive biases can be incorporated into machine learning algorithms. Unlike loss functions, which can be evaluated on data, it seems necessary that interpretability is evaluated in user studies. Thus, we need to establish appropriate evaluation procedures for

---

[4] Since our experiments were based on subjective comparisons of pairs of rules, a more precise formulation would be, "comparatively more relevant than the most relevant condition in an alternative rule".

interpretability, and develop appropriate heuristic surrogate functions that can be quickly evaluated and optimized in learning algorithms.

Acknowledgements. We would like to thank Frederik Janssen and Julius Stecher for providing us with their code, Eyke Hüllermeier, Frank Jäkel, Niklas Lavesson, Nada Lavrač and Kai-Ming Ting for interesting discussions and pointers to related work, and Jilles Vreeken for pointing us to Munroe (2013). We are also grateful for the insightful comments of the reviewers of (Fürnkranz et al., 2018), which helped us considerably to focus our paper. TK was supported by grant IGA 33/2018 of the Faculty of Informatics and Statistics, University of Economics, Prague.

References

Allahyari, H., Lavesson, N.: User-oriented assessment of classification model understandability. In: Kofod-Petersen, A., Heintz, F., Langseth, H. (eds.) Proceedings of the 11th Scandinavian Conference on Artificial Intelligence (SCAI-11), pp. 11–19 (2011)

Bensusan, H.: God doesn't always shave with Occam's Razor — learning when and how to prune. In: Nédellec, C., Rouveirol, C. (eds.) ECML 1998. LNCS, vol. 1398, pp. 119–124. Springer, Heidelberg (1998). https://doi.org/10.1007/BFb0026680

Blumer, A., Ehrenfeucht, A., Haussler, D., Warmuth, M.K.: Occam's razor. Inf. Process. Lett. **24**, 377–380 (1987)

Cohen, W.W.: Fast effective rule induction. In: Prieditis, A., Russell, S. (eds.) Proceedings of the 12th International Conference on Machine Learning (ML-95), pp. 115–123. Morgan Kaufmann, Lake Tahoe (1995)

Domingos, P.: The role of Occam's Razor in knowledge discovery. Data Min. Knowl. Discov. **3**(4), 409–425 (1999)

Freitas, A.A.: Comprehensible classification models: a position paper. SIGKDD Explor. **15**(1), 1–10 (2013)

Fürnkranz, J., Flach, P.A.: ROC 'n' rule learning - towards a better understanding of covering algorithms. Mach. Learn. **58**(1), 39–77 (2005)

Fürnkranz, J., Kliegr, T., Paulheim, H.: On cognitive preferences and the interpretability of rule-based models. arXiv preprint arXiv:1803.01316 (2018)

Ganter, B., Wille, R.: Formal Concept Analysis. Springer, Heidelberg (1999). https://doi.org/10.1007/978-3-642-59830-2

Goldstein, D.G., Gigerenzer, G.: The recognition heuristic: how ignorance makes us smart. Simple Heuristics That Make Us Smart, pp. 37–58. Oxford (1999)

Gordon, D.F., DesJardins, M.: Evaluation and selection of biases in machine learning. Mach. Learn. **20**(1–2), 5–22 (1995)

Grünwald, P.D.: The Minimum Description Length Principle. MIT Press, Cambridge (2007)

Hahn, H.: Überflüssige Wesenheiten: Occams Rasiermesser. Veröffentlichungen des Vereines Ernst Mach, Wien (1930)

Hertwig, R., Benz, B., Krauss, S.: The conjunction fallacy and the many meanings of and. Cognition **108**(3), 740–753 (2008)

Huysmans, J., Dejaeger, K., Mues, C., Vanthienen, J., Baesens, B.: An empirical evaluation of the comprehensibility of decision table, tree and rule based predictive models. Decis. Support Syst. **51**(1), 141–154 (2011)

Kemeny, J.G.: The use of simplicity in induction. Philos. Rev. **62**(3), 391–408 (1953)

Kliegr, T., Bahník, Š., Fürnkranz, J.: A review of possible effects of cognitive biases on interpretation of rule-based machine learning models. arXiv preprint arXiv:1804.02969 (2018)

Kodratoff, Y.: The comprehensibility manifesto. KDD Nuggets, 94(9) (1994)

Kononenko, I.: Inductive and Bayesian learning in medical diagnosis. Appl. Artif. Intell. **7**, 317–337 (1993)

Li, M., Vitányi, P.: An Introduction to Kolmogorov Complexity and Its Applications. TCS. Springer, New York (2008). https://doi.org/10.1007/978-0-387-49820-1

Mehta, M., Rissanen, J., Agrawal, R.: MDL-based decision tree pruning. In: Fayyad, U., Uthurusamy, R. (eds.) Proceedings of the 1st International Conference on Knowledge Discovery and Data Mining, pp. 216–221. AAAI Press (1995)

Michalski, R.S.: A theory and methodology of inductive learning. Artif. Intell. **20**(2), 111–162 (1983)

Michie, D.: Machine learning in the next five years. In: Proceedings of the 3rd European Working Session on Learning (EWSL-88), pp. 107–122. Pitman (1988)

Mitchell, T.M., The need for biases in learning generalizations. Technical report, Computer Science Department, Rutgers University, New Brunswick (1980)

Mitchell, T.M.: Version spaces: a candidate elimination approach to rule learning. In: Reddy, R. (ed.) Proceedings of the 5th International Joint Conference on Artificial Intelligence (IJCAI-77), pp. 305–310. William Kaufmann (1977)

Mitchell, T.M.: Machine Learning. McGraw Hill, New York (1997)

Muggleton, S.H., Schmid, U., Zeller, C., Tamaddoni-Nezhad, A., Besold, T.: Ultra-strong machine learning: comprehensibility of programs learned with ILP. Mach. Learn. 1–22 (2018)

Munroe, R. Kolmogorov directions. www.xkcd.com, A webcomic of romance, sarcasm, math, and language (2013)

Murphy, P.M., Pazzani, M.J.: Exploring the decision forest: an empirical investigation of Occam's Razor in decision tree induction. J. Artif. Intell. Res. **1**, 257–275 (1994)

Paulheim, H.: Generating possible interpretations for statistics from linked open data. In: Simperl, E., Cimiano, P., Polleres, A., Corcho, O., Presutti, V. (eds.) ESWC 2012. LNCS, vol. 7295, pp. 560–574. Springer, Heidelberg (2012). https://doi.org/10.1007/978-3-642-30284-8_44

Paulheim, H., Fürnkranz, J.: Unsupervised generation of data mining features from linked open data. In: Proceedings of the International Conference on Web Intelligence and Semantics (WIMS'12) (2012)

Piltaver, R., Luštrek, M., Gams, M., Martinčić-Ipšić, S.: What makes classification trees comprehensible? Expert Syst. Appl. **62**, 333–346 (2016)

Pohl, R.: Cognitive Illusions: A Handbook on Fallacies and Biases in Thinking, Judgement and Memory, 2nd edn. Psychology Press, London (2017)

Post, H.: Simplicity in scientific theories. Br. J. Philos. Sci. **11**(41), 32–41 (1960)

Quinlan, J.R.: Learning logical definitions from relations. Mach. Learn. **5**, 239–266 (1990)

Rissanen, J.: Modeling by shortest data description. Automatica **14**, 465–471 (1978)

Schaffer, C.: Overfitting avoidance as bias. Mach. Learn. **10**, 153–178 (1993)

Stecher, J., Janssen, F., Fürnkranz, J.: Separating rule refinement and rule selection heuristics in inductive rule learning. In: Calders, T., Esposito, F., Hüllermeier, E., Meo, R. (eds.) ECML PKDD 2014. LNCS (LNAI), vol. 8726, pp. 114–129. Springer, Heidelberg (2014). https://doi.org/10.1007/978-3-662-44845-8_8

Stecher, J., Janssen, F., Fürnkranz, J.: Shorter rules are better, aren't they? In: Calders, T., Ceci, M., Malerba, D. (eds.) DS 2016. LNCS (LNAI), vol. 9956, pp. 279–294. Springer, Cham (2016). https://doi.org/10.1007/978-3-319-46307-0_18

Stumme, G., Taouil, R., Bastide, Y., Pasquier, N., Lakhal, L.: Computing iceberg concept lattices with Titanic. Data Knowl. Eng. **42**(2), 189–222 (2002)

Tversky, A., Kahneman, D.: Belief in the law of small numbers. Psychol. Bull. **76**(2), 105–110 (1971)

Tversky, A., Kahneman, D.: Judgment under uncertainty: heuristics and biases. Science **185**(4157), 1124–1131 (1974)

Tversky, A., Kahneman, D.: Extensional versus intuitive reasoning: the conjunction fallacy in probability judgment. Psychol. Rev. **90**(4), 293–315 (1983)

Valmarska, A., Lavrač, N., Fürnkranz, J., Robnik-Sikonja, M.: Refinement and selection heuristics in subgroup discovery and classification rule learning. Expert Syst. Appl. **81**, 147–162 (2017)

Vreeken, J., van Leeuwen, M., Siebes, A.: Krimp: mining itemsets that compress. Data Min. Knowl. Discov. **23**(1), 169–214 (2011)

Wallace, C.S., Boulton, D.M.: An information measure for classification. Comput. J. **11**, 185–194 (1968)

Webb, G.I.: Further experimental evidence against the utility of Occam's razor. J. Artif. Intell. Res. **4**, 397–417 (1996)

Wille, R.: Restructuring lattice theory: an approach based on hierarchies of concepts. In: Rival, I. (ed.) Ordered Sets, pp. 445–470. Reidel, Dordrecht-Boston (1982)

Zaki, M.J., Hsiao, C.-J.: CHARM: An efficient algorithm for closed itemset mining. In: Grossman, R.L., Han, J., Kumar, V., Mannila, H., Motwani, R. (eds.) Proceedings of the 2nd SIAM International Conference on Data Mining (SDM-02), Arlington (2002)

Selected Contributions

Open Data Science

Leo Lahti$^{(\boxtimes)}$ (iD)

University of Turku, Turku, Finland
leo.lahti@iki.fi
http://www.iki.fi/Leo.Lahti

Abstract. The increasing openness of data, methods, and collaboration networks has created new opportunities for research, citizen science, and industry. Whereas openly licensed scientific, governmental, and institutional data sets can now be accessed through programmatic interfaces, compressed archives, and downloadable spreadsheets, realizing the full potential of open data streams depends critically on the availability of targeted data analytical methods, and on user communities that can derive value from these digital resources. Interoperable software libraries have become a central element in modern statistical data analysis, bridging the gap between theory and practice, while open developer communities have emerged as a powerful driver of research software development. Drawing insights from a decade of community engagement, I propose the concept of *open data science*, which refers to the new forms of research enabled by open data, open methods, and open collaboration.

Keywords: Algorithmic data analysis · Open data science
Open collaboration · Open research software

1 Introduction

Openly licensed data sets from scientific, governmental, institutional, and other sources are now increasingly accessible online and can be used to support academic research. Deriving value from data depends critically on the availability of appropriate data analytical methods, and on research communities that are capable of taking advantage of these emerging opportunities in the overall research workflow.

Research software plays an essential role in bridging the gap between data, theoretical models and application expertise. Access to open data on various areas ranging from biomedical measurements and geospatial information to demographics, government activities, and historical records has opened new opportunities for research but there is a persisting shortage of algorithmic tools to access, process and analyse open data resources. Domain-specific tools are often missing, and researchers can put remarkable effort on building custom scripts that never become widely distributed, utilized, and verified despite their broader research potential. Thriving virtual research communities have formed

© Springer Nature Switzerland AG 2018
W. Duivesteijn et al. (Eds.): IDA 2018, LNCS 11191, pp. 31–39, 2018.
https://doi.org/10.1007/978-3-030-01768-2_3

around statistical programming environments, such as R, Python, or Julia, to address these needs. These rapidly growing ecosystems of research software and algorithms have provided the means to standardize many routine tasks in data analysis that can be used as building blocks in complex data science workflows.

The role of community is fundamental to academic research. In the context of data science, developer communities can provide social and technical incentives to promote long-term development and maintenance of open research software and collaboration networks when immediate academic incentives are lacking. This helps to avoid duplicated effort and channel resources to collective quality control. The open development model has emerged as a predominant mode for research algorithm development in natural sciences during the past decade, and is now rapidly gaining ground in the social sciences and humanities. The research potential of collective initiatives exceeds far beyond the capacities of any single research group or institution. Virtual and often informal research networks have emerged as powerful drivers of open research. Open collaboration platforms such as the rOpenSci[1] and Bioconductor [5] are further helping to expand the scope of these efforts towards increased standardization and domain-specific algorithms.

The field of *open data science*, proposed in this perspective article, refers to the new forms of research and research quality enabled by open data, algorithms, and collaboration networks. In many practical situations, these components of research are open only partially. Open data science emphasizes the possibilities of open research practices, hence being a field that is both taking advantage of and furthering the development towards more open and collaborative research through standardization and collective verification of common analysis tasks.

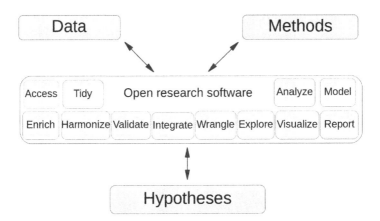

Fig. 1. Role of research software in the open data science workflow. Open research software mediates the community efforts and interaction based on shared data, methods, and hypotheses defined by the research community at each stage of an open data science project. Open collaboration facilitates standardization and reproducibility, and the overall quality of research.

---

[1] https://ropensci.org.

2   Elements of Open Data Science

The three pillars of open data science include open data, open algorithms, and open collaboration (Fig. 1). Research software has a central role in mediating the interaction between these elements, helping to simplify, standardize, and automate research. Open collaboration networks can play a key role by providing peer support, collective quality control, and collaborative development opportunities [2, 4]. Techniques from the machine learning and artificial intelligence can support various steps of algorithmic data analysis from raw data access through analysis to final reporting [15]. Open data science emphasizes data and methods sharing through open infrastructures and virtual collaboration networks that have been enabled by digitalization and the push towards openness in government and academia.

2.1   Open Data

A number of data repositories have been opened by academic, governmental, and industrial parties, and have been integrated with data analytical workflows in research and commercial applications. Eurostat, the statistical office of the European Union, is one example of the many institutions that are sharing vast open data resources online[2]. The Eurostat database contains thousands of contemporary and longitudinal data sets on demography, economics, health, infrastructure, traffic and other topics at the European level, often with fine spatial and temporal resolution spanning several years or decades. Open data sharing differs from more traditional data services that provide access only to limited subsets of the data, and limit data analysis options on tools that are readily implemented in the query interface rather than letting the researcher decide which tools and analyses to execute. Such limitations form severe bottlenecks for research that relies on access to the full raw data.

The research use of open data, on the other hand, has been limited by the shortage of efficient tools to access, process, and integrate such data sets. The data sources and formats are scattered, and the methods for handling such data are heterogeneous, requiring a multitude of expertise and skills due to variability in data formats and interfaces. Research communities can benefit from shared programmatic tools that can seamlessly integrate initial data retrieval with downstream algorithms for statistical analysis and reporting. Standardized software libraries have been developed to facilitate fluent retrieval of open data from within statistical programming environments such as R, Python, or Julia. Collaborative development and automation of the open data retrieval is a central element in open data science.

For instance, the *eurostat* R package [6] is specifically tailored to retrieve data in the R environment from Eurostat open data portal. The package includes custom tools to query, download, manipulate, and visualize these data sets in a

---

[2] http://ec.europa.eu/eurostat/data/database.

smooth, automated and reproducible manner. Standard features, such as compliance with tidy data principles [18], support the integration with other tools of open data science. Significant portions of the package documentation have been published as open and reproducible case studies based on the Eurostat open data, providing concrete examples of possible research use, and a straightforward starting point for further adjustments. In the case of eurostat, also many generic database packages, such as *datamart* [17], *quandl* [12], *pdfetch* [13], and *rsdmx* [1], could be used to retrieve the open data sets. However, these more generic database packages are not dedicated to Eurostat data access, and do not therefore fully support the full spectrum of Eurostat open data services and their research use. This highlights the need to complement generic database tools with targeted algorithms that are specifically tailored to access particular data sources, and facilitate their integration with other data sets and statistical tools (Fig. 2).

Community projects, such as rOpenSci[3] and our own project, the rOpenGov [10][4], have emerged to provide various algorithmic tools and software packages for accessing open data portals. Many such packages are now distributed by open data science initiatives such as Bioconductor, CRAN, and rOpenSci. Such tools are typically created by the user communities, and facilitate data access independently of the original data provider.

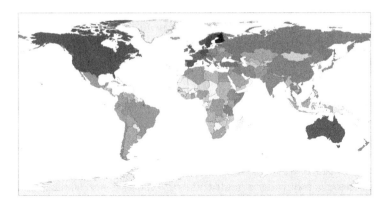

Fig. 2. Migration to (red) and from (blue) Finland in 2011 according to data from Statistics Finland as retrieved with the *pxweb* R package. The visualization relies on openly developed custom methods in the R statistical programming environment, from raw data access to harmonization, statistical analysis, and visualization (color figure online).

---

[3] https://ropensci.org.
[4] http://ropengov.github.io.

2.2   Open Algorithms

The increased availability of open data has potential to support and renew research but the methodological basis of open data science is still shaping up. Open data retrieval tools need to complemented by statistical data exploration, analysis, and modeling algorithms (Fig. 3). Statistical programming environments provide access to a vast body of advanced techniques for data analysis, including techniques such as (generalized) linear models, machine learning, probabilistic programming [3,14], and visualization [19].

Many research projects rely on rich combinations of spatio-temporal, textual, personal, demographic, and other types of data that may require remarkable amounts of dedicated custom processing before reliable statistical analysis becomes possible. Hence, general-purpose methods need to be complemented by targeted data processing and analysis algorithms. Most methods for advanced statistical analysis assume that data is readily available in a clean or tidy format. This does not hold in most real research situations. Hence, data cleaning and harmonization often forms a major component in research projects. Projects such as the *tidyverse* [20] have emerged to harmonize and organize research data before and during various stages of statistical analysis. Such general-purpose data wrangling methods can be complemented by domain-specific tools for data subsetting and manipulation (see e.g. [11]). Our experience is in line with the frequently encountered statement that the majority of the effort in data science projects is spent on organizing and harmonizing data before it is amenable for research use. In practice, data cleaning and harmonization often rely on combinations of automation and manual work. Intelligent algorithms for data analysis can greatly benefit from domain-specific tools for data wrangling, subsetting and visualization.

Our recent work on the historical development of print press provides an example [7], where we developed algorithmic tools to clean up bibliographic metadata collections in a scalable manner. This is now allowing a quantitative analysis of historical book production across Europe. In order to estimate paper consumption, for instance, we extracted information on books heights, widths, and page counts. This included converting various standard book formats into the SI system, summing up information on cover pages, special pages, and so forth. Furthemore, we could augment the data and analyses with open data on name-gender mappings, author metadata, and other sources of public information. The open algorithms can be verified and further improved when potential inconsistencies are observed, and the data sets can be gradually refined over time when new information arrives. Replacing manual curation by supervised machine learning techniques is now helping to scale up this research to cover millions of print products. We anticipate that the demand for such open and customized analysis methods and workflows will increase rapidly in this field when research libraries start to share these data resources more openly [7]. Open availability of methods and collaboration networks can potentially help to facilitate shifts towards increased data availability.

Finally, data harmonization and statistical analysis need to be complemented with high-quality visualization and reporting. Published visualizations often rely on geospatial maps or demographic data that are available from multiple governmental and international institutions. The eurostat package, for instance, can be used to download custom administrative boundaries by EuroGeographics, thus supporting seamless data visualization on the European map. Similar geospatial tools are also available for specific countries and cities[5].

Collaboratively developed tools to access, harmonize, integrate, and analyse large data collections are needed to pool scarce resources and increase the efficiency of data-intensive research. Open collaboration networks can gradually accumulate and refine collections of targeted algorithms in open statistical programming environments, as demonstrated by Bioconductor, rOpenSci, and other open data science projects. Hence, intelligent data analysis is often critically dependent on the overall data analytical infrastructures that provide the fundamental context for the application of state-of-the-art analysis algorithms. Moreover, in our experience academic teaching can also benefit from well-documented and reproducible workflows and reproducible notebooks as interactive learning tools.

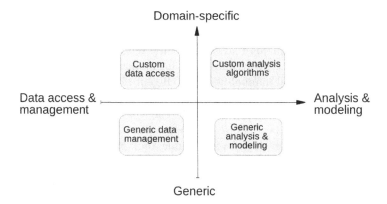

Fig. 3. Tradeoffs in open data science. The emphasis in methods development is shifting from standard data management towards intelligent algorithms for data analysis and modeling (horizontal axis). At the same, general-purpose tools are increasingly complemented by targeted domain-specific algorithms (vertical axis). Open data science aims at standardization but this is contrasted with the constant tendency to drift towards vast flexibility in the development of alternative methods and innovative combinations of the shared data and software components. Increasing openness of data and algorithm is bringing up new opportunities for research and collaborative methods development.

---

[5] The gisfin and helsinki packages; see http://ropengov.github.io.

2.3   Open Collaboration

Whereas open data science emphasizes the role of collaborative methods development and refinement [2,9], the efforts to standardize data analytical methods are balanced by a constant drift towards flexibility and custom methods (Fig. 3). Open and institutional community projects have emerged to balance these needs based on R, Python, and other programming languages, resulting in vast networks of developers and users of open research software from natural sciences to humanities. Related examples include the The OpenML [16] that provides tools to bring together data, algorithms and analysis results for open evaluation, and Project Open Data[6], which promotes the development and use of tools on open government data. We have made many such tools available within the rOpenGov project for computational social science and digital humanities. This is an example of a community-driven open data analytical ecosystem, which is now facilitating research use of many open institutional data resources based on a collection of over 20 R packages in varying stages of development. The eurostat package, for instance, evolved gradually from the earlier work by the same authors. Over time, multiple contributors joined in, and the package was extensively being developed and tested by various users before its eventual release. Open developer communities can also organize software review, promote data and software citation best practices, develop improved methods for authorship determination, and gain additional visibility for the projects. Moreover, open access to research publications in the form of pre-prints, post-prints, and openly licensed peer-reviewed literature can also be viewed as a component of open collaboration, as it facilitates the collective research efforts.

3   Conclusion

This brief perspective introduced the concept of open data science. This new paradigm is emerging at the intersection of open data, methods, and collaboration networks. Open research practices are now transforming the way we understand and share research outputs [8,9]. Open developer communities can provide social and technical incentives to promote open, collaborative work when academic incentives are lacking. Social aspects remain among the greatest challenges towards further development of open data science, as balancing the collaborative need for long-term development and maintenance with the prevailing authorship and incentive structures in academia remains a constant challenge. Given the enormous significance of high-quality open source software in modern data-intensive research, academic institutions and funding bodies should continue to develop and experiment with new ways to support sustainable development of open data science for instance by providing funding and recognition for the developers, maintainers and contributors of open research software, which is a key mediator between the key elements of open data science.

---

[6] https://project-open-data.cio.gov.

Statistical programming environments facilitate open participation, and allow full flexibility in constructing custom workflows in order to harness the full potential of modern data analysis and visualization arsenal. Open methods can be used and further tested and refined by the user communities, contributing to the growing open source ecosystems in natural sciences, social sciences, and digital humanities. Emphasis on open research practices will help the research communities to avoid replication and pool scarce research resources, and find improved methods for collective analysis and verification of research hypotheses.

Acknowledgements. I am grateful to the rOpenGov contributors, in particular Joona Lehtomäki, Markus Kainu, and Juuso Parkkinen, and our close collaborator Mikko Tolonen. The work has been partially funded by Academy of Finland (decisions 295741, 307127).

References

1. Blondel, E.: rsdmx: Tools for Reading SDMX Data and Metadata (2018). https://doi.org/10.5281/zenodo.1173229 (R package)
2. Boettiger, C., Chamberlain, S., Hart, E., Ram, K.: Building software, building community: lessons from the rOpenSci project. J. Open Res. Softw. **3** (2015). https://doi.org/10.5334/jors.bu
3. Carpenter, B., et al.: Stan: a probabilistic programming language. J. Stat. Softw. **76** (2017). https://doi.org/10.18637/jss.v076.i01
4. Gandrud, C.: Reproducible research with R and R Studio. Chapman & Hall/CRC, Boca Raton (2013)
5. Huber, W., et al.: Orchestrating high-throughput genomic analysis with Bioconductor. Nat. Methods **12**, 115–121 (2015). https://doi.org/10.1038/nmeth.3252
6. Lahti, L., Huovari, J., Kainu, M., Biecek, P.: Retrieval and analysis of eurostat open data with the eurostat package. R J. **9**, 385–392 (2017). https://journal.r-project.org/archive/2017/RJ-2017-019/index.html
7. Lahti, L., Ilomäki, N., Tolonen, M.: A quantitative study of history in the english short-title catalogue (ESTC) 1470–1800. LIBER Q. **25**, 87–116 (2015). https://doi.org/10.18352/lq.10112
8. Lahti, L., da Silva, F., Laine, M.P., Lhteenoja, V., Tolonen, M.: Alchemy & algorithms: perspectives on the philosophy and history of open science. RIO J. **3**, e13593 (2017). https://doi.org/10.3897/rio.3.e13593
9. Laine, H., Lahti, L., Lehto, A., Ollila, S., Miettinen, M.: Beyond open access - the changing culture of producing and disseminating scientific knowledge. In: Proceedings of the 19th International Academic Mindtrek Conference in Tampere, Finland, September 22–24. AcademicMindTrek'15: Proceedings of the 19th International Academic Mindtrek Conference, ACM, ACM New York, NY, USA (2015). http://dl.acm.org/citation.cfm?id=2818187
10. Leo, L., Juuso, P., J.L., Kainu, M.: rOpenGov: open source ecosystem for computational social sciences and digital humanities (2013). http://ropengov.github.io, ICML/MLOSS workshop (Int'l Conf. on Machine Learning - Open Source Software workshop)
11. McMurdie, J., Holmes, S.: phyloseq: an R package for reproducible interactive analysis and graphics of microbiome census data. PLoS ONE **8**, e61217 (2013). https://doi.org/10.1371/journal.pone.0061217

12. McTaggart, R., Daroczi, G., Leung, C.: Quandl: API wrapper for quandl.com (2015). http://CRAN.R-project.org/package=Quandl, R package version 2.7.0
13. Reinhart, A.: pdfetch: fetch economic and financial time series data from public sources (2015). http://CRAN.R-project.org/package=pdfetch, R package version 0.1.7
14. Salvatier, J., Wiecki, T., Fonnesbeck, C.: Probabilistic programming in Python using PyMC3. PeerJ Comput. Sci. **2**, e55 (2016). https://doi.org/10.7717/peerj-cs.55
15. Toivonen, H., Gross, O.: Data mining and machine learning in computational creativity. Wiley Int. Rev. Data Min. Knowl. Disc. **5**, 265–275 (2015). https://doi.org/10.1002/widm.1170
16. Vanschoren, J., van Rijn, J.N., Bischl, B., Torgo, L.: OpenML: networked science in machine learning. SIGKDD Explor. Newsl. **15**, 49–60 (2014)
17. Weinert, K.: datamart: unified access to your data sources (2014). http://CRAN.R-project.org/package=datamart, R package version 0.5.2
18. Wickham, H.: Tidy data. J. Stat. Softw. **59** (2014). https://doi.org/10.18637/jss.v059.i10
19. Wickham, H.: ggplot2: Elegant Graphics for Data Analysis. Springer, New York (2016). http://ggplot2.org
20. Wickham, H.: tidyverse: easily install and load the 'Tidyverse' (2017). https://CRAN.R-project.org/package=tidyverse, R package

Automatic POI Matching Using an Outlier Detection Based Approach

Alexandre Almeida[1(✉)], Ana Alves[1,2], and Rui Gomes[1]

[1] Universidade de Coimbra, CISUC, Coimbra, Portugal
{acalmeida,ana,ruig}@dei.uc.pt
[2] Instituto Politécnico de Coimbra, ISEC, Coimbra, Portugal

Abstract. Points of Interest (POI) are widely used in many applications nowadays mainly due to the increasing amount of related data available online, notably from volunteered geographic information (VGI) sources. Being able to connect these data from different sources is useful for many things like validating, correcting and also removing duplicated data in a database. However, there is no standard way to identify the same POIs across different sources and doing it manually could be very expensive. Therefore, automatic POI matching has been an attractive research topic. In our work, we propose a novel data-driven machine learning approach based on an outlier detection algorithm to match POIs automatically. Surprisingly, works that have been presented so far do not use data-driven machine learning approaches. The reason for this might be that such approaches need a training dataset to be constructed by manually matching some POIs. To mitigate this, we have taken advantage of the Crosswalk API, available at the time we started our project, which allowed us to retrieve already matched POI data from different sources in US territory. We trained and tested our model with a dataset containing Factual, Facebook and Foursquare POIs from New York City and were able to successfully apply it to another dataset of Facebook and Foursquare POIs from Porto, Portugal, finding matches with an accuracy around 95%. These are encouraging results that confirm our approach as an effective way to address the problem of automatically matching POIs. They also show that such a model can be trained with data available from multiple sources and be applied to other datasets with different locations from those used in training. Furthermore, as a data-driven machine learning approach, the model can be continuously improved by adding new validated data to its training dataset.

Keywords: Machine learning · Outlier detection · Point-Of-Interest
GIS

1 Introduction

POI is a term referring to a point in a map that might represent a relevant location depending on a specific context or interest in a geographic area. With more and more applications using maps or any sort of geographic data, POIs have become increasingly common to represent any potential place of interest in a map to a given user. Another

© Springer Nature Switzerland AG 2018
W. Duivesteijn et al. (Eds.): IDA 2018, LNCS 11191, pp. 40–51, 2018.
https://doi.org/10.1007/978-3-030-01768-2_4

thing that contributes to the increasing utilization of POI information is the amount of related data that has been made available from different sources, notably from VGI and social media applications which provide application programming interfaces (API) to access their data. Although these sources have very useful information, they lack a standard way to identify the same POIs across different sources. Therefore, POI matching emerges as a way to connect POI information from different datasets. This is useful for many applications like confirming or correcting data, enriching the data by complementing it with different information from different sources or removing duplicated data in a database.

Our work is a part of a project called URBY. Sense which aims to study individual's mobility for mining non-routine mobility patterns from multiple data sources. The city we are studying is Porto, Portugal. In the data analysis task of the project we aimed at producing a richer knowledge to understand the choices of mobility. We collected event data from websites that gather events in Porto city and POI data from Facebook, Foursquare and Factual.com. When analyzing this information, one question emerged: are all POIs and events equally important? The answer is that it may depend on their online popularity. Most of the collected events had a link to a Facebook event which, in turn, had a link to a Facebook place. Although this provided us with some popularity information about the places of events, the Foursquare dataset could complement this with more information about popularity as its check-in counts. We also wanted to connect all the POIs from the three different sources in our database for future analyses. But we needed an automatic way to do this connection.

Although an important task, POI matching is difficult, time-consuming and expensive if done manually. Thus, research in automatic approaches of matching POIs have increased in the last years. Contrary to other works, we approach the POI matching problem with a novel data-driven strategy based on a machine learning outlier detection model. By using this approach, instead of experimenting with different weights and rules to create a POI matching algorithm, we create a model that can learn on its own how to match POIs from available data, using previous matched data from different sources as training data. This way, we can also keep improving the model by feeding it with more data as soon as it becomes available. To do this, we take advantage of data collected with the Factual Crosswalk API, an API that was available at the time we started this work and allowed one to translate how place entities are represented across different 3rd party APIs [1]. As the Crosswalk API was available in United States only, we used a dataset of Factual POIs from New York City to create the training dataset for our model. The goal was to create a model that could learn how to match POIs of different sources independently of the country of the data it was trained with, considering only features non-dependent of a country's native-language. Our strategy uses only the metadata that is commonly present in most POI datasets such as name, website, address, category and geographic coordinates, to make it possible to use the model with as many datasets as possible from different sources and locations. Furthermore, it handles missing values, in case that metadata is still not present. In addition, the model was successfully used to connect POIs from Porto in our database, which represents not only a validation of the model but attests its ability to generalize and match POIs of datasets from countries other than the one used to train the model.

We also make publicly available all the datasets and describe the model configuration used in this work so other researchers may benefit from it. All classification tasks such as model train and test are done using the Weka workbench tool [2].

The remainder of this paper is structured as follows. The next section gives a review about related work from POI matching to outlier detection. Section 3 provides a description of the datasets used in this work. Section 4, describes the model created and its experiments. Section 5, discusses the validation of the model. Finally, Sect. 6 concludes this work and provides directions for future research.

2   Related Work

2.1   POI Matching

Users have been contributing useful information about POIs to services and social media applications for some years. This VGI data has become increasingly appealing to explore, but it also brings concerns about its quality and lack of standardization across different datasets. POI matching emerges to address some of this concerns by giving the possibility to correct, complete and enrich information of one POI across different datasets. This makes POI matching an important task in urban studies and applications that rely on POI information and, as a result, many approaches to this problem have been proposed in the literature.

Scheffler et al. [3], presented an algorithm to match POIs from Qype and Facebook Places to their counterparts in Open Street Map. The algorithm had several steps that combined the geographic distance and string similarity of POIs, deciding whether two POIs are a match based on some defined thresholds. They achieved an overall accuracy of 79% for Qype and 64% for Facebook. McKenzie et al. [4], proposed three distinct weighted POI matching models based on multiple attributes like name, category, geographic location and descriptive text of POIs from Foursquare and Yelp, achieving a match-accuracy of 97% in their model evaluation. They have also showed that individually the name outperformed all other attributes. Novack et al. [5], presented a graph-based matching of POIs from OpenStreetMap and Foursquare in the city of London, approaching the issue of one-to-none and one-to-many matches. Their best matching result achieved an overall accuracy of 91%. Li et al. [6] proposed an entropy-weighted approach to POI matching by integrating heterogeneous attributes with the allocation of suitable attribute weights via information entropy. They showed that their best model had a F1 value between 0.8 and 0.9. Dalvi et al. [7] presented a language model that encapsulated both domain knowledge as well as local geographical knowledge and introduced an unsupervised learning problem to assign weights to words in POI names to remove duplicated entries from a database of places. They were able to achieve an accurate deduplication with a recall of 90% at a precision of 90%. Yu et al. [8] used an approach based on semantic technologies to automate the geospatial data conflation process for use in the emergency services response domain. They considered only shopping center POIs and showed a conflation accuracy of 98%.

Although they may use some unsupervised or supervised learning methods to generate attributes or weights for a model, to the best of our knowledge, there is no study that tries to use a data-driven machine learning approach to build a decision or classification model that can learn to automatically predict POI matches based on training datasets with previously matched POIs.

2.2 Outlier Detection

Although there is no universally accepted definition, an outlier could be defined as an observation outside the limits of a well characterized population. Therefore, by characterizing normal observations we decide what is considered abnormal. Sometimes, depending on the domain and approach used, authors describe their various approaches to outlier detection as novelty detection, anomaly detection, noise detection, deviation detection or exception mining, all being fundamentally identical [9]. Outlier detection has thus been found to be applicable in a large number of domains like intrusion detection, fraud detection, industrial damage detection, image processing, medical and pharmaceutical research, among many others [9–11]. Outlier detection algorithms have also been used for automatic verification and identifying wrong links between datasets [12, 13] as a post-process step to entity linking systems, but to the best of our knowledge, they have not been used as an approach to create the actual links.

Outlier detection algorithms based on machine learning need a training dataset to build an explicit predictive model. If the training dataset has no labels we have an unsupervised learning problem. Often, unsupervised algorithms assume that data instances with a frequently occurring pattern or closely related are normal examples while the remaining are considered outliers. In semi-supervised learning, only one class of the training dataset is labeled which represents a special case of one class classification also known as novelty detection [14]. Such techniques model only the available class and then test if further observations can fit to the initial population. When both the normal and abnormal classes are labeled in the training dataset we have a supervised scenario. If both classes are balanced, we have a binary classification problem and an accurate model can be created. But that is often not the case, which originates a highly unbalanced classification problem. In such a scenario both one-class and binary classifiers can be used. Bellinger et al. [15], conducted experiments on various datasets to investigate the performance of binary and one-class classifiers as the level of imbalance and uncertainty increased by purposely decreasing the size of the outlier class. They concluded that as the level of imbalance increases, the performance of binary classifiers decreases, whereas one-class classifiers stay relatively stable. Despite this, they state that their findings do not imply that binary classifiers should not be used if there is imbalance present as, even with a decent level of imbalance, certain binary classifiers can come up with effective decision boundaries. In the case of our work, our concern with the outlier examples is more related with their quality rather than their quantity. That is because we have examples of matching POIs for the target class but would have to find a strategy to generate the outlier examples. One strategy could be to generate random pairs of POIs and confirm that they are not matches. However, the generated examples might not be good outlier representatives, which is important in case of binary classification to avoid over-fitting. Therefore, using an algorithm that can use only the matching examples to train seems a better approach to this kind of problem.

3   Description of the Datasets

In this section we describe the datasets created to train, test and validate our POI matching model. For each POI we have selected five attributes: name, website, address, category and geographic coordinates (latitude and longitude). Because we want the model to be able to match POIs from any dataset, these attributes were chosen for being the most commonly available attributes in a POI dataset. Since the datasets used in the model refer to POI pairs, each attribute of the datasets will be a partial distance between each attribute of two POIs, which results in a total of five attributes or features. The datasets also include POI ids, for each source, which are ignored by the classifier algorithm. This is done to track the POIs of each pair later in the validation phase. The detailed constitution of the datasets is described in Table 1.

Table 1. Number of instances for each attribute in each dataset.

Attribute	Training dataset (NY)		Testing dataset (NY)	Validation dataset (Porto)
	All	No missing		
Name	8004	2473	16008	394944
Website	2547	2473	4461	19224
Address	7094	2473	14146	175938
Category	7791	2473	15562	394944
Geographic distance	7961	2473	15925	394944
Target	8004	2473	8004	–
Outlier	0	0	8004	–
Total	8004	2473	16008	394944

3.1   New York Dataset

In order to create our model's training dataset, we have used the Factual Crosswalk API to connect POIs from Factual with their counterparts in Facebook and Foursquare. Using a Factual ID, the API gave us the ID of the POI in other sources, when available. By doing so, we retrieved a sample of Factual POIs connected with Facebook and/or Foursquare and stored that information in the crosswalk table of our database. Then we used each source API to retrieve the necessary metadata for each POI of the table, storing that metadata in separate tables. Finally, we create the dataset by adding pairs from each Factual and Foursquare connection, as well as from each Factual and Facebook connection and from each Foursquare and Facebook connection. The only requirement for forming a pair of POIs was that both had at least a name. This resulted in a dataset with 8004 instances, being 5798 Factual and Foursquare pairs, 1703 Factual and Facebook pairs and 503 Foursquare and Facebook pairs. These instances represent the "target" or matching examples that will train our POI matching model. We have also created a training dataset with no missing values by removing each instance with one or more missing attributes. This resulted in a dataset with 2473 instances, with all attributes having the same number of instances.

We have also generated an equal number of non-matching POI pairs (the outlier instances) to test the model. To do this, we opted for a simple approach of forming POI pairs from two random POIs of the crosswalk table and then confirm if the pair was not a match in table. This way, we generated a dataset with a total of 16008 instances, 8004 matching pairs and 8004 non-matching pairs for testing purposes.

3.2 Porto Dataset

In order to create the dataset to validate the POI matching model, we have combined the facebook places table with the foursquare venues table of our database. The facebook places table has 132 entries that represent the places of events in Porto city collected for our project for a given month of study. This represents the number of events that provided links to a Facebook Place. We used the Facebook API to obtain the required metadata for those places. The foursquare venues table has 2992 entries that represent venues around certain geographic coordinates of Porto city and were collected using the foursquare API. Combining those two resulted in a dataset with 394944 POI pairs. This is the dataset used to automatically test matches between our Facebook and Foursquare database tables and validate the trained model in Porto city.

4 Model Description

In our classification model, we use the Isolation Forest (iForest) algorithm [16] available in Weka (3.19) with its default parameters. iForest works by assuming that outliers are few and different and, for that reason, easier to isolate than normal examples. It is by nature an unsupervised machine learning method as it does not require one to label the training data. Despite this, we can use it in cases where the training dataset only has "target" instances like we would do with a semi-supervised method. We preferred this method for two main reasons. First, although we assume that the crosswalk data used is correct (only has matching examples), it is possible that some outliers exist in the dataset. We cannot confirm this as it would be extremely costly to do so. But either if they are or not, the good thing about iForest is that it can handle the two scenarios very well. Therefore, it is ideal for our training dataset. Second, the iForest algorithm has demonstrated to have very good performance in outlier detection as the results of several comparative studies showed [16–18]. Furthermore, it has high computational efficiency, having a linear time complexity with a low constant and a low memory requirement.

One drawback of iForest is that it does not handle missing values. To address this, we use the Expectation Maximization (EM) Imputation method [19] also available in Weka. An EM method should be better than simple methods like mean imputation because it preserves the relationship between variables, using other variables to impute an expected value and maximize its likelihood. EM imputation methods have also shown good results in previous works against other imputation methods [20, 21].

4.1 Feature Engineering

In order to derive the partial distance between POIs, the model is based on five dimensions: name, website, address, category and geographic coordinates. We have computed the 2D Cartesian distance between the geographic coordinates, directly from our PostgreSQL database to generate the geographic distance between the POIs. We have also used and compared several string similarity methods available in different python libraries [22–24] to compute the distances between the name, website, address and category. To make the model language independent, we have only used string similarity methods, avoiding phonetic algorithms like soundex or metaphone and other methods that make use of lexic databases like wordnet. The methods used range from classic distance measures like Levenshtein [25], Jaccard [26], Sorensen [27] and Jaro-Winkler [28, 29] to fuzzy methods like the Ratio, Partial Ratio, Token Sort Ratio (TSoR) and Token Set Ratio (TSeR) [30]. We use two variants of the Jaro-Winkler method, one uses only the Jaro measure (jarowinkler_f) and the other uses the Winkler addition with a scale of 0.1 (jarowinkler_t). Complementing our list, we have computed the average between a case insensitive partial ratio and a sort ratio (avg partial sort ratio or APSR) which tries to emphasize partial matches between strings without giving it total merit and the average between the sort ratio and set ratio (avg sort set ratio) which tries to balance this two methods as the later might be too flexible.

After computing all the above distances, we have tested them individually with the iForest classifier, to select which distances we should use for each attribute. Although accuracy is a common measure when evaluating supervised classification algorithms, it might not be the best in other scenarios like outlier detection problems. In these cases, the area under the Receiver Operating Characteristic (ROC) curve seems to be a much more utilized and accepted measure to evaluate the performance of outlier and novelty detection algorithms [16–18, 31]. When a model has a ROC of 0.5 it is similar to a random guess classifier. When it achieves a ROC of 1 it means that it can clearly distinguish between targets and outliers. Thus, to produce the best model we tried to maximize its ROC value. In Table 2, we show the resulting best distance in terms of ROC for each attribute. These results indicate how each attribute can contribute to the model. As can be seen, the name attribute obtains the best results with a ROC of 0.99. Category is the worst performing attribute which might be explained by the lack of standardization between sources for representing POI categories. With a ROC near 0.55, the category attribute seems to be ineffective to do any meaningful decision on its own. This also means that simple string similarity is not enough to extract relevant information for the category attribute. The geographic distance is the second best performing attribute. The fact that it was surpassed by the name attribute might indicate that the geographic information contributed to these platforms often have more inaccuracies than the POI name. This might be due to the inaccuracy of mobile devices or inaccuracies when introducing information that later is geocoded. The address and website attributes are the third and fourth best results respectively. Despite the good results these two attributes have greater percentage of missing values. This means that their contribution when combining them with other attributes might be diminished as the model will not have their information in most cases.

Table 2. Individual attribute performance.

Attribute	Best distance	Accuracy	ROC
Name	Avg partial sort ratio	0.727	0.990
Website	Avg partial sort ratio	0.769	0.927
Address	Partial ratio	0.892	0.953
Category	Sorensen	0.516	0.545
Geographic distance		0.928	0.968

After computing the best performing distances for each attribute individually, we have created a model with them together. Although this should give good results, selecting the attributes that individually give the best ROC might not create the model with the best ROC. For that reason, we decided to test all possible combinations of each distance for each attribute, choosing the combination that produced the model with the best ROC. This way we can ensure that the resulting model uses the combination of attributes that best maximizes its ROC value. Besides testing all combinations, we have also tested two different training approaches for each combination. In the first approach, we used the entire training dataset. In the second approach we use the training dataset without instances with missing values. This means that only 2473 instances were used for training in the second approach instead of 8004, but testing was done with the full testing dataset which has 16008 instances for both approaches. Table 3 shows the performance of the models.

Table 3. Performance of different models.

Model	Attribute distances (besides geo distance)				Training dataset	Accuracy	ROC
	Name	Website	Address	Category			
Each best individual attribute combination	APSR	APSR	Partial ratio	Sorensen	All	0.925	0.990
					No miss	0.882	0.994
Best attribute combination for all instances	Token set ratio	Partial ratio	Partial ratio	Jarowinkler_f	All	0.927	0.995
					No miss	0.906	0.996
Best attribute combination for no missing instances	Token set ratio	Token sort ratio	APSR	Token set ratio	All	0.925	0.992
					No miss	0.883	0.997

Not surprisingly, the best combination of attributes obtained by computing all possible combinations is different from the combination using the best individual attributes. One interesting finding is that the models trained only with instances with no missing values performed better than the ones trained with all instances for any of the feature combinations used. The degradation of the model's performance when using all instances might be due to the lack of quality resulting from artificially filling the missing values with the EM imputation method or due to the lack of quality of the remaining available values of POI examples that have missing values. Either case, these results seem to indicate that POI examples with missing values are less reliable than the ones with all attributes available and should be avoided in training. The model that achieves the best ROC is the best combination of features for the training dataset without missing values (3rd Model). Therefore, it is the model we choose to proceed with the validation in our Porto dataset.

5 Model Validation

Once we have trained and tested our model we performed its validation using the already described Porto dataset. By using such a different dataset from the training one we are not only validating the model's ability to match POIs from different sources but also its ability to match POIs from different geographic areas from those used in training, while using it to connect our database of POIs from the city of Porto.

The process of validation was done by manually analyzing the classification results given by the model by verifying if two POIs where correctly predicted as match (True Positive – TP) or outlier (True Negative – TN). The model returned 141 matches from 394944 POI pairs present in the validation dataset. Besides reviewing these matches, we selected outliers with a geographic distance below or equal 100 meters and then select the 1000 outliers with the higher name similarity. This resulted in a dataset with 1141 instances to review.

When manually reviewing these instances, we decided to consider 3 validation scenarios. In the first scenario we consider to be a match only POIs that correspond exactly to each other. In a second scenario we also consider to be a match a place that is included in the other. In a third scenario we also consider to be a match places that are related and nearby. Examples of the second scenario might be: a university department matching the university to which it belongs; a bar, shop or theater matching a shopping center that contains them. As for scenario 3 it might be: a match between a region or street and places in that region or street; a match between a bus stop nearby a particular place it serves.

In the Table 4 we present the results for our 3 validation scenarios. Depending on the matching scenario, one need to consider which approach is more suitable to one's needs, a stricter definition of a match or a broader one. In our case, we ended up using the broader matching results (scenario 3) as it might also be useful to connect places that are related and nearby an event. Despite this, the best results for the model were obtained when considering the stricter scenario 1, while the worst results were obtained when considering the broader scenario 3. Nonetheless, all scenarios present very good validation results for the model, as Table 4 shows.

Besides showing good overall matching results, the model also shows a natural capacity to identity related places and POIs represented multiple times. As can be seen in Fig. 1, when considering the validation scenario 1, we have a higher percentage of one-to-one (1 − 1) matches and less one-to-many (1 − N) matches. When considering scenario 2 and 3 we can observe an increase in the number of 1 − N matches being detected but also much higher matches being falsely detected as outliers which might

Table 4. Validation results for the model according to the 3 validation methodologies used

Validation scenario	Match		Outlier		Accuracy	ROC
	TP	FP	TN	FN		
1	85	56	995	5	0.947	0.975
2	112	29	929	71	0.912	0.848
3	122	19	919	81	0.912	0.846

explain the worse results obtained by scenario 2 and 3. Despite this, these two scenarios obtain more true matches (TP) which in some cases is better even though we also get more false outliers (FN).

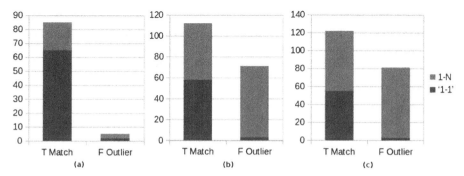

Fig. 1. Validation results per matching relation one-to-one $(1 - 1)$ and one-to-many $(1 - N)$ for validation scenario 1(a), scenario 2(b) and scenario 3(c).

6 Conclusions and Future Work

In this paper we presented a data-driven approach to automatically match POIs from different sources based on an outlier detection machine learning model. To do this we have taken advantage of the Crosswalk API available at the time we started our work and were able to retrieve matching POIs from different sources in US territory. We trained our model with a dataset of Factual, Facebook and Foursquare POIs from New York and were able to successfully apply it to our dataset of Facebook and Foursquare POIs from Porto, finding matches with an accuracy close to 95%.

We think that the results presented in this work support our approach as an effective way to tackle the problem of automatically matching POIs. They show that such a model can be trained with data available from different sources and be applied to other datasets even from different locations. Furthermore, as this is a data-driven machine learning approach, the model can be continuously improved by adding new validated data to its training dataset. Although manual validation of POI matches could be expensive, it is many times inevitable. Therefore, taking advantage of already validated data to create or improve a model that can automatically match POIs seems to be a good idea. Besides strictly matching exact or same POIs, we find that the model is very good at finding related POIs when we accept matches with less certainty outputs. This can be useful in many scenarios like, for example, POI search engines, suggesting other relevant POIs, etc. In these cases, such a model can also produce good results.

Nevertheless, there is room for improvement to this approach. We need to take in consideration that the data we used for training the model might have errors. As these models rely heavily on the quality of the data used for training them, we believe that with a reduced but hand validated dataset the results would be even better. In future work it could be interesting to not only ensure the quality of the training data but also add more validated data from different sources and locations to the training dataset. Besides that, experimenting with more POI metadata and better methods to extract relevant information from them should be very beneficial to improve the model performance. Experimenting with different outlier detection algorithms should also be considered.

Acknowledgement. The authors would like to thank the funding by URBY.SENSE project (POCI-01-0145-FEDER-016848). URBY.SENSE is co-financed by COMPETE 2020, Portugal 2020 - Programa Operacional Competitividade e Internacionalização (POCI), Fundo Europeu de Desenvolvimento Regional (FEDER) and Fundação para a Ciência e a Tecnologia (FCT).

References

1. Factual| Crosswalk API. https://www.factual.com/blog/crosswalk-api/
2. Hall, M., Frank, E., Holmes, G., Pfahringer, B., Reutemann, P., Witten, I.H.: The WEKA data mining software: an update. SIGKDD Explor. Newsl. **11**, 10–18 (2009)
3. Scheffler, T., Schirru, R., Lehmann, P.: Matching points of interest from different social networking sites. In: Glimm, B., Krüger, A. (eds.) KI 2012. LNCS (LNAI), vol. 7526, pp. 245–248. Springer, Heidelberg (2012). https://doi.org/10.1007/978-3-642-33347-7_24
4. McKenzie, G., Janowicz, K., Adams, B.: A weighted multi-attribute method for matching user-generated points of interest. Cartogr. Geogr. Inf. Sci. **41**, 125–137 (2014)
5. Novack, T., Peters, R., Zipf, A.: Graph-based matching of points-of-interest from collaborative geo-datasets. ISPRS Int. J. Geo-Inf. **7**, 117 (2018)
6. Li, L., Xing, X., Xia, H., Huang, X.: Entropy-weighted instance matching between different sourcing points of interest. Entropy **18**, 45 (2016)
7. Dalvi, N., Olteanu, M., Raghavan, M., Bohannon, P.: Deduplicating a places database. In: Proceedings of the 23rd International Conference on World Wide Web, WWW 2014, pp. 409–418 (2014)
8. Yu, F., McMeekin, David A., Arnold, L., West, G.: Semantic web technologies automate geospatial data conflation: conflating points of interest data for emergency response services. In: Kiefer, P., Huang, H., Van de Weghe, N., Raubal, M. (eds.) LBS 2018. LNGC, pp. 111–131. Springer, Cham (2018). https://doi.org/10.1007/978-3-319-71470-7_6
9. Hodge, V., Austin, J.: A survey of outlier detection methodologies. Artif. Intell. Rev. **22**, 85–126 (2004)
10. Chandola, V., Banerjee, A., Kumar, V.: Outlier detection: a survey (2007)
11. Beldar, Alka P., Wadne, Vinod S.: The detail survey of anomaly/outlier detection methods in data mining. Int. J. Multidiscip. Curr. Res. (2015)

12. Heinzerling, B., Strube, M., Lin, C.-Y.: Trust, but verify! Better entity linking through automatic verification. In: Proceedings of the 15th Conference of the European Chapter of the Association for Computational Linguistics: Volume 1, Long Papers, pp. 828–838. Association for Computational Linguistics, Valencia, Spain (2017)

13. Paulheim, H.: Identifying wrong links between datasets by multi-dimensional outlier detection. In: CEUR Workshop Proceedings, vol. 1162, pp. 27–38 (2014)

14. Pimentel, M.A.F., Clifton, D.A., Clifton, L., Tarassenko, L.: A review of novelty detection. Signal Process. **99**, 215–249 (2014)

15. Bellinger, C., Sharma, S., Japkowicz, N.: One-class versus binary classification: which and when? In: 2012 11th International Conference on Machine Learning and Applications, pp. 102–106 (2012)

16. Liu, F.T., Ting, K.M., Zhou, Z.-H.: Isolation-based anomaly detection. ACM Trans. Knowl. Discov. Data. **6**, 1–39 (2012)

17. Domingues, R., Filippone, M., Michiardi, P., Zouaoui, J.: A comparative evaluation of outlier detection algorithms: experiments and analyses. Pattern Recognit. **74**, 406–421 (2018)

18. Tun, J.S.: Semi-supervised outlier detection algorithms. https://escholarship.org/uc/item/1f03f6hb (2018)

19. Schafer, J.L.: Analysis of Incomplete Multivariate Data. CRC Press (1997)

20. Alkan, B.B., Alkan, N., Atakan, C., Terzi, Y.: Use of biplot technique for the comparison of the missing value imputation methods. Int. J. Data Anal. Tech. Strat. **7**, 217–230 (2015)

21. Ghorbani, S., Desmarais, M.C.: Performance comparison of recent imputation methods for classification tasks over binary data. Appl. Artif. Intell. **31**, 1–22 (2017)

22. Doukremt: Levenshtein and Hamming distance computation. https://github.com/doukremt/distance

23. Ratté, J.-B.: Jaro-winkler-distance: find the Jaro Winkler distance which indicates the similarity score between two strings. https://github.com/nap/jaro-winkler-distance

24. Fuzzywuzzy: fuzzy string matching in Python. https://github.com/seatgeek/fuzzywuzzy

25. Levenshtein, V.I.: Binary codes capable of correcting deletions. Inser. Reversals. Sov. Phys. Dokl. **10**, 707 (1966)

26. Jaccard, P.: Étude comparative de la distribution florale dans une portion des Alpes et des Jura. Bull. del la Société Vaud. Sci. Naturelles **37**, 547–579 (1901)

27. Sørensen, T.J.: A method of establishing groups of equal amplitude in plant sociology based on similarity of species content and its application to analyses of the vegetation on Danish commons. I kommission hos E. Munksgaard, København (1948)

28. Jaro, M.A.: Advances in record-linkage methodology as applied to matching the 1985 census of Tampa, Florida. J. Am. Stat. Assoc. **84**, 414–420 (1989)

29. Winkler, W.E.: String comparator metrics and enhanced decision rules in the Fellegi-Sunter model of record linkage (1990)

30. FuzzyWuzzy: fuzzy string matching in Python – ChairNerd. http://chairnerd.seatgeek.com/fuzzywuzzy-fuzzy-string-matching-in-python/

31. Ratle, F., Kanevski, M., Terrettaz-Zufferey, A.-L., Esseiva, P., Ribaux, O.: A comparison of one-class classifiers for novelty detection in forensic case data. In: Yin, H., Tino, P., Corchado, E., Byrne, W., Yao, X. (eds.) IDEAL 2007. LNCS, vol. 4881, pp. 67–76. Springer, Heidelberg (2007). https://doi.org/10.1007/978-3-540-77226-2_8

Fact Checking from Natural Text with Probabilistic Soft Logic

Nouf Bindris[✉], Saatviga Sudhahar, and Nello Cristianini

Department of Computer Science, University of Bristol, Bristol, UK
{nouf.bindris,saatviga.sudhahar,nello.cristianini}@bristol.ac.uk

Abstract. We demonstrate a method to support fact-checking of statements found in natural text such as online news, encyclopedias or academic repositories, by detecting if they violate knowledge that is implicitly present in a reference corpus. The method combines the use of information extraction techniques with probabilistic reasoning, allowing for inferences to be performed starting from natural text. We present two case studies, one in the domain of verifying claims about family relations, the other about political relations. This allows us to contrast the case where ground truth is available about the relations and the rules that can be applied to them (families) with the case where neither relations nor rules are clear cut (politics).

Keywords: Fact checking · Information extraction · Probabilistic soft logic

1 Introduction

The vast availability of information on the web, its incompleteness, inconsistencies and the speed with which it spreads, have recently brought the need for identifying fake information. Detecting if an assertion is true or false is a tall order for an algorithm, as it may also be for a person, except for special cases where the assertion directly contradicts a known fact. Yet we expect algorithms to help us weed out fake news stories from online media [7,18]. Fact checking, once the domain of journalists and editors, and now the realm of specialists, remains a time consuming and specialised task. We are interested in the situation where assertions must be assessed by an algorithm, without requiring an authoritative source of truth (a controversial requirement in the case of the press).

We will focus on assertions that we consider "implausible" because they implicitly conflict with a number of other statements present in a corpus of reference. For example, if all newspapers report various statements placing Hillary Clinton in the "pro-choice" camp of a debate, a single news item placing her in the "pro-life" camp would require further fact checking, and be deemed implausible, but not necessarily false. This approach allows us to handle statements that

W. Duivesteijn et al. (Eds.): IDA 2018, LNCS 11191, pp. 52–61, 2018.
https://doi.org/10.1007/978-3-030-01768-2_5

contain some degree of judgement, and not just expressions of facts, because we focus on the compatibility or internal consistency of large numbers of claims. In this paper we take the view that human fact checkers can benefit from a method which flags statements that do not naturally fit with a knowledge base, a corpus, or a set of rules, and are therefore implausible, or surprising. This could provide at least some degree of protection in the news ecosystem. Note that similar tools can be useful in many other scenarios, besides screening news in social media, for example they can be used to help curate large projects like Wikipedia, identifying claims in one page that conflict with claims in other pages.

The technical question of this paper is: how can we use techniques from information extraction and probabilistic reasoning to check facts that are implicit in a set of documents written in natural language? How can we decide if a claim is compatible with other claims, i.e. can it be true when the others are also true? Another way to formulate this question is: can we extract information that is not explicitly stated, but is implicitly present, in a set of documents?

We use two case studies to demonstrate the approach: one based on statements of fact and the other based on judgements. In the first case, we rely on natural language descriptions of the British Royal Family, and on facts about family relations, to extract the actual relations between members of the family, and use them to fact-check claims about further family relations (e.g. Who is whose cousin?). In the second case, we rely on news accounts of the 2012 US Elections, and general assumptions about how political relations work, to extract or check information about the political position of certain actors (e.g. Who supports which issue in the debate?). Technically, we make use of GATE [4] for information extraction, and Probabilistic Soft Logic [9] for inference. The documents are parsed, the named entities and their relations are extracted from natural language, then they are provided to the reasoning module that uses a knowledge base to see if a given claim is compatible with the rest.

In Sect. 2 we discuss related work in the domain of fact checking. In Sect. 3 we present Probabilistic Soft Logic (PSL) as a method of inference. In Sect. 4 we demonstrate our approach in the case of checking Family Relations. In Sect. 5 we demonstrate the approach in the case of checking Political Relations and in Sect. 6 we discuss limitations and future work.

2   Related Work

Several automated fact-checking systems [1,6,7,18] have been developed and used in real-world scenarios, such as monitoring false claims during the primary and general election debates throughout the 2016 U.S. elections. Given a claim, it is checked by first collecting supporting or opposing evidence from knowledge bases and the web, generate questions/queries related to the claim and a final answer derived and presented to the user based on discrepancies between the returned answers and the claim.

Fact checking numerical claims has also been studied in recent times. For example, Vlachos and Riedel [16] focused on fact checking simple numerical claims such as "population of Germany in 2015 was 80 million". They used distant supervision for identification and verification of claims to fact check 16 numerical properties of countries (such as population etc.). Input claims were matched with entries in a knowledge base and verdicts were deduced. In the follow-up work, they extended the system to include temporal expressions, so that the temporal context of the claim could be taken into account [15].

Recent work has used Markov Logic Networks to reason about the world under uncertainty, answering questions such as "According to sources A and B, is Mr. Doe euro-sceptic?" [10,11]. Their algorithms support the task of extracting information about the facts from various sources and fact checking the claims against background data although it was not tested on real-world data. Work by Patwari et al. [12] discusses a system to identify check-worthy statements in political debates which needs to be fact-checked using a multi-classifier system that models latent groupings in data. These statements may not be explicitly mentioned in the text but they are check-worthy. From the statement, "We need the private sectors help, because government is not innovating" they identify a check-worthy claim such as "the U.S. government is not innovating". Natural language summaries of relational databases have also been fact-checked in a semi-automatic way using probabilistic modelling that identifies erroneous claims in articles from major newspapers [8]. The limitation in their work is that it requires humans to check the interpretations of the system and correct it if it was wrong.

In contrast, we check claims that are not explicitly stated in the text corpus. Using a knowledge base of extracted facts from various sources and first order logic rules we infer information that is implicit in text. We focus on detecting claims that can be considered as not plausible, in that they implicitly contradict background knowledge, assumptions or other claims contained in a reference corpus.

3   Probabilistic Soft Logic

Probabilistic soft logic (PSL) [9] is a framework that allows users to specify rich probabilistic models over continuous-valued random variables using first-order logic to describe features that define a Markov network similar to statistical relational learning languages such as Markov Logic Networks (MLNs). User-defined predicates model relationships and attributes and first-order logic rules model dependencies or constraints on these predicates in a PSL program. A PSL program consists of a set of predicates, weighted rules involving these predicates, and known truth values of ground atoms derived from observed data. Inference for the PSL program is over the remaining unknown truth values. PSL uses the most probable explanation (MPE) inference which is to find the most probable interpretation given evidence, that is, the most likely interpretation extending a given partial interpretation [9]. Given a set of atoms $l = \{l_1, ...l_n\}$, we call the mapping $I : l \rightarrow \{0,1\}^n$ from atoms to *soft truth* values an *interpretation*.

Soft logic is mathematically represented in PSL using the Lukasiewicz t-norm as the relaxation of the logical AND and OR, respectively. These relaxations are exact at points, when variables are either true(1.0) or false (0.0), and provide a consistent interpretation for values in-between. The probability distribution defined by a PSL program measures the overall distance to satisfaction, which is a function of all ground rules truth values.

A PSL program containing a set of rules and ground atoms induces a distribution over interpretations I given by,

$$f(I) = \frac{1}{Z} exp[-\sum_{r \in R} \lambda_r (d_r(I))^p] \tag{1}$$

where λ_r is the weight of the rule r, Z is a normalization constant and $p \in \{1, 2\}$ provides a choice of two different loss functions. $p = 1$ refers to satisfying one rule while $p = 2$ refers to satisfying all rules to some extent. These probabilistic models are said to be instances of Hinge-loss Markov random fields [2]. In our work, we use PSL because it's proven to be scalable and it works with continuous truth values which is useful for different modelling problems.

4   Fact Checking Family Relations

In this study we use a long BBC news article describing kinship of the members in the royal family[1]. This includes a Royal Family tree and line of succession beginning from Queen Elizabeth II to Prince George. We automatically extract information from this article about family relations from the Royal Family such as Parent and Spouse. For example we extract,

Charles is the **Parent** of William
William is the **Spouse** of Kate

We build a knowledge base with the facts extracted and use logical rules in PSL to infer relationships not mentioned in text. How we extract facts is explained in Sect. 4.1. We then fact check claims about the Royal Family. PSL is a system for collective inference and therefore it can collectively infer new relationships according to logical rules specified. Eventually, we can check our claims against the system. If the result for the claim was already inferred by PSL the system returns the verdict, a binary value 0 (False) or 1 (True). If not the fact from the claim is added to PSL targets and the result is inferred. In the following sections we explain how we automatically extract facts from text, infer new relations not mentioned in text and then fact check similar claims.

4.1   Fact Extraction

We use ANNIE, a Nearly-New IE system in GATE [4], an open source platform for text engineering in order to extract named entities with their gender from text. We chose to use GATE since its simple, scalable and easily customisable

---

[1] Royal Family tree and line of succession: http://www.bbc.co.uk/news/uk-23272491.

with the use of JAPE grammars and Gazetteer lists. We do co-reference resolution, which is the process of determining whether two expressions in natural
language refer to the same entity in the world [13]. For example, Queen Elizabeth
II and Queen refer to the same entity. The Orthomatcher module in the ANNIE
Information extraction system in GATE [13] is used to perform this task. We
resolve pronouns to their referring entity names using the Pronominal resolution
module. The system resolves pronouns such as 'he', 'she', 'his', 'him' and 'her'
to their referring entity names. JAPE grammars are used to extract patterns of
Parent and Spouse relations. For example, the grammar shown below says if a
Person entity is followed by the word 'child' or 'son' or 'daughter' which is then
followed by the word 'of' followed by a Person entity, the first person refers to
a Parent entity. Therefore, the system annotates the relation as Parent relation.
{Tokens} refer to pronouns and stop words that could occur inbetween.

$$Person, \{Tokens\}, Token == (\text{``child''} \mid \text{``son''} \mid \text{``daughter''}),$$
$$Token == \text{``of''}, Person$$

Similarly we annotate Spouse relations if a Person entity is followed by the word
'married' or 'wife' or 'husband' which is then followed by another Person entity.

$$Person, \{Tokens\}, Token == (\text{``married''} \mid \text{``wife''} \mid \text{``husband''}),$$
$$\{Tokens\}, Person$$

We extracted 16 female names, 12 male names, 10 Parent relations and 7
Spouse relations from the article and this information was added to our knowledge base in PSL. In the next step we use logical rules to infer relations not
explicitly mentioned in text.

4.2   Inferring Relations

From the extracted family relations, we infer relations that were not explicitly
mentioned in text such as Cousins, Sisters, Brothers, Siblings, Uncle, Aunt, Niece
and Nephew. Examples of a few logical rules we used to infer relations Cousins,
Siblings, Uncle, Aunt and Nephew are shown below.

$$Parent(X, B) \wedge Parent(X, A) \wedge (A \neg = B) \Rightarrow Siblings(A, B)$$
$$Parent(X, B) \wedge Parent(Y, A) \wedge Siblings(X, Y) \Rightarrow Cousins(A, B)$$
$$Parent(X, B) \wedge Siblings(X, Y) \wedge Female(Y) \Rightarrow Aunt(Y, B)$$
$$Parent(X, B) \wedge Siblings(X, Y) \wedge Male(Y) \Rightarrow Uncle(Y, B)$$
$$Parent(X, B) \wedge Siblings(X, Y) \wedge Male(B) \Rightarrow Nephew(B, Y)$$

The first rule infers Siblings, saying that if X is the Parent of B and X is
also the Parent of A and A and B are different people then B and A should be
Siblings. The second rule says A and B are Cousins if X is the Parent of B, and
Y is the Parent of A, X and Y are siblings. The third rule says if X is the Parent
of B and X is the sibling of Y and Y is a Female then Y is the Aunt of B. The
fourth rule infers Uncle relation and fifth Nephew relation.

PSL uses MPE inference to infer information, which is to find the most probable interpretation given evidence but also provides a lazy implementation of the algorithm. We use the Lazy MPE inference in PSL which allows to specify only the required targets for inference and uses less memory.

4.3   Fact Checking

In total the system inferred the following number of relations from text: 10 Cousins, 7 Uncles, 3 Aunts, 11 Siblings, 4 Nephews and 6 Nieces. We checked if the inferred relations were correct by manually checking the family tree given in the article, and all of them were correct.

When a new fact needs to be checked about family relations, it is checked against relations that are inferred already by PSL. If it was already inferred, the Verdict True or False is returned. Otherwise the fact is added to the target list in PSL, which then initiates the inference process and returns a result. Following examples show how a claim regarding Cousins and Nephew relation is converted to a target, added to PSL and how the Verdict True or False is returned.

Claim : " Is Prince William the Cousin of Princess Euginie"
Target : Cousin(Prince William, Princess Euginie)
Verdict : 1.0/True

Claim : "Is Prince William the Nephew of Princess Beatrice"
Target : Nephew(Prince William, Princess Beatrice)
Verdict := 0.0/False

5   Fact Checking Political Relations

In this study we infer and fact check political relations among actors in a political network generated from 130,213 English news articles about 2012 US Elections. This involves fact checking supporting or opposing views of Political actors towards other actors and issues. Data collection was done via extraction of news articles using a modular media content analysis system [5] containing US and International media and training a topic classifier to classify election articles.

5.1   Fact Extraction

We extract subject-verb-object (SVO) triplets from the election news collection via a fully automated pipeline [14] that performs named entity detection, co-reference and anaphora resolution before the triplet extraction. In the triplets, subjects and objects are named entities or noun phrases (issues) and the verb expresses a positive or negative attitude between the subjects and objects in the political discourse. The number of triplets are reduced in size after filtering high confidence triplets and they are used to create positively and negatively weighted relations between actors. We make use of positive and negative verb lists to count a triplets as a vote in favour of a positive or negative attitude and calculate a weight for the relation between actors. Verb lists denoting political support/opposition were manually created by going through actions in triplets that were extracted from the elections corpus and labelling then positive or negative. When quantifying the weight of a relation between actors a and b a confidence interval [17] around the estimate of the value is also considered. Based on computed confidence intervals, we extract relations that are sufficiently supported by the corpus, calculate positive and negative weights and use them to assemble a network consisting nodes representing actors/issues and edges representing the weights ranging from $[-1 +1]$. From this network we use structural balance [3] rules to infer political relations among actors and between actors and issues using PSL.

Structural balance can at most give us plausibility of a claim, as it is not an exact relation like family relations. An inferred political relation will have a weight corresponding to the level of support or opposition between actors in the relation conveying how plausible it is.

5.2   Inferring Relations

In order to prove that we could infer political relations among actors from the network, we remove a few links from it and use the remaining relations to predict the removed links. We want to see when 5%, 10% or even 20% of the links are removed from the network can we still infer them using the remaining observed relations. Since we have the truth values for the removed links we also evaluate the performance of the system. The network used for this study contains 169 nodes and 238 links with weights in the interval $[-1,1]$. To make this appropriate for the PSL framework, weights were normalized to $[0,1]$ interval. First, we carefully select the number of links that should be removed from the network. This involves the links that connect nodes with a degree greater than or equal to 2 so that we do not introduce singletons in the network when links are removed. In total we quantify 126 links as removable.

We then remove 5% (12 links), 10% (24 links) and 20% (48 links) of the links from the whole network randomly selected from the 126 removable links identified and predict them using PSL. The logical rules created for predicting links are based on the structural balance theory [3] with a binary predicate Rel (relations between actors). A few logical rules are shown below.

$$Rel(A, B) \wedge Rel(B, C) \Rightarrow Rel(A, C)$$
$$Rel(A, B) \wedge \neg Rel(B, C) \Rightarrow \neg Rel(A, C)$$
$$\neg Rel(A, B) \wedge Rel(B, C) \Rightarrow \neg Rel(A, C)$$
$$\neg Rel(A, B) \wedge \neg Rel(B, C) \Rightarrow Rel(A, C)$$

The first four rules adapt to structural balance in transitive triads in the network that state a friend of my friend is my friend, a friend of my enemy is my enemy, an enemy of my friend is my enemy and the enemy of my enemy is my friend. Political relations are not always transitive and therefore in future we plan to add more rules that can better explain the relationships between political entities. The outcome is a set of truth values assigned by PSL for links predicted and this relies on the input relations that are highly confident. Since we also know the truth values for the links predicted, in each case we measure the Mean Absolute Error (MAE) over all the links predicted in 100 iterations.

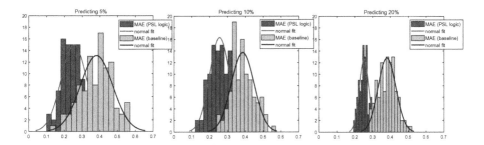

Fig. 1. MAE distribution with normal fitted curve over 100 iterations for the predictions with PSL and random (baseline) when predicting 5% (left), 10% (middle) and 20% (right) of the links from the network

The MAE over all predictions is given by,

$$MAE = \frac{\mid y^i - x^i \mid}{n} \tag{2}$$

where y^i refers to the prediction of the ith link, x^i refers to the truth value of the ith link and n, the total number of links predicted.

We compute the MAE over 100 iterations when removing 5%, 10% and 20% of the links from the network and predicting them with PSL. To compare this with a baseline and prove its better than random, in each experiment we randomly pick a value from the whole link weight distribution of the network as the prediction and compute the MAE as before. Figure 1 shows the MAE distribution with a normal fitted curve over 100 iterations for the predictions with PSL and random predictions (baseline) when predicting 5%, 10% and 20% of the links from the network. The most common MAEs lie in the range 0.19–0.27 (5%), 0.22–0.28 (10%), 0.25–0.28 (20%) for PSL predictions and 0.33–0.41 (5%), 0.33–0.39 (10%) and 0.34–0.39 (20%) for the baseline. Therefore the test does show that PSL does better than random in predicting relations.

5.3 Fact Checking

Now since we have proven that political relations could be inferred given a set of political relations between actors, we can use this to check facts about political relations.

For example given a claim/fact such as,

Claim : "Hillary Clinton opposes Abortion".

the system adds this fact to the PSL target list and runs the inference process to fact check the truth. The weight of this relation could be assigned to 0 since oppose is a negative verb in the context of elections and the most negative weights are mapped to 0 values in PSL. The target is comprised of Hillary Clinton, Abortion and the negative weight associated with the relation.

Target : (HillaryClinton, Abortion)
ClaimWeight : 0.0
InferredWeight : 0.85
Verdict := 0.0/False

The inferred weight for the given target is 0.85 indicating that there is a reasonably high support for Abortion from Hillary Clinton. Comparing to the weight of Claim (0.0) the system returns the Verdict False. It is also possible to reason out this decision saying that Hillary Clinton supports Obama and Obama supports Abortion, therefore Clinton supports Abortion violating the first logical rule given to PSL which says if A supports B and B supports C, then A supports C.

6   Conclusion and Future Work

This paper has demonstrated an automated system to detect claims that can be considered as not plausible, in that they implicitly contradict background knowledge, assumptions or other claims contained in a reference corpus. The key is that the claim we are checking is not explicitly stated in the reference corpus, and the necessary knowledge to verify it is potentially distributed across many documents. We address this by combining information extraction with probabilistic reasoning, to see if a claim can follow from other known facts showing two examples, fact checking Family relations for which ground truth is available and Political relations where neither relations nor rules are clearly available. We check the implausibility of claims in that domain. We expect this kind of approach to be useful for projects like Wikipedia, or to provide support to news fact checkers, but always in the form of assisting the job of humans. We are planning to deploy these tools to very large corpora combining information from multiple sources such as those created by digital humanities and computational social sciences as well as to applications that can lead to Q/A systems based on news content. The main challenge lies in scaling up the probabilistic reasoning to work with large amounts of facts while also having the ability to provide explanations to the verdicts given by the system.

Acknowledgements. NC and SS were supported by ERC, NB was supported by a grant from KSU, Saudi Arabia.

References

1. Ba, M.L., Berti-Equille, L., Shah, K., Hammady, H.M.: Vera: A platform for veracity estimation over web data. In: Proceedings of the 25th International Conference Companion on World Wide Web, International World Wide Web Conferences Steering Committee, pp. 159–162 (2016)
2. Bach, S., Huang, B., London, B., Getoor, L.: Hinge-loss Markov random fields: convex inference for structured prediction. arXiv preprint arXiv:1309.6813 (2013)
3. Cartwright, D., Harary, F.: Structural balance: a generalization of Heider's theory. Psychol. Rev. **63**(5), 277 (1956)
4. Cunningham, H., Wilks, Y., Gaizauskas, R.J.: Gate: a general architecture for text engineering. In: Proceedings of the 16th Conference on Computational Linguistics, vol. 2, pp. 1057–1060. Association for Computational Linguistics (1996)
5. Flaounas, I., Lansdall-Welfare, T., Antonakaki, P., Cristianini, N.: The anatomy of a modular system for media content analysis. arXiv preprint arXiv:1402.6208 (2014)
6. Hassan, N., et al.: The quest to automate fact-checking. World (2015)
7. Hassan, N., et al.: Claimbuster: the first-ever end-to-end fact-checking system. Proc. VLDB Endow. **10**(12), 1945–1948 (2017)
8. Jo, S., Trummer, I., Yu, W., Liu, D., Mehta, N.: The factchecker: verifying text summaries of relational data sets. arXiv preprint arXiv:1804.07686 (2018)
9. Kimmig, A., Bach, S., Broecheler, M., Huang, B., Getoor, L.: A short introduction to probabilistic soft logic. In: Proceedings of the NIPS Workshop on Probabilistic Programming: Foundations and Applications, pp. 1–4 (2012)
10. Leblay, J.: A declarative approach to data-driven fact checking. In: AAAI, pp. 147–153 (2017)
11. Leblay, J., Chen, W., Lynden, S.: Exploring the veracity of online claims with backdrop. In: Proceedings of the 2017 ACM on Conference on Information and Knowledge Management, pp. 2491–2494. ACM (2017)
12. Patwari, A., Goldwasser, D., Bagchi, S.: Tathya: A multi-classifier system for detecting check-worthy statements in political debates. In: Proceedings of the 2017 ACM on Conference on Information and Knowledge Management, pp. 2259–2262. ACM (2017)
13. Soon, W.M., Ng, H.T., Lim, D.C.Y.: A machine learning approach to coreference resolution of noun phrases. Comput. Linguist. **27**(4), 521–544 (2001)
14. Sudhahar, S., De Fazio, G., Franzosi, R., Cristianini, N.: Network analysis of narrative content in large corpora. Nat. Lang. Eng. **21**(1), 81–112 (2015)
15. Thorne, J., Vlachos, A.: An extensible framework for verification of numerical claims. In: Proceedings of the Software Demonstrations of the 15th Conference of the European Chapter of the Association for Computational Linguistics, pp. 37–40. Association for Computational Linguistics (2017)
16. Vlachos, A., Riedel, S.: Identification and verification of simple claims about statistical properties. In: Proceedings of the 2015 Conference on Empirical Methods in Natural Language Processing, pp. 2596–2601. Association for Computational Linguistics (2015)
17. Wilson, E.B.: Probable inference, the law of succession, and statistical inference. J. Am. Stat. Assoc. **22**(158), 209–212 (1927)
18. Wu, Y., et al.: iCheck: computationally combating lies, d-ned lies, and statistics. In: Proceedings of the 2014 ACM SIGMOD International Conference on Management of Data, pp. 1063–1066. ACM (2014)

ConvoMap: Using Convolution to Order Boolean Data

Thomas Bollen, Guillaume Leurquin, and Siegfried Nijssen[✉]

ICTEAM, UCLouvain, Louvain-la-Neuve, Belgium
siegfried.nijssen@uclouvain.be

Abstract. Heatmaps, also called matrix visualisations, are a popular technique for visualising boolean data. They are easy to understand, and provide a relatively loss-free image of a given dataset. However, they are also highly dependent on the order of rows and columns chosen. We propose a novel technique, called *ConvoMap*, for ordering the rows and columns of a matrix such that the resulting image represents data faithfully. ConvoMap uses a novel optimisation criterion based on convolution to obtain a good column and row order. While in this paper we focus on the creation of images for exploratory data analysis in binary data, the simplicity of the ConvoMap optimisation criterion could allow for the creation of images for many other types of data as well.

1 Introduction

Data visualisation is an important step in exploratory data analysis: information that is provided in a visual manner can often be processed more easily. For these reasons, there is a large literature on data visualization and related areas, including visual analytics and visual data mining, and there is a need for techniques that visualize data well. Popular types of visualisation include line graphs, bar charts, pie charts, histograms, boxplots and scatter plots, often in combination with dimensionality reduction techniques; they are used both in the initial stages of the data mining process, to gain a better understanding in data, and in later stages of the process to display results in an insightful manner. While these popular techniques have clear benefits for many types of data analysis, they also have drawbacks: they only provide summaries of underlying data; they do not allow to visualize the complete data itself.

Heatmaps, also called *matrix visualisations* [1], are a visualisation technique that does not have this disadvantage. They excel in showing certain types of patterns, work well on discrete data, and provide a complete view on data. For this reason, they are popular in many areas, including bioinformatics, ecology, and web mining.

The key idea behind the heatmap is simple: given a data matrix $\mathbf{M}$, we treat this data matrix as an image, such that entry $\mathbf{M}_{ij}$ of the data matrix directly determines the color of the pixel at coordinate (i,j) in the image. In the boolean case, we use black to indicate values in the matrix that are one, and white to indicate values that are zero.

© Springer Nature Switzerland AG 2018
W. Duivesteijn et al. (Eds.): IDA 2018, LNCS 11191, pp. 62–74, 2018.
https://doi.org/10.1007/978-3-030-01768-2_6

A heatmap provides a lossless image for a given dataset in the following sense: there is a one-to-one correspondence between pixels in the image and entries in the data matrix. The only information that may not be visible in the heatmap, is the name of the attributes of the matrix. Hence, for a modern screen with a resolution of $\approx 4000 \times 2000$, a data matrix of similar dimensions is shown completely to the analyst, except for the names of the attributes.

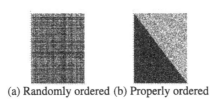

(a) Randomly ordered (b) Properly ordered

Fig. 1. Two heatmaps for the same data, using different orders for the rows and the columns

It is well-known, however, that the usefulness of a heatmap strongly depends on the order that is chosen for visualising the rows and the columns of the data. Figure 1 provides an example for boolean data. In this figure, two heatmaps are shown for the same underlying dataset; the only difference between the two figures is the ordering of the rows and the columns.

Clearly, the first image provides little information about the data; the second image is informative and reveals that that the data has a clear triangular pattern. Hence, a key challenge when creating heatmaps is the *data seriation problem*, that is, the problem of ordering rows and columns such that the resulting order is useful and reveals patterns.

The key contribution of this paper is a new approach for choosing a data seriation, even if patterns in the data are not rectangular in structure and the data has a high level of noise, as in the image above. The key novel idea in this method is the use of *convolution* to evaluate the quality of a data order. A benefit of convolution is that it is a well-known image processing technique. An example of convolution is *blurring*: a blurred version of an image can be obtained by applying a Gaussian convolution kernel to an image.

We propose to use convolution as follows. Given a data matrix, we aim to order its rows and columns such that for the resulting matrix $\mathbf{M}$ the following holds:

$$error(\mathbf{M}, \mathbf{M} * \mathbf{K}) \text{ is minimal,}$$

where $\mathbf{M} * \mathbf{K}$ denotes the application of a convolution kernel, such as a blurring kernel, on the matrix $\mathbf{M}$, and *error* measures the distance between two matrices. Hence, we are looking for an order of rows and columns, such that for the resulting image it is the case that blurring does not change the image too much. As we will see, such an order has a number of desirable properties.

We will refer to a matrix that optimizes this scoring function as a *ConvoMap*, a heatmap obtained under optimization for a given convolution kernel. We will argue that this scoring function can be used to select a useful order among a given number of different orders, and to build a new algorithm for finding a good ordering.

The work in this paper may only represent a first step in the use of convolution in data seriation. In our conclusions we will point out that many possible extensions of the ideas presented in this article are possible.

This paper is organized as follows. In Sect. 2 we discuss related work in more detail. In Sect. 3 we will introduce the ConvoMap optimization criterion in more detail, and we will study its properties. In Sect. 4 we provide a high-level overview of a search algorithm. Given the NP-hard nature of the problem, this algorithm is a local search algorithm that combines a number of heuristics introduced in this section. In Sect. 5 we perform experiments. In Sect. 6 we conclude and provide directions for future research.

This article skips a number of details to keep its length limited. These details can be found in a master's thesis available online [2].

2   Related Work

Existing methods for data seriation can be separated into two classes: methods that aim to order columns and rows based on pairwise similarities between the columns and rows, and methods that order rows and columns such that the resulting image most closely resembles a desirable structure.

Distance-based Methods. The key idea in distance-based seriation methods is to put rows (resp. columns) next to each other that are similar to each other.

Arguably the most common such techniques are based on a *hierarchical clustering* of the rows and columns of a matrix. Standard implementations of heatmaps based on hierarchical clustering are available for a number of data analytics languages and systems, including R[1], Matlab[2], Python[3], and KNIME; these packages are in particular popular for the visualisation of gene expression data in bioinformatics.

A relationship with traveling salesman problems was first identified by Hubert in 1974 [3]. The key idea is here that we wish to order rows (or columns) such that the sum of pairwise distances between the rows is as small as possible.

Related are also techniques based on *spectral ordering* [4]. Given a distance matrix with pairwise distances (for instance, between the rows of a given matrix), these techniques consider all pairs of rows and aim to put more similar rows closer to each other. The same process can be used to reorder columns.

A wide range of seriation techniques based on pairwise distances is available in the R seriation package [5]. A historical overview of seriation techniques can be found in work by Liiv [6].

---

[1] https://cran.r-project.org/web/packages/heatmap3/index.html.

[2] https://www.mathworks.com/help/bioinfo/ref/clustergram.html.

[3] http://seaborn.pydata.org/generated/seaborn.clustermap.html.

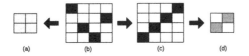

Fig. 2. (b) A 4x4 original dataset; (c) reordering of its columns and rows; (a) an averaged, zoomed-out version for order (a); (d) a zoomed-out version of order (c)

However, the use of pairwise distances does not always yield insightful orders. An extreme example is given in Fig. 2, where all columns and rows in Fig. 2(b) are equidistant. Methods based on pairwise distances would have no reason to prefer one order over another. Still, showing an arbitrary order, such as in Fig. 2(b) can be undesirable. One argument is that this data has a strong *banded* structure; the order shown in Fig. 2(c) would make this structure clear. Another argument is that users will typically look at such images from a certain distance, which effectively amounts to a certain level of zoom-out in which details are lost. When averaging is used to create a zoomed-out picture, all detail is lost for an incorrect order, as illustrated in Fig. 2(a). A proper order, such as in Fig. 2(c) would return the structure at other levels of zoom.

While this example is an extreme case, it makes clear that methods based on pairwise distances do not take into account more distant similarities along diagonals. Our method will provide an elegant solution to this problem; our method will not only consider similarities with direct horizontal and vertical neighbors, but also neighbors at a larger distance, including those along diagonals.

Structure-based Methods. The second class of methods aims to reorder both the rows and columns of a matrix such that the resulting matrix has a desirable structure. Two types of structures in particular have attracted significant attention in the data mining literature: *nested structures* [7] and *banded structures* [8]. These methods are popular in biology as well, as it is known that binary data regarding the occurrence of species in geographic regions, has a nested structure: some regions have less diversity than others. One can reorder data to match this specific property. This has led to a number of different techniques that we will perform further experimental comparisons with.

A basic technique for finding nested orders [9] is based on the observation that a perfect nested order would have its columns and rows sorted by the number of ones. The idea behind this method is therefore to count the number of ones in each row (resp. column) and then reorder the rows (resp. columns) according to those counts. We will refer to this technique as the *Nested* algorithm.

A simple technique for finding banded orders is the barycentric method [10]. The barycentric measure is a measure that determines the average position of ones in a row/column, and can be used in an algorithm that iteratively optimizes the row and column order. We will refer to this technique as the *Barycentric* method.

An alternative method for finding banded orders is the *bidirectional ordering method* [8], which uses an alternating method as well. First, it determines for each row the smallest number of modifications that need to be done to obtain a *consecutive one* row, i.e., a row in which all ones are consecutive. The next step is to resolve the *Sperner* conflicts between rows, which leads to a new row order. A similar process is executed for the columns. We will refer to this technique as the *Bidirectional* technique.

Clearly, a disadvantage of this class of methods is that each method works best on data that has a very specific structure; an analyst needs to have a certain level of understanding in her data before the analysis starts, or an additional method is required for making a choice between different possible images; our method does not assume that such knowledge is available apriori.

Biclustering Methods and Itemset Mining Methods. Other problems distantly related to data seriation are clustering, co-clustering and boolean matrix factorisation. While these techniques could be used as a step in a data seriation algorithm, they do not solve the problem of finding a total order for all rows and columns in data, and do not provide a solution for the problem of identifying the best order of rows and columns.

3   Definition of the ConvoMap Optimization Criterion

We limit our attention to boolean matrices. Hence, we assume given a boolean $m \times n$ matrix M with $M_{i,j} \in \mathcal{D}$ where $\mathcal{D} = \{0, 1\}$. A *kernel* matrix K (also called a *convolution matrix*) is a $k_m \times k_n$ matrix, where both k_m and k_n are odd. In this paper, for reasons of simplicity we assume that $K_{i,j} \in [0, 1]$ and that $\sum_{i,j} K_{i,j} = 1$. Furthermore, for reasons of notational simplicity, we assume that the value of the kernel is zero whenever $(i, j) \notin \{1, \ldots, k_m\} \times \{1, \ldots, k_n\}$.

We define the *convolution* of a data matrix with a kernel as follows:

$$(M * K)_{i,j} = \sum_{x=1}^{k_m} \sum_{y=1}^{k_n} M_{i+x-\lceil k_m/2 \rceil, j+y-\lceil k_n/2 \rceil} \cdot K_{x,y}. \tag{1}$$

Hence, in the convoluted matrix a pixel is replaced by a weighted average of the neighborhood of the original pixel. The kernel defines the weights that are used. Note that in this definition we ignore border effects; in our experiments, we will address these by padding the data with a border that is as large as half the kernel size. As we will see, the choice of values used to pad the image will allow us to bias the search towards certain images.

$$\begin{pmatrix} \frac{1}{16} & \frac{2}{16} & \frac{1}{16} \\ \frac{2}{16} & \frac{4}{16} & \frac{2}{16} \\ \frac{1}{16} & \frac{2}{16} & \frac{1}{16} \end{pmatrix} \qquad \begin{pmatrix} \frac{1}{10} & \frac{1}{10} & \frac{1}{10} \\ \frac{1}{10} & \frac{2}{10} & \frac{1}{10} \\ \frac{1}{10} & \frac{1}{10} & \frac{1}{10} \end{pmatrix} \qquad \begin{pmatrix} 0 & b & 0 \\ b & a & b \\ 0 & b & 0 \end{pmatrix}$$
$$\text{Exponential} \qquad\qquad \text{Linear} \qquad\qquad \text{Exponential Cross}$$

Fig. 3. Examples of different convolution kernels

The effect of the convolution depends on the kernel that is used. The following are a number of kernels that we will consider in this work; examples for the 3×3

case of these kernels can be found in Fig. 3. In these formulas, we assume an an arbitrary odd size $k_m \times k_n$, center of the rows $c_{row} = \lfloor k_m/2 \rfloor$, center of the columns $c_{col} = \lfloor k_n/2 \rfloor$ and center $c_{max} = max(c_{row}, c_{col})$.

The Exponential blur kernel, defined by $K_{r,c} = \frac{2^{2c_{max}}}{2^{|r-c_{row}|+|c-c_{col}|}}$.

The Linear blur kernel, defined using $K_{r,c} = \frac{c_{max}-max(|c_{row}-r|,|c_{col}-c|)+1}{C}$,
where C is a normalisation constant.

The Exponential Cross blur kernel, which is simar to the exponential blur kernel, except that any value that is not on its middle row or middle column is equal to 0.

All these kernels have the effect that they *blur* an image; they differ in which neighbors are considered when calculating the blur; moreover, the size of the kernel has an important impact on the level of blur.

The following properties are relevant for kernels. A kernel is *square* if its number of rows equals its number of columns. A kernel is *row symmetric* if reversing the order of the rows does not yield a different matrix. Similarly, it is *column symmetric* if reversing the column order has no effect. A kernel is *symmetric* if it is row and column symmetric. In this paper we will limit our attention to symmetric kernels.

When we convolve a data matrix with a kernel, the order of rows and columns is clearly important. For a different order of columns and rows we would find a different corresponding convoluted matrix. The optimization problem that we study in this paper is hence the following.

Definition 1. (ConvoMap). *Given a binary data matrix* $\boldsymbol{M}$*, a kernel matrix* $\boldsymbol{K}$*, an error function error between two matrices of equal size, find a permutation of the rows and columns of* $\boldsymbol{M}$*, such that if we order the columns and rows of* $\boldsymbol{M}$ *according to these permutations, the resulting matrix* $\boldsymbol{M}'$ *minimizes the score* $error(\boldsymbol{M}', \boldsymbol{M}' * \boldsymbol{K})$.

In this paper, we will focus on an L1-norm, i.e.,

$$error(\boldsymbol{M}', \boldsymbol{M}' * \boldsymbol{K}) = \sum_{x=1}^{m}\sum_{y=1}^{n}|\boldsymbol{M}'_{x,y} - (\boldsymbol{M}' * \boldsymbol{K})_{x,y}|, \tag{2}$$

as we obtained slightly better results with an L1-norm. Other distance functions can however also be considered, such as an L2-norm.

Intuitively, our optimisation criterion favors orders of the rows and columns such that the resulting image is similar to its blurred version; typically, this is the case if the image has relatively little black-white transitions, and the matrix is clearly partitioned into black and white regions.

For a good understanding of the ConvoMap problem, we will now study some of its properties.

First, we will observe that for symmetric kernels, we can rewrite the error as a sum over *weighted pairwise disagreements* between entries in the matrix.

Definition 2. *Given two entries* (x, y) *and* (x', y') *in ordered data matrix* $\boldsymbol{M}$, *their pairwise weight according to kernel* $\boldsymbol{K}$ *is* $w_{\boldsymbol{K}}((x, y), (x', y')) = \boldsymbol{K}_{\lfloor k_m/2 \rfloor + x - x', \lfloor k_n/2 \rfloor + y - y'}$.

Note that in this definition we use our notational convention that entries outside the range of the kernel matrix are assumed to be zero. Note furthermore that under this definition for a symmetric kernel it holds that $w_{\boldsymbol{K}}((x, y), (x', y')) = w_{\boldsymbol{K}}((x', y'), (x, y))$.

Theorem 1. *For given matrix* $\boldsymbol{M}$ *and kernel* $\boldsymbol{K}$ *it holds that:*

$$error(\boldsymbol{M}, \boldsymbol{M} * \boldsymbol{K}) = 2 \sum_{M_{x,y} \neq M_{x',y'}} w_{\boldsymbol{K}}((x', y'), (x, y)),$$

where we sum over all pairs of entries (x, y) *and* (x', y') *in the data matrix exactly once.*

Hence, the convolution error score matches the intuition that it counts the number of disagreements between entries in the matrix, where the distance between the entries determines the weight that is given to the disagreement.

This observation has specific consequences for 3×3 cross kernels; arguably these are the simplest types of kernels that can be used within our framework. We can show that methods for solving the Traveling Salesman Problem can be used to solve ConvoMap for 3×3 cross kernels.

Let us define the total number of 0–1 transitions in a boolean matrix as follows:

$$\tau(\boldsymbol{M}) = \sum_{i=0}^{m} \sum_{j=1}^{n} |\boldsymbol{M}_{i,j} - \boldsymbol{M}_{i+1,j}| + \sum_{i=1}^{m} \sum_{j=0}^{n} |\boldsymbol{M}_{i,j} - \boldsymbol{M}_{i,j+1}|, \quad (3)$$

where the first term counts the vertical zero-one transitions and the second term counts the horizontal zero-one transitions.

Corollary 1. *For the cross kernel it holds that*

$$error(\boldsymbol{M}, \boldsymbol{M} * \boldsymbol{K}) = 2b\tau(\boldsymbol{M}),$$

where b *is the value in the* 3×3 *cross kernel on the spokes of the cross.*

As a consequence of this observation, we can solve the ConvoMap problem for 3×3 cross kernels as follows. (1) For every pair of rows, calculate their Hamming distance, i.e. calculate the number of entries that are different between these two rows; (2) Solve the TSP on the resulting distance matrix. (3) Repeat this process for the columns. The correctness of this algorithm follows from Corollary 1 and Eq. 3: the sum over j in Eq. 3 corresponds to a Hamming distance calculation; the sum over i sums consecutive Hamming distances. Hence, the problem of finding a ConvoMap can be seen as a generalization of the TSP approach towards data seriation.

A practical issue with this approach is that TSPs are well-known NP-complete problems; however, as Hamming distances satisfy the triangle inequality, a reasonably good approximation algorithm can be used: the Christofides algorithm has an approximation factor of $3/2$ [11].

Even though we can hence reduce one specific instance of ConvoMap to a TSP problem, an important question is whether ConvoMap is NP-hard as well. We can proof the following, using a reduction of the Hamiltonian path problem.

Theorem 2. *The ConvoMap problem with a 3×3 cross kernel is NP-hard.*

Spectral ordering methods can be related to ConvoMap by using cross kernels of a larger size than 3×3.

4   Algorithm

Given that our optimisation problem is NP-hard, we cannot expect an exact algorithm to find optimal solutions within reasonable time.

We can however use our scoring function in two alternative ways:

– to select an order from a given set of orders produced by other algorithms;
– to build a heuristic algorithm for finding a good, although not necessarily optimal, solution under our scoring function.

In this section, we provide a sketch of a local search algorithm that falls in the second category. The aim of this algorithm is to determine whether it makes sense to optimize the ConvoMap scoring function directly.

Our local search algorithm consists of a combination of randomized local search and Traveling Salesman Problem solving; the integration of other types of algorithms specific for banded and nested structures is left as future work.

Local search and TSP solving have different tasks in our optimisation algorithm. The focus of the local search algorithm is to optimize data within *blocks*. A block is here a set of rows (or columns) that are next to each other. The TSP solver, on the other hand, is responsible for rearranging different blocks of data globally. To this aim, we iteratively split the rows and the columns of the data in different blocks, where the local search algorithm is applied to optimize each individual block, and the TSP solver optimizes the order of the blocks.

The local search algorithm is based on *moves*. At random we execute one of these moves, accepting the result if it improves our score:

Swap Given 4 row indexes $a < b < c < d$, this moves creates a new matrix M' in which the rows of matrix M occur in the following order:

$$M_1, \ldots, M_{a-1}, \underline{M_c, \ldots, M_{d-1}}, M_b, \ldots M_{c-1}, \underline{M_a, \ldots, M_{b-1}}, M_d, \ldots M_m, \tag{4}$$

i.e. two *blocks* of rows are exchanged.

Reverse Given 2 row indexes $a < b$, we create a new matrix M' in which the order of rows $a, \ldots, b-1$ is reversed, i.e., we create the matrix with rows

$$M_1, \ldots, M_{a-1}, \underline{M_{b-1}, \ldots, M_a}, M_b, \ldots M_m. \tag{5}$$

The advantage of these moves is that the error score can efficiently be recalculated for these moves. Let k_m be the number of rows in the kernel; then for any row that has a distance of more than $\lfloor m/2 \rfloor$ to a, b, c or d the error will not change due to the move, as its relevant neighborhood does not change. As a consequence, to update the error, we only need to recalculate the error for regions of the data around a, b, c and d.

In practice, we determined that choosing a, b, c and d uniformly at randoms leads to slow convergence; the local search algorithm is unlikely to select moves that lead to an improvement of the initial solution. We address this by limiting the choice of a, b, c and d. We omit the details of these choices here.

Afterwards, the order of blocks is optimized using a TSP solver, in which we use a distance measure between the blocks that is derived from the kernel. The new order is followed by another round of local search, for a different block size; this process is repeated till convergence. We skip the details here as well.

5   Experimental Evaluation

The aim of our experiments is to evaluate whether (1) our novel scoring function indeed prefers orders that reveal hidden structure in data, for different types of patterns; (2) the choice of convolution kernel has a large impact on the results, (3) our new optimization algorithm is able to find an order that optimizes our criterion well, and that reflects the imputed patterns well.

In this paper we restrict ourselves to artificial data, in which we hide 4 types of patterns in the data: banded matrices, nested matrices, matrices with blocks on the diagonal, and matrices with a number of blocks not necessarily on the diagonal[4]. We created data as follows:

1. we generate an initial 300×300 boolean matrix that possesses a given pattern;
2. we add random noise by flipping each boolean in the matrix with a given probability (25% in the experiments reported here, although the reports are similar for 10% noise);
3. we shuffle the rows and columns of the matrix until the pattern is no longer visible.

The data shown in Fig. 1(a) of the introduction is an example of data that is the result of this process.

Different algorithms can then be used to order the rows and the columns of the resulting matrix. Our first goal is to determine whether the ConvoMap scoring function successfully selects an order that reveals the underlying pattern.

---

[4] Results on real-world data can be found in [2].

To this aim, we will first evaluate the error score that the ConvoMap scoring function obtains for different orders created by the Bidirectional, Barycentric, Hierarchical Clustering (abbreviated as HClus), Nested, and TSP methods discussed in the related work section. We use our own implementations of these algorithms, except for Hierarchical Clustering, where we use the R Heatmap3 package. We use our own implementations as for the alternative methods there are no publicly available implementations. We consider these methods to be representative for a class of related methods.

In our experiments, we pad the right-hand border and the bottom border with ones, and the left-hand and top border with zeros. As algorithms in the literature are not aware of this preference, in our experiments we have flipped the outcome of an alternative algorithm if for that orientation we obtain a lower score for our scoring function.

The images created for the different methods, as well as the error scores for different choices of convolution kernel, are provided in Table 1. Note that despite the side-by-side visualisation, the original order is not necessarily the best one.

We consider two different approaches for evaluating the quality of the scoring function: (1) the scoring function gives the lowest score to the original order of the data, that is, the order before shuffling the data; (2) among the orders calculated by algorithms in the literature, it selects the order that matches the intended pattern the best.

For this purpose, we have indicated in our results for each different choice of kernel (1) whether the original data obtains the lowest score for that kernel, and (2) which algorithm in the literature receives the lowest score when that kernel is used.

Considering the size of the kernel, the worst results are obtained for 3x3 kernels, which select the TSP solution: (1) the original order never scores best; (2) in cases where the pattern is not rectangular in structure, such as banded and nested matrices, it prefers orders that clearly do not reflect the underlying pattern.

Larger kernel sizes perform better. The Linear 29×29 kernel always selects the original order as the best one, and prefers the algorithm that yields the desired shape. The 49×49 kernel has a slight preference for images that are more blurry, but the differences between 29×29 and 49×49 kernels are small, which makes it easy to fix the parameter.

We evaluate our local search algorithm next. Is this algorithm able to find orders that perform better than those found using existing algorithms?

Table 2 shows the outcome of our algorithm for different kernel sizes, using the Linear kernel. In this experiment the 49×49 kernel size provides better results than the 25×25 kernel size. We found in further experiments that the 49×49 kernel size provides better results and use this kernel in our final experiment.

In Table 3 it can be observed that in all cases our local search algorithm identifies a solution that has a better error score than that obtained by the other algorithms. In two cases, the error scores obtained are lower than those

Table 1. Errors for a number of different datasets and kernel choices; for each kernel, the result for the original order is indicated in **bold** if the kernel obtains the lowest error for that order. The result for an algorithm is <u>underlined</u> if its error is the lowest, as calculated using the indicated kernel. Bold and underlined results are highlighted.

Config		Original	Nested	Baryc.	Bidir.	TSP	HClus
Nested, 25% noise							
Linear	49x49	**16981**	<u>17311</u>	22242	17396	18820	18341
Linear	29x29	**16898**	17330	22148	<u>17301</u>	18387	18029
Linear	3x3	13480	13958	17294	13687	<u>12937</u>	13415
Exp.	49x49	**16979**	<u>17356</u>	22169	17366	18541	18142
Exp.	29x29	**15027**	15494	19137	15253	<u>15192</u>	15270
Exp.	3x3	12642	13068	15975	12812	<u>11924</u>	12417
Cross	49x49	13534	13906	16497	13668	<u>13211</u>	13360
Cross	29x29	13533	13905	16497	13667	<u>13211</u>	13360
Cross	3x3	11246	11585	13776	11352	<u>10235</u>	10754
Banded, 25% noise							
Linear	49x49	**17533**	21193	18969	<u>18202</u>	19269	18872
Linear	29x29	**17229**	21274	18804	<u>17777</u>	18708	18410
Linear	3x3	13515	17053	14892	13833	<u>13104</u>	13557
Exp.	49x49	**17374**	21293	18861	<u>17914</u>	18912	18554
Exp.	29x29	15118	18968	16552	<u>15429</u>	15348	15454
Exp.	3x3	12672	15955	13907	12935	<u>12088</u>	12557
Cross	49x49	13598	16978	14722	13798	<u>13364</u>	13523
Cross	29x29	13598	16978	14722	13798	<u>13364</u>	13523
Cross	3x3	11269	14126	12267	11438	<u>10393</u>	10891
Blocks, 25% noise							
Linear	49x49	**17640**	17940	18416	<u>17655</u>	17728	17814
Linear	29x29	**17319**	17975	18267	17465	<u>17419</u>	17450
Linear	3x3	13555	14458	14417	13670	<u>12645</u>	13042
Exp.	49x49	**17415**	17994	18323	<u>17538</u>	17540	17576
Exp.	29x29	15152	15987	16057	15249	<u>14690</u>	14822
Exp.	3x3	12708	13484	13461	12784	<u>11663</u>	12087
Cross	49x49	13603	14178	14251	13613	<u>12838</u>	13010
Cross	29x29	13603	14178	14251	13613	<u>12838</u>	13010
Cross	3x3	11296	11859	11867	11308	<u>10026</u>	10495
Banded Blocks, 25% noise							
Linear	49x49	**17822**	20019	18717	<u>17831</u>	18088	17888
Linear	29x29	**17461**	20144	18610	<u>17486</u>	17667	17515
Linear	3x3	13590	16336	14798	13579	<u>12726</u>	13100
Exp.	49x49	**17569**	20155	18659	<u>17593</u>	17806	17638
Exp.	29x29	15196	18146	16427	15200	<u>14795</u>	14894
Exp.	3x3	12733	15307	13805	12712	<u>11743</u>	12138
Cross	49x49	13631	16341	14571	13599	<u>12925</u>	13063
Cross	29x29	13631	16341	14571	13599	<u>12925</u>	13063
Cross	3x3	11304	13593	12149	11266	<u>10104</u>	10533

Table 2. Results for our local search algorithm, for different kernel sizes

Config	Original	3x3	11x11	25x25	49x49
Nested, 25% noise					
Banded, 25% noise					

calculated for the original order. Due to the large kernel size, the chosen orders make a more blurred impression.

A major concern of our algorithm is its run time. In general, we found that we need to run the local search algorithm for a significant amount of time to identify solutions that score better than the initial solution identified by an alternative algorithm. As a result, this algorithm is currently not applicable in settings that require fast visualisation.

6 Conclusions

In this paper, we proposed a new approach for evaluating the quality of a data seriation. The key idea in this approach is to compare an image before and after the application of a blurring filter. We argued that this approach allows to consider similarities at larger distances, as well as along diagonals; this is beneficial in particular if we take into account that users may consider such

Table 3. Results for the local search algorithm using a 49×49 Linear kernel; error scores are shown for a 49×49 kernel size, as well as run times for the local search algorithm.

Nested		Banded		Blocks		B. Blocks	
Original	Ordered	Original	Ordered	Original	Ordered	Original	Ordered
16981	17111	17533	17586	17640	16953	17822	17438
	21354s		21782s		45856s		43511s

images at varying levels of zoom. Results confirmed potential benefits of our scoring function on artificial data.

Many directions for future research remain. An important question is how we can the performance of data seriation algorithms based on our scoring function. Possibilities include the use of GPUs, the development of better local search algorithms and the exploitation of other data seriation algorithms to jump start the search. Other extensions of interest may include constraint-based data seriation, data seriation for data that is not boolean, combinations of data seriation with segmentation, approaches for visualising sparse data, a more detailed consideration of the impact of zooming, learning convolution kernels, the consideration of kernels that are not square, and the application of pipelines of kernels, e.g., the application of sharpening filters after blurring.

References

1. Chen, C-h, Härdle, W., Unwin, A.: Handbook of Data Visualization. Springer, Berlin (2008). https://doi.org/10.1007/978-3-540-33037-0
2. Bollen, T., Leurquin, G.: Faithful visualization of categorical data. Master's thesis (2017). Université catholique de Louvain, Louvain-la-Neuve
3. Hubert, L.J.: Some applications of graph theory and related nonmetric techniques to problems of approximate seriation: the case of symmetric proximity measures. Br. J. Math. Stat. Psychol. **27**, 133–153 (1974)
4. Atkins, J.E., Boman, E.G., Hendrickson, B.: A spectral algorithm for seriation and the consecutive ones problem. SIAM J. Comput. **28**, 297–310 (1998)
5. Hahsler, M., Hornik, K. Buchta, C.: Getting things in order: an introduction to the R package seriation. J. Stat. Softw. Artic. 25(3) (2008)
6. Liiv, I.: Seriation and matrix reordering methods: an historical overview. Stat. Anal. Data Min. **3**(2), 70–91 (2010)
7. Kaski, P., Junttila, E.: Segmented nestedness in binary data. In: Proceedings of the Eleventh SIAM International Conference on Data Mining, pp. 235–246 (2011)
8. Garriga, G.C., Junttila, E., Mannila, H.: Banded structure in binary matrices. Knowl. Inf. Syst. **28**(1), 197–226 (2011)
9. Junttila, E.: Patterns in permuted binary matrices. PhD thesis, University of Helsinki (2011)
10. Mäkinen, E., Siirtola, H.: The barycenter heuristic and the reorderable matrix. Inf. (Slov.) **29**(3), 357–364 (2005)
11. Christofides, N.: Worst-case analysis of a new heuristic for the travelling salesman problem, Report 388, Graduate School of Industrial Administration, CMU (1976)

Training Neural Networks to Distinguish Craving Smokers, Non-craving Smokers, and Non-smokers

Christoph Doell[1][(✉)], Sarah Donohue[2], Cedrik Pätz[3], and Christan Borgelt[1,3]

[1] Dept of Computer and Information Science, University of Konstanz,
Universitätsstraße 10, 78457 Konstanz, Germany
christoph.doell@uni.kn
[2] Department of Behavioral Neurology, Leibnitz-Institute for Neurobiology,
Brenneckestraße 6, 39118 Magdeburg, Germany
[3] Institute for Intelligent Cooperating Systems, University of Magdeburg,
Universitätsplatz 2, 39106 Magdeburg, Germany

Abstract. In the present study, we investigate the differences in brain signals of craving smokers, non-craving smokers, and non-smokers. To this end, we use data from resting-state EEG measurements to train predictive models to distinguish these three groups. We compare the results obtained from three simple models – majority class prediction, random guessing, and naive Bayes – as well as two neural network approaches. The first of these approaches uses a channel-wise model with dense layers, the second one uses cross-channel convolution. We therefore generate a benchmark on the given data set and show that there is a significant difference in the EEG signals of smokers and non-smokers.

Keywords: Smoker · Craving · EEG · Neural network · Classification

1 Introduction

Substance abuse and addiction have many negative effects on the health of the addicted individual, and society as a whole, with the resulting health care costs alone being staggeringly high. Understanding how addiction works in the brain is therefore of utmost importance, as it is the first step in determining the best ways to treat addiction. Nicotine is legally used worldwide and provides an excellent opportunity to study addiction in the brain for multiple reasons. First, nicotine, like other drugs, has chemical effects on the brain, which can be measured (e.g., [10]). Second, after only few hours of abstinence, smokers start to crave the next cigarette – a hallmark of addiction, the neural underpinnings of which are little understood. Third, the legality and prevalence of nicotine provides an available subject population, without the ethically and legally questionable issues that can be present when examining addiction in illegal substance abuse. Fourth,

S. Donohue—This work was partially funded by DFG SFB 779 TP A14N.

© Springer Nature Switzerland AG 2018
W. Duivesteijn et al. (Eds.): IDA 2018, LNCS 11191, pp. 75–86, 2018.
https://doi.org/10.1007/978-3-030-01768-2_7

the study of addiction in humans avoids the ethically questionable administration of drugs to animal models, which may or may not respond in similar ways to the drugs as humans do.

In the present study, use neural networks to classify the data from smokers who have just smoked (non-craving), smokers who have abstained from smoking for four hours (craving), and non-smokers. The data format used, electroencephalography (EEG), measures the millisecond-by-millisecond changes in electrical potentials on the scalp, providing a measure of the neural activity over time. We used resting-state data here, in which the participants fixated on a cross for approximately 10 min, to determine if the patterns present in this basic data could be detected and used to classify our subject groups.

2   Related Work

Previous research on addiction has generally used functional magnetic resonance imaging (fMRI) to examine differences in resting-state data between craving and sated smokers [9], or between smokers and non-smokers [17,19], with frontal, executive-control-related regions such as the insula or dorsolateral prefrontal cortex (DLPFC) being implicated in differences present. Previous modeling techniques used machine learning to determine smoking status in fMRI data [12]. FMRI is, however, an expensive method to use, with low temporal resolution and restrictions in subject populations due to its necessary metal-free environment.

Measuring EEG Signals

EEG is a cost-effective and non-invasive technique, which can be used to assess changes in neural activity over time. The data are measured at various electrodes (in the current study, 32) relative to a reference electrode, and the electrodes cover the head in a way (see Fig. 1) to optimally pick up neural signals, presumably generated from local field potentials [11]. Each electrode measures the signal representing one channel of the dataset.

Event Related Analysis

One more traditional way to analyze EEG data is to conduct an event-related analysis. In this form, a subject is given a task, and every time an event is presented (e.g., a picture), a code signal is added to the data, which can be used for time-locked selective averaging. Using this method on a partially overlapping population with the present study, Donohue and colleagues [3] found that when smokers were craving, they showed generally more arousal in their neural activity in response to all stimuli presented,

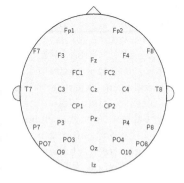

Fig. 1. EEG electrode locations.

and, regardless of whether the image was nicotine-related or non-nicotine related.

It is an open question, however, if overall enhanced arousal would be present in resting-state data, and if the differences observed in the event-related study are great enough to be captured by a machine learning algorithm.

Resting State Analysis

For many other big-data tasks, the important patterns are known. For example the p300 [18] shows a specific reaction to stimuli after 300 ms, which has been widely used since its discovery. One difficulty of using resting-state signals is that these patterns are unknown in our case. Previous studies using EEG measures disagree on the frequency bands in which significant differences occur. For smokers, Brown [2] found reduced alpha and increased rhythmic high frequency, Rass [13] detected reduced alpha as well, but also reduced delta and Knott [6] reports reduced delta and increased beta.

EEG Analysis using Neural Networks

The recent developments in feature extraction using neural networks offers a novel way to examine brain data, to find patterns, which may be highly meaningful and would otherwise remain undiscovered. Schirrmeister [15] applied deep convolutional neural networks (CNNs) on EEG data. They share connection weights to find specific local patterns within the given data. With pictures, CNNs have proven to be very successful for object recognition on the Imagenet competition [7]. As objects in pictures are represented by groups of nearby pixels, convolutions are perfectly tailored for this task. However, it is not clear that the patterns we are looking for in the EEG are also local.

3   Data Description and Preprocessing

The experimental methods and procedures used in this study were authorized by the Ethics Committee at the Otto-von-Guericke University of Magdeburg. From all participants of the study written, informed consent was given prior the participation. All subjects were financially compensated for their time.

Initially, EEG data from 30 smokers and 9 non-smokers were measured by 32 electrodes positioned on the scalp in the frequently-used 10-20-system as depicted in Fig. 1. Smokers were measured in two sessions: In the non-craving session they had recently smoked a cigarette, in the craving session they had not smoked for at least 4 h. For non-smokers, only one session was obtained. Each recording session consists of 9.5 min resting state with a recording frequency of 508 Hz. Specifically, one measurement contains $508 \text{ Hz} \times 60 \text{ s} \times 9.5 \text{ min} \approx 290.000$ dimensions per channel.

Preprocessing

EEG electrodes not only measure signals arising from the brain, but they also pick up various forms of noise. As a first preprocessing step, we applied a low-pass filter at 30 Hz and a high-pass filter at 0.5 Hz. This removed high frequency noise, including power line interference, some muscle artifacts, slow-drift related

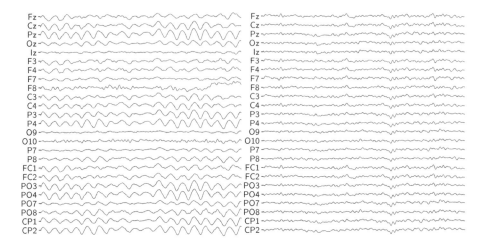

Fig. 2. Data snippet from non-smoker

Fig. 3. Data snippet from craving smoker

movements, respiration and sweat artifacts. Subsequently, we removed physiological artifacts using Independent Component Analysis (ICA). This algorithm uses the sensor signals and creates independent components. From these, we manually selected and removed components containing eye blinks, eye movements and heart beat. The selection of the components was conservative, as the removal of a noise-like component also removes some brain signals, and it is not possible to remove only the noisy parts of a component.

We verified visually that the ICA had successfully removed these artifacts, but it had also created high frequency noise, which is why we filtered again, keeping only the signal between 0.5 Hz and 30 Hz. To additionally exclude any remaining physiological noise present in the data, we excluded channels Fp1 and Fp2 (eye artifacts) and T7 and T8 (muscle artifacts) from subsequent analysis.

We had to exclude three participants: One had fallen asleep during recording, and two more were rejected, as we could not successfully remove the artifacts without removing most of the signal as well. For the subsequent analysis, we used data from a final set of 27 smokers and 9 non-smokers, each with 25 channels. Sample snippets of approximately two seconds of preprocessed data are shown for a non-smoker in Fig. 2 and for a craving smoker in Fig. 3. We chose snippets that can be distinguished as easy as possible. We performed the preprocessing using the MNE framework [4].

Effects Hypothesized to be Inherent

EEG data is well known to have a bad signal-to-noise ratio, even when carefully preprocessed. We suppose that two effects could be inherent, an effect of addiction and an effect of craving. We investigate both effects by creating models for classifying two or three classes. Considering *craving smokers vs. non-smokers* should measure both effects, which, if these effects sum up, would be indicated by a high predictability. *Non-craving smokers vs. non-smokers* only measures the effect of addiction and *craving vs. non-craving* takes the effect of craving into account. The most difficult problem uses data from all three classes and tries to distinguish them all.

The measurements for craving and non-craving subjects were taken from the same subjects. This means, for training of the models containing craving and non-craving measurements, a problem with the assumption of test sets and training sets being independent and identically distributed (i.i.d) occurs if data from the same subject are used in both sets simultaneously. For a detailed description, we refer to the work of Le Boudec [8]. Although this seems like a theoretical problem, it is possible that our models find and learn person-specific patterns (i.e., identifying a specific subject) [14]. These patterns could confuse the model when a subject was in both data sets at the same time. This can cause difficulties for the model, as it gets the opportunity to learn subject-specific patterns in the EEG signals, which might be used to identify the person. To mitigate this problem, for all subjects both measurements (craving and non-craving) were used either for training or for testing. In this case it is still possible that the model learns person-specific patterns, but these will not directly affect the results.

4   Methodology

The data set contains measurements from 36 participants, which is a lot for medical studies, as measurements are expensive, but is very small for data analysis. Therefore the general reliability of the results is low, and results should be verified with more data, when available. This also motivates the need for a methodology that adds as little variance as possible.

With data from only 36 participants, a classification is prone to over-fit the training data and needs a good feature extraction, especially since our input space has ≈ 290.000 dimensions per channel. We focus here on neural network models, which are known for their ability to automatically detect features that are relevant for the task at hand. To reduce the problem of few measurements, bootstrapping methods exist, which generate more training examples by re-sampling the data. All samples generated from one measurement have to be considered statistically dependent on each other. This means, in order to keep the independence assumption, they may not be used in both the training and the testing set at the same time.

In our case we apply bootstrapping by taking time windows of fixed size from a measurement and use these windows instead of the whole measurement. This leads to two advantages: First, it reduces the dimensionality, second it increases the number of training samples. But it also raises questions: Which length should the window have and should windows be allowed to overlap?

A larger window length gives the model a longer signal to process and therefore more information, which might help to distinguish the classes, but it also increases the time to process the data. On the other hand a smaller window length makes it possible to generate more training samples.

Another important topic is the validation method. With few samples it is common to reuse data several times in independent tests in order to get an estimate of the quality, for an unknown, unseen data set. A good overview of cross-validation procedures was written by Arlot [1].

In the Leave-One-Out Cross-Validation *(LOO-CV)* one measurement is used for validation, while all others are used for training. For 36 subjects, the number of different splits with *LOO-CV* is only 36, which causes limited computational costs, but also lacks the possibility to perform more independent runs. This method maximizes the number of training samples but is known to return optimistic results.

The random shuffle split cross-validation copes with these problems: We split our data into training and test data at a certain arbitrarily chosen ratio. We choose 7 out of every 9 subjects for the training data and the remaining 2 for testing, i.e. 28 for training, 8 for testing in total. This means we randomly choose two non-smokers and six smokers out of the 36 subjects as test set. To minimize variance during the testing we apply stratification. This guarantees that for any random split, those ratios hold for all classes. As the numbers of smokers and non-smokers are multiples of 9 in all classes (27 craving, 27 non-craving and 9 non-smoker), no rounding is needed here. The random choice has the advantage that it can easily be repeated often to generate more reliable results. In this example, there are $\binom{27}{6}$ possibilities to choose smokers and another $\binom{9}{2}$ for non-smokers, which adds up to 10.656.360 possibilities.

With 3 times as many smokers as non-smokers, our classes are unbalanced. We handle this by balancing the class weights during the training and the validation process. To score our results, we use the class-balanced accuracy in all our experiments. Note that this score is equivalent to the class-balanced F_1-Score [16] with micro-averaging.

5   Experimentation and Results

We performed two series of experiments. In the first one we wanted to start simple. We focused on the problem to distinguish non-smokers (ns) from craving smokers (c), as we expected it to be the easiest. We looked for possibly small networks and a set of parameters that generates results better than guessing. We performed various experiments on network structures, network parameters as optimizers and number of epochs and we also varied the window length.

The second experimentation series was meant to check the other problems, to improve the results, to correct possible weaknesses and to try a different network structure. Here, we were aiming for reliable and statistically significant results, so we needed to repeat the experiments several times.

5.1   First Series of Experiments

We found the following experiment set-up to be working. We used *LOO-CV*, non-overlapping windows of length 1000, which corresponds to pieces of approximately two seconds. Thus, we created 290.000/1.000 = 290 training samples per

Table 1. Network Structures of Dense Networks

Name	Structure
Dense 1	(25 × 5) merge × 64 × 2
Dense 2	(25 × 10) merge × 128 × 64 × 2
Dense 3	(25 × 20) merge × 256 × 128 × 64 × 2

measurement. Using one measurement per subject, we received 10.440 samples in 25.000 dimensions.

Our neural networks used mostly dense layers and dropout. We experimented with three different models, which contain mainly dense layers and dropout. Our smallest model is Dense 1. It starts with an independent dense layer with 5 neurons for each of the 25 channels. Their outputs are then merged into one layer of 125 neurons. Next follows a dropout (rate: .2) and another dense layer with 64 neurons. Finally, we add again dropout (rate: .1) and softmax with one neuron per class.

All three variants are summarized in Table 1. For networks Dense 2 and Dense 3 we increased the number of neurons in the layer before the merge and added further dense layers (each of them accompanied by a dropout of .2) after the merge.

Results of the First Series

Dense 1 reached 60.9%, Dense 2 59.7% and Dense 3 65,9% as average class-weighted prediction accuracy. As random guessing would achieve 50%, these results indicate that it is possible to find the combined effects of smoking and craving within EEG data.

Our analysis of the first experiment series indicated that our models have a tendency to predict the craving class. As there are three times as many craving subjects as non-smokers, this imbalance occurs as well in the test set of the *LOO-CV* and could result in overly optimistic results. Hence, in the second experiment series, we repeat these experiments with random shuffle split cross-validation. (Note: As we show detailed results for shuffle split, we omit the detailed results here.)

5.2   Second Series of Experiments

In the second series of experiments we consider all four classification problems (three 2-class problems and the 3-class problem) in order to investigate the effects of smoking and of craving separately and in combination. We use shuffle-split cross-validation with 100 repetitions in order to get unbiased and reliable results. To overcome the limited number of possible samples, we now sample random pieces with replacement permitting overlapping. In this way the number of possible pieces per measurement increases to 290.000 minus the window length. We fix the number of samples per epoch to 10.000. We also compare our results to those of the simple models: predicting the majority class, random guessing, and naive Bayes. Finally, we perform t-tests to show that our models perform significantly better than the simple models. As Schirrmeister [15] recommended, we also try a convolutional network which applies a convolution over the channels. We start with a convolutional layer with 512 filters, followed by a max-pooling by Factor 2. Then again a convolution layer with 512 filters, followed by a max-pooling by Factor 2. It follows a flatten and a dense layer with 1024 neurons. The final layer uses softmax.

Results of the Second Series

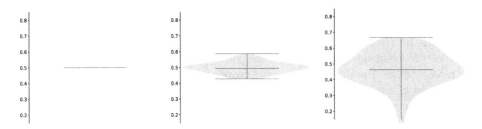

Fig. 4. Majority class   **Fig. 5.** Random guessing   **Fig. 6.** Naive Bayes

For analyzing the results, we use violin plots of the average class-weighted prediction accuracy. They visualize the distribution of results and therefore show more than just mean and standard deviation. Figures 4, 5, 6 show the violin plots when predicting the majority class, when randomly guessing, and when using a naive Bayes predictor to distinguish craving and non-smokers. The first shows zero variance at a mean of 0.5. Random guessing imports some variance at the same mean value. The Bayes model has the highest variance and even a worse mean value. It is unable to detect the relevant features.

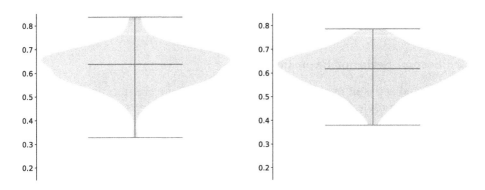

Fig. 7. C vs NS: Dense 3   **Fig. 8.** C vs NS: CNN

Craving vs. Non-Smoker

In contrast to the simple models, our neural networks are able to find the combined effects of smoking and craving. Figure 7 shows with 63.7% even better results than the Convolutional Network in Fig. 8. Yet, the earlier 65.9% of Dense 3 were indeed optimistic.

Craving vs. Non-Craving

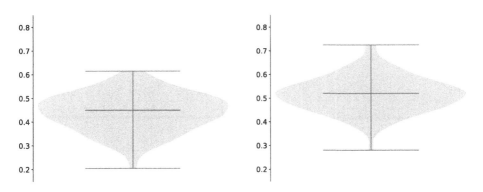

Fig. 9. C vs NC: Dense 3   **Fig. 10.** C vs NC: CNN

The effect of craving in EEG data seems to be very small. In Fig. 9 we see the performance of the Dense 3 network. With a median accuracy of 45% it is worse than random guessing. The convolutional network has a median accuracy of 52%. A t-test for different means comparing with random guessing returned a p-value of 0.156. This means our models are unable to predict the craving effect significantly better than guessing.

Non-craving vs. Non-smoker

The Dense model is able to detect the effect of smoking with a median accuracy of 61.8% (Fig. 11) and outperforms the convolutional network (see Fig. 12), which achieves only 57.8%. This shows that the effect of smoking (without craving) can be found in EEG signals.

3-Class-Problem

For the three class problem, the convolutional network has a median accuracy of 37.6% and outperforms the dense network (Fig. 13), which reaches only 33.1% – the level of random guessing. So compared to craving vs. non-smoker, the non-craving data reduced the prediction ability of Dense 3. The convolutional network shows again (Fig. 14) predictions that are significantly better than guessing ($p < 0.0001$).

Finally, we look at the confusion matrix for the 3-class case. The entries contain the average normalized values and their variance as numbers and more

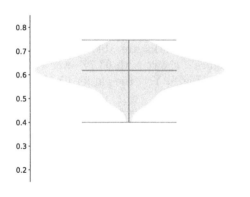

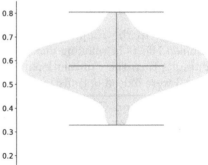

Fig. 11. NC vs NS: Dense 3

Fig. 12. NC vs NS: CNN

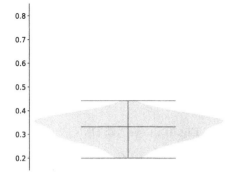

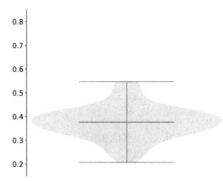

Fig. 13. 3class: Dense 3

Fig. 14. 3class: Convolutional Network

reddish color indicates a higher mean. Figures 15 and 16 show that both models are good at correctly predicting the craving class, while both have a low quality identifying non-smokers. Also both frequently predict craving, when non-craving is correct. Therefore, this confirms that the craving effect – if existent – is difficult to find. The CNN has higher rates for all correct predictions and is clearly the better model. Nevertheless, it shows more variance in most of the cases.

6   Conclusion and Future Work

In this work, we created models to distinguish craving smokers, non-craving smokers and non-smokers. Our models are able to successfully distinguish smokers from non-smokers. Nevertheless, we found no model able to find a significant effect of craving within the data. Models distinguishing all three classes showed the same weakness.

We have shown that resting-state EEG measurements contain information on the smoking status of a person. This is a great result, especially since EEG data are known to have a low signal-to-noise ratio and thus a good classification

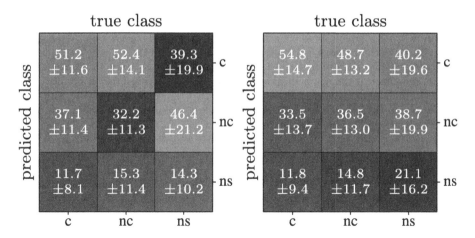

Fig. 15. Dense 3 Confusion Matrix   **Fig. 16.** CNN Confusion Matrix

cannot be expected. This promising finding builds the basis of future research with many implications for the study of addiction in cognitive neuroscience.

For our future work, we plan to investigate recurrent networks like the Long-Short-Term-Memory (LSTM) [5]. These units have shown good results when modeling multivariate time series, such as EEG signals. Further, we aim for visualizing the network's features in order to gain insights what are the patterns that differ in the brains of smokers and non-smokers.

References

1. Arlot, Sylvain, Celisse, Alain: A survey of cross-validation procedures for model selection. Stat. Surv. **4**, 40–79 (2010)
2. Brown, Barbara B.: Some characteristic EEG differences between heavy smoker and non-smoker subjects. Neuropsychologia **6**(4), 381–388 (1968)
3. Donohue, S.E., Woldorff, M.G., Hopf, J.-M., Harris, J.A., Heinze, H.-J., Schoenfeld, M.A.: An electrophysiological dissociation of craving and stimulus-dependent attentional capture in smokers. Cogn. Affect. Behav. Neurosci. **16**(6), 1114–1126 (2016)
4. Gramfort, A., et al.: MEG and EEG data analysis with MNE-Python. Front. Neurosci. **7** (2013)
5. Hochreiter, Sepp, Schmidhuber, Jürgen: Long short-term memory. Neural Comput. **9**(8), 1735–1780 (1997)
6. Knott, Verner, Cosgrove, Meaghan, Villeneuve, Crystal, Fisher, Derek, Millar, Anne, McIntosh, Judy: EEG correlates of imagery-induced cigarette craving in male and female smokers. Addict. Behav. **33**(4), 616–621 (2008)
7. Krizhevsky, A., Sutskever, I., Hinton, G.E.: Imagenet classification with deep convolutional neural networks. Adv. Neural Inf. Process. Syst. 1097–1105 (2012)
8. Le Boudec, Jean-Yves: Performance Evaluation of Computer and Communication Systems. EPFL Press, Lausanne (2010)

9. Lerman, C., Gu, H., Loughead, J., Ruparel, K., Yang, Y., Stein, E.A.: Large-scale brain network coupling predicts acute nicotine abstinence effects on craving and cognitive function. JAMA psychiatry **71**(5), 523–530 (2014)
10. Logemann, H.N.A., Böcker, K.B.E., Deschamps, P.K.H., Kemner, C., Kenemans, J.L.: The effect of the augmentation of cholinergic neurotransmission by nicotine on EEG indices of visuospatial attention. Behav. Brain Res. **260**, 67–73 (2014)
11. Luck, S.J.: An introduction to the event-related potential technique (cognitive neuroscience). A Bradford Book (2005)
12. Pariyadath, V., Stein, E.A., Ross, T.J.: Machine learning classification of resting state functional connectivity predicts smoking status. Front. Hum. Neurosci. **8**, 425 (2014)
13. Rass, O., Ahn, W.Y., O'Donnell, B.F.: Resting-state EEG, impulsiveness, and personality in daily and nondaily smokers. Clin. Neurophys. **127**(1), 409–418 (2016)
14. Schetinin, V., Jakaite, L., Nyah, N., Novakovic, D., Krzanowski, W.: Feature extraction with gmdh-type neural networks for EEG-based person identification. Int. J. Neural Syst. 1750064 (2017)
15. Schirrmeister, R.T., et al.: Deep learning with convolutional neural networks for brain mapping and decoding of movement-related information from the human EEG. arXiv preprint arXiv:1703.05051 (2017)
16. Sebastiani, Fabrizio: Machine learning in automated text categorization. ACM Comput. Surv. (CSUR) **34**(1), 1–47 (2002)
17. Stoeckel, L.E., Chai, X.J., Zhang, J., Whitfield-Gabrieli, S., Evins, A.E.: Lower gray matter density and functional connectivity in the anterior insula in smokers compared with never smokers. Addict. Biol. **21**(4), 972–981 (2016)
18. Sutton, Samuel, Braren, Margery, Zubin, Joseph, John, E.R.: Evoked-potential correlates of stimulus uncertainty. Science **150**(3700), 1187–1188 (1965)
19. Weiland, B.J., Sabbineni, A., Calhoun, V.D., Welsh, R.C., Hutchison, K.E.: Reduced executive and default network functional connectivity in cigarette smokers. Hum. Brain Mapp. **36**(3), 872–882 (2015)

Missing Data Imputation via Denoising Autoencoders: The Untold Story

Adriana Fonseca Costa, Miriam Seoane Santos, Jastin Pompeu Soares,
and Pedro Henriques Abreu[(✉)]

CISUC, Department of Informatics Engineering, University of Coimbra,
Coimbra, Portugal
{adrianaifc,miriams,jastinps}@student.dei.uc.pt, pha@dei.uc.pt

Abstract. Missing data consists in the lack of information in a dataset and since it directly influences classification performance, neglecting it is not a valid option. Over the years, several studies presented alternative imputation strategies to deal with the three missing data mechanisms, Missing Completely At Random, Missing At Random and Missing Not At Random. However, there are no studies regarding the influence of all these three mechanisms on the latest high-performance Artificial Intelligence techniques, such as Deep Learning. The goal of this work is to perform a comparison study between state-of-the-art imputation techniques and a Stacked Denoising Autoencoders approach. To that end, the missing data mechanisms were synthetically generated in 6 different ways; 8 different imputation techniques were implemented; and finally, 33 complete datasets from different open source repositories were selected. The obtained results showed that Support Vector Machines imputation ensures the best classification performance while Multiple Imputation by Chained Equations performs better in terms of imputation quality.

Keywords: Missing data · Missing mechanisms · Data imputation
Denoising autoencoders

1 Introduction

Missing Data is a common problem that appears in real-world datasets and is an important issue since it affects the performance of classifiers [20]. Over the past decades, many methods have been proposed to impute the missing values. In the research community, three main missing mechanisms are recognised – Missing Completely At Random (MCAR), Missing At Random (MAR) and Missing Not At Random (MNAR) – and adjusting the imputation method to the missing mechanism is crucial, since an improper choice can bias the classification performance [23]. Deep Learning techniques are currently a hot topic in Machine Learning literature [2], although their application for imputation purposes remains an understudied topic.

This work analyses the appropriateness of Stacked Denoising Autoencoders (SDAE) to impute the different data mechanisms, considering univariate and

© Springer Nature Switzerland AG 2018
W. Duivesteijn et al. (Eds.): IDA 2018, LNCS 11191, pp. 87–98, 2018.
https://doi.org/10.1007/978-3-030-01768-2_8

multivariate scenarios. The performance of SDAE is then compared to the performance of state-of-the-art imputation techniques. To achieve that, we selected 33 complete datasets from different open source repositories and simulated the missing mechanisms using 6 different configurations. Then, 8 different imputation techniques are evaluated in terms of F-measure and Root Mean Squared Error (RMSE). Summing up, the contributions of this research are the following: (i) presenting a comparative study that considers several missing data mechanisms, imputation methods and missing rates (5, 10, 15, 20, 40%), (ii) proposing an imputation approach based on SDAE and (iii) simultaneously evaluating the quality of imputation (similarly to related work) and the benefits for classification performance (mostly overlooked in related work). Our experiments show that the imputation methods (and consequently the classification performance) are influenced by missing mechanisms and configurations. Furthermore, we conclude that SDAE do not show a significant advantage over other standard imputation algorithms: regarding the quality of imputation, Multiple Imputation by Chained Equations (MICE) seems to be a better approach while Support Vector Machines (SVM) provides the best imputation for the classification stage. This document is organised as follows: Sect. 2 presents several research works that considered different configurations to generate the missing mechanisms and studied well-know imputation techniques and some recent deep learning approaches. Then, Sect. 3 describes the different stages of the experimental setup while Sect. 4 discusses the obtained results. Finally, Sect. 5 concludes the paper and presents some possibilities for future work.

2   Background Knowledge and Related Work

In this section, we provide some background on missing data mechanisms and imputation methods, also including a thorough explanation on the procedure of SDAE. Along with some background information, we refer to previous work on both topics, highlighting their main objectives and conclusions.

2.1   Missing Mechanisms

There are three mechanisms under which missing data can occur [15]: MCAR, MAR and MNAR [10]. MCAR occurs when the reason why data is missing is unrelated to any observed or unobserved value from the dataset (e.g. a survey participant had a flat tire and misses his appointment). In the case of MAR, the cause of the missing data is unrelated to the missing values but it is related with observed values from the dataset (e.g. an investigator finds that women are less likely to reveal their weight) and finally, in the case of MNAR, the probability of a value to be missing is related to the value itself (e.g. obese subjects are less likely to reveal their weight).

These mechanisms could be generated in various ways and several different examples could be found in the literature [9,12,18,23,26,28]. Twala et al. [23] investigated the robustness and accuracy of techniques for handling incomplete data for different mechanisms of missing data. Three suites of data were created corresponding to MCAR, MAR and MNAR. For each of them, univariate (one feature only) and multivariate (several features) generation of missing data was performed using 21 datasets. These approaches were implemented for 3 missing rates (15, 30 and 50%). Rieger et al. [18] performed an extensive study covering both classification and regression problems and a variety of missing data mechanisms. Four different types of MAR generation are proposed as well as a mechanism for MCAR generation. Garciarena et al. [12] studied the interaction between missing data mechanisms, imputation methods and supervised classification algorithms. The authors generated missing values for the three different mechanisms and present two different versions of MNAR. In total, 4 missing data configurations are created for 6 different missing rates (5, 10, 20, 30, 40 and 50%) on 10 datasets from UCI Machine Learning Repository.

2.2   Imputation Algorithms

Imputation methods aim to find a plausible value to replace one that is missing and are mainly divided into statistical-based or machine learning-based methods [11]. Statistical methods consist in substituting the missing observations with the most similar ones among the training data, without the need of constructing a predictive model to evaluate their "similarity" (e.g. Mean imputation – Meanimp, MICE, Expectation-Maximization – EM). Machine learning-based techniques, construct a predictive model with the complete available data to estimate values for substituting those that are missing (e.g. k-Nearest Neighbours imputation – kNNimp, SVM imputation – SVMimp, DAE imputation).

Garciarena et al. [12] compared the performance of 8 different imputation techniques including MICE, Meanimp and EM. The classification results (evaluated with F-measure) showed that MICE was the best technique. García-Laencina et al. [9] proposed an approach that achieves a balance between classification and imputation by using Multi-Task Learning perceptrons. This approach is compared with 4 well-known imputation methods (including kNNimp) using classification accuracy. The results show that the proposed method outperforms the other well-known techniques. Twala et al. [23] studied the effect of different imputation techniques in classification accuracy of a decision tree. The authors used 7 imputation methods including EM and Meanimp. The results show that EM works well on small datasets, particularly for numeric attributes. Xia et al. [26] compared their proposed algorithm with 5 imputation methods, including Meanimp and kNNimp. They used accuracy and Area Under the ROC Curve (AUC) as evaluation metric for the classification process (using a Random Forest classifier).

General neural network-based methods have been increasingly used for missing data imputation; however, deep learning architectures especially designed for missing data imputation has not yet been explored to its full potential. Denoising Autoencoders (DAE) [24] are an example of deep architectures that are designed to recover noisy data ($\tilde{\mathbf{x}}$), which can exist due to data corruption via some additive mechanism or by missing data. DAE are a variant of

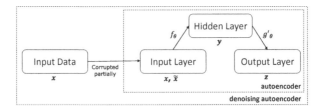

Fig. 1. Differences between autoencoder and denoising autoencoder structures.

autoencoders (AE) – Fig. 1 – which is a type of neural network that uses back-propagation to learn a representation for a set of data. Each autoencoder is composed by three layers (input, hidden and output layer) which can be divided into two parts: encoder (from the input layer to the output of the hidden layer) and decoder (from the hidden layer to the output of the output layer). The encoder part maps an input vector $\mathbf{x}$ to a hidden representation $\mathbf{y}$, through a nonlinear transformation $f_\theta(\mathbf{x}) = s(\mathbf{x}\mathbf{W}^T + \mathbf{b})$ where θ represents $\mathbf{W}$ (weight matrix) and $\mathbf{b}$ (bias vector) parameters. The resulting $\mathbf{y}$ representation is then mapped back to a vector $\mathbf{z}$ which have the same shape of $\mathbf{x}$, where $\mathbf{z}$ is equal to $g'_\theta(\mathbf{y}) = s(\mathbf{W'y} + \mathbf{b'})$. The train of an autoencoder consists in optimising the model parameters ($\mathbf{W}$, $\mathbf{W'}$, $\mathbf{b}$ and $\mathbf{b'}$), minimising the reconstruction error between $\mathbf{x}$ and $\mathbf{z}$. Vincent et al. [25] proposed a strategy to build deep networks by stacking layers of Denoising Autoencoders – SDAE. The results have shown that stacking DAE improves the performance over the standard DAE. In two recent works, Gondara et al. studied the appropriateness of SDAE for multiple imputation [13] and their application to imputation in clinical health records (recovering loss to followup information) [14]. In these works, the proposed algorithm is compared with MICE using the Predictive Mean Matching method. In the first work, authors consider only MCAR and MNAR mechanisms. The imputation results of both mechanisms are compared using sum of Root Mean Squared Error ($RMSE_{sum}$). Additionally, MNAR mechanism is also evaluated in terms of classification error, using a Random Forest classifier. In the second work, authors propose a SDAE model to handle imputation in healthcare data, using datasets under MCAR and MNAR mechanisms. The simulation results showed that their proposed approach surpassed the state-of-the-art methods. In both previous works, although authors prove the advantages of SDAE for imputation, a complete study under all missing mechanisms is not provided, since in both cases, MAR generation is completely disregarded. Furthermore, they only compare two imputation methods (MICE and SDAE) and the classification performance is only evaluated for one mechanism (MNAR). Beaulieu et al. [4] used SDAE to impute data in electronic health records. This approach is compared with five other imputation strategies (including Meanimp and kNNimp) and evaluated with RMSE. The results show that the proposed SDAE-based approach outperforms MICE. Duan et al. [7,8] used SDAE for traffic data imputation. In the first work [7], the proposed approach is compared with another one that uses artificial neural networks with the same set of layers and nodes as the ones used in SDAE. In the second work [8] another imputation method is used (ARIMA – AutoRegressive Integrated Moving-Average) for comparison. To evaluate the imputation process authors used RMSE, Mean Absolute Error (MAE) and Mean Relative Error (MRE). Ning et al. [17] proposed an algorithm based on SDAE for dealing with big data of quality inspection. The proposed approach is compared with two other imputation algorithms (GBWKNN [19] and MkNNI [16]) that are both based on the k-nearest neighbour algorithm. The results are evaluated through d_2 (the suitability between the imputed value and the actual value) and RMSE. The above-mentioned works show that the proposed imputation methods outperform the ones used for comparison, showing that deep learning based techniques are promising in the field of imputation. Sánchez-Morales et al. [22] proposed an imputation method that uses a SDAE. The main goal of their work was to understand how the proposed approach can improve the results obtained in the pre-imputation step. They used three state of the art methods for the pre-imputation: Zero Imputation, kNNimp and SVMimp. The results, for three datasets from UCI, are evaluated in terms of MSE. Authors concluded that the SDAE is capable of improving the final results for a pre-imputed dataset. To summarise, most of related work does not address all three missing data mechanisms and mostly evaluates the results in terms of quality of imputation rather than also evaluating the usefulness of an imputation method to generate quality data for classification. Furthermore, none of the reviewed works studies the effect of different missing data mechanisms on imputation techniques (including DAE) for several missing rates.

3   Experiments

We start our experiments by collecting 33 publicly available real-world datasets (UCI Machine Learning Repository, KEEL, STATLIB) to analyse the effect of different missing mechanisms (using different configurations) on imputation methods. Some of the original datasets were preprocessed in order to remove instances containing small amounts of missing values. In the case of multiclass datasets, they were modified in order to represent a binary problem. Afterwards, we perform the missing data generation, inserting missing values at five missing rates (5, 10, 15, 20 and 40%) following 6 different scenarios ($MCAR_{univa}$, $MCAR_{unifo}$, MAR_{univa}, MAR_{unifo}, $MNAR_{univa}$ and $MNAR_{unifo}$) based on state-of-the-art generation methods. Five runs were performed for each missing generation, per dataset and missing rate. To provide a clear explanation of all the generation methods it is important to establish some basic notation. Therefore, let us assume a dataset $\mathbf{X}$ represented by a $n \times p$ matrix, where $i = 1, ..., n$ patterns and $j = 1, ..., p$ attributes. The elements of $\mathbf{X}$ are denoted by x_{ij}, each individual feature in $\mathbf{X}$ is denoted by x_j and each pattern is referred to as $\mathbf{x}_i = [x_{i,1}, x_{i,2}, ..., x_{i,j}, ..., x_{i,p}]$. For the univariate configuration, $univa$, the feature that will have the missing values, x_m, will always be the one most correlated with the class labels and the determining feature x_d is the one most correlated with x_m. Regarding multivariate configurations, $unifo$, there are several alternatives to choose the missing values positions which will be detailed later.

Missing Completely at Random. For the univariate configuration of MCAR, $MCAR_{univa}$, we consider the method proposed by Rieger et al. [18] and Xia et al. [26]. This configuration chooses random locations in x_m to be missing, i.e., random values of $x_{i,m}$ are eliminated. The multivariate configuration of MCAR is proposed in the work of Garciarena et al. [12]. $MCAR_{unifo}$ chooses random locations, $x_{i,j}$, in the dataset to be missing until the desired MR is reached.

Missing at Random. The univariate configuration of MAR is based on ranks of x_d: the probability of a pattern $x_{i,m}$ to be missing is computed by dividing the rank of $x_{i,m}$ in the determining feature x_d by the sum of all ranks for x_d – this configuration method is herein referred to as MAR_{univa}. Then, the patterns to have missing values are sampled according to such probability, until the desired MR is reached [18,26]. The multivariate configuration of MAR, MAR_{unifo}, starts by defining pairs of features which include a determining and a missing feature $\{x_d, x_m\}$. This pair selection was based on high correlations among all the features of the dataset. In the case of having an odd number of features, the unpaired feature may be added to the pair which contains its most correlated feature. For each pair of correlated features, the missing feature will be the one most correlated with the labels. In the case of having a triple of correlated features, there will be two missing features which will also be those most correlated with the class labels. x_m will be missing for the observations that are below the MR percentile in the determining feature x_d. This means that the lowest observations of x_d will be deleted on x_m.

Missing Not at Random. $MNAR_{univa}$ was proposed by Twala et al. [23]: for this method the feature x_m itself is used as determining feature, i.e., the MR percentile of x_m is determined and values of x_m lower than a cut-off value are removed. The multivariate configuration of MNAR, $MNAR_{unifo}$, was also proposed by Twala et al. [23] and is called *Missingness depending on unobserved Variables (MuOV)*, where each feature of the dataset has the same number of missing values for the same observations. The missing observations are randomly chosen.

Nine imputation methods were then applied to the incomplete data: Mean imputation (Meanimp), imputation with kNN (kNNimp), imputation with SVM (SVMimp), MICE, EM imputation and SDAE-based imputation. Meanimp imputes the missing values with the mean of the complete values in the respective feature [12,23,26], while kNNimp imputes the incomplete patterns according to the values of their k-nearest neighbours [9,26]. For kNNimp we considered the euclidean distance and a set of closest neighbours (1, 3 and 5). SVMimp was implemented considering a gaussian kernel – Radial Basis Function (RBF) [11]: the incomplete feature is used as target, while the remaining features are used to fit the model. The search for optimal parameters C and γ of the kernel was performed through a grid search for each dataset (different ranges of values were tested: 10^{-2} to 10^{10} for C and 10^{-9} to 10^3 for γ, both ranges increasing by a factor of 10). MICE is a multiple imputation technique that specifies a separate conditional model for each feature with missing data [3]. For each model, all other features can be used as predictors [13,14]. EM is a maximum-likelihood-based missing data imputation method which estimates parameters by maximising the expected log-likelihood of the complete data [6]. The above methods were applied using open-source python implementations: `scikit-learn` for SVMimp and Meanimp, `fancyimpute` for kNNimp and MICE and `impyute` for EM.

Regarding the SDAE, we propose a model based on stacked denoising autoencoders, for the complete reconstruction of missing data. It was implemented using Keras library with a Theano backend. SDAE require complete data for initialisation so missing patterns are pre-imputed using the well-known Mean/Mode imputation method. We also apply z-score standardisation to the input data in order to have a faster convergence. There are two types of representations for an autoencoder [5]: overcomplete, where the hidden layer has more nodes than input layer and undercomplete, where the hidden layer is smaller than the input layer.

Our architecture is overcomplete, which means that the encoder block has more units in consecutive hidden layers than the input layer. This architecture of the SDAE is similar to the one proposed by Gondara et al. [13]. The model is composed by an input layer, 5 hidden layers and an output layer which form the encoder and the decoder (both constructed using regular densely-connected neural network layers). The number of nodes for each hidden layer was set to 7, as it has proven to obtain good results in related work [13]. For the encoding layers we chose hyperbolic tangent (`tanh`) as activation function due to its greater gradients [5]. Rectified Linear Units function (`reLu`) was used as activation function in the decoding layers. We have performed experiments with two different configurations for the training phase: the first one was adapted from Gondara et al. [13] while for the second one we have decided to study a different optimisation function – Adadelta optimisation algorithm – since it avoids the difficulties of defining a proper learning rate [27]. At the end, we have decided to use Adadelta since it proved to be most effective. Therefore, our final SDAE is trained with 100 epochs using Adadelta optimisation algorithm [27] and mean squared error as loss function. Our model has an input dropout ratio of 50%, which means that half of the network inputs are set to zero in each training batch. To prevent the training data from overfitting we add a regularization function named $L2$ [5]. Our imputation approach based on this SDAE considers the creation of three different models (for three different training sets), for which three runs will be made (multiple imputation). This approach is illustrated in Algorithm 1 and works as follows: (1) the instances of each dataset are divided in three equal-size sets; (2) each set is used as test set, while the remaining two are used to feed the SDAE in the training phase; (3) 3 multiple runs will be performed for each one of these models; (4) the output mean of the three models is used to impute the unknown values of the test set. After the imputation step

---

Algorithm 1 Multiple imputation using SDAE

Input: Pre-imputed dataset X, p data partitions, k multiple imputations
1: **for** $i = 1 \rightarrow p$ **do**
2:     Consider all partitions (except partition i) as training set
3:     Consider partition i as test set
4:     **for** $j = 1 \rightarrow k$ **do**
5:         Perform dropout (50%) in training set
6:         Initialise the SDAE with random weights
7:         Fit the imputation model to the training set
8:         Apply the trained model to test set i and save its imputed version j
9:     **end for**
10:    Reconstruct test set i by averaging over all its j versions
11: **end for**
12: **return** Complete dataset X

---

is concluded, we move towards the classification stage. We perform classification with a SVM with linear kernel (considering a value of $C = 1$) and considered two different metrics to evaluate two key performance requirements for imputation techniques: their efficiency on retrieving the true values in data (quality of imputation) [21] and their ability to provide quality data for classification [11]. The quality of imputation was assessed using RMSE, given by $\sqrt{\frac{1}{n} \sum_{i=1}^{n} (x_i - \tilde{x}_i)^2}$, where $\tilde{x}$ are the imputed values of a feature, x are the corresponding original values and n is the number of missing values. The classification performance was assessed using F-measure which consists of an harmonic mean of precision and recall [1], defined as F-measure $= \frac{2 \times \text{precision} \times \text{recall}}{\text{precision} + \text{recall}}$.

4   Results and Discussion

Our work consists of a missing value generation phase followed by imputation and classification. Thus, we evaluate both the imputation quality and its impact on the classification performance. The results are divided by metric (F-measure and RMSE), missing mechanism (MCAR, MAR and MNAR), type of configuration (univariate and multivariate) and missing rate (5, 10, 15, 20 and 40%). Table 1 presents the average results obtained for all the datasets used in this study. As expected, the increase of missing rate leads to a decrease in the performance of classifiers (F-measure) and the quality of imputation (RMSE).

Quality of Imputation (RMSE). For *univa* configurations, MICE proved to be the best approach in most of the scenarios: for MNAR mechanism and a higher MR (40%), SDAE seems to be the best method. For the *unifo* configurations, MICE is the best imputation method for MCAR mechanism, regardless of the MR. Considering MAR mechanism, MICE is also the best method in most of scenarios, except for a higher MR (40%) – SDAE seems to be the best approach. In the case of MNAR mechanism and for lower MRs (5 and 10 %), MICE is also the best approach. However, for higher MRs, the SDAE-based

Table 1. Simulation results by imputation method: average F-measure and RMSE is shown regarding each configuration, missing data mechanism and missing rate. The best results for each configuration and missing mechanism are marked in bold, considering both metrics.

		F-measure						RMSE					
		Univa			Unifo			Univa			Unifo		
MR	Methods	MCAR	MAR	MNAR	MCAR	MAR	MNAR	MCAR	MAR	MNAR	MCAR	MAR	MNAR
5%	Mean	0.7626 (7)	0.7648 (7)	0.7628 (7)	0.7593 (6)	0.7675 (3)	0.7759 (5)	0.2202 (6)	0.2291 (6)	0.3691 (6)	0.2206 (5)	0.2613 (6)	0.3621 (5)
	kNN1	0.7630 (5)	0.7671 (4)	0.7673 (3)	0.7587 (7)	0.7630 (8)	0.7535 (8)	0.2180 (4)	0.2187 (4)	0.3169 (4)	0.2339 (6)	0.2391 (4)	0.3748 (6)
	kNN3	0.7642 (4)	0.7680 (2)	0.7679 (2)	0.7646 (4)	0.7672 (5)	0.7765 (2)	0.1802 (3)	0.1872 (3)	0.2932 (3)	0.1986 (3)	0.2050 (3)	0.3518 (3)
	kNN5	0.7645 (3)	0.7672 (3)	0.7654 (4)	0.7671 (2)	0.7674 (4)	0.7763 (4)	0.1736 (2)	0.1813 (2)	0.2869 (2)	0.1917 (2)	0.1985 (2)	0.3451 (2)
	SVM	**0.7676** (1)	**0.7693** (1)	**0.7715** (1)	**0.7686** (1)	0.7676 (2)	**0.7871** (1)	0.4918 (8)	0.5857 (8)	0.5622 (8)	0.5094 (8)	0.5285 (8)	0.6300 (8)
	EM	0.7591 (8)	0.7634 (8)	0.7618 (8)	0.7460 (8)	0.7648 (7)	0.7654 (7)	0.2979 (7)	0.2998 (7)	0.4064 (7)	0.2947 (7)	0.3173 (7)	0.4016 (7)
	MICE	0.7656 (2)	0.7665 (5)	0.7644 (5)	0.7659 (3)	**0.7692** (1)	0.7751 (6)	**0.1701** (1)	**0.1736** (1)	**0.2805** (1)	**0.1806** (1)	**0.1887** (1)	**0.3143** (1)
	SDAE	0.7627 (6)	0.7651 (6)	0.7630 (6)	0.7595 (5)	0.7666 (6)	0.7763 (3)	0.2191 (5)	0.2245 (5)	0.3679 (5)	0.2202 (4)	0.2547 (5)	0.3605 (4)
10%	Mean	0.7618 (7)	0.7631 (7)	0.7592 (5)	0.7490 (6)	0.7676 (4)	0.7682 (3)	0.3070 (5)	0.3255 (6)	0.4997 (6)	0.3144 (4)	0.3530 (5)	0.4891 (3)
	kNN1	0.7646 (5)	0.7656 (4)	0.7612 (4)	0.7494 (5)	0.7626 (7)	0.7614 (5)	0.3104 (6)	0.3155 (4)	0.4362 (4)	0.3420 (6)	0.3536 (6)	0.5268 (6)
	kNN3	**0.7677** (1)	0.7664 (3)	0.7615 (3)	0.7538 (4)	0.7685 (2)	0.7563 (7)	0.2565 (3)	0.2760 (3)	0.3960 (3)	0.2897 (3)	0.2859 (3)	0.4949 (5)
	kNN5	0.7677 (2)	0.7674 (2)	**0.7622** (1)	0.7558 (3)	0.7668 (5)	0.7602 (6)	0.2474 (2)	0.2664 (2)	0.3919 (2)	0.2795 (2)	0.2749 (2)	0.4878 (2)
	SVM	0.7668 (3)	**0.7702** (1)	0.7620 (2)	**0.7655** (1)	0.7679 (3)	**0.7801** (1)	0.6793 (8)	0.6784 (8)	0.6194 (8)	0.7005 (8)	0.5958 (8)	0.8301 (8)
	EM	0.7592 (8)	0.7592 (8)	0.7589 (7)	0.7333 (8)	0.7557 (8)	0.7483 (8)	0.4165 (7)	0.4299 (7)	0.5411 (7)	0.4187 (7)	0.4285 (7)	0.5384 (7)
	MICE	0.7661 (4)	0.7652 (5)	0.7583 (8)	0.7586 (2)	**0.7690** (1)	0.7693 (2)	**0.2435** (1)	**0.2477** (1)	**0.3786** (1)	**0.2599** (1)	**0.2631** (1)	**0.4467** (1)
	SDAE	0.7625 (6)	0.7646 (6)	0.7589 (6)	0.7485 (7)	0.7654 (6)	0.7676 (4)	0.3057 (4)	0.3178 (5)	0.4755 (5)	0.3144 (5)	0.3314 (4)	0.4933 (4)
15%	Mean	0.7589 (6)	0.7581 (7)	0.7597 (6)	0.7381 (5)	0.7514 (5)	0.7317 (4)	0.3934 (6)	0.3937 (6)	0.6075 (6)	0.3879 (4)	0.4381 (6)	0.5849 (3)
	kNN1	0.7624 (5)	0.7635 (4)	0.7612 (3)	0.7335 (7)	0.7651 (2)	0.7205 (8)	0.3843 (4)	0.3822 (5)	0.5259 (4)	0.4365 (6)	0.4195 (5)	0.6534 (7)
	kNN3	0.7655 (2)	0.7647 (2)	0.7604 (4)	0.7451 (4)	0.7531 (4)	0.7324 (6)	0.3268 (3)	0.3168 (3)	0.4802 (3)	0.3698 (3)	0.3721 (3)	0.6162 (5)
	kNN5	0.7647 (3)	0.7643 (3)	0.7593 (7)	0.7503 (3)	0.7509 (6)	0.7374 (5)	0.3136 (2)	0.3074 (2)	0.4707 (2)	0.3551 (2)	0.3624 (2)	0.6088 (4)
	SVM	**0.7691** (1)	**0.7678** (1)	**0.7658** (1)	**0.7672** (1)	**0.7789** (1)	**0.7872** (1)	0.9742 (8)	0.7884 (8)	0.8418 (8)	0.8628 (8)	0.8873 (8)	1.0848 (8)
	EM	0.7548 (8)	0.7539 (8)	0.7582 (8)	0.7085 (8)	0.7332 (8)	0.7230 (7)	0.5189 (7)	0.5154 (7)	0.6584 (7)	0.5157 (7)	0.5229 (7)	0.6311 (6)
	MICE	0.7630 (4)	0.7607 (5)	0.7612 (2)	0.7528 (2)	0.7504 (7)	0.7611 (3)	**0.3054** (1)	**0.3021** (1)	**0.4502** (1)	**0.3262** (1)	**0.3494** (1)	0.5404 (2)
	SDAE	0.7585 (7)	0.7583 (6)	0.7602 (5)	0.7378 (6)	0.7561 (3)	0.7633 (2)	0.3907 (5)	0.3802 (4)	0.5482 (5)	0.3886 (5)	0.3950 (4)	**0.5305** (1)
20%	Mean	0.7587 (6)	0.7573 (7)	0.7553 (6)	0.7219 (5)	0.7335 (7)	0.7317 (4)	0.4479 (6)	0.4595 (6)	0.7067 (6)	0.4479 (4)	0.5094 (6)	0.6700 (3)
	kNN1	0.7554 (7)	0.7583 (5)	0.7564 (4)	0.7185 (7)	0.7408 (4)	0.7062 (7)	0.4438 (4)	0.4386 (4)	0.5979 (4)	0.5094 (6)	0.5077 (5)	0.7541 (7)
	kNN3	0.7609 (3)	0.7607 (4)	0.7570 (3)	0.7381 (3)	0.7414 (3)	0.7228 (6)	0.3717 (3)	0.3759 (3)	0.5686 (3)	0.4346 (3)	0.4359 (3)	0.7185 (6)
	kNN5	0.7613 (2)	0.7620 (3)	0.7556 (5)	0.7380 (4)	0.7395 (5)	0.7296 (5)	0.3581 (2)	0.3618 (2)	0.5613 (2)	0.4189 (2)	0.4243 (2)	0.7114 (5)
	SVM	**0.7661** (1)	**0.7714** (1)	**0.7627** (1)	**0.7643** (1)	**0.7582** (1)	**0.7896** (1)	1.1028 (8)	0.9814 (8)	0.9409 (8)	1.0050 (8)	1.5731 (8)	1.2533 (8)
	EM	0.7547 (8)	0.7533 (8)	0.7536 (7)	0.6861 (8)	0.7146 (8)	0.6976 (8)	0.5966 (7)	0.5974 (7)	0.7395 (7)	0.5938 (7)	0.5950 (7)	0.7101 (4)
	MICE	0.7599 (4)	0.7632 (2)	0.7515 (8)	0.7431 (2)	0.7425 (2)	0.7499 (3)	**0.3484** (1)	**0.3511** (1)	**0.5329** (1)	**0.3806** (1)	**0.4009** (1)	0.6326 (2)
	SDAE	0.7589 (5)	0.7577 (6)	0.7591 (2)	0.7210 (6)	0.7363 (6)	0.7515 (2)	0.4448 (5)	0.4416 (5)	0.6045 (5)	0.4484 (5)	0.4435 (4)	**0.6101** (1)
40%	Mean	0.7478 (6)	0.7431 (7)	0.7448 (3)	0.6676 (3)	0.6801 (6)	0.6710 (3)	0.6387 (6)	0.6682 (6)	1.0326 (7)	0.6357 (2)	0.7553 (5)	0.9590 (3)
	kNN1	0.7469 (7)	0.7441 (6)	0.7415 (7)	0.6387 (7)	0.6855 (5)	0.5867 (7)	0.6364 (5)	0.6502 (5)	0.9124 (5)	0.7798 (6)	0.7817 (6)	1.0844 (7)
	kNN3	0.7512 (4)	0.7464 (4)	0.7440 (4)	0.6621 (5)	0.6973 (4)	0.5836 (8)	0.5404 (3)	0.5492 (3)	0.8883 (3)	0.6701 (5)	0.7163 (4)	1.0379 (6)
	kNN5	0.7541 (2)	0.7480 (3)	0.7428 (5)	0.6581 (6)	0.6988 (3)	0.5948 (6)	0.5229 (2)	0.5302 (2)	0.8951 (4)	0.6497 (4)	0.6987 (3)	1.0274 (5)
	SVM	**0.7649** (1)	**0.7695** (1)	0.7532 (2)	**0.7618** (1)	**0.7670** (1)	**0.7385** (1)	1.1565 (8)	1.4194 (8)	1.8521 (8)	1.3355 (8)	3.7205 (8)	1.4128 (8)
	EM	0.7407 (8)	0.7392 (8)	0.7416 (6)	0.6105 (8)	0.6585 (8)	0.5954 (5)	0.8460 (7)	0.8408 (7)	0.9938 (6)	0.8355 (7)	0.8270 (7)	0.9483 (2)
	MICE	0.7526 (3)	0.7491 (2)	0.7393 (8)	0.6988 (2)	0.7025 (2)	0.6344 (4)	**0.5027** (1)	**0.5094** (1)	0.8396 (2)	**0.5648** (1)	0.6975 (2)	0.9758 (4)
	SDAE	0.7479 (5)	0.7453 (5)	**0.7552** (1)	0.6652 (4)	0.6781 (7)	0.7330 (2)	0.6347 (4)	0.6256 (4)	**0.7078** (1)	0.6366 (3)	**0.5890** (1)	**0.6687** (1)

approach guarantees a better imputation quality. Furthermore, there are some datasets where SDAE is the top winner, especially for MR 40% (*dermatology, hcc-data-survival, hcc-data-mortality, lung-cancer,* among others), although this is not generalisable for all datasets.

Impact on classification (F-measure). The results show that SVMimp seems to be the best imputation method in terms of classification performance, regardless the missing mechanism and configuration considered. This is shown in Table 1, where for the three highest MRs (15, 20 and 40%) SVMimp is the winner approach for most of the studied scenarios, although for MNAR *univa* configuration and under a MR of 40%, SDAE is the best approach. For the lowest MRs (5 and 10%) there is no standard, suggesting that small amounts of missing values have little influence on the quality of the dataset for classification purposes – there is an exception for the *univa* configurations under 5% of MR: in this case, SVM is the winner approach. Regarding the classification performance of the SDAE-based approach, it belongs to the top 3 imputation approaches for MNAR configurations under higher MRs (20 and 40%) .

We continue this section by referring to the results obtained by Gondara et al.[13], who used a similar benchmarking of datasets (although smaller, with only 15 datasets) and a SDAE approach. Gondara et al.[13] proposed a SDAE based model for imputation but only compare its results with MICE. Therefore, we also perform this comparison, only for *unifo* configuration, and present the respective results in Fig. 2. The SDAE seems to perform better than MICE for MNAR data - this is always the case for higher missing rates (15, 20 and 40%), regardless of the used metric.

We also performed a statistical test (*Wilcoxon rank-sum*) in order to verify if there were significant differences between the results obtained by the SDAE and the best method for the classification and imputation (MICE for RMSE and SVMimp for F-measure). In terms of RMSE and for most of the studied scenarios, the p-value reveals strong evidence against the null hypothesis, so we reject it - meaning that there are significant differences between the two methods, MICE and SDAE. For some scenarios where SDAE seems to be superior – MNAR *unifo* under 15 and 20% of MR – the p-value reveals weak evidence against the null hypothesis and therefore we can not ensure that there are significant differences between SDAE and MICE. Regarding F-measure and for almost all of the studied scenarios, we obtained a p-value that indicates strong evidence against the null hypothesis, so we reject it, meaning that there are significant differences between the two methods, SVMimp and SDAE. Since SVMimp has a higher performance, it does not seem that using SDAE brings any advantage in terms of classification performance.

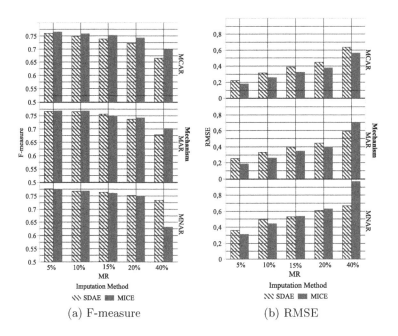

(a) F-measure   (b) RMSE

Fig. 2. Comparison between the results obtained from the SDAE-based approach and from MICE (multivariate configuration).

5   Conclusions and Future Work

This work investigates the influence of different missing mechanisms on imputation methods (including a deep learning-based approach) under several missing rates. This influence is evaluated in terms of imputation quality (RMSE) and classification performance (F-measure). Our experiments show that MICE performs well in terms of imputation quality while SVMimp seems to be the method that guarantees the best classification results.

We also compare the behaviour of SDAE with well-established imputation techniques included in related work: for standard datasets, such as those we have used, SDAE does not seem to be superior to the remaining approaches, since the obtained results do not outperform all of the state-of-the-art methods. Furthermore, the simulations become more complex with the use of deep networks due to both computational time and space/memory required.

As future work, we will investigate the usefulness of SDAE when handling more complex datasets (higher number of samples and dimensionality). Also, as the advantage of SDAE seems to be more clear for higher missing rates (40%), a smoother step of missing rates (between 20% and 40%) could bring new insights.

References

1. Abreu, P.H., Santos, M.S., Abreu, M.H., Andrade, B., Silva, D.C.: Predicting breast cancer recurrence using machine learning techniques: a systematic review. ACM Comput. Surv. (CSUR) **49**(3), 52 (2016)
2. Amorim, J.P., Domingues, I., Abreu, P.H., Santos, J.: Interpreting deep learning models for ordinal problems. In: 26th European Symposium on Artificial Neural Networks, Computational Intelligence and Machine learning (ESANN), pp. 373–378 (2018)
3. Azur, M.J., Stuart, E.A., Frangakis, C., Leaf, P.J.: Multiple imputation by chained equations: what is it and how does it work? Int. J. Methods Psychiatr. Res. **20**, 40–49 (2011)
4. Beaulieu-Jones, B.K., Moore, J.H.: Missing data imputation in the electronic health record using deeply learned autoencoders. In: Altman, R.B., Dunker, A.K., Hunter, L., Ritchie, M.D., Klein, T.E. (eds.) PSB, pp. 207–218 (2017)
5. Charte, D., Charte, F., García, S., del Jesus, M.J., Herrera, F.: A Practical Tutorial on Autoencoders for Nonlinear Feature Fusion: Taxonomy, Models, Software and Guidelines, vol. 44, pp. 78–96. Elsevier (2018)
6. Dempster, A.P., Laird, N.M., Rubin, D.B.: Maximum likelihood from incomplete data via the EM algorithm. **39**, 1–22 (1977)
7. Duan, Y., Lv, Y., Kang, W., Zhao, Y.: A deep learning based approach for traffic data imputation. In: ITSC, pp. 912–917. IEEE (2014)
8. Duan, Y., Lv, Y., Liu, Y.L., Wang, F.Y.: An efficient realization of deep learning for traffic data imputation. Transp. Res. Part C: Emerg. Technol. **72**, 168–181 (2016)
9. García-Laencina, P.J., Sancho-Gómez, J.L., Figueiras-Vidal, A.R.: Classifying patterns with missing values using multi-task learning perceptrons. Expert Syst. Appl. **40**, 1333–1341 (2013)

10. García-Laencina, P.J., Abreu, P.H., Abreu, M.H., Afonso, N.: Missing data imputation on the 5-year survival prediction of breast cancer patients with unknown discrete values. Comput. Biol. Med. **59**, 125–133 (2015)
11. García-Laencina, P.J., Sancho-Gómez, J.L., Figueiras-Vidal, A.R.: Pattern classification with missing data: a review. Neural Comput. Appl. **19**, 263–282 (2009)
12. Garciarena, U., Santana, R.: An extensive analysis of the interaction between missing data types, imputation methods, and supervised classifiers. Expert Syst. Appl. **89**, 52–65 (2017)
13. Gondara, L., Wang, K.: Multiple imputation using deep denoising autoencoders. Department of Computer Science, Simon Fraser University (2017)
14. Gondara, L., Wang, K.: Recovering loss to followup information using denoising autoencoders. Simon Fraser University (2017)
15. Little, R.J., Rubin, D.B.: Statistical Analysis with Missing Data. Wiley, New York (1987)
16. Man-long, Z.: MkNNI: new missing value imputation method using mutual nearest neighbor. Mod. Comput. **31**, 001 (2012)
17. Ning, X., Xu, Y., Gao, X., Li, Y.: Missing data of quality inspection imputation algorithm base on stacked denoising auto-encoder. In: 2017 IEEE 2nd International Conference on Big Data Analysis (ICBDA), pp. 84–88. IEEE (2017)
18. Rieger, A., Hothorn, T., Strobl, C.: Random forests with missing values in the covariates. Department of Statistics, University of Munich (2010)
19. Sang, G., Shi, K., Liu, Z., Gao, L.: Missing data imputation based on grey system theory. Int. J. Hybrid Inf. Technol. **27**(2), 347–355 (2014)
20. Santos, M.S., Abreu, P.H., García-Laencina, P.J., Simão, A., Carvalho, A.: A new cluster-based oversampling method for improving survival prediction of hepatocellular carcinoma patients. J. Biomed. Inform. **58**, 49–59 (2015)
21. Santos, M.S., Soares, J.P., Henriques Abreu, P., Araújo, H., Santos, J.: Influence of data distribution in missing data imputation. In: ten Teije, A., Popow, C., Holmes, J.H., Sacchi, L. (eds.) AIME 2017. LNCS (LNAI), vol. 10259, pp. 285–294. Springer, Cham (2017). https://doi.org/10.1007/978-3-319-59758-4_33
22. Sánchez-Morales, A., Sancho-Gómez, J.-L., Figueiras-Vidal, A.R.: Values deletion to improve deep imputation processes. In: Ferrández Vicente, J.M., Álvarez-Sánchez, J.R., de la Paz López, F., Toledo Moreo, J., Adeli, H. (eds.) IWINAC 2017. LNCS, vol. 10338, pp. 240–246. Springer, Cham (2017). https://doi.org/10.1007/978-3-319-59773-7_25
23. Twala, B.: An empirical comparison of techniques for handling incomplete data using decision trees. Appl. Artif. Intell. **23**, 373–405 (2009)
24. Vincent, P., Larochelle, H., Bengio, Y., Manzagol, P.A.: Extracting and composing robust features with denoising autoencoders. In: International Conference on Machine Learning proceedings (2008)
25. Vincent, P., Larochelle, H., Lajoie, I., Bengio, Y., Manzagol, P.A.: Stacked denoising autoencoders: learning useful representations in a deep network with a local denoising criterion. J. Mach. Learn. Res. **11**, 3371–3408 (2010)
26. Xia, J., Zhang, S., Cai, G., Li, L., Pan, Q., Yan, J., Ning, G.: Adjusted weight voting algorithm for random forests in handling missing values. Pattern Recognit. **69**, 52–60 (2017)
27. Zeiler, M.D.: Adadelta: an adaptive learning rate method. arXiv preprint arXiv:1212.5701 (2012)
28. Zhu, B., He, C., Liatsis, P.: A robust missing value imputation method for noisy data. Appl. Intell. **36**(1), 61–74 (2012)

Online Non-linear Gradient Boosting in Multi-latent Spaces

Jordan Frery[1,2(✉)], Amaury Habrard[1], Marc Sebban[1], Olivier Caelen[2], and Liyun He-Guelton[2]

[1] Université de Lyon, Université Saint-Étienne Jean-Monnet, UMR CNRS 5516, Laboratoire Hubert-Curien, 42000 Saint-Étienne, France
{jordan.frery,amaury.habrard,marc.sebban}@univ-st-etienne.fr
[2] Worldline, 95870 Bezons, France
{jordan.frery,olivier.caelen,liyun.he-guelton}@worldline.com

Abstract. Gradient Boosting is a popular ensemble method that combines linearly diverse and weak hypotheses to build a strong classifier. In this work, we propose a new Online Non-Linear gradient Boosting (ONLB) algorithm where we suggest to jointly learn different combinations of the same set of weak classifiers in order to learn the idiosyncrasies of the target concept. To expand the expressiveness of the final model, our method leverages the non linear complementarity of these combinations. We perform an experimental study showing that ONLB (i) outperforms most recent online boosting methods in both terms of convergence rate and accuracy and (ii) learns diverse and useful new latent spaces.

1 Introduction

Ensemble learning aims at combining diverse hypotheses to generate a strong classifier and has been shown to be very effective in many real life applications. Several categories of ensemble methods have been proposed in the literature, like *bagging* (e.g. random forest [1]), *stacking* [2], *cascade generalization* [3], *boosting* [4], etc. Those state of the art methods essentially differ by the way they generate diversity and combine the base hypotheses. In this paper, we focus on gradient boosting [5] which - unlike many other machine learning methods - performs an optimization in the *function* space rather than in the *parameter* space. This opens the door to the use of any loss function expanding the spectrum of applications that can be covered by this method. Moreover, the popularity of gradient boosting has been increased by recent implementations showing the scalability of the method even with billions of examples [6,7].

Despite these advantages, real world applications such as fraud detection, click prediction or face recognition are often subject to uninterrupted data flow which is completely ignored in the batch gradient boosting setting. This brings up a major concern: How to train models over always increasing volumes of data that need more memory and more storage? While big data centers can partially solve the problem, training the model from scratch each time new instances arrive remains unrealistic.

© Springer Nature Switzerland AG 2018
W. Duivesteijn et al. (Eds.): IDA 2018, LNCS 11191, pp. 99–110, 2018.
https://doi.org/10.1007/978-3-030-01768-2_9

To overcome this problem, online boosting has received much attention during the past few years [8–14]. In these methods, the boosted model is updated after seing each example. While they can process efficiently large amount of data, their practical limitations include: (i) an edge assumption usually made on the asymptotic accuracy (*i.e.* the edge over random guessing) of the weak learners making some approaches hard to tune, (ii) the absence of a weighting scheme of the weak learners that depends on their performance and (iii) for some of them a lack of adaptiveness (despite the fact that it was a strong point of Adaboost [4]).

Moreover, all the previous online methods face another issue: they usually perform a linear combination over a finite number of learned hypotheses which may limit the expressiveness of the final model to reach complex target concepts. While the batch setting would allow us to add step by step new hypotheses and capture the complexity of the underlying problem, an online algorithm keeps the same set of weak learners all along the process. This remark prompted us to investigate the way to develop a **non linear** gradient boosting algorithm with an enhanced expressiveness. To the best of our knowledge, there is only one work specific to non-linear boosting [15] but only usable in a batch setting. This is why the main contribution of this paper takes the form of a new algorithm, called ONLB - for Online Non Linear gradient Boosting. Inspired from previous research in domain adaptation [16], boosted-multi-task learning [17] and boosting in concept drift [18], ONLB resorts to the same set of boosted weak learners, projects their outputs in different latent spaces and takes advantage of their complementarity to learn non linearly the idiosyncrasies of the underlying concept. ONLB is illustrated in Fig. 1. At first glance, it looks similar to boosted neural networks, as done in [19,20], where the embedding layer is learned with boosting in order to infer more diversity. However, our method aims at learning the weak hypotheses iteratively, the next weak learner trying to minimize the error made by the network restricted to the previous hypotheses (see the solid lines in Fig. 1). The other main difference comes from the back-propagation that is performed at each step only on the parameters related to the weak learner subject to an update (see the red lines in Fig. 1). Thanks to the non-linear function brought by the last layer to combine the different representation output, ONLB converges much faster than the other state of the art online boosting algorithms.

The paper is organized as follows: Sect. 2 is devoted to the presentation of the related work. Our new non-linear online gradient boosting algorithm ONLB is presented in Sect. 3. Section 4 is dedicated to a large experimental comparison with the state of the art methods. We conclude the paper in Sect. 5.

2 Related Work

Online boosting methods have been developed soon after their batch counterpart. The first one introduced in [8] uses a resampling method based on a Poisson distribution and was applied in computer vision by [9] for feature selection. Theoretical justifications were developed later in [10] where they notably discuss

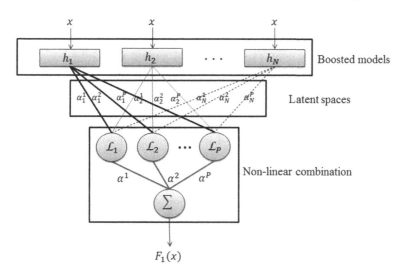

Fig. 1. Graphical representation of our Online Non-Linear gradient Boosting method: the first top layer corresponds to the learned weak classifiers; the second layer represents different linear combinations of their outputs; the bottom layer proceeds a non linear transformation of those combinations. The thickest lines show the needed activated path to learn a given classifier (here h_2). The red lines show the update performed only on the parameters concerned by this weak learner. The dashed lines are not taken into account at this iteration.

the number of weak learners needed in an online boosting framework. This is indeed a major concern since having too many of them could lead to predictions dominated by redundant weak learners that perform poorly. On the other hand, too few weak learners could make the boosting process itself irrelevant, as the goal is still to improve upon the performance of a simple base learner. More recently, [11] extends this previous work to propose an optimal version of boosting in terms of the number of weak learners for classification. An adaptation of this framework to multi-class online boosting was proposed in [12]. While these methods come with a solid theory, the assumption usually made on the asymptotic accuracy (*i.e.* the edge over random guessing) of the weak learners leads to two main practical limitations. The first one is the undeniable difficulty to estimate this edge without prior knowledge on the task at hand. The second comes from the fact that the edge of each weak learner might be very different depending on their own performance. And it turns out that the latter is never taken into consideration and might impact the overall performance of boosting.

Online gradient boosting was introduced by [21] allowing one to use more general loss functions but without any theoretical guarantees. Later, [13] and its extension to non smooth losses [14], propose online gradient boosting algorithms with theoretical justifications. These are the closest approaches to ours but they do not weight the weak learners based on their own performance. Moreover, the linear aspect of these methods limit strongly their expressiveness.

Another series of related works is the use of boosting in neural network methods. Recently, neural networks were used with incremental boosting [19] to train a specific layer. In [20], the authors reused [13] to optimize and increase the diversity of their embedding layer. Our work is related in the sense that we boost a layer to build a new feature space. However, we do not aim at learning a general neural network. This layer is rather used to make connections between our different weak learners. This is why our back-propagation procedure differs by focusing only on the parameters of the weak learner to be optimize at each step.

Apart from online boosting methods, our work is also related to non-linear boosting. However, as far as we know, only [15] tackled this topic by proposing a non-linear boosting projection method where, at each iteration of boosting, they build a new neural network only with the examples misclassified during the previous round. They finally take the new feature space induced by the hidden layer and feed it as the input space for the next learner. Nonetheless, it is very expensive and unsuitable to online learning.

3   Online Non-linear Gradient Boosting

In this study, we consider a binary supervised online learning setting where at each time step $t = 1, 2, ..., T$ one receives a labeled example $(x_t, y_t) \in \mathcal{X} \times \{-1, 1\}$ where $\mathcal{X}$ is a feature space. In this setting, the learner makes a prediction $f(x_t)$, the true label y_t is then revealed and it suffers a loss $\ell(f(x_t), y_t)$.

Boosting aims at combining different weak hypotheses. In batch gradient boosting, weak learners are learned sequentially while in the online setting, they are not allowed to see all examples at once. Thus, it is not possible to simply add new models iteratively in the combination as in batch boosting. In fact, online boosting maintains a sequence of N weak online learning algorithms $\mathcal{A}_1, ..., \mathcal{A}_N$ such that each weak learner h_i is updated by $\mathcal{A}_i$ in an online fashion. Note that every $\mathcal{A}_i$ considers hypotheses from a given restricted hypothesis class $\mathcal{H}$. The final model corresponds to a weighted linear combination of the N weak learners:

$$F(x) = \sum_{i=1}^{N} \alpha_i h_i(x), \tag{1}$$

where α_i stands for the weight of the weak learner h_i.

We now present our Online Non-Linear gradient Boosting, ONLB. As shown in Fig. 1, our method maintains P different representations that correspond to different combinations of the N learned weak learners, projecting their outputs into different latent spaces. Every representation p is updated right after a weak learner is learned. The outputs given by the p representations are then merged together to build a strong classifier, $F(x)$. To capture non linearities during this process, we propose to pass the output of each representation p into a non linear function $\mathcal{L}_p$. We define the prediction of our model $F(x)$ as follows:

$$F(x) = \sum_{p=1}^{P} \alpha^p \mathcal{L}_p \left(\sum_{i=1}^{N} \alpha_i^p h_i(x) \right), \tag{2}$$

where α_i^p are the weights projecting the outputs of the weak learner h_i in the latent space p and α^p the weight of this representation. Equation (2) illustrates clearly the difference with linear boosting formulation of Eq. (1). We denote by F_k the classifier restricted to the first k weak learners: $F_k(x) = \sum_{p=1}^{P} \alpha^p \mathcal{L}_p \left(\sum_{i=1}^{k} \alpha_i^p h_i(x) \right)$.

Our method aims thus at combining the same set of classifiers into different latent spaces. A key point here relies in making these classifiers diverse while still being relevant in the final decision. To achieve this goal, we update every weak learner h_i to decrease the error of the already learned models in F_{i-1} such that:

$$h_i = argmin_h \sum_{t=1}^{T} \ell_c \left(\sum_{p=1}^{P} \alpha^p \mathcal{L}_p \left(\sum_{k=1}^{i-1} \alpha_k^p h_k(x_t) + h(x_t) \right), y_t \right), \tag{3}$$

where $\ell_c(F(x), y)$ is a classification loss. In other words, we look for a learner h_i that improves over the learned combination, F_{i-1}.

In gradient boosting [5], one way to learn the next weak learner is to approximate the negative gradient (residuals) of F_{i-1} by minimizing the square loss between these residuals and the weak learner predictions. We define r_i^t the residual at iteration i for the example x_t as follows:

$$r_i^t = -\frac{\partial \ell_c(F_{i-1}(x_t), y_t))}{\partial F_{i-1}(x_t)}. \tag{4}$$

In fact, from this functional gradient descent approach, we can define a greedy approximation of Eq. (3) by using a regression loss ℓ_r on the residuals computed in Eq. (4) with respect to the classification loss ℓ_c:

$$h_i = argmin_h \sum_{t=1}^{T} \ell_r(h(x_t), r_i^t). \tag{5}$$

As stated above, when a weak learner h_i is updated, we need: (i) to update the weights α_t^p associated to this learner in each representation p and (ii) update the representation weights α^p in the final decision as follows:

$$\alpha^p := \alpha_p - \eta \frac{\partial \ell_c(F_i(x_t), y_t)}{\partial \alpha^p}; \quad \alpha_i^p := \alpha_t^p - \eta \frac{\partial \ell_c(F_i(x_t), y_t)}{\partial \alpha_i^p}.$$

All the steps of our ONLB training process are summarized in Algorithm 1.

In practice, we instantiate our losses with the square loss for the regression and the logistic loss for the classification as follows:

$$\ell_c(f(x_t), y_t) = log(1 + e^{-y_t F_i(x_t)}); \quad \ell_r(f(x_t), r_i^t) = (r_i^t - f(x_t))^2.$$

The choice of the logistic loss is motivated by the need to have bounded gradients in order to avoid their exponential growth with the boosting iterations, which can happen for noisy instances for example. The square loss is the main loss function for regression tasks and has demonstrated superior computational and theoretical properties for the online setting [22]. Then, according to Eq. (5), the weak classifiers are updated as follows:

$$h_i = argmin_h \sum_{t=1}^{T} (h(x_t) - r_i^t)^2. \tag{6}$$

Equation (6) suggests a fairly simple update of each weak learner: each weak online learning algorithm $\mathcal{A}_i$ uses a simple stochastic gradient descent with respect to one example at each step. The residuals can be obtained thanks to a straight forward closed form:

$$r_i^t = \frac{-y_t}{1 + e^{y_t F_{i-1}(x_t)}}.$$

Finally, we used a *relu* activation function such that $\mathcal{L}(x) = \begin{cases} x \text{ if } x > 0, \\ 0 \text{ otherwise.} \end{cases}$ The weights of the latent spaces α_i^p and α^p are now updated as follows:

$$\alpha_i^p := \alpha_i^p + \eta \begin{cases} \frac{y_t \alpha^p h_i(x_t)}{1 + e^{y_t F_i(x_t)}} \text{ if } \alpha_i^p h_i(x_t) > 0, \\ 0 \quad\quad\quad \text{otherwise} \end{cases} ; \quad \alpha^p := \alpha^p + \eta \frac{y_t \mathcal{L}_p\left(\sum_{i=1}^{N} \alpha_i^p h_i(x_t)\right)}{1 + e^{y_t F_i(x_t)}}.$$

At test time, our model learned using Algorithm 1 predicts as follows:

$$F^*(x) = sign\left(F(x)\right) = sign\left(\sum_{p=1}^{P} \alpha^p \mathcal{L}_p\left(\sum_{i=1}^{N} \alpha_i^p h_i(x)\right)\right).$$

Algorithm 1 Online Non-Linear gradient Boosting (ONLB)

1: INPUT: N online weak learners, a learning rate η and P latent spaces.
2: Initialize $h_0 = 0$
3: **for** $t = 1$ to T **do**
4:     Receive example x_t
5:     Predict $F_0(x_t) = h_0 = 0$
6:     **for** $i = 1$ to N **do**
7:         Reveal y_t the label of example x_t
8:         Compute the residual $r_i^t = \frac{\partial \ell_c(F_{i-1}(x_t), y_t)}{\partial F_{i-1}(x)}$
9:         Predict $h_i(x_t)$
10:        $\mathcal{A}_i$ suffers loss $\ell_r(r_i^t, h_i(x_t))$ and updates the hypothesis h_i
11:        **for** $p = 1$ to P **do**
12:            $\alpha^p := \alpha^p - \eta \frac{\partial \ell_c(F_i(x_t), y_t)}{\partial \alpha^p}$; $\alpha_i^p := \alpha_t^p - \eta \frac{\partial \ell_c(F_i(x_t), y_t)}{\partial \alpha_i^p}$
13:        **end for**
14:    **end for**
15: **end for**

Table 1. Properties of the datasets used in the experiments.

	#Examples	Positives ratio	#Features
Covtype	$581,012$	51.2%	54
Poker	$1,025,010$	49.88%	10
MNIST	$70,000$	49%	718
Abalone	$4,177$	49%	8
Pima	767	34.9%	8
Adult	$42,842$	23.9%	14
HIV	$6,590$	13.3%	8
w8a	64000	3%	300
Shuttle	$58,000$	21.4%	9
Wine	$6,497$	20.64%	12

4   Experiments

In this section, we provide an experimental evaluation of our non-linear online boosting method ONLB in terms of both quantitative and qualitative analysis. First, we perform a comparative study with different state-of-the-art online boosting algorithms on public datasets. Second, we present an analysis of the learned representations.

4.1   Classification Results

We use 10 public datasets from the UCI repository by considering binary classification problems (multi-class datasets were converted into binary problems as indicated in parenthesis): Poker (0 vs [1,9]), MNIST ([0,4] vs [5,9]), Wine ([3,6] vs [7,9]), Abalone ([0,9] vs [10,29]), Covtype (2 vs all), Shuttle (1 vs all), Pima, Adult, HIV, w8a. A summary of these datasets is presented in Table 1.

Our experimental setup is defined as follows. For every dataset, we apply a 3-fold cross validation. For tuning the hyper-parameters, we perform in each fold a progressive validation [23] on the training set as proposed in [11]: This validation process uses every new example to evaluate the model and then use it for training. Note that we simulate the online learning setting by giving the examples according to a random order to the algorithm. We train different models in parallel with respect to their hyper-parameter values (i.e. the number of weak learners N, the learning rate η and γ the weak learner edge) and we select the one achieving the lowest progressive validation error. The selected model is then evaluated on the test set.

We compare our method to different online boosting algorithms from current state-of-the-art: the four algorithms online.BBM, Adaboost.OL,

Adaboost.OL.W, OGB from [11,13] and streamBoost from [14][1]. For all the algorithms, we choose as a relatively weak classifier a neural network with one hidden layer and two units that we update in an online learning fashion using stochastic gradient descent. We report the classification error obtained for each algorithm in Table 2.

ONLB achieves competitive results with the state of the art online boosting methods and even outperforms them on most datasets. In some cases, such as for MNIST or Poker, we clearly see that, while using much more weak learners (see Fig. 2), the other methods were not able to capture the target concept as much as ONLB did. Note that, a mandatory condition in our experiments was $T > 1$ such that the boosting takes part in the learning process but in some cases, the online boosting algorithms were not able to do better than the baseline on the test set. For example, on the Adult database, only ONLB and OGB achieved an average error lower than the base learner.

In Table 3, we present the average number of weak learners chosen with respect to the progressive validation process for each model. While being an online linear boosting algorithm, online.BBM achieves its performances with a significantly smaller number of weak learners compared to the other linear boosting methods. As mentioned in [11], this algorithm is optimal in the sense that no online linear boosting algorithm can achieve the same error rate with fewer weak learners or examples asymptotically. That being said, ONLB algorithm achieves, on average, better performances with more than twice less weak learners than online.BBM.

Finally, in Fig. 2, we plot the convergence curves with respect to the increasing number of examples used for two datasets: MNIST and Abalone. For all algorithms, each curve corresponds to the evolution of the error rate according to the progressive validation error measured during training. We observe that ONLB still achieves the best convergence rate for both datasets. A similar behavior has been observed for the other datasets and exhibits the nice fast convergence property of our algorithm which needs less weak learners to converge to its optimum.

4.2   Analysis of the Learned Multi-latent Representations

In this section, we present two different qualitative analyses on the latent representations learned by our algorithm. First, we show that given a sufficiently large number of weak base learners, the representations obtained tend to be rather uncorrelated. This provides an evidence that ONLB can generate some diversity. Then, we show that these representations contribute in a comparable way to the final decision. For our study, we use the following setup. We consider a model with 100 representations (*i.e.* $P = 100$). We use two base learners: a relatively weak neural network with one hidden layer composed of 2 units (2-NN) and a

---

[1] We used the implementations available in Vowpal Wabbit and re-implemented the streamBoost and OGB algorithms.

Table 2. Error rate reported for different online boosting algorithms.

Dataset	Base learner	ONLB	online.BBM	Adaboost.OL	Adaboost.OL.W	OGB	StreamBoost
Covtype	0.2401	**0.2057**	0.2242	0.2273	0.2313	0.2264	0.2128
Poker	0.4182	**0.0497**	0.2375	0.1234	0.0953	0.3880	0.2668
MNIST	0.1105	**0.0561**	0.1029	0.1557	0.0830	0.1139	0.0655
Abalone	0.2673	0.2523	0.2831	**0.2487**	0.2531	0.2669	0.2720
Pima	0.2992	**0.2795**	0.2913	0.2952	0.2835	0.2874	0.2953
Adult	0.1523	**0.1465**	0.1530	0.1530	0.1526	0.1476	0.1586
HIV	0.1986	0.1393	**0.1273**	0.1360	0.1291	0.1540	0.1526
Shuttle	0.0211	**0.0024**	0.0173	0.0061	0.0058	0.0133	0.0050
w8a	0.0189	0.0148	0.0158	**0.0146**	0.0167	0.0178	0.0155
Wine	0.1979	**0.1687**	0.1921	0.1931	0.1931	0.1743	0.1833

Table 3. Average number of weak learners (N) selected by progressive validation.

Dataset	ONLB	online.BBM	Adaboost.OL	Adaboost.OL.W	OGB	StreamBoost
Covtype	6	60	79	59	282	63
Poker	52	222	348	311	320	285
MNIST	14	66	147	207	431	131
Abalone	5	6	12	3	166	8
Pima	65	64	109	141	437	174
Adult	13	6	18	17	161	119
HIV	6	6	94	188	32	16
Shuttle	30	43	243	108	121	159
w8a	4	7	54	42	132	40
Wine	5	8	112	91	97	118
Average	20	49	121	116	218	111

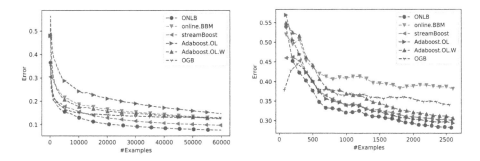

Fig. 2. Progressive validation error with respect to the learning examples for MNIST on the left and Abalone on the right.

stronger learner consisting of a neural network with 500 units in its unique hidden layer (500-NN). All representation weights are initialized following a uniform distribution such that the different representations are highly uncorrelated. We consider one training file of a fold of the MNIST dataset used above for learning.

Our first analysis aims at showing that the learned representations tend to be uncorrelated when using a weak learner. For this purpose, we compute a correlation matrix C between all the representations such that $C_{nm} = \frac{cov_{nm}}{\sqrt{cov_{nn} * cov_{mm}}}$ measures the correlation between the latent representations n and m, cov is the covariance matrix computed with respect to the input weights $\{\alpha_i^m\}_{i=1}^N$ and $\{\alpha_i^n\}_{i=1}^N$ of these representations. We show, in Fig. 3, the C matrix for the latent space representations obtained after convergence with the 2-NN base learners. We can see that most of the representations tend to be uncorrelated or weakly correlated. In contrast, Fig. 4 presents the C matrix using the 500-NN base learners. We see here that most of the representations are highly correlated. This experiment shows that by using sufficiently weak base learners, we are able to learn diverse and uncorrelated representations.

In our second analysis, we want to confirm that the uncorrelated latent representations are informative enough to contribute in a comparable way to the final strong model. We propose to compute, for each representation p, a relative importance coefficient Ω_p by taking the absolute values of the predictions of p right before they are merged together with the other representation outputs to form the final prediction. We average this coefficient over $\{x_t\}_{t=1}^K$ examples taken from a validation set independent from the learning sample as follows:

$$\Omega_p = \frac{1}{K} \sum_{t=1}^K |\alpha^p \mathcal{L}_p \left(\sum_{i=1}^N \alpha_i^p h_i(x_t) \right)|. \tag{7}$$

We expect for important representations a high Ω_p (*i.e.* having a high impact in the final decision) and a low Ω_p for irrelevant ones (*i.e.* having low impact in the final decision).

We consider then the models learned with the 2-NN and 500-NN base learners as previously. For each model, we plot the importance coefficient Ω_p (y-axis) against the average correlation of each representation (x-axis) that we define as $\widehat{C}_p = \frac{1}{P} \sum_{i=1}^P C_{pi}$. This illustrates the importance of each representation in the final decision with respect to their correlation level.

Figure 5 gives the plot for the model using the 2-NN base learners. We see here that all the representations are involved in the final decision and that their relative importance coefficients are rather comparable. This is in opposition to the plot of Fig. 6 that provides the results for the model using the 500-NN base learners. First, we see that many representations are not used in the final decision and these correspond to the ones that are uncorrelated. In fact, representations involved in the final decision are the ones that are all highly correlated with an average correlation coefficient around 0.75. Clearly, since these representations have a high correlation level, actually only one representation is really useful at the end. But note that this representation can in fact be learned by a standard linear gradient boosting.

From this experiment, we see that complex models are hard to diversify in online boosting. Moreover, tuning their hyperparameters is harder making the probability of overfitting higher and they require a significant larger amount of training time which makes such complex models useless for online boosting.

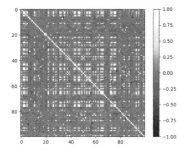

Fig. 3. Correlation matrix of the representations with 2-NN learners.

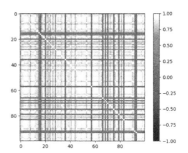

Fig. 4. Correlation matrix of the representations with the 500-NN learners.

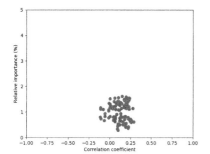

Fig. 5. Importance of each latent representation with the 2-NN learners.

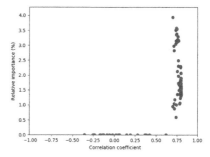

Fig. 6. Importance of each latent representation with the 500-NN learners.

5   Conclusion

In this paper, we presented a new Online Non-Linear Boosting algorithm. In this method, we combine different representations of the same set of weak classifiers to produce a non-linearly boosted model in order to learn the idiosyncrasies of the target concept. Our experimental results showed a general improvement over current state of the art online boosting methods. Additionally, the non-linear architecture of the model allows the method to use less weak learners and to obtain faster convergence in terms of examples. Our approach has also the interesting property to produce efficiently diverse latent spaces contributing actively to the model predictions. This property makes our model adaptive by giving more importance to the best current representations.

Perspectives of this work include adapting our method to the multi-class setting, to study the impact of delayed feedback (i.e. labels arriving only after some time delay) and to investigate possible adaptations for transfer learning and continuous learning in the online setting.

References

1. Breiman, L.: Random forests. Mach. Learn. **45**(1), 5–32 (2001)
2. Wolpert, D.H.: Stacked generalization. Neural Netw. **5**(2), 241–259 (1992)
3. Gama, J., Brazdil, P.: Cascade generalization. Mach. Learn. **41**(3), 315–343 (2000)
4. Freund, Y., Schapire, R.E.: A decision-theoretic generalization of on-line learning and an application to boosting. J. Comput. Syst. Sci. **55**(1), 119–139 (1997)
5. Friedman, J.H.: Greedy function approximation: a gradient boosting machine. Ann. Stat. 1189–1232 (2001)
6. Chen, T., Guestrin, C.: Xgboost: a scalable tree boosting system. In: SIGKDD, pp. 785–794. ACM (2016)
7. Ke, G., et al.: LightGBM: a highly efficient gradient boosting decision tree. In: NIPS (2017)
8. Oza, N.C.: Online bagging and boosting. In: 2005 IEEE International Conference on Systems, Man and cybernetics, vol. 3, pp. 2340–2345. IEEE (2005)
9. Grabner, H., Bischof, H.: On-line boosting and vision. In: CVPR, vol. 1, pp. 260–267. IEEE (2006)
10. Chen, S.T., Lin, H.T., Lu, C.J.: An online boosting algorithm with theoretical justifications. In: ICML (2012)
11. Beygelzimer, A., Kale, S., Luo, H.: Optimal and adaptive algorithms for online boosting. In: ICML (2015)
12. Jung, Y.H., Goetz, J., Tewari, A.: Online multiclass boosting. In: Advances in Neural Information Processing Systems, pp. 920–929 (2017)
13. Beygelzimer, A., Hazan, E., Kale, S., Luo, H.: Online gradient boosting. In: Advances in Neural Information Processing Systems, pp. 2458–2466 (2015)
14. Hu, H., Sun, W., Venkatraman, A., Hebert, M., Bagnell, J.A.: Gradient boosting on stochastic data streams. In: AISTATS, pp. 595–603 (2017)
15. García-Pedrajas, N., García-Osorio, C., Fyfe, C.: Nonlinear boosting projections for ensemble construction. J. Mach. Learn. Res. **8**, 1–33 (2007)
16. Becker, C.J., Christoudias, C.M., Fua, P.: Non-linear domain adaptation with boosting. In: Advances in Neural Information Processing Systems, pp. 485–493 (2013)
17. Chapelle, O., Shivaswamy, P., Vadrevu, S., Weinberger, K., Zhang, Y., Tseng, B.: Boosted multi-task learning. Mach. Learn. **85**(1–2), 149–173 (2011)
18. Scholz, M., Klinkenberg, R.: Boosting classifiers for drifting concepts. Intell. Data Anal. **11**(1), 3–28 (2007)
19. Han, S., Meng, Z., Khan, A.S., Tong, Y.: Incremental boosting convolutional neural network for facial action unit recognition. In: NIPS, pp. 109–117 (2016)
20. Opitz, M., Waltner, G., Possegger, H., Bischof, H.: Bier-boosting independent embeddings robustly. In: CVPR, pp. 5189–5198 (2017)
21. Leistner, C., Saffari, A., Roth, P., Bischof, H.: On robustness of on-line boosting - a competitive study. In: 3rd ICCV Workshop on On-line Computer Vision (2009)
22. Gao, W., Jin, R., Zhu, S., Zhou, Z.H.: One-pass AUC optimization. In: International Conference on Machine Learning, pp. 906–914 (2013)
23. Blum, A., Kalai, A., Langford, J.: Beating the hold-out: bounds for k-fold and progressive cross-validation. In: COLT, pp. 203–208. ACM (1999)

MDP-based Itinerary Recommendation using Geo-Tagged Social Media

Radhika Gaonkar[1], Maryam Tavakol[2(✉)], and Ulf Brefeld[2]

[1] Stony Brook University, Stony Brook, NY, USA
rgaonkar@cs.stonybrook.edu
[2] Leuphana Universität Lüneburg, Lüneburg, Germany
{tavakol,brefeld}@leuphana.de

Abstract. Planning vacations is a complex decision problem. Many variables like the place(s) to visit, how many days to stay, the duration at each location, and the overall travel budget need to be controlled and arranged by the user. Automatically recommending travel itineraries would thus be a remedy to quickly converge to an individual trip that is tailored to a user's interests. While on a trip, users frequently share their experiences on social media platforms e.g., by uploading photos of specific locations and times of day. Their uploaded data serves as an asset when it comes to gathering information on their journey. In this paper, we leverage social media, more explicitly photo uploads and their tags, to reverse engineer historic user itineraries. Our solution grounds on Markov decision processes that capture the sequential nature of itineraries. The tags attached to the photos provide the factors to generate possible configurations and prove crucial for contextualising the proposed approach. Empirically, we observe that the predicted itineraries are more accurate than standard path planning algorithms.

Keywords: Itinerary recommendation · MDP · Personalisation

1 Introduction

The Web has become an effective resource for travelers. In addition to an increasing number of travel blogs, verticals providing reviews and recommendations of places, restaurants and hotels, prove useful tools for planning trips and night outs. However, common resources do not exhaustively cover a wide range of aspects but often focus on narrow scopes to maintain a clear segregation to other content providers. Users who seek different types of information thus need to query various sites and aggregate the pieces of information themselves, which requires significant amount of time and effort.

At the same time, the rise of digital photography through widespread use of mobile devices and digital cameras has resulted in a great deal of photos being shared on the Web. Uploaded photos are mostly tagged by users with information snippets and key words to share the location, emotion, people, etc.

ⓒ Springer Nature Switzerland AG 2018
W. Duivesteijn et al. (Eds.): IDA 2018, LNCS 11191, pp. 111–123, 2018.
https://doi.org/10.1007/978-3-030-01768-2_10

with others. A remarkable way of understanding itineraries is to study the photo streams of tourists in touristic zones.

In this paper, we showcase how freely available user-tagged information on the Web can be aggregated to recover trajectories of tourists in cities. Our analysis is based on the online photo streams of users that reflect (a possibly incomplete) sequence of visited locations during a trip, and we assume those sequences indicate overall trip satisfaction of users. We thus turn photo-sharing sites into useful resources to reconstruct a user's trips. We use Flickr[1] as our main source to acquire such photo streams. Flickr proves useful to generate candidate lists of Points of Interest (POIs) for any city. Moreover, many photos already come with geographic, temporal, and/or semantic annotations. Photos annotated with geo-coordinates can be accurately placed on a map and if the user also provided semantic tags, the content can be indexed and further processed by Natural Language Processing techniques.

A touristic trip is considered a sequential problem. At each stage of travel, a user chooses her next destination from a list of touristic points in the city. Additionally, the data provides implicit feedback on the user's preference of a touristic site by the photographs she uploads on Flickr. This partial labeling of the data fits well to the problem setting of Reinforcement Learning (RL)-based approaches where the uncertainty of taking different actions and the resulting transitions is minimised by trading off exploration and exploitation [20]. We thus reconstruct sequences of POI visits using reverse engineering of historic user itineraries.

In our proposed approach [2], we take into account both the sequential nature of POI visits and the user's overall satisfaction. We learn a model of the traveler behavior as a Markov Decision Process (MDP) and extend it to make personalised travel recommendations. The system learns the optimal recommendation policy by observing the consequences of visiting different places by the travelers in the city and the traveler's personal preferences. Using the MDP, the user is recommended a place corresponding to the place category, which is nearest to her, both in distance and personal taste, and receives an immediate reward for taking that action. We empirically compare our approach to various path planning algorithms on data from three European touristic cities - Munich, Paris and London.

2   Related Work

Many systems have been developed to extract user-generated multimedia content and infer meaningful information for travel planning. Crandall et al. [4] is one of the earlier works in exploring the association of Flickr photos to physical locations, and apply their techniques to extract landmarks at various granularity levels that correspond to a geo-spatial hierarchy. Cao et al. [3] introduce a method that uses both logistic regression and kernel canonical correlation to

---

[1] www.flickr.com.

[2] https://github.com/RGaonkar/MDP-based-Itinerary-Recommendation.

enrich semantic information and location information based on image content. The tags assigned to Flickr photographs are further employed to extract place names, coordinates, and categories as well as popularity values [15,18]. Baba et al. [2] use co-occurrences between textual tags and geolocations to represent places related to a tag by probability distributions.

The growing surge of travel data on social media platforms has resulted in many recent works on touristic place recommendations. Jiang et al. [7] enhance collaborative filtering recommendations with author topic models that consider different types of user preferences to exploit textual metadata associated with geo-tagged pictures on Flickr. Zhang et al. [24] present an extension of the collaborative retrieval model (CRM) for POI recommendation, taking temporal information and social relations into account. Rakesh et al. [17] use Foursquare data to build a probabilistic generative framework that recommends tours based on user's preference, peer circle, travel transitions and popularity of venues. Lim [10] and Quercia et al. [16] also restrict their work to the geo-tagged points on Flickr to find shortest routes with the highest satisfaction.

While all these models capture many different aspects of tourist movement, they fail to address sequentiality in travel itineraries. Shani et al. [20] and Tavakol and Brefeld [22] propose sequential approaches to recommender systems using MDPs [21]. Accordingly, probabilistic sequential approaches are used in recommending the next POI either based on location services [14,19], or social networks [6]. In *WhereNext* [12] a T-pattern decision tree is designed to classify the trajectory patterns, and Muntean et al. [13] rank POIs using Gradient Boosted Regression Trees and Ranking SVM. Ashbrook et al. [1] apply a Markov model to GPS data in an attempt to model travel behavior. Kurashima et al. [8] combines user preference and current location into a probabilistic behavior model by combining topic and Markov models. Zhang et al. [23] goes one step further to prune the search space and recommend sequential POIs considering their time constraints. In this paper, we propose a recommendation approach which additionally encodes the history of visited POIs into the Markov model in order to better understand the sequential patterns.

3   Data Extraction and Analysis

In order to automate the acquisition of tourist information, we make use of geo-temporal data from Flickr. The advent of digital photography and its continually increasing features of spatially and temporally annotated images in real time, has enriched photographs with useful metadata. This results in augmenting the photographs with geographical coordinates specifying the location of the picture, as well as its date and time. Flickr consists of over 5 billion photographs, and many of them are time stamped. In addition, photos are annotated with semantic data such as tags and titles associated with them. A small fraction of the photographs are annotated with geographical coordinates. Our system focuses on extracting and discovering a large number of trips from Flickr metadata and using these to deduce novel methods of itinerary recommendation.

3.1   Data Acquisition

Using the public API of Flickr, we collect 44051, 22970, 42104 photographs of three popular cities, Munich, London and Paris, along with their metadata. However, a significant portion of the photographs are without geo-coordinates. Restricting ourselves to only the geo-referenced pictures would significantly decrease the coverage of our approach. Therefore, we utilise the metadata associated with photographs to infer their locations. Nonetheless, working with such open data poses several key challenges. Most of the photographs have linguistically noisy tags or tags with no location information. For instance, the tags might only include the details of photography techniques, weather, city name, or contains semantic ambiguities. Hence, inferring POI names requires using both, the location coordinates and the information gleaned from the textual tags. We propose approaches for data pre-processing which result in a significant increase in the performance of our system.

3.2   From Coordinates to Places of Interest

In order to maintain a high quality mapping from geo-coordinates of photo to place names, we query the free version of Google Places API and obtain a list of POIs in each city. This is with the assumption that many touristic points are already available on Google Maps. We furthermore collect the textual tags of multiple photographs having the same location coordinates in the Flickr dataset. The tags are then cleaned, of stopwords, city names and Flickr specific stopwords such as camera and weather details. The place name and place category (e.g., museum, church, etc.) of the location coordinate is obtained by calling the API with *latitude, longitude, ranking criteria* and *search radius* around the location coordinates. To get the best place name candidate from the returned list, a fuzzy string match using Levenshtein distance [9] is used and the place with the highest fuzzy matching similarity with the textual tags of the location coordinates is assigned to that location. Despite these techniques, a small fraction of the coordinates never get a place name from the Google Places API. We thus assign their place name manually using the Google Maps interface.

3.3   Location Mapping with Tags

The user provided textual tags often contain event and geospatial information which could be used for inferring the location of non-geotagged data. Since users may define arbitrary tags, finding the relevant ones is not trivial. In addition, there is no sequential structure that could be exploited to support possibly contained geographical information using the concept of named-entity recognition or relation extraction in the text. We exploit the co-occurrence statistics of words in low dimensional vector space by using the Latent Semantic Analysis (LSA) [5] similarity between tags of a target non-geotagged photograph and each of the geo-tagged photographs. The LSA model is learned on the geo-tagged *(location tags*) co-occurrence matrix. Using this, each new tag of a non-geotagged photograph is assigned a location from the highest similarity score, provided it is above a certain similarity threshold. The data points without a place information in the tags are dropped for further analysis.

3.4 Itinerary Inference

After obtaining the POI names, we use the Flickr data to emulate tourist behavior. The first step is to remove all travel points falling outside the bounding box of a city. Our model aims to recommend only single-day itineraries. Therefore, the sequences of photographs for more than one day are split by their datetime into single day sequences. Additionally, it is important to differentiate between the resident and tourist in a city by checking the number of POIs covered by her. A resident would exhibit travel movements slower than a tourist. Therefore, we discard travel paths consisting of less than 3 unique POIs. Lastly, some photographers on Flickr add photographs with invalid datetime value or incorrect format. This hampers our modeling of the recommender system and is ergo removed. As a result, a total of 17904, 6000 and 9032 photographs are left for Munich, London and Paris, respectively.

4 MDP-based POI Recommendation

4.1 Preliminaries

The photos are uploaded by a set of users U in different cities. Each city c contains n_c POIs where $L_c = \{l_1, l_2, l_3, ..., l_{n_c}\}$ represents the set of POIs for that city. The photos are characterised by a set of attributes containing the timestamp of capture, the latitude and longitude of photo location, the title, the textual tag and description attached to the picture. Furthermore, the category vector $\boldsymbol{cat}_l \in \mathbb{R}^m$ for each POI l indicates which categories are assigned to the place, i.e., for a certain category a, $\boldsymbol{cat}_l(a) = 1$ if l belongs to category a, and is zero otherwise. Our goal is to recommend an itinerary $I = (l_1, l_2, ..., l_k)$ for each user that tries to maximise her overall trip satisfaction.

An MDP is defined by a four tuple: (S, A, R, T), where S is the set of states, A is the set of actions, $R(s, a) : S \times A \rightarrow \mathbb{R}$ is the reward function that assigns a real value to each (state, action) pair, and $T(s, a, s') : S \times A \times S \rightarrow [0, 1]$ is the state-transition function, which provides the probability of a transition between every pair of states given an action from the available set. The goal of an MDP is to obtain the optimal policy, $\pi^* : S \rightarrow A$, that gives the best action for every state in order to maximise the sum of discounted reward.

In our problem, the *states* represent the history of user travels. State s_t is given by the sequence of at most k places the user has visited up to time t, $s_t = (l_1, ..., l_k)$. The *actions* are all POI categories present in the city where the user is visiting. *Transition probability* function models the probability of going to another place given the current location and the recommended place category. Each state that the user enters on taking a particular action, she gets an immediate reward from the *reward* function. A higher reward is awarded when the transition is present in the sequence of places in the training set.

4.2   The Predictive Model

We begin with a simple Markov chain model to estimate the state-transition function. The transition function gives the probability of going to the next place l_{k+1}, for a user whose k recent POI visits are $(l_1, ..., l_k)$. A maximum-likelihood method is used to estimate this transition function based on the user travel data

$$N(s, s') = \frac{count(s')}{count(s)}, \tag{1}$$

where s and s' are $(l_1, l_2, ..., l_k)$ and $(l_1, l_2, ...l_{k+1})$, respectively. The *count* function gives the frequency of occurrences. We expand this model to an MDP framework which gives the probability of visiting a new POI l_{k+1} after choosing some action a, where $cat_{l_{k+1}}(a) = 1$. The visit to this new POI depends on the place category recommended to the user at the current POI. The non-zero transitions occur when (s, s') occurs in the dataset and a is a place category of s'. For each set of $\{s, a, s'\}$ transition probability is defined as

$$T(s, a, s') = \frac{N(s, s')}{\sum_{s'' \in S'} N(s, s'')}, \quad \sum_{s' \in S'} T(s, a, s') = 1, \tag{2}$$

where S' signifies the set of states that can be reached from s when action a is taken. The reward after taking action a in state s is given by the reward function $R(s, a)$, which is simply inferred by the number of occurrence of state-action sequences in the training data.

$$R(s, a) = \frac{count(s, a)}{count(s)}. \tag{3}$$

4.3   Optimisation

The resulting MDP can be optimised using reinforcement learning methods such as value iteration. Value iteration learns the state-value function, $V(s)$, and converges to an optimal policy in a discounted finite MDP [21]. The policy is defined as the category recommendation for the traveller. An optimal policy π^* gives the highest expected utility through the traveller's movements. The utility of a state $V(s)$ is defined as the expected sum of discounted rewards that the agent obtains by starting from state s and following policy π. The standard update rule of value iteration with discount factor γ is given by:

$$V(s) = max_{a \in A(s)}[R(s, a) + \gamma \times \sum_{s'} T(s, a, s')V(s')]. \tag{4}$$

When the value function $V(s)$ converges to an optimal value function $V^*(s)$, the state-action values $Q(s, a)$ is derived

$$Q(s, a) = R(s, a) + \gamma \sum_{s'} T(s, a, s') V^*(s'). \tag{5}$$

The Q-values are proportional to the probability that the user visits a POI of place category a, given the sequence of visited POIs in s. Hence, a high $Q(s, a)$ indicates a higher likelihood of observing the transition from s with action a.

4.4   Multi-step Place Recommendations

We use the *softmax* function to approximate a probability distribution over the place categories from the Q-values

$$P(A = a|s) = \frac{exp\{Q(s, a)\}}{\sum_{a'} exp\{Q(s, a')\}}. \tag{6}$$

The action with the highest probability $a^* = \arg\max_a P(A = a|s)$, is recommended at each state. However, the system must consider various places associated with this category to recommend a specific place. We include the distance factor of POIs to predict the next place. Considering all places corresponding to the optimal policy, the recommended place l_{rec} is the place closest in distance to the current state. Since each state consists of a sequence of places $(l_1, l_2, ..., l_k)$, the distance from the last place l_k is considered. The recommendation score is calculated by the Euclidean distance between the last place l_k and the places in L_c corresponding to the place category of the optimal action.

$$l_{rec} = \arg \min_{\substack{l_x \in L_c \\ cat_{l_x}(a^*)=1}} dist(l_k, l_x), \tag{7}$$

4.5   Online Personalisation

In order to personalise the recommendation model, we apply two techniques for inferring user preferences from her travel history; duration based user interests as introduced in [11] and frequency based user interests.

Duration Based User Preference. Each location l_x in the user travel history contains an arrival time $t_{l_x}^a$ and departure time $t_{l_x}^d$. The duration-based user preference $\rho_u^{dur}(a)$, for user $u \in U$ and category a, is given by the fraction of time she spent at each of the POIs from category a in her travel history,

$$\rho_u^{dur}(a) = \sum_{\substack{l_x \in L_u \\ cat_{l_x}(a)=1}} (t_{l_x}^d - t_{l_x}^a), \tag{8}$$

where L_u contains all the locations visited by user u. These preferences are then normalised to $[0, 1]$ for each user. The more time a user spends at a POI of a place category, the more likely it is that the user is interested in that category.

Frequency Based User Preference. In this method, the user preferences are inferred from the number of times a user visited POIs of a certain category [11]

$$\rho_u^{frq}(a) = \sum_{\substack{l_x \in L_u \\ cat_{l_x}(a)=1}} count(l_x),$$

Table 1. Variation of partial path accuracy@7 with user history

Path Length	1	2	3	4	5	6
History 1	0.041	0.041	0.042	0.042	0.041	0.034
History 2	0.098	0.090	0.096	0.106	0.100	0.103
History 3	0.097	0.090	0.093	0.105	0.090	0.087
History 4	0.089	0.084	0.083	0.094	0.077	0.060
History 5	0.074	0.071	0.058	0.072	0.070	0.058

which is also normalised for each user.

The preference values obtained from either of techniques, form a preference vector for each user, e.g., $\rho_u = \{a_1 : 0.6, a_2 : 0.01, \cdots, a_m : 0.3\}$. We incorporate the individual preferences into our model at the time of recommending places for the optimal category a^*. We assign a score to each place proportional to the weighted sum of distance and the preference associated with its other categories,

$$l_{rec} = \arg \max_{\substack{l_x \in L_c \\ cat_{l_x}(a^*)=1}} \left((1 - \alpha) \times \frac{1}{dist(l_k, l_x)} + \alpha \times (\rho_u \cdot cat_{l_x}) \right),$$

where α is the personalisation coefficient. A place is recommended which is closer in distance and belongs to the categories that are preferred by the user.

5   Empirical Study

In this section, we first analyse the path accuracy of our recommended path by varying the amount of user history encoded in each state. On obtaining the optimal length of user history, we further compare the performance across three cities against several baselines. Moreover, we compute accuracy@k when the recommended places are among the top-k closets places to the current POI. All the experiments are conducted first without the effects of user preference and then when user preferences are included.

We use a time-series leave-one-out cross-validation for tuning the parameters of our model. For the users with multi-day itineraries, we use the last day's travel sequence as the test set and the remaining as training set. For users that have only traveled on one day, the travel sequence is split into 60%-20%-20% of

POIs into training, validation, and test sets. For evaluation, paths of length z are obtained from the test set, where $z \in \{1, 2, 3, 4, 5, 6\}$. A path of length 1 would contain two place locations (l_1, l_2) and so on. The performance criteria evaluate how many of the recommended places are present in the test paths. The exact match accuracy of total n paths from test set is given by

$$Acc_{exact} = \frac{1}{n} \sum_{x=path_1}^{path_n} \sum_{z=1}^{length(x)} \frac{h(z)}{length(x)}, \tag{9}$$

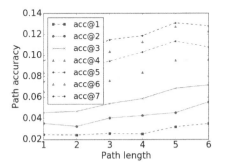

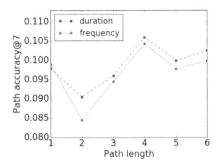

Fig. 1. Variation in partial path accuracy with k in accuracy@k

Fig. 2. Partial path accuracy for personalisation techniques

where $h(z) = 1$ if subpath of size z from path x is predicted correctly from the model, and is zero otherwise. The overall accuracy is given by averaging the accuracy of all the n paths. Additionally, we compute the partial path accuracy which assigns a score of 100% if at least one subpath of test path matches the recommended pair

$$Acc_{partial} = \frac{1}{n} \sum_{x=path_1}^{path_n} \sum_{z=1}^{length(x)} \frac{\psi(h(z))}{length(x)}, \quad \psi(h(z)) = \begin{cases} length(x), & \exists z \quad h(z) \geq 1 \\ 0, & otherwise \end{cases}$$

5.1 Baseline Comparison

We compare our approach with standard graph search algorithms as baselines and the non-personalised MDP policy. We start from the simplest, Breadth First Search (BFS) and evaluate more sophisticated algorithms of Dijkstra, Heuristic Search and A^*. For Dijkstra and A^*, the edge cost is given by the distance between the locations. For each of the baseline algorithms, we look for paths starting from l_{start} corresponding to the starting POI in the test set and iteratively choose a next POI to visit, till the last POI l_{end} in the itinerary is found. The heuristic used in A^* and heuristic search is the *Manhattan Distance* between the current place node and the goal node.

5.2   Results and Discussion

We first study the impact of path history on the prediction accuracy. Note that history length is the number of visited POIs encoded in the state, while path length is the number of next consecutive POIs to recommend. Path length of one hence stands for step-by-step recommendation. Table 1 captures the relation of path history to the performance of the system. There is a jump in performance as we change the path history from 1 to 2. Nonetheless, the performance shows very less improvement as the path history is increased up to length 5. This is primarily due to the fact that many of the travel sequences do not cover places more than three on a single day. Moreover, we observe that, as the path history increases, the number of successors in the transition decreases.

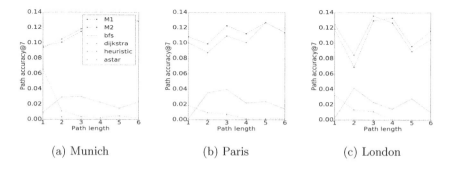

(a) Munich   (b) Paris   (c) London

Fig. 3. Personalised Recommendation vs Baselines (Partial path accuracy)

In addition, we demonstrate the increase in performance by recommending the k closest places in Fig. 1. All these places correspond to the optimal place category obtained through value iteration. Thus, the more flexible a traveler is to multiple recommendation options at her current POI, the higher the likelihood to recommend the best possible place entailing her travel preferences. We also compare the performance of the two personalisation techniques, i.e., duration- and frequency-based user interest as shown in Fig. 2. The former consistently outperforms its counterpart and proves more accurate w.r.t. real-life tours of users, compared to the frequency-based personalisation. Additionally, the personalisation factor α can be varied to balance the distance from the current state and the user personal interest. A value of $\alpha = 0.35$ gave the highest partial path accuracy during cross validation.

Furthermore, Figs. 3 and 4 show the performance compare to baselines in terms of partial and exact accuracy, respectively. M1 denotes the personalised itinerary recommender system and M2 its non-personalised counterpart. Partial path accuracy@7 is used as evaluation measure. There is an average improvement of 10.5% of M1 over the path planning baselines, across the three cities. The effects of personalisation in M1 over the non-personalised recommendations in M2 is still not very significant in our experiments. However, there is a slight improvement for the shorter tour recommendations in Paris. Note that the overall low accuracy is due to the limited quality data, sparsity of transitions, and minimal manual intervention in data processing. Nevertheless, the computationally inexpensive MDP-based personalised recommender system outperforms the robust path planning algorithms and serves as a promising technique for modeling user behavior for travel recommendation.

6   Conclusion

We presented an MDP-based itinerary recommendation approach which took the sequential travel histories and preferences of users into account. Our system used both photo-sharing sites (Flickr) as well as the large abundance of geographical information on web-mapping services to extract supplementary knowledge. As opposed to many existing systems proposed earlier, our model was not restricted to the geo-tagged pictures on Flickr but tracked tourist movements from the time-stamps extracted from data; recommended travel plans emulated the trip plan of tourists. The empirical study showed that our proposed approach outperforms standard path planning algorithms.

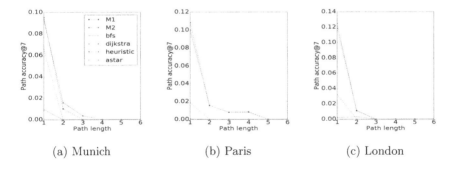

(a) Munich   (b) Paris   (c) London

Fig. 4. Personalised Recommendation vs Baselines (Exact path accuracy)

References

1. Ashbrook, D., Starner, T.: Using GPS to learn significant locations and predict movement across multiple users. Pers. Ubiquitous Comput. **7**(5), 275–286 (2003)
2. Baba, Y., Ishikawa, F., Honiden, S.: Extraction of places related to flickr tags. In: Proceeding of the 2010 conference on ECAI 2010: 19th European Conference on Artificial Intelligence, pp. 523–528. IOS Press (2010)
3. Cao, L., Yu, J., Luo, J., Huang, T.S.: Enhancing semantic and geographic annotation of web images via logistic canonical correlation regression. In: Proceedings of the 17th ACM International Conference on Multimedia, pp. 125–134. MM '09, ACM, New York, NY, USA (2009)

4. Crandall, D.J., Backstrom, L., Huttenlocher, D., Kleinberg, J.: Mapping the world's photos. In: Proceedings of the 18th International Conference on World Wide Web, pp. 761–770. WWW '09, ACM, New York, NY, USA (2009)
5. Dumais, S.T.: Latent semantic analysis. Annu. Rev. Inf. Sci. Technol. **38**(1), 188–230 (2004)
6. Feng, S., Li, X., Zeng, Y., Cong, G., Chee, Y.M., Yuan, Q.: Personalized ranking metric embedding for next new poi recommendation. In: IJCAI, pp. 2069–2075 (2015)
7. Jiang, S., Qian, X., Shen, J., Fu, Y., Mei, T.: Author topic model-based collaborative filtering for personalized poi recommendations. IEEE Trans. Multimed. **17**(6), 907–918 (2015)
8. Kurashima, T., Iwata, T., Irie, G., Fujimura, K.: Travel route recommendation using geotags in photo sharing sites. In: Proceedings of the 19th ACM International Conference on Information and Knowledge Management, pp. 579–588. CIKM '10, ACM, New York, NY, USA (2010)
9. Levenshtein, V.: Binary codes capable of correcting spurious insertions and deletions of ones. Probl. Inf. Transm. **1**(1), 8–17 (1965)
10. Lim, K.H.: Recommending and planning trip itineraries for individual travellers and groups of tourists. In: The 26th International Conference on Automated Planning and Scheduling,p. 115 (2016)
11. Lim, K.H., Chan, J., Leckie, C., Karunasekera, S.: Personalized tour recommendation based on user interests and points of interest visit durations. In: IJCAI, pp. 1778–1784 (2015)
12. Monreale, A., Pinelli, F., Trasarti, R., Giannotti, F.: WhereNext: a location predictor on trajectory pattern mining. In: Proceedings of the 15th ACM SIGKDD International Conference on Knowledge Discovery and Data Mining, pp. 637–646. ACM (2009)
13. Muntean, C.I., Nardini, F.M., Silvestri, F., Baraglia, R.: On learning prediction models for tourists paths. ACM Trans. Intell. Syst. Technol. (TIST) **7**(1), 8 (2015)
14. Noulas, A., Scellato, S., Lathia, N., Mascolo, C.: Mining user mobility features for next place prediction in location-based services. In: 2012 IEEE 12th international conference on Data mining (ICDM), pp. 1038–1043. IEEE (2012)
15. Popescu, A., Grefenstette, G., Moëllic, P.: Gazetiki: automatic construction of a geographical gazetteer. In: Proceedings of JCDL (2008)
16. Quercia, D., Schifanella, R., Aiello, L.M.: The shortest path to happiness: recommending beautiful, quiet, and happy routes in the city. In: Proceedings of the 25th ACM conference on Hypertext and Social Media, pp. 116–125. ACM (2014)
17. Rakesh, V., Jadhav, N., Kotov, A., Reddy, C.K.: Probabilistic social sequential model for tour recommendation. In: Proceedings of the Tenth ACM International Conference on Web Search and Data Mining, pp. 631–640. WSDM '17, ACM, New York, NY, USA (2017)
18. Rattenbury, T., Good, N., Naaman, M.: Towards automatic extraction of event and place semantics from Flickr tags. In: Proceedings of the 30th Annual International ACM SIGIR Conference on Research and Development in Information Retrieval, pp. 103–110. ACM (2007)
19. Sang, J., Mei, T., Sun, J.T., Xu, C., Li, S.: Probabilistic sequential POIs recommendation via check-in data. In: Proceedings of the 20th International Conference on Advances in Geographic Information Systems, pp. 402–405. ACM (2012)
20. Shani, G., Brafman, R.I., Heckerman, D.: An MDP-based recommender system. In: Proceedings of the Eighteenth Conference on Uncertainty in Artificial Intelligence, pp. 453–460. Morgan Kaufmann Publishers Inc. (2002)

21. Sutton, R.S., Barto, A.G.: Reinforcement learning: An introduction, vol. 1. MIT Press, Cambridge (1998)
22. Tavakol, M., Brefeld, U.: Factored MDPs for detecting topics of user sessions. In: Proceedings of the 8th ACM Conference on Recommender Systems, pp. 33–40. ACM (2014)
23. Zhang, C., Liang, H., Wang, K., Sun, J.: Personalized trip recommendation with poi availability and uncertain traveling time. In: Proceedings of the 24th ACM International on Conference on Information and Knowledge Management, pp. 911–920. ACM (2015)
24. Zhang, W., Wang, J.: Location and time aware social collaborative retrieval for new successive point-of-interest recommendation. In: Proceedings of the 24th ACM International on Conference on Information and Knowledge Management, pp. 1221–1230. ACM (2015)

Multiview Learning of Weighted Majority Vote by Bregman Divergence Minimization

Anil Goyal[1,2]([✉]), Emilie Morvant[1], and Massih-Reza Amini[2]

[1] Laboratoire Hubert Curien UMR 5516, Université de Lyon, UJM-St-Etienne,
CNRS, Institut d'Optique Graduate School, 42023 St-Etienne, France
`anil.goyal@univ-st-etienne.fr`
[2] Laboratoire d'Informatique de Grenoble, AMA, Université Grenoble Alps, 38058
Grenoble, France

Abstract. We tackle the issue of classifier combinations when observations have multiple views. Our method jointly learns view-specific weighted majority vote classifiers (*i.e.* for each view) over a set of base voters, and a second weighted majority vote classifier over the set of these view-specific weighted majority vote classifiers. We show that the empirical risk minimization of the final majority vote given a multiview training set can be cast as the minimization of Bregman divergences. This allows us to derive a parallel-update optimization algorithm for learning our multiview model. We empirically study our algorithm with a particular focus on the impact of the training set size on the multiview learning results. The experiments show that our approach is able to overcome the lack of labeled information.

Keywords: Multiview learning · Bregman divergence · Majority vote

1 Introduction

In many real-life applications, observations are produced by more than one source and are so-called multiview [22]. For example, in multilingual regions of the world, including many regions of Europe or in Canada, documents are available in more than one language. The aim of multiview learning is to use this multi-modal information by combining the predictions of each classifier (or the models themselves) operating over each view (called view-specific classifier) in order to improve the overall performance beyond that of predictors trained on each view separately, or by combining directly the views [21].

Related works. The main idea here follows the conclusion of the seminal work of *Blum and Mitchell* [3] which states that correlated yet not completely redundant views contain valuable information for learning. Based on this idea, many studies on multiview learning have been conducted and they can be grouped in three main categories. These approaches exploit the redundancy in different

© Springer Nature Switzerland AG 2018
W. Duivesteijn et al. (Eds.): IDA 2018, LNCS 11191, pp. 124–136, 2018.
https://doi.org/10.1007/978-3-030-01768-2_11

representations of data, either by projecting the view-specific representations in a common canonical space [10,25,29], or by constraining the classifiers to have *similar* outputs on the same observations; for example by adding a disagreement term in their objective functions [20], or lastly by exploiting diversity in the views in order to learn the final classifier defined as the majority vote over the set of view-specific classifiers [17,18,24]. While the two first families of approaches were designed for learning with labeled and unlabeled training data, the last one, were developed in the context of supervised learning. In this line, most of the supervised multiview learning algorithms dealt with the particular case of two view learning [9,12,28], and some recent works studied the general case of multiview learning with more than two views under the majority vote setting. *Amini et al.* [1] derived a generalization error bound for classifiers learned on multiview examples and identified situations where it is more interesting to use all views to learn a uniformly weighted majority vote classifier instead of single view learning. *Koço et al.* [13] proposed a Boosting-based strategy that maintains a different distribution of examples with respect to each view. For a given view, the corresponding distribution is updated based on view-specific *weak* classifiers from that view and all the other views with the idea of using all the view-specific distributions to weight hard examples for the next iteration. *Peng et al.* [17,18] enhanced this idea by maintaining a single weight distribution among the multiple views in order to ensure consistency between them. *Xiao et al.* [24] proposed a multiview learning algorithm where they boost the performance of view-specific classifiers by combining multiview learning with Adaboost.

Contribution. In this work, we propose a multiview Boosting-based algorithm, called $\text{M}\omega\text{MvC}^2$, for the general case where observations are described by more than two views. Our algorithm combines previously learned view-specific classifiers as in [1] but with the difference that it jointly learns two sets of weights for, first, combining view-specific *weak classifiers*; and then combining the obtained view-specific weighted majority vote classifiers to get a final weighted majority vote classifier. We show that the minimization of the classification error over a multiview training set can be cast as the minimization of Bregman divergences allowing the development of an efficient parallel update scheme to learn the weights. Using a large publicly available corpus of multilingual documents extracted from the Reuters RCV1 and RCV2 corpora as well as MNIST_1 and MNIST_2 collections, we show that our approach consistently improves over other methods, in the particular when there are only few training examples available for learning. This is a particularly interesting setting when resources are limited, and corresponds, for example, to the common situation of multilingual data.

Organization of the paper. In the next section, we present the double weighted majority vote classifier for multiview learning. Section 3 shows that the learning problem is equivalent to a Bregman-divergence minimization and describes the Boosting-based algorithm we developed to learn the classifier. In Sect. 4, we present experimental results obtained with our approach. Finally, in

Sect. 5 we discuss the outcomes of this study and give some pointers to further research.

2   Notations and Setting

For any positive integer N, $[N]$ denotes the set $[N] \doteq \{1, \ldots, N\}$. We consider binary classification problems with $V \geq 2$ input spaces $\mathcal{X}_v \subset \mathbb{R}^{d_v}; \forall v \in [V]$, and an output space $\mathcal{Y} = \{-1, +1\}$. Each *multiview observation* $\mathbf{x} \in \mathcal{X}_1 \times \cdots \times \mathcal{X}_V$ is a sequence $\mathbf{x} \doteq (x^1, \cdots, x^V)$ where each *view* x^v provides a representation of the same observation in a different vector space $\mathcal{X}_v$ (each vector space are not necessarily of the same dimension). We further assume that we have a finite set of *weak classifiers* $\mathcal{H}_v \doteq \{h_{v,j} : \mathcal{X}_v \to \{-1, +1\} \mid j \in [n_v]\}$ of size n_v. We aim at learning a two-level weighted majority vote classifier where at the first level a weighted majority vote is built for each view $v \in [V]$ over the associated set of weak classifiers $\mathcal{H}_v$, and the final classifier, referred to as the Multiview double ωeighted Majority vote Classifier ($M\omega MvC^2$), is a weighted majority vote over the previous view-specific majority vote classifiers (see Fig. 1 for an illustration). Given a training set $\mathcal{S} = (\mathbf{x}_i, y_i)_{1 \leq i \leq m}$ of size m drawn *i.i.d.* with respect to a fixed, yet unknown, distribution $\mathcal{D}$ over $(\mathcal{X}_1 \times \cdots \times \mathcal{X}_V) \times \mathcal{Y}$, the learning objective is to train the weak view-specific classifiers $(\mathcal{H}_v)_{1 \leq v \leq V}$ and to choose two sets of weights; $\boldsymbol{\Pi} = (\boldsymbol{\pi}_v)_{1 \leq v \leq V}$, where $\forall v \in [V]$, $\boldsymbol{\pi}_v = (\pi_{v,j})_{1 \leq j \leq n_v}$, and $\boldsymbol{\rho} = (\rho_v)_{1 \leq v \leq V}$, such that the $\boldsymbol{\rho\Pi}$-weighted majority vote classifier $B_{\boldsymbol{\rho\Pi}}$

$$B_{\boldsymbol{\rho\Pi}}(\mathbf{x}) = \sum_{v=1}^{V} \rho_v \sum_{j=1}^{n_v} \pi_{v,j} \, h_{v,j}(x^v) \tag{1}$$

has the smallest possible generalization error on $\mathcal{D}$. We follow the Empirical Risk Minimization principle [23], and aim at minimizing the 0/1-loss over $\mathcal{S}$:

$$\hat{\mathcal{L}}_m^{0/1}(B_{\boldsymbol{\rho\Pi}}, \mathcal{S}) = \frac{1}{m} \sum_{i=1}^{m} \mathbb{1}_{y_i B_{\boldsymbol{\rho\Pi}}(\mathbf{x}_i) \leq 0},$$

where $\mathbb{1}_p$ is equal to 1 if the predicate p is true, and 0 otherwise. As this loss function is non-continuous and non-differentiable, it is typically replaced by an appropriate convex and differentiable proxy. Here, we replace $\mathbb{1}_{z \leq 0}$ by the logistic upper bound $a \log(1 + e^{-z})$, with $a = (\log 2)^{-1}$. The misclassification cost becomes

$$\hat{\mathcal{L}}_m(B_{\boldsymbol{\rho\Pi}}, \mathcal{S}) = \frac{a}{m} \sum_{i=1}^{m} \ln \left(1 + \exp\left(-y_i B_{\boldsymbol{\rho\Pi}}(\mathbf{x}_i)\right)\right), \tag{2}$$

and the objective would be then to find the optimal combination weights $\boldsymbol{\Pi}^\star$ and $\boldsymbol{\rho}^\star$ that minimize this surrogate logistic loss.

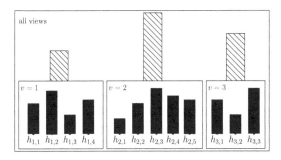

Fig. 1. Illustration of MωMvC² with $V=3$. For all views $v \in \{1,2,3\}$, we have a set of view-specific weak classifiers $(\mathcal{H}_v)_{1 \leq v \leq V}$ that are learned over a multiview training set. The objective is then to learn the weights $\boldsymbol{\Pi}$ (black histograms) associated to $(\mathcal{H}_v)_{1 \leq v \leq V}$; and the weights $\boldsymbol{\rho}$ (hatched histograms) associated to weighted majority vote classifiers such that the $\boldsymbol{\rho\Pi}$-weighted majority vote classifier $B_{\rho\Pi}$ (Eq. 1) will have the smallest possible generalization error.

3   An Iterative Parallel Update Algorithm to Learn MωMvC²

In this section, we first show how the minimization of the surrogate loss of Eq. (2) is equivalent to the minimization of a given Bregman divergence. Then, this equivalence allows us to employ a parallel-update optimization algorithm to learn the weights $\boldsymbol{\Pi}=(\boldsymbol{\pi}_v)_{1 \leq v \leq V}$ and $\boldsymbol{\rho}$ leading to this minimization.

3.1   Bregman-Divergence Optimization

We first recall the definition of a Bregman divergence [4,14].

Definition 1 (Bregman divergence). *Let $\Omega \subseteq \mathbb{R}^m$ and $F : \Omega \to \mathbb{R}$ be a continuously differentiable and strictly convex real-valued function. The Bregman divergence D_F associated to F is defined for all $(\mathbf{p},\mathbf{q}) \in \Omega \times \Omega$ as*

$$D_F(\mathbf{p}\|\mathbf{q}) \doteq F(\mathbf{p}) - F(\mathbf{q}) - \langle \nabla F(\mathbf{q}), (\mathbf{p} - \mathbf{q}) \rangle, \tag{3}$$

where $\nabla F(\mathbf{q})$ is the gradient of F estimated at $\mathbf{q}$, and the operator $\langle \cdot, \cdot \rangle$ is the dot product function.

The optimization problem arising from this definition that we are interested in, is to find a vector $\mathbf{p}^\star \in \Omega$—that is the closest to a given vector $\mathbf{q}_0 \in \Omega$—under the set $\mathcal{P}$ of V linear constraints

$$\mathcal{P} \doteq \{\mathbf{p} \in \Omega | \forall v \in [V], \ \rho_v \mathbf{p}^\top \mathbf{M}_v = \rho_v \tilde{\mathbf{p}}^\top \mathbf{M}_v\},$$

where $\tilde{\mathbf{p}} \in \Omega$ is a specified vector, and $\mathbf{M}_v$ is a $m \times n_v$ matrix with $n_v=|\mathcal{H}_v|$ the number of weak classifiers for view $v \in [V]$. Defining the Legendre transform as

$$L_F\left(\mathbf{q}, \sum_{v=1}^V \rho_v \mathbf{M}_v \boldsymbol{\pi}_v\right) \doteq \arg\min_{\mathbf{p} \in \Omega} \left\{ D_F(\mathbf{p}\|\mathbf{q}) + \sum_{v=1}^V \langle \rho_v \mathbf{M}_v \boldsymbol{\pi}_v, \mathbf{p} \rangle \right\}.$$

the dual optimization problem can be stated as finding a vector $\mathbf{q}^*$ in $\bar{\mathcal{Q}}$, the closure of the set

$$\mathcal{Q} \doteq \left\{ \mathbf{q} = L_F \left(\mathbf{q}_0, \sum_{v=1}^{V} \rho_v \mathbf{M}_v \boldsymbol{\pi}_v \right) \middle| \rho \in \mathbb{R}^V; \forall v, \boldsymbol{\pi}_v \in \mathbb{R}^{n_v} \right\},$$

for which $D_F(\tilde{\mathbf{p}}||\mathbf{q}^*)$ is the lowest. It can be shown that both of these optimization problems have the same unique solution [8,14], with the advantage of having parallel-update optimization algorithms to find the solution of the dual form in the mono-view case [6–8], making the use of the latter more appealing.

According to our multiview setting and to optimize Eq. (2) through a Bregman divergence, we consider the function F defined for all $\mathbf{p} \in \Omega = [0, 1]^m$ as

$$F(\mathbf{p}) \doteq \sum_{i=1}^{m} p_i \ln(p_i) + (1 - p_i) \ln(1 - p_i),$$

which from Definition 1 and the definition of the Legendre transform, yields that for all $(\mathbf{p}, \mathbf{q}) \in \Omega \times \Omega$ and $\mathbf{r} \in \Omega$

$$D_F(\mathbf{p}||\mathbf{q}) = \sum_{i=1}^{m} p_i \ln \left(\frac{p_i}{q_i} \right) + (1 - p_i) \ln \left(\frac{1 - p_i}{1 - q_i} \right), \tag{4}$$

$$and \forall i \in [m], \ L_F(\mathbf{q}, \mathbf{r})_i = \frac{q_i e^{-r_i}}{1 - q_i + q_i e^{-r_i}}, \tag{5}$$

with a_i the ith characteristic of $\mathbf{a} = (a_i)_{1 \leq i \leq m}$ ($\mathbf{a}$ being $\mathbf{p}$, $\mathbf{q}$, $\mathbf{r}$ or $L_F(\mathbf{q}, \mathbf{r})$).

Now, let $\mathbf{q}_0 = \frac{1}{2} \mathbf{1}_m$ be the vector with all its components set to $\frac{1}{2}$. For all $i \in [m]$, we define $L_F(\mathbf{q}_0, \mathbf{v})_i = \sigma(v_i)$ with $\sigma(z) = (1 + e^z)^{-1}$, $\forall z \in \mathbb{R}$. We set the matrix $\mathbf{M}_v$ as for all $(i, j) \in [m] \times [n_v]$, $(\mathbf{M}_v)_{ij} = y_i h_{v,j}(x_i^v)$. Then using Eqs. (4) and (5), it comes

$$D_F \left(\mathbf{0} \middle\| L_F \left(\mathbf{q}_0, \sum_{v=1}^{V} \rho_v \mathbf{M}_v \boldsymbol{\pi}_v \right) \right) = \sum_{i=1}^{m} \ln \left(1 + \exp \left(-y_i \sum_{v=1}^{V} \rho_v \sum_{j=1}^{n_v} \pi_{v,j} h_{v,j}(x_i^v) \right) \right). \tag{6}$$

As a consequence, minimizing Eq. (2) is equivalent to minimizing $D_F(\mathbf{0}||\mathbf{q})$ over $\mathbf{q} \in \bar{\mathcal{Q}}_0$, where for $\Omega = [0, 1]^m$

$$\mathcal{Q}_0 = \left\{ \mathbf{q} \in \Omega \middle| q_i = \sigma \left(y_i \sum_{v=1}^{V} \rho_v \sum_{j=1}^{n_v} \pi_{v,j} h_{v,j}(x_i^v) \right); \rho, \boldsymbol{\Pi} \right\}. \tag{7}$$

For a set of weak-classifiers $(\mathcal{H}_v)_{1 \leq v \leq V}$ learned over a training set $\mathcal{S}$; this equivalence allows us to adapt the parallel-update optimization algorithm described in [6] to find the optimal weights $\boldsymbol{\Pi}$ and ρ defining $\text{M}\omega\text{MvC}^2$ of Eq. (1), as described in Algorithm 1.

Algorithm 1 Learning $\text{M}\omega\text{MvC}^2$

Input: Training set $\mathcal{S} = (\mathbf{x}_i, y_i)_{1 \leq i \leq m}$, where $\forall i, \mathbf{x}_i = (x_i^1, \ldots, x_i^V)$ and $y_i \in \{-1, 1\}$; and a maximal number of iterations T.

Initialization: $\rho^{(1)} \leftarrow \frac{1}{V}\mathbf{1}_V$ and $\forall v, \boldsymbol{\pi}_v^{(1)} \leftarrow \frac{1}{n_v}\mathbf{1}_{n_v}$

Train the weak classifiers $(\mathcal{H}_v)_{1 \leq v \leq V}$ over $\mathcal{S}$

For $v \in [V]$ set the $m \times n_v$ matrix $\mathbf{M}_v$ such that $\forall i \in [m]$, $\forall j \in [n_v]$, $(\mathbf{M}_v)_{ij} = y_i h_{v,j}(x_i^v)$

1: **for** $t = 1, \ldots, T$ **do**
2:     **for** $i = 1, \ldots, m$ **do**
3:         $q_i^{(t)} = \sigma\left(y_i \sum_{v=1}^{V} \rho_v^{(t)} \sum_{j=1}^{n_v} \pi_{v,j}^{(t)} h_{v,j}(x_i^v)\right)$
4:     **for** $v = 1, \ldots, V$ **do**
5:         **for** $j = 1, \ldots, n_v$ **do**
6:             $W_{v,j}^{(t)+} = \sum_{i:\text{sign}((\mathbf{M}_v)_{ij})=+1} q_i^{(t)}|(\mathbf{M}_v)_{ij}|$
7:             $W_{v,j}^{(t)-} = \sum_{i:\text{sign}((\mathbf{M}_v)_{ij})=-1} q_i^{(t)}|(\mathbf{M}_v)_{ij}|$
8:             $\delta_{v,j}^{(t)} = \frac{1}{2}\ln\left(\frac{W_{v,j}^{(t)+}}{W_{v,j}^{(t)-}}\right)$
9:         $\boldsymbol{\pi}_v^{(t+1)} = \boldsymbol{\pi}_v^{(t)} + \boldsymbol{\delta}_v^{(t)}$
10:     **Set** $\rho^{(t+1)}$, as the solution of :

$$\min_{\rho} \quad -\sum_{v=1}^{V} \rho_v \sum_{j=1}^{n_v}\left(\sqrt{W_{v,j}^{(t)+}} - \sqrt{W_{v,j}^{(t)-}}\right)^2 \tag{8}$$

$$\text{s.t.} \quad \sum_{v=1}^{V} \rho_v = 1, \quad \rho_v \geq 0 \quad \forall v \in [V]$$

Return: Weights $\rho^{(T)}$ and $\boldsymbol{\Pi}^{(T)}$.

3.2   A Multiview Parallel Update Algorithm

Once all view-specific *weak classifiers* $(\mathcal{H}_v)_{1 \leq v \leq V}$ have been trained, we start from an initial point $\mathbf{q}^{(1)} \in \mathcal{Q}_0$ (Eq. 7) corresponding to uniform values of weights $\rho^{(1)} = \frac{1}{V}\mathbf{1}_V$ and $\forall v \in [V]$, $\boldsymbol{\pi}_v^{(1)} = \frac{1}{n_v}\mathbf{1}_{n_v}$. Then, we iteratively update the weights such that at each iteration t, using the current parameters $\rho^{(t)}, \boldsymbol{\Pi}^{(t)}$ and $\mathbf{q}^{(t)} \in \mathcal{Q}_0$, we seek new parameters $\rho^{(t+1)}$ and $\boldsymbol{\delta}_v^{(t)}$ such that for

$$\mathbf{q}^{(t+1)} = L_F\left(\mathbf{q}_0, \sum_{v=1}^{V} \rho_v^{(t+1)}\mathbf{M}_v(\boldsymbol{\pi}_v^{(t)} + \boldsymbol{\delta}_v^{(t)})\right), \tag{9}$$

we get $D_F(0\|\mathbf{q}^{(t+1)}) \leq D_F(0\|\mathbf{q}^{(t)})$.

Following [6, Theorem 3], it is straightforward to show that in this case, the following inequality holds:

$$D_F(\mathbf{0}||\mathbf{q}^{(t+1)}) - D_F(\mathbf{0}||\mathbf{q}^{(t)}) \leq A^{(t)}, \tag{10}$$

$$where \quad A^{(t)} = -\sum_{v=1}^{V} \rho_v^{(t+1)} \sum_{j=1}^{n_v} \left(W_{v,j}^{(t)+}(e^{-\delta_{v,j}^{(t)}} - 1) - W_{v,j}^{(t)-}(e^{\delta_{v,j}^{(t)}} - 1) \right)^2,$$

with $\forall j \in [n_v]; W_{v,j}^{(t)\pm} = \sum_{i:\text{sign}((\mathbf{M}_v)_{ij})=\pm 1} q_i^{(t)} |(\mathbf{M}_v)_{ij}|$.

By fixing the set of parameters $\rho^{(t+1)}$; the parameters $\delta_v^{(t)}$ that minimize $A^{(t)}$ are defined as $\forall v \in [V], \forall j \in [n_v]; \delta_{v,j}^{(t)} = \frac{1}{2} \ln \left(\frac{W_{v,j}^{(t)+}}{W_{v,j}^{(t)-}} \right)$. Plugging back these values into the above equation gives

$$A^{(t)} = -\sum_{v=1}^{V} \rho_v^{(t+1)} \sum_{j=1}^{n_v} \left(\sqrt{W_{v,j}^{(t)+}} - \sqrt{W_{v,j}^{(t)-}} \right)^2. \tag{11}$$

Now by fixing the set of parameters $(W_{v,j}^{(t)\pm})_{v,j}$, the weights $\rho^{(t+1)}$ are found by minimizing Eq. (11) under the linear constraints $\forall v \in [V], \rho_v \geq 0$ and $\sum_{v=1}^{V} \rho_v = 1$. This alternating optimization of $A^{(t)}$ bears similarity with the block-coordinate descent technique [2], where at each iteration, variables are split into two subsets—the set of the active variables, and the set of the inactive ones—and the objective function is minimized along active dimensions while inactive variables are fixed at current values.

Convergence of Algorithm. The sequences of weights $(\boldsymbol{\Pi}^{(t)})_{t\in\mathbb{N}}$ and $(\boldsymbol{\rho}^{(t)})_{t\in\mathbb{N}}$ found by Algorithm 1 converge to the minimizers of the multiview classification loss (Eq. 2), as with the resulting sequence $(\mathbf{q}^{(t)})_{t\in\mathbb{N}}$ (Eq. 9), the sequence $(D_F(\mathbf{0}||\mathbf{q}^{(t)}))_{t\in\mathbb{N}}$ is decreasing and since it is lower-bounded (Eq. 6), it converges to the minimum of Eq. (2).

3.3 A Note on the Complexity of Algorithm

For each view v, the complexity of learning decision tree classifiers is $O(d_v\, m log(m))$. We learn the weights over the views by optimizing Eq. (11) (Step 10 of our algorithm) using SLSQP method which has time complexity of $O(V^3)$. Therefore, the overall complexity is $O(V\, d_v\, m.log(m) + T\, (V^3 + \sum_{v=1}^{V} m\, n_v))$. Note that it is easy to parallelize our algorithm: by using V different machines, we can learn the view-specific classifiers and weights over them (Steps 4 to 9).

4 Experimental Results

We present below the results of the experiments we have performed to evaluate the efficiency of Algorithm 1 to learn the set of weights $\boldsymbol{\Pi}$ and $\boldsymbol{\rho}$ involved in the definition of the $\boldsymbol{\rho\Pi}$-weighted majority vote classifier $B_{\rho\Pi}$ (Eq. (1)).

4.1 Datasets

MNIST. is a publicly available dataset consisting of $70,000$ images of handwritten digits distributed over 10 classes [15]. For our experiments, we created 2 multi-view collections from the initial dataset. Following [5], the first dataset (MNIST_1) was created by extracting 4 no-overlapping quarters of each image considered as its 4 views. The second dataset (MNIST_2) was made by extracting 4 overlapping quarters from each image as its 4 views. We randomly split each collection by keeping $10,000$ images for testing and the remaining images for training.

Reuters RCV1/RCV2. is a multilingual text classification data extracted from Reuters RCV1 and RCV2 corpus[1]. It consists of more than $110,000$ documents written in five different languages (English, French, German, Italian and Spanish) distributed over six classes. In this paper we consider each language as a view. We reserved 30% of documents for testing and the remaining for training.

Table 1. Test classification accuracy and F_1-score of different approaches averaged over all the classes and over 20 random sets of $m = 100$ labeled examples per training set. Along each column, the best result is in bold, and second one in italic. $^\downarrow$ indicates that a result is statistically significantly worse than the best result, according to a Wilcoxon rank sum test with $p < 0.02$.

Strategy	MNIST_1		MNIST_2		Reuters	
	Accuracy	F_1	Accuracy	F_1	Accuracy	F_1
Mono	$.7827 \pm .008^\downarrow$	$.4355 \pm .009^\downarrow$	$.7896 \pm .008^\downarrow$	$.4535 \pm .011^\downarrow$	$.7089 \pm .017^\downarrow$	$.4439 \pm .007^\downarrow$
Concat	$.7988 \pm .011^\downarrow$	$.4618 \pm .015^\downarrow$	$.7982 \pm .017^\downarrow$	$.4653 \pm .021^\downarrow$	$.6918 \pm .029^\downarrow$	$.4378 \pm .015^\downarrow$
Fusion	$.8167 \pm .017^\downarrow$	$.4769 \pm .018^\downarrow$	$.8244 \pm .019^\downarrow$	$.4955 \pm .027^\downarrow$	$.7086 \pm .029^\downarrow$	$.4200 \pm .021^\downarrow$
MVMLsp	$.7221 \pm .021^\downarrow$	$.3646 \pm .019^\downarrow$	$.7669 \pm .032^\downarrow$	$.4318 \pm .025^\downarrow$	$.6037 \pm .020^\downarrow$	$.3181 \pm .022^\downarrow$
MV-MV	$.8381 \pm .009^\downarrow$	$.5238 \pm .015^\downarrow$	$.8380 \pm .010^\downarrow$	$.5307 \pm .016^\downarrow$	$.7453 \pm .023^\downarrow$	$.4979 \pm .012^\downarrow$
MVWAB	$.8470 \pm .015^\downarrow$	$.5704 \pm .012^\downarrow$	$.8331 \pm .016^\downarrow$	$.5320 \pm .011^\downarrow$	$.7484 \pm .017^\downarrow$	$.5034 \pm .016^\downarrow$
rBoost.SH	$.7580 \pm .011^\downarrow$	$.4067 \pm .009^\downarrow$	$.8247 \pm .009^\downarrow$	$.5148 \pm .015^\downarrow$	$.7641 \pm .014$	$.5093 \pm .010^\downarrow$
$\text{M}\omega\text{MvC}^2$	$.8659 \pm .011$	$.5914 \pm .015$	$.8474 \pm .012$	$.5523 \pm .018$	$.7662 \pm .010$	$.5244 \pm .012$

4.2 Experimental Protocol

In our experiments, we set up binary classification tasks by using all multiview observations from one class as positive examples and all the others as negative examples. We reduced the imbalance between positive and negative examples by subsampling the latter in the training sets, and used decision trees as view specific weak classifiers. We compare our approach to the following seven algorithms.

- Mono is the best performing decision tree model operating on a single view.
- Concat is an early fusion approach, where a mono-view decision tree operates over the concatenation of all views of multiview observations.

---

[1] https://archive.ics.uci.edu/ml/datasets/Reuters+RCV1+RCV2+Multilingual,
+Multiview+Text+Categorization+Test+collection.

- **Fusion** is a late fusion approach, sometimes referred to as stacking, where view-specific classifiers are trained independently over different views using 60% of the training examples. A final multiview model is then trained over the predictions of the view-specific classifiers using the rest of the training examples.
- **MVMLsp** [11] is a multiview metric learning approach, where multiview kernels are learned to capture the view-specific information and relation between the views. We kept the experimental setup of [11] with Nyström parameter 0.24.[2]
- **MV-MV** [1] is a multiview algorithm where view-specific classifiers are trained over the views using all the training examples. The final model is the uniformly weighted majority vote.
- **MVWAB** [24] is a Multiview Weighted Voting AdaBoost algorithm, where multiview learning and ababoost techniques are combined to learn a weighted majority vote over view-specific classifiers but without any notion of learning weights over views.
- **rBoost.SH** [17,18] is a multiview boosting approach where a single distribution over different views of training examples is maintained and, the distribution over the views are updated using the multiarmed bandit framework. For the tuning of parameters, we followed the experimental setup of [17].

Fusion, MV-MV, MVWAB, and rBoost.SH make decision based on some majority vote strategies, as the proposed $M\omega MvC^2$ classifier. The difference relies on how the view-specific classifiers are combined. For MVWAB and rBoost.SH, we used decision tree model to learn view-specific weak classifiers at each iteration of algorithm and fixed the maximum number of iterations to $T = 100$. To learn $M\omega MvC^2$, we generated the matrix $\mathbf{M}_v$ by considering a set of weak decision tree classifiers with different depths (from 1 to $\max_d -2$, where $\max_d$ is maximum possible depth of a decision tree). We tuned the maximum number of iterations by cross-validation which came out to be $T = 2$ in most of the cases and that we fixed throughout all of the experiments. To solve the optimization problem for finding the weights ρ (Eq. 8), we used the Sequential Least SQuares Programming (SLSQP) implementation of scikit-learn [16], that we also used to learn the decision trees. Results are computed over the test set using the accuracy and the standard F_1-score [19], which is the harmonic average of precision and recall. Experiments are repeated 20 times by each time splitting the training and the test sets at random over the initial datasets.

4.3   Results

Table 1 reports the results obtained for $m=100$ training examples by different methods averaged over all classes and the 20 test results obtained over 20 random experiments[3]. From these results it becomes clear that late fusion and other multiview approaches (except MVMLsp) provide consistent improvements over training independent mono-view classifiers and with early fusion, when the size of

---

[2] We used the Python code available from https://lives.lif.univ-mrs.fr/?page_id=12.
[3] We also did experiments for Mono, Concat, Fusion, MV-MV using Adaboost. The performance of Adaboost for these baselines is similar to that of decision trees.

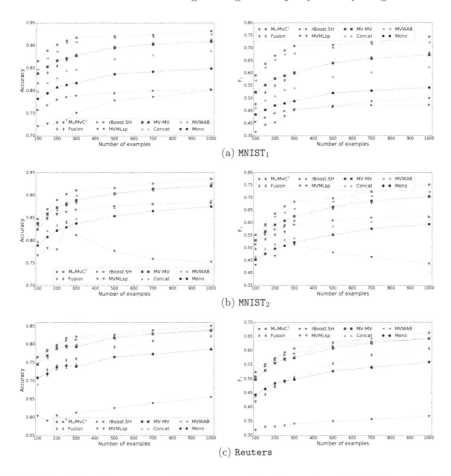

Fig. 2. Evolution of accuracy and F_1-score $w.r.t$ to the number of labeled examples in the initial labeled training sets on MNIST$_1$, MNIST$_2$ and Reuters datasets.

the training set is small. Furthermore, MωMvC^2 outperforms the other approaches and compared to the second best strategy the gain in accuracy (*resp.* F_1-score) varies between 0.2% and 2.2% (*resp.* 2.2% and 3.8%) across the collections. These results provide evidence that majority voting for multiview learning is an effective way to overcome the lack of labeled information and that all the views do not have the same strength (or do not bring information in the same way) as the learning of weights, as it is done in MωMvC^2, is much more effective than the uniform combination of view-specific classifiers as it is done in MV-MV.

We also analyze the behavior of the algorithms for growing initial amounts of labeled data. Figure 2 illustrates this by showing the evolution of the accuracy and the F_1-score with respect to the number of labeled examples in the initial labeled training sets on MNIST$_1$, MNIST$_2$ and Reuters datasets. As expected, all performance curves increase monotonically (except MVMLsp) $w.r.t$ the additional labeled data. When there are sufficient labeled examples, the performance increase of all algorithms actually begins to slow, suggesting that the labeled data carries sufficient information and that the different views do not bring additional information.

An important point here is that `rBoost.SH`—which takes into account both view-consistency and diversity between views—provides the worst results on $MNIST_1$ where there is no overlapping between the views, while the weighted majority vote as it is performed in $M\omega MvC^2$ still provides an efficient model. Furthermore, `MVMLsp`—which learns multiview kernels to capture views-specific informations and relation between views—performs worst on all the datasets. We believe that the superior performance of our method stands in our two-level framework. Indeed, thanks to this trick, we are able to consider the view-specific information by learning weights over view-specific classifiers, and to capture the importance of each view in the final ensemble by learning weights over the views.

5   Conclusion

In this paper, we tackle the issue of classifier combination when observations have different representations (or have multiple views). Our approach jointly learns weighted majority vote view-specific classifiers (*i.e.* at the view level) over a set of base classifiers, and a second weighted majority vote classifier over the previous set of view specific weighted majority vote classifiers. We show that the minimization of the multiview classification error is equivalent to the minimization of Bregman divergences. This embedding allowed to derive a parallel-update optimization boosting-like algorithm to learn the weights of the double weighted multiview majority vote classifier. Our results show clearly that our method allows to reach high performance in terms of accuracy and F_1-score on three datasets in the situation where few initial labeled training documents are available. It also comes out that compared to the uniform combination of view-specific classifiers, the learning of weights allows to better capture the strengths of different views.

As future work, we would like to extend our algorithm to the *semi-supervised* case, where one has access to an additionally unlabeled set during the training. One possible way is to learn a view-specific classifier using pseudo-labels (for unlabeled data) generated from the classifiers trained from other views, *e.g.* [27]. Moreover, the question of extending our work to the case where all the views are not necessarily available or not complete (*missing views* or *incomplete views*, *e.g.* [1,26]), is very exciting. One solution could be to adapt the definition of the matrix M_v to allow to deal with incomplete data; this may be done by considering a notion of diversity to complete M_v.

Acknowledgment. This work is partially funded by the French ANR project LIVES ANR-15-CE23-0026-03 and the "Région Rhône-Alpes".

References

1. Amini, M.R., Usunier, N., Goutte, C.: Learning from multiple partially observed views - an application to multilingual text categorization. In: NIPS (2009)
2. Bertsekas, D.P.: Nonlinear Programming. Athena Scientific, Belmont (1999)
3. Blum, A., Mitchell, T.M.: Combining labeled and unlabeled data with co-training. In: COLT, pp. 92–100 (1998)
4. Bregman, L.: The relaxation method of finding the common point of convex sets and its application to the solution of problems in convex programming. USSR Comput. Math. Math. Phys. **7**(3), 200–217 (1967)
5. Chen, M., Denoyer, L.: Multi-view generative adversarial networks. In: ECML-PKDD, pp. 175–188 (2017)
6. Collins, M., Schapire, R.E., Singer, Y.: Logistic regression, adaboost and bregman distances. Mach. Learn. **48**(1–3), 253–285 (2002)
7. Darroch, J.N., Ratcliff, D.: Generalized iterative scaling for log-linear models. Ann. Math. Stat. **43**, 1470–1480 (1972)
8. Della Pietra, S., Della Pietra, V., Lafferty, J.: Inducing features of random fields. IEEE TPAMI **19**(4), 380–393 (1997)
9. Farquhar, J., Hardoon, D., Meng, H., Shawe-taylor, J.S., Szedmák, S.: Two view learning: Svm-2k, theory and practice. In: NIPS, pp. 355–362 (2006)
10. Gönen, M., Alpayd, E.: Multiple kernel learning algorithms. JMLR **12**, 2211–2268 (2011)
11. Huusari, R., Kadri, H., Capponi, C.: Multi-view metric learning in vector-valued kernel spaces. In: AISTATS (2018)
12. Janodet, J.C., Sebban, M., Suchier, H.M.: Boosting classifiers built from different subsets of features. Fundam. Inf. **94**(2009), 1–21 (2009)
13. Koço, S., Capponi, C.: A boosting approach to multiview classification with cooperation. In: Gunopulos, D., Hofmann, T., Malerba, D., Vazirgiannis, M. (eds.) ECML PKDD 2011. LNCS (LNAI), vol. 6912, pp. 209–228. Springer, Heidelberg (2011). https://doi.org/10.1007/978-3-642-23783-6_14
14. Lafferty, J.: Additive models, boosting, and inference for generalized divergences. In: COLT, pp. 125–133 (1999)
15. Lecun, Y., Bottou, L., Bengio, Y., Haffner, P.: Gradient-based learning applied to document recognition. In: Proceedings of the IEEE, pp. 2278–2324 (1998)
16. Pedregosa, F., et al.: Scikit-learn: machine learning in python. JMLR **12**, 2825–2830 (2011)
17. Peng, J., Aved, A.J., Seetharaman, G., Palaniappan, K.: Multiview boosting with information propagation for classification. IEEE Trans. Neural Netw. Learn. Syst. **99**, 1–13 (2017)
18. Peng, J., Barbu, C., Seetharaman, G., Fan, W., Wu, X., Palaniappan, K.: Shareboost: boosting for multi-view learning with performance guarantees. In: ECML-PKDD, pp. 597–612 (2011)
19. Powers, D.M.: Evaluation: from precision, recall and F-measure to ROC, informedness, markedness and correlation. J. Mach. Learn. Technol. **1**(2), 37–63 (2011)
20. Sindhwani, V., Rosenberg, D.S.: An RKHS for multi-view learning and manifold co-regularization. In: ICML, pp. 976–983 (2008)
21. Snoek, C., Worring, M., Smeulders, A.W.M.: Early versus late fusion in semantic video analysis. In: ACM Multimedia, pp. 399–402 (2005)
22. Sun, S.: A survey of multi-view machine learning. Neural Comput. Appl. **23**(7–8), 2031–2038 (2013)

23. Vapnik, V.N.: The Nature of Statistical Learning Theory. Springer, Berlin (1999)
24. Xiao, M., Guo, Y.: Multi-view Adaboost for multilingual subjectivity analysis. In: COLING, pp. 2851–2866 (2012)
25. Xu, C., Tao, D., Xu, C.: Large-margin multi-viewinformation bottleneck. IEEE TPAMI **36**(8), 1559–1572 (2014)
26. Xu, C., Tao, D., Xu, C.: Multi-view learning with incomplete views. IEEE Trans. Image Process. **24**(12), 5812–5825 (2015)
27. Xu, X., Li, W., Xu, D., Tsang, I.W.: Co-labeling for multi-view weakly labeled learning. IEEE TPAMI **38**(6), 1113–1125 (2016)
28. Xu, Z., Sun, S.: An algorithm on multi-view Adaboost. In: Wong, K.W., Mendis, B.S.U., Bouzerdoum, A. (eds.) ICONIP 2010. LNCS, vol. 6443, pp. 355–362. Springer, Heidelberg (2010). https://doi.org/10.1007/978-3-642-17537-4_44
29. Zhang, J., Zhang, D.: A novel ensemble construction method for multi-view data using random cross-view correlation between within-class examples. Pattern. Recogn. **44**(6), 1162–1171 (2011)

Non-negative Local Sparse Coding
for Subspace Clustering

Babak Hosseini$^{(\boxtimes)}$ and Barbara Hammer

CITEC centre of excellence, Bielefeld University, Bielefeld, Germany
{bhosseini,bhammer}@techfak.uni-bielefeld.de

Abstract. Subspace sparse coding (SSC) algorithms have proven to be beneficial to the clustering problems. They provide an alternative data representation in which the underlying structure of the clusters can be better captured. However, most of the research in this area is mainly focused on enhancing the sparse coding part of the problem. In contrast, we introduce a novel objective term in our proposed SSC framework which focuses on the separability of data points in the coding space. We also provide mathematical insights into how this local-separability term improves the clustering result of the SSC framework. Our proposed non-linear local SSC algorithm (NLSSC) also benefits from the efficient choice of its sparsity terms and constraints. The NLSSC algorithm is also formulated in the kernel-based framework (NLKSSC) which can represent the nonlinear structure of data. In addition, we address the possibility of having redundancies in sparse coding results and its negative effect on graph-based clustering problems. We introduce the link-restore post-processing step to improve the representation graph of non-negative SSC algorithms such as ours. Empirical evaluations on well-known clustering benchmarks show that our proposed NLSSC framework results in better clusterings compared to the state-of-the-art baselines and demonstrate the effectiveness of the link-restore post-processing in improving the clustering accuracy via correcting the broken links of the representation graph.

Keywords: Machine learning · Data mining · Subspace clustering
Sparse coding

1 Introduction

Clustering is one of the challenging problems in the area of machine learning and data analysis [24], for which unsupervised methods try to discover the hidden structure of the data. On the other hand, sparse coding algorithms aim for finding a latent representation of data points based on a weighted combination of

---

This research was supported by the Cluster of Excellence Cognitive Interaction Technology 'CITEC' (EXC 277) at Bielefeld University, which is funded by the German Research Foundation (DFG).

W. Duivesteijn et al. (Eds.): IDA 2018, LNCS 11191, pp. 137–150, 2018.
https://doi.org/10.1007/978-3-030-01768-2_12

sparsely selected base vectors [18]. Such a sparse representation has the potential to capture the essential characteristics of the data including its hidden structure [10]. Therefore, in recent years, several studies have tried and succeeded in using sparse coding models for clustering purposes [14,25,27]. Calling the weighting coefficients sparse codes, the clustering phase is applied to the learned sparse codes using common clustering methods such as spectral clustering [26].

An important group of sparse coding methods for clustering is called sparse subspace clustering algorithms (SSC) [6]. Assuming the data is distributed on a union of linear subspaces, SSC methods focus on obtaining self-expressive representations, such that each data point could be represented by using other samples from its cluster (subspace) [5,14]. There are considerable variations in the structure of existing SSC algorithms [7,20,27], which leads to different optimization schemes.

From another point of view, some of the sparse coding approaches restrict the sparse codes to non-negative values to obtain a more interpretable representation for the data, especially when the data is related to biological models [9]. Such non-negativity also often results in a better construction of the subsequent clustering graph [23,28].

Benefiting from kernel functions, it could be possible to transfer data to a high-dimensional space in which clusters are more separable. Hence, a subset of SSC algorithms focused on developing kernel-based SSC methods [2,17,23] which typically achieve higher clustering accuracies in comparison to their vectorial versions.

Contributions: In this work, we propose a non-negative SSC algorithm with a unique structure. The method combines nuclear-norm with a local-separability objective term. In addition, it preserves the affine representation of data in the latent space in accordance with an affine assumption about the underlying subspaces. Accordingly, our explicit contributions are as follows:

- We introduce and add a novel objective term to the problem which focuses on increasing local separability of data. This term is used in an unsupervised way, and it affects the sparse representation of data to have a better cluster separability.
- An efficient post-processing method is introduced regarding the negative effect of sparse coding redundancies on clustering performance.
- Our algorithm is also extended to the nonlinear version via incorporating a kernel function in its framework.

In the next section, we briefly review SSC algorithms. Afterward, we present our proposed approaches in Sect. 3 and the optimization procedure in Sect. 4. Then, we carry out empirical evaluations in Sect. 5, and make the conclusion in the final section.

2   Related Works

Consider the data matrix $\mathbf{X} = [\vec{x}_1, ..., \vec{x}_N] \in \mathbb{R}^{d \times N}$ which lies in the union of n linear subspaces $\cup_{l=1}^{n} \mathcal{S}_l$ each with the dimension of $\{d_l\}_{l=1}^{n}$. Subspace clustering tries to cluster the data such that each cluster i contains samples lying in one individual subspace $\mathcal{S}_i$. Therefore, each data point $\vec{x}_i$ can be represented by other data points in $\mathbf{X}$ as a linear combination $\vec{x}_i \approx \mathbf{X}\vec{\gamma}_i$. Focusing on the sparseness of the coding vectors $\vec{\gamma}_i$, subspace sparse clustering [6] can be formulated as

$$\min_{\mathbf{\Gamma}}\|\mathbf{\Gamma}\|_0 \quad s.t. \quad \mathbf{X} = \mathbf{X}\mathbf{\Gamma}, \gamma_{ii} = 0 , \ \forall i \tag{1}$$

where $\mathbf{\Gamma}$ is the matrix of sparse codes, γ_{ii} points to diagonal elements of $\mathbf{\Gamma}$, and $\|.\|_0$ denotes the cardinality norm. It is assumed each resulting $\vec{\gamma}_i$ from Eq. 1 represents $\vec{x}_i$ using only data points from the subspace in which $\vec{x}_i$ lies as well. In that case, computing an affinity matrix $\mathbf{A} = |\mathbf{\Gamma}|^\top + |\mathbf{\Gamma}|$ which represents the pairwise similarities of data points, and using it in graph-based methods such as spectral clustering should identify the clusters. However, the problem in Eq. 1 is NP-hard to solve [6] in its original format. As a solution, $\|.\|_0$ can be relaxed into other norms. For instance [2,6,7,17] use the $l1$-norm to achieve sparse $\mathbf{\Gamma}$, while [27] aims for the approximate solution of Eq. 1 while having $\|\vec{\gamma}_i\|_0 \leq T_0$. Another group of SSC methods [14,20,23,28] focuses on shrinking the nuclear norm $\|\mathbf{\Gamma}\|_*$ and making $\mathbf{\Gamma}$ low-rank to better represent the global structure of data. Among SSC algorithms, [6,17] enforced $\mathbf{\Gamma}$ to provide affine representations by using the constraint $\mathbf{\Gamma}^\top\vec{1} = \vec{1}$ based on the idea of having the data points lying on an affine combination of subspaces. Despite continuous improvements in clustering results of aforementioned SSC methods, there is no direct link between the quality of the sparse coding part and the subsequent clustering goal. Consequently, they suffer from performance variations across different datasets and high sensitivity of their results to the choice of parameters.

On the other hand, another group of algorithms called Laplacian sparse coding encourage the sparse coefficient vectors $\vec{\gamma}_i$ related to each cluster to be as similar as possible [7,26]. In their SSC formulation (Eq. 2) they employ a similarity matrix $\mathbf{W}$ in which each w_{ij} measures the pair-wise similarity between a pair $(\vec{x}_i, \vec{x}_j)$.

$$\min_{\mathbf{\Gamma}} \|\mathbf{X} - \mathbf{X}\mathbf{\Gamma}\|_F^2 + \lambda\|\mathbf{\Gamma}\|_1 + \tfrac{1}{2}\sum_{i,j} w_{ij}\|\vec{\gamma}_i - \vec{\gamma}_j\|_2^2 \qquad s.t. \ \gamma_{ii} = 0 , \ \forall i \tag{2}$$

Nevertheless, the optimization frameworks like this suffer from two issues:

1. Columns of $\mathbf{\Gamma}$ are forced to become similar to each other while the similarity matrix is used as the weighting coefficients. Hence, at best the sparse codes $\vec{\gamma}_i$ obtain a distribution similar to the neighborhoods in $\mathbf{W}$. Consequently, their performance is comparable to kernel-based clustering with direct use of the kernel information.
2. Although Eq. 2 tries to decrease the intra-cluster distances, the inter-cluster structure of data is ignored in such frameworks; however, typically both of these terms have to be adopted when focusing on the separability of clusters.

Contrary to the previous works, our algorithm benefits from a clustering-based objective term in its framework. Therefore, its resulting sparse codes are more suitable for the clustering purpose. In addition, our post-processing technique can contribute to non-negative SSC methods such as [13,23,28] to improve their latent representations.

3 Proposed Non-Negative SSC algorithm

In this section, we introduce our proposed SSC algorithms NLSSC and NKLSSC. Although they are explained in individual subsections, NKLSSC is the kernel extension of NLSSC which is optimized similarly to NLSSC's optimization.

3.1 Non-Negative Local Subspace Sparse Clustering

We formulate our non-negative local SSC algorithm (NLSSC) using the following self-representative framework:

$$\min_{\mathbf{\Gamma}} \|\mathbf{\Gamma}\|_* + \frac{\lambda}{2}\|\mathbf{X} - \mathbf{X}\mathbf{\Gamma}\|_F^2 + \mu\mathcal{E}_{lsp}(\mathbf{\Gamma}, \mathbf{X}) \tag{3}$$
$$\text{s.t} \quad \mathbf{\Gamma}^\top \vec{\mathbf{1}} = \vec{\mathbf{1}}, \gamma_{ij} \geq 0, \quad \gamma_{ii} = 0 \ , \ \forall ij$$

where $\gamma_{ii} = 0$ prevents data points from being represented by own contributions. The constraint $\mathbf{\Gamma}^\top \vec{\mathbf{1}} = \vec{\mathbf{1}}$ focuses on the affine reconstruction of data points which coincides with having the data lying in an affine union of subspaces $\mathcal{S}_l$. The nuclear norm regularization term $\|\mathbf{\Gamma}\|_* = trace(\sqrt{\mathbf{\Gamma}^*\mathbf{\Gamma}})$ is employed to ensure the sparse coding representations are low-rank. This helps the sparse model to better capture the global structure of data distribution. The non-negativity constraint on γ_{ij} is employed to enforce the data combinations to happen mostly between similar samples. The novel term $\mathcal{E}_{lsp}(\mathbf{\Gamma}, \mathbf{X})$ is a loss function which focuses on the local separability of data points in the coding space based on values of $\mathbf{\Gamma}$. Accordingly, scalars λ and μ are constants which control the contribution of the objective terms. The goal of having $\mathcal{E}_{lsp}(\mathbf{\Gamma}, \mathbf{X})$ in the SSC model is to reduce intra-cluster distance and increase inter-cluster distance. To do so in an unsupervised way, we define

$$\mathcal{E}_{lsp}(\mathbf{\Gamma}, \mathbf{X}) := \frac{1}{2}\sum_{i,j}\left[w_{ij}\|\vec{\gamma}_i - \vec{\gamma}_j\|_2^2 + b_{ij}(\vec{\gamma}_i^\top\vec{\gamma}_j)\right] \tag{4}$$

in which the binary regularization weighting matrices $\mathbf{W}$ and $\mathbf{B}$ are computed as

$$w_{ij} = \begin{cases} 1, & \text{if } \vec{x}_j \in \mathcal{N}_i^k \\ 0, & \text{otherwise} \end{cases}, \qquad b_{ij} = \begin{cases} 1, & \text{if } \vec{x}_j \in \mathcal{F}_i^k \\ 0, & \text{otherwise} \end{cases} \tag{5}$$

The two sets $\mathcal{N}_i^k$ and $\mathcal{F}_i^k$ refer to the k-nearest and k-farthest data points to $\vec{x}_i$, and are determined via computing Euclidean distance $\|\vec{x}_i - \vec{x}_j\|_2$ between each $\vec{x}_i$ and $\vec{x}_j$. Defining $\mathcal{D}(\mathbf{W}, \mathbf{\Gamma}) := \sum_{i,j} w_{ij}\|\vec{\gamma}_i - \vec{\gamma}_j\|_2^2$ and $\mathcal{H}(\mathbf{B}, \mathbf{\Gamma}) := \sum_{i,j} b_{ij}(\vec{\gamma}_i^\top\vec{\gamma}_j)$, the first part reduces the distance between $(\vec{\gamma}_i, \vec{\gamma}_j)$ if they belong to $\mathcal{N}_i^k$ while the latter focuses on incoherency of each pair of $(\vec{\gamma}_i, \vec{\gamma}_j)$ if they are members of $\mathcal{F}_i^k$. The following explains the effect of $\mathcal{E}_{lsp}$ on the separability of the clusters in the coding space.

Assuming there exist the labeling scalars $\{l_i\}_{i=1}^N \in \mathbb{R}$, we prefer $\vec{x}_i$ and members of $\mathcal{N}_i^k$ to belong to the same class while the set $\mathcal{F}_i^k$ to contain data from other clusters. We define $\mathbf{W}_c$ and $\mathbf{W}_m$ such that $\mathbf{W} = \mathbf{W}_c + \mathbf{W}_m$, and they

respectively denote the correct and wring assignments regarding the label information $\vec{l}$. more precisely, if $w(i, j) = 1$ then in case $l_i = l_j$ we have $w_c(i, j) = 1$,
otherwise $w_m(i, j) = 1$. The rest of the entries in $(\mathbf{W}_c, \mathbf{W}_m)$ are set to zero.

Definition 1. *The neighborhoods in* $\mathbf{X}$ *are cluster representative to the order
of* o_r, *if* $\exists k \in \mathbb{N} : \|\mathbf{W}_c\|_0 / \|\mathbf{W}_m\|_0 = o_r \wedge o_r < 1$.

Definition 1 means that in the neighborhoods of data samples in $\mathbf{X}$ there are
more points of the same class than of different ones.

Proposition 1. *Minimizing* $\mathcal{E}_{lsp}$ *in Eq. (4) makes columns of* $\mathbf{\Gamma}$ *to be better
locally separable regarding the underlying classes, if the neighborhoods in* $\mathbf{X}$ *are
cluster representative with a sufficiently small* o_r.

Proof. {*sketch*} *Eq. 4 can be rewritten as*

$$\mathcal{E}_{lsp} = \mathcal{D}(\mathbf{W}_c, \mathbf{\Gamma}) + \mathcal{D}(\mathbf{W}_m, \mathbf{\Gamma}) + \mathcal{H}(\mathbf{B}, \mathbf{\Gamma})$$

Therefore, $\mathbf{\Gamma}^* = \arg\min_{\mathbf{\Gamma}} \mathcal{E}_{lsp}$ *generally works in favor of decreasing* $\mathcal{D}(\mathbf{W}_c, \mathbf{\Gamma})$
and $\mathcal{H}(\mathbf{B}, \mathbf{\Gamma})$ *compared to an initial* $\mathbf{\Gamma}^0$.
Consequently, a small $\mathcal{D}(\mathbf{W}_c, \mathbf{\Gamma})$ *leads to compact same-label neighborhoods in*
$\mathbf{\Gamma}^*$, *and decreasing* $\mathcal{H}(\mathbf{B}, \mathbf{\Gamma})$ *generally increases* $\mathcal{D}(\mathbf{B}, \mathbf{\Gamma})$ *and more provides a
more localized structure for* $\mathbf{\Gamma}^*$.
Denoting $\Delta\mathcal{D}(\mathbf{W}, \mathbf{\Gamma}^*) := \mathcal{D}(\mathbf{W}, \mathbf{\Gamma}^*) - \mathcal{D}(\mathbf{W}, \mathbf{\Gamma}^0)$, *according to the definition 1,*
$\Delta\mathcal{D}(\mathbf{W}_m, \mathbf{\Gamma}^*) / \Delta\mathcal{D}(\mathbf{W}_c, \mathbf{\Gamma}^*)$ *is a decreasing function of* $1/o_r$.
Hence, the smaller o_r *becomes the more columns of* $\mathbf{\Gamma}^*$ *can be locally separated
from data samples of the other classes* $(\mathbf{W}_m)$ *in their neighborhoods.*

Proposition 1 shows the effect of minimizing the loss term $\mathcal{E}_{lsp}$ on having
localized and condense neighborhoods in the sparse codes $\mathbf{\Gamma}$ by making the sparse
codes of the neighboring samples more similar (identical in ideal case) while
making those of far away points incoherent (orthogonal in ideal case). It also
provides the desired condition by which the local neighborhoods in $\mathbf{\Gamma}$ can better
respect the class labels $\vec{l}$ and leading to a better alignment between $\mathbf{\Gamma}$ and the
underlying subspaces. **Note:** Here we referred to $\vec{l}$ only to explain the reason
behind our specific model design; however, the algorithm does need the labeling
information in any of its steps.

3.2   Clustering Based on $\mathbf{\Gamma}$

Similar to other SSC algorithms, the resulted sparse coefficients are used to
construct an adjacency matrix $\mathbf{A} = \mathbf{\Gamma} + \mathbf{\Gamma}^\top$ defining a a sparse representation
graph $\mathcal{G}$. This undirected graph consists of weighted connections between pairs
of $(\vec{x}_i, \vec{x}_j)$. Therefore, $\mathbf{A}$ is used as the affinity matrix in the spectral clustering
algorithm [26] to find the data clusters.

3.3 Link-Restore

After constructing the affinity matrix based on the resulting $\mathbf{\Gamma}$, it is desired to have positive weights in the representation graph $\mathcal{G}$ between every two points of a cluster. However, in practice, it is possible to see non-connected nodes (broken links) even inside condense clusters. This happens due to the redundancy issue related to sparse coding algorithms. In Eq. 3, $\mathbf{X}$ is used as an over-complete dictionary for reconstruction of each $\vec{x}_i$, therefore we can assume $\vec{x}_i \approx \mathbf{X}\vec{\gamma}_i$. Nevertheless, as a common observation in sparse coding models the solution for the value of $\vec{\gamma}_i$ is suboptimal because of the utilized $\|\vec{\gamma}_i\|_p$ relaxations. Thus for $\vec{x}_s$ as a close data point to $\vec{x}_i$, it is possible to have $\vec{x}_s \approx \mathbf{X}\vec{\gamma}_s$, but with a big $\vec{\gamma}_i^\top \vec{\gamma}_s$. This means $\vec{\gamma}_i$ and $\vec{\gamma}_s$ are not similar in the entries. Consequently, a_{ij} can be small resulting from dissimilar $\vec{\gamma}_i$ and $\vec{\gamma}_s$, albeit $\vec{x}_i$ and $\vec{x}_s$ are very similar. As a workaround to the mentioned issue, we propose the Link-Restore method (Algorithm 1) as an effective step regarding these situations. It acts as a post-processing step on the obtained $\mathbf{\Gamma}$ before application of spectral clustering. Link-restore corrects entries of each $\vec{\gamma}$ by restoring the broken connections between $\vec{x}$ and other points in the dataset. To do so, it first obtains the current set of data points connected to $\vec{x}$ as $I = \{i \mid \gamma_i \neq 0\}$, where γ_i denotes i-th entry in vector $\vec{\gamma}$. Then for each $\vec{\gamma}_i$ that $i \in I$, the algorithm collects the indices $\bar{I}$ of data points which are close to $\vec{x}_i$ but not used in the sparse code of $\vec{x}$ (line 1). To that aim, for each $\vec{x}_s \in \bar{I}$ the criterion $\|\vec{x}_i - \vec{x}_s\|_2^2 / \|\vec{x}_i\|_2^2 < \tau$ should be fulfilled, where $0 \leq \tau \leq 1$. Then in order to incorporate members of $\bar{I}$ into $\vec{\gamma}$, the entry γ_i is projected to $\bar{I} \cup i$ based on the value of $\vec{x}_i^\top \vec{x}_s / \vec{x}_i^\top \vec{x}_i \ \forall s \in \bar{I}$ while also maintaining the affinity constraint on $\vec{\gamma}$ (lines 2–3). It is important to point out that the pre-assumption for the above is that $\gamma_i \geq 0 \ \forall i$. Therefore link-restore method can be assumed as a proper post-processing method for *non-negative* subspace clustering algorithms.

3.4 Kernel Extension of NLSSC

Assume $\Phi : \mathbb{R}^d \to \mathbb{R}^m$ is an implicit nonlinear mapping to a Reproducing Kernel Hilbert Space (RKHS) such that $m \gg d$. Thus, there exists a kernel function $\mathcal{K}(\vec{x}_i, \vec{x}_j) = \Phi(\vec{x}_i)^\top \Phi(\vec{x}_j)$. Doing so, we can benefit from the non-linear characteristics of this implicit mapping to obtain better representation for the data.

Algorithm 1: Link-Restore post-processing

Input: Sparse code $\vec{\gamma}$, data matrix $\mathbf{X}$, threshold $\tau \in [0, 1]$
Output: Corrected $\vec{\gamma}$ by restoring its connections to other data points
Initialization: $I = \{i \mid \gamma_i \neq 0\}$ (except index of $\vec{x}$)
Loop: {over all elements $i \in I$ }

1 $\hat{\vec{\gamma}} = \vec{\gamma}, \quad \bar{I} := \{s \mid (\vec{x}_s^\top \vec{x}_s - 2\vec{x}_i^\top \vec{x}_s) < (\tau - 1)\vec{x}_i^\top \vec{x}_i \ , \ \gamma_s = 0\}$

2 $\hat{\gamma}_i = \gamma_i(\vec{x}_i^\top \vec{x}_i / \sum_{s \in \{\bar{I} \cup i\}} \vec{x}_i^\top \vec{x}_s)$

3 $\hat{\gamma}_s = \hat{\gamma}_i(\vec{x}_i^\top \vec{x}_s / \vec{x}_i^\top \vec{x}_i) \ , \ \forall s \in \bar{I}$

4 $\vec{\gamma} = \hat{\vec{\gamma}}, \quad I = I \backslash \{i\}$

Accordingly, we can reformulate our NLSSC method (Eq. 3) into its kernel extension as the non-negative local kernel SSC algorithm (NLKSSC):

$$\min_{\mathbf{\Gamma}} \|\mathbf{\Gamma}\|_* + \tfrac{\lambda}{2}\|\Phi(\mathbf{X}) - \Phi(\mathbf{X})\mathbf{\Gamma}\|_F^2 + \mu\mathcal{E}_{lsp}(\mathbf{\Gamma}, \Phi(\mathbf{X}))$$
$$\text{s.t} \quad \mathbf{\Gamma}^\top\vec{\mathbf{1}} = \vec{\mathbf{1}},\ \gamma_{ij} \geq 0,\ \gamma_{ii} = 0,\ \forall ij \tag{6}$$

Comparing to Eq. 3, the second term in the objective of Eq. 6 means a self-representation in the feature space, and the local-separability term ($\mathcal{E}_{lsp}$) is equivalent to the one used in Eq. 3. However, $\mathbf{W}$ and $\mathbf{W}_m$ in $\mathcal{E}_{lsp}$ are computed based on the entries $\mathcal{K}(\vec{x}_i, \vec{x}_j)$ which directly indicate the pair-wise similarity of each data $\vec{x}_i$ to its surrounding neighborhood. The benefit of having a kernel representation of $\mathbf{X}$ is that a proper kernel function facilitates the validity of the pre-assumption for Proposition 1, which leads to the more efficient role of $\mathcal{E}_{lsp}$. As we see in Sect. 4, we can use the same optimization regime for both NLSSC and NLKSSC. In addition, the lines 1–3 of the link-restore algorithm can be implemented using the above dot-product rule.

4   Optimization Scheme of Proposed Methods

Putting Eq. 4 into Eq. 3 the following optimization framework is derived

$$\min_{\mathbf{\Gamma}} \|\mathbf{\Gamma}\|_* + \tfrac{\lambda}{2}\|\mathbf{X} - \mathbf{X}\mathbf{\Gamma}\|_F^2 + \tfrac{\mu}{2}\sum_{i,j}\left[w_{ij}\|\vec{\gamma}_i - \vec{\gamma}_j\|_2^2 + b_{ij}(\vec{\gamma}_i^\top\vec{\gamma}_j)\right]$$
$$\text{s.t} \quad \mathbf{\Gamma}^\top\vec{\mathbf{1}} = \vec{\mathbf{1}},\ \gamma_{ij} \geq 0,\ \gamma_{ii} = 0,\ \forall ij \tag{7}$$

To simplify the 3rd loss term in (7), we symmetrize $\mathbf{W} \rightarrow \frac{\mathbf{W}+\mathbf{W}^\top}{2}$ and do the same for $\mathbf{B}$. Then according to [21] we compute the Laplacian matrix $\mathbf{L} = \mathbf{D} - \mathbf{W}$, where $\mathbf{D}$ is a diagonal matrix such that $d_{ii} = \sum_j w_{ij}$. Then, with simple algebric operations we can rewrite $\mathcal{E}_{lsp}(\mathbf{\Gamma}, \mathbf{X}) = \text{Tr}(\mathbf{\Gamma}\mathbf{L}\mathbf{\Gamma}^\top) + \tfrac{1}{2}\text{Tr}(\mathbf{\Gamma}\mathbf{B}\mathbf{\Gamma}^\top)$, and reformulate Eq. 7 as:

$$\min_{\mathbf{\Gamma}} \|\mathbf{\Gamma}\|_* + \tfrac{\lambda}{2}\|\mathbf{X} - \mathbf{X}\mathbf{\Gamma}\|_F^2 + \mu\text{Tr}(\mathbf{\Gamma}\hat{\mathbf{L}}\mathbf{\Gamma}^\top)$$
$$\text{s.t} \quad \mathbf{\Gamma}^\top\vec{\mathbf{1}} = \vec{\mathbf{1}},\ \gamma_{ij} \geq 0,\ \gamma_{ii} = 0,\ \forall ij \tag{8}$$

where $\text{Tr}(.)$ is the trace operator and $\hat{\mathbf{L}} = (\mathbf{L} + \tfrac{1}{2}\mathbf{B})$. The objective of Eq. 8 is sum of convex functions (trace, inner-product, and convex norms), therefore the optimization problem is a constrained convex problem and can be solved using the alternating direction method of multipliers (ADMM) [3] as presented in Algorithm 2. Optimizing Eq. 8 coincides with minimizing the following augmented Lagrangian which is derived by adding its constraints as penalty terms in the objective function.

$$\mathcal{L}_\rho\left(\mathbf{\Gamma}, \mathbf{\Gamma}_+, \mathbf{U}, \alpha_+, \alpha_U, \vec{\alpha_1}\right) = \|\mathbf{U}\|_* + \lambda\mathcal{E}_{rep}(\mathbf{X}, \mathbf{\Gamma}) + \mu\mathcal{E}_{lsp}(\mathbf{X}, \mathbf{\Gamma})$$
$$+\tfrac{\rho}{2}\|\mathbf{\Gamma} - \mathbf{\Gamma}_+\|_F^2 + \text{Tr}(\alpha_+^\top(\mathbf{\Gamma} - \mathbf{\Gamma}_+)) + \tfrac{\rho}{2}\|\mathbf{\Gamma} - \mathbf{U}\|_F^2$$
$$+\text{Tr}(\alpha_U^\top(\mathbf{\Gamma} - \mathbf{U})) + \tfrac{\rho}{2}\|\mathbf{\Gamma}^\top\vec{\mathbf{1}} - \vec{\mathbf{1}}\|_2^2 + \langle\vec{\alpha_1}, \mathbf{\Gamma}^\top\vec{\mathbf{1}} - \vec{\mathbf{1}}\rangle \tag{9}$$

in which $\mathcal{E}_{rep} := \frac{1}{2}\|\mathbf{X} - \mathbf{X}\boldsymbol{\Gamma}\|_F^2$, and matrices $(\boldsymbol{\Gamma}_+, \mathbf{U})$ are axillary matrices related the non-negativity constraint and the term $\|\boldsymbol{\Gamma}\|_*$. Equation 9 contains the Lagrangian multipliers $\alpha_+, \alpha_U \in \mathbb{R}^{N \times N}$ and $\vec{\alpha_1} \in \mathbb{R}^N$, and the penalty parameter $\rho \in \mathbb{R}^+$. Minimizing $\mathcal{L}_\rho$ Eq. 9 is carried out in an alternating optimization framework, such that at each step of the optimization all of the parameters $\{\boldsymbol{\Gamma}, \boldsymbol{\Gamma}_+, \mathbf{U}, \alpha_+, \alpha_U, \vec{\alpha_1}\}$ are fixed except one. Therefore, the updating steps are described as follows.

Updating $\boldsymbol{\Gamma}$: At iteration t of ADMM, via fixing $\boldsymbol{\Gamma}_+^t, \mathbf{U}^t, \alpha_+^t, \alpha_U^t, \vec{\alpha_1}^t$, the matrix $\boldsymbol{\Gamma}^{t+1}$ is updated as the solution to this Sylvester linear system of equations [11]

$$[2\lambda\mathbf{X}^\top\mathbf{X} + 2\rho\mathbf{I} + \vec{1}\vec{1}^\top]\boldsymbol{\Gamma}^{t+1} + \boldsymbol{\Gamma}^{t+1}[2\mu\hat{\mathbf{L}}] = \rho[\boldsymbol{\Gamma}_+^t + \mathbf{U}^t + \vec{1}\vec{1}^\top] - \alpha_\mathbf{U}^t - \alpha_+^t - \vec{1}\vec{\alpha_1}^{t\top} \quad (10)$$

Updating $\mathbf{U}$: Updating $\mathbf{U}^{t+1}$ which is associated with $\|\boldsymbol{\Gamma}\|_*$ can be done via fixing other parameters and using the singular value thresholding method [4] as $\mathbf{U}^{t+1} = \mathcal{T}_{1/\rho}(\boldsymbol{\Gamma})$ where term $\mathcal{T}(.)$ is the thresholding operator from [4](Eq. 2.2).

Updating $\boldsymbol{\Gamma}_+, \alpha_+, \alpha_U, \vec{\alpha_1}, \rho$: The matrix $\boldsymbol{\Gamma}_+$ and the multipliers are updated using the following projected gradient descent and gradient ascent steps respectively

$$\begin{aligned}
\boldsymbol{\Gamma}_+^{t+1} &= max(\boldsymbol{\Gamma} + \tfrac{1}{\rho}\alpha_+, 0), & \alpha_+^{t+1} &= \alpha_+^t + \rho(\boldsymbol{\Gamma} - \boldsymbol{\Gamma}_+) \\
\vec{\alpha_1}^{t+1} &= \vec{\alpha_1}^t + \rho(\boldsymbol{\Gamma}^\top\vec{1} - \vec{1}), & \rho^{t+1} &= min(\rho^t(1 + \Delta_\rho), \rho_{max})
\end{aligned} \quad (11)$$

in which $(\Delta_\rho, \rho_{max})$ are the update step and higher bound of ρ respectively.

Convergence Criteria: The algorithm reaches its convergence point when for a fixed $\epsilon > 0$, $\|\boldsymbol{\Gamma}^t - \boldsymbol{\Gamma}^{t-1}\|_\infty \leq \epsilon$, $\|\boldsymbol{\Gamma}_+^t - \boldsymbol{\Gamma}^t\|_\infty \leq \epsilon$, $\|\mathbf{U}^t - \boldsymbol{\Gamma}^t\|_\infty \leq \epsilon$, and $\|\boldsymbol{\Gamma}^{t\top}\vec{1} - \vec{1}\|_\infty \leq \epsilon$.

Optimizing NLKSSC: The kernel-based algorithm (NLKSSC) is optimized also using Algorithm 2 while the kernel trick $\Phi(\vec{x}_i)^\top\Phi(\vec{x}_j) = \mathcal{K}(\vec{x}_i, \vec{x}_j)$ is applied to replace $\mathbf{X}^\top\mathbf{X}$ by $\mathcal{K}(\mathbf{X}, \mathbf{X})$ in Eq. 10, and to kernelize the link-restore algorithm as well.

Algorithm 2: Optimization Scheme of NLSSC
Input: $\mathbf{X}, \lambda, \mu, k, \Delta_\rho = 0.1, \rho_{max} = 10^6$
Output: Sparse coefficient matrix $\boldsymbol{\Gamma}$
Initialization: Compute $\mathbf{W}, \mathbf{B}$ and $\hat{\mathbf{L}}$. Set all $\{\boldsymbol{\Gamma}_+, \boldsymbol{\Gamma}, \mathbf{U}, \alpha_+, \alpha_U, \vec{\alpha_1}\}$ to zero
repeat
Updating $\boldsymbol{\Gamma}$ by solving Eq. 10
Updating $\mathbf{U}$ based on [4](Eq. 2.2)
Updating $\boldsymbol{\Gamma}_+, \alpha_+, \alpha_U, \vec{\alpha_1}$ based on Eq. 11
until Convergence Criteria is fulfilled;

5   Experiments

For empirical evaluation of our proposed NNLSSC and NLKSSC algorithms, we implement them on 4 different widely-used benchmarks of clustering datasets:

- Hopkins155 [19]: Segmentation of 156 video sequences with a setup similar to [6].
- COIL-20 [16]: A dataset of 1440 gray-scale images of 20 different objects with the pixel size of 32×32.
- Extended YaleB[8]: Contains frontal face images taken from 38 subjects with the average of 64 samples per subject. Feature extraction is done based on [20].
- AR-Face [15]: An image dataset including more than 4000 frontal faces of 126 different subjects. We use 2600 images from 100 subjects and use the pre-processing procedure from [23].

The basis of evaluation is the clustering error as $CE = \frac{\#\text{of miss-clustered samples}}{\#\text{of data samples}}$ using the posterior labeling of the clusters and the normalized mutual information (NMI) [1]. For each method, an average CE is calculated over 10 runs of the algorithm. NMI measures the amount of information shared between the clustering result and the ground-truth which lays in range of $[0, 1]$ with the ideal score of 1. Based on the common practice in the literature, we use average CE along with its median value for the Hopkin155 dataset.

We compare our algorithms' performance to baseline methods SSC [6], LRSC [20], SSOMP [27], S^{3}C [12], GNLMF [13], KSSC [17] KSSR [2] and RKNNLRS [23]. These algorithms are selected from major sparse coding-based clustering approaches, among which KSSC, KSSR, and RKNNLRS are kernel-based methods. The spectral clustering step of the baselines is performed via using the correct number of clusters.

To compute the kernels required for kernel-based we use Histogram Intersection Kernel (HIK) as in [22] for AR dataset as it is a proper choice regarding its frequency-based features [23]. For the implementations on the rest of the datasets we adopted the Gaussian kernel $\mathcal{K}(x, y) = exp(-\frac{\|x-y\|^2}{\sigma})$, where δ is the average of $\|\vec{x}_i - \vec{x}_j\|^2$ over all data samples.

5.1   Parameter Settings

In order to tune the parameters λ, μ, k we utilize a grid-search method. We do the search for λ in the range of $\{1, 1.5, ..., 7\}$, for μ in the range of $\{0.1, 0.2, ..., 1\}$ and k in $\{3, 4, ..., 8\}$. We implement a similar parameter search for the baselines to find their best settings. Although for the link-restore parameter, $\tau = 0.2$ generally works well, one can do a separate grid-search for τ.

5.2   Clustering Results

According to the results summarized in Table 1, the proposed methods outperformed the benchmarks regarding the clustering error. Comparing NLKSSC

Table 1. Average clustering error (CE) and NMI for YALE, COIL20, AR datasets. CE and its median value for Hopkins155-(2 motions and 3 motions) datasets.

Methods	YALE B		COIL20		AR-Face		Hopkins-2m		Hopkins-3m	
	CE	NMI	CE	NMI	CE	NMI	CE	med.	CE	med.
SSC [6]	0.1734	0.8902	0.1737	0.9104	0.1065	0.9103	0.0289	0	0.0663	0.0114
LRSC [20]	0.3136	0.7340	0.2943	0.7838	0.0938	0.9037	0.0369	0.2127	0.0746	0.0245
SSOMP [27]	0.3214	0.6792	0.7652	0.5274	0.1012	0.8353	0.1432	0.0328	0.1973	0.1504
S³C [12]	0.1565	0.9104	0.1635	0.9063	0.0897	0.9117	0.0263	0	0.0527	0.0089
GNLMF [13]	0.3074	0.4172	0.3972	0.6421	0.1544	0.8769	0.1052	0.0216	0.1239	0.0841
KSSC [17]	0.1504	0.8907	0.1833	0.9039	0.0678	0.9241	0.0275	0	0.0584	0.0096
KSSR [2]	0.1598	0.8864	0.1983	0.9027	0.0742	0.8983	0.0437	0.6121	0.0756	0.0151
RKNNLRS [23]	0.1493	0.9035	0.1672	0.9126	0.0886	0.9131	0.0254	0	0.0512	0.0087
NLSSC(Proposed)	0.1242	0.9146	**0.1409**	**0.9254**	0.0832	0.9125	0.0189	0	0.0427	0.0079
NLKSSC(Proposed)	**0.1107**	**0.9163**	0.1528	0.9147	**0.0542**	**0.9364**	**0.0122**	0	**0.0331**	**0.0065**

to NLSSC, the kernel-based algorithm resulted in a smaller CE compared to NLSSC (except for COIL20), which shows that the kernel-based framework was able to better represent cluster distributions. Regarding the COIL20 dataset, via comparing kernel-based methods to other baselines, it can be concluded that the utilized kernel function was not strongly effective for cluster-based representation of the dataset. However, NLKSSC still outperformed other baselines due to the effectiveness of its sparse subspace model.

Among other methods, S³C, RKNNLRS, and KSSC have comparable results, especially for the Hopkins dataset. This means, although KSSC and RKNNLRS benefited from kernel representation, the S³C algorithm was relatively effective regarding capturing the data structure. However, KSSR presented low performance even in comparison to vectorial methods such as SSC and LRSC. This behavior is due to lack of having any strong regularization term in its model regarding the subspace structure of data. Among non-negative methods, GNLMF performance is relatively below average. This may suggest that its NMF-based structure is not suitable for grasping cluster distribution in comparison to self-representative methods. On the other hand, RKNNLRS performance shows that its non-negative model is more effective for clustering purposes compared to NMF-based models. Comparing NLSSC (the proposed algorithm) to other baselines with low-rank regularizations in their models, we can conclude that proper combination of the locality term and the affine constraints aided NLSSC to obtain higher performance. The same conclusion can be derived via comparing NLSSC/NLKSSC to KSSC as an affine subspace clustering algorithm.

5.3   Effect of Link-Restore

To investigate the effect of the proposed link-restore algorithm we apply it on GNLMF, RKNNLRS, NLSSC, and NLKSSC as a post-processing step. This selection is based on the fact that link-restore is designed based on the non-negativity assumption about columns of $\boldsymbol{\Gamma}$. Also regarding its application on

Table 2. Application of the link-restore method on the non-negative approaches

Methods	YALE		COIL20		AR		Hopkins-2m		Hopkins-3m	
	CE	NMI	CE	NMI	CE	NMI	CE	median	CE	median
GNLMF-link [13]	0.2514	0.6564	0.2674	0.7161	0.1251	0.8846	0.0793	0.0147	0.1025	0.0649
RKNNLRS-link [23]	0.1237	0.9103	0.1602	0.9137	0.0823	0.9135	0.0230	0	0.0469	0.0081
NLSSC-link	0.1027	0.9182	**0.1409**	**0.9254**	0.0776	0.9153	0.0189	0	0.0392	0.0064
NLKSSC-link	**0.0842**	**0.9326**	0.1523	0.9148	**0.0482**	**0.9381**	**0.0122**	0	**0.0301**	**0.0054**

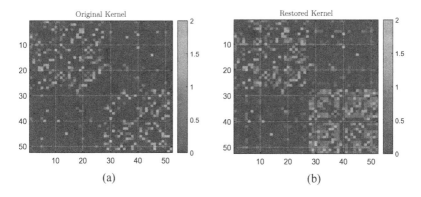

(a)   (b)

Fig. 1. A subset of the affinity matrix resulted by the implementation of NLKSSC on the AR dataset: (a) Before application of link-restore. (b) After application of link-restore

GNLMF and NLSSC, we use the kernel matrix $\mathcal{K}(\mathbf{X}, \mathbf{X})$ related to the kernel baselines. According to Table 2, the application of link-restore was effecting regarding almost all the cases. It reduced the clustering error of all the relevant methods to some extent, which demonstrates its ability to correct broken links in the representation graph $\mathcal{G}$. Nevertheless, the amount of improvements in NLSS/NLKSSC methods vary among datasets. For the 2-motions subset of Hopkins and for COIL20 datasets it did not add any important link to graph $\mathcal{G}$ which consequently did not change the value of CE. However, for YALE and AR datasets the amount of decreases in CE shows the effectiveness of link-restore in correcting the missing connections in $\mathcal{G}$.

Figure 1 visualizes the affinity matrix for implementation of NKLSSC on the AR dataset. The figure is zoomed in on two of the clusters showing that the representation graph contains more intra-cluster connections after applying link-restore (Fig. 1-b).

5.4   Sensitivity to the Parameter Settings

Due to the space limits, we study the sensitivity of NLKSSC to the choice of parameters only for the AR dataset considering 3 different experiments. In each experiment, we fix two of λ, μ, k and change the other one and study the effect of

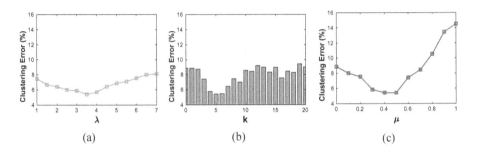

Fig. 2. Sensitivity analysis of NLKSSC to parameter selection (a)λ, (b)μ and (c)k for AR dataset

this variation on clustering error (CE). Based on Fig. 2, the algorithm sensitivity to λ is acceptable when $2 \leq \lambda \leq 4.5$. Having $\lambda \geq 6$ does not change CE since it makes the loss term $\mathcal{E}_{rep} := \|\Phi(\mathbf{X}) - \Phi(\mathbf{X})\mathbf{\Gamma}\|_F^2$ more dominant in optimization problem of Eq. 6.

By choosing $0.25 \leq \mu \leq 0.5$, the algorithm's performance does not change drastically. However, NLKSSC shows a considerable sensitivity if μ goes beyond 0.6. High values of μ weaken the role of $\mathcal{E}_{rep}$ (the main loss term) in the sparse coding model.

Studying the sensitivity curve of k, its starting point has a similar CE to the start of μ sensitivity curve, as in both cases effect of $\mathcal{E}_{lsp}$ becomes zero in the optimization. Figure 2-b shows that $k \in \{3, 4, 5\}$ is a good choice. However, with $k \leq 3$ the objective term $\mathcal{E}_{lsp}$ is not effective enough and with $k \geq 10$ the CE curve does not follow any constant pattern, but generally becomes worse because it increases $\frac{\|W_w\|_0}{\|W_c\|_0}$ and it may infringe the pre-assumption of Proposition 1. It is important to note that even a small neighborhood radius (e.g. $k = 4$) could have a wide impact on the global representation if the local neighborhoods can have overlapping. Generally, similar sensitivity behaviors are also observed for the other datasets.

6 Conclusion

In this work, we proposed a novel subspace sparse coding framework regarding data clustering. Our non-negative local subspace clustering (NLSSC) benefits from a novel locality objective in its formulation which focuses on improving the separability of data points in the coding space. In addition, NLSSC also obtains low-rank and affine sparse codes for the representation of the data. Implementations on real clustering benchmarks showed that this locality constraint is effective when performing a clustering based on the obtained representation graph. In addition, the kernel extension of the algorithm (NLKSSC) is also provided in order to benefit from kernel-based representations of data. Furthermore, we introduced the link-restore algorithm as an effective solution to the sparse coding redundancy issue when it has negative effects on clustering performance.

This post-processing algorithm which is suitable for non-negative sparse representations corrects the broken links between close data points in the representation graph. Empirical evaluations demonstrated that link-restore can act as an effective post-processing step for different types of SSC methods which use non-negative sparse coding models. As a future step, we are interested in combining our framework with dimension reduction strategies to better deal with multi-dimensional data types.

References

1. Ana, L., Jain, A.K.: Robust data clustering. In: IEEE Conference on Computer Vision and Pattern Recognition. vol. 2, pp. II-128. IEEE (2003)
2. Bian, X., Li, F., Ning, X.: Kernelized sparse self-representation for clustering and recommendation. In: SIAM International Conference on Data Mining, pp. 10–17 (2016)
3. Boyd, S., Parikh, N., Chu, E., Peleato, B., Eckstein, J.: Distributed optimization and statistical learning via the alternating direction method of multipliers. Found. Trends® Mach. Learn. **3**(1), 1–122 (2011)
4. Cai, J.F., Candès, E.J., Shen, Z.: A singular value thresholding algorithm for matrix completion. SIAM J. Optim. **20**(4), 1956–1982 (2010)
5. Cheng, B., Yang, J., Yan, S., Fu, Y., Huang, T.S.: Learning with l1-graph for image analysis. Trans. Img. Proc. **19**(4), 858–866 (2010). Apr
6. Elhamifar, E., Vidal, R.: Sparse subspace clustering: algorithm, theory, and applications. IEEE Trans. Pattern Anal. Mach. Intell. **35**(11), 2765–2781 (2013)
7. Gao, S., Tsang, I.W.h., Chia, L.t.: Laplacian sparse coding, hypergraph laplacian sparse coding, and applications. IEEE TPAMI 35(1), 92–104 (2012)
8. Georghiades, A.S., Belhumeur, P.N., Kriegman, D.J.: From few to many: illumination cone models for face recognition under variable lighting and pose. IEEE Trans. Pattern Anal. Mach. Intell. **23**(6), 643–660 (2001)
9. Hoyer, P.O.: Modeling receptive fields with non-negative sparse coding. Neurocomputing **52**, 547–552 (2003)
10. Kim, T., Shakhnarovich, G., Urtasun, R.: Sparse coding for learning interpretable spatio-temporal primitives. In: NIPS'10, pp. 1117–1125 (2010)
11. Kirrinnis, P.: Fast algorithms for the sylvester equation ax- xbt= c. Theor. Comput. Sci. **259**(1–2), 623–638 (2001)
12. Li, C.G., Vidal, R., et al.: Structured sparse subspace clustering: a unified optimization framework. In: CVPR, pp. 277–286 (2015)
13. Li, X., Cui, G., Dong, Y.: Graph regularized non-negative low-rank matrix factorization for image clustering. IEEE Trans. Cybern. **47**(11), 3840–3853 (2017)
14. Liu, G., Lin, Z., Yan, S., Sun, J., Yu, Y., Ma, Y.: Robust recovery of subspace structures by low-rank representation. IEEE TPAMI **35**(1), 171–184 (2013)
15. Martinez, A.M.: The AR face database. CVC Technical Report 24 (1998)
16. Nene, S.A., Nayar, S.K., Murase, H., et al.: Columbia object image library (coil-20) (1996)
17. Patel, V.M., Vidal, R.: Kernel sparse subspace clustering. In: 2014 IEEE International Conference on Image Processing (ICIP), pp. 2849–2853. IEEE (2014)
18. Rubinstein, R., Zibulevsky, M., Elad, M.: Efficient implementation of the k-svd algorithm using batch orthogonal matching pursuit. Cs Tech. **40**(8), 1–15 (2008)

19. Tron, R., Vidal, R.: A benchmark for the comparison of 3-d motion segmentation algorithms. In: CVPR'07, pp. 1–8. IEEE (2007)
20. Vidal, R., Favaro, P.: Low rank subspace clustering (lrsc). Pattern Recog. Lett. **43**, 47–61 (2014)
21. Von Luxburg, U.: A tutorial on spectral clustering. Stat. Comput. 17(4), 395–416 (2007)
22. Wu, J., Rehg, J.M.: Beyond the Euclidean distance: creating effective visual codebooks using the histogram intersection kernel. In: ICCV 2009. pp. 630–637. IEEE (2009)
23. Xiao, S., Tan, M., Xu, D., Dong, Z.Y.: Robust kernel low-rank representation. IEEE Trans. Neural Netw. Learn. Syst. **27**(11), 2268–2281 (2016)
24. Xu, R., Wunsch, D.: Survey of clustering algorithms. IEEE Trans. Neural Netw. **16**(3), 645–678 (2005)
25. Xu, S., Chan, K.S., Zhou, T., Gao, J., Li, X., Hua, X.: A novel cluster ensemble approach effected by subspace similarity. Intell. Data Anal. **20**(3), 561–574 (2016)
26. Yang, Y., Wang, Z., Yang, J., Wang, J., Chang, S., Huang, T.S.: Data clustering by laplacian regularized l1-graph. In: AAAI, pp. 3148–3149 (2014)
27. You, C., Robinson, D., Vidal, R.: Scalable sparse subspace clustering by orthogonal matching pursuit. In: Computer Vision and Pattern Recognition (CVPR), pp. 3918–3927 (2016)
28. Zhuang, L., Gao, H., Lin, Z., Ma, Y., Zhang, X., Yu, N.: Non-negative low rank and sparse graph for semi-supervised learning. In: CVPR 2012, pp. 2328–2335. IEEE (2012)

Pushing the Envelope in Overlapping Communities Detection

Said Jabbour[1], Nizar Mhadhbi[1], Badran Raddaoui[2], and Lakhdar Sais[1(✉)]

[1] CRIL-CNRS UMR 8188, Université d'Artois, 62307 Lens Cedex, France
{jabbour,mhadhbi,sais}@cril.fr
[2] SAMOVAR, Télécom SudParis, CNRS, Université Paris-Saclay, Evry, France
badran.raddaoui@telecom-sudparis.eu

Abstract. Discovering the hidden community structure is a fundamental problem in network and graph analysis. Several approaches have been proposed to solve this challenging problem. Among them, detecting overlapping communities in a network is a usual way towards understanding the features of networks. In this paper, we propose a novel approach to identify overlapping communities in large complex networks. It makes an original use of a new community model, called *k-clique-star*, to discover densely connected structures in social interactions. We show that such model allows to ensure a minimum density on the discovered communities and overcomes some weaknesses of existing cohesive structures. Experimental results demonstrate the effectiveness and efficiency of our overlapping community model in a variety of real graphs.

Keywords: Community detection · Overlapping community detection · Social networks · Graph analysis

1 Introduction

One of the most important tasks when studying networks (or graphs [1]) is that of identifying *network communities*. Fundamentally, community detection aims to partition a network into communities (clusters), typically thought of as a group of nodes with more and/or better interactions amongst its members than between its members and the remainder of the network. The problem of community detection has been extensively studied in many fields, and many algorithms have been proposed. Discovering communities in networks is a crucial step in studying the structure and dynamics of social, technological, and biological systems. For example, community detection allows us to gain insights into metabolic and protein-protein interactions (PPIs), ecological food webs, social networks, collaboration networks, information networks of interlinked documents, and even networks of co-purchased products, etc.

Identifying network communities can be viewed as a problem of finding dense subgraphs, e.g., finding groups of nodes that are densely connected, where a

---

[1] In this paper, we use network and graph interchangeably.

© Springer Nature Switzerland AG 2018
W. Duivesteijn et al. (Eds.): IDA 2018, LNCS 11191, pp. 151–163, 2018.
https://doi.org/10.1007/978-3-030-01768-2_13

node can belong to multiple subgraphs at once. Therefore, different mathematical models have been studied over years as basis for extracting communities in networks. The most intuitive model for social network analysis is the clique [12] in which every node is adjacent to every other node. Such structure, preferably maximal clique, is really the ideal community structure, that one would like to find. Unfortunately, generating communities with such structural property is computationally intractable. Additionally, the clique structure is too restrictive. Cliques in small size are highly frequent in real-world networks, while larger cliques are expected to be rare (e.g. [5]). Indeed, graphs that occur in many real-world networks have instead a "small word" topology in which nodes are highly clustered yet the path length between them is small [22]. In other words, a small-world network is a type of graph in which most nodes are not neighbors of one another, but the neighbors of any given node are likely to be neighbors of each other and most nodes can be reached from every other node by a small number steps. Moreover, Watts and Strogatz [22] have shown that many real-world networks such as the collaboration graph of actors in feature films and the electrical power grid of the western United States, all have a small world topology.

The arguments mentioned above reveal the clique is too strict to be helpful. Consequently, other more relaxed forms of cohesive subgraphs were proposed. Luce introduced a distance-based model called k-*clique* [11], and Alba proposed a diameter-based model called k-*club* [2]. Generally speaking, these models relax the reachability among vertices from 1 to k. However, they do not remove either the problems of enumeration or computational intractability. Furthermore, other proposals focus on the degree constraint of the clique, like k-*plex* [16] and k-*core* [17]. The k-plex is still NP-Complete since it restricts the subgraph size, while k-core further relaxes it to achieve the linear time complexity with respect to the number of edges. However, the k-core method is usually not powerful enough for uncovering the detailed community structure although it is computationally quite efficient [15]. Recently, a new direction based on the edge triangle model, like DN-Graph [20] and truss decomposition [2] [19], is more suitable for social network analysis since it captures the tie strength between actors inside the subgroup. Notice that in [18], the authors have shown that k-truss is better than k-core from the point of view of cohesiveness.

Our paper follows this research issue. We first highlight some limitations of the k-truss graph structure in providing meaningful communities.

To address these difficulties, we propose a new community model, called k-*clique-star*, which can be roughly seen as a hybrid subgraph class combining both cliques and star structures. In other words, the clique can be seen as the centroid of the star structure conditionally linked to other nodes outside that clique. From the arguments about the real-world networks and the computational complexity issue mentioned above, the initial clique part might be of reasonable

---

[2] For the k-truss structure, the idea is introduced independently by Saito et al. [15] (as k-dense), Cohen [5] (as k-truss), Zhang and Parthasarathy [27] (as triangle k-core), and Verma and Butenko [21] (as k-community).

size. Such centroid clique is incrementally augmented with nodes strongly connected to that clique. In addition, we show that this new structure allows to overcome some shortcomings of k-truss concept while maintaining a reasonable (lower bound) density of the communities in networks. Finally, our approach can scale community detection to large graphs and outperforms several popular algorithms.

2   Background Information

In this paper, we focus on an *undirected graph* $G = (V, E)$, where V is a set of nodes and $E \subseteq V \times V$ is a set of edges. We denote by n (resp. m) the number of nodes (resp. edges) in G. For a node $u \in V$, we denote by N_u the set of neighbors of u, i.e., $N_u = \{v \in V : (u, v) \in E\}$. The *degree* of a node $u \in V$, denoted d_u, is equal to $|N_u|$. In graph theory, *communities* are defined as groups of nodes that are closely knit together relative to the rest of the network. In real-world networks, nodes are organized into densely linked sets of nodes that are commonly referred to as *network communities*, clusters or modules. Notice that in many social and information networks, communities naturally overlap as nodes can belong to multiple communities at once. Network *overlapping community detection* problem consists in dividing a network of interest into (overlapping) communities for intelligent analysis. It has recently attracted significant attention in diverse application domains. In fact, identifying the community structure is crucial for understanding structural properties of the real-world networks. Various methods have been proposed to identify the community structure of complex networks (see [24] for an overview). These existing methods can be roughly categorized into three classes: *(1) optimization-based methods*: these approaches aim to partition the network in communities by maximizing a goodness metric as modularity, conductance, density-isolation, etc.; *(2) seed set expansion methods:* starting from a seed, such methods greedily expand a community around that seed until they reach a local optima of the community detection objective; and, *(3) cohesive subgraphs based methods:* these method aim to partition the network into dense subgraphs by using some cohesive graph structures. Specifically, various definitions of communities based on different notions of dense subgraphs have been proposed and studied. Our approach follows this third class and it is designed for overlapping community detection based on dense subgraphs.

Let us start with some subgraph structures used to discover communities.

Definition 1 (k-clique). *A graph $G = (V, E)$ is a k-clique if G is a clique and $|V| = k$.*

Next, less restricted but also inspired from the clique structure, the k-core is motivated by the property that every node has degree $k - 1$ in a k-clique. The k-core also needs to satisfy the degree condition, but the restriction on subgraph size is not required.

Definition 2 (k-core). *A graph $G = (V, E)$ is a k-core if $\forall u \in V$, $d(u) \geq k$.*

Obviously, a k-clique is also a k-1-core. In the worst case, the number of k-core subgraphs can be exponential in the size of the graph. Therefore, a maximal k-core subgraph is defined to avoid redundancy.

Similarly to k-core, the k-dense structure defined bellow is inspired by the fact that in a k-clique each edge is belonging to $k - 2$ triangles. More formally,

Definition 3 (k-dense). *A graph $G = (V, E)$ is a k-dense if $\forall (u, v) \in E$, $|N_u \cap N_v| \geq k - 2$.*

One can see that a k-clique is also k-dense, while a k-dense graph is also k-core. Obviously, the converse does not hold. This relationships can be deduced by relating the number of triangles sharing an edge and the degree of the nodes.

Independently, in [5], Cohen introduced a similar structure as k-dense, called k-truss. This structure is motivated by a simple observation on social networks, stating that if two individuals are strongly tied, it is likely that they also share ties to others.

Definition 4 (k-truss). *The k-truss of a graph G is the largest connected subgraph in which every edge is a part of (reinforced by) at least $(k - 2)$ triangles within the subgraph.*

As we can observe, the difference between k-truss and k-dense is tiny. Indeed, an edge (u, v) shares at least $k - 2$ triangles if and only if $|N_u \cap N_v| \geq k - 2$. The two definitions differ only in the fact that k-truss corresponds to a connected subgraph, while the k-dense may be disconnected. With this additional condition, a k-truss subgraph is also k-dense. Obviously the converse is not true. Note that in the experimental part of [15], the authors have explicitly mentioned that the required communities are the connected components of the resulting k-dense structures. To obtain more cohesive communities in networks, Huang et al. introduced an extension of k-truss, called k-truss community [8], defined as the maximal k-truss subgraph with an additional constraint on edge connectivity, i.e., any two edges in a community either belong to the same triangle, or are reachable from each other through a series of adjacent triangles. Here two triangles are defined as adjacent if they share a common edge.

3 k-Clique-Star Based Community Discovery

In this section, we first show some limitations of k-truss and k-truss community concepts so that they are not appropriate to find meaningful communities of a graph. Then, we propose a novel structure aiming to overcome these drawbacks. Before proceeding further, let us consider the graphs G and G' of Fig. 1. G contains two cliques sharing one node v_1, while G' is obtained from G with an additional edge (v_2, v_9) connecting the two cliques. By the k-truss definition, the whole graph G is considered as a unique community for $k > 2$. In contrast, the k-truss community structure allows to divide G into two communities, i.e., each clique is a community. Indeed, there is no adjacent set of triangles allowing to connect an edge from the first clique to the second one. Now, consider the second graph G'. Due to the triangle adjacency condition in the k-truss community concept, both k-truss and k-truss community allow to group the cliques of G' in the same community whatever the size of the cliques. This is clearly a problem, since the two cliques do not share enough edges and nodes. So the k-truss and k-truss community subgraphs may not correspond to a meaningful communities. To cope with these difficulties, in the sequel, we design a novel structure which we call k-*clique-star* that allows to detect more intuitive communities in a graph.

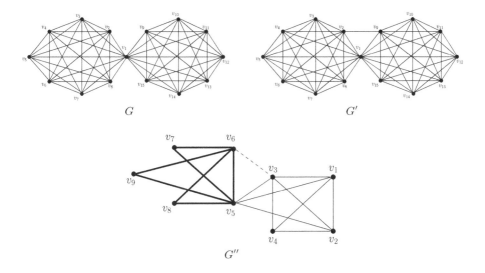

Fig. 1. Three undirected graphs

The intuition behind our structure is that a k-clique can be seen as a $(k-1)$-clique with an additional node connected to all nodes of the $(k-1)$-clique. By generalizing this condition, a k-clique can be seen as two disjoints cliques n-clique and m-clique such that $n + m = k$ and each node of n-clique is connected to all nodes of m-clique. Now, we can relax these conditions by considering one clique instead of two, which gives us the definition of k-clique-star.

Definition 5 (k-clique-star). *A graph* $G = (V, E)$ *is called a k-clique-star* *($k > 1$) if there exists a subgraph* $G' = (V', E')$ *of G such that G' is a k-clique,* *and* $\forall\ u \in V \setminus V',\ \forall\ v \in V',\ (u, v) \in E.$ *G' is called the centroid of G.*

A k-clique-star G is a graph containing a centroid subgraph G', that is, G' is a k-clique and the remaining nodes of G are connected to each node of G'.

Specifically, a k-clique is a k-clique-star with $V = V'$ and $E = E'$. Also, let us mention that $\forall\ k' < k$, a k-clique-star subgraph is a k'-clique-star.

Example 1. Let us consider the graph G'' depicted in Fig. 1. The subgraph $G''(X)$ associated to the set of nodes $X = \{v_1, v_2, v_3, v_4, v_5\}$ is a 3-clique-star whereas the subgraph $G''(Y)$ associated to the set of nodes $Y =$

$\{v_5, v_6, v_7, v_8, v_9\}$ is a 2-clique-star. Note that the addition of the edge (v_3, v_6) to G'' leads to the 3-truss community G''. Indeed, such additional edge ensures the triangles adjacency among all the edges of G''.

Interestingly, the requirements imposed to the k-clique-star guarantee a lower bound on the density of the graph. In fact, for $k = 2$, it is straightforward to conclude that G contains at least $(2 \times |V| - 3)$ edges and $(2 \times |V| - 2)$ triangles. When k increases, the set of edges and triangles increases too, making the subgraph more dense. In the following, we characterize the k-clique-star subgraph in the light of k-truss structure and edge connectivity.

Proposition 1. *If G is a k-clique-star subgraph, then G is k-truss and edge connected.*

Proof. If $G = (V, E)$ is a k-clique-star, then G contains a k-clique $G' = (V', E')$ as a centroid. Let (u, v) be an edge of G. We can distinguish three cases.

1. $u, v \notin V'$: In this case, each u and v are connected to each edges of G'. As G' contains k nodes, and the nodes of $V \setminus V'$ are connected to all nodes of G', then (u, v) belongs to k triangles.
2. $u, v \in V'$: In this case, for each $w \in V' \setminus \{u, v\}$, $\{u, v, w\}$ forms a triangle. Consequently, (u, v) belongs to $|V'| - 2 = k - 2$ triangles.
3. $u \in V'$ and $v \notin V'$: In this case for each $w \in V' \setminus \{u\}$, $\{u, v, w\}$ is a triangle. Consequently, the number of triangles sharing (u, v) is equal to $|V'| - 1 = k - 1$.

From the three cases considered above, we deduce that G is k-truss as each edge is reinforced by at least $k - 2$ triangles.

Let us now prove the edge connectivity condition. Let $e = (u, v)$ and $e' = (u', v')$ two edges of G. 1) If $e, e' \in E'$, it is straightforward to conclude that e and e' are adjacent since G' is a clique. 2) If $e = (u, v) \notin E'$ and $u \in V'$ and $v \notin V'$, thanks to the edges of G', $e = (u, v)$ is adjacent to each edge $e' \in E \setminus \{e\}$, by definition of the k-clique-star structure. Indeed, v is connected to each node $w \in V'$, which is connected to each node in $V \setminus V'$. 3) Finally, let $e = (u, v) \notin E'$ and $e' = (u', v') \notin E'$. Let $e'' = (u'', v'') \in E'$, then $\{u, v, u'', v''\}$ and $\{u', v', u'', v''\}$ are two cliques sharing the edge e''. Consequently, e, e' are edge connected.

Consequently, a k-clique-star is a k-truss community without the maximality condition. Let us also mention that a k-truss community is not necessarily a k-star-clique. In fact, consider the graph G'' of Fig. 1 as a counter-example. Clearly, G'' with the additional doted edge (v_3, v_6) is 3-truss community. However, there is no integer k making the whole graph a k-clique-star.

Given a large network and an integer k, the number of k-clique-star subgraphs can be exponential in the original graph size in the worst case. Therefore, we further define the maximal k-clique-star subgraph to avoid redundancy.

Definition 6 (Maximal k-clique-star). *A graph $G = (V, E)$ is a maximal k-clique-star subgraph if there is no $G' \supset G$ such that G' is a k-clique-star.*

Example 2 Let us consider the graphs depicted in Fig. 1. For the graph G, there are two maximal 2-clique-star, namely $C_1 = \{v_1, v_2, v_3, v_4, v_5, v_6, v_7, v_8\}$ and $C_2 = \{v_1, v_9, v_{10}, v_{11}, v_{12}, v_{13}, v_{14}, v_{15}\}$. For the graph G' there are also two maximal 2-clique-star $C'_1 = \{v_1, v_2, v_3, v_4, v_5, v_6, v_7, v_8\}$ and $C'_2 = \{v_1, v_9, v_{10}, v_{11}, v_{12}, v_{13}, v_{14}, v_{15}\}$. Let us remark that in contrast to k-truss community, where the whole graph G forms a unique community, our approach derives more meaningful communities. More interestingly, for $k > 2$, the two possible maximal communities are the two cliques for both G and G'.

Next, we describe the computation process of maximal k-clique-star subgraphs. This set of communities can be detected in two steps. Once the detection of the set of centroids according to the fixed value k is performed. The simplest case is obtained when k is set to 2. In this case, the set of initial communities is obtained by considering for each edge (u, v) the community $C_{(u,v)} = \{u, v\} \cup \bigcap_{x \in \{u,v\}} N_x$. When k is fixed to 3, the centroid is a triangle. Then, this requires the enumeration of all triangles. Various algorithms have been proposed to efficiently enumerate triangles in large graphs. Afterward, each initial community is built starting from each triangle $\{u, v, w\}$ and considering $C_{u,v,w} = \{u, v, w\} \cup \bigcap_{x \in \{u,v,w\}} N_x$. When, k exceeds 3, the efficient algorithm [6] for extracting k-cliques can be used. Notice that the goal of our new concept is precisely to avoid enumerating large cliques by considering small cliques as centroids, since for real-world networks, small cliques are more frequent contrary to larger cliques [18]. As the worst-case complexity of our algorithm is in $O(n^k)$, in the experimental evaluation, we perform our tests with $k \in \{2, 3\}$. Finally, to obtain the final communities, we have to remove the set of redundant ones. The following Algorithm 1 summarizes the computation process $\forall k$.

Algorithm 1: k-clique-star based communities detection

Input: A network $\mathcal{G} = (V, E)$ and k an integer
Output: A set of overlapping communities $\mathcal{S}$
1 $\mathcal{C} \leftarrow k$-cliques(G);
2 $\mathcal{S} \leftarrow \emptyset$;
3 **for** $C = (V_C, E_C) \in \mathcal{C}$ **do**
4    $\quad \mathcal{S} \leftarrow \mathcal{S} \cup (V_C \cup \bigcap_{u \in V_C} N_u)$;
5 **end**
6 Remove-redundancy($\mathcal{S}$);
7 **return** $\mathcal{S}$

---

4   Experimental Evaluation

Our experimental evaluation was conducted on five small networks and four big networks to show the scalability of our model. These instances cover a variety of application areas. All these networks have ground-truth communities as presented in column 3 of Table 1.

We evaluate the performance of our approach by comparing it against the following most prominent state-of-the-art (overlapping) community detection algorithms: (i) *Community finding using Model-based Overlapping Seed Expansion* (MOSES) [14]: a local approach that search a set of seed nodes and look for the local view of each node to expand them in order to form communities; (ii) *Clique Percolation Method* (CPM) [1]: a local approach consisting of deriving the local neighborhood of each node. In this method, each node is described by the cliques it is a member of; (iii) *Cluster Affiliation Model for Big Networks* (BIGCLAM) [25]; and (iv) *Communities from Edge Structure and Node Attributes* (CESNA) [26]. For the CPM algorithm, we use the cliques of size 3. For BIGCLAM method, user can specify the number of communities to detect, or let the program determine the number of communities from the topology of the network. We opt for the case where the number of communities is not fixed.

Table 1. Datasets description

Small datasets			
Dataset	Nodes/Edges	#Truth communities	Source
Dolphin	62/159	2	[13]
Karate	34/78	2	[23]
Risk map	42/83	6	[4]
Railway	301/1 224	21	[3]
Football	115/613	12	[7]
Big datasets			
Dataset	Nodes/Edges	#Truth communities	Source
Amazon	334 863/925 872	75 149	[10]
dblp	317 080/1 049 866	13 477	[10]
Youtube	1 134 890/2 987 624	8 385	[10]
Live-journal	3 997 962/34 681 189	287 512	[10]

The proposed system, referred to as K-CLIQUE-STAR, was written in C. Given an input network as a set of edges and an integer k, our algorithm starts by generating the most dense part of each community called centroid. Such centroid contains k interconnected nodes. The next step consists of expanding the centroids by adding all nodes that are connected to all of the nodes of the centroids. Our final communities are the maximal k-clique-star subgraphs. Notice that each community is a one connected component.

For our experimental study, all algorithms have been run on a PC with an Intel Core 2 Duo (2 GHz) processor and 2 GB memory. We imposed 1 h time limit for all the methods. Missing histogram bars in Fig. 4 indicate that the algorithm was not able to scale on the considered network under the time limit.

4.1   Size of the Centroids

As argued previously, in our k-clique-star based model, the value of k must be set to a small value. So we run our approach on two different types of networks from real-world data, namely small and big datasets, while varying k from 2 to 3, and generate the communities for each value of k. Figure 2 shows some statistics related to the communities obtained on `dblp` and `youtube` networks. What we can see from these statistics is that starting from a small clique of size 2 or 3 our approach can find communities of large size. Also, in Fig. 2 for each of the two networks we show the community size distribution when increasing the size k of the clique. As can be seen, when k increases from 2 to 3 fewer communities of small size are found for both `dblp` and `youtube` datasets.

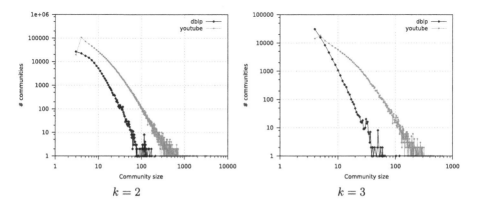

Fig. 2. Communities size distributions

4.2   Impact of k on Quality Metrics

To further investigate the impact of the size of the centroids in our k-clique-star based model, we look at the relationship between k and quality metrics (see Fig. 3). We recall that, several measures have been proposed for quantifying the quality of communities in networks. Here, we adopt two popular metrics, F1 score [25] and NMI score [9], to assess the performance of our method. Figure 3(a) (respectively Fig. 3(b)) shows the relationship between F1 score and k (respectively between NMI score and k). As Fig. 3 reveals, for some big datasets, the best F1 scores (respectively NMI score) are obtained for $k = 2$. For example, for `amazon`, `youtube` and `live-journal` datasets, $k = 2$ gives an important improvement against $k = 3$. We also observe that these F1 scores are relatively close for the `dblp` network. Now, these performances are relatively close for small datasets except the `karate` network. More precisely, the F1 and NMI scores are very close for `dolphin`, `railway` and `football` networks.

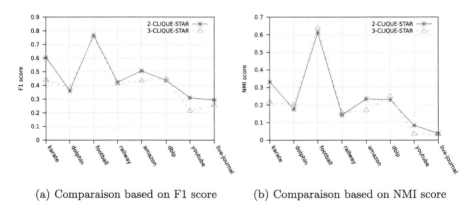

(a) Comparaison based on F1 score   (b) Comparaison based on NMI score

Fig. 3. Results for $k = 2$ and $k = 3$

4.3 Experiments on Recovering Ground-Truth Communities

We evaluate the performance of K-CLIQUE-STAR for $k = 2$ and baselines in terms of the agreement between the ground-truth communities and the detected communities.

Results on Big Networks: After finding communities in big networks, we can gauge the performance of each community that an algorithm has discovered and whether a ground-truth community has been successfully identified. Figure 4 reports the performance comparison between our approach and the baseline algorithms.

Experiments shows that our method outperforms every baseline for both F1 and NMI scores. We also note that our approach shows a high margin in performance gain against all baselines in two large networks youtube and live-journal. MOSES is the closest one to our approach for amazon, and dblp. Interestingly, on amazon and dblp, K-CLIQUE-STAR outperforms CESNA and BIGCLAM with a bigger margin of F1 and NMI scores. In terms of average F1 performance, we have 0.389, 0.200, 0.065, 0.060 and 0.241 for K-CLIQUE-STAR, CPM, BIGCLAM, CESNA and MOSES, respectively. From the average of F1 score our approach outperforms CPM by 94.5%, BIGCLAM by 498, 46%, CESNA by 548, 33% and MOSES by 61, 41%.

Similarly, we also observe that our approach, in terms of NMI score average, gives an important improvement against the baselines in all the large networks.

Results on Small Networks:

Figure 5 displays the F1 and NMI based performance of the methods over all five small networks.

Compared to baseline algorithms, our approach performs better on karate graph and relatively close on dolphin, risk map, railway and football datasets for both F1 and NMI metrics. On average, the F1 performance is 0.566, 0.441, 0.434, 0.532 and 0.438 for K-CLIQUE-STAR, CPM, BIGCLAM, CESNA and MOSES, respectively. The average value of NMI over the 5 networks is 0.441,

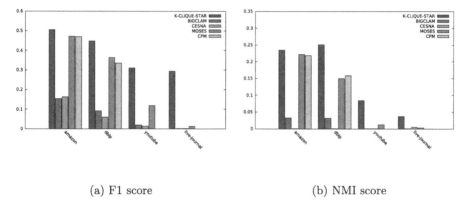

(a) F1 score   (b) NMI score

Fig. 4. Results for big networks

0.272, 0.252, 0.391 and 0.281 for K-CLIQUE-STAR, CPM, BIGCLAM, CESNA and MOSES, respectively. Overall, K-CLIQUE-STAR outperforms the baselines on average among the two scores.

As a summary, experimental results show that our approach outperforms the baselines in every measure and every big network, and it achieves competitive performance on small datasets and is able to find the ideal communities as same as the known communities.

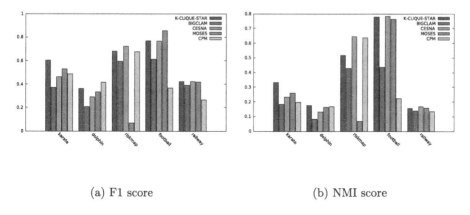

(a) F1 score   (b) NMI score

Fig. 5. Results on small networks

5 Conclusion

In this paper, we proposed a novel overlapping community detection model based on the k-clique-star concept which is shown to have cohesive community structure. Such structure has a centered set of nodes forming a clique and a set of additional nodes connected to all the nodes of that clique. We showed that this hybrid structure allows to avoid some k-truss limitations. Experiments on real-world networks demonstrate the effectiveness and the efficiency of our proposed algorithm. As a future work, detecting communities using other hybrid graph classes is an interesting issue that we plan to further investigate.

References

1. Adamcsek, B., Palla, G., Farkas, I.J., Derényi, I., Vicsek, T.: CFinder: locating cliques and overlapping modules in biological networks. Bioinformatics **22**(8), 1021–1023 (2006)
2. Alba, R.D.: A graph-theoretic definition of a sociometric clique **3**, 113–126 (1973)
3. Chakraborty, T., Srinivasan, S., Ganguly, N., Mukherjee, A., Bhowmick, S.: On the permanence of vertices in network communities. In: SIGKDD, pp. 1396–1405 (2014)
4. Cheng, J., Leng, M., Li, L., Zhou, H., Chen, X.: Active semi-supervised community detection based on must-link and cannot-link constraints. PLoS **9**(10), 1–18 (2014)
5. Cohen, J.: Trusses: cohesive subgraphs for social network analysis. In: Technical report, National Security Agency (2008)
6. Danisch, M., Balalau, O.D., Sozio, M.: Listing k-cliques in sparse real-world graphs. In: WWW, pp. 589–598 (2018)
7. Girvan, M., Newman, M.E.J.: Community structure in social and biological networks. Proc. Natl. Acad. Sci. **99**, 7821 (2002)
8. Huang, X., Cheng, H., Qin, L., Tian, W., Yu, J.X.: Querying k-truss community in large and dynamic graphs. In: SIGMOD, pp. 1311–1322 (2014)
9. Lancichinetti, A., Fortunato, S., Kertesz, J.: Community detection algorithms: a comparative analysis. New J. Phys. **11** (2009)
10. Leskovec, J., Krevl, A.: SNAP datasets: stanford large network dataset collection (2014). http://snap.stanford.edu/data
11. Luce, R.D.: Connectivity and generalized cliques in sociometric group structure. Psychometrika **15**(2), 169–190 (1950)
12. Luce, R.D., Perry, A.D.: A method of matrix analysis of group structure. Psychometrika **14**(2), 95–116 (1949)
13. Lusseau, D., Schneider, K., Boisseau, O., Haase, P., Slooten, E., Dawson, S.: The bottlenose dolphin community of doubtful Sound features a large proportion of long-lasting associations. Behav. Ecol. Sociobiol. **54**(4), 396–405 (2003)
14. McDaid, A.F., Hurley, N.J.: Detecting highly overlapping communities with model-based overlapping seed expansion. In: ASONAM, pp. 112–119 (2010)
15. Saito, K., Yamada, T., Kazama, K.: Extracting communities from complex networks by the k-dense method. IEICE Trans. **91**(A11), 3304–3311 (2008)
16. Seidman, S.B.: A graph-theoretic generalization of the clique concep. J. Math. Sociol. **5**(3), 139–154 (1978)
17. Seidman, S.B.: Network structure and minimum degree. Soc. Netw. **5**(3), 269–287 (1983)
18. Shao, Y., Chen, L., Cui, B.: Efficient cohesive subgraphs detection in parallel. In: SIGMOD, pp. 613–624 (2014)
19. Wang, J., Cheng, J.: Truss decomposition in massive networks. PVLDB **5**(9), 812–823 (2012)

20. Wang, N., Zhang, J., Tan, K., Tung, A.K.H.: On triangulation-based dense neighborhood graphs discovery. PVLDB **4**(2), 58–68 (2010)
21. Wasserman, S., Faust, K.: Social Network Analysis: Methods and Applications. Cambridge University Press, Cambridge (1994)
22. Watts, D.J., Strogatz, S.H.: Collective dynamics of small-world networks. Nature **393**(6684), 440–442 (1998)
23. Zachary, W.W.: An information flow model for conflict and fission in small groups. J. Anthropol. Res. **33**, 452–473 (1977)
24. Xie, J., Kelley, S., Szymanski, B.K.: Overlapping community detection in networks: the state-of-the-art and comparative study. ACM Comput. Surv. **45**(4), 43:1–43:35 (2013)
25. Yang, J., Leskovec, J.: Overlapping community detection at scale: a nonnegative matrix factorization approach. In: WSDM, pp. 587–596 (2013)
26. Yang, J., McAuley, J.J., Leskovec, J.: Community detection in networks with node attributes. CoRR abs/1401.7267 (2014)
27. Zhang, Y., Parthasarathy, S.: Extracting analyzing and visualizing triangle k-core motifs within networks. In: ICDE, pp. 1049–1060 (2012)

Right for the Right Reason: Training Agnostic Networks

Sen Jia, Thomas Lansdall-Welfare[(✉)], and Nello Cristianini

Intelligent Systems Laboratory, University of Bristol, Bristol BS8 1UB, UK
{sen.jia,thomas.lansdall-welfare,nello.cristianini}@bris.ac.uk

Abstract. We consider the problem of a neural network being requested to classify images (or other inputs) without making implicit use of a "protected concept", that is a concept that should not play any role in the decision of the network. Typically these concepts include information such as gender or race, or other contextual information such as image backgrounds that might be implicitly reflected in unknown correlations with other variables, making it insufficient to simply remove them from the input features. In other words, making accurate predictions is not good enough if those predictions rely on information that should not be used: predictive performance is not the only important metric for learning systems. We apply a method developed in the context of domain adaptation to address this problem of "being right for the right reason", where we request a classifier to make a decision in a way that is entirely 'agnostic' to a given protected concept (*e.g.* gender, race, background etc.), even if this could be implicitly reflected in other attributes via unknown correlations. After defining the concept of an 'agnostic model', we demonstrate how the Domain-Adversarial Neural Network can remove unwanted information from a model using a gradient reversal layer.

Keywords: Agnostic models · Explainable AI · Fairness in AI · Trust

1 Introduction

Data-driven Artificial Intelligence (AI) is behind the new generation of success stories in the field, and is predicated not just on a few technological breakthroughs, but on a cultural shift amongst its practitioners: namely the belief that predictions are more important than explanations, and that correlations count more than causations [4,8]. Powerful black-box algorithms have been developed to sift through data and detect any possible correlation between inputs and intended outputs, exploiting anything that can increase predictive performance. Computer vision (CV) is one of the fields that has benefited the most from this choice, and therefore can serve as a test bed for more general ideas in AI.

This paper targets the important problem of ensuring trust in AI systems. Consider a case as simple as object classification. It is true that exploiting contextual clues can be beneficial in CV and generally in AI tasks. After all, if an

© Springer Nature Switzerland AG 2018
W. Duivesteijn et al. (Eds.): IDA 2018, LNCS 11191, pp. 164–174, 2018.
https://doi.org/10.1007/978-3-030-01768-2_14

algorithm thinks it is seeing an elephant (the object) in a telephone box (the context), or Mickey Mouse driving a Ferrari, it is probably wrong. This illustrates that even though your classifier might have an opinion about the objects in an image, the context around it can be used to improve your performance (*e.g.* telling you that it is unlikely to be an elephant inside a telephone box), as shown in many recent works [3,13,14].

However, making predictions based on context can also lead to problems and creates various concerns, one of which is the use of classifiers in "out of domain" situations, a problem that leads to research questions in domain adaptation [6,18]. Other concerns are also created around issues of bias, *e.g.* classifiers incorporating biases that are present in the data and are not intended to be used [2], which run the risk of reinforcing or amplifying cultural (and other) biases [20]. Therefore, both predictive accuracy and fairness are heavily influenced by the choices made when developing black-box machine-learning models.

Since the limiting factor in training models is often sourcing labelled data, a common choice is to resort to reusing existing data for a new purpose, such as using web queries to generate training data, and employing various strategies to annotate labels, *i.e.* using proxy signals that are expected to be somewhat correlated to the intended target concept [5,11]. These methods come with no guarantees of being unbiased, or even to reflect the deployment conditions necessarily, with any data collected "in the wild" [8,10] carrying with it the biases that come from the wild.

To address these issues, a shift in thinking is needed, from the aforementioned belief that predictions are more important than explanations, to ideally developing models that make predictions that are right for the right reason, and consider other metrics, such as fairness, transparency and trustworthiness, as equally important as predictive performance. This means that we want to ensure that certain protected concepts are not used as part of making critical decisions (*e.g.* decisions about jobs should not be based on gender or race) for example, or that similarly, predictions about objects in an image should not be based on contextual information (gender of a subject in an image should not be based on the background).

In this direction, we demonstrate how the Domain-Adversarial Neural Network (DANN) developed in the context of domain adaptation [6] can be modified to generate 'agnostic' feature representations that do not incorporate any implicit contextual (correlated) information that we do not want, and is therefore unbiased and fair. We note that this is a far stronger requirement than simply removing protected features from the input that might otherwise implicitly remain in the model due to unforeseen correlations with other features.

We present a series of experiments, showing how the relevant pixels used to make a decision move from the contextual information to the relevant parts of the image. This addresses the problem of relying on contextual information, exemplified by the Husky/Wolf problem in [15], but more importantly shows a way to de-bias classifiers in the feature engineering step, allowing it to be applied generally for different models, whether that is word embeddings, support vector machines, or deep networks etc.

Ultimately, this ties into the current debate about how to build trust in these tools, whether this is about their predictive performance, their being right for the right reason, their being fair, or their decisions being explainable.

2   Agnostic Models

Methods have previously been proposed to remove biases, based on various principles, one of which is distribution matching [20]: ensuring that the ratio between protected attributes is the same in the training instances and in the testing instances. However, this does not avoid using the wrong reasons in assessing an input but simply enforces a post-hoc rescaling of scores, to ensure that the outcome matches the desired statistical requirements of fairness.

In our case, we do not want to have an output distribution that only looks as if it has been done without using protected concepts. We actually want a model that cannot even represent them within its internal representations, where we call such a model *agnostic*. This is a model that does not represent a protected concept internally, and therefore cannot use it even indirectly. Of course this kind of constraint is likely to lead to lower accuracy. However, we should keep in mind that this reduction in accuracy is a direct result of no longer using contextual clues and correlations that we explicitly wish to prevent.

In this direction, we consider classification tasks where X is the input space and $Y = \{0, 1, \ldots, L - 1\}$ is the set of L possible labels. An agnostic model (or feature representation) $G_f : X \to \mathbb{R}^D$, parameterized by θ_f, maps a data example $(\mathbf{x}_i, \mathbf{y}_i)$ into a new D-dimensional feature representation $\mathbf{z} \in \mathbb{R}^D$ such that for a given label $p \in Y$, there does not exist an algorithm $G_y : \mathbb{R}^D \to [0, 1]^L$ which can predict p with better than random performance.

3   Domain-Adversarial Neural Networks

One possible way to learn an agnostic model is to use a DANN [6], recently proposed for domain adaptation, which explicitly implements the idea raised in [1] of learning a representation that is unable to distinguish between training and test domains. In our case, we wish for the model to be able to learn a representation that is agnostic to a protected concept.

DANNs are a type of Convolutional Neural Network (CNN) that can achieve an agnostic representation using three components. A feature extractor $G_f(\cdot; \theta_f)$, a label prediction output layer $G_y(\cdot; \theta_y)$ and an additional protected concept prediction layer $G_p : \mathbb{R}^D \to [0, 1]$, parameterized by θ_p. During training, two different losses are then computed: a target prediction loss for the i-th data instance $\mathcal{L}_y^i(\theta_f, \theta_y) = \mathcal{L}_y(G_y(G_f(\mathbf{x}_i; \theta_f); \theta_y), \mathbf{y}_i)$ and a protected concept loss $\mathcal{L}_p^i(\theta_f, \theta_p) = \mathcal{L}_p(G_p(G_f(\mathbf{x}_i; \theta_f); \theta_p), p_i)$, where $\mathcal{L}_y$ and $\mathcal{L}_p$ are both given by the cross-entropy loss and p_i is the label denoting the protected concept we wish to be unable to distinguish using the learnt representation.

Training the network then attempts to optimise

$$E(\theta_f, \theta_y, \theta_p) = (1 - \alpha)\frac{1}{n}\sum_{i=1}^{n}\mathcal{L}_y^i(\theta_f, \theta_y) - \alpha\left(\frac{1}{n}\sum_{i=1}^{n}\mathcal{L}_p^i(\theta_f, \theta_p) + \frac{1}{n'}\sum_{i=n+1}^{N}\mathcal{L}_p^i(\theta_f, \theta_p)\right),$$
(1)

where $n' = N - n$ and α is the hyper-parameter for the trade-off between the two losses, finding the saddle point $\hat{\theta}_f, \hat{\theta}_y, \hat{\theta}_p$ such that

$$(\hat{\theta}_f, \hat{\theta}_y) = \operatorname{argmin}_{\theta_f, \theta_y} E(\theta_f, \theta_y, \hat{\theta}_p),$$
(2)

$$\hat{\theta}_p = \operatorname{argmax}_{\theta_p} E(\hat{\theta}_f, \hat{\theta}_y, \theta_p).$$
(3)

As further detailed in [6], introducing a *gradient reversal layer* (GRL) between the feature extractor G_f and the protected concept classifier G_p allows (1) to be framed as a standard stochastic gradient descent (SGD) procedure as commonly implemented in most deep learning libraries.

The network can therefore be learnt using a simple stochastic gradient procedure, where updates to θ_f are made in the opposite direction of the gradient for the maximizing parameters, and in the direction of the gradient for the minimizing parameters. Stochastic estimates of the gradient are made, both for the target concept and for the protected concept, using the training set. We can see this as the two parts of the neural network (target classifier G_y and protected concept classifier G_p) are competing with each other for the control of the internal representation. DANN will attempt to learn a model G_f that maps an example into a representation allowing the target classifier to accurately classify instances, but crippling the ability of the protected concept classifier to discriminate inputs by their label for the protected concept.

4   Experiments

To test the use of DANNs for learning representations that can be used to make predictions for the right reasons, we ran two different experiments. In Experiment 1, we first demonstrate the issue of using contextual information to make predictions in a cross-domain classification task, before using a DANN in Experiment 2, showing that the network can learn an agnostic representation that allows us to make predictions on a target concept without using information from a correlated contextual concept (the protected concept in this case), such as the image background.

4.1   Data Description

In this work, we combine two datasets, making use of the 'Jaguar' and 'Killer whale' categories from the ImageNet dataset [16], as well as the 'Forest path' and 'Coast' categories from the Places dataset [21].

A two-part training set was constructed containing 2,524 images from the 'Jaguar' category, and the same number for the 'Killer whale' category from

Fig. 1. Example images taken from the 'Jaguar', 'Killer whale', 'Forest path' and 'Coast' categories of the ImageNet and Places datasets respectively (left-right).

ImageNet (the target concept training set). This was further supplemented with 5,000 images from each of the two categories ('Forest path' and 'Coast') from the Places dataset (the contextual concept training set), for a total of 15,048 images in the combined training set. Two separate hold-out sets were also created, one for the target concept containing 50 hold-out images from each of the 'Jaguar' and 'Killer whale' categories, and one for the contextual concept containing 50 hold-out images from each of the 'Forest path' and 'Coast' categories.

Data augmentation was performed on the training set to increase the number of instances by creating new images that are multi-crops of 224 × 224 pixels and horizontally flipping copies of the training set images. All images in our experiments were also pre-processed to be 256 × 256 pixels by a process of multi-cropping where each image is resized before cropping the final size from the centre region, as in [9,12]. Example images from the training set used for the experiments can be seen in Fig. 1.

4.2 Network Structure

The network structure used for our experiments in this paper are based upon a simplified version of the VGG-net CNN used in [17], where the feature extraction layers G_f consist of five convolutional layers: conv3-64[1], conv3-128, conv3-256, conv3-512 and conv3-512, with ReLU activation and max-pooling layers inserted after each convolutional layer. The output prediction classifiers G_y and G_p are each composed of four fully connected layers, fc-1024, with ReLU and dropout layers with a dropout of 0.5 after each fully connected layer.

---

[1] conv$a$-b denotes a convolutional layer consisting of b filters of size $a \times a$.

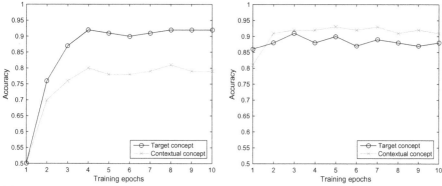

(a) CNN trained on the target concept training set (animals)

(b) CNN trained on the contextual concept training set (backgrounds)

Fig. 2. Results from Experiment 1, showing that a standard CNN model trained on the target concept will also learn how to classify in the contextual concept and vice versa.

4.3   Experiment 1: Cross-domain Classification

In this first experiment, we motivate our approach by demonstrating the problem we wish to address, namely that contextual information can be used to make classification decisions about our target concept that is not related to the target that we actually wish to learn.

We began by training from scratch two independent CNNs with the same network architecture, one on the target concept training set and one on contextual concept training set. The layers of the network are described in Sect. 4.2 with a single output prediction classifier G_y per model, *i.e.* each CNN is composed of five convolution layers, followed by four fully connected layers with no shared features across the models. Each model was trained for 10 epochs using the following model parameters: a batch size of 32, a starting learning rate of $\eta = 0.01$ that decays every three epochs by a factor of 10, a momentum of 0.5 and a weight decay of $5e^{-4}$.

The accuracy of each model was measured on both the target and contextual test sets after each epoch as shown in Fig. 2. As one might expect, we can see that the model trained on the target concept achieves an accuracy of 92% on the target test set, while the contextual concept model achieves an accuracy of 91% on the contextual test set. More problematically, we can see that the target concept model, trained only on images of animals, also has good performance at classifying images of forest paths and coastlines from the contextual test set, with an accuracy of 79%. Similarly, the contextual concept model, trained only on images of forest paths and coastlines can correctly identify animals with an accuracy of 88%.

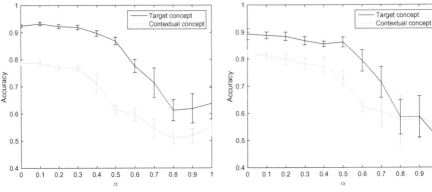

(a) Performance of G_y in the DANN trained for the target concept (animals)

(b) Performance of G_p in the DANN trained for the contextual concept (backgrounds)

Fig. 3. Accuracy of the two independent classifiers in the DANN using the shared feature space on the test sets for different values of α.

4.4   Experiment 2: Learning with Domain-Adversarial Neural Networks

In this next experiment, we show that with our proposed use of DANNs maximises its performance on the target concept whilst following the constraint that it should not learn useful features for the protected contextual concept. We further examine the most informative pixels (*e.g.* those pixels which have the strongest response in the feature map) used for classification [7,19], showing that the most informative pixels are no longer found in the image background.

Keeping all the model parameters, apart from a new learning rate ($\eta = 0.001$), the same as in Experiment 1, we trained a single DANN model on the combined training set, with the network layers outlined in Sect. 4.2, with the target prediction output layers G_y predicting the target concept, and the protected concept prediction layers predicting the contextual concept. By doing so, we force the model to learn a shared data representation (feature space) that maximises performance on the target while incorporating no knowledge of features which are useful for classifying the contextual concept images. This process was repeated for different gradient trade-offs in the range $\alpha = [0, 0.1, \ldots, 1]$ using a grid-search procedure, where $\alpha = 0$ represents simply training the shared feature space on the target concept, and $\alpha = 1$ represents training the shared feature space to maximise the loss for the contextual concept. We repeated this process 10 times, reporting the average accuracy for each run, along with the standard deviation.

In Fig. 3, we can see the accuracy of the DANN for varying gradient trade-off values on the target and contextual concept test sets. Our results show that as α increases and is further constrained in its use of information from the contextual concept, the performance on the target concept decreases, suggesting

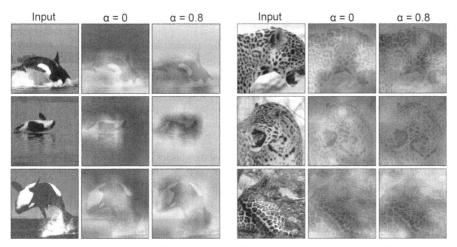

(a) Activation maps for the 'Killer whale' category

(b) Activation maps for the 'Jaguar' category

Fig. 4. Activation maps based on the strongest response of the shared feature representation. Examples selected are those with the least correlation between the activation maps for $\alpha = 0$ and $\alpha = 0.8$ as shown in the images.

that the performance on the intended target concept was indeed being helped by the contextual background information. Our results show that once we have removed features which are useful for predicting the contextual concept, our target classifier achieves an accuracy of 64%, while the contextual classifier can only maintain an accuracy close to random guessing.

We further investigated whether after applying the minimax procedure of the DANN that the most informative pixels for prediction corresponded with the location of the target concept in the image, or whether they were focused on the background scene of the image. Figure 4 shows activation maps for the feature representation shared between the independent classifiers on a set of three images for each target concept category. Examples were selected as those with the least correlation between the activation maps for the contrasting α values of 0 and 0.8 shown, where α values were chosen as the two extremes in the classification accuracy.

We can observe that for the 'Killer whale' category, the most informative pixels for $\alpha = 0$ are indeed found in the background of the image, while for $\alpha = 0.8$ the activation maps show that the network is focusing on the actual body of the animal instead, as desired. For the 'Jaguar' category, analysis of the most informative pixels is less clear, with activation generally being spread widely across the image. However, we do see some evidence of a stronger activation response to parts of the jaguar's body overall.

5   Discussion

In our experiments, we found that as the model learns the shared features with increasingly less contextual information, accuracy of the target classifier decreases. This is exactly what we expect and directly addresses our main argument, that previously the classifier was relying on the protected contextual background information that should not be used to make its predictions.

At one extreme, where $\alpha = 1$, the network is using no information from the target concept in its data representation, instead trying to maximise its loss on the protected concept in the shared feature space G_f, while minimising its loss in the protected classifier G_p. This tension between the two parts of the network leads to a minimax scenario where if there is any information which can be exploited to correctly predict in the protected concept, it is subsequently removed from the data representation.

We note that ideally α should be set to 1 for similar experiments, given that for any other setting the learning system would still be exploiting forbidden information from the protected concept, and would not be satisfying the original requirements of the task: to learn to predict without the contextual information. However, since in this scenario the shared feature space would not rely on the target domain at all, α needs to be slowly increased as training progresses until reaching its maximum. In this way, the features will be guided by the target domain as well, forming a saddle point in the exploration of the feature space as required.

Results from investigating the most informative pixels for classification at differing levels of α revealed that the constraint of the contextual concept appears to have been more successful for the 'Killer whale' and 'Coast' images than for the 'Jaguar' and 'Forest path' pairing. This can perhaps be best explained by how closely the contextual concept training images represent the contextual concept found in the target concept training images, $i.e.$ the whales are always pictured next to or in the ocean, whereas jaguars will sometimes be found outside of the jungle with different backgrounds, and therefore the 'Forest path' category does not match 'Jaguar' backgrounds as closely as 'Coast' does for the 'Killer whale' category.

Further theoretical and experimental analysis of additional minimax architectures is needed to explain the phenomena of the target classifier accuracy increasing on both target and contextual test sets for values of $\alpha \geq 0.8$.

6   Conclusions

The creation of a new generation of AI systems that can be trusted to make fair and unbiased decisions is an urgent task for researchers. As AI rapidly conquers technical challenges related to predictive performance, we are discovering a new dimension to the design of such systems that must be addressed: the fairness and trust in the system's decisions.

In this paper, we address this critical issue of trust in AI by not only proposing a new high standard for models to meet, being agnostic to a protected concept, but also proposing a method to achieve such models. We define a model to be agnostic with respect to a set of concepts if we can show that it makes its decisions without ever using these concepts. This is a much stronger requirement than in distributional matching or other definitions of fairness. We focus on the case where a small set of protected concepts should not be used in decisions, and can be exemplified by samples of data. We have demonstrated how ideas developed in the context of domain adaptation can deliver agnostic representations that are important to ensure fairness and therefore trust.

Our experiments demonstrate that the DANN successfully removes unwanted contextual information, and makes decisions for the right reasons. While demonstrated here by ignoring the physical background context of an object in an image, the same approach can be used to ensure that other protected information does not make its way into black-box classifiers deployed to make decisions about people in other domains and classification tasks.

Acknowledgements. SJ, TLW and NC are support by the FP7 Ideas: European Research Council Grant 339365 - ThinkBIG.

References

1. Ben-David, S., Blitzer, J., Crammer, K., Pereira, F.:. Analysis of representations for domain adaptation. In: Advances in Neural Information Processing Systems, pp. 137–144 (2007)
2. Caliskan, A., Bryson, J.J., Narayanan, A.: Semantics derived automatically from language corpora contain human-like biases. Science **356**(6334), 183–186 (2017)
3. Chu, W., Cai, D.: Deep feature based contextual model for object detection. Neurocomputing **275**, 1035–1042 (2018)
4. Cristianini, N.: On the current paradigm in artificial intelligence. AI Communications **27**(1), 37–43 (2014)
5. Deng, J., Dong, W., Socher, R., Li, L.-J., Li, K., Fei-Fei, L.: Imagenet: a large-scale hierarchical image database. In: IEEE Conference on Computer Vision and Pattern Recognition, 2009. CVPR 2009, pp. 248–255. IEEE (2009)
6. Ganin, Y., Ustinova, E., Ajakan, H., Germain, P., Larochelle, H., Laviolette, F., Marchand, M., Lempitsky, V.: Domain-adversarial training of neural networks. J. Mach. Learn. Res. **17**(1), 2030–2096 (2016)
7. Girshick, R.B., Donahue, J., Darrell, T., Malik, J.: Rich feature hierarchies for accurate object detection and semantic segmentation. CoRR, arXiv:abs/1311.2524 (2013)
8. Halevy, A., Norvig, P., Pereira, F.: The unreasonable effectiveness of data. IEEE Intell. Syst. **24**(2), 8–12 (2009)
9. He, K., Zhang, X., Ren, S., Sun, J.: Deep residual learning for image recognition. arXiv preprint arXiv:1512.03385 (2015)
10. Huang, G.B., Ramesh, M., Berg, T., Learned-Miller, E.: Labeled faces in the wild: a database for studying face recognition in unconstrained environments. Technical report, Technical Report 07–49, University of Massachusetts, Amherst (2007)
11. Jia, S., Lansdall-Welfare, T., Cristianini, N.: Gender classification by deep learning on millions of weakly labelled images. In: 2016 IEEE 16th International Conference on Data Mining Workshops (ICDMW), pp. 462–467. IEEE (2016)

12. Krizhevsky, A., Sutskever, I., Hinton, G.E.: Imagenet classification with deep convolutional neural networks. In: Pereira, F., Burges, C.J.C., Bottou, L., Weinberger, K.Q. (eds.) Advances in Neural Information Processing Systems, vol. 25, pp. 1097–1105. Curran Associates Inc. (2012)
13. Li, J., Wei, Y., Liang, X., Dong, J., Tingfa, X., Feng, J., Yan, S.: Attentive contexts for object detection. IEEE Trans. Multimed. **19**(5), 944–954 (2017)
14. Redmon, J., Divvala, S., Girshick, R., Farhadi, A.: You only look once: Unified, real-time object detection. In: Proceedings of the IEEE Conference on Computer Vision and Pattern Recognition, pp. 779–788 (2016)
15. Ribeiro, M.T., Singh, S., Guestrin, C.: Why should i trust you? Explaining the predictions of any classifier. In: Proceedings of the 22nd ACM SIGKDD International Conference on Knowledge Discovery and Data Mining, pp. 1135–1144. ACM (2016)
16. Russakovsky, O., Deng, J., Hao, S., Krause, J., Satheesh, S., Ma, S., Huang, Z., Karpathy, A., Khosla, A., Bernstein, M., Berg, A.C., Fei-Fei, L.: ImageNet large scale visual recognition challenge. Int. J. Comput. Vis. (IJCV) **115**(3), 211–252 (2015)
17. Simonyan, K., Zisserman, A.: Very deep convolutional networks for large-scale image recognition. Eprint Arxiv (2014)
18. Wulfmeier, M., Bewley, A., Posner, I.: Addressing appearance change in outdoor robotics with adversarial domain adaptation. arXiv preprint arXiv:1703.01461 (2017)
19. Zeiler, M.D., Fergus, R.: Visualizing and Understanding convolutional networks. In: Fleet, D., Pajdla, T., Schiele, B., Tuytelaars, T. (eds.) ECCV 2014. LNCS, vol. 8689, pp. 818–833. Springer, Cham (2014). https://doi.org/10.1007/978-3-319-10590-1_53
20. Zhao, J., Wang, T., Yatskar, M., Ordonez, V., Chang, K.-W.: Men also like shopping: Reducing gender bias amplification using corpus-level constraints. arXiv preprint arXiv:1707.09457 (2017)
21. Zhou, B., Lapedriza, A., Khosla, A., Oliva, A., Torralba, A.: Places: A 10 million image database for scene recognition. IEEE Trans. Pattern Anal. Mach. Intell. (2017)

Link Prediction in Multi-layer Networks and Its Application to Drug Design

Maksim Koptelov$^{(\boxtimes)}$ ⬤, Albrecht Zimmermann⬤, and Bruno Crémilleux

Normandie Univ, UNICAEN, ENSICAEN, CNRS - UMR GREYC, Caen, France
{maksim.koptelov, albrecht.zimmermann, bruno.cremilleux}@unicaen.fr

Abstract. Search of valid drug candidates for a given target is a vital part of modern drug discovery. Since the problem was established, a number of approaches have been proposed that augment interaction networks with, typically, two compound/target similarity networks. In this work we propose a method capable of using an arbitrary number of similarity or interaction networks. We adapt an existing method for random walks on heterogeneous networks and show that adding additional networks improves prediction quality.

Keywords: Chemoinformatics · Link prediction · Multi-layer graphs

1 Introduction

Predicting links between biological or chemical compounds, and targets, such as therapeutic targets, binding sites or disease phenotypes, is an integral part of research in biology and medicinal chemistry. While the main approach to reliably identifying such links still depends on *in vitro* testing, computational methods are employed more and more frequently to fine-tune the set of candidates to be tested *in silico*, cutting down on time and money invested in real-world testing.

A number of methods have been introduced since the problem was first formulated in this form. A straight-forward manner consists of formulating a classification problem: given a particular target, and a number of compounds that have been tested against it, one decides on a representation for the compounds and creates a binary prediction problem that can be solved using any number of existing machine learning techniques. The problem can also be turned around, treating a compound as the class, and targets as data instances, or learning on both entities' representation [13].

A problem such approaches have to overcome is sparsity: whether it is because a target has only recently been identified, because a disease is rare (hence commercially unattractive), or because the relation between certain compounds and targets has not been evaluated for plausible biological reasons, the total space of possible links remains largely under-explored. Concretely, this means that *negative examples* are often not available, ruling certain techniques out.

A semantically similar problem setting that also faces the sparsity problem is that of product recommendation, and recommender systems have therefore been

© Springer Nature Switzerland AG 2018
W. Duivesteijn et al. (Eds.): IDA 2018, LNCS 11191, pp. 175–187, 2018.
https://doi.org/10.1007/978-3-030-01768-2_15

adapted for the problem setting [7]. A simple recommender system-like approach implements, for instance, the reasoning that if two compounds are both linked with several shared targets, and one of them is linked to an additional one, it is reasonable to assume that the other one should be as well. Such an approach has the advantage of exploiting information that is not directly linked to the chosen target yet is still faced with a sparsity problem since, as mentioned, most compounds do not have many links to start with. This makes some approaches to recommendation, such as matrix factorization, difficult or impossible to use.

One relatively recent proposal to address this problem consists of using network data: vertices represent entities, i.e. compounds and targets, and edges between them their relation. While this does not solve the sparsity problem per se, it allows to introduce additional information: chemical or genetic similarity, for instance, or drug-drug/target-target interactions reported in the literature. There are two obvious question related to this idea: (1) Which information sources should one use? (2) How can different networks be integrated?

Current solutions often limit themselves to a single similarity network for both compounds and targets, choosing a single similarity measure such as the Tanimoto, Cosine, Simcomp [4] similarity, or Smith-Waterman scores [11] (typically based on empirical validation). In addition, networks are not integrated as such but typically treated separately, with the similarity networks inducing new edges in the interaction network.

In our work, we propose to use a multi-layer network to solve this problem. We illustrate our proposal in the context of ligand-protein interactions, ligands being organic compounds, and proteins biological targets identified as relevant for diseases. Instead of picking and choosing between different sources of information, we propose to use **all of them**, exploiting different similarity measures and interaction information available. Our main contribution is an improvement on the previously introduced NRWRH method [2] that allows us to exploit multi-layer networks assembled from an **arbitrary** number and type of layers. As we show in the experimental evaluation, the algorithm effectively exploits the combination of different types of incomplete data to perform drug-target prediction.

The rest of the paper is organized as follows. Section 2 provides basic notations and problem formulation. Section 3 discusses related work in the given field. Section 4 describes how we adapt existing algorithms to the multi-layer setting. Section 5 describes how we prepare and integrate different data sources, the experimental setup, and presents empirical results. Finally, Sect. 6 concludes and outlines future work.

2   Definitions and Problem Formulation

2.1   Basic Notations

The most important concept in our work is that of a graph.

Definition 1 *(**Labeled Graph**). A labeled graph is a tuple $\langle V, E, \lambda_v, \lambda_e \rangle$, with V a set of vertices, $E \subseteq V \times V$ a set of edges, $\lambda_v : V \mapsto \mathcal{A}_v$ a labeling function* *mapping vertices to elements of an alphabet of possible vertex labels, and λ_e : $E \mapsto \mathcal{A}_e$ a labeling function for edges. We call the degree of a vertex the number of edges in which it is involved: $deg(v) = |\{(u, w) \in E \mid u = v \lor w = v\}|.$*

We exploit this representation in two ways: First, ligands are represented by their *molecular 2D-structure*, with $\mathcal{A}_v$ a subset of atoms, and $\mathcal{A}_e = \{$single covalent bond, double covalent bond, triple covalent bond$\}$. For example, *Pyridin-4-amine* has chemical equation $C_5H_6N_2$ and can be presented as in Fig. 1.

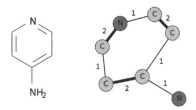

Fig. 1. Example of a molecule 2D representation (left) and its corresponding graph in hydrogen suppressed form (right)

Second, the relationships between ligands, proteins, or between ligands and proteins, are represented as *networks*. These include ligand-ligand (ll) and protein-protein (pp) similarity networks, in which $\mathcal{A}_v$ is the set of ligand/protein identifiers, respectively, and $\mathcal{A}_e = [0, 1]$. The other type of network are interaction networks, both ligand-ligand/protein-protein interaction networks derived from the literature, with $\mathcal{A}_e = \{0, 1\}$, and ligand-protein (lp) interaction networks, which contain two set of vertices V_l, V_p and edges $\forall (u, v) \in E : u \in V_l, v \in V_p$, and $\mathcal{A}_e = \{0, 1\}$ or $\mathcal{A}_e = \mathbb{R}$. The former labeling is usually derived from the latter by thresholding. An example of relationships between ligands and/or proteins as networks is presented in Fig. 2.

Definition 2 *(Connected component). Given a graph G, we call a subgraph $G' = \langle V', E', \lambda_v, \lambda_e \rangle, V' \subseteq V, E' \subseteq E$ a connected component (CC) iff for any two vertices $u, v \in V$, there exists a path $\{(v_1, v_2), \ldots, (v_{m-1}, v_m)\}, v_i \in V, (v_i, v_{i+1}) \in E$, such that $v_1 = u, v_m = v$ and there is no supergraph of G', $G'' = \langle V'', E'', \lambda_v, \lambda_e \rangle, V'' \supset V', E'' \supset E'$ that is a CC.*

Definition 3 *(Multi-layer graph). A multi-layer graph is a tuple $\langle V, E, \lambda_v, \lambda_e \rangle$, with V a set of vertices, E a multi-set of edges, i.e. tuples $(u, v), u, v \in V$. In a multi-layer graph, E can be decomposed into disjunct sets $E_l \subseteq V \times V$, called layers, $E = \bigcup_i E_{l_i}$.*

As becomes clear from this definition, an arbitrary number of networks can be aggregated into a multigraph, as long as there is overlap in their vertex sets. Trivially, even networks with disjunct vertex sets can be aggregated but since such vertices will not have any edges in the graphs from which they are missing, this will probably be of little use.

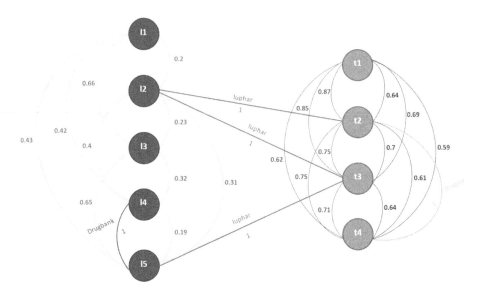

Fig. 2. An example of a multi-layer graph with 6 networks: ligand-protein network is in deep blue (IUPHAR), ligand-ligand networks are in light blue (ligand similarity network) and violet (DrugBank), protein-protein networks are in green (BioGrid), grey (protein similarity network based on substrings) and brown (protein similarity network based on motifs)

Definition 4 *(Motif). Protein motifs are patterns defined using biochemical background knowledge, often expressed in the form of regular expressions.*[1]

Definition 5 *(Tanimoto coefficient). The Tanimoto coefficient of two vectors* $x, y \in \{0,1\}^d$ *is calculated as: coeff$_{Tanimoto}(x, y) = \frac{x \cdot y}{||x||^2 + ||y||^2 - x \cdot y}$.*

2.2   Problem Formulation

The problem setting we address in this paper is one of link prediction between ligands (drug candidates) and proteins (biological targets).

Definition 6 *(Ligand-protein activity prediction). For a given number of ligand-protein activity networks* $G_{lp}^i = \langle V_l \cup V_p, E_i, \lambda_v, \lambda_{e_i} \rangle$, *with* $u \in V_l$ *labeled with ligands identifiers,* $v \in V_p$ *labeled with protein identifiers,* $\forall (u,v) \in E, u \in V_l, v \in V_l$, *and* $\mathcal{A}_e = \{0,1\}$, *ligand-ligand networks* $G_l^i = \langle V_l, E_l^i, \lambda_v, \lambda_{e_l^i} \rangle$, *protein-protein networks* $G_p^i = \langle V_p, E_p^i, \lambda_v, \lambda_{e_p^i} \rangle$ *and a given* $(u,v) \notin E, u \in V_l, v \in V_p$ *predict, whether* $\lambda_e((u,v)) = 1$.

We limit ourselves to the relatively easier task of predicting whether there is activity or not, leaving the prediction of its *strength* as future work.

---

[1] An open-access database is available at http://prosite.expasy.org.

3   Related Work

The literature on compound-target activity prediction, even using networks, is too vast to discuss here. We therefore present a number of works illustrating the characteristics we discussed in the introduction. Ligand-protein activity, the use case we explore here, has been addressed in [13], which selects a ligand and target similarity measure each, and multiplies activity vectors of known ligands/targets with the similarity to new ligands/targets to derive predictions. In [14], the same group used ligand structural and pharmacological similarity, as well as genetic protein similarity, mapped ligands and targets into a shared feature space and predicted activity. The authors of [3] used three networks: ligand-ligand similarity, target-target similarity, ligand-target activity, evaluated four ligand similarity measures, settling on Tanimoto distance. The proposed method, NWNBI, exploits similarity weights and log-values of activity measurements to perform four-step network traversals. In [2], ligand similarity is calculated as weighted average of *two* similarity measures, and combined with a target similarity, and the interaction network into a three-layer network, which they refer to as "heterogeneous". They simulate random walk with restart by matrix multiplication, and show that only using a single similarity measure or ignoring the interaction network deteriorates results. Three networks are also used in [7], the authors discuss different options for similarity measures, and perform low-rank matrix factorization on the adjacency/similarity matrices. They address sparsity by giving non-existing links a small non-negative weight. Ligand-protein activity is also the subject of [1], which exploits the three-layer network to perform weighted nearest-neighbor classification. Gene-disease interactions have been considered in [12], using three layers, simulating random walk by matrix multiplication, using different numbers of steps for the two similarity networks. Using a similar bi-random walk idea, [9] consider microRNA-disease interactions, exploiting a three-layer network. The random walk with restart in [8] is symmetric (and functionally the same as in [2]), with the similarity networks constructed by averaging two similarity measures. They evaluate different parameter settings.

4   Exploring a Multi-layer Graph

As the preceding section shows, the standard setting employed consists of three networks, and to adhere to this setting, authors either choose a single similarity measure empirically, or combine similarity measures via user-specified weights. Instead, we propose to combine all available networks into a multi-graph having more than three layers. Once we have such a network, the question is how to exploit it, however, and here we hew close to the literature.

4.1   The Random Walk Model

A long-established method for exploring a network is the random walk [10], which proceeds roughly as follows: starting from a randomly selected node, it performs walks along edges of the graph at random. In every step, the edge to follow is chosen uniformly from all outgoing links (in the case of an unweighted graph) or proportional to link weights (in the case of a weighted graph). Node importance is based on how frequently the walker visits the node: a node with higher frequency is considered more important than a node with a low value (Fig. 3). This idea can be modified in a number of ways to improve network exploration: the walker can be constrained to perform at most *max_steps* steps, to not visit any of the last c vertices it encountered, or with small probability $1 - \beta$ the process can be restarted at any time to avoid getting trapped by those vertices it mustn't visit. The product of the probabilities of edges the walker traversed gives the cumulative probability of a path between two nodes and can be used to *predict* a link between a starting node and an end node: if the path probability is greater than a given threshold, a new edge is predicted.

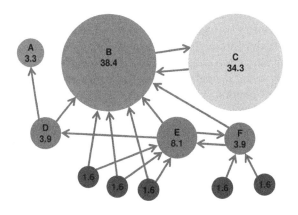

Fig. 3. Nodes importance example in a graph, taken from [6]

To extend this approach to multi-layer graphs, one needs to add how to choose the layer to walk in. We propose to select a network uniformly at random from the set of networks, and multiply the path strength by $\frac{1}{|\{G_l^i\}|+|\{G_p^j\}|+|\{G_{lp}^k\}|}$. Repeat the process until a user-defined target vertex is reached or the maximum number of steps have been performed. Due to the randomized nature, random walks are usually repeated several times to derive more robust estimates.

4.2   Network-Based Random Walk on Multi-layer Network

Instead of explicitly random walking as described above, random walks are often simulated via matrix multiplication of transition matrices. This is notably the approach proposed in [2], abbreviated as NRWRH. They define a transition matrix $M = \begin{bmatrix} M_{pp} & M_{pl} \\ M_{lp} & M_{ll} \end{bmatrix}$, in the manner described above, i.e. uniform probabilities for lp/pl-transitions, proportional probabilities for similarities, with an additional user-specified parameter $\lambda \in [0, 1]$ affecting moves from ligands to proteins and vice versa. Given a ligand l_i, a starting vector $v_0 \in [0,1]^{|V_l|+|V_p|}$ is initialized with 1 at the position for $v \in V_l, \lambda_v(v) = l_i, \frac{1}{|\{(v,u) \in E_{l_p}\}|}$ at the positions for the proteins linked to it, 0 otherwise. Protein entries in v_0 are multiplied with $1 - \eta$, ligand entries with η, a user-defined parameter to bias the walk towards proteins ($\eta < 0.5$), or ligands ($\eta > 0.5$). The vector representing the probabilities that a walker starting with l_i finds itself in any of the nodes is calculated iteratively as $p_{t+1} = (1-\beta)M^T p_t + \beta p_0$ until $|p_{t+1} - p_t| < 10^{-10}$. This can be understood as the random walker walking "in all directions at the same time". The approach can be considered a simplified version of Personalized PageRank [5], simplified because edges are undirected and there is only a single starting vertex. Removing the starting vertices from the final state vector, and ranking entries gives predicted edges. We adapt this approach to a setting with $|\{G_l^i\}| + |\{G_p^j\}| + |\{G_{lp}^k\}| \geq 3$. While the algorithm stays essentially the same, we decompose the transition matrix into a matrix M for within-network/layer transitions, and a matrix N for between-network/layer transitions. We also do away with the user-dependent λ. Explicitly creating M in the manner shown above is easy for three layers but becomes much harder when different numbers can be involved. We hence con-

$$\text{struct } M = \begin{bmatrix} M_{G_p} & 0 & 0 \\ 0 & M_{G_l} & 0 \\ 0 & 0 & M_{G_{lp}} \end{bmatrix}, \text{ with } M_{G_p} = \begin{bmatrix} M_{G_p}^1 & 0 & \cdots & 0 \\ 0 & M_{G_p}^2 & \cdots & 0 \\ 0 & 0 & \cdots & M_{G_p}^{|\{G_p^i\}|} \end{bmatrix} \text{ derived}$$

from protein-protein similarity networks (M_{G_l}, $M_{G_{lp}}$ accordingly). The tran-

$$\text{sition matrix } N = \begin{bmatrix} N_{G_p^1 \to G_p^1} & N_{G_p^2 \to G_p^1} & \cdots & N_{G_{lp}^i \to G_p^1} \\ \cdots & \cdots & \cdots & \cdots \\ N_{G_p^1 \to G_{lp}^i} & N_{G_p^2 \to G_{lp}^i} & \cdots & N_{G_{lp}^i \to G_{lp}^i} \end{bmatrix} \text{ explicitly models}$$

possible layer transitions, with 1s on the main diagonal of a submatrix $N_{G_j \to G_i}$ for all nodes present in both layers, 0s otherwise. Note that this means that transition matrixes from ligand to protein layers (and vice versa) have zeros everywhere including the main diagonal. The initial state vector v_0 has dimensionality ($|V_p| \cdot |\{G_{p_i}\}| + |V_l| \cdot |\{G_{l_i}\}| + |V_l \cup V_p| \cdot |\{G_{lp_i}\}|$) with entries for *all* vertices in *all* layers. It is initialized by setting the entry for the starting ligand and each linked protein to 1 in every network they are present. Matrices and state vectors are column-normalized – the entries of a column must sum to 1.

Our algorithm, NEtWork-basEd Random walk on MultI-layered NEtwork (NEWERMINE), is summarized in Algorithm 1. $(M_{norm}N)_{norm}$ can be precomputed, giving us a matrix that is functionally equivalent to M as defined in NRWRH, and used on every iteration of NEWERMINE to save computation time. At the end, v_{final} needs to be summarized by summing up for each vertex all corresponding entries, leading to a vector with dimensionality $|V_l \cup V_p|$ from which the edge ranking can be derived.

5   Experimental Evaluation

In order to allow reproducibility of our work, we evaluated our approach on publicly available data. In this part we provide a description of the data used

---

Algorithm 1: The NEWERMINE algorithm

Input   : adjacency matrix M, transition matrix N, *starting_vertex*,
          max_steps, η, β, *max_diff*
Output: Probability scores v_{final}
$V_{0_l} \leftarrow$ initialize *starting_vertex*
$V_{0_p} \leftarrow$ initialize targets for which an interaction with *starting_vertex* is known
$V_0 \leftarrow (1 - \eta) \cdot V_{0_l\,norm} + \eta \cdot V_{0_p\,norm}$
step $\leftarrow 0$
repeat
    | *step* $\leftarrow$ *step* $+ 1$
    | $V_{step} \leftarrow \beta \cdot (M_{norm} N)_{norm} V_{step-1} + (1 - \beta) \cdot V_0$
until $(|v_{step} - v_{step-1}| \leq$ *max_diff*$) \vee ($*step* $>$ *max_steps*$)$
return v_{step}

---

and the details of the experimental protocol. This is followed by the results and the discussion.

5.1   Experimental Settings

Datasets. In total we have used 4 datasets:

1. IUPHAR – an open-access database of ligands, biological targets and their interactions. We used version 2017.5 (released on 22/08/2017). The full dataset has 8978 ligands, 2987 proteins, and 17198 interactions (edges) between them[2]. In order to satisfy the designed setting conditions, we removed duplicate interactions (based on different affinity measures), leaving 12456 interactions in total. For existing interactions, we label an edge with 1 if the negative logarithm of the affinity measure is ≥ 5, non-interacting otherwise.[3] We treat all affinity measures available in the data (pKi, pIC50, pEC50, pKd, pA2, pKB) as equivalent.
2. DrugBank (DB) – an open-access database of drug-drug interactions. We used version 5.0.11 (released 20-12-2017). It has 658079 interactions of 3138 distinct drugs. 242922 of these interactions involve 1254 distinct ligands that are present in IUPHAR. The database was also used as a source of 2D representations of ligands to compute ligand similarities.
3. BioGrid (BG) – an open-access database of protein-protein interactions mined from a corpus of biomedical literature. We used version 3.4.154 (25/10/2017). It has 1482649 interactions of 67372 distinct proteins. Only 15410 of these interactions involve proteins present in IUPHAR (1925 distinct proteins).
4. NCBI Protein database – The National Center for Biotechnology Information proteins database[4] was used to obtain amino acids sequences to represent targets. The data was parsed from the website of NCBI and mapped to IUPHAR

---

[2] in ligands.csv, interactions.csv, and targets_and_families.csv, respectively.

[3] Cutoff proposed by researchers from CERMN (http://cermn.unicaen.fr).

[4] https://www.ncbi.nlm.nih.gov/protein/.

Table 1. Data set and network characteristics

Data set	Entities	Relations	Sparsity	Network			
				Vertices	Edges	Sparsity	CC
IUPHAR	11965	12456	0.00017	11965	12456	0.00017	443
DrugBank	3138	658079	0.1337	1254	122808	0.15631	1
BioGrid	67372	1482649	0.00065	1898	8658	0.0048	11
Ligand similarity	6821	23259610	1	6821	23259610	1	1
NCBI	1818	1651653	1	1818	1651653	1	1

using the RefSeq attribute (human protein sequence identifier) available in IUPHAR. The database was accessed 20/12/2017.

Ligands were mapped between networks by numerical identifiers provided by IUPHAR as well as by INN (International Non-proprietary Name) and Common name attributes. Proteins were mapped by IUPHAR identifiers as well as by Human Entrez Gene attribute.[5] In total we have built 6 networks:

1. a drug interaction network based on DrugBank,
2. a drug similarity network based on similarities calculated using the Tanimoto coefficient on binary vectors constructed by frequent subgraphs,
3. the drug-target interaction network based on IUPHAR,
4. a target interaction network based on BioGrid, and
5. two target similarity networks calculated using the Tanimoto coefficient on feature vectors constructed by *frequent substrings* and *Prosite motifs*.

Similarity networks' edges were labeled with labels $\in [0, 1]$, interaction networks with labels $\in \{0, 1\}$. Table 1 shows the characteristics of the data sets, and of the networks we derived from them. It is noticeable how sparse the data is, and also how this sparsity translates into disconnected parts of the network. Sparsity might result in a low performance of the traditional recommender systems approaches, while disconnected networks are challenging for random walker approaches.

Evaluation Protocol. To evaluate our approach, we used leave-one-out cross-validation: for each of the 12456 edges in the IUPHAR network, we remove it from the network, set the ligand as starting vertex, infer strengths for all possible ligand-target paths, remove ligand-target edges contained in the training data, and check whether the removed edge is found in the top-20 remaining paths[6] according to their strengths. If this is the case for an interacting edge, we consider it a *true positive*, otherwise a *false negative*. For negative examples, the relationship is inverse.

---

[5] Global Query Cross-Database Search System gene identifiers: https://www.ncbi. nlm.nih.gov/gene.

[6] Precision at 20.

Quality Measures. To evaluate our methods we use several performance measures:

- Accuracy: the ratio of true positives (TP) – drug-target links correctly classified as positives – and true negatives (TN) – drug-target links correctly classified as negatives – over all predictions: $Acc = \frac{TP+TN}{TP+FP+TN+FN}$.
- Area under receiver operating curve (AUC): evaluates whether true positives are usually ranked above or below false positives when sorting predictions by confidence.
- Precision: the ratio of TP over all drug-target links classified as positives: $Prec = \frac{TP}{TP+FP}$. Precision measures whether a model is specific enough to mainly classify links of the positive class as positive. This gives additional insight into the accuracy score.
- Recall: the ratio of TP over all positive links in the test data: $Rec = \frac{TP}{TP+FN}$. Recall measures whether a model is general enough to classify a large proportion of the positive class as positive.

In addition to this, we also report weighted versions of accuracy, precision, and recall that give us a more accurate assessment for unbalanced datasets. Due to the fact that the number of negative examples are smaller than that of the positives in our data, we assign a classification cost of 1 to positives and cost neg_cost to negatives, derived by: $neg\_cost = \frac{|D|}{2 \times |N|}$, where $|D|$ – number of examples, $|N|$ – number of negative examples. We then perform evaluation based on the costs defined: FN and TN receive score neg_cost for every negative example w.r.t. its real class, while FP and TP receives score 1 for positives.

Implementation. We implemented NEWERMINE in Python[7]. We used the networkx library to model the multi-layer network, the NumPy library to perform all matrix computations and the sklearn library for cost-based evaluation.

5.2   Experimental Results

Using Three-Layer Graphs. We first use NEWERMINE on a number of multigraphs aggregated from three networks each, the ligand-target network, one ligand-ligand network, and one target-target network. This is the setting used in the papers discussed in Sect. 3.

For the experiments we defined 6 possible combinations with IUPHAR, only ligand-target interaction network we have: (1) DrugBank + BioGrid, (2) DrugBank + Target similarity (TS) (substrings:str), (3) DrugBank + TS (motifs:mot), (4) Ligand similarity (LS) + BioGrid, (5) LS + TS (str), (6) LS + TS (mot). The basic properties of the combinations compared to the full graph are presented in Table 2. The results of the use of NEWERMINE with parameters $\eta = 0.2$, $\beta = 0.7$ (taken from [2]) are presented in Fig. 4. This is a rather conservative setting, equivalent to relatively few steps before the walker restarts.

---

[7] https://zimmermanna.users.greyc.fr/supplementary-material.html.

Table 2. Basic properties of different combinations of networks

Combination	Ligands	Targets	$|V|$	$|E|$	Sparsity	CC
DB + BG	7025	2307	9332	143922	0.003	87
DB + TS (str)	7025	2101	9126	1786917	0.042	103
DB + TS (mot)	7025	2101	9126	1786917	0.042	103
LS + BG	8056	2307	10363	23280724	0.434	21
LS + TS (str)	8056	2101	10157	24923719	0.4832	22
LS + TS (mot)	8056	2101	10157	24923719	0.4832	22
Six layers	8137	2502	10639	26706838	0.4719	1

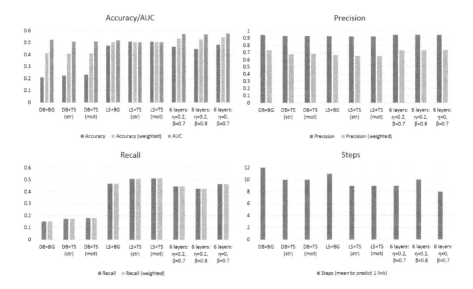

Fig. 4. Evaluation results of NEWERMINE for different combinations of three networks and the six-layer graph

The number of vertices in different networks depend on available IDs and structural information. In any case, the networks are sparse and they are not fully connected. Using similarity networks alleviates this situation somewhat and combining *all* networks leads to a single connected component (bottom row).

Figure 4 shows that using different three-layer graphs leads to rather different results. The arguably most notable result is that using ligand structural similarity instead of DrugBank network significantly improves accuracy and recall.

Using the Full, Six-Layer Graph. The results for NEWERMINE on the full multi-layer graph are also presented in the Fig. 4. We show additional values for η and β: $\eta = 0$ strongly biases the walk towards targets, we also consider $\beta = 0.8$

for $\eta = 0.2$. Using more layers decreases recall somewhat, but improves weighted accuracy (taking the lower proportion of negative examples into account), AUC score and precision. Different parameter values do not have a large effect on the results but change running times: increasing β also increases the number of steps necessary for convergence, and decreasing η decreases this number.

6   Conclusion and Perspectives

We have presented an approach for exploiting an arbitrary number of networks combined into a multi-layer network, proposing general matrix formulations to form intra- and inter-network transitions.

As we have demonstrated experimentally, combining different networks improves vertex reachability and therefore interaction prediction. So far, we have only exploited more than one protein similarity network, already achieving very good results. In future work, we intend to also integrate different ligand similarity semantics, and different databases indicating ligand-protein activity. Additionally, we intend to employ our approach for different target settings, e.g. for miRNG-disease links. Finally, we aim to move from the "active"/"inactive" setting to one where we predict the strength of the activity.

References

1. Buza, K., Peska, L.: ALADIN: a new approach for drug–target interaction prediction. In: Ceci, M., Hollmén, J., Todorovski, L., Vens, C., Džeroski, S. (eds.) ECML PKDD 2017. LNCS (LNAI), vol. 10535, pp. 322–337. Springer, Cham (2017). https://doi.org/10.1007/978-3-319-71246-8_20
2. Chen, X., Liu, M.X., Yan, G.Y.: Drug-target interaction prediction by random walk on the heterogeneous network. Mol. BioSyst. **8**(7), 1970–1978 (2012)
3. Cheng, F., Zhou, Y., Li, W., Liu, G., Tang, Y.: Prediction of chemical-protein interactions network with weighted network-based inference method. PloS One **7**(7), e41064 (2012)
4. Hattori, M., Okuno, Y., Goto, S., Kanehisa, M.: Development of a chemical structure comparison method for integrated analysis of chemical and genomic information in the metabolic pathways. JACS **125**(39), 11853–11865 (2003)
5. Haveliwala, T.H.: Topic-sensitive pagerank: a context-sensitive ranking algorithm for web search. TKDE **15**(4), 784–796 (2003)
6. Leskovec, J., Rajaraman, A., Ullman, J.D.: Mining of Massive Datasets. Cambridge University Press, Cambridge (2014)
7. Lim, H., Gray, P., Xie, L., Poleksic, A.: Improved genome-scale multi-target virtual screening via a novel collaborative filtering approach to cold-start problem. Sci. Rep. **6**, 38860 (2016)
8. Liu, Y., Zeng, X., He, Z., Zou, Q.: Inferring microrna-disease associations by random walk on a heterogeneous network with multiple data sources. TCBB **14**(4), 905–915 (2017)
9. Luo, J., Xiao, Q.: A novel approach for predicting microrna-disease associations by unbalanced bi-random walk on heterogeneous network. J. Biomed. Inform. **66**, 194–203 (2017)

10. Pearson, K.: The problem of the random walk. Nature **72**(1867), 342 (1905)
11. Smith, T., Waterman, M.: Identification of common molecular subsequences. Mol. Biol. **147**, 195–197 (1981)
12. Xie, M., Hwang, T., Kuang, R.: Prioritizing disease genes by bi-random walk. In: Tan, P.-N., Chawla, S., Ho, C.K., Bailey, J. (eds.) PAKDD 2012. LNCS (LNAI), vol. 7302, pp. 292–303. Springer, Heidelberg (2012). https://doi.org/10.1007/978-3-642-30220-6_25
13. Yamanishi, Y., Araki, M., Gutteridge, A., Honda, W., Kanehisa, M.: Prediction of drug-target interaction networks from the integration of chemical and genomic spaces. Bioinformatics **24**(13), i232–i240 (2008)
14. Yamanishi, Y., Kotera, M., Kanehisa, M., Goto, S.: Drug-target interaction prediction from chemical, genomic and pharmacological data in an integrated framework. Bioinformatics **26**(12), i246–i254 (2010)

A Hierarchical Ornstein-Uhlenbeck Model for Stochastic Time Series Analysis

Ville Laitinen$^{(\boxtimes)}$ ⓘ and Leo Lahti ⓘ

Department of Mathematics and Statistics, University of Turku, Turku, Finland
velait@utu.fi

Abstract. Longitudinal data is ubiquitous in research, and often complemented by broad collections of static background information. There is, however, a shortage of general-purpose statistical tools for studying the temporal dynamics of complex and stochastic dynamical systems especially when data is scarce, and the underlying mechanisms that generate the observation are poorly understood. Contemporary microbiome research provides a topical example, where vast cross-sectional and longitudinal collections of taxonomic profiling data from the human body and other environments are now being collected in various research laboratories world-wide. Many classical algorithms rely on long and densely sampled time series, whereas human microbiome studies typically have more limited sample sizes, short time spans, sparse sampling intervals, lack of replicates and high levels of unaccounted technical and biological variation. We demonstrate how non-parametric models can help to quantify key properties of a dynamical system when the actual data-generating mechanisms are largely unknown. Such properties include the locations of stable states, resilience of the system, and the levels of stochastic fluctuations. Moreover, we show how limited data availability can be compensated by pooling statistical evidence across multiple individuals or studies, and by incorporating prior information in the models. In particular, we derive and implement a hierarchical Bayesian variant of Ornstein-Uhlenbeck driven t-processes. This can be used to characterize universal dynamics in univariate, unimodal, and mean reversible systems based on multiple short time series. We validate the model with simulated data and investigate its applicability in characterizing temporal dynamics of human gut microbiome.

Keywords: Longitudinal analysis · Hierarchical models ·
Ornstein-Uhlenbeck process · Resilience · Stochastic processes

1 Introduction

Many natural and social systems are complex and cannot be studied in isolation. The underlying data-generating mechanisms are often largely unknown in such cases, and the observed dynamics can be characterized only indirectly [8]. Non-parametric models that focus on characterizing observed data properties, rather

© Springer Nature Switzerland AG 2018
W. Duivesteijn et al. (Eds.): IDA 2018, LNCS 11191, pp. 188–199, 2018.
https://doi.org/10.1007/978-3-030-01768-2_16

than modeling the underlying mechanisms, can provide valuable information on the system behavior. In the context of human microbiome dynamics, for instance, such non-parametric models have been used to describe and infer the presence of alternative ecosystem states [13], periodicity, stochasticity, and chaos [5,6]. In many real applications, the data is scarce, and new methods are needed in order to derive maximal information from limited observations.

Our study is motivated by the analysis of temporal dynamics of human gut microbiome. This refers to the totality of microbial communities living on skin, gastrointestinal tract and other body sites. Contemporary human microbiome research has largely focused on cross-sectional cohorts with limited follow-ups, providing information on the composition and inter-individual variation of the microbiome. The dynamics of these systems are yet, however, not well understood despite their clinical importance [1,10]. As understanding of these systems is accumulating, the research focus is beginning to shift from general descriptions towards actionable clinical applications and manipulation.

In this work, we show how key dynamical properties of poorly understood dynamical systems can be inferred from limited time series by pooling information can across multiple individuals. In the present work, we focus specifically on mean-reversible stochastic processes. Such dynamic behavior is frequently observed in the human gut microbiome. Many bacterial species in the human gut ecosystem have been reported to exhibit characteristic abundance levels around which they tend to fluctuate over time (see e.g. [13]). It has been reported that the average abundance levels of many gut bacteria remain relatively stable over long time periods but on a shorter (daily) time scale the abundances can exhibit considerable fluctuations [3]. Mean-reverting stochastic processes, in particular the Ornstein-Uhlenbeck (OU) process, provide well-established means to characterize key properties of such systems, including the location and resilience of the potential wells, speed of mean reversion, and volatility of abundance levels, even when the underlying mechanisms regulating those dynamics are unknown. Stochastic processes and generative probabilistic models provide a rigorous framework for the characterization of the observed dynamics in such cases, with wide applicability across different application domains [9,11,16,18].

We adapt and apply these techniques to model human gut microbiome dynamics. A key practical limitation of the existing methods in our application is that the available implementations of the OU process depend on the availability of long time series with dozens of time points or more. The currently available longitudinal data sets in typical human microbiome studies have more limited sample sizes and time series lengths, or sparse sampling intervals. Combined with high levels of variation and limited knowledge of the data-generating processes, these limitations form considerable challenges for the application of previously established stochastic models, such as the the OU process, in contemporary human microbiome research. In order to address these limitations, we derive, implement, and validate a hierarchical extension to the OU process. This can be used to recover key information of the system dynamics from limited data by aggregating information across short time series from multiple individuals. Further potential advantages of the probabilistic formulation include the opportunities to model individual variation, and to incorporate of prior information from the cross-sectional background collections in the model. We validate the implementation with simulated data, investigate its robustness to varying modeling assumptions including the numbers, lengths and densities of the time series, and ranges of parameter values, and finally explore the applicability of this model on topical human gut microbiome data sets.

In order to maximize the flexibility we have constructed the implementation so that the number of observation per time series and the observation times do not have to be identical. Thus, our implementation of the OU process provides a rigorous and justified method for modeling dynamics of single potential wells.

2   Preliminaries

This section outlines the statistical model and the relevant technical derivations.

2.1   The Ornstein-Uhlenbeck Process

Many natural processes can be modeled by a combination of deterministic drift and stochastic fluctuations. These assumptions naturally lead to stochastic differential equations, which are commonly encountered in literature in the form:

$$dX_t = f(X, t)dt + L(X, t)dZ_t.$$

Here, X_t is the system state at time t, Z is a stochastic process and f, and L are called the *drift* and *dispersion* terms, respectively. The drift defines the deterministic behavior, whereas dispersion characterizes the stochastic component of the system. Unlike the solutions of ordinary differential equations, the solutions of the stochastic counterparts are non-unique and nowhere differentiable as they are different for different realizations of the noise term. The deterministic solution can be recovered by averaging over these solutions.

The Ornstein-Uhlenbeck (OU) process, also known as the Langevin equation in physics and Vasicek model in finance, is a stochastic process with a wide range of applications [12]. It is frequently used to model systems that have a steady state, and a tendency to recover from perturbations by gradually returning, or drifting, towards the long-term mean value. The OU process is the continuous-time extension of autoregressive AR(1) model and is defined as the solution to the stochastic differential equation with drift function $f(X, t) = \lambda(\mu - X)$ and constant dispersion $L(X, t) = \sigma$. The parameters $\lambda \in [0, 1]$, $\mu \in \mathbb{R}$ and $\sigma \geq 0$ have natural interpretations as mean-reversion rate, long-term mean and size of stochastic fluctuations, respectively. The OU process can be formulated as a Gaussian process on the real line $GP(\mu, K)$ with a covariance function $K = \text{Cov}(X_{t_1}, X_{t_2}) = \frac{\sigma^2}{2\lambda}e^{-\lambda\Delta t}$, and as all diffusion processes, is also a Markov process [12].

2.2   The Ornstein-Uhlenbeck Driven t-Process

We adopt the Student's t-process, instead of the traditionally used Wiener process as the driving process of the OU process. This choice is more robust to outliers and short term volatility, with little if any additional computational cost as the critical analytical equations are available in both cases.

Although the stochastic process in OU process is often modeled as white noise, requiring Z_t to have Gaussian transition density is often a too limiting assumption for practical purposes as it does not allow large enough fluctuations. Thus, robustness against outliers is compromised and a more general process would be preferred [15]. The Student's t-process is a non-Gaussian alternative to a prior over functions that allows more flexibility and room for outliers. Using t-processes is a convenient choice also in the sense that the Gaussian process can be obtained as a special case by taking the limit $\nu \to \infty$ [15]. Thus we will adopt t-processes as the driver of dispersion of the OU process. See Fig. 1 for an example of simulated OU process time series and corresponding parameter estimates. The t-process has recently been studied in e.g. [14,15] and the following definition can be found in these references.

Definition 1. *A vector $\bar{y} \in \mathbb{R}^n$ is multivariate Student-t distributed with ν degrees of freedom, mean parameter μ and shape matrix Σ, $\bar{y} \sim \mathcal{ST}_n(\nu, \mu, \Sigma)$, if it has density*

$$p(\bar{y}) = \frac{\Gamma(\frac{\nu+n}{2})}{((\nu-2)\pi)^{\frac{n}{2}}\Gamma(\frac{\nu}{2})}|\Sigma|^{-\frac{1}{2}} \times \left(1 + \frac{(\bar{y}-\bar{\mu})^T\Sigma^{-1}(\bar{y}-\bar{\mu})}{\nu-2}\right)^{-\frac{\nu+n}{2}} \tag{1}$$

Definition 2. *The process f is a Student-t process, $f \sim \mathcal{ST}(\nu, \mu, \Sigma)$, if any finite set of values is multivariate t-distributed.*

The covariance matrix K is related to the shape matrix via $\Sigma = \frac{\nu-2}{\nu}K$.

2.3   Hierarchical Extension

The model outlined above describes the Ornstein-Uhlenbeck driven t-process as implemented in [9]. Our novel contribution that we present now is to equip the model with hierarchical structure and testing the robustness of the extended implementation. Let $\mathcal{X} = \{\bar{X}_i, i \in \{1, \ldots, N\}\}$ be a set of OU process values, with n_i observations in each, each i representing e.g. a different measurement site. We assume a hierarchical structure for the parameters λ, μ and σ,

$$dX_{j,t} = \lambda_j(\mu_j - X_{j,t})dt + \sigma_j dZ_t,$$

for all $j \in \{1, \ldots, n_i\}$. As the OU process is a Markov process the generative model for the data can be described as in 2. We have implemented the model using the multivariate t-distribution formulation but it is possible to implement the model using transition densities between consecutive observations.

Adding a level of hierarchy to the implementation for a single series can be obtained by modifying the model likelihood in the extended version so that it

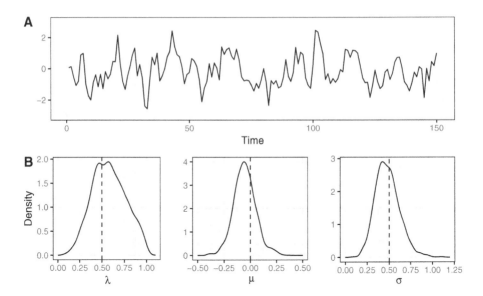

Fig. 1. **A** A simulated OU driven t-process time series with $\nu = 7$ and parameter values $\lambda, \sigma = 0.5$, $\mu = 0$. **B** Posterior estimates of the model parameters. Dashed lines mark the simulation values used to generate the data.

equals the product of likelihoods of individual series. In addition priors have to be assumed to follow some distribution. We have used normal distributions for μ and σ and inverse gamma distribution for λ. Hyperpriors for the hyperparameters ϕ were chosen to be uninformative but still strong enough to guide the parameter estimates to practically reasonable ranges. We can now write the generative model for the hierarchical OU process with partially pooled estimates

$$
\begin{aligned}
X_i &\sim \mathrm{MVT}_n(\nu, \mu_i, \Sigma_i) \\
\mu_i &\sim \mathcal{N}(\mu_{\mu,i}, \sigma_{\mu,i}) \\
\sigma_i &\sim \mathcal{N}(\mu_{\sigma,i}, \sigma_{\sigma,i}) \\
\lambda &\sim \Gamma^{-1}(\alpha_i, \beta_i) \\
\phi &\sim \mathcal{N}(\phi_\mu, \phi_\sigma),
\end{aligned}
\tag{2}
$$

where $i = \{1, \ldots, N\}$ and ϕ represents all hyperpriors.

The model can also be specified so that both the prior shape and hyperparameters are fixed. This version corresponds to no pooling between distinct observations. It does not share information as it assumes that the differences between series are too large to be modeled together. The other extreme is complete pooling in which all data are assumed to be generated by identical parameters. Partial pooling assumes some, but not full, similarity between time series and thus represents a compromise between the other two alternatives. These models are compared in Subsect. 3.1 below.

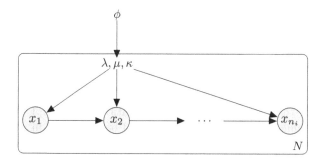

Fig. 2. Bayesian graph representation of the hierarchical OU process. Hyperparameters are denoted with ϕ.

For a general and simplified treatment of the OU process we assumed that our observations are directly generated from the OU process and use uniform time intervals in the following simulations. The model can, however, incorporate unequal time intervals and varying numbers of observations per time series. Alternative models of observation noise represent opportunities for further extension. In ecological studies that motivate the present work, the observation noise is often modeled with a Gaussian or Poisson distribution, where the rate parameter is obtained from the OU process by exponentiation. This so called stochastic Gompertz model is frequently used in ecological time-series analysis [4]. For OU process implementation of the Gompertz model in the context of a single time series, see [9].

3   Model Validation

Next, we tested the implementation with simulation experiments. The simulations were motivated by recent human microbiome studies that are introduced in more detail in Sect. 4. The data sets in these studies have considerable differences in sample sizes and in this respect represent the scope of the currently available human microbiome data.

In the simulations the values for λ, σ and μ were sampled separately for each series from priors $\Gamma^{-1}(6,4)$, $\mathcal{N}(0,1)$ and $\mathcal{N}(3,1)$ respectively. The degrees of freedom in the multivariate Student's t-distribution was set to 7. These distributions and parameter values were chosen as they generate values and variation resembling those encountered in (log-transformed and centered) human gut microbiome time series. Hyperprior distributions for the model parameters were chosen to be vague as no prior understanding of these parameters exists in this context. Normal distributions with relatively large variance were used.

Parameter estimates are obtained by coding the model in rstan [2]. Stan requires the user to specify data, parameters and model in the corresponding code blocks and uses Hamiltonian Monte Carlo and No-U-Turn Sampler techniques to sample from the posterior distribution. To minimize the amount of divergent transitions in HMC sampling we have used a non-centered parameterization for μ and σ. This is in agreement with [17] where it is mentioned that hierarchical models often perform better with non-centered parameterizations, especially when the sample size is limited. Non-centering λ led to additional divergences so its parameterization was kept centered. We encountered no divergences of other pathologies in the MCMC diagnostics, which yields additional confirmation for the validity of our implementation. In principle the degrees of freedom of the multivariate t-distribution could be estimated in addition to the other model parameters. In our experiments we were, however, unable to reliably recover this parameter so the implementation assumes it to be fixed and input to the model. The source code for the Stan model is available at https://github.com/velait/OU_IDA.

3.1   Model Comparison

To demonstrate the differences between the three basic model variants available for multiple observation units (complete, partial and no pooling) we now compare the estimates they provide. We use a single simulated test set with sample size similar to [7]: 30 time series, 30 samples each with 3 time units between observations. The parameter values were sampled from prior distributions individually for each series and parameter.

Maximum a posteriori (MAP) estimates for the parameter λ from each model as well as their distance to simulation values and widths of the 50% interquartile ranges are displayed in 3. The MAP estimates of the partially pooled model are on average closer to the simulation values, although some individual estimates are farther as they get shrunk towards the estimate from completely pooled model (dashed line). The IQRs are shorter compared to the model with no pooling, which yields additional confirmation for the models improved accuracy. Similar results were obtained for the other parameters.

One of the advantages of a hierarchical model with partially pooled parameters is that the prior distributions can be estimated as well. This provides information on the parameters' population level variation. In Fig. 4 the simulation and estimated priors are compared. Prior of μ is recovered best and lambda on a relatively satisfactory level as well. The prior of the variation parameter σ, however, is not very well estimated as the mode and variance are clearly different from the target. The reason for less than ideal estimates may lie in the low number of values simulated in the first place, as only 30 values are drawn from each distribution. Thus there is plenty of room for stochastic variation. Additional uncertainties may arise due to possibly challenging regions in the (λ, σ) space. As these parameters are intertwined it is possible that certain combinations (e.g. small λ, large σ) pose challenges beyond the capabilities of our implementation.

4   Application to Human Microbiome Time Series

Next, we demonstrate the use of these models in analyzing the dynamics of microbial ecosystems in the human body.

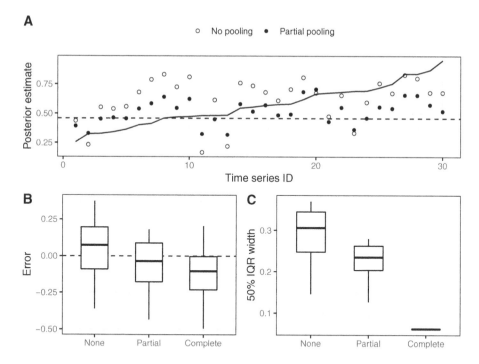

Fig. 3. A MAP estimates from different model variants. Dashed line marks the completely pooled estimate and solid line the simulation values, sorted in increasing order. **B** Distribution of estimates error, defined as difference between MAP and simulation value. **C** Distribution of 50% IQR widths.

In the first case study, two healthy volunteers were followed over a year and provided hundreds of stool samples [3]. During the study the gut ecosystem of one of the individuals experienced a dramatic change in composition due to a *Salmonella* infection. This perturbation is beyond the capacities of the OU process model and for this reason we have limited our analysis to the samples prior to the infection, leaving 125 samples covering 4.5 months for a closer analysis. The sample size in this study is large in the human gut microbiome context, consisting of nearly daily samples from two individuals over several months. In total 387 different genus level taxonomic units were observed out of which we chose to focus on the symmetric and unimodal *abundance types* as their observed dynamics roughly corresponds to the model assumptions. For demonstration purposes, we limit the analysis to a single genus-level taxonomic unit, *Bacteroides*, which is highly abundant and prevalent in human gut at least in the Western populations. We explored the estimates given by our implementation with the first 120 samples and subsets of these to assess how many samples are required for estimates close to the full sample size. Figure 5 A displays the MAP estimates for various samples sizes, where values on the x-axis correspond the first n samples of the full 120 time points. The estimates level after sufficient amounts of time

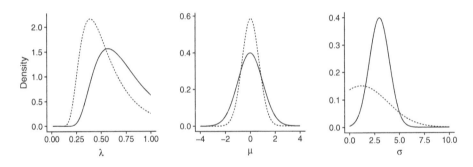

Fig. 4. Prior distributions used for data simulations (solid line) and posterior estimates of these distributions (dashed line) based on MAP estimates of the hyperparameters.

points suggesting that a there is little increase in accuracy after enough samples. We also experimented with randomly removing observations and discovered that roughly half of the samples can be removed without significant loss of accuracy compared to the full sample size, see B.

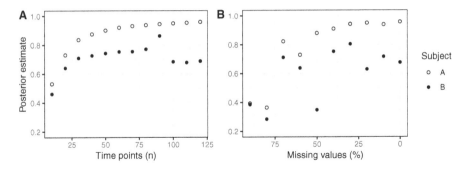

Fig. 5. MAP estimates for parameter λ against length of time series **A** and proportion of randomly removed samples **B**.

We also carried out preliminary analyses on the HITChip Atlas data set [13], which has considerably shorter time series but from a larger number of individuals. The HITChip Atlas data set consists of stool samples from 1006 healthy western adults. Multiple (2–5) follow-up samples were available from 78 subjects with weeks or months between samples. We performed preliminary experiments on this data and data simulated with similar abundance, variation and sparsity profiles but recovered only unreliable and inaccurate results. The posterior estimates had high levels of uncertainty, the model inference had convergence issues, and the results were sensitive to initialization and changes in the data, indicating that the 2–5 sparse time points will not suffice to distinguish the effects of the mean reversion and stochastic drift parameters in the hierarchical OU model.

5   Discussion

The main objective of this work has been to propose new general-purpose methods to characterize key properties of poorly understood dynamical systems based on scarce longitudinal data, and demonstrate their applicability in the topical research area of human microbiome studies.

We have extended the previously proposed Ornstein-Uhlenbeck (OU) driven t-process by deriving hierarchical version, which allows the pooling of information across multiple time series and parameter inference of the shared stochastic process. This is specifically motivated by topical problems in human microbiome research, where time series are often as short as 2–3 time points per individual, but available for a potentially large number of individuals. In such case, the traditional variants of the OU process are not applicable, and a hierarchical extension can potentially help to aggregate information across multiple experiments. We have implemented this model by adding a new level of hierarchy to the standard OU driven t-process [9]. Importantly, we designed the model so that the number of samples and observation times in each time series is flexible, allowing efficient utilization of real time series where the number and timings of the observations may differ across the available time series. This removes the need to impute missing values, or force synchronized observation times, thus facilitating application in many real-life scenarios. Following the work by [9], our model takes advantage of the Student's t-process based version of the OU process, rather than the Wiener process which is more common in the OU process literature, in order to increase robustness for outliers. This comes with little additional computational cost.

In simulation experiments we have demonstrated the advantage of partially pooling the parameters over the variants with complete and no pooling. In addition to increased accuracy the hierarchical OU process model offers information on the population level variation of the model parameters as it learns the prior distribution by estimating the hyperpriors. The model performance was satisfactory when tested on a simulated data set with moderate amounts of samples and series but failed to produce reliable estimates for very sparse and short time series. We anticipate that this failure could be explained by the narrow width of observation intervals compared to the simulated dynamics. Naturally observations need to be sufficiently dense and cover a large enough interval to be able to capture dynamics at of a particular scale. We also demonstrated the use of this model on longitudinal time series from human gut microbiome [3]. These experiments clearly demonstrate how the model parameters converge towards a saturation point with increasing time series lengths and densities. Regarding technicalities of he model fitting, the MCMC sampling converged well, also supporting the validity of the implementation. For a more complete view on the robustness of parameter inference, a more extensive probing of the parameter ranges, alternative priors, observation noise and data with uneven and sparse sampling intervals should be undertaken. Alternative parameterizations should be tested to see if some perform better with higher sample sizes.

The hierarchical OU process provides several promising opportunities for future extensions that are directly applicable to microbial ecological time series. In particular, the standard OU process, which assumes unimodal and symmetrically distributed data, could be generalized to model other abundance types [13] of the human-associated microbial taxa abundance distributions. In particular, the analysis of alternative community states of dynamical systems, frequently observed the human vaginal microbiome[7], for instance, provides interesting challenges for further research and model extensions. Our current implementation of the hierarchical OU process currently only handles time series with unimodal density profiles. Moreover, generalizations of the hierarchical model to the multivariate setting would be valuable. These depend on the development of computationally more efficient implementations, for instance based on variational learning of simulation-based methods. Apart from [9] we are not aware of applications of these models, in particular its hierarchical extension that we develop here, in the context of human microbiome studies.

Whereas the focus in our current analysis is limited to investigating the applicability of the model to readily available real observations from a single taxonomic group, further studies could provide a systematic comparison of the stochastic, mean and drift parameters across different taxonomic units in order to characterize differences in the dynamical variation in the abundance level of various gut bacteria. By classifying the individuals to larger groups based on health status, life style factors, age or other meta data, clinically and biologically interesting connection could be learned. The methodology and the challenges of overcoming the limitations of scarce, noisy, and poorly understood observations that these models help to solve are very generic, and the potential applications naturally reach beyond population dynamics.

Acknowledgments. The work has been partially funded by Academy of Finland (grants 295741, 307127).

References

1. Bashan, A., Gibson, T.E., Friedman, J.: Universality of human microbial dynamics. Nature **534**(7606), 259–262 (2016). https://doi.org/10.1038/nature18301
2. Carpenter, B., Gelman, A., Hoffman, M.D., et al.: Stan: a probabilistic programming language. J. Stat. Softw. **76**, 1–32 (2017). https://doi.org/10.18637/jss.v076.i01
3. David, L.A., Materna, A.C., Friedman, J.: Host lifestyle affects human microbiota on daily timescales. Genome Biol. **15**, R89 (2014). https://doi.org/10.1186/gb-2014-15-7-r89
4. Dennis, B., Ponciano, J.M.: Density dependent state space model for population abundance data with unequal time intervals. Ecology **95**(8), 2069–2076 (2014). https://doi.org/10.1890/13-1486.1
5. Faust, K., Bauchinger, F., Laroche, B., de Buyl, S., Lahti, L.: Signatures of ecological processes in microbial community time series. Microbiome **6**, 120 (2018). https://doi.org/10.1186/s40168-018-0496-2

6. Faust, K., Lahti, L., Gonze, D., de Vos, W.M., Raes, J.: Metagenomics meets time series analysis: unraveling microbial community dynamics. Curr. Opin. Microbiol. **25**(Supplement C), 56–66 (2015). https://doi.org/10.1016/j.mib.2015.04.004
7. Gajer, P., Brotman, R.M., Bai, G., et al.: Temporal dynamics of the human vaginal microbiota. Sci. Transl. Med. **4**(132), 132ra52 (2012). https://doi.org/10.1126/scitranslmed.3003605
8. Gonze, D., Coyte, K.Z., Lahti, L., Faust, K.: Microbial communities as dynamical systems. Curr. Opin. Microbiol. **44**, 41–49 (2018). https://doi.org/10.1016/j.mib.2018.07.004
9. Goodman, A.: Fitting ornstein-uhlenbeck-type student's t-processes in stan with applications for population dynamics data (2018). https://doi.org/10.5281/zenodo.1284346
10. Halfvarson, J., Brislawn, C.J., Lamendella, R.: Dynamics of the human gut microbiome in inflammatory bowel disease. Nat. Microbiol. **2**(5), 17004 (2017). https://doi.org/10.1038/nmicrobiol.2017.4
11. Heinonen, M., Yildiz, C., Mannerström, H., et al.: Learning unknown ODE models with Gaussian processes, March 2018. http://arxiv.org/abs/1803.04303
12. Iacus, S.M.: Simulation and Inference for Stochastic Differential Equations: with R Examples. Springer Series in Statistics, 1st edn. Springer, New York (2008). https://doi.org/10.1007/978-0-387-75839-8
13. Lahti, L., Salojärvi, J., Salonen, A., Scheffer, M., de Vos, W.M.: Tipping elements in the human intestinal ecosystem. Nat. Commun. **5**, 4344 (2014). https://doi.org/10.1038/ncomms5344
14. Shah, A., Wilson, A.G., Ghahramani, Z.: Student-t processes as alternatives to gaussian processes. In: The Seventeenth International Conference on Artificial Intelligence and Statistics (AISTATS) (2014)
15. Solin, A., Särkkä, S.: State space methods for efficient inference in student-t process regression. In: Proceedings of the 18th International Conference on Artificial Intelligence and Statistics (AISTATS) 38 (2015)
16. Srokowski, T.: Multiplicative levy noise in bistable systems. Eur. Phys. J. B **85**(2), 65 (2012). https://doi.org/10.1140/epjb/e2012-30003-9
17. Stan Development Team: modeling language user's guide and reference manual, version 2.17.0 (2017). http://mc-stan.org
18. Yildiz, C., Heinonen, M., Intosalmi, J., et al.: Learning stochastic differential equations with gaussian processes without gradient matching, July 2018. http://arxiv.org/abs/1807.05748

Analysing the Footprint of Classifiers in Overlapped and Imbalanced Contexts

Marta Mercier[1], Miriam S. Santos[1], Pedro H. Abreu[1(✉)], Carlos Soares[2],
Jastin P. Soares[1], and João Santos[3]

[1] CISUC, Department of Informatics Engineering, University of Coimbra, Coimbra,
Portugal
{mmercier, miriams, jastinps}@student.dei.uc.pt, pha@dei.uc.pt
[2] INESC TEC, Faculty of Engineering, University of Porto, Porto, Portugal
csoares@fe.up.pt
[3] IPO-Porto Research Centre (CI-IPOP), Porto, Portugal
joao.santos@ipoporto.min-saude.pt

Abstract. It is recognised that the imbalanced data problem is aggravated by other difficulty factors, such as class overlap. Over the years, several research works have focused on this problematic, although presenting two major hitches: the limitation of test domains and the lack of a formulation of the overlap degree, which makes results hard to generalise. This work studies the performance degradation of classifiers with distinct learning biases in overlap and imbalanced contexts, focusing on the characteristics of the test domains (shape, dimensionality and imbalance ratio) and on to what extent our proposed overlapping measure (*degOver*) is aligned with the performance results observed. Our results show that MLP and CART classifiers are the most robust to high levels of class overlap, even for complex domains, and that KNN and linear SVM are the most aligned with *degOver*. Furthermore, we found that the dimensionality of data also plays an important role in explaining performance results.

Keywords: Imbalanced data · Class overlap · Machine learning classifiers

1 Introduction

Data imbalance occurs when there is a considerable difference between the class priors of a given problem and, for a binary classification scenario, is commonly described by the Imbalance Ratio, IR $= \frac{n_{maj}}{n_{min}}$, where n_{maj} and n_{min} represent the number of majority and minority examples in the domain [2]. Prediction models built from imbalanced datasets are most often biased towards the

This article is a result of the project NORTE-01-0145-FEDER-000027, supported by Norte Portugal Regional Operational Programme (NORTE 2020), under the POR-TUGAL 2020 Partnership Agreement, through the European Regional Development Fund (ERDF).

© Springer Nature Switzerland AG 2018
W. Duivesteijn et al. (Eds.): IDA 2018, LNCS 11191, pp. 200–212, 2018.
https://doi.org/10.1007/978-3-030-01768-2_17

majority concept [9], which is especially critical when there is a higher cost of misclassifying the minority examples, such as diagnosing rare diseases, preventing fraud or detecting faulty systems [4,14]. However, data imbalance is not the sole factor that affects the performance of classifiers. As stated in recent literature, there are several others that combined with data imbalance, create a rather chaotic setting [12]. These are frequently referred to as *data difficulty factors* and commonly include: class overlap, small data set size/lack of density, the presence of small disjuncts and the existence of different types of minority examples (e.g. safe, borderline, rare and outlier examples) [16].

The problem of class overlap in imbalanced domains has been previously discussed in related work, although not with the required depth. The main objective of related work is to show that class imbalance is not the sole factor that affects classification performance, and that overlap plays an important role as well. However, authors often fail to provide some insights on how both problems act together and affect well-established classifiers, and to what extent one problem is more critical than the other for different learning biases. Furthermore, related work is also limited in the following aspects:

- **Definition of overlapping degree:** Some authors define the overlapping degree as a distance between minority and majority classes [3,10,13], which is only appropriate for specific data structures/shapes, while others define it as an intersection region of the majority and minority class, although without presenting a clear formulae to the define the degree of overlapping [5–7]. Other authors approximate the overlapping degree by considering the overlap of individual features (e.g. Fisher Discriminant Ratio – F1 measure) [11] or by identifying minority borderline examples [12,15], which may not completely capture the overall overlapping of the domains.
- **Tested domains:** Most research works consider artificial domains where the data structure is limited and unlikely to be found in real-world scenarios [5–7], besides being limited to two to five dimensions [3,13]. Others consider more complex shapes (e.g. linear versus non-linear shapes), however, limited to a two-dimensional space [12,15].
- **Nature of data and classifiers:** In the majority of works, only one or two/three classifiers are tested. The research of García et al. [5–7] is an exception, where different inductive biases are discussed, and it is possible to distinguish the behaviour of local versus global classifiers, although not in depth. Furthermore, performance results are most often discussed from a general perspective, rather than attending to the characteristics of the tested domains.

We have replicated several imbalanced scenarios with different characteristics found in related work and compare them altogether. These scenarios are generated for different degrees of imbalance and overlap, and the performance of standard classifiers is analysed. We also put an effort to fill in the gaps in related work by defining and evaluating a measure of the overlapping degree (*degOver*), considering artificial domains with different shapes and dimensionality (2–40 dimensions). Our experiments are focused on studying the behaviour of classifiers with distinct learning biases to determine whether some are more affected than others. This study is furthermore taken from different perspectives: focusing on the properties of the tested domains (shape and dimensionality), and focusing on to what extent the proposed overlapping measure is aligned with the performance results of the studied classifiers.

2   Related Work

The work of Prati et al. was one of the first studies on the impact of overlap in imbalanced domains [13]. Their domains consisted of two 5-dimensional clusters (Fig. 1a), where the distribution of minority and majority examples, as well as the distance between cluster centroids, could be changed (1–9 standard deviations). The classification results (C4.5) showed that the influence of the degree of imbalance becomes weaker as the distance between centroids increases.

García et al. [7] performed a similar experiment with 2-dimensional domains, where the majority and minority classes start well-separated and, for a fixed IR, the majority class moves towards the minority class, increasing the amount of overlap (Fig. 1b). Similarly to Prati et al. [13], authors concluded that the increasing overlap deteriorated the performance of classifiers. In a later work [5], authors distinguish between typical and atypical domains (Figs. 1b/d and c, respectively).

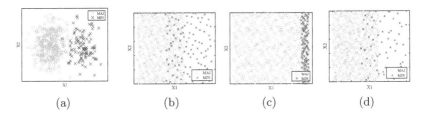

(a)   (b)   (c)   (d)

Fig. 1. Artificial domains generated by Prati et al. [13] (a) and García et al. [7] (b–d).

Authors found that for typical domains, classifiers with a local nature (e.g. KNN) were more subjected to loss in performance for the majority class than classifiers with a more global learning. Regarding atypical domains, the classification results suggested that the recognition rate of the minority class improved as the minority class became denser. Denil and Trappenberg [3] also studied the joint-effect of class imbalance and overlap: they generated two-dimensional domains where both the class overlap and class imbalance could be changed. Their analysis was focused on the performance of SVM, showing that as the training size increases, the influence of class imbalance is negligible and that overlap is the main responsible for performance degradation.

The research of Luengo et al. [11] was not focused on the effects of class imbalance and overlap, although authors found that one measure of overlap between classes (F1 measure) proved to be informative of good/bad behaviour of classifiers.

Finally, we refer to the line of research of Napierala and Stefanowski [12,15], where class overlap is defined via the percentage of borderline minority examples. Napierala and Stefanowski studied the influence of disturbing minority class borders in three different 2-dimensional domains with different characteristics, *paw*, *clover* and *subclus*, (Fig. 2) and concluded that increasingly adding borderline examples degraded the classification performance [12].

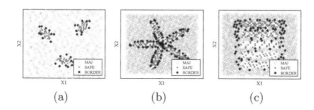

Fig. 2. Artificial domains generated according to Napierala and Stefanowski [12,15].

As stated in the Introduction, a common limitation of related work is in the way class overlap is measured. In the research work of Prati et al. [13], increasing the distance between cluster centroids guarantees that the overlap is being reduced, although it is not possible to quantify the exact degree of overlap in each configuration. In García et al. [5–7], authors generate an artificial domain represented by a square of length 100 where both classes are defined uniformly in a rectangle of 50 × 100 (typical domain). The IR was fixed to 4:1, while the overlapping degree was controlled through the distance between the square centres. Initially, the majority and minority squares start well separated by a line orthogonal to $X1$ axis, and increasing amounts of class overlap are produced by moving the majority square towards the minority square in a stepwise manner: [0..50], [10..60], [20..70], [30..80], [40..90] and [50..100] for 0, 20, 40, 60, 80 and 100% overlap. Let us consider the example given in Fig. 1b, for a typical domain with IR 4:1 and 40% overlap. Since no formulae is presented in the original papers [5–7], we may assume that the calculation of the overlap degree was performed as a fraction of the area that is overlapped (A_{inter}) over the total minority area (A_{min}) (or majority area, since they are equal). In that way we would obtain $overlap = \frac{A_{inter}}{A_{min}} = \frac{2000}{5000} = 40\%$. If the IR was defined arbitrarily, then Fig. 1d, with an IR of 8:1, would also illustrate a scenario with 40% class overlap. However, if we consider the definition of class overlap as regions in the data space with similar priors [10], this does not seem correct, since the number of points that occupies the same region is lower in Fig. 1d. Basing our reasoning on the similarity of class priors, a 8:1 configuration should produce a lower degree of overlap.

For atypical situations, the majority examples are always uniformly distributed in a square of length 100, while the minority examples are condensed in ranges [75..100], [80..100], [85..100], [90..100] and [95..100]. If the same rationale as above is applied to atypical domains (Fig. 1c), the percentage of overlap would be 100%, since the minority area is completely embedded in the majority area. In their paper [5], authors do not elaborate on the percentage of overlap present in each configuration – no percentages or any other values are presented for the overlapping amount. Instead, these domains are evaluated in terms of global imbalance, local imbalance and the size of the overlapping region: the notion of overlap gets somewhat lost, which complicated the discussion of results. According to the definition of class overlap as "regions in the data space with similar priors" [3,10], we believe that the "local imbalance in the overlap region" implies the existence of an overlap degree. For instance, since the distribution of examples is uniform, a [75..100] range of minority examples over the majority class square means that both classes have the same number of patterns (100 points of each class) in the overlap region, thus, there is no local imbalance in the overlap region. In this situation, the priors of both classes are the same, and therefore the overlap degree should be maximum. As the minority class becomes denser, the local imbalance increases because the size of the overlapping region is decreased, meaning that the class priors are uneven, and therefore the overlap, in fact, is decreasing. From this perspective, we could evaluate the results as follows: as the minority class becomes denser, the overlapping degree is decreasing and therefore the classification performance improves.

Regarding the F1 measure used in the research of Luengo et al. [11], it measures the highest discriminative power in all the features in the data. Essentially, F1 is measured for all the features in the dataset according to $F1 = \frac{(\mu_1 - \mu_2)^2}{\sigma_1^2 + \sigma_2^2}$, and the highest value among all features is returned. Therefore, F1 measures the overlapping of individual features, not the "overall overlapping of data". If two domains have the same structure (features have the same range and spread), F1 assumes the same or similar value, although they might be different in classification terms.

Finally, regarding the typology defined by Napierala and Stefanowski [12], as only the minority class is considered, borderline examples from the majority class (that contribute to class overlapping) are not identified. Also, as the percentage is determined over the total minority examples, majority regions where there are no examples from the minority class are not taken into account.

An overlapping degree should attend to regions with the same class priors (rather than considering distances between classes or the size of overlapping areas only), consider the overall overlap (rather than the overlap of individual features or focusing solely on the minority class examples) and focus on the characteristics of data space: structure and class decomposition, distribution of examples (implying that class imbalance could affect class overlap) and data dimensionality. In a recent work, Lee and Kim propose a hybrid classifier based on a fuzzy support vector machine and k-nearest neighbour algorithm to address class imbalance and overlapping simultaneously [8]: the data space is divided into soft and hard overlap regions so that each is handled separately. Although the focus of the work is not to analyse the joint-impact of these problems, authors define overlap-sensitive costs, where each example is classified as being part of an overlapping or a non-overlapping region, through a k neighbourhood-based function. This approach is advantageous since it considers the factors mentioned above and therefore we have decided to adapt it in order to formulate a degree of overlap and analyse its behaviour when applied to several data characteristics and imbalance ratios.

3   Experiments

All datasets contained 1500 examples and were generated with increasing levels of imbalance, namely 1:1, 2:1, 4:1, 6:1, 8:1 and 10:1, and increasing number of dimensions, namely 2, 3, 5, 10, 15, 20, 30 and 40D. The datasets further considered several overlap degrees and data structures (shapes), resulting in different levels of complexity for classifiers: *clusters* and *garcia* (less complex shapes) and *clover*, *paw* and *subclus* (more complex shapes).

The *clusters* domains, *clusters-vo* (Fig. 1a) and *clusters-va*, consist of two normal distributions (one for each class) where each cluster has unitary standard deviation. For *clusters-vo* only one of the attributes is changed and the overlap region decreases as the separation in the $X1$ axis between cluster centres increases. For *clusters-va*, all the attributes are changed and the separation is increased in all axis, according to the number of dimensions. The *garcia* domains, *garcia-va* and *garcia-vo* (Fig. 1b), follow a rectangular shape where both class are centred in the same point, being overlapped. The distance between the centres is then increased in steps of 10 units until 3×radius for *garcia-va* or 4×radius for *garcia-vo* is reached, guaranteeing no overlap. The *paw*, *clover* and *subclus* scenarios (Figs. 2a, b and c, respectively) are composed by different shapes of the minority class, and the remaining space is filled by the majority class. The minority class is formed by two types of examples – safe (located in homogeneous regions of the class) and borderline (located in the boundary between both classes). For each imbalance ratio and dimension, the ratio of safe/borderline examples varies from 100/0 to 0/100.

We measured the degree of overlap using a neighbourhood function. For each example x_i in data (considering both classes), its 5-nearest neighbours are found: if x_i and all its 5-nearest neighbours are from the same class, then example x_i belong to a non-overlapping region; otherwise, it belongs to an overlapping region. The number of examples (considering both classes) that belong to overlapping regions (n_{min_over} and n_{maj_over}) are then divided by the total number of examples, n. Thus, $degOver = (n_{min\_over} + n_{maj\_over})/n$ measures the percentage of examples comprised in overlapping regions. Measuring the degree of overlap as a neighbourhood-based function has two main advantages: it can be applied to d-dimensional data with different structures/shapes and takes the imbalance ratio (IR) into account. Besides considering the IR as a fraction of n_{maj}/n_{min}, we have normalised this ratio to measure the severity of the imbalance ratio. The degree of imbalance is defined as $degIR = 1 - \frac{n_{min}}{n/2}$. The value of n_{min} is naturally affected by the IR, and for a particular IR (e.g. $IR = 4$) and total number of examples (e.g. $n = 500$), is computed as $n_{min} = n/(IR + 1)$, (for IR = 4:1, $n_{min} = 500/(4 + 1) = 100$ minority examples and $degIR = 1 - 100/(500/2) = 0.6$). This degree of imbalance reflects how much a particular scenario is affected by class imbalance on a normalised scale between 0 and 1. We analysed seven classifiers with distinct inductive biases [1]: Classification and Regression Trees (CART), k-Nearest Neighbour (KNN), Fisher Linear Discriminant (FLD), Naive Bayes Classifier (NB), Multilayer Perceptron (MLP), Support Vector Machine with a linear kernel (SVM-linear) and Support Vector Machine with radial basis kernel (SVM-rbf). Regarding the evaluation of the classification performance, similarly to previous work [5,16], we use Sensitivity (SENS) and Specificity (SPEC).

4   Results and Discussion

We start by analysing the performance degradation of each classifier according to the properties of the test domains (IR, structure/shape and dimensionality). To analyse this degradation, we first tuned the parameters of all classifiers (k for KNN, C for SVM-linear, C and γ for SVM-rbf and number of neurons and layers for MLP) on the configuration with the least amount of overlap, for each domain, IR and dimensionality. Then, we analysed how much the defined model is affected by increasing levels of overlap. The Sensitivity results for the minority class are presented in Table 1, as well as the *degOver* for all the presented domains (due to space restrictions, we report only the Sensitivity, although the Specificity was analysed as well). Overall, CART, MLP and KNN show the lowest degradation in classification performance (considering both Sensitivity and Specificity) for all the test domains, whereas FLD and SVM-linear suffer the most with the increase of class overlap. These latter two classifiers also seem to be critically affected by the IR and data structure: the Sensitivity of FLD becomes 0 for 4:1 ratios and higher (*clover* and *subclus* domains), while SVM-linear struggles with both higher IR and higher dimensions (for *clover* and *subclus*) with Sensitivity results of 0 for ratios higher than 4:1 in higher dimensions (15 and 40D). Thus, linear classifiers seem to be affected by all four components of the problem (IR, dimensionality, class overlap and data structure), where the data structure seems to be the most prominent factor.

CART, MLP and KNN, although with different classification paradigms, are able to "adapt" to the data structure more easily, handling data that is not linearly separable: CART by recursively partitioning the input space, MLP by using multiple layers with non-linear activation functions and KNN through its neighbourhood function. These three classifiers have only achieved a poor performance for *clusters-va* and *garcia-va*, when both clusters/squares are centred at the same coordinates, respectively. These poor results are consistent with higher values of *degOver* (between 0.4 and 0.97), although *degOver* is not capable of explaining this effect entirely: in *clover* and *subclus* domains, there are some scenarios achieving the same overlapping values, where KNN, MLP and CART perform well. This may be mostly due to the structure of the domain

Table 1. Sensitivity of classifiers for different domains, overlap levels, IR and dimensionality.

		degOver				CART				FLD				SVM-linear				SVM-rbf				NB				MLP				KNN			
Dimensions	Overlap	1:1	4:1	6:1	10:1	1:1	4:1	6:1	10:1	1:1	4:1	6:1	10:1	1:1	4:1	6:1	10:1	1:1	4:1	6:1	10:1	1:1	4:1	6:1	10:1	1:1	4:1	6:1	10:1	1:1	4:1	6:1	10:1
clover																																	
	S100-B0	0.201	0.221	0.205	0.162	0.91	0.78	0.70	0.66	0.48	0.00	0.00	0.00	0.69	0.47	0.50	0.46	1.00	0.95	0.93	0.88	0.91	0.23	0.05	0.00	0.99	0.93	0.91	0.79	1.00	0.91	0.81	0.66
2D	S50-B50	0.261	0.301	0.274	0.214	0.94	0.73	0.67	0.36	0.47	0.00	0.00	0.00	0.66	0.31	0.41	0.40	1.00	0.92	0.85	0.66	0.88	0.18	0.05	0.00	0.99	0.91	0.86	0.74	1.00	0.79	0.65	0.49
	S0-B100	0.290	0.339	0.277	0.228	0.94	0.71	0.53	0.44	0.48	0.00	0.00	0.00	0.68	0.31	0.46	0.44	1.00	0.97	0.93	0.73	0.88	0.26	0.10	0.00	1.00	0.94	0.90	0.79	1.00	0.80	0.62	0.39
	S100-B0	0.044	0.047	0.040	0.042	0.99	0.98	0.99	0.94	0.51	0.00	0.00	0.00	0.97	0.36	0.43	0.15	1.00	1.00	1.00	1.00	1.00	1.00	1.00	1.00	1.00	1.00	0.91	0.99	1.00	1.00	1.00	1.00
5D	S50-B50	0.043	0.043	0.046	0.044	1.00	0.98	0.96	0.96	0.52	0.00	0.00	0.00	0.93	0.21	0.20	0.19	1.00	0.99	1.00	1.00	1.00	1.00	1.00	1.00	1.00	0.99	1.00	0.99	1.00	1.00	1.00	0.99
	S0-B100	0.045	0.046	0.045	0.052	1.00	0.97	0.97	0.93	0.48	0.00	0.00	0.00	0.98	0.37	0.19	0.39	1.00	0.97	1.00	1.00	1.00	1.00	1.00	1.00	1.00	0.99	1.00	0.98	1.00	1.00	1.00	0.99
	S100-B0	0.140	0.095	0.089	0.082	1.00	0.99	0.96	0.95	0.52	0.00	0.00	0.00	1.00	0.06	0.00	0.00	1.00	1.00	0.99	1.00	1.00	1.00	1.00	1.00	1.00	1.00	1.00	1.00	1.00	1.00	1.00	1.00
15D	S50-B50	0.148	0.090	0.081	0.073	1.00	0.98	0.99	0.96	0.53	0.00	0.00	0.00	1.00	0.05	0.00	0.00	1.00	1.00	0.98	1.00	1.00	1.00	1.00	1.00	1.00	1.00	1.00	1.00	1.00	1.00	1.00	1.00
	S0-B100	0.140	0.098	0.083	0.079	0.99	0.96	0.96	0.93	0.50	0.00	0.00	0.00	1.00	0.05	0.00	0.00	1.00	1.00	0.99	1.00	1.00	1.00	1.00	1.00	1.00	1.00	1.00	1.00	1.00	1.00	1.00	1.00
	S100-B0	0.499	0.095	0.089	0.082	1.00	1.00	1.00	1.00	0.92	0.00	0.00	0.00	1.00	0.00	0.00	0.00	1.00	1.00	1.00	1.00	1.00	1.00	1.00	1.00	1.00	1.00	1.00	1.00	1.00	1.00	1.00	1.00
40d	S50-B50	0.499	0.090	0.081	0.073	1.00	0.99	1.00	0.99	1.00	0.00	0.00	0.00	1.00	0.00	0.00	0.00	1.00	1.00	1.00	0.99	1.00	1.00	1.00	1.00	1.00	1.00	1.00	1.00	1.00	1.00	1.00	1.00
	S0-B100	0.500	0.098	0.083	0.079	1.00	0.99	0.99	0.99	0.65	0.00	0.00	0.00	1.00	0.00	0.00	0.00	1.00	1.00	1.00	1.00	1.00	1.00	1.00	1.00	1.00	1.00	1.00	1.00	1.00	1.00	1.00	1.00
subclus																																	
	S100-B0	0.202	0.230	0.208	0.169	1.00	0.98	0.97	0.93	0.63	0.00	0.00	0.00	0.74	0.48	0.38	0.33	1.00	0.90	0.78	0.69	1.00	0.53	0.27	0.00	0.98	0.80	0.88	0.81	1.00	0.85	0.79	0.65
2D	S50-B50	0.340	0.317	0.266	0.229	0.98	0.90	0.86	0.73	0.65	0.00	0.00	0.00	0.72	0.40	0.31	0.12	0.00	0.85	0.69	0.54	1.00	0.46	0.10	0.00	0.97	0.00	0.67	0.57	0.98	0.66	0.56	0.48
	S0-B100	0.353	0.340	0.307	0.248	0.97	0.89	0.85	0.70	0.67	0.00	0.00	0.00	0.69	0.24	0.22	0.00	0.01	0.79	0.71	0.36	1.00	0.35	0.02	0.00	0.90	0.00	0.63	0.49	0.99	0.66	0.45	0.35
	S100-B0	0.251	0.253	0.236	0.199	1.00	0.97	0.96	0.96	0.64	0.00	0.00	0.00	0.73	0.48	0.48	0.41	1.00	0.96	0.92	0.84	1.00	1.00	1.00	0.96	0.99	0.89	0.88	0.77	1.00	0.99	0.96	0.83
5D	S50-B50	0.300	0.283	0.259	0.219	1.00	0.97	0.97	0.89	0.64	0.00	0.00	0.00	0.72	0.47	0.42	0.35	1.00	0.94	0.90	0.75	1.00	1.00	0.99	0.93	0.98	0.83	0.86	0.69	0.99	0.97	0.93	0.78
	S0-B100	0.295	0.315	0.303	0.241	0.99	0.98	0.96	0.90	0.65	0.00	0.00	0.00	0.70	0.40	0.49	0.34	1.00	0.94	0.89	0.79	1.00	1.00	1.00	0.82	0.98	0.81	0.75	0.65	1.00	0.94	0.83	0.69
	S100-B0	0.493	0.661	0.625	0.575	1.00	0.98	0.95	0.93	0.64	0.00	0.00	0.00	0.72	0.08	0.07	0.00	1.00	1.00	0.98	1.00	1.00	1.00	1.00	1.00	0.99	0.96	0.94	0.93	1.00	1.00	1.00	1.00
15D	S50-B50	0.495	0.671	0.655	0.593	1.00	0.99	0.96	0.90	0.64	0.00	0.00	0.00	0.72	0.09	0.08	0.00	1.00	0.99	0.97	0.99	1.00	1.00	1.00	1.00	0.98	0.92	0.96	0.84	1.00	1.00	1.00	0.99
	S0-B100	0.494	0.677	0.661	0.599	1.00	0.99	0.99	0.95	0.63	0.00	0.00	0.00	0.73	0.12	0.07	0.00	0.90	1.00	1.00	1.00	1.00	1.00	1.00	1.00	0.98	0.93	0.91	0.79	1.00	1.00	1.00	0.99
	S100-B0	0.500	0.800	0.857	0.909	1.00	0.98	0.96	0.90	0.64	0.00	0.00	0.00	0.72	0.00	0.00	0.00	1.00	1.00	1.00	1.00	1.00	1.00	1.00	1.00	1.00	0.99	0.99	0.96	1.00	1.00	1.00	1.00
40D	S50-B50	0.500	0.800	0.857	0.909	1.00	0.95	0.92	0.93	0.64	0.00	0.00	0.00	0.71	0.00	0.00	0.00	1.00	1.00	1.00	1.00	1.00	1.00	1.00	1.00	1.00	0.97	0.98	0.98	1.00	1.00	1.00	1.00
	S0-B100	0.500	0.800	0.857	0.909	1.00	0.99	0.98	0.92	0.64	0.00	0.00	0.00	0.70	0.00	0.00	0.00	1.00	1.00	1.00	1.00	1.00	1.00	1.00	1.00	1.00	0.99	0.99	0.96	1.00	1.00	1.00	1.00
clusters-va																																	
	8 std	0.000	0.000	0.000	0.000	1.00	1.00	1.00	1.00	1.00	1.00	1.00	1.00	1.00	1.00	1.00	0.43	0.72	1.00	1.00	1.00	1.00	1.00	1.00	1.00	1.00	1.00	0.80	0.90	1.00	1.00	1.00	1.00
2D	4 std	0.007	0.007	0.005	0.001	1.00	0.99	0.99	0.98	1.00	0.99	1.00	1.00	1.00	0.99	0.99	0.96	0.23	0.44	0.00	0.00	1.00	0.99	1.00	1.00	1.00	0.99	1.00	1.00	1.00	0.99	1.00	1.00
	0 std	0.961	0.741	0.580	0.427	0.51	0.18	0.08	0.08	0.49	0.00	0.00	0.00	0.49	0.00	0.00	0.00	0.86	0.00	0.00	0.00	0.45	0.00	0.00	0.00	0.15	0.01	0.01	0.00	0.50	0.20	0.15	0.09
	8 std	0.000	0.000	0.000	0.000	1.00	1.00	1.00	1.00	1.00	1.00	1.00	1.00	1.00	1.00	1.00	1.00	1.00	1.00	1.00	1.00	1.00	1.00	1.00	1.00	1.00	1.00	1.00	1.00	1.00	1.00	1.00	1.00
5D	4 std	0.000	0.000	0.000	0.000	1.00	0.99	0.98	0.98	1.00	1.00	1.00	1.00	1.00	1.00	1.00	1.00	0.97	1.00	1.00	0.25	1.00	1.00	1.00	1.00	1.00	1.00	1.00	1.00	1.00	1.00	1.00	1.00
	0 std	0.971	0.731	0.598	0.448	0.49	0.17	0.13	0.05	0.52	0.00	0.00	0.00	0.48	0.00	0.00	0.00	0.22	0.00	0.00	0.00	0.59	0.00	0.01	0.00	0.46	0.02	0.04	0.01	0.50	0.17	0.14	0.10
	8 std	0.000	0.000	0.000	0.000	1.00	1.00	1.00	1.00	1.00	1.00	1.00	1.00	1.00	1.00	1.00	1.00	0.70	1.00	1.00	1.00	1.00	1.00	1.00	1.00	1.00	1.00	1.00	1.00	1.00	1.00	1.00	1.00
15D	4 std	0.000	0.000	0.000	0.000	1.00	0.98	0.99	0.99	1.00	1.00	1.00	1.00	1.00	1.00	1.00	1.00	1.00	1.00	1.00	1.00	1.00	1.00	1.00	1.00	1.00	1.00	1.00	1.00	1.00	1.00	1.00	1.00
	0 std	0.973	0.735	0.603	0.416	0.47	0.22	0.21	0.11	0.50	0.00	0.00	0.00	0.39	0.00	0.00	0.00	0.80	0.00	0.00	0.00	0.48	0.00	0.01	0.02	0.45	0.15	0.13	0.09	0.50	0.22	0.13	0.07
	8 std	0.000	0.000	0.000	0.000	1.00	1.00	1.00	0.99	1.00	1.00	1.00	1.00	1.00	1.00	1.00	1.00	1.00	1.00	1.00	1.00	1.00	1.00	1.00	1.00	1.00	1.00	1.00	1.00	1.00	1.00	1.00	1.00
40D	4 std	0.000	0.000	0.000	0.000	0.99	0.99	0.96	0.95	1.00	1.00	1.00	1.00	1.00	1.00	1.00	1.00	0.80	1.00	1.00	1.00	1.00	1.00	1.00	1.00	1.00	1.00	1.00	1.00	1.00	1.00	1.00	1.00
	0 std	0.961	0.751	0.603	0.445	0.52	0.22	0.16	0.08	0.50	0.00	0.00	0.00	0.54	0.00	0.00	0.00	0.99	0.00	0.00	0.00	0.52	0.05	0.02	0.01	0.48	0.24	0.14	0.11	0.49	0.23	0.12	0.10
garcia-va																																	
	step-100	0.000	0.000	0.000	0.000	1.00	1.00	1.00	1.00	1.00	1.00	1.00	1.00	1.00	1.00	1.00	1.00	1.00	1.00	1.00	1.00	1.00	1.00	1.00	1.00	0.90	1.00	1.00	1.00	1.00	1.00	1.00	1.00
2d	step-50	0.106	0.089	0.081	0.056	0.94	0.91	0.91	0.91	0.96	0.90	0.87	0.84	0.96	0.90	0.87	0.83	0.94	0.00	0.00	0.84	0.90	0.87	0.86	0.83	0.96	0.90	0.89	0.86	0.93	0.90	0.90	0.88
	step-0	1.000	0.887	0.775	0.555	0.20	0.01	0.00	0.00	0.46	0.00	0.00	0.00	0.46	0.00	0.00	0.00	0.29	0.00	0.00	0.00	0.43	0.00	0.00	0.00	0.28	0.00	0.00	0.00	0.23	0.04	0.00	0.00
	step-100	0.000	0.000	0.000	0.000	1.00	1.00	1.00	1.00	1.00	1.00	1.00	1.00	1.00	1.00	1.00	1.00	1.00	1.00	1.00	1.00	1.00	1.00	1.00	1.00	0.90	1.00	1.00	1.00	1.00	1.00	1.00	1.00
5d	step-50	0.011	0.013	0.007	0.005	1.00	0.98	0.99	0.96	1.00	1.00	0.99	0.99	1.00	1.00	0.99	0.99	1.00	0.93	0.47	0.00	1.00	1.00	0.99	0.99	1.00	0.99	0.99	0.98	1.00	0.99	1.00	0.98
	step-0	0.999	0.826	0.691	0.547	0.33	0.05	0.02	0.01	0.44	0.00	0.00	0.00	0.43	0.00	0.00	0.00	0.17	0.00	0.00	0.00	0.35	0.00	0.00	0.00	0.45	0.00	0.01	0.00	0.19	0.05	0.03	0.01
	step-100	0.000	0.000	0.000	0.000	1.00	1.00	1.00	1.00	1.00	1.00	1.00	1.00	1.00	1.00	1.00	1.00	1.00	1.00	1.00	1.00	1.00	1.00	1.00	1.00	1.00	1.00	1.00	1.00	1.00	1.00	1.00	1.00
15d	step-50	0.000	0.000	0.000	0.000	1.00	0.98	0.95	0.95	1.00	1.00	1.00	1.00	1.00	1.00	1.00	1.00	1.00	1.00	1.00	0.14	1.00	1.00	1.00	1.00	1.00	1.00	1.00	1.00	1.00	1.00	1.00	1.00
	step-0	0.993	0.800	0.631	0.500	0.51	0.14	0.03	0.05	0.36	0.00	0.00	0.00	0.42	0.00	0.00	0.00	0.36	0.00	0.00	0.00	0.24	0.00	0.00	0.00	0.91	0.55	0.38	0.38	0.54	0.12	0.09	0.08
	step-100	0.000	0.000	0.000	0.000	1.00	1.00	1.00	1.00	1.00	1.00	1.00	1.00	1.00	1.00	1.00	1.00	1.00	1.00	1.00	1.00	1.00	1.00	1.00	1.00	1.00	1.00	1.00	1.00	1.00	1.00	1.00	1.00
40d	step-50	0.000	0.000	0.000	0.000	1.00	1.00	0.98	0.96	1.00	1.00	1.00	1.00	1.00	1.00	1.00	1.00	1.00	1.00	1.00	1.00	1.00	1.00	1.00	1.00	1.00	1.00	1.00	1.00	1.00	1.00	1.00	1.00
	step-0	0.911	0.775	0.554	0.399	0.80	0.50	0.52	0.28	0.34	0.00	0.00	0.00	0.33	0.00	0.00	0.00	0.57	0.00	0.00	0.00	0.18	0.00	0.00	0.00	0.98	0.62	0.74	0.53	0.58	0.20	0.24	0.25

and the way overlap is generated. In *clover* and *subclus*, the structure of data is not changed (when the overlap increases, more borderline examples are added, but the core structure of the domain remains the same – Fig. 2). In *clusters-va* and *garcia-va*, the structure of data changes with the increase of overlap, since the cluster/square centres become closer (Figs. 1a and b). For these particular scenarios (*clusters-va* and *garcia-va*) it is also noticeable that higher IR ratios deteriorate the classification performance (for all dimensions), which is not observed for the remaining domains. Therefore, it is not possible to infer clearly what is more severe for these classifiers, since they seem to be affected by a combination of data structure, IR and class overlap, though not as severely by data dimensionality. Finally, although SVM-rbf seems to be more affected by class overlap than class imbalance, where the decrease in Sensitivity results was especially noticed in lower dimensions (2D) for most scenarios. Kernel methods are known to ease non-linear problems by mapping the input data to an "improved" feature space, but this largely depends on data itself. Furthermore, we also observed that this classifier has obtained poor Specificity results: it was not possible to define a clear decision hyperplane without compromising the classification of the majority class. On the contrary, NB suffered the most from higher IR, which is consistent with its bias to favour the most prevalent class, adjusting its decision threshold accordingly.

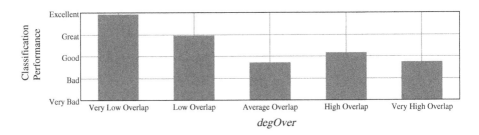

Fig. 3. Alignment between *degOver* and classification performance of KNN.

We now perform an analysis on the alignment of *degOver* and classification performance. As previously discussed, *degOver* may not be able to fully characterise the behaviour of all classifiers, although it may provide interesting insights in some cases. Of note is the ability of *degOver* to "adapt" to different IR levels: class overlap is not measured independently of class imbalance, and *degOver* generally assumes lower values as the IR increases, as discussed in Sect. 2. An exception occurs for the *subclus* domain for higher dimensions (15 and 40D), which shows that both the shape of domain and dimensionality may impact the results in certain scenarios. We then transformed *degOver* and classification performance to categories to ease the interpretation of results: *degOver* values were divided in five intervals from 0 to 1: *very low overlap* (VLO), *low overlap* (LO), *average overlap* (AO), *high overlap* (HO) and *very high overlap* (VHO),

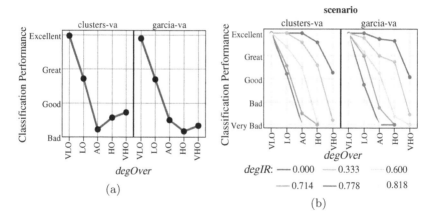

Fig. 4. (a) Alignment between *degOver* and classification performance of FLD (*clusters* and *garcia*); (b) Lines representing different levels of *degIR*.

while Sensitivity and Specificity results were combined to produce also five categories of performance: *very bad, bad, good, great* and *excellent*. Figure 3 shows the relationship between *degOver* and KNN, which was found to be the classifier most aligned with *degOver* (as expected, since their underlying principles are the same – they are based on neighbourhood functions). Overall, the performance of classifiers deteriorates with higher values of *degOver*, although this decrease is not linear: maximum levels of overlap do not necessarily correspond to minimum performance results. This suggests, as previously discussed, that there are other factors (namely, data structure) affecting the performance of classifiers, as will be discussed in what follows.

For *clusters* and *garcia*, classification performance and *degOver* are aligned for all classifiers: an example of this alignment is presented in Fig. 4a for FLD. The slight increase in performance for higher *degOver* values (HO and VHO) may be explained by the IR values (Fig. 4b): the blue line (normalised IR of 0) indicates that there is no class imbalance – in this scenario, although the overlap is high, the performance results are also high, causing the slight increase of performance for the high overlap levels in Fig. 4a. Again, these results suggest that all these properties of data (IR, class overlap and data structure) should be analysed together to better understand the performance of classifiers. For more complex scenarios, as *clover, subclus* and *paw*, the alignment with *degOver* varies for different classifiers. None of them presents the expected behaviour (a performance decrease for higher values of *degOver*) for all three domains, although KNN and SVM-linear present a better alignment than the remaining classifiers, being KNN clearly the most aligned (Fig. 5a). Figure 5a also presents the results for FLD and SVM-rbf, two of the classifiers that do not present a good alignment between *degOver* and classification performance for complex domains. We hypothesise that this mismatch can be related to the structure of data, which may be influenced by data dimensionality. Some classifiers (SVM-

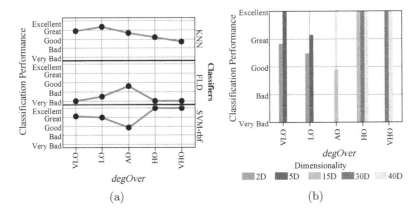

Fig. 5. (a) Alignment between *degOver* and classification performance of KNN, FLD and SVM-rbf considering only more complex shapes (*paw*, *clover* and *subclus*); (b) Dimensionality discrimination for SVM-rbf.

rbf, CART, NB and MLP) are able to classify datasets with higher overlap levels in higher dimensions (Fig. 5b): the *subclus* domain is such an example (Table 1) where high *degOver* values occur in 40D, and the mentioned classifiers obtain better results than for lower dimensions (sometimes with lower *degOver* values as well). These results suggest that data dimensionality is especially relevant for more complex domains and that *degOver* may have to be adjusted according to the number of dimensions and number of examples in data in order to give more insights on properties of the domain.

5   Conclusions

Class overlap is one of the difficulty factors that deteriorates the performance of classifiers and is even more critical in imbalanced contexts, as discussed in related work. However, most authors study class overlap without providing a clear formula to measure its degree: overlap is often perceived as a distance between majority and minority concepts or as an area of intersection between majority and minority classes, without considering the IR nor the structure of data, which may limit the conclusions derived from such setups. From our perspective, a measure of the degree of overlap should take the IR and structure of data into account. Therefore, we evaluate the usefulness of *degOver* to quantify the overlapping degree and its relationship with the classification performance of standard classifiers in several domains with different shapes, IRs and dimensionality. Our results revealed that MLP and CART are less prone to suffer from high levels of overlap and show good performance even in the presence of more complex domains. Furthermore, in simpler scenarios, *degOver* is aligned with classification performance for all classifiers, even for varying amounts of imbalance. However, this alignment varies significantly in more complex domains and seems to be influenced by data dimensionality. In sum, although *degOver* takes the imbalance ratio into account and can be measured for any data structure and dimensionality, it needs to be adjusted to better represent these properties of data so that it may provide more useful insights for more complex domains.

References

1. Abreu, P.H., Santos, M.S., Abreu, M.H., Andrade, B., Silva, D.C.: Predicting breast cancer recurrence using machine learning techniques: a systematic review. ACM Comput. Surv. (CSUR) **49**(3), 52 (2016)
2. Ali, A., Shamsuddin, S.M., Ralescu, A.L.: Classification with class imbalance problem: a review. Int. J. Adv. Soft Compu. Appl. **7**(3), 176–204 (2015)
3. Denil, M., Trappenberg, T.: Overlap versus imbalance. In: Farzindar, A., Kešelj, V. (eds.) AI 2010. LNCS (LNAI), vol. 6085, pp. 220–231. Springer, Heidelberg (2010). https://doi.org/10.1007/978-3-642-13059-5_22
4. Domingues, I., Amorim, J.P., Abreu, P.H., Duarte, H., Santos, J.: Evaluation of oversampling data balancing techniques in the context of ordinal classification, pp. 5691–5698 (2018)
5. García, V., Mollineda, R.A., Sánchez, J.S.: On the k-nn performance in a challenging scenario of imbalance and overlapping. Pattern Anal. Appl. **11**(3–4), 269–280 (2008)
6. García, V., Mollineda, R.A., Sánchez, J.S., Alejo, R., Sotoca, J.M.: When overlapping unexpectedly alters the class imbalance effects. In: Martí, J., Benedí, J.M., Mendonça, A.M., Serrat, J. (eds.) IbPRIA 2007. LNCS, vol. 4478, pp. 499–506. Springer, Heidelberg (2007). https://doi.org/10.1007/978-3-540-72849-8_63
7. García, V., Sánchez, J., Mollineda, R.: An empirical study of the behavior of classifiers on imbalanced and overlapped data sets. In: Rueda, L., Mery, D., Kittler, J. (eds.) CIARP 2007. LNCS, vol. 4756, pp. 397–406. Springer, Heidelberg (2007). https://doi.org/10.1007/978-3-540-76725-1_42
8. Lee, H.K., Kim, S.B.: An overlap-sensitive margin classifier for imbalanced and overlapping data. Expert Syst. Appl. **98**, 72–83 (2018)
9. Longadge, R., Dongre, S.: Class imbalance problem in data mining review. arXiv preprint arXiv:1305.1707 (2013)
10. López, V., Fernández, A., García, S., Palade, V., Herrera, F.: An insight into classification with imbalanced data: empirical results and current trends on using data intrinsic characteristics. Inf. Sci. **250**, 113–141 (2013)
11. Luengo, J., Fernández, A., García, S., Herrera, F.: Addressing data complexity for imbalanced data sets: analysis of smote-based oversampling and evolutionary undersampling. Soft Comput. **15**(10), 1909–1936 (2011)
12. Napierała, K., Stefanowski, J., Wilk, S.: Learning from imbalanced data in presence of noisy and borderline examples. In: Szczuka, M., Kryszkiewicz, M., Ramanna, S., Jensen, R., Hu, Q. (eds.) RSCTC 2010. LNCS (LNAI), vol. 6086, pp. 158–167. Springer, Heidelberg (2010). https://doi.org/10.1007/978-3-642-13529-3_18
13. Prati, R.C., Batista, G.E.A.P.A., Monard, M.C.: Class imbalances *versus* class overlapping: an analysis of a learning system behavior. In: Monroy, R., Arroyo-Figueroa, G., Sucar, L.E., Sossa, H. (eds.) MICAI 2004. LNCS (LNAI), vol. 2972, pp. 312–321. Springer, Heidelberg (2004). https://doi.org/10.1007/978-3-540-24694-7_32

14. Santos, M.S., Abreu, P.H., García-Laencina, P.J., Simão, A., Carvalho, A.: A new cluster-based oversampling method for improving survival prediction of hepatocellular carcinoma patients. J. Biomed. Inf. **58**, 49–59 (2015)
15. Stefanowski, J.: Overlapping, rare examples and class decomposition in learning classifiers from imbalanced data. Emerging Paradigms in Machine Learning, pp. 277–306. Springer, Berlin (2013). https://doi.org/10.1007/978-3-642-28699-5_11
16. Wojciechowski, S., Wilk, S.: Difficulty factors and preprocessing in imbalanced data sets: an experimental study on artificial data. Found. Comput. Decis. Sci. **42**(2), 149–176 (2017)

Tree-Based Cost Sensitive Methods for Fraud Detection in Imbalanced Data

Guillaume Metzler[1,2(✉)], Xavier Badiche[2], Brahim Belkasmi[2], Elisa Fromont[3], Amaury Habrard[1], and Marc Sebban[1]

[1] Univ. Lyon, UJM-Saint-Etienne, CNRS, Institut d'Optique Graduate School, Laboratoire Hubert Curien UMR 5516, 42023 Saint-Etienne, France
{guillaume.metzer,amaury.habrard,marc.sebban}@univ-st-etienne.fr
[2] Blitz Business Service, 265 Rue Denis Papin, 38090 Villefontaine, France
{gmetzler,xbadiche,bbelkasmi}@blitzbs.com
[3] Univ. Rennes 1, IRISA/Inria, 35042 Rennes Cedex, France
efromont@irisa.fr

Abstract. Bank fraud detection is a difficult classification problem where the number of frauds is much smaller than the number of genuine transactions. In this paper, we present cost sensitive tree-based learning strategies applied in this context of highly imbalanced data. We first propose a cost sensitive splitting criterion for decision trees that takes into account the cost of each transaction and we extend it with a decision rule for classification with tree ensembles. We then propose a new cost-sensitive loss for gradient boosting. Both methods have been shown to be particularly relevant in the context of imbalanced data. Experiments on a proprietary dataset of bank fraud detection in retail transactions show that our cost sensitive algorithms allow to increase the retailer's benefits by 1,43% compared to non cost-sensitive ones and that the gradient boosting approach outperforms all its competitors.

Keywords: Cost sensitive learning · Imbalance learning · Binary classification

1 Introduction and Related Work

Imbalanced data are ubiquitous in many real world applications, e.g. in medical domains [13], bank transactions [2,16] or industrial processes [1]. Supervised machine learning tasks are challenging in this context because algorithms struggle to focus on the important class (e.g. fraud, disease, failure, etc.) which is under-represented in the data. Classical approaches tend to tackle the problem by rebalancing the data [7] or optimizing different performance measures than the classical accuracy [15] which would otherwise lead to predict all instances in the over-represented classes. Ensemble methods such as random forests [5] or boosting algorithms [9,17] have been shown to be particularly successful in this context because they can combine local decisions taken in areas where the imbalance is (made) less prominent.

© Springer Nature Switzerland AG 2018
W. Duivesteijn et al. (Eds.): IDA 2018, LNCS 11191, pp. 213–224, 2018.
https://doi.org/10.1007/978-3-030-01768-2_18

In some application domains such as fraud/anomaly detection, additional precise information can be given to favor one class from other ones in the learning process. This can for example be done by cost-sensitive learning approaches [8] which can take into account user preferences (in terms of the importance of the classes or of the attributes). For example, [2] proposes a cost-sensitive decision tree stacking algorithm to tackle a fraud detection task in a banking context. The authors provide a cost matrix that assigns costs to each decision made by the model and define an optimization function that takes this matrix into account. In Decision Tree learning the splitting criterion is made according to these costs method and not according to the usual impurity measures (such as entropy or Gini). This allows them to better target the rare classes. [17] presents a cost-sensitive version of the Adaboost boosting algorithm [9] and also shows its relevance in this imbalanced scenario. [18] gives a general study of the cost-sensitive learning methods in the context of imbalanced data. They categorise the methods into two sets: those which fix the error costs in each class and apply it *a posteriori* to make a decision, and those which tune *a priori* the cost matrix depending on the local distribution of the data (this category seems more successful). [16] tackles the problem of credit card fraud detection. The approach, similar to [2] and to the first one we present in this paper, proposes to induce decision trees by splitting each node according to a cost matrix associated to each example. However, as in [16], they focus on the actual money losses losses but not on possible benefits of better classifications and they apply their method to ranking problems. Other methods like [13] have focused on the cost of the attributes (here in the context of medical data). They consider that acquiring the exact value of a given attribute is costly and try to find a good compromise between the classification errors and the total feature acquisition costs.

In this paper, we also propose different cost sensitive tree-based learning approaches in the highly imbalanced context of bank fraud detection. The first approach, similar to [2] and [16] and presented in Sect. 3, uses a cost sensitive splitting criterion for decision trees that takes into account the costs (as well as the benefits) of each transaction. But it differs from [2] and [16] in the combinaison strategy for building an ensemble method. The second one presented in Sect. 4 is a new cost-sensitive proper loss [6] for gradient boosting. Section 2 presents our notations, the gain/cost matrix we are working with and the associated weighted miss-classification loss we want to optimize. The experiments and results are presented in Sect. 5. We illustrate the different methods using both the retailer margin and the F-Measure (F_1) as performance measures. The experiments are made on a proprietary dataset of the *Blitz* company. We finally conclude in Sect. 6.

2   Notations and Problem Formulation

2.1   Notations

We focus in this paper on binary supervised classification problems. Let $S = (\mathbf{X}, \mathbf{Y}) = ((\boldsymbol{x}_1, y_1), ...(\boldsymbol{x}_m, y_m))$ be a set of m training instances where $\boldsymbol{x}_i \in \mathbb{R}^d$

and $y_i \in \{0,1\}^m$ are their corresponding labels. The notation x_i^j is used to denote the value of the jth variable of the instance i. The label 0 will be used for the negative or majority class (i.e. the genuine transactions) and the label 1 will be used for the positive or rare class (i.e. the fraudulent transactions). We will further denote by S_+ the set of m_+ positive examples and S_- the set of m_- negative examples (here $m_- >> m_+$). We will also note $\hat{y}_i$ the label predicted by our learned model for the instance i. We use the notation p for the predicted probability that an example belongs to the minority class, F will be used to design the learned model, i.e. $p_i = F(x_i)$ is the probability that the transaction is fraudulent. A threshold is then used to get its label.

2.2   Problem Formulation

Our goal is to maximize the profits of the retailers by predicting, online, with decision trees [4] which transactions, made by a customer are genuine or not. While training the trees offline, the company might like to introduce some costs assigned to the training examples, according to the adequacy between the actual label of the transaction and the predicted one (see Table 1). For instance, the retailers will gain money by accepting a genuine transaction, i.e. $c_{TN_i} > 0$, where TN stands for *True Negative* or genuine transactions correctly classified. However, if the retailers accept a fraudulent one, they will loose the amount of the transaction $c_{FN_i} < 0$, where FN stands for *False Negative* or fraudulent transaction predicted as a genuine one.

Table 1. Cost Matrix associated to each example of the training set.

	Predicted positive (fraud)	Predicted negative (genuine)
Actual positive (fraud)	c_{TP_i}	c_{FN_i}
Actual negative (genuine)	c_{FP_i}	c_{TN_i}

In this paper, we use a similar approach as the one presented in [2]. However, instead of only minimizing the money loss due to an acceptation of a fraudulent transaction, we rather focus on maximizing the retailers profits, i.e. we aim at maximizing the loss function L defined as follows:

$$L(y \mid \hat{y}) = \sum_{i=1}^{m} [y_i(\hat{y}_i c_{TP_i} + (1 - \hat{y}_i)c_{FN_i}) + (1 - y_i)(\hat{y}_i c_{FP_i} + (1 - \hat{y}_i)c_{TN_i})].$$

(1)

Talking about profits instead of classical "costs" is more meaningful for the retailers. Furthermore, if we simply focus on the error made by the algorithm, a correctly classified instance will have no influence on the learned model.

In the next section, we show how this loss function can be optimized while learning decision trees.

3   Cost Sensitive Decision Trees

A classic decision tree induction algorithm proceeds in a top-down recursive divide-and-conquer manner. At each step, the best (according to a given criterion) attribute A is chosen as a new test (internal node) in the tree and the set of examples is splitted according to the outcome of the attribute for each of the instance (there is one child node v per possible outcomes for a given attribute). Then, the same procedure is applied recursively to each new created subset of examples S_v until reaching a given stopping criterion. Classification trees (e.g. [4]) usually split the nodes according to an "impurity" measure. One such measure is the Gini index of a set of m instances $(\boldsymbol{x}_i, \boldsymbol{y}_i)$ defined as follows: $Gini = 1 - \sum_{k=1}^{C} p_k^2$, where p_k denotes the probability to belong to the class k and C is the number of classes ($C = 2$ in our case). In this paper, the splitting criterion is based on the cost matrix defined above. We do not want to minimize an impurity but to *maximize the retailer profits* according to the cost matrix.

3.1   Splitting Criterion and Label Assignment

Our splitting criterion Γ_S on a given set of training instances S of size m (as defined in Sect. 2) is:

$$\Gamma_S = \sum_{i \in S_-} \left(\frac{m_+}{m} c_{FP_i}(\boldsymbol{x}_i) + \frac{m_-}{m} c_{TN_i}(\boldsymbol{x}_i) \right) + \sum_{i \in S_+} \left(\frac{m_+}{m} c_{TP_i}(\boldsymbol{x}_i) + \frac{m_-}{m} c_{FN_i}(\boldsymbol{x}_i) \right), \quad (2)$$

where the first term corresponds to the profits due to genuine transactions and the second to the fraudulent transactions.

Note that this quantity depends on the amount of the transaction of each example in S through the costs c. The best attribute A is the one which *maximizes* the quantity:

$$(\frac{1}{n + \varepsilon}) \sum_{v \in Children(A)} \Gamma_{S_v} - \Gamma_S.$$

Note that this quantity is very similar to the splitting criterion used to minimize to minimize the Gini impurity up to the number of examples in the parent node. We simply take the opposite of the classical gain and divide it by the number of instances in the parent node, so that this criterion becomes convex.

The values Γ_{S_v} are computed using Eq. (2) on each set S_v. It differs from the splitting criterion used in [2] where the splits minimize the cost of wrongly accepting or blocking the transactions.

Once the induction tree stopping criterion is reached (ours is defined in Sect. 5), a class label is associated to each leaf of the tree. For the sake of clarity we introduce the following notations:

$\gamma_0(l)$: the average profit associated to the leaf l if all the instances are predicted as genuine:

$$\gamma_0(l) = \frac{1}{|l|} \left(\sum_{i:\boldsymbol{x}_i \in l \cap S_-} c_{TN_i} + \sum_{i:\boldsymbol{x}_i \in l \cap S_+} c_{FN_i} \right),$$

$\gamma_1(t)$: the average profit associated to the leaf l if all instances are predicted as frauds:

$$\gamma_1(l) = \frac{1}{|l|} \left(\sum_{i:\boldsymbol{x}_i \in l \cap S_-} c_{FP_i} + \sum_{i:\boldsymbol{x}_i \in l \cap S_-} c_{TP_i} \right),$$

where $|l|$ denotes the number of examples in the leaf l and $i : \boldsymbol{x}_i \in l \cap S$ denotes the index i of the example $\boldsymbol{x}_i$ both in leaf l and in the set S.

A leaf is assigned the label 1 if $\gamma_1 > \gamma_0$, i.e. all the transactions in a given leaf are predicted fraudulent if the associated average profit is greater than one associated when all instances are predicted genuine.

Note that this strategy can be easily extended to ensembles of trees [5]. In this case, a standard decision rule consists in applying a majority vote over the whole set of the T learned decision trees. However, this decision rule does not take into account the probability score that can be associated to each tree prediction using the class distribution of the examples in the leaf $l(\boldsymbol{x}_i)$ (as in [16]). Following this idea, we suggest here to label an instance as positive if the average $\bar{\gamma}_1(\boldsymbol{x})$ of the average profits $\gamma_1(l^j(\boldsymbol{x}_i))$ over the T trees is greater than $\bar{\gamma}_0(\boldsymbol{x})$, where $l^j(\boldsymbol{x}_i)$ is the leaf of the jth tree containing $\boldsymbol{x}_i$:

$$\bar{\gamma}_1(\boldsymbol{x}) = \frac{1}{T} \sum_{j=1}^{T} \gamma_1(l(\boldsymbol{x})) \geq \frac{1}{T} \sum_{j=1}^{T} \gamma_0(l(\boldsymbol{x})) = \bar{\gamma}_0(\boldsymbol{x}).$$

4   Cost Sensitive Gradient Boosting

In this section, we briefly present the gradient boosting framework introduced in [11]. Then we present a proper cost-sensitive loss function in order to implement it in a gradient boosting algorithm in an efficient way.

4.1   Generalities about Gradient Boosting

Gradient boosting has been shown to be very efficient to deal with classification problems, and a very good candidate to address issues due to imbalance data [3,12]. Unlike the well known Adaboost algorithm [9], gradient boosting performs an optimization in the *function* space rather than in the *parameter* space. At each iteration, a weak learner f_t is learned using the *residuals* (or the errors) obtained by the linear combination of the previous models. The linear combination F_t at time t is defined as follows:

$$F_t = F_{t-1} + \alpha_t f_t, \tag{3}$$

where F_{t-1} is the linear combination of the first $t-1$ models and α_t is the weight given to the tth weak learner. The weak learners are trained on the residuals $r_i = y_i - F_{t-1}(x_i)$ of the current model. These residuals are given by the negative gradient, $-g_t$, of the used loss function L with respect to the current prediction $F_{t-1}(x_i)$:

$$r_i = g_t = -\left[\frac{\partial L(y, F_{t-1}(x_i))}{\partial F_{t-1}(x_i)}\right].$$

Once the residuals r_i are computed, the following optimization problem is solved:

$$(f_t, \alpha_t) = \underset{\alpha, f}{argmin} \sum_{i=1}^{m}(r_i - \alpha f(x_i))^2.$$

Finally, the update rule (3) is applied.

4.2   Cost Sensitive Loss for Gradient Boosting

In this section we aim to use the framework presented in [6] to give a proper formulation of our loss function of Eq. (1) in the context of a boosting algorithm, using the gain matrix presented in Table 1.

Using a Bayes rule for classification [8], an instance i is predicted fraudulent if $\gamma_1 > \gamma_0$, i.e:

$$p_i c_{TP_i} + (1 - p_i)c_{FP_i} - p_i c_{FN_i} - (1 - p_i)c_{TN_i} > 0,$$

where p_i denotes the probability of the instance to be a genuine transaction. It gives us a threshold over which the transaction is declined (or predicted fraudulent):

$$p_i > \frac{c_{TN_i} - c_{FP_i}}{c_{TP_i} - c_{FN_i} + c_{TN_i} - c_{FP_i}} = s_i$$

Using the threshold s_i, our cost-weighted miss-classification loss can be rewritten as:

$$L(y \mid p) = -\frac{1}{m}\sum_{i=1}^{m}(y_i c_{TP_i} + (1 - y_i)c_{FP_i})\,\mathbb{1}_{p_i > s_i} + (y_i c_{FN_i} + (1 - y_i)c_{TN_i})\mathbb{1}_{p_i \leq s_i}.$$
$$(4)$$

Then, following the framework presented in [6], $L(y \mid p)$ can be rewritten as follows:

$$L(y \mid p) = \frac{1}{m}\sum_{i=1}^{m}\xi_i\left[y_i(1 - s_i)\mathbb{1}_{p_i \leq s_i} + (1 - y_i)s_i\mathbb{1}_{p_i > s_i}\right]$$

$$-\frac{1}{m}\sum_{i=1}^{m}(y_i c_{TP_i} + (1 - y_i)c_{TN_i}),   (5)$$

where $\mathbb{1}$ is an indicator function and where we use the fact that $s = s\mathbb{1}_{p>s} + s\mathbb{1}_{p\leq s}$ and set $\xi_i = c_{TN_i} - c_{FP_i} + c_{TP_i} - c_{FN_i}$ which is positive in our context. In fact, $c_{TN} > c_{FP}$, we earn more if we correctly classify a genuine transaction. Furthermore, if we accept a fraudulent transaction then we loose money and we earn nothing if we declined it, i.e. $0 = c_{TP} > c_{FN}$.

The first part of Eq. (5), which we will note L_{s_i} corresponds to the cost-sensitive loss introduced in [6] with $s_i \in [0,1]$. Each term of the sum is multiplied by a constant ξ_i which depends on the data. The second term represents the maximum that our loss can reach if the predictions were perfect. Note that this second term does not depend on p_i. Therefore, we want to minimize:

$$\underset{p\in[0,1]}{argmin}\ \mathbb{E}_y[L(y\mid p)] = \underset{p\in[0,1]}{argmin}\ \mathbb{E}_y\left[\frac{1}{m}\sum_{i=1}^{m}\xi_i L_{s_i}(y_i\mid p_i)\right].$$

However it has been shown that in the context of Boosting, it is more convenient to use an exponential approximation [11]. We adapt it to consider the output of a prediction model F directly in our approach as follows [1]:

$$\ell_{s_i} = (1-s_i)y_i e^{-F(\boldsymbol{x}_i)} + s_i(1-y_i)e^{F(\boldsymbol{x}_i)}.$$

Solving $\dfrac{\partial \mathbb{E}_{\mathbf{Y}}[\ell_{s_i}]}{\partial F(\boldsymbol{x}_i)} = 0$, we obtain the link function ψ_i between p_i and $\hat{F}_i = F(\boldsymbol{x}_i)$:

$$p_i = \psi_i(\hat{F}_i) = \frac{1}{1 + \dfrac{1-s_i}{s_i}e^{-2\hat{F}_i}},$$

and its inverse ψ_i^{-1} is given by:

$$e^{\hat{F}_i} = \left(\frac{1-s_i}{s_i}\right)^{1/2}\left(\frac{p_i}{1-p_i}\right)^{1/2}. \qquad (6)$$

The way to transform the output of a boosting model into a probability (the calibration process) plays a key role in the performance of the predictive algorithm. It has been shown that we can achieve at least the same performance with well calibrated boosting model than with one which is cost sensitive [14]. However, we think that our cost sensitive approach gives us a good transformation of the output of the model into a probability.

It is worth noticing that we can make use of Eq. (6) to provide a smooth approximation of the indicator function, such that:

$$\mathbb{1}_{p_i>s_i} \leq \left(\frac{1-s_i}{s_i}\right)^{1/2}\left(\frac{p_i}{1-p_i}\right)^{1/2} = e^{\hat{F}_i}.$$

---

[1] Note that it exists a direct link between a predicted probability and the output of a model (see Sect. 3 of [10] and Sect. 4 of [6] for further details).

Note that: $p_i > s_i \iff \psi_i(\hat{F}_i) > s_i \iff e^{\hat{F}_i} > 1 \iff \hat{F}_i > 0$. So it is enough to check the sign of the score to predict the label of each transaction. Finally we are minimizing an upper bound $\tilde{L}$ of L:

$$L(y \mid p) \leq \tilde{L}(y \mid F) = \frac{1}{m} \sum_{i=1}^{m} (1 - s_i) y_i e^{-\hat{F}_i} + s_i(1 - y_i) e^{\hat{F}_i}.$$

To use it in a gradient boosting algorithm, it remains to compute the first and second order derivative of $\tilde{L}$ for each instance i with respect to $\hat{F}_i$. They are given by:

$$\frac{\partial \tilde{L}}{\partial \hat{F}_i} = \xi_i \left[-(1 - s_i) y_i e^{-\hat{F}_i} + s_i(1 - y_i) e^{\hat{F}_i} \right],$$

and

$$\frac{\partial^2 \tilde{L}}{\partial \hat{F}_i^2} = \xi_i \left[(1 - s_i) y_i e^{-\hat{F}_i} + s_i(1 - y_i) e^{\hat{F}_i} \right].$$

5   Experiments

In this section, we evaluate the decision rule presented in Sect. 3 and the loss function presented in Sect. 4. We compare the results of our method on the retailer profits compared to using a classic Random Forest (RF) algorithm based on the Gini impurity criterion (baseline). The experiments are performed on a private dataset own by the *Blitz* company which can not be entirely described and made available for privacy reasons.

5.1   Dataset and Experiments

The *Blitz* dataset consists of 10 months of bank transactions of a retailer. The first six months are used as the training set ($1,663,009$ transactions) and the four remaining ones as test set ($1,012,380$ transactions). The data are described by 17 features and are labeled as *fraud* or *genuine*. The Imbalance Ratio (IR) of the dataset is equal to 0.33%.

The first series of experiments compares the random forest baseline (**RF**) to the tree ensemble algorithm which uses the decision rule presented in Sect. 3 (**RF$_X$**). We made different variants of the decision rule:

1. **RF$_{maj}$**: each leaf is labeled according to the majority class of the examples that fall into the leaf, thus the output of each tree is in $\{0,1\}$. The voting criterion is detailed below.
2. **RF$_{maj-mar}$**: each leaf is labeled to maximize the profit (also called margin) over the set of all examples in the leaf (the label is 0 if $\gamma_0 > \gamma_1$ and 1 otherwise). We then use a majority vote to predict the label of each transaction.
3. **RF$_{mean-mar}$**: this model is the one described in Sect. 3

For each tree ensemble algorithm, we have used 24 trees with the same maximum depth. Furthermore, for the models $\mathbf{RF}, \mathbf{RF_{maj}}$ and $\mathbf{RF_{maj-mar}}$, the ensemble classifies a transaction as "fraud" if at least 9 trees agree on this positive class (this threshold is coherent with the one currently used in the *Blitz* company).

The second series of experiments is dedicated to the analysis of the gradient boosting approaches. We compare our approach $\mathbf{GB_{margin}}$, presented in Sect. 4.2, with three gradient boosting algorithms which aim to minimize the logistic loss:

1. $\mathbf{GB_{tune-Pre}}$: the threshold has been chosen so that we have the same precision on the validation set as the model $\mathbf{RF}$ in the training phase.
2. $\mathbf{GB_{tune-mar}}$: the threshold has been chosen to maximize the margin on the validation dataset.
3. $\mathbf{GB_{tune-F1}}$: the threshold has been chosen to maximize the F-Measure F_1 on the validation dataset.

For each of these three experiments we needed a validation data set to choose the optimal threshold over which a transaction is predicted as fraudulent. For this purpose, the training set is splitted in two sets, the first one is used to train the model and the other as a validation set, to find the best threshold for the given criterium we want to optimize. To do so, the first four months of transactions constitute the training set, the two remaining months are used as the validation set. Finally these three experiments have been conducted on the same *training/validation* set and the $\mathbf{R}$ software[2].

For privacy reasons, the explicit expressions of $c_{TP_i}, c_{FP_i}, c_{TN_i}, c_{FN_i}$ of the cost matrix can not be given. Note that they are simple functions of the amount M of the transaction. For example, we define c_{FP_i} as follows $c_{FP_i} = h(M) - \zeta$, where ζ is a parameter used to translate in financial terms, the dissatisfaction of the customer whose transaction has been declined.

5.2   Results

To measure the performance of each algorithm, we measure the gap between the maximum profits, i.e. the profits obtained if no errors are made, and the profits given by the algorithms. We use classic performance measures that are often used in an imbalanced setting such as the Precision, Recall and F_1-Measure defined as follows:

$$Precision = \frac{TP}{TP + FP}, \quad Recall = \frac{TP}{TP + FN}, \quad F_1 = \frac{2\,Precision \times Recall}{Precision + Recall}.$$

All the experiments have been conducted with the same cost matrix where $\zeta = 5$. The results are presented in Table 2. We first notice that we get a reduction of the gap of profits of 1.43%, with the gradient boosting model $\mathbf{GB}_{margin}$ compared to the baseline $\mathbf{RF}$. To give an idea to the reader, having a gap of 1%

---

[2] https://www.r-project.org/ and using the package $\mathbf{XGBoost}$.

Table 2. Gap to the maximal margin of each algorithm. In this table, the value of ζ was set to 5. The results are separated into two groups: Random Forest models and Gradient Boosting models.

Experiments	Gap max profits	Precision	Recall	F_1
RF	2.99%	68.1%	5.66%	10.5%
RF_{maj}	2.88%	73.8%	4.71%	8.86%
$RF_{maj-mar}$	1.81%	30.2%	10.6%	15.7%
$RF_{mean-margin}$	1.87%	30.3%	9.52%	14.5%
$GB_{tune-Pre}$	3.01%	**61.0%**	6.49%	11.7%
$GB_{tune-mar}$	2.26%	19.1%	**16.6%**	**17.8%**
$GB_{tune-F1}$	2.70%	45.4%	9.24%	15.4%
GB_{margin}	**1.56%**	18.8%	13.3%	15.6%

to the maximum profits represents a loss of $43,000$ euros. So, by reducing the gap of 1.43% we increase the profits of the retailer by $60,000$ euros.

Regarding the Random Forest models, we note that the proposed approaches are able to improve the profits of the retailer compared to the model **RF**. However, we note that **RF$_{maj}$**, which uses the number of examples and their label to predict the class of the examples in the leaf, gives similar performance as **RF** even if it is built differently. This means that the way to label the leaves has, at least, the same importance as the way to build the trees. The models **RF$_{maj-mar}$** and **RF$_{mean-mar}$** which directly use the notion of average profits in each leaf are the two models that give the best results, in terms of both profits, recall and F-Measure even if the precision is reduced. This is explained by the fact that refusing a genuine transaction will have small impact on the margin of the retailers while accepting a fraudulent transaction will represent a loss for the retailers that is close to the amount of the transaction. Using only our proposed method of Random Forest algorithm, we are able to reduce the gap of 1.18.

If we focus now on gradient boosting models, we first note that the model **GB$_{tune-Pre}$** is the one with the highest precision. On the other hand, the other models have a significantly smaller precision but exhibits a higher recall: by maximizing the margin they actually try to find the most fraudulent transactions. As mentioned previously, our cost-sensitive approach **GB$_{margin}$** is the one that achieves the best results in terms of margin. But it has also the worst precision (18.8%) for the reason given in the previous paragraph. This model provides also better results than **GB$_{tune-mar}$** which emphasizes the interest of a cost-sensitive approach compared to a simple classification model. However, we note that the model **GB$_{tune-F1}$** is not the one achieving the best F-Measure at test time. Let us also note that F_1 score remains low for each presented algorithms. We think that low values are observed because of the complexity of the data and the problem. Frauds are rare and spread in the all data set.

In a second part, we want to analyze the effect of the parameter ζ. Indeed, some retailers, for marketing reasons, do not want to refuse the transaction of good customers, i.e. they prefer to have a higher precision on their predictions. A simple way to take this into account in our model is to artificially increase the value of ζ. Figure 1 shows the impact of the parameter ζ on the *Precision*, *Recall* and F_1, while the Gap Margin is still evaluated with $\zeta = 5$. Recall that some retailers do not want to refuse the payment of the good customers, however, the model which maximized is the one with the lowest precision (16.6%). So, it can be interesting to propose to the retailers several models using different values of ζ and give them the choice of the compromise between profits and precision.

We first notice that the higher the value of ζ, the higher the precision and the smaller the recall. However, we see that it possible to reach a precision which is twice superior than the **GB$_{margin}$** one by setting $\zeta = 20$ and the gap will still be low with a value of 1.94%.

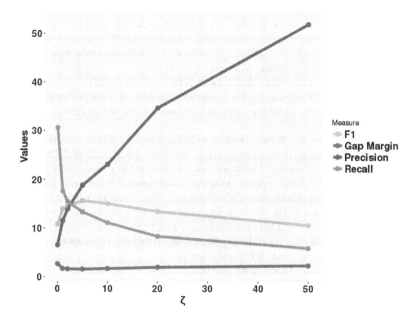

Fig. 1. Study of the influence of the parameter ζ in the definition of the gain of false positive C_{FP_i}. We illustrate the behaviour of the Precision, Recall and F_1 according to ζ. We also represent the gap to the maximum margin with respect to ζ, but we set $\zeta = 5$ to compute the gap.

6   Conclusion

We have presented different cost sensitive tree-based learning strategies to detect frauds in imbalanced retail transaction data. The first strategy is a tree ensemble algorithm which uses a new decision rule which tries to directly optimize the retailer profit. The second one is a gradient boosting algorithm which optimizes a new cost-sensitive loss function. Experiments show that our cost sensitive algorithms allow to increase the retailer's benefits by 1,43% compared to non cost-sensitive ones and that the gradient boosting approach outperforms all its competitors. We plan to focus on how to combine different types of models that may capture different modalities of the data. Furthermore, due to our industrial context, we also want to work on the notion of *concept drift* and study how the distribution of frauds is evolving in order to take it into account in our models. This opens the door to the development of new domain adaptation methods.

References

1. Aggarwal, C.C.: Outlier Analysis. Springer, Cham (2013). https://doi.org/10.1007/978-3-319-14142-8_8
2. Bahnsen, A.C., Villegas, S., Aouada, D., Ottersten, B., Correa, A.M., Villegas, S.: Fraud detection by stacking cost-sensitive decision trees. DSCS (2017)
3. Beygelzimer, A., Hazan, E., Kale, S., Luo, H.: Online gradient boosting. In: Advances in Neural Information Processing Systems (NIPS), pp. 2458–2466 (2015)
4. Breiman, L., Friedman, J., Olshen, R., Stone, C.: Classification and Regression Trees. Wadsworth and Brooks, Monterey (1984)
5. Breiman, L.: Random forests. Mach. Learn. **45**(1), 5–32 (2001)
6. Buja, A., Stuetzle, W., Shen, Y.: Loss functions for binary class probability estimation and classification: structure and applications, manuscript (2005). www-stat.wharton.upenn.edu/buja
7. Chawla, N.V., Bowyer, K.W., Hall, L.O., Kegelmeyer, W.P.: Smote: synthetic minority over-sampling technique. J. Artif. Int. Res. **16**(1), 321–357 (2002)
8. Elkan, C.: The foundations of cost-sensitive learning. In: Proceedings of the 17th International Joint Conference on Artificial Intelligence - Volume 2, IJCAI 2001, pp. 973–978. Morgan Kaufmann Publishers Inc., San Francisco (2001)
9. Freund, Y., Schapire, R.E.: A short introduction to boosting. In: Proceedings of the Sixteenth IJCAI, pp. 1401–1406. Morgan Kaufmann, San Francisco (1999)
10. Friedman, J., Hastie, T., Tibshirani, R.: Additive logistic regression: a statistical view of boosting. Ann. Stat. **28**, 2000 (1998)
11. Friedman, J.H.: Greedy function approximation: a gradient boosting machine. Ann. Stat. **29**, 1189–1232 (2000)
12. Li, P., Burges, C.J.C., Wu, Q.: Mcrank: Learning to rank using multiple classification and gradient boosting. In: Proceedings of the 20th International Conference on Neural Information Processing Systems, NIPS 2007, pp. 897–904 (2007)
13. Ling, C., Sheng, V., Yang, Q.: Test strategies for cost-sensitive decision trees. IEEE Trans. Knowl. Data Eng. **18**(8), 1055–1067 (2006)
14. Nikolaou, N., Edakunni, N., Kull, M., Flach, P., Brown, G.: Cost-sensitive boosting algorithms: do we really need them? Mach. Learn. **104**(2), 359–384 (2016)
15. Parambath, S.P., Usunier, N., Grandvalet, Y.: Optimizing f-measures by cost-sensitive classification. In: NIPS, pp. 2123–2131 (2014)
16. Sahin, Y., Bulkan, S., Duman, E.: A cost-sensitive decision tree approach for fraud detection. Expert Syst. Appl. **40**(15), 5916–5923 (2013)
17. Sun, Y., Kamel, M.S., Wong, A.K., Wang, Y.: Cost-sensitive boosting for classification of imbalanced data. Pattern Recognit. **40**(12), 3358–3378 (2007)
18. Thai-Nghe, N., Gantner, Z., Schmidt-Thieme, L.: Cost-sensitive learning methods for imbalanced data. In: The 2010 International Joint Conference on Neural Networks (IJCNN). IEEE, July 2010

Reduction Stumps for Multi-class Classification

Felix Mohr, Marcel Wever[(✉)], and Eyke Hüllermeier

Heinz Nixdorf Institute, Department of Computer Science, Paderborn University,
Paderborn, Germany
`marcel.wever@uni-paderborn.de`

Abstract. Multi-class classification problems are often solved via *reduction*, i.e., by breaking the original problem into a set of presumably simpler subproblems (and aggregating the solutions of these problems later on). Typical examples of this approach include decomposition schemes such as one-vs-rest, all-pairs, and nested dichotomies. While all these techniques produce reductions to purely binary subproblems, which is reasonable when only binary classifiers ought to be used, we argue that reductions to other multi-class problems can be interesting, too. In this paper, we examine a new type of (meta-)classifier called *reduction stump*. A reduction stump creates a binary split among the given classes, thereby creating two subproblems, each of which is solved by a multi-class classifier in turn. On top, the two groups of classes are separated by a binary (or multi-class) classifier. In addition to simple reduction stumps, we consider ensembles of such models. Empirically, we show that this kind of reduction, in spite of its simplicity, can often lead to significant performance gains.

Keywords: Multi-class classification · Reduction · Ensembles
Automated machine learning

1 Introduction

Reduction of a multi-class classification problem means breaking down the original problem into other presumably simpler subproblems. Typical examples include one-vs-rest and all-pairs decomposition [6], as well as nested dichotomies [5]. One-vs-rest creates one binary problem for each class, in which the class is separated from the rest, whereas all-pairs creates a binary problem for each pair of classes. Nested dichotomies reduce the given problem by recursively splitting the set of classes, which yields a binary tree structure where each leaf has one class and each inner node is meant to separate the classes occurring under the left child from the classes occurring under the right child. In general, the subproblems created by reduction are all binary. Thus, reduction makes multi-class problems amenable to binary classifiers, which can be seen as their main merit.

© Springer Nature Switzerland AG 2018
W. Duivesteijn et al. (Eds.): IDA 2018, LNCS 11191, pp. 225–237, 2018.
https://doi.org/10.1007/978-3-030-01768-2_19

Fig. 1. A multi-class problem with five classes.

While a complete reduction to binary problems is necessary when only binary classifiers can be used, reductions to other multi-class problems might be interesting as well. A priori, one cannot exclude that modifying an underlying multi-class problem by reducing it to other multi-class problems (on less but possibly more than two classes) is beneficial for a learner, even if the latter is principally able to solve multi-class problems right away. For example, one may suspect that a multi-class learner like a random forest or a neural network could benefit from an explicit reduction of the problem shown in Fig. 1.

An interesting area of research where such reductions can be important is automated machine learning (AutoML). AutoML aims at automatically finding a machine learning "pipeline" (including methods for data preprocessing, model induction, etc.) that optimizes a performance measure of interest for a given learning task (typically specified by a dataset). A couple of approaches to AutoML have been proposed [4,10–12] in the recent past. Currently, however, reduction is hardly considered by these approaches, although its potential benefit is completely unclear.

In this paper, we examine a new classifier that we call *reduction stumps*. Reduction stumps split the given set of classes into two subsets and then solve the resulting problems with a multi-class classifier. Separating instances of the two subsets is achieved by a third (and possibly binary) classifier. The motivation for looking at this type of classifier is that it offers a middle-ground solution between native multi-class classifiers and a complete reduction to binary problems as in nested dichotomies. Therefore, reduction stumps achieve a reasonable compromise between simplification and complexity.

Due to this property, reduction stumps offer an interesting means to achieve performance gains in AutoML. However, the effort to determine such reductions needs to be moderate, as AutoML tools must consider many different machine learning pipelines and cannot spend too much time on a single decision, such as whether or not reduction should be used. Besides, each of the reduced problems gives rise to a new AutoML problem itself, so again for reasons of complexity, one should avoid creating too many of them.

Empirically, we show that (ensembles of) reduction stumps indeed lead to significant performance gains over *many* other classification algorithms in a significant number of cases. More precisely, we compare reduction stumps against several standard classification algorithms, including multi-class logistic regression, neural networks, nearest neighbors, support vector machines via all-pairs reduction, decision tress, and random forests. We find that reduction stumps or ensembles of them are better than *any* of the other algorithms in more than half of the 21 examined datasets from the UCI repository [1]. Even though the improvement over the best non-reduction-based classifier is often only small, we thus provide a strong justification for the consideration of reduction stumps when solving multi-class classification problems.

2   Background: Nested Dichotomies

Nested dichotomies (NDs) reduce a multi-class classification problem to a set of (presumably easier to solve) binary problems. To this end, the original set of classes (as long as comprising more than one element) is recursively split into two nonempty subsets. Thus, an ND defines a binary tree, in which every node is labeled with a set of classes, such that every leaf is labeled with a distinct class, and every inner node with the union of labels of its children. Figure 2 shows two example dichotomies for the case of four classes.

To each inner node of an ND, a classifier is attached and fitted for the task of discriminating the two sets of classes (meta-classes) assigned to its children. These classifiers are trained using a base learner, which is typically supposed to produce probabilistic predictions. For a given instance, the class with the highest probability is predicted, where the probability for a leaf is obtained by multiplying the probabilities predicted by the base learners along the path from the root to the respective leaf node.

Of course, the performance of an ND critically depends on the structure of the binary tree, as it determines the complexity of the induced binary classification problems, as well as the type of classifier attached to the inner nodes. Usually, the type of classifier is fixed, and one is interested in finding the most beneficial structure [9]. The criterion that is commonly optimized is the overall predictive accuracy (percentage of correct classifications), which depends on the quality of the binary classifiers, and therefore on the structure of the ND. Approaches to finding suitable dichotomies are based on random sampling [5,9], greedy error minimization [8], clustering [3], and evolutionary optimization [13].

A *partial* nested dichotomy is an ND in which the leaf nodes may be labeled with more than only one class. Therefore, partial NDs need to be equipped with multi-class classifiers in their leaf nodes. Of course, other reduction techniques such as one-vs-rest or all-pairs [6] could be used here as well. To our knowledge, partial dichotomies have only occurred during the construction process of complete nested dichotomies, but have never been used as classifiers themselves.

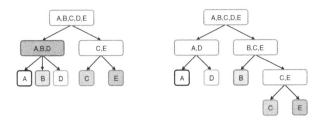

Fig. 2. A partial (left) and a complete (right) nested dichotomy for five classes.

3 Reduction Stumps and Reduction Stump Ensembles

In this paper, we focus on partial NDs of depth 1, which we refer to as *reduction stumps*. Reduction stump have exactly one inner node, which is the root, and two child nodes with an arbitrary number of classes. Of course, just like NDs, reduction stumps are multi-class classifiers.

3.1 Motivation and Overview

The main goal of classical reduction techniques is to make multi-class problems amenable to binary classification. Therefore, techniques such as one-vs-rest, all-pairs [6], ECOC [7], and nested dichotomies [2,5] reduce the original problem in such a way that *all* induced subproblems are binary. As opposed to this, the distinguishing feature of reduction stumps is their partiality. In fact, reduction stumps have a different use case and aim at *distributing* smaller and presumably easier subproblems among two multi-class classifiers. For instance, this can be advantageous because the multi-class classifier, despite being principally able to treat an arbitrary number of classes, does not scale well for larger numbers of classes. Furthermore, it might be interesting to consider different types of base learners at the inner nodes, as one classifier might be able to separate one group of classes well, while another one may prove beneficial for separating the remaining classes.

In contrast to previous approaches, we allow different classifiers to be used as base learners in reduction stumps. The flexibility of adopting different classifiers for (different parts of) the same problem is precisely one of the supposed strengths of reduction stumps. We call reduction stumps with different classifiers *heterogeneous*. Analogously, reduction stumps with the same classifier for all subproblems are called *homogeneous*. One reason for considering homogeneous reduction stumps may be that only one classification algorithm is available; for example, in medical data analysis, often only decision trees are accepted for reasons of interpretability.

In addition to single reduction stumps, we also consider ensembles. It has been observed that ensembling often improves predictive accuracy, provided there is a reasonable variety among the classifiers within the ensemble. For reduction stumps, there are two sources of variety, which makes them especially suitable for being used in an ensemble. First, there is randomness in the choice of the splits of a reduction stump, which can be averaged out using ensembles; for the same reason, it is common to consider ensembles of nested dichotomies instead of only single dichotomies [5,8]. Second, the topology of a reduction stump strongly depends on the choice of the base learner. Hence, the ensemble effect might even be amplified when heterogeneous reduction stumps are used.

3.2   Training a Reduction Stump and Obtaining Predictions

Training a reduction stump requires two decisions. First, one must choose a split of the set of classes, i.e., decide which classes belong to the left and which to the right child of the root node. Second, one must choose the classifiers for (i) the binary split and (ii) the rest problems associated with the left and the right child, respectively. Obviously, there is an interaction between these two choices.

Even though the number of reduction stumps is *much* smaller than the number of nested dichotomies, it is still infeasible to enumerate all possible reduction stumps. Given a problem with n classes, there are $2^{n-1} - 1$ different splits. We *may* enumerate these candidates for small n, but we cannot reasonably build a general algorithm on this basis. However, there is reason to believe that near-optimal splits can be found without extensive search. First, a number of heuristics for finding good splits has been proposed [8]. Second, it has been shown that even randomly sampling a relatively small number of splits and taking the best of them often yields at least as good results [9].

Moreover, it is possible to conduct a grid-search over the possible classifiers for the binary problem and the two child nodes, i.e., to enumerate all options for the second choice. A full nested dichotomy has $n - 1$ inner nodes, where n is the number of classes. If m classification algorithms are eligible, this leads to m^{n-1} possible combinations of classifiers over the inner nodes, which is generally not feasible. For the reduction stump, however, we have at most m^3 many combinations[1]. For example, we shall consider $m = 23$ classifiers, which leads to over 10^{12} combinations in a full nested dichotomy for a 10-class problem, whereas we only have 12,167 possible combinations for a reduction stump.

As a consequence, we design the reduction stump as a meta-classifier that can be parametrized with a *set* of base classifiers. Given such a set C of classifiers, it iterates over all active classifier combinations $R \subseteq C^3$, where $R = C^3$ in the heterogeneous case and $R = \{(c, c, c) \mid c \in C\}$ in the homogeneous case. For each classifier combination $r \in R$, depending on the split technique, one or more splits are identified and evaluated. The algorithm then associates the classifier combination r with the best determined split $s(r)$ and the respective validation score $t(r)$. The stump eventually selects $\text{argmin}_{r \in R} t(r)$ as the classifier combination and uses $s(r)$ as the split.

The split is computed by drawing splits (uniformly) at random and evaluating them against a validation set. To this end, the set of classes is organized in a

---

[1] If the split separates a single class from the rest, then we even have only m^2 many combinations.

shuffled list, and a position within that list is drawn uniformly at random. We draw k such splits and, for each of them, we also split the given training data into a reduced training set and a validation set. The reduced training set is used to train the reduction stump, and the validation set is used to validate it. We do neither conduct cross-validation nor a holdout method here, but only use single evaluations. First, conducting a sophisticated evaluation would be costly and further reduce the data available for training the stump. Second, since the sampling routine itself considers different splits of both data and classes, an averaging effect over different data is still achieved.

We also experimented with another interesting split technique called *random pairs*. The random-pair selection heuristic (RPND) was proposed by Leathart et al. [8] for the construction of nested dichotomies and suggests to build the two subsets by randomly choosing two classes as "seeds", training a classifier to separate them, and adding each of the other classes to the seed to which most of its instances are assigned by the trained classifier. Our experiments showed that RPND does not perform significantly better than the above best-of-k random sampling, so we do not include it in the experiments for space reasons; this also conforms to the observations of [9]. However, the results are available with the implementation.

The inference for reduction stumps is straight forward. Given a new instance, the root classifier decides whether the instance should belong to the first or the second subset of classes. Based on this decision, the respective classifier for the subproblem is used to make a final decision for the class of the instance. For probabilistic predictions, each of the three classifiers computes a probability for the instance to belong to its covered classes. The class distribution for an instance is computed by multiplying the class probabilities produced by the base learners at the child nodes with the probability for the respective child as obtained from the root node's base learner.

3.3 Ensembles of Reduction Stumps

As already said, in addition to single reduction stumps, we are interested in *ensembles* of such models. Yet, in this paper, we only consider ensembles of homogeneous reduction stumps. Although we conjecture that heterogeneous ensembles can be much more powerful, a training procedure needs to make more decisions and would have to be more sophisticated than the straight forward approach as described below. To reduce the computational cost, an effective heuristic would be required. Since this work is more concerned with the fundamental question of whether a reduction is beneficial at all, designing such a heuristic is left for future work.

For ensembles of homogeneous reduction stumps, the training method is quite straight forward. Given a set C of available base classifiers, the algorithm iterates over all $c \in C$, using c as the base learner at each inner node. The algorithm constructs an ensemble of a given size by creating the structure of the reduction stumps at random. Furthermore, instead of performing a best-of-k selection for each ensemble member, we apply the best-of-k heuristic to the entire ensemble.

That is, we build k ensembles of reduction stumps and select the ensemble with the best score. For computing the score, the training data is again split into a reduced training set and a validation set, and the ensemble is trained on the former and evaluated on the latter. This evaluation procedure is repeated several times to obtain a stable estimate for the ensemble (which is not changed over the iterations), resulting in a holdout validation of the ensembles. After having selected all $|C|$ ensembles, the algorithm chooses the one with the best score to be used for future predictions and trains it on the entire training data.

The prediction routine for ensembles is implemented as a majority vote. Each reduction stump votes for a class, and the prediction of the ensemble is the class that collects the highest number of votes.

4   Experimental Evaluation

In our experimental evaluation, we compare the proposed (ensembles of) reduction stumps to (ensembles of) single classifiers to analyze the potential benefit of reducing the original problem to a set of simpler problems (with fewer classes). Recalling our motivation of reduction as a possible means to improve automated machine learning, note that, as part of an AutoML toolbox, reduction stumps would serve as an *option* rather than a *default choice*. Correspondingly, including them in the toolbox seems warranted if they provide the best choice in a *sufficient* portion—but not necessarily the *majority*—of the cases.

We subdivide our analysis into two main aspects. First, we carry out a detailed analysis of (ensembles of) homogeneous reduction stumps, comparing them to the single classifier and a bagged ensemble of the latter. Second, we additionally consider heterogeneous reduction stumps, comparing the best models using any classifier as a base learner.

4.1   Experimental Setup

In total, we evaluate the four methods on 21 datasets (as shown in Table 1) from different domains, including image recognition, biology, and audio. To estimate the predictive accuracy of each method, we used a 20-holdout (also known as Monte-Carlo cross-validation), splitting the data into 70% training data and 30% test data. As learning algorithms, which were also used as base learners for the reduction stumps, we considered BayesNet (BN), NaiveBayes (NB), NaiveBayesMultinomial (NBM), Logistic (L), MultilayerPerceptron (MP), SimpleLogistic (SL), SMO (SMO), IBk (IB), KStar (KS), JRip (JR), PART (PART), DecisionStump (DS), J48 (J48), LMT (LMT), RandomForest (RF), and RandomTree (RT).

To build ensembles of reduction stumps, we used the Best-of-k strategy. To this end, we used another internal stratified split of 70% data for building the reduction stumps and 30% validation data for selection, and set $k = 10$.

We have implemented both reduction stumps and ensembles as WEKA classifiers. The code, the data used to conduct the experiments, and the database

Table 1. Datasets used in the evaluation

Dataset	#instances	#attributes	#classes
audiology	226	69	24
autoUnivau6750	750	40	8
car	1728	6	4
cnae9	1080	856	9
fbis.wc	2463	2000	17
kropt	28056	6	18
letter	20000	16	26
mfeat-factors	2000	216	10
mfeat-fourier	2000	76	10
mfeat-karhunen	2000	64	10
mfeat-pixel	2000	240	10
optdigits	5620	64	10
pendigits	10992	16	10
page-blocks	5473	10	5
segment	2310	19	7
semeion	1593	256	10
vowel	990	13	11
waveform	5000	40	3
winequality	4898	11	11
yeast	1484	8	10
zoo	101	17	7

with the presented results are publicly available[2]. The computations were executed on (up to) 150 Linux machines in parallel, each of which with a resource limitation of 2 cores (Intel Xeon E5-2670, 2.6 Ghz) and 16 GB memory. The total run-time was over 30 k CPU hours (more than 3 years).

4.2   Analysis of Homogeneous Reduction Stumps

Table 2 shows the error rate averaged over 20 train/test splits of single classifiers (SC), homogeneous reduction stumps (RS), bagged ensembles of classifiers (BA), and majority vote ensembles of homogeneous reduction stumps (EN) for different classifiers and datasets. In the last column of the table, a statistic of wins/ties/losses (W/T/L) is provided comparing RS to SC and EN to BA. Missing values indicate that the respective algorithm was either not applicable to the problem or that it did not finish in a given timeout of 1h.

---

[2] https://github.com/fmohr/ML-Plan/tree/ida2018.

Considering the results for RS, we can indeed see that the performance of *every* classifier can sometimes be increased when wrapped into a reduction stump. Although RS is not an overall dominating strategy, except for SL and LMT, there are at least 3 datasets for each classifier where a reduction stump performs better than the single classifier. This indicates that reduction in principle can be beneficial in terms of performance improvement.

Comparing BA to EN, for some datasets, the overall picture is quite similar to the comparison of RS and SC. Neglecting the classifiers BN and NBM, there are at least 8 datasets for which EN yields a better performance. In particular, EN seems to yield improved results for DS, LMT, RT, and RF rather frequently. For 13 of 16 classifiers, EN wins more often than it loses against BA. We conclude that reduction stumps might be more suitable for being used in ensembles.

4.3   Analysis of Heterogeneous Reduction Stumps

In the second part of our evaluation, we consider heterogeneous reduction stumps. Since we cannot compare heterogeneous stumps in the context of a single base classifier, we now consider the overall best performance achieved with *any* classifier of the respective class. From the perspective of AutoML, this is the most interesting part of the evaluation, because it answers the questions whether (ensembles of) reduction stumps can be superior to *any* other classification algorithm (either by itself or used within a (bagging) ensemble).

The results are summarized in Table 3, where we now distinguish between RS-hom for homogeneous and RS-het for heterogeneous reduction stumps. Note that with EN we still only refer to ensembles of homogeneous reduction stumps. Significant differences are determined using a t-test with $p = 0.05$. While significant improvements of reduction stumps over the baseline (single classifier respectively bagged ensemble) are indicated by •, significant degradations are indicated by ○. Best performances within one row are highlighted in bold. Results that are not significantly worse than the best result are underlined.

Regarding RS-hom, in this table, it becomes even clearer that homogeneous reduction stumps do not perform that strong and in this context never achieve the best performance for any of the datasets. Nevertheless, if used in an ensemble, the homogeneous reduction stumps yield the best result in 5 cases. Furthermore, compared to BA, EN achieves 9 significant improvements. A significant degradation, in turn, is observed only once.

However, the most remarkable observations are made for heterogeneous reduction stumps that clearly outperform the other approaches. RS-het yields 6 significant improvements over SC while being significantly worse in only two cases. Furthermore, it turns out to achieve the best performance in 15 of 21 cases. From these results, we conclude that reduction stumps represent an interesting approach for decomposing multi-class classification problems to a set of simpler subproblems.

The results also motivate the investigation of ensembles of heterogeneous reduction stumps. On one hand, it would be interesting to design a heuristic for building such ensembles as a standalone classifier. On the other hand, instead

Table 2. Mean error rate of base learners on 21 UCI datasets. (see Footnote 2)

		audiology	autoUnivau6750	car	cmae9	kropt	letter	mfeat-factors	mfeat-fourier	mfeat-karhunen	mfeat-pixel	optdigits	page-blocks	pendigits	segment	semeion	vowel	waveform	winequality	yeast	zoo	fbis.wc	
BN	SC	**27.2**	77.1	13.5	**11.7**	63.7	26.0	7.6	23.5	8.5	6.5	8.1	6.6	**12.1**	**8.6**	14.4	42.3	20.0	52.4	42.1	5.7	29.7	
BN	RS	30.3	**75.8**	**12.0**	12.8	**63.4**	27.8	–	–	–	–	–	6.3	13.8	9.2	–	41.4	**18.9**	**49.7**	43.2	7.1	–	7/0/7
BN	BA	29.3	77.0	14.0	12.1	63.8	**25.8**	7.4	23.2	7.4	6.3	8.0	**5.9**	12.3	8.8	14.0	**37.1**	19.5	50.9	**40.9**	6.1	28.6	
BN	EN	28.8	77.4	13.8	12.1	63.9	26.1	–	–	–	–	–	6.3	12.6	8.7	–	38.0	22.9	52.0	41.2	**4.5**	–	4/1/9
NB	SC	**28.8**	80.1	13.7	8.4	63.7	35.9	8.1	**23.5**	6.5	6.8	9.1	10.7	14.2	19.6	13.8	37.6	19.9	56.3	**42.1**	4.8	37.7	
NB	RS	31.4	**79.5**	**12.4**	9.8	**63.7**	38.1	9.9	24.5	8.2	8.7	10.5	**6.4**	15.8	**18.6**	15.4	40.4	**17.6**	**51.2**	42.8	6.3	38.9	6/1/14
NB	BA	33.1	80.7	14.4	7.9	63.9	**35.8**	7.7	23.7	**6.4**	**6.5**	9.2	10.2	14.3	19.2	**13.6**	**36.6**	19.8	55.2	42.9	5.7	**32.7**	
NB	EN	30.7	79.7	13.9	**7.6**	64.0	36.2	7.6	24.1	6.8	7.2	**9.0**	10.8	14.3	19.8	14.0	38.0	22.2	55.7	42.3	**3.9**	37.5	8/1/12
NBM	SC	–	–	–	5.9	–	**44.7**	15.4	25.3	–	–	**9.4**	8.7	**19.4**	–	**15.4**	–	–	60.1	66.3	–	23.3	
NBM	RS	–	–	–	6.7	–	45.8	21.3	**24.7**	–	–	12.0	**8.0**	22.3	–	17.3	–	–	**56.2**	66.4	–	25.0	3/0/8
NBM	BA	–	–	–	6.8	–	44.8	**15.1**	26.0	–	–	9.4	8.2	19.5	–	15.5	–	–	59.4	**66.2**	–	**22.2**	
NBM	EN	–	–	–	**5.6**	–	45.3	15.4	25.3	–	–	**9.5**	8.5	19.6	–	15.9	–	–	60.2	66.5	–	23.1	2/0/9
L	SC	22.6	81.6	6.3	8.3	–	22.6	2.8	29.0	6.9	–	6.7	3.4	**4.5**	4.9	29.8	20.0	**13.1**	46.1	40.7	10.9	–	
L	RS	22.4	–	–	7.7	–	24.7	3.3	25.8	8.4	–	6.4	3.2	5.1	–	17.6	23.4	16.5	**45.9**	–	–	–	7/0/6
L	BA	25.7	84.1	6.4	7.6	59.7	22.7	2.2	24.8	**5.2**	–	**3.6**	3.0	4.5	4.6	**9.7**	21.9	13.1	46.3	41.3	12.2	–	
L	EN	**19.7**	80.7	6.1	**6.6**	–	–	**2.1**	21.9	5.3	5.8	3.7	3.4	4.7	4.5	12.3	15.3	16.1	46.1	40.9	5.6	–	11/0/6
MP	SC	**18.1**	83.9	1.1	–	37.3	17.7	2.5	17.6	4.1	–	1.8	3.7	5.6	3.8	7.8	9.1	16.6	44.0	40.9	4.8	–	
MP	RS	22.4	–	–	–	17.9	–	–	1.8	3.5	5.2	–	1.9	3.3	**1.6**	–	–	5.7	16.9	44.5	–	–	3/0/7
MP	BA	22.8	82.1	1.8	29.3	33.8	14.3	2.5	17.8	4.1	0.0	1.9	**3.2**	4.9	3.7	7.3	9.1	**13.8**	**42.6**	39.4	6.1	0.0	
MP	EN	20.1	81.7	0.4	–	–	16.7	3.5	–	–	–	1.4	3.3	1.8	3.0	–	**3.6**	16.5	44.1	39.7	4.2	–	10/0/4
SMO	SC	21.2	80.3	**6.6**	7.2	56.3	18.4	2.4	**15.9**	3.8	2.6	1.7	7.2	**2.2**	7.6	6.7	32.8	**13.6**	47.4	43.1	4.4	22.1	
SMO	RS	22.4	**79.3**	6.8	8.6	57.3	23.0	2.6	15.9	4.1	3.1	2.1	**6.6**	2.6	7.1	7.3	34.7	16.0	**47.4**	44.0	4.3	23.0	4/2/15
SMO	BA	28.1	81.4	7.0	7.3	**56.1**	19.0	**2.3**	16.9	3.6	2.6	**1.7**	6.8	2.3	8.3	6.7	38.9	13.8	47.6	44.4	6.1	23.4	
SMO	EN	21.3	79.6	7.0	**6.7**	56.9	–	2.4	16.7	**3.5**	**2.5**	2.1	6.8	4.3	**7.1**	7.3	**28.6**	16.1	47.5	**43.0**	**3.8**	**20.5**	12/2/6
SL	SC	16.4	77.2	6.7	8.0	**59.4**	22.7	2.7	18.0	4.6	4.4	3.1	3.4	4.7	5.1	9.3	19.8	13.0	**46.2**	40.6	7.0	18.2	
SL	RS	21.3	–	–	9.2	60.1	24.7	2.9	18.8	5.1	4.7	3.2	**3.3**	6.3	–	9.5	20.9	16.1	46.3	–	–	18.2	1/1/14
SL	BA	19.3	81.7	7.0	8.1	59.7	22.8	**2.2**	18.1	3.9	3.9	3.0	3.4	**4.6**	5.2	**7.7**	19.5	**13.0**	46.4	41.2	9.1	**15.2**	
SL	EN	–	78.8	6.8	**7.2**	59.6	–	**2.2**	17.3	**3.7**	3.6	**2.8**	3.5	5.1	4.9	8.4	16.1	16.0	46.4	42.6	6.2	15.6	12/2/5
IB	SC	22.2	84.3	8.3	16.6	**29.7**	4.6	4.4	20.8	3.8	3.9	1.5	4.1	0.8	**3.4**	10.0	1.8	26.4	**37.6**	48.5	3.9	50.3	
IB	RS	20.7	84.1	**7.2**	17.7	29.8	4.8	4.5	20.4	**3.7**	3.8	1.4	**3.8**	0.8	3.5	9.5	**1.7**	26.6	37.8	49.5	4.6	51.0	10/1/10
IB	BA	25.0	84.4	8.0	**15.8**	32.5	4.8	**3.8**	19.8	4.0	**3.8**	1.5	3.8	0.8	4.1	9.8	4.7	**24.7**	39.6	**47.0**	5.2	49.1	
IB	EN	23.4	**83.6**	7.3	16.2	32.3	–	4.2	**17.4**	4.1	4.2	1.4	4.0	**0.7**	3.4	**9.2**	2.0	26.9	37.9	48.0	**3.7**	**49.1**	11/1/8
KS	SC	**19.1**	84.7	12.4	11.4	41.3	4.8	84.1	15.2	6.4	3.9	2.4	3.3	**0.9**	3.1	9.7	2.8	27.3	37.3	47.2	3.5	–	
KS	RS	19.3	–	–	12.5	**41.1**	–	–	23.9	6.5	**3.8**	2.5	**2.9**	1.0	–	9.0	2.6	27.6	**37.3**	–	–	–	6/1/6
KS	BA	21.6	85.8	13.1	**11.1**	42.0	4.8	83.9	24.9	**6.3**	3.8	2.3	3.2	1.0	3.2	9.4	4.7	24.4	39.1	46.7	4.3	62.4	
KS	EN	21.3	84.8	12.5	11.2	41.2	–	–	–	6.4	4.1	**2.2**	3.1	0.9	3.3	**8.7**	**2.5**	–	37.6	46.9	4.0	–	11/0/5
JR	SC	31.0	73.4	15.1	15.3	61.5	15.8	13.9	27.6	20.5	15.5	10.0	3.0	4.3	5.7	29.0	33.1	21.0	46.7	42.5	12.2	25.6	
JR	RS	31.0	74.0	**11.6**	14.9	48.7	15.5	12.4	28.8	20.4	15.2	9.0	2.8	4.3	5.6	25.7	28.1	20.9	46.2	42.9	10.9	25.7	15/2/4
JR	BA	27.8	78.1	13.2	**10.1**	**46.8**	8.4	5.7	21.6	9.4	6.5	3.9	**2.5**	1.8	**3.2**	14.5	20.0	**16.0**	**42.0**	41.1	**9.6**	20.6	
JR	EN	–	**72.7**	12.4	11.6	58.7	–	**4.6**	19.5	7.6	4.9	3.4	2.8	1.4	3.5	**12.6**	**15.5**	19.7	45.2	**40.7**	10.8	**20.3**	12/0/7
PART	SC	24.1	82.2	4.3	13.1	48.8	12.4	11.4	26.4	16.2	17.3	8.0	3.1	3.4	4.1	22.7	23.8	22.6	43.1	46.0	5.7	26.1	
PART	RS	24.1	83.6	**3.8**	13.8	43.8	13.1	11.8	26.6	18.3	14.9	8.0	2.7	3.6	4.5	21.7	26.0	22.3	42.6	45.5	9.0	25.8	9/2/10
PART	BA	22.2	80.8	4.0	**10.9**	41.7	7.8	6.4	20.6	10.1	10.9	4.2	**2.4**	1.9	3.5	14.6	17.6	**16.3**	**37.5**	**40.0**	7.0	**20.0**	
PART	EN	**21.6**	**79.6**	4.2	11.6	**38.1**	–	**5.9**	19.4	**8.2**	**6.7**	3.1	2.7	1.5	**3.0**	**11.4**	**13.7**	21.9	38.9	41.5	**5.5**	20.3	13/0/7
DS	SC	50.0	78.0	**29.4**	79.6	81.1	92.9	80.2	80.4	80.5	80.2	80.2	6.6	79.6	71.5	80.2	82.4	43.1	55.0	59.0	30.4	63.4	
DS	RS	**44.8**	**76.2**	29.4	70.5	**76.4**	88.2	67.8	65.8	68.1	66.4	68.5	**5.3**	63.1	46.6	69.7	75.5	**34.5**	**49.4**	**54.3**	**17.9**	**51.2**	20/1/0
DS	BA	50.0	77.4	29.4	65.2	78.5	90.4	63.9	80.5	79.9	79.0	76.2	6.6	79.5	43.6	79.8	72.1	42.0	55.0	59.3	25.7	63.4	
DS	EN	**46.2**	77.5	**29.4**	50.3	78.5	**82.1**	14.8	61.5	56.7	**55.6**	68.5	5.8	**55.4**	**34.9**	64.0	**66.3**	36.6	55.0	57.0	19.7	63.4	16/3/2
J48	SC	22.9	83.3	9.5	11.8	46.5	13.3	12.0	25.5	19.0	23.0	10.2	3.0	3.9	3.5	27.0	22.2	24.8	43.3	45.8	6.1	26.9	
J48	RS	22.4	82.2	**8.2**	12.4	45.1	13.7	12.3	27.9	21.3	20.2	9.3	2.8	4.1	4.1	25.1	25.4	24.5	43.2	44.7	8.2	27.4	11/0/10
J48	BA	**21.2**	80.5	8.3	10.9	43.9	9.0	7.1	21.1	10.4	17.0	5.1	**2.6**	2.4	3.5	17.7	16.4	17.6	**38.2**	**40.0**	7.0	**21.4**	
J48	EN	21.5	**78.2**	8.4	11.2	**43.6**	**6.5**	**6.3**	**20.3**	10.0	**12.7**	3.7	2.9	1.8	**3.2**	**13.2**	**15.1**	24.6	39.9	42.1	**5.7**	23.6	13/0/8
LMT	SC	16.4	77.1	3.5	8.0	–	9.1	2.7	18.2	4.6	4.4	2.8	3.0	1.6	3.6	9.3	7.9	**13.0**	43.6	40.6	7.0	–	
LMT	RS	20.7	–	–	9.2	–	–	3.2	17.9	5.4	5.4	2.9	2.7	1.7	–	10.1	12.4	16.0	44.9	–	–	–	2/0/11
LMT	BA	19.3	82.5	3.9	8.1	32.2	6.1	2.2	17.4	3.9	3.9	2.9	**2.6**	1.2	3.1	**7.7**	8.1	**14.3**	**37.8**	41.3	9.1	15.1	
LMT	EN	–	**78.7**	2.9	**7.1**	29.4	3.9	**2.2**	**16.5**	**3.6**	**3.6**	1.9	2.8	0.9	2.8	7.9	**5.2**	16.0	39.2	40.5	6.3	–	14/1/4
RF	SC	22.8	74.6	6.2	6.6	32.8	4.2	3.7	**16.2**	4.4	4.4	2.0	2.5	1.0	**2.2**	6.7	3.9	14.8	32.3	39.6	**3.9**	23.6	
RF	RS	22.4	75.2	**4.7**	7.2	29.8	4.4	3.8	17.5	4.4	4.1	2.1	2.4	1.0	2.6	6.4	4.2	14.8	**32.3**	39.8	5.2	**22.3**	7/4/10
RF	BA	23.6	73.5	6.6	7.8	33.4	4.8	3.8	17.3	4.0	4.2	2.1	**2.4**	1.2	2.8	6.6	6.7	**14.2**	**33.5**	**38.4**	7.0	26.1	
RF	EN	**21.9**	**73.3**	5.4	**6.2**	–	3.8	3.4	16.6	**3.8**	3.4	1.8	2.5	1.0	2.2	**5.9**	**3.3**	14.8	32.5	38.5	4.0	23.0	17/0/3
RT	SC	34.0	85.2	16.6	25.8	52.0	15.4	16.6	37.0	30.4	36.5	14.3	3.8	4.7	**5.0**	34.5	20.2	27.6	40.3	**49.8**	27.8	56.8	
RT	RS	36.6	83.9	13.6	24.6	49.7	16.1	16.9	35.9	30.6	34.7	15.4	3.6	5.2	5.3	35.3	19.9	27.6	39.8	49.3	23.9	53.7	12/1/8
RT	BA	27.6	81.5	**7.2**	11.5	39.6	7.6	6.1	**21.5**	10.4	11.1	4.2	**2.9**	1.7	3.1	16.0	9.7	**18.2**	**36.7**	**42.5**	**8.3**	34.6	
RT	EN	**26.4**	**80.9**	10.9	**11.3**	**37.4**	**5.7**	**5.6**	21.6	**9.1**	**10.4**	3.7	3.1	1.4	**3.0**	**12.5**	**7.1**	24.9	37.6	43.8	22.5	**29.8**	14/0/7

Table 3. Averaged error rate (mean±standard deviation) using best base learners.

Dataset	SC	RS-hom	RS-het	BA	EN
audiology	16.38±3.01	19.31±3.99	**14.22±0.75**	19.31±1.86	19.68±0.96
autoUnivau6750	73.4±2.77	74.02±2.17	**70.05±0.24** •	73.54±1.75	72.72±0.38
car	1.13±0.58	3.84±0.75 ○	**0.10±0.10** •	1.75±0.70	0.42±0.12 •
cnae9	5.90±1.16	5.80±1.20	**4.60±0.16** •	6.83±1.46	5.61±0.53 •
fbis.wc	18.19±1.05	18.23±1.93	19.99±1.19	**15.13±1.25**	15.62±0.40
kropt	29.74±0.38	29.77±0.59	30.17±0.11 ○	32.22±0.46	**29.36±0.43** •
letter	4.22±0.28	4.35±0.19	4.13±0.07	4.80±0.22	**3.84±0.07** •
mfeat-factors	2.41±0.50	2.60±0.62	**1.95±0.42**	2.20±0.28	2.09±0.20
mfeat-fourier	15.88±1.21	16.84±1.42	**15.76±0.51**	16.93±1.11	16.48±0.52
mfeat-karhunen	3.76±0.34	3.81±0.42	**2.97±0.25**	3.61±0.57	3.46±0.24
mfeat-pixel	2.59±0.47	2.88±0.39	**2.46±0.25**	2.58±0.48	2.48±0.11
optdigits	1.51±0.26	1.50±0.35	**1.11±0.15**	1.50±0.26	1.38±0.08
page-blocks	2.51±0.38	2.44±0.25	**2.00±0.15** •	2.37±0.31	2.45±0.09
pendigits	0.77±0.13	0.75±0.12	0.73±0.18	0.84±0.16	**0.70±0.03** •
segment	2.16±0.49	2.58±0.48 ○	**2.04±0.44**	2.76±0.65	2.19±0.19 •
semeion	6.65±0.96	6.52±0.92	6.77±0.10	6.61±0.64	**5.92±0.28** •
vowel	1.78±0.98	2.20±1.23	**1.05±0.55**	4.69±2.23	2.02±0.23 •
waveform	13.04±0.78	14.82±0.56 ○	13.08±0.17	**13.01±0.58**	14.75±0.31 ○
winequality	32.29±1.48	32.54±1.09	**31.12±0.71**	33.53±1.12	32.49±0.30 •
yeast	39.58±2.09	39.79±2.75	**36.46±0.81** •	38.38±2.25	38.51±0.63
zoo	3.48±2.61	4.35±4.86	**0.00±0.00** •	4.35±3.37	3.67±0.68

of only choosing classifiers from a portfolio, the results motivate to actively decompose multi-class problems in the context of AutoML, and further tailoring the base learners to the respective subproblems. From an AutoML perspective, homogeneous reduction stumps are less attractive, as they seem to never achieve globally the best performance; thus, the effort for considering them would not be justifiable. In contrast to this, it is worth considering ensembles of reduction stumps, which in some cases perform best, especially since the effort for building them is relatively low.

5   Conclusion

In this paper, we proposed a meta-classifier called reduction stump, which can be seen as the simplest reduction scheme for multi-class classification problems: the original problem is decomposed into three subproblems of smaller size, two multi-class problems on subsets of the original set of classes, and one binary problem on the two respective meta-classes. In spite of their simplicity, reduction stumps show promising performance in our experiments, especially in their heterogeneous version.

Our main motivation for analyzing reduction stumps originates from the field of automated machine learning. For the reasons already explained, reduction can be useful in AutoML, but should be applied with caution, in order to keep the complexity manageable. Encouraged by the results of this paper, our next step is to incorporate reduction stumps into the toolbox of AutoML. An additional interesting research question that arises from the observation that some datasets are more amenable to reduction than others is whether one can predict the benefit of applying reduction based on the properties of a dataset.

Acknowledgements. This work was partially supported by the German Research Foundation (DFG) within the Collaborative Research Center "On-The-Fly Computing" (SFB 901).

References

1. Dheeru, D., Karra Taniskidou, E.: UCI machine learning repository (2017). http://archive.ics.uci.edu/ml
2. Dong, Lin, Frank, Eibe, Kramer, Stefan: Ensembles of balanced nested dichotomies for multi-class problems. In: Jorge, Alípio Mário, Torgo, Luís, Brazdil, Pavel, Camacho, Rui, Gama, João (eds.) PKDD 2005. LNCS (LNAI), vol. 3721, pp. 84–95. Springer, Heidelberg (2005). https://doi.org/10.1007/11564126_13
3. Duarte-Villaseñor, Miriam Mónica, Carrasco-Ochoa, Jesús Ariel, Martínez-Trinidad, José Francisco, Flores-Garrido, Marisol: Nested dichotomies based on clustering. In: Alvarez, Luis, Mejail, Marta, Gomez, Luis, Jacobo, Julio (eds.) CIARP 2012. LNCS, vol. 7441, pp. 162–169. Springer, Heidelberg (2012). https://doi.org/10.1007/978-3-642-33275-3_20
4. Feurer, M., Klein, A., Eggensperger, K., Springenberg, J.T., Blum, M., Hutter, F.: Efficient and robust automated machine learning. In: Advances in Neural Information Processing Systems 28: Annual Conference on Neural Information Processing Systems 2015, Montreal, Quebec, Canada, 7–12 December 2015, pp. 2962–2970 (2015)
5. Frank, E., Kramer, S.: Ensembles of nested dichotomies for multi-class problems. In: Proceedings ICML, 21st International Conference on Machine Learning. Banff, Alberta, Canada (2004)
6. Fürnkranz, J.: Round robin classification. J. Mach. Learn. Res. **2**, 721–747 (2002). http://www.jmlr.org/papers/v2/fuernkranz02a.html
7. Kajdanowicz, T., Kazienko, P.: Multi-label classification using error correcting output codes. Appl. Math. Comput. Sci. **22**(4), 829–840 (2012). http://www.degruyter.com/view/j/amcs.2012.22.issue-4/v10006-012-0061-2/v10006-012-0061-2.xml
8. Leathart, Tim, Pfahringer, Bernhard, Frank, Eibe: Building Ensembles of adaptive nested dichotomies with random-pair selection. In: Frasconi, Paolo, Landwehr, Niels, Manco, Giuseppe, Vreeken, Jilles (eds.) ECML PKDD 2016. LNCS (LNAI), vol. 9852, pp. 179–194. Springer, Cham (2016). https://doi.org/10.1007/978-3-319-46227-1_12
9. Melnikov, V., Hüllermeier, E.: On the effectiveness of heuristics for learning nested dichotomies: an empirical analysis. Mach. Learn. **107**(8), 1537–1560 (2018)
10. Mohr, F., Wever, M., Hüllermeier, E.: Ml-Plan: automated machine learning via hierarchical planning. Mach. Learn. **107**(8), 1495–1515 (2018)

11. Olson, R.S., Moore, J.H.: TPOT: A tree-based pipeline optimization tool for automating machine learning. In: Proceedings of the 2016 Workshop on Automatic Machine Learning, AutoML 2016, Co-located with 33rd International Conference on Machine Learning (ICML 2016), New York City, NY, USA, 24 June 2016, pp. 66–74 (2016)

12. Thornton, C., Hutter, F., Hoos, H.H., Leyton-Brown, K.: Auto-WEKA: combined selection and hyperparameter optimization of classification algorithms. In: The 19th ACM SIGKDD International Conference on Knowledge Discovery and Data Mining, KDD 2013, Chicago, IL, USA, 11–14 August 2013, pp. 847–855 (2013)

13. Wever, M., Mohr, F., Hüllermeier, E.: Ensembles of evolved nested dichotomies. In: Proceedings of the Genetic and Evolutionary Computation Conference, GECCO 2018, Kyoto, Germany, 15–19 July 2018 (2018)

Decomposition of Quantitative Gaifman Graphs as a Data Analysis Tool

José Luis Balcázar, Marie Ely Piceno$^{(\boxtimes)}$, and Laura Rodríguez-Navas

Universitat Politècnica de Catalunya, Barcelona, Spain
mpiceno@cs.upc.edu

Abstract. We argue the usefulness of Gaifman graphs of first-order relational structures as an exploratory data analysis tool. We illustrate our approach with cases where the modular decompositions of these graphs reveal interesting facts about the data. Then, we introduce generalized notions of Gaifman graphs, enhanced with quantitative information, to which we can apply more general, existing decomposition notions via 2-structures; thus enlarging the analytical capabilities of the scheme. The very essence of Gaifman graphs makes this approach immediately appropriate for the multirelational data framework.

1 Introduction

First-order (finite) relational structures (see e.g. [9]) are the conceptual essence of the relational database model. Gaifman graphs are a well-known, quite natural theoretical construction that can be applied to any relational structure [9]. They have provided very interesting progress in the theory of these logical models.

Given a first-order relational structure, or relational database, with relations (or tables) R_i, where the values in the tuples come from a fixed universe U, the corresponding Gaifman graph has the elements of U as vertices; and there is an edge (x, y), for $x \neq y$, exactly when x and y appear together in some tuple $t \in R_i$ for some table R_i. That is, Gaifman graphs record co-occurrence (or lack thereof) among every pair of universe items.

Hence, a clique in a Gaifman graph would group items that, pairwise, appear together somewhere in the relational structure: co-occurrence patterns; a clique in its complement would reveal an incompatibility pattern. Of course, finding maximal cliques is NP-complete; but there are less demanding ways to study graphs that identify efficiently both sorts of patterns in a recursive decomposition: namely, the modular decomposition and its generalization, the decomposition of 2-structures.

This paper proposes to employ these decompositions as avenues for exploratory data analysis on relational data (whether single- or multi-relational):

This research was supported by grant TIN2017-89244-R from Ministerio de Economia, Industria y Competitividad, and by Conacyt (México); and we acknowledge recognition 2017SGR-856 (MACDA) from AGAUR (Generalitat de Catalunya).

W. Duivesteijn et al. (Eds.): IDA 2018, LNCS 11191, pp. 238–250, 2018.
https://doi.org/10.1007/978-3-030-01768-2_20

by applying them on the Gaifman graph of a dataset, we can obtain valuable information that would not be readily observable directly on the data.

Modular decompositions suffice to treat standard Gaifman graphs. However, we extend the capabilities of our approach by generalizing, in very natural ways, the notion of Gaifman graph so as to handle quantitative information (a must in many data analysis applications). Hence, we develop our work using the more general decomposition of 2-structures [4]: again a notion that has been very fruitfully developed in their theoretical form, and in a number of applications (such as [8]), but not yet imported, to our knowledge, into data analysis frameworks.

2   Decomposing Standard Gaifman Graphs

As already mentioned, the basic notion of Gaifman graph is pretty simple: on all items that appear along all the tuples of a single- or multi-relational dataset, edges join pairs of items that appear together in some tuple.

Example 1. As a running example, let us consider a very small, single-relation database on the universe $\{a, b, c, d, e\}$, with three attributes and three tuples:

t_1: a b c
t_2: a d e
t_3: a c d

Then, the Gaifman graph is as shown in Fig. 1 (left).

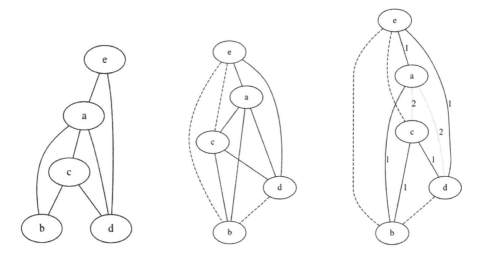

Fig. 1. A Gaifman graph, its natural completion, and a labeled variant.

2.1   2-Structures and Their Decompositions

The very classical notion called "modular decomposition" [6] suffices to implement our approach on plain Gaifman graphs; this notion has been rediscovered many times and described under several different names[1]. However, it is insufficient to handle adequately the generalizations that we will propose below. Therefore, we develop our approach directly on top of the more general notion of 2-structures and their clans [4].

First, we describe some "cosmetics" on our Gaifman graphs: they will be seen as a complete graph with two sorts of (nonreflexive) edges. One sort corresponds to edges present in the graph (solid lines in our diagrams); the other corresponds to absent (nonreflexive) edges (broken lines). We call this graph the "natural completion" of the original graph. In our example, this process is illustrated in Fig. 1 (center).

Additionally, we can label each edge with its multiplicity, that is, the number of tuples that contain the pair of items linked by the edge. The previous example then becomes as in Fig. 1 (right): pairs appear either zero times together (dashed edges), once (black lines, labeled 1) or, in two cases, twice (gray lines, labeled 2).

Now, in general terms, a 2-structure is simply the complete graph on some universe U, plus an equivalence relation E among the edges. Figure 1 (right) serves as an example, where there are three equivalence classes of edges: the broken edges, the black edges, and the gray edges; of course, Fig. 1 (center) is also an example, with just two equivalence classes of edges. We will restrict ourselves to undirected edges, and will employ the common, very graphical and intuitive representation of coloring in the same way edges belonging to the same equivalence class.

Observe that the type of the equivalence relation E is $E \subseteq ((U \times U) \times (U \times U))$ because E tells us whether two arbitrary edges (x, y) and (u, v) are equivalent.

For a 2-structure given by the set of vertices U and the equivalence relation E among the edges of the complete graph on U, we say that a subset $C \subseteq U$ is a clan, informally, if all the members of C are indistinguishable among them by non-members. That is: whenever some $x \notin C$ "can distinguish" between $y \in C$ and $z \in C$, in the sense that the edge (x, y) is not equivalent to the edge (x, z), then C is *not* a clan. Formally (see [4]):

Definition 1. *Given U and an equivalence relation $E \subseteq ((U \times U) \times (U \times U))$ on the edges of the complete graph on U, $C \subseteq U$ is a clan when*

$$\forall x \notin C \, \forall y \in C \, \forall z \in C \, ((x, y), (x, z)) \in E.$$

Note that different vertices outside the clan might see the clan differently: for $x \notin C$ and $x' \notin C$, and $y \in C$, the edges (x, y) and (x', y) may well be nonequivalent. We only require that each fixed x does not distinguish between the clan members.

---

[1] See https://en.wikipedia.org/wiki/Modular_decomposition for some of the alternative names that the concept has received.

Basic examples of clans are the so-called trivial clans: all the singletons $\{x\}$ for $x \in U$, as well as U itself, are vacuously clans. There may be other clans. For instance, consider the natural completion of the Gaifman graph obtained from Example 1, depicted in Fig. 1 (center). Edges are split into two equivalence classes (existing or nonexisting edges in the original Gaifman graph). Then, one can see that there would be exactly one nontrivial clan, formed by $\{b, c, d, e\}$: all vertices not in the clan (that is, vertex a, the single one not in the clan) are connected to each vertex inside the clan through edges of the same color, namely solid black. Any other candidate turns out not to be a clan. For instance, any set including a and b but excluding e is not a clan, as e "distinguishes" between a and b; then, any set including b and e must include c and d, which can distinguish between them. All in all, any clan including a and b ends up including all the vertices, that is, becoming a trivial clan. Analogous reasoning applies if we start by pairing a with other vertices.

On the other hand, it is not difficult to see that the labeled, colored version of the Gaifman graph of Example 1, as depicted in Fig. 1 (right), does not have nontrivial clans. Equivalence is given by the same multiplicity label (that is, edges drawn in the same "color"): the extra distinction between gray and black edges allows for external vertices to distinguish between some vertices inside every candidate proper subset. Further examples come later as clans are the key tool for our proposal of a data analysis method.

2.2   Prime Clans and Tree Decompositions

It is known [4] that certain clans, called prime clans, allow us to decompose a 2-structure into a tree-like form.

Definition 2. *For a fixed universe U, we say that two subsets of U overlap if neither is a subset of the other, but they are not disjoint. That is, for $S \subseteq U$ and $T \subseteq U$, they overlap if the three sets $S \cap T$, $S \setminus T$, and $T \setminus S$ are all three nonempty. Then, prime clans are those clans that do not overlap any other clan.*

Of course, trivial clans are also immediately prime clans. Thus, by definition, any two sets in the family of prime clans are either disjoint, or a subset of one another: they provide us with a so-called "decomposable set family" [11] that can be pictured in a tree form, by displaying every prime clan (except U itself) as a child of the smallest prime clan that properly contains it.

There are studies that report how these decompositions look like. Specifically, at each node of the tree we have again a 2-structure, whose vertices correspond to the clans that fall as children of the node. In the case of our constructions out of Gaifman graphs, it is known that all the 2-structures that appear as nodes of such a tree decomposition are of one of two well-defined sorts: either "complete" (all edges are equivalent) or "primitive" (only having trivial clans). This is due to our graphs being undirected, because 2-structures on directed graphs may exhibit a third basic component in their tree decomposition ("linear" 2-structures). Further information on this topic appears in [4]. This reference contains, as well, often far-from-trivial proofs of theorems that ensure that things are as we have described.

Example 2. Continuing Example 1, the tree decomposition of the 2-structure in Fig. 1 (center) is displayed in Fig. 2 (left). Boxes correspond to clans: here, the topmost box corresponds to the trivial clan containing all the vertices and, inside it, each dot corresponds to a prime subclan. All along the whole decomposition, trivial clans are indicated by a link to the vertex they consist of, represented with an elliptic node; nontrivial ones are linked instead to a new box describing the internal structure of the clan, in terms of the prime clans it has as proper subsets. Then, as a set, each clan is formed by all the elements in the leaves of the subtree rooted at it.

A "brute-force", exhaustive search attempt was employed in [12] to identify all prime clans. A couple of published algorithms [10,11] can be adapted for implementing a system computing this sort of tree decompositions. However, as we envision an analysis support system able to add Gaifman nodes in an incremental manner, we have implemented a somewhat different, incremental algorithm. Due to the space limit, the details of our algorithmic contributions will be presented in a follow-up paper (or in an expanded version of this one), together with some comparisons against other algorithms.

2.3   Limits to the Visualization of Complex Clans

Our experimentation shows that, unsurprisingly, the visualization of large Gaifman graphs is unadvisable. Actually, sometimes the clans lead to large primitive 2-structures, whose mathematical study gets pretty complicated [5]. We set up some relatively arbitrary limits, trying to get understandable diagrams. Let us consider a more realistic example to explain them.

In Fig. 2 (right) we display (a fragment of) the decomposition of the Gaifman graph of the well-known Zoo dataset from the UC Irvine repository [2]; it contains 17 attributes of 100 animal species. We have preprocessed it slightly so that the semantics of each item is clearly identifiable (e. g. predator_False or toothed_True). We will return to this dataset below in Sect. 4.2.

For the time being, we just discuss the decomposition of its standard Gaifman graph. The topmost node of this decomposition is, as always, the trivial clan with the whole universe; in this case, it turns out to decompose as a set of many trivial clans, set up in the form of a primitive 2-structure that we choose not to draw complete; however, one nontrivial clan also appears: "mammal" and 'milk_True" are indistinguishable from the perspective of all the other elements in the dataset. That is, for every other piece of information, either it goes together with each in some tuples (one such item could be "hair_True"), or it does not go together with any of them ever (for instance: "feathers_True").

In our diagrams, as we do here, clans containing more than a handful of nontrivial clans are not drawn in detail: just the clan type label ("primitive" or "complete") is shown. Besides, if there are few nontrivial clans, but many trivial

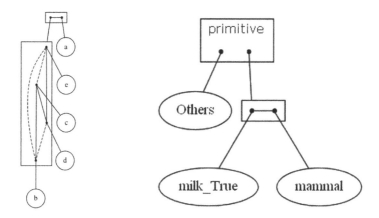

Fig. 2. Decompositions of the Gaifman graphs for Example 1 and for the Zoo dataset.

ones, then the trivial clans are grouped in a single node labeled Others, sort of a merge of them all. The reader must keep in mind that this particular node actually represents together a number of unstructured items.

This approach of limiting the size of the substructures that become fully spelled-out was taken also in [8], where also a "zooming" capability was introduced (we may consider adding one such option to our system in the future).

2.4   Isolated Vertex Elision

As we move on, later, into quantitative generalizations of Gaifman graphs, one case turns out to be common in our experiments. Whereas Gaifman graphs do not have isolated vertices (except in limit, artificial cases such as relations with a single attribute), in our generalizations this is no longer true: many datasets will lead to 2-structures exhibiting many vertices that are endpoints only of broken edges; that is, they are isolated vertices in the corresponding (generalized) Gaifman graph. The set of those isolated vertices forms a sometimes quite large clan that clutters the diagram but contributes nothing to the analysis beyond "all these vertices are actually isolated". We use again the label "Others" to represent these items, all alike from the decomposition perspective, as a single vertex, as indeed this is a particular case of the usage of the "Others" label as per the previous Sect. 2.3.

3   Interpreting a Decomposition of a Gaifman Graph

We move on to explain another example of our analysis strategy. We present and discuss the outcome of a tree decomposition of the Gaifman graph of a simple, famous, and relatively small dataset often used for teaching introductory data analysis courses. It comes from data of each of the passengers of the Titanic. Among several existing variants of this dataset, some of them pretty complete, we choose a reduced variant on which we illustrate the interpretation of our decompositions. This variant we use keeps four attributes, one of them (age) discretized. To describe the details of this dataset, we quote:

"The titanic dataset gives the values of four categorical attributes for each of the 2201 people on board the Titanic when it struck an iceberg and sank. The attributes are social class (first class, second class, third class, crewmember), age (adult or child), sex, and whether or not the person survived."

(http://www.cs.toronto.edu/~delve/data/titanic/desc.html)

(As indicated in that website, this variant of the data was originally compiled by Dawson [1] and converted for use in the DELVE data analysis environment by Radford Neal.)

The decomposition via its standard Gaifman graph is depicted in Fig. 3. Recall that broken edges represent pairs that never appear together in any tuple, whereas solid edges are edges of the original Gaifman graph and thus join universe elements that appear together in some tuple.

The clans for sex and survival are clear and intuitive: as they are different possible values for the same attribute, they never appear together. On the other hand, every possibility for these attributes does appear somewhere, as does every possible pairing with all other items in the universe, so that the top node is a complete 2-structure consisting on all solid edges.

Likewise, one might expect a clan with the four alternative values of traveling class, namely, 1st, 2nd, 3rd or Crew. However, that clan only has actual passenger classes. The value Crew migrates to the parent "ages" clan, where we find some interesting fact: a small primitive 2-structure arising from the interaction of the ages values and the Crew value, where of course being an adult is incompatible with being a child, and both are compatible to all the traveling classes (the top node in the middle clan); however, being in the crew is only compatible with being an adult. This calls our attention to the fact that the crew included, of course, no children, a fact that we might overlook in a non-systematic analysis. That is: even if the traveling classes and the "Crew" label are employed as values in the same column, the data tells us, through our decomposition procedure, that they have different semantics!

4   Generalizations of Gaifman Graphs

We move on to discuss tree decompositions based on generalized Gaifman graphs. The aim is to keep track of quantitative information that the standard Gaifman graph lacks. In our context, many ideas present themselves to complement Gaifman graphs and clan decompositions with quantitative considerations. For the time being, we contemplate just some very simple cases: we let the number of occurrences of each pair play a role.

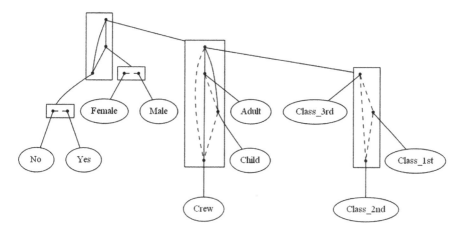

Fig. 3. Decomposing the standard Gaifman graph of the Titanic dataset.

4.1 Thresholded Gaifman Graphs

Our first variant is as follows.

Definition 3. *For a threshold k (a nonzero natural number) a thresholded Gaifman graph is a completion of a Gaifman graph in which each labeled edge is classified according to its number of occurrences, as follows. We still have two equivalence classes of edges. If the number in the label is above the threshold k, the edge goes into one equivalence class (represented in our diagrams by a solid line); whereas if the number of occurrences of the edge is less than or equal to the threshold, then the edge belongs to the other equivalence class (and a broken line is used to represent it).*

Figure 4 provides an alternative analysis of the Titanic dataset described before. There, we decompose a thresholded Gaifman graph, aiming at uncovering very common co-occurrences, that is, high multiplicities. We set the threshold rather arbitrarily at the quite high value of 1000 (out of 2201 tuples). We see at work the effect of isolated vertex elision, as many attribute values to not reach multiplicity 1000 with any other value: the elision process, as described in Sect. 2.4, replaces all of them by a single node, playing the same role all of them play, that is, broken lines among themselves and to all the surviving values. The new decomposition is interesting in that it very clearly reflects the Birkenhead Drill: "Women and children first".

4.2 Quantitative Gaifman Graphs

The *linear colored Gaifman graph* is a (completion of a) Gaifman graph in which the equivalence classes of the edges are directly defined by the label, that is, the number of occurrences. All pairs occurring once would lead to one class, those

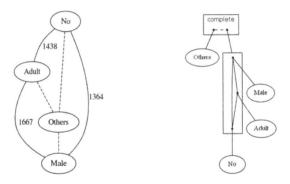

Fig. 4. Titanic dataset: thresholded Gaifman graph, at 1000, and its decomposition.

occurring twice to another, and so on; up to some limit, beyond which we do not keep the distinction. Figure 1 (right) corresponds to this case.

A natural variation is to have each color stand for some interval of values, with linearly growing limits; the case just described would correspond to intervals of width 1. Figure 5 shows one such case: we apply intervals of width 25 over the Zoo dataset. Broken lines mark less than 25 occurrences, solid lines less than 50, and the gray line appearing inside one of the clans goes beyond that limit because it gathers all birds and all fish and all insects into the oviparous clan.

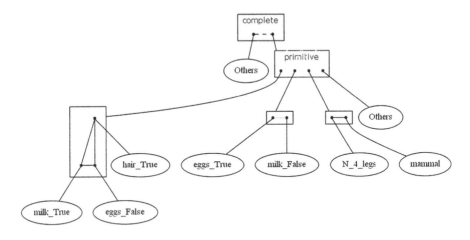

Fig. 5. Decomposing the linear Gaifman graph of Zoo with 25 as interval width.

This notion can be combined naturally with the previous one: instead of broken lines being simply the first interval, we can apply a different value as threshold and leave as broken lines all occurrence multiplicities below it, and then use the colors for the values at the threshold or above it, at linearly growing intervals of fixed width. Likewise, an upper threshold can be imposed. For instance, on the Titanic data, we used colors by width 1 intervals up to an upper threshold of 10: this approach is able to point out for us, with no particular user guidance, the fact that the number of children among the first-class travelers was surprisingly small: as it happened to Crew, the first-class node migrates from the traveling-class clan to the age clan.

We expect usefulness also from the *exponential colored Gaifman graph*: while similar in spirit to the intervals in linear graphs, here the interval width grows exponentially: each equivalence class (or color) represents an exponentially growing interval of occurrence multiplicities. On one hand, this frees the user from having to bet on a specific interval width. On the other, there are cases where the Gaifman graph multiplicities turn out to be approximately Zipfian, and the exponential coloring is likely to be adequate. Again, as with the linear case, we can also impose a user-defined threshold below which, or over which, the occurrences are not considered different; then, one runs the exponential count between them.

Even though the black-and-white printed version of this paper will not show it, we chose to provide an example of application of the exponential graph to the ("people" table within the) UW-CSE dataset from the Relational Dataset Repository (http://relational.fit.cvut.cz) at threshold 3. The items have been renamed for better understanding; also, we have manually edited out a small part of the diagram to fit the page size and to focus on the three different colors in the pairs of equivalent items: these colors tell us that the amount of Students (and thus NotProfessors) is largish (specifically 216), the quantity of year zero cases clearly smaller (namely 138) and the amount of Professors even smaller (62 in total).

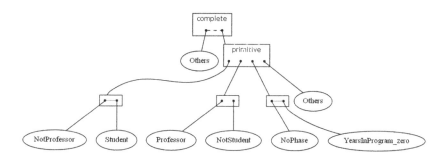

Fig. 6. UW-CSE: part of the decomposition via the exponential Gaifman graph.

5   Discussion and Subsequent Work

We have described a data analysis approach based on the prime tree decomposition of variations of the Gaifman graph of a dataset. We have illustrated the process with some relatively successful cases. Technologically, we have resorted to a relatively simple implementation in Python, https://github.com/MelyPic/ PrimeTreeDecomposition, relying on the standard graph module NetworkX and on the graphical capabilities of the `pydot` interface to the Dot engine of Graphviz [7]. We have not compared the available algorithms: there is no room left for that study in this submission, and it will be the subject of forthcoming write-ups.

Many possibilities of further development remain. First and foremost, we must discuss a clear limitation. Like in so many other exploratory data analysis frameworks, for a given dataset we may not be lucky: it may happen that a given selection of Gaifman graph, once decomposed, has no nontrivial clans, or decomposes into just a few quite large primitive substructures that provide little or no insight about the data. For one, the linear Gaifman graph of the well-known toy dataset Weather (discussed e.g. in [13]) has only trivial clans and, if fully displayed, leads to just a large box of colored spaghetti. Useful advice to choose properly sorts of Gaifman graphs, thresholds, and interval widths remains to be found. After all, parameter tuning is a black art in many data mining approaches.

One natural variant consists of combining the constraints defining clans with those of standard frequent-set mining; we explored that avenue and, unfortunately, in all our attempts, we never found a single case of nontrivial clans.

Also, we can run this sort of processes on multirelational datasets or, even, directly on graphs. For the first case, our examples so far fall into the very common and standard "single table" perspective. However, from their earliest inception, Gaifman graphs were a multirelational concept by essence. Applying tree decompositions of generalized Gaifman graphs to multirelational datasets is, therefore, conceptually immediate, and indeed our example in Fig. 6 comes from a well-known multirelational benchmark. However, there, we have not taken into account the foreign key phenomenon: would it be appropriate to denormalize before computing the Gaifman graph? If so, can one compute the graph directly, efficiently, without actually denormalizing the data?

For the second case, graphs are, so to speak, their own Gaifman graph, so we can simply apply the tree decomposition on the given graph. A couple of extra possibilities naturally arise. For instance, we could decompose a 2-structure where the equivalence classes come from the lengths of the shortest paths between vertices, or from thresholding these lengths; or from the vertex- or edge-connectivity (equivalently, min-cuts, by Menger's theorem), again possibly thresholded. Along this line, there may be interesting connections with the topic known as "blockmodeling" in social networks, which uses a notion similar to that of clan, although relaxed through allowing exceptions.

The multiplicity-based generalizations we have proposed are quite basic; more sophisticate approaches to define the equivalence relation between edges might be advantageous. In particular, we believe now that some advances might come from the study of the applicability of unsupervised discretization methods [3]. Indeed, the actual multiplicities appearing as labels of the edges of the Gaifman graph form a set of integers that is to be discretized in a number of intervals in an unsupervised manner. A few existing algorithms for unsupervised discretization can be applied to try and automatize parts of the transformation of the labeled Gaifman graph into the starting 2-structure.

Besides the theoretical developments, improving the software tool is also a desirable endeavor. Initially, we found the very notion of exploratory data analysis via 2-structure decompositions of quantitative versions of Gaifman graphs risky enough, and were not eager to compute very fast, nor in a very usable way by other people, results that, in principle, were candidates to be fully useless. However, we found our initial results clearly sufficient to consider that this approach is worth of further effort: we did design better algorithms than the ones initially employed [12], and we are confident that our tool will see considerable improvements along several facets in the coming months: the exploration of alternative tree visualizations, the implementation of additional control like zooming, or the possibility of importing the data directly from databases; this last extension is actually crucial in order to try our methods on the usual multirelational benchmarks.

References

1. Dawson, R.J.M.: The 'unusual episode' data revisited. J. Stat. Educ. 3(3) (1995)
2. Dheeru, D., Karra Taniskidou, E.: UCI machine learning repository (2017). http://archive.ics.uci.edu/ml
3. Dougherty, J., Kohavi, R., Sahami, M.: Supervised and unsupervised discretization of continuous features. In: Prieditis, A., Russell, S.J. (eds.) Machine Learning, Proceedings of the Twelfth International Conference on Machine Learning, Tahoe City, California, USA, 9–12 July 1995, pp. 194–202. Morgan Kaufmann (1995)
4. Ehrenfeucht, A., Harju, T., Rozenberg, G.: The Theory of 2-Structures - A Framework for Decomposition and Transformation of Graphs. World Scientific, Singapore (1999). http://www.worldscibooks.com/mathematics/4197.html
5. Ehrenfeucht, A., Rozenberg, G.: Primitivity is hereditary for 2-structures. Theor. Comput. Sci. **70**(3), 343–358 (1990). https://doi.org/10.1016/0304-3975(90)90131-Z
6. Gallai, T.: Transitiv orientierbare graphen. Acta Mathematica Academiae Scientiarum Hungarica **18**(1), 25–66 (1967). http://dx.doi.org/10.1007/BF02020961
7. Gansner, E.R., North, S.C.: An open graph visualization system and its applications to software engineering. Softw. - Pract. Exp. **30**(11), 1203–1233 (2000)
8. Larraz, D.: Aplicación de las 2-estructuras a las gramáticas del lenguaje humano y representación gráfica de ambas. Graduation Project, Universidad de Zaragoza (2010). http://zaguan.unizar.es/record/5000
9. Libkin, L.: Elements of Finite Model Theory. Texts in Theoretical Computer Science. An EATCS Series. Springer, Berlin (2004). https://doi.org/10.1007/978-3-662-07003-1
10. McConnell, R.M.: An $O(n^2)$ incremental algorithm for modular decomposition of graphs and 2-structures. Algorithmica **14**(3), 229–248 (1995). https://doi.org/10.1007/BF01206330
11. McConnell, R.M., Spinrad, J.P.: Modular decomposition and transitive orientation. Discrete Mathematics **201**(1), 189–241 (1999). http://www.sciencedirect.com/science/article/pii/S0012365X98003197

12. Rodríguez-Navas, L.: Estructures de grafs amb equivalències d'arestes aplicades a l'anàlisi de dades relacionals. Graduation Project, FIB, UPC (2017)
13. Witten, I.H., Eibe, F., Hall, M.A.: Data Mining: Practical Machine Learning Tools and Techniques, 3rd edn. Morgan Kaufmann, Elsevier, Burlington (2011). http://www.worldcat.org/oclc/262433473

Exploring the Effects of Data Distribution in Missing Data Imputation

Jastin Pompeu Soares[1], Miriam Seoane Santos[1], Pedro Henriques Abreu[1(✉)],
Hélder Araújo[2], and João Santos[3]

[1] CISUC, Department of Informatics Engineering, University of Coimbra,
Coimbra, Portugal
{jastinps,miriams}@student.dei.uc.pt, pha@dei.uc.pt
[2] ISR, Department of Electrical and Computer Engineering,
University of Coimbra, Coimbra, Portugal
helder@isr.uc.pt
[3] IPO-Porto Research Centre (CI-IPOP), Porto, Portugal
joao.santos@ipoporto.min-saude.pt

Abstract. In data imputation problems, researchers typically use several techniques, individually or in combination, in order to find the one that presents the best performance over all the features comprised in the dataset. This strategy, however, neglects the nature of data (data distribution) and makes impractical the generalisation of the findings, since for new datasets, a huge number of new, time consuming experiments need to be performed. To overcome this issue, this work aims to understand the relationship between data distribution and the performance of standard imputation techniques, providing a heuristic on the choice of proper imputation methods and avoiding the needs to test a large set of methods. To this end, several datasets were selected considering different sample sizes, number of features, distributions and contexts and missing values were inserted at different percentages and scenarios. Then, different imputation methods were evaluated in terms of predictive and distributional accuracy. Our findings show that there is a relationship between features' distribution and algorithms' performance, and that their performance seems to be affected by the combination of missing rate and scenario at state and also other less obvious factors such as sample size, goodness-of-fit of features and the ratio between the number of features and the different distributions comprised in the dataset.

Keywords: Missing data · Data imputation · Data distribution

1 Introduction

Missing data imputation refers to the process of finding plausible values to replace those who are missing in a dataset and is a common data preprocessing technique applied in several fields [14]. Most often, imputation is performed using a brute force strategy, where a set of algorithms is used to impute all the features

© Springer Nature Switzerland AG 2018
W. Duivesteijn et al. (Eds.): IDA 2018, LNCS 11191, pp. 251–263, 2018.
https://doi.org/10.1007/978-3-030-01768-2_21

in a dataset. Then, the imputed datasets pass to the classification stage, where the imputation performance is evaluated through the classification error (CE) [1]. Although this is a standard approach to the missing data problem, it raises some important hitches: first, since all techniques must be implemented for all features, its computational cost is high; secondly, it assumes that the same technique should perform well for all or the great majority of features, which could be an over-assumption for features with different characteristics and finally, it uses the CE to evaluate the imputation quality, which for contexts other than classification, could be inappropriate. In general classification scenarios, the objective is to efficiently solve a classification problem, and therefore imputation is considered a required step to produce quality data. When imputation, rather than classification, is the focus, the use of CE is controversial. Some authors strongly defend that "imputation is not prediction" [22], and that the imputation method that minimises the classification error may produce biased estimates and affect the original data distribution.

Imputation methods should ideally be able to reproduce the true values in data – Predictive Accuracy (PAC) – and preserve the distribution of those true values – Distributional Accuracy (DAC) [6]. However, in the majority of imputation works, the nature of data (data distribution) is completely neglected and the above-mentioned properties are disregarded in favour of CE. Taking into account the distribution of data could be relevant to guide the choice of an appropriate imputation method: it considers the intrinsic characteristics of data and avoids the need to test a large set of methods for datasets where the features' distributions are known. Thus, studying the influence of data distribution in imputation presents a new challenge for missing data research and may provide a heuristic on the most appropriate imputation strategy for each feature in the study, allowing researchers to address missing data problems more easily and effectively.

This work follows from the initial research of Santos et al. [18], where authors showed that there was a relation between imputation methods and data distribution, when missing data is generated completely at random (MCAR mechanism). In this work, we extend their experimental set up to consider more datasets (15 datasets) and missing not at random (MNAR) mechanism, created in 6 different ways (scenarios T_1 to T_6, as will be explained in Sect. 3). Our experiments show that regardless of the missing data generation scenario, the imputation methods are in fact influenced by data distribution, with the exception of Support Vector Machine (SVM). Aside for SVM, that achieves the best PAC and DAC results for the great majority of distributions, Self-Organizing Map (SOM) is the overall winner in both metrics. However, the choice of the best imputation method depends also on the scenario and missing rate at state, besides other less obvious aspects as the Goodness of Fit (GoF), sample size and ratio of features per distribution.

The remainder of this document is structured as follows: Sect. 2 discusses related works regarding missing data imputation in several contexts. Sections

3 and 4 describe the experimental setup used in this work and report on the achieved results, while Sect. 5 presents the conclusions and suggests some possibilities for future work.

2   Related Work

Nanni et al. [13] compared the performance of standard imputation techniques (including MMimp and KNNimp) and their proposed imputation method for classification purposes, by generating missing values on 5 health related datasets at different rates (10–50%). The researchers concluded that their imputation techniques, based on clustering and random sub-spaces, present better behaviour than all the others (in terms of CE), achieving a satisfactory performance for MR greater than 30%. Aisha et al. [2] studied the effects of data imputation (including MMimp, KNNimp and SVMimp) on the classification of an incomplete health dataset (MR of 48%). SVMimp, along with Local Least Squares, outperformed the remaining techniques (in terms of CE). Rahman and Davis [15], investigated the classification performance of several imputation methods (such as SVMimp, MMimp, DTimp) using CE metrics, on a real incomplete medical dataset with 0–30% MR per feature. The results showed that all imputation methods based on machine learning improved the sensibility (and in some cases accuracy) of the classification task, in relation to MMimp. García-Laencina et al. [7] studied the influence of imputation (including KNNimp and SOMimp) on classification accuracy, using synthetic and real datasets. In this work, the authors start by evaluating the imputation quality using PAC (Pearson's r) and DAC (Kolmogorov–Smirnov distance) metrics, but just applied KNNimp (with different k values) on the first feature of synthetics datasets (MR 5–40%). However, this approach was discarded in favour of CE metrics, since the main objective of the experiments was to solve a classification problem. Rahman and Islam [16] propose imputation techniques based on DT and compare them in terms of PAC - coefficient of determination (R^2), Mean Squared Error (MSE) and Mean Absolute Error (MAE). DAC metrics are, however, neglected. This work used 9 real datasets from different contexts, where missing values were generated (1–10%). The proposed imputation techniques outperformed the others. Amiri and Jensen [3] introduced three imputation methods based on Fuzzy Rough Sets and compared their performances with 11 standard techniques (including KNNimp and SVMimp), in terms of RMSE (PAC analysis). In this work, the authors used 27 complete and real datasets from different contexts and inserted missing values varying from 5 to 30%. The simulations showed that SVMimp, KNNimp and the three proposed techniques obtained the best results.

In the above-mentioned works, imputation techniques are frequently evaluated in terms of CE, and the effects they may have in data distribution are most often ignored. Moreover, in these approaches, the same technique is used to impute all features, without considering the possibility that different features may be more properly imputed with different techniques. This work conducts a study on the influence of data distribution in missing data imputation, aiming to assess how different imputation techniques perform across different feature distributions and missing generation types, extending the work of Santos et al. [18].

3   Experimental Setup

Our experimental setup consisted in 4 main stages: Data Collection, Distribution Fitting and Missing Data Generation, Data Imputation and Evaluation (Fig. 1).

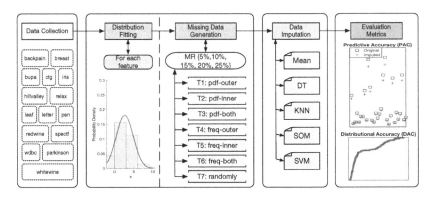

Fig. 1. Experimental Setup Architecture, comprising Data Collection, Distribution Fitting and Missing Data Generation, Data Imputation and Evaluation.

Data Collection comprised the selection of several publicly available datasets, from UCI Machine Learning Repository (http://archive.ics.uci.edu/ml) and Kaggle Datasets (https://www.kaggle.com/datasets), attending to different contexts, sample sizes, number of features and number of different distributions (Table 1).

After the datasets were collected, the Distribution Fitting and Missing Data Generation follows. Each feature of each dataset is fitted against a comprehensive set of distributions (beta, birnbaum-saunders, exponential, extreme value, gamma, generalized extreme value, generalized pareto, inverse gaussian, logistic, loglogistic, lognormal, nakagami, normal, rayleigh, rician, t location-scale and weibull) and the Goodness of Fit (GoF) statistic is used to determine the distribution that best fits the data—GoF values vary from $-\infty$ (bad fit) to 1 (perfect fit). Then, based on the best fitting distribution, the probability density function (pdf) is determined and used to define several scenarios from which the missing values are introduced at different rates (5, 10, 15, 20 and 25%). Missing values are inserted following 7 distinct methods: the simplest method (T_7) consists on randomly selecting values to remove from each feature (MCAR mechanism); the remaining methods follow MNAR mechanism and are based on the probability density function (pdf-based methods: T_1 to T_3) and on the frequency distribution ($freq$-based methods: T_4 to T_6) of each feature. For each of these methods,

Table 1. Summary of datasets' characteristics.

Dataset	Context	Sample size	No. of features	No. of distributions (no. of features)	No. features/No. distributions^2
Backpain	Detect abnormal back pain	310	12	Beta(1), Gamma(2), Generalized Pareto(5) Normal(1), Nakagami(1), tLocationScale(2)	0.333
Breast	Identify breast carcinomas	106	9	Birnbaum-saunders(2), Generalized Extreme Value(4), Generalized Pareto(2), Lognormal(1)	0.563
Bupa	Detect alcoholism problems	345	6	Birnbaum-saunders(1), Exponential(1), Generalized Extreme Value(1), Inverse Gaussian(1), Loglogistic(2)	0.240
ctg	Detect pathologic fetal cardiotocograms	2126	21	Birnbaum-saunders(1), Gamma(4), Generalized Extreme Value(3) Generalized Pareto(2), Inverse Gaussian(1), Logistic(2) Normal(3), Nakagami(1), tLocationscale(2), Weibull(2)	0.210
Hillvalley	Detect hills and valleys	1212	100	Birnbaum-saunders(94), Generalized Extreme Value(6)	25
Iris	Distinguish between different types of iris plants	150	4	Extreme Value(1), Generalized Extreme Value(2), Inverse Guassian(1)	0.444
Leaf	Distinguish between different species of leafs	340	14	Beta(3), Birnbaum-saunders(1), Generalized Extreme Value(2) Generalized Pareto(5), Nakagami(1), Lognormal(1), Rayleigh(1)	0.286
Leaf	Identify the alphabet letters (A-Z)	5000	16	Exponential(1), Gamma(9), Generalized Pareto(2) Normal(2), Rayleigh(2)	0.640
Parkinson	Diagnose cases of parkinson's disease	195	22	Beta(1), Gamma(1), Generalized Extreme Value(14), Generalized Pareto(2), Inverse Gaussian(2), Loglogistic(1), Weibull(1)	0.449
Pen	Identify handwritten digits (0-9)	3498	16	Extreme Value(1), Gamma(2), Generalized Extreme Value(4) Generalized Pareto(1), Logistic(8)	0.640
Redwine	Classify red wine quality	1599	11	Birnbaum-saunders(2), Generalized Extreme Value(4) Logistic(1), Loglogistic(1), Nakagami(1), tLocationScale(2)	0.306
Relax	Distinguish between relaxed state and motor imagery state	182	12	Generalized Extreme Value(1), Logistic(3) Normal(1), tLocationScale(7)	0.750
Spectf	Detect abnormal SPECTF images	267	44	Extreme Value(30), Logistic(3), Weibull(11)	4.889
Wdbc	Diagnose breast cancer cases	569	30	Birnbaum-saunders(1), Gamma(5), Generalized Extreme Value(17), Generalized Pareto(1), Inverse Gaussian(1), Loglogistic(2), Lognormal(2), tLocationScale(1)	0.469
Whitewine	Classify white wine quality	4898	11	Generalized Extreme Value(4), Generalized Pareto(1) Loglogistic(3), Nakagami(2), tLocationScale(1)	0.440

the missing values are selected considering 3 different scenarios: removing from the inner areas, outer areas, or both. Inner and outer areas refer to high and low values of the *pdf* and *freq* histograms, respectively. Figure 2 depicts each of these methods and variations.

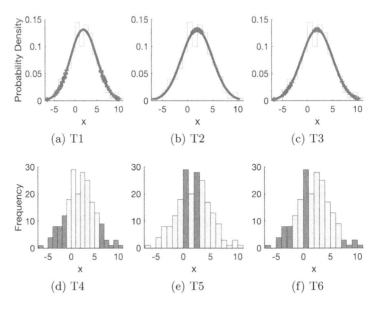

(a) T1   (b) T2   (c) T3

(d) T4   (e) T5   (f) T6

Fig. 2. Strategies for missing data generation: T_1 to T_3 are *pdf*-based methods while T_4 to T_6 are *freq*-based methods.

The Data Imputation stage considers the top five strategies used in recent works, attending also to different paradigms: statistical-based (Mean imputation - MMimp), tree-based models (Decision Trees - DTimp), neural networks-based (Self-Organizing Maps - SOMimp), similarity-based methods (k-Nearest Neighbours - KNNimp) and kernel-based methods (Support Vector Machines - SVMimp), which we briefly describe herein. MMimp is the most common and simple of imputation techniques: it imputes the missing values with the mean of the complete values on the respective features [8,13,19]. KNN imputes the incomplete patterns by finding its k nearest neighbours, found by minimising a similarity measure. Once those k neighbours are found, the missing values are imputed according to the type of feature [17]. The KNN implementation used in this work considers a weighted average of the k neighbours (1–20 neighbours) to determine the substitute value to impute. In DTimp, each incomplete feature is used as target, while the remaining features are used to fit the model: missing values are determined as if they were class labels [5]. SOMimp determines each incomplete pattern's Best Matching Unit (BMU) and imputes its missing values according to the BMU's weights on the incomplete features [11]. In this work, several network sizes were tested for SOMimp: 10–100 nodes. Support Vector

Machines can also be used for imputation (SVMimp), considering the feature to be imputed as the target. In this work, SVMimp was implemented considering both a linear (SVMlinear) and a gaussian (radial basis function, RBF) kernel (SVMrbf) [7]. For the linear kernel, we considered a value of $C = 1$, while for the gaussian kernel, different values of C and γ were tested ($1e^{-5}$ to $1e^5$, increasing by a factor of 10).

Finally, the quality of imputation is evaluated regarding two imputation properties proposed by Chambers [6]: Predictive Accuracy (PAC) and Distributional Accuracy (DAC). The former refers to a procedure's efficiency on retrieving the true values in data while the latter refers to its ability to preserve the original data distribution. PAC properties were assessed using the well-known coefficient of determination (R^2) and Mean Squared Error (MSE) [10] and DAC was assessed using the Kolmogorov–Smirnov distance (D_{KS}) [12]. R^2 provides a measure of the correlation between the original and imputed values (efficient imputations should have a value closer to 1), MSE measures the average squared deviation of the imputed values from the true values (values closer to 0 suggest more accurate imputations) and D_{KS} measures the distance between the cumulative distribution functions of the imputed values of a feature and its original values where better imputations are represented by smaller distance values.

4   Experimental Results and Discussion

Considering all imputation methods, our experiments have shown that SVMimp is the winning method for the great majority of distributions, with an overall ratio of victories over 80%, regarding both PAC and DAC metrics. Considering all distributions, SVMimp obtains the highest mean value for R^2 – 0.765 versus 0.723 obtained with the remaining methods – and the lowest mean values for MSE and D_{KS} – 0.015 and 0.106 versus 0.019 and 0.136 of the remaining methods, for the respective measures, showing that it is not affected by data distribution and surpassing the remaining methods. However, a preliminary analysis of the results indicated that, if SVMimp was not considered, the remaining methods performed differently across different distributions, metrics, scenarios and missing rates. Therefore, we have investigated how the remaining methods behave in different configurations.

Overall, KNNimp and SOMimp are responsible for the highest performance results, with a percentage of wins of 46.8% and 43.2%, respectively. Regarding each individual metric, this tendency is maintained for R^2 (Fig. 3a), although it is slightly different for D_{KS} and MSE: KNNimp is more appropriate to keep the data distribution (Fig. 3b), while SOMimp is responsible for the best MSE values (Fig. 3c).

Figure 4a shows the victories and draws, altogether, for each range of considered missing rates (5–10, 15–20 and 25%). SOMimp and MMimp show a similar behaviour, where they surpass the other methods for increasing percentages of missing data. Contrariwise, DTimp and KNNimp tend to perform worse as the MRs increase. To further study this behaviour, Fig. 4b shows the overall victories and draws of each method, considering each specific metric (R^2, D_{KS} and

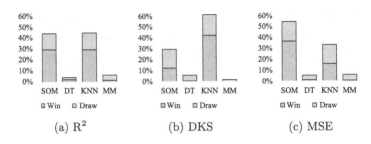

Fig. 3. Overall results (divided by wins and draws) for each metric: R^2, D_{KS} and MSE.

MSE). For low MRs (5–10%), KNN outperforms all other methods in terms of both PAC and DAC, being considered the most frequent winner in all metrics (50%, 75.2% and 68.6% for MSE, R^2 and D_{KS}, respectively). When the MR increases (15–20%), KNNimp loses its podium to SOMimp in terms of PAC (R^2 and MSE), though not DAC, where KNN appears as winner in 57.2% of times. When the missing rate increases to 25%, the previous behaviour is respected, although the differences between SOM and KNN are more accentuated. In terms of PAC, SOMimp's superiority becomes clearer (66.9% and 59.6% of wins for MSE and R^2), while KNNimp's dominance in terms of D_{KS} decreases to 49%.

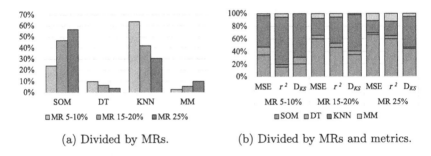

Fig. 4. Overall results (wins and draws altogether) for each imputation method, divided by MRs (a) and further specified by each metric (b).

The observed results are in agreement with the characteristics of the considered algorithms. Although MMimp is a rapid and simple solution to impute missing data, it is known to ignore the relations between the features, disturbing the original data variance [9]. As such, MMimp tends to have a poor performance compared to the other methods, in terms of DAC. Regarding KNNimp, previous works have shown that it has a robust behaviour even for large amounts of missing data [4,21]. The fact that it uses the information of the most similar cases rather than all the cases makes it superior to MMimp, being stronger in maintaining the distribution of data (DAC). DTimp is resilient to outliers and has the ability to cope with skewed distributions; however, the higher the amount of missing data, the more difficult is to have a good decision tree to estimate the missing values [22]. SOM imputation somehow approximates a clustering solution, in the sense that the imputations are made in clusters, activation groups constituted by the k-closest BMUs of a given incomplete pattern. This type of mapping allows SOM to preserve the data topology, which is one of the factors that may contribute to its robust behaviour [20].

Out of these four methods, MMimp serves as a baseline, and behaved as expected, deteriorating the data distribution. DTimp does not seem to be a general good approach for imputation in terms of PAC and DAC: it estimates missing values based on the information of the remaining features and therefore it produces good estimates when the correlation is high. However, for low correlations between features it can lead to poor performances, which could be on the origin of its discouraging behaviour. Finally, imputation algorithms that approached a clustering-based solution (KNNimp and SOMimp) seem to be generally appropriate to keep the PAC and DAC properties of data: this fact could be related to the fact that both these methods properly address the similarity between patterns, using only resembling data points to impute the missing values.

Figure 5 specifies the overall victories and draws of each imputation by metric (MSE, R^2 and D_{KS}), for each scenario. It is clear that KNNimp achieves the best results for DAC, regarding all generation types. In terms of PAC, SOMimp seems to be the preferable approach for all scenarios except T_2, where the supremacy of KNN is noticeable both in terms of MSE and R^2.

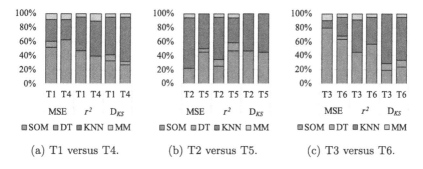

(a) T1 versus T4.   (b) T2 versus T5.   (c) T3 versus T6.

Fig. 5. Comparison between analogous pairs: *freq*-based versus *pdf*-based generations types.

From Fig. 5 it is also possible to compare the analogous pairs of *freq*-based and *pdf*-based generation types. There are not relevant differences to point out, except for the imbalance between SOM's and KNN's results for PAC metrics in T_2 versus T_5 pairs. T_2 generation is most often better imputed with KNN for all metrics, with KNN gaining a clear advantage over SOM; in T_5, this gap is not so clear.

Since this work considers an extensive set of configurations (distributions, missing data rates, scenarios and metrics), summarising the conclusions to provide a clear heuristic is not a trivial process. Thus, we have decided to build a dataset including each existing variable from each studied dataset to analyse all the available information. Specifically, the produced dataset includes information on the name of distribution, missing rates, metrics, generation type, feature ratio, number of features, number of features with the same distribution included in the dataset, sample size, goodness-of-fit of the feature and the best imputation method, as the target class. An excerpt of such dataset is shown on Listing 1.1.

```
 1  @relation LowLevelInfoT1T2T3T4T5T6T7
 2
 3  @attribute Distribution_class {Beta,BirnbaumSaunders,Exponential,
        ExtremeValue,Gamma,GeneralizedExtremeValue,GeneralizedPareto,
        InverseGaussian,Logistic,Loglogistic,Lognormal,Nakagami,Normal,
        Rayleigh,Weibull,tLocationScale}
 4  @attribute MissingRate {5,10,15,20,25}
 5  @attribute Metric_class {ksdistance,mse,pearson}
 6  @attribute GenType_class {T1,T2,T3,T4,T5,T6,T7}
 7  @attribute FeatureRatio numeric
 8  @attribute FeatureNo numeric
 9  @attribute SameFeature numeric
10  @attribute SampleSize numeric
11  @attribute GoF numeric
12  @attribute bestMethod_class {DT,KNN,Mean/Mode,SOM}
13
14  @data
15  Gamma,5,mse,T1,0.33333,12,2,310,0.91288,SOM
16  Gamma,5,pearson,T1,0.33333,12,2,310,0.91288,SOM
17  Gamma,5,ksdistance,T1,0.33333,12,2,310,0.91288,DT
```

Listing 1.1. Produced dataset regarding all the available information.

With the help of Waikato Environment for Knowledge Analysis (WEKA) software, we then started by analysing the simplest rules (ZeroR and OneR) that allowed a general classification of the data. ZeroR suggested classifying all instances as SOM (AUC of 0.5) and OneR used GoF to produce a larger set of rules for classification (AUC of 0.608). These results show that SOM is generally the overall winner for the great majority of configurations and suggest that GoF has a high discriminative power. Motivated by these results, we performed an attribute selection based on Information Gain, which revealed that GoF (0.229), Sample Size (0.165) and Feature Ratio (0.158) are the top three most discriminative features. We also ran a sequential forward selection to determine the subset of features that more accurately traduced the best imputation method for each input variable. This search returned a subset including the missing generation scenario (Generation Type), Sample Size and GoF, for which a 10-fold cross-validation of a C4.5 decision tree returned an average AUC of 0.725, decreasing just by 0.027 relatively to the AUC results including all information (0.752).

However, these features did not provide any insights regarding the different distributions. Therefore, we have tested several decision trees in order to obtain a model that included the most information possible, but without compromising the interpretability of the model: we looked for subsets of features that enabled a clear interpretation of a decision tree with a minimum performance drop, in order to produce meaningful rules. The subset of features that enable the most clear decision tree is the distribution of the feature (Distribution), MR, the metric considered (Metric) and Generation Type, with a mean AUC of 0.675, showing a decrease of 0.077 relatively to the best AUC achieved (considering all features). Despite this drop in performance, this model allows the construction of general, heuristic rules that may be useful for researchers that know the distribution of data and want to select the best imputation method: an example branch of such a decision tree is shown in Fig. 6. From this heuristic, some imputation methods stood out for particular Distribution and Generation Types, e.g.: SOMimp for Birnbaum-saunders ($T_{1,2,3,4,5,6}$), Extreme Value ($T_{1,2,3,6}$) and Weibull ($T_{1,3,4,6}$); KNNimp for Logistic ($T_{1,2,3,4,5}$).

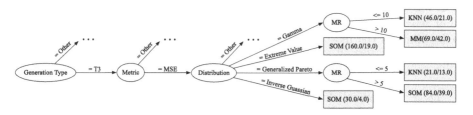

Fig. 6. Example of a branch of the decision tree generated from the considered subset of features. An example of a rule obtained by the presented model is: `Generation Type = T3 and Metric = MSE and Distribution = Gamma and Missing Rate <= 10: KNN(46,21)`

5   Conclusions and Future Work

This research follows from Santos et al. [18], where authors found a relation between data distribution and imputation quality, showing that the latter is influenced by the missing rate and the ratio of features per distribution, when missing data is generated completely at random. Herein, we extend the work of Santos et al. to more extreme setups, where missing values affect specific areas of features' frequency histograms and probability density functions. To this end, a set of comprehensive experiments were conducted in order to study the effect of several data distributions on well-known imputation algorithms. We collected several datasets with different characteristics, fitted the data to determine the best distribution that describes each feature and then inserted missing data in 7 different approaches (T_1 to T_7). After the insertion of missing values, five imputation methods were used to reproduce the original values and the results were evaluated in terms of PAC and DAC metrics.

From the results gathered we can summarise the following conclusions:

- SVMimp is the winning method for nearly all distributions in both PAC and DAC metrics, unaffected by data distribution;
- Overall, imputation algorithms that followed clustering-based solutions (KNNimp and SOMimp) seem to be generally appropriate to keep the PAC and DAC properties;

- KNNimp is more appropriate in terms of DAC and SOMimp seems preferable in terms of PAC;
- KNNimp outperforms all methods regarding both PAC and DAC metrics for MRs < 15%, However, for MRs ≥ 15% SOMimp is generally the best approach for PAC, though for DAC, KNNimp still maintains its superiority.

With more detail on the heuristic analysis we have the following conclusions:

- Overall, SOMimp is the most robust approach across several scenarios;
- GoF, Sample Size, Feature Ratio and Generation Type seem to be relevant features to determine appropriate imputation algorithms, although they do not provide insights regarding the different distributions;
- It was possible to obtain a clear decision tree model that allows the extraction of general rules comprising Generation Type, Metric, Distribution and MR;
- SOMimp is the most appropriate method for Birnbaum-saunders, Extreme Value and Weibull distributions. Logistic distributions tend to be better imputed with KNNimp.

There are several directions for future work. One is the extension of this methodology for datasets comprising also discrete features, fitting discrete distributions and investigating how the studied imputation techniques perform in each scenario. Also, from a classification perspective, it would be interesting to assess whether the best imputation techniques regarding PAC and DAC metrics would also achieve good results in terms of classification error. An ongoing work is focused on a sensibility analysis of SVMimp, studying the best set of parameters that achieve high PAC and DAC results and looking for the absolute most missing data rate for which SVMimp is still able to maintain the original data values and distribution.

Acknowledgments. This article is a result of the project NORTE-01-0145-FEDER-000027, supported by Norte Portugal Regional Operational Programme (NORTE 2020), under the PORTUGAL 2020 Partnership Agreement, through the European Regional Development Fund (ERDF).

References

1. Abreu, P.H., Santos, M.S., Abreu, M.H., Andrade, B., Silva, D.C.: Predicting breast cancer recurrence using machine learning techniques: a systematic review. ACM Comput. Surv. (CSUR) **49**(3), 52 (2016)
2. Aisha, N., Adam, M.B., Shohaimi, S.: Effect of missing value methods on bayesian network classification of hepatitis data. Int. J. Comput. Sci. Telecommun. **4**(6), 8–12 (2013)
3. Amiri, M., Jensen, R.: Missing data imputation using fuzzy-rough methods. Neurocomputing **205**, 152–164 (2016)
4. Batista, G.E., Monard, M.C.: A study of k-nearest neighbour as an imputation method. HIS **87**(251–260), 48 (2002)
5. Breiman, L., Friedman, J., Stone, C.J., Olshen, R.A.: Classification and Rregression Trees. CRC Press, Boca Raton (1984)

6. Chambers, R.: Evaluation criteria for statistical editing and imputation, national statistics methodological series no. 28. University of Southampton (2001)
7. García-Laencina, P.J., Sancho-Gómez, J.L., Figueiras-Vidal, A.R.: Pattern classification with missing data: a review. Neural Comput. Appl. **19**(2), 263–282 (2010)
8. García-Laencina, P.J., Sancho-Gómez, J.L., Figueiras-Vidal, A.R.: Classifying patterns with missing values using multi-task learning perceptrons. Expert Syst. with Appl. **40**(4), 1333–1341 (2013)
9. Howell, D.C.: The treatment of missing data. The Sage Handbook of Social Science Methodology, pp. 208–224. Sage Publications, Thousand Oaks (2007)
10. Junninen, H., Niska, H., Tuppurainen, K., Ruuskanen, J., Kolehmainen, M.: Methods for imputation of missing values in air quality data sets. Atmos. Enviro. **38**(18), 2895–2907 (2004)
11. Kohonen, T.: Self-Organizing Maps. Springer, Berlin (1995)
12. Lopes, R.H.: Kolmogorov-smirnov test. International Encyclopedia of Statistical Science, pp. 718–720. Springer, New York (2011)
13. Nanni, L., Lumini, A., Brahnam, S.: A classifier ensemble approach for the missing feature problem. Artif. Intell. Med. **55**(1), 37–50 (2012)
14. Pigott, T.D.: A review of methods for missing data. Educ. Res. Eval. **7**(4), 353–383 (2001)
15. Rahman, M.M., Davis, D.N.: Fuzzy unordered rules induction algorithm used as missing value imputation methods for k-mean clustering on real cardiovascular data. In: Proceedings of the World Congress on Engineering I, pp. 391–394 (2012)
16. Rahman, M.G., Islam, M.Z.: Missing value imputation using decision trees and decision forests by splitting and merging records: two novel techniques. Knowledge-Based Syst. **53**, 51–65 (2013)
17. Santos, M.S., Abreu, P.H., García-Laencina, P.J., Simão, A., Carvalho, A.: A new cluster-based oversampling method for improving survival prediction of hepatocellular carcinoma patients. J. Biomed. Inf. **58**, 49–59 (2015)
18. Santos, M.S., Soares, J.P., Henriques Abreu, P., Araújo, H., Santos, J.: Influence of data distribution in missing data imputation. In: Artificial Intelligence in Medicine, pp. 285–294. Springer International Publishing, Cham (2017)
19. Sivapriya, T., Kamal, A.N.B., Thavavel, V.: Imputation and classification of missing data using least square support vector machines-a new approach in dementia diagnosis. Int. J. Adv. Res. Artif. Intell. **1**(4), 29–33 (2012)
20. Sorjamaa, A., Corona, F., Miche, Y., Merlin, P., Maillet, B., Séverin, E., Lendasse, A.: Sparse linear combination of soms for data imputation: application to financial database. In: Príncipe, J.C., Miikkulainen, R. (eds.) WSOM 2009. LNCS, vol. 5629, pp. 290–297. Springer, Heidelberg (2009). https://doi.org/10.1007/978-3-642-02397-2_33
21. Troyanskaya, O., Cantor, M., Sherlock, G., Brown, P., Hastie, T., Tibshirani, R., Botstein, D., Altman, R.B.: Missing value estimation methods for dna microarrays. Bioinformatics **17**(6), 520–525 (2001)
22. Van Buuren, S.: Flexible Imputation of Missing Data. CRC Press, Boca Raton (2012)

Communication-Free Widened Learning of Bayesian Network Classifiers Using Hashed Fiedler Vectors

Oliver R. Sampson$^{(\boxtimes)}$, Christian Borgelt, and Michael R. Berthold

Chair for Bioinformatics and Information Mining, Department of Computer
and Information Science, University of Konstanz, Konstanz, Germany
`oliver.sampson@uni-konstanz.de`

Abstract. *Widening* is a method where parallel resources are used to
find better solutions from greedy algorithms instead of merely trying to
find the same solutions more quickly. To date, every example of Widening has used some form of communication between the parallel workers
to maintain their distances from one another in the model space. For
the first time, we present a communication-free, widened extension to a
standard machine learning algorithm. By using Locality Sensitive Hashing on the Bayesian networks' Fiedler vectors, we demonstrate the ability
to learn classifiers superior to those of standard implementations and to
those generated with a greedy heuristic alone.

1 Introduction

Moore's Law has begun to run up against harder physical limits, and parallel
processing has taken over the continuing increases in computing performance.
Whether it is from multiple cores in potentially multiple CPUs on desktops or
thousands of individual cores available in GPGPUs (general-purpose graphics
processing units) to seemingly unlimited parallel computing resources available
from commercial cloud computing providers, little research [2] has been performed on applying those parallel resources to finding better quality solutions.
WIDENING [1] has demonstrated an ability to describe parallelized versions of
greedy machine learning algorithms, while using *diversity* between the parallel
workers, that are able to find better solutions than their standard counterparts.
The guiding philosophy is "Better. Not Faster." Although the demonstrated
examples, such as WIDENED KRIMP [24], WIDENED HIERARCHICAL CLUSTER-
ING [11], WIDENED BAYESIAN NETWORKS [25] and BUCKET SELECTION [12]
have been able to find superior solutions, i.e., "better," they have been unable
to demonstrate this ability in a run-time that is comparable to the standard versions of the greedy algorithms. "Not faster" is not intended to mean "slower."

This is because all of the demonstrated examples have used some form of
communication between the parallel workers to enforce a distance between them
while they move through the model space. In this paper we present the first

© Springer Nature Switzerland AG 2018
W. Duivesteijn et al. (Eds.): IDA 2018, LNCS 11191, pp. 264–277, 2018.
https://doi.org/10.1007/978-3-030-01768-2_22

example of WIDENING that enables the workers to traverse the model/solution space without communication between them–*communication-free widening*.

Communication-free widening can be realized through the use of a hash function, where each model and its refinements form a potential path through the model space only when they have all been hashed to the same hash value. The sets of models that hash to the same values form a partitioning of the model space and are the mechanism WIDENING uses to maintain diversity between the parallel workers in the model space.

The hash function used here is a variant of a LOCALITY SENSITIVE HASHING [13] hash family and is used to hash the Fiedler vectors of the matrix representations of Bayesian networks which are evaluated for use as classifiers.

2   Background

2.1   Learning Bayesian Networks

A Bayesian network is a probabilistic graphical model that represents conditional dependencies between features of a dataset. More formally, given a dataset, $\mathcal{D}$, with features, $\mathcal{X}$, a Bayesian network, B, is a pair $\langle G, \Theta \rangle$, where $G = \langle \mathcal{X}, \mathcal{E} \rangle$ is a pair representing a directed acyclic graph, where the nodes of the graph are represented by $\mathcal{X}$, $\mathcal{E}$ are the edges, and Θ is the set of conditional probability tables for each of the features. Each edge, $E = \langle X_i, X_j \rangle$, where $E \in \mathcal{E}$ and $X_i, X_j \in \mathcal{X}$, is an ordered pair reflecting the conditional dependency of one feature on another, where a *child node*, X_j, is conditionally dependent a *parent node*, X_i.

Algorithms for learning the structure of Bayesian networks are, at their core, search algorithms that vary in how they score changes to a network's structure along the search path in the super-exponentially sized, i.e., $\mathcal{O}(|\mathcal{X}|!2^{\binom{|\mathcal{X}|}{2}})$, model space. Largely, they vary in the starting network configuration and in the assumptions they make about the relationships between the features of the Bayesian network and in their method of scoring the network. The algorithms can be divided into four categories: *constraint-based*, *search-and-score*, *hybrid*, [15] and *evolutionary algorithms* [17]. Constraint-based algorithms derive network structure based on dependency relationships between features. Search-and-score algorithms refine the network topology by adding, deleting, or reversing the edges in the network and then score and select the network in a greedy manner. Hybrid algorithms integrate techniques from both of the search-and-score and constraint-based methods; a partially-directed-acyclic graph is created using constraint-based techniques, and the network is evaluated using search-and-score methods, while giving a direction to each undirected edge. These methods usually use either Bayesian methods, by calculating the posterior probability of a network given the dataset or likelihood-based information theoretic scores. Evolutionary algorithms follow a typical evolutionary algorithmic pattern of mutation, reproduction, selection, and random sampling, where the classification performance accuracy for classification is often used for the selection (fitness) function.

When using a Bayesian network as a classifier, the calculated probabilities are solely influenced by the *Markov blanket*, i.e., the target variable, its parents, its children, and the other parents of its children [22]. To calculate the predicted target variable value, each value of the target variable is evaluated using a vector, $\mathbf{x}$, of instantiated values for all of the other features in the dataset, i.e., $\mathcal{X} \setminus C$, using Eq. 1 [3],

$$\hat{c} = \underset{u=1,\dots,|C|}{\text{argmax}} \; P(c_u, \mathbf{x}) = \underset{u=1,\dots,|C|}{\text{argmax}} \; P(c_u | \boldsymbol{pa}(C)) \prod_{v=1}^{|\mathbf{x}|} P(x_v | \boldsymbol{pa}(X_v)) \qquad (1)$$

where $C \in \mathcal{X}$ is the target variable, c_u are the values that C may assume, X_v is the variable corresponding to the value $x_v \in \mathbf{x}$, and $\boldsymbol{pa}(\cdot)$ is the set of parents of a given node. The target variable value, $\hat{c}$, with the highest probability is the predicted value.

2.2   Widening

WIDENING is a framework that describes a method for using parallel resources for potentially finding better solutions with greedy algorithms than the algorithms would find using their standard implementation.

Given an initial model, $m_0 \in \mathcal{M}$, from the set of all models in a model space, a refinement operator, $r(\cdot)$, and a selection operator based on a performance metric, $s(\cdot)$, a greedy algorithm can be defined as a series of iterations, $m_{i+1} = s(r(m_i))$, which continues until a stopping criterion is met. More exactly, m_i is refined to a set of derivative models, $\boldsymbol{M}_i' = r(m_i)$, and from this set one model is selected, $m_{i+1} = s(\boldsymbol{M}_i')$. A simple extension to this is BEAM SEARCH, where the top k models are selected at each iteration. The widening framework terms this *Top-k-widening*, i.e., $\boldsymbol{M}_{i+1} = s_{Top-k}(r(\boldsymbol{M}_i)) : |\boldsymbol{M}_{i+1}| = k$. WIDENING begins to widen the search paths beyond a simple greedy mechanism when diversity is brought into play. The notion of diversity can be implemented in either the refining step as in [24,25] or in the selection step as in [11,12]. Given a diverse refinement operator, $r_\Delta(\cdot)$, as in [24,25], where a diversity function, Δ, is imposed on the output, DIVERSE TOP-K WIDENING is described by $\boldsymbol{M}_{i+1} = s_{Top-k}(r_\Delta(\boldsymbol{M}_i))$.

Depending on how this diversity is imposed, it can either be communication-free or not. WIDENED KRIMP evaluated the best models from all parallel workers at the end of each iteration. The P-DISPERSION-MIN-SUM measure [21] is used by WIDENED BAYESIAN NETWORKS to find maximally disperse, i.e., diverse, members of the refined sets at each refinement step. WIDENED HIERARCHICAL CLUSTERING, in contrast, uses a clustering method to find diverse subsets and selected a top member from each of the clusters. BUCKET SELECTION uses a hashing mechanism and transfers models between the parallel workers. All four examples require non-parallelized communication between the parallel workers for a comparison of their results.

2.3   Communication-Free Widening

Communication-free widening can be thought of as a partitioning of the model space, where a refinement operator either yields only models that are part of the partition, or yields models to many partitions and discards those that do not belong to the partition.

Many problems have large model spaces that are characterized as having large plateau-like structures that are difficult for greedy algorithms to progress within. Often there are many local optima distributed throughout the solution space. Given a partitioning of such a model space, which restricts the search of each parallel worker within a partition (See Fig. 1), we hypothesize (1) that as the number of partitions increases, i.e., as the width increases, that WIDENING will be able to find better solutions, and (2) that with too many partitions, the solutions will deteriorate as more of the partitions do not cover a better solution or will not cover a complete path to a solution.

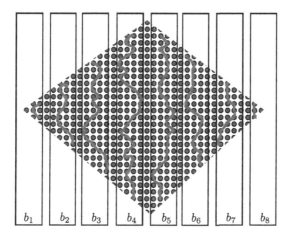

Fig. 1. Solution paths (red) are limited to regions of the model space defined by the output of a hash function, i.e., buckets, denoted by $b_1, \ldots, b_8$.

Partitioning the model space introduces a potential problem to the greedy search–*reachability*. The problem of reachability describes when the parallel worker is unable to find any better solution in a partition or, in the extreme case, any better solution in any partition. It also describes when a good or best solution path is not *complete* under any given partition and would need to "jump" partitions.

A hash function, $H(\cdot)$, is a natural method for partitioning a model space. (See Fig. 1.) The refined models are hashed with $H(\cdot)$, where refined models with different hash values from the original model are discarded. The best of these models are in turn selected by a selection operator for the next iteration. Continuing with the notation from above, each parallel path, denoted by j, is described by WIDENING as $M_{j,i+1} = s(\{m' \in r(M_{j,i})|H(m') = j\})$ where j is the output of the hash function $H(\cdot)$.

2.4 Locality Sensitive Hashing

LOCALITY SENSITIVE HASHING (LSH) has shown excellent results in similarity search, with applications in image retrieval [16], genetic sequence comparison [5], melody-based audio retrieval [20], among others. LSH reduces the dimensionality of a dataset by hashing the dataset's entries with a hash function, $h(\cdot) \in \mathcal{F}$, from a hash family $\mathcal{F}$, which has a high probability of giving the same value to similar examples [6].

Several different hash families, $\mathcal{F}$, are found in the literature including datapoints on a unit hypersphere [28], angle-based distance [6], and p-stable distributions [9].

In the R-NEAREST NEIGHBOR (R-NN) problem, LSH is used with a number, L, of sets of concatenated hash functions from $\mathcal{F}$ in order to increase the probability of a collision between a query example and examples already hashed from the database. Typically, the results of g different examples of each hash function, $\{h_1(\cdot), \ldots, h_g(\cdot)\}$, are concatenated together to create a hash value for one hash function, $H(\cdot)$. L hash functions are used to hash each example, $x \in \mathcal{D}$, into L hash tables. When there is a collision between examples, a collision list is kept for each hash entry in the appropriate hash table. When searching for R-NN examples, a query item x_q is hashed using each of the L hash functions, and the previously bucketed values from each of L hash tables are retrieved. These are then compared to x_q with a standard similarity measure. Those falling within some distance, r, of x_q are considered to be matches for R-NN [9].

The L2 Gaussian hash family [9] hashes an example, $\mathbf{v}$, of dimension d using the function $h(\mathbf{v}) = \lfloor \frac{\mathbf{v} \cdot \mathbf{a} + b}{w} \rfloor$, where $\mathbf{a}$ is a d-dimensional vector whose elements are randomly sampled from a Gaussian distribution with $\mu = 0$ and $\sigma = 1$ and b is a value randomly sampled from a linear distribution between $[0, w)$, where w is an input parameter. g different examples of $h(\cdot)$ derived from g different vectors $\mathbf{a}$ and values b are concatenated together to compose $H(\cdot)$. In this work we only use one $(L = 1)$ set of hash functions, as opposed to the larger number used for R-NEAREST NEIGHBOR in [9], because we are only interested in testing a single partitioning of the model space.

2.5 Fiedler Vectors

An *adjacency matrix*, $\mathbf{A}$, of an undirected network graph is defined to be an $n \times n : n = |\mathcal{X}|$ matrix with entries, $a_{ij} \in \{0, 1\} : i, j \in \{1, \ldots, |\mathcal{X}|\}$. a_{ij} is set to 1 if there is an edge between nodes i and j in the network, and to 0 where no edge exists. A *node degree matrix*, $\mathbf{D}$, is an $n \times n$ diagonal matrix where the diagonal, i.e., the entries d_{ii}, are set to the number of edges incident to the node $i \in \{1, \ldots, |\mathcal{X}|\}$; all other entries are set to 0. The unnormalized *Laplacian matrix* of the undirected graph is simply $\mathbf{L} = \mathbf{D} - \mathbf{A}$, which, when $deg(i)$ is the node degree, gives [7]:

$$\mathbf{L}_{UN} = \begin{cases} deg(i) & \text{if } i = j, \\ -1 & \text{if } i \neq j \text{ and } X_i, X_j \text{ are adjacent,} \\ 0 & \text{otherwise.} \end{cases} \tag{2}$$

Normalized Laplacian matrices exist, such as the *symmetric norm* from Chung [7]

$$\mathbf{L}_{SN} = \begin{cases} 1 & \text{if } i = j \text{ and } deg(i) \neq 0, \\ -\frac{1}{\sqrt{deg(i)deg(j)}} & \text{if } i \neq j \text{ and } X_i, X_j \text{ are adjacent,} \\ 0 & \text{otherwise.} \end{cases} \tag{3}$$

and the *random walk* from Doyle and Snell [10], $\mathbf{L}_{RW}$, which differs from that of Chung by the value for adjacent nodes: $-\frac{1}{deg(i)}$.

The eigenvalues of symmetric matrices are both real and positive, with the number of eigenvalues equal to 0 reflecting the number of connected components in the graph. The *Fiedler vector* is the eigenvector associated with the second smallest, i.e., first non-zero, eigenvalue, or *Fiedler value*, of a connected graph's Laplacian matrix [7]. The Fiedler value is associated with a graph's algebraic connectivity; the Fiedler vector reflects graph's structure, in that graphs cannot be isomorphic if they do not have the same Fiedler vector. If the graphs do have the same Fiedler vector, then the probability of their being isomorphic is very high and seems to trend to 100% as $|\mathcal{X}| \to \infty$ [29].

Table 1. Dataset Characteristics. $|\mathcal{D}|$ is the number of entries in the dataset, $|\mathcal{X}|$ is the number of features including the target feature, $|C|$ is the number of target classes, and max $|H(\cdot)|$ is the width where refined models are more likely to be refined to the same hash than random, obtained from the experiments as depicted in Figs. 3a and 3b.

Dataset	$|\mathcal{D}|$	$|\mathcal{X}|$	$|C|$	max $|H(\cdot)|$
Car	1728	7	4	22
Connect4	67556	43	3	29
Ecoli	336	8	8	23
Glass	214	10	7	24
Ionosphere	351	35	2	28
Pima	768	9	2	24
Waveform	5000	22	3	28

Assuming the property that the Fiedler vector approximates a unique identifier for a graph,[1] we hypothesize (3) that the LSH function as described

---

[1] Isomorphic graphs have similar Fiedler vectors. The converse is not necessarily true.

above, when hashing the Fiedler vector allows similar Bayesian networks to stay together in a partition, and that the disparate refinement paths will lead to a superior solution, thereby realizing COMMUNICATION-FREE WIDENING.

2.6   Related Work

This work relies implicitly on work related to the SUBGRAPH ISOMORPHISM PROBLEM, which is an area of active research into efficient methods for finding common subgraphs. The use of graph spectra is a popular method with applications in clustering [26], chemistry [30], and image retrieval [23], among others. Luo et al. in [19] used spectral properties with other graph theoretical values for graph clustering. Qiu and Hancock in [23] used graph spectral properties, and the Fiedler vector in particular, for graph matching by decomposing a graph into subgraphs.

Zhang et al. in [31] used LSH on graphs for K-NEAREST NEIGHBOR SIMI-LARITY SEARCH. Their method is based on using a hash function of differences between graphs in the database and prototypes either randomly selected beforehand or calculated by clustering. Variants of LSH exist that use only one hash function, such as the Single Hash MINHASH [4]. To our knowledge no examples exist in the literature of implementing LSH for graphs with the Fiedler vector as the value to be hashed.

3   Experimental Setup

The datasets used for the experiments were chosen for their wide variety of dimensionality and number of target classes and for their lack of missing values (See Table 1). They are all available from the UCI Machine Learning Repository [18] and were discretized using the LUCS-KDD DN software [8].

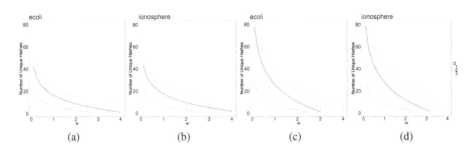

| (a) | (b) | (c) | (d) |

Fig. 2. Number of hash values related to w and g. The number of different initial hash values measured for two datasets (`ecoli` and `ionosphere`) with two different sizes of sets of initial models, $|M_0| = 40$ in Fig. 2a and 2b, and $|M_0| = 80$ in Fig. 2c and 2d, are plotted with values for $g \in \{1, 2, 3\}$ and $w \in \{0.1, 0.2, 0.4, 0.8, 1.0, 2.0, 3.0, 4.0\}$. Small values of w result in a large number of hashes quickly approaching the number of initial values.

Each experiment tested the response to WIDENING by varying the input variables w, which controls the number of different output values for each function $h_g(\cdot)$ and g, which is the number of hash values concatenated together. Experiments with every combination of w and g for each dataset were conducted using 5-fold cross-validation and repeated five times, resulting in 25 individually scored trials with different random values for the hash functions $h(\cdot)$ for each trial. The 5-fold cross-validation is naturally an 80/20 train/test split. The iterative refine-score-select steps in each of the five training folds are also learned and scored using an 80/20 partitioning, resulting in an overall 64/16/20 train/validate/test split. All experiments were conducted using KNIME v3.5.

3.1   Initialization

In the experiments presented here, the initial models are single-component networks with up to two edges being added from every node to other random node(s). All experiments were performed with an initial model set, M_0, with $|M_0| = 40$ initial models and with $w \in \{0.5, 0.6, 0.7, 0.8, 0.9, 1.0, 1.5, 2, 3, 4\}$ and $g \in \{1, 2, 3\}$. For each initial model, the Fiedler vector for the Markov blanket is calculated and hashed. The number of initial hashes for the experiment is determined from the initial set of hashed values.

Because of the stochastic nature of the hashing scheme, it is impossible to predict exactly how many different partitions will be created from the initial set of models, but we can measure the response for the number of generated hash values. What is certain is that, in our application as w decreases and g increases there will be a tendency for the number of hash values to increase (See Fig. 2).

For applications where the exact width needs to be known beforehand, several different rounds of initialization are performed, and the round with the model(s) with the correct number of unique hashes is used as the starting point for WIDENING. The primary relationship being evaluated here is that between

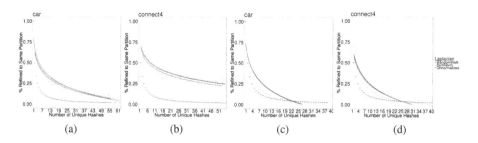

(a)   (b)   (c)   (d)

Fig. 3. Percentage of refined models with Fiedler vector/LSH to the same hash value for two datasets: `car` and `connect4` and three Laplacian normalizations: SymNorm (green), RandomWalk (purple), Unnormalized (blue). Figure 3a and 3b show the percentage of models refined to the same partition when comparing the Fiedler vector for the entire network. Figure 3c and 3d show the percentage of models refined to the same partition when using the Fiedler vector only for the network's Markov blanket.

the amount of widening, i.e., the number of unique hash values, and the resulting classification performance of the derived Bayesian networks. When there is no widening, i.e., there is no hashing and partitioning of the model space, the refined model path is a simple, greedy search.

3.2   Refinement

Because the Markov blanket is the portion of the network that, when changed, can cause changes in classification accuracy, the refinement strategy first attempts to add or delete edges from non-Markov blanket nodes to the Markov blanket, depending on the constraints of the network's being acyclic and a single component. If that fails, similar attempts for any edge in the network are made. Because this work is interested in demonstrating WIDENING via the use of the Fiedler vector as a good hashable descriptor of a Bayesian network, and how its use with an LSH-based hashing scheme will find better solutions than standard greedy algorithms, only one model is refined per iteration—this corresponds to the use of $l = 1$ in [25]. The number of parents for any given node in a model is limited to 5, because conditioned probabilities can degrade to 0 for datasets where $|\mathcal{D}|$ is insufficiently large.

The Fiedler vector for the refined model is filled with zeroes for the nodes that are not included in the Markov blanket, and hashed using g concatenated values of $h(\cdot)$. Any refined model with a hash value differing from its preceding model is discarded. The preceding model may have a differing set of nodes in the Markov blanket.

3.3   Partitioning

To determine the efficacy of the Fiedler vector/LSH method of refining models within the same partition, we performed some preliminary experiments. Twenty-five repetitions of $|\mathbf{M}_0| = \{40, 80\}$ initialized models were refined through 50 iterations as described above. The new model's hash value is compared to the previous model's hash value. When equal, the new model is kept for further refinement; when unequal, it is discarded. No scoring of the resulting Bayesian network is performed, so in this case, the only difference considered between datasets is the number of features.

Figure 3 shows how well the Fiedler Hash/LSH technique performs with refining models to the same hash value for three different types of normalization for the Laplacian matrix compared to a $1/n$ baseline, which would be expected with a purely random hashing scheme. Two different Fiedler vector/LSH hashing schemes are shown in Fig. 3 to illustrate the effect of using just the Markov blanket compared to the entire network. In the cases (Fig. 3a and 3b) where the Fiedler vector from the entire network is hashed, the larger datasets have a higher number of hashes for which the models are refined to the same partition, and a higher number of hashes which perform better than the baseline. This is because small perturbations to the larger network can have smaller effects on the Fiedler vector. In the cases (Fig. 3c and 3d), where only the Markov blanket is

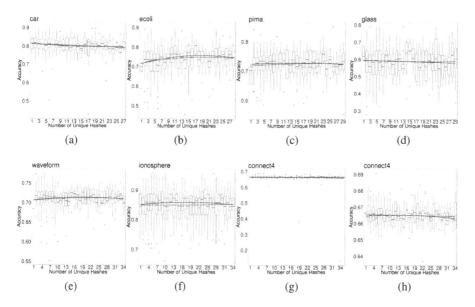

Fig. 4. COMMUNICATION-FREE WIDENED BAYES accuracy versus the number of unique hashes. The red and blue lines are second degree polynomials fitted to the mean (red dots) and median accuracy, respectively, for each value of the number of unique hashes (width). When the lines are concave facing down, it supports the hypothesis of better performance with WIDENING to a certain point with worsening performance thereafter. `connect4` is shown twice (Fig. 4g and 4h, once each with and without outliers ($\sigma \geq 3$), to better show the trend.) The x-axis shows the max number of hashes from Table 1 plus 20% thereof allowing for a decline in accuracy afterwards.

considered, the Markov blanket is (usually) smaller than the total network, and small changes may eliminate a node or nodes entirely from the Markov blanket resulting in larger changes to the Fiedler vector and its hash value. The crossover to performance worse than the baseline is between 23 hash values for smaller datasets, e.g., `car` and 29 for larger datasets, e.g., `connect4`. This value (max $|H(\cdot)|$ in Table 1) is used for the maximal widening in later experiments.

Additionally, the different Laplacian matrix normalizations described in Sect. 2.5 were compared with an unnormalized Laplacian matrix in these experiments. The three different types of Laplacian matrix normalization performed similarly to one another, but Chung's $\mathbf{L}_{SN}$ (See Eq. 3) slightly yet consistently outperformed $\mathbf{L}_{RW}$ and $\mathbf{L}_{UN}$ (See Eq. 2), and is therefore used in the classification evaluation experiments.

3.4   Scoring and Selection

At each iteration, the model is scored using 20% of the training data subset. For WIDENING in general, the best models are selected, but, here only a single model is being evaluated—this corresponds to the use of $k = 1$ in [25]. If the

Table 2. Experimental results comparing simple greedy search (one partition) to the best results from COMMUNICATION-FREE WIDENED BAYES and three algorithms from the **R** bnlearn package. The p-values are for Student's t-test, two-tailed, 95% confidence level with equal variances assumed, comparing COMMUNICATION-FREE WIDENED BAYES NETWORKS to the purely greedy variant.

Dataset	R:HILL-CLIMBING	R:MMHC	R:TABU	GREEDY	COMM.-FREE WIDENED BAYES	Best number of Partitions	p-value
car	0.715 ± 0.037	0.700 ± 0.002	0.718 ± 0.035	0.682 ± 0.125	**0.816 ± 0.029**	2	<0.01
connect4	0.678 ± 0.012	0.658 ± 0.000	**0.684 ± 0.002**	0.589 ± 0.152	0.669 ± 0.006	23	<0.01
ecoli	0.632 ± 0.044	0.495 ± 0.088	0.602 ± 0.109	0.677 ± 0.100	**0.803 ± 0.032**	17	<0.01
glass	0.501 ± 0.112	0.388 ± 0.036	0.500 ± 0.057	0.532 ± 0.107	**0.649 ± 0.079**	15	<0.01
ionosphere	0.807 ± 0.055	0.641 ± 0.011	0.810 ± 0.057	0.826 ± 0.055	**0.869 ± 0.037**	17	<0.01
pima	0.706 ± 0.053	0.716 ± 0.065	**0.760 ± 0.027**	0.693 ± 0.050	0.745 ± 0.051	23	<0.01
waveform	0.504 ± 0.119	0.339 ± 0.000	0.612 ± 0.016	0.630 ± 0.058	**0.725 ± 0.017**	15	<0.01

performance score is better than that of the model from the previous iteration, the model is passed into the next iteration, otherwise the old model is kept and refined anew. The iterations stop when the improvement in performance is less than 0.01%. A Laplacian correction of 1 is added to the entries in the conditional probability table when a count is 0.

4   Results

A summary of the experimental results for the seven datasets is shown in Table 2. COMMUNICATION-FREE WIDENED BAYES was able to find superior solutions when compared to three standard Bayesian network learning algorithms (HILL-CLIMBING (both **perturb** and **restart** = 100)), MAX-MIN HILL-CLIMBING (MMHC) (**perturb** = 100), and TABU from the **R** bnlearn v4.2 package [27]) for five of seven datasets. However, for all seven datasets COMMUNICATION-FREE WIDENED BAYES was able to demonstrate, as hypothesized, finding better solutions when compared to a purely greedy learning method.

As depicted in Fig. 4, five of the seven datasets, (**ecoli**, **pima**, **waveform**, **ionosphere**, and **connect4**) show the predicted curves for both the mean and the median with the exception of **ionospheres**'s mean. **ecoli** and **pima** show the clearest examples whereas **glass** shows a sharp peak in the middle that the smoothing lines oversmooth. **connect4** shows minimal variation in response to WIDENING, and its results from the different algorithms differ relatively little, indicating that good solutions are relatively easy to find along the solution surface; we do not expect all datasets to respond equally well, either because of the nature of the dataset, or because of the reachability problem described in Sect. 2.2. `car` found the best solutions with only two partitions, but, like `connect4` showed little variability overall.

5   Conclusion and Future Work

The results demonstrate for the first time the successful implementation of a communication-free, widened version of a class of popular machine learning algorithms. Additionally, the experiments compared two methods of normalizing the Laplacian matrix and the unnormalized Laplacian matrix, and while no large differences between the three were found, Chung's symmetric normalization [7] slightly outperformed the other two. The results verify the Fiedler vector as a viable descriptor of mixed-sized Markov blankets from Bayesian networks for use with LOCALITY SENSITIVE HASHING.

A drawback to these experiments is the use of the undirected adjacency matrix for calculating the Laplacian matrix. Hashing the complex values that are the result of the eigendecomposition of skew-symmetric adjacency matrices or of a Hermitian adjacency matrix [14], or even of variations to the Laplacian matrix calculated with them could result in a stricter partitioning. Furthermore, within each hash region, a *Top-k* could be used to find slightly better models at each refinement step, thereby accelerating the search. Schemes that affect the refining step, such as preventing an edge that has contributed to a better score from being deleted in the next refining step, could also speed up the search. Experiments involving other LSH hash families could also be useful.

References

1. Akbar, Zaenal, Ivanova, Violeta N., Berthold, Michael R.: Parallel data mining revisited. Better, not faster. In: Hollmén, Jaakko, Klawonn, Frank, Tucker, Allan (eds.) IDA 2012. LNCS, vol. 7619, pp. 23–34. Springer, Heidelberg (2012). https://doi.org/10.1007/978-3-642-34156-4_4
2. Akl, S.G.: Parallel real-time computation: sometimes quantity means quality. In: Proceedings of International Symposium on Parallel Architectures, Algorithms and Networks, 2000. I-SPAN 2000, pp. 2–11. IEEE (2000)
3. Bielza, Concha, Larrañaga, Pedro: Discrete Bayesian network classifiers: a survey. ACM Comput. Surv. (CSUR) **47**(1), 5 (2014)
4. Andrei Z. Broder. On the resemblance and containment of documents. In: Proceedings of Compression and Complexity of Sequences 1997, pp. 21–29. IEEE (1997)
5. Buhler, Jeremy: Efficient large-scale sequence comparison by locality-sensitive hashing. Bioinformatics **17**(5), 419–428 (2001)
6. Charikar, M.S.: Similarity estimation techniques from rounding algorithms. In: Proceedings of the Thiry-Fourth Annual ACM Symposium on Theory of Computing, pp. 380–388. ACM (2002)
7. Fan-Roon Kim Chung. Spectral Graph Theory. Number 92 in Regional Conference Series in Mathematics. American Mathematical Society, 1997
8. Coenen, F.: LUCS-KDD DN software (2003)

9. Datar, M., Immorlica, N., Indyk, P., Mirrokni, V.S.: Locality-sensitive hashing scheme based on p-stable distributions. In: Proceedings of the Twentieth Annual Symposium on Computational Geometry, pp. 253–262. ACM (2004)

10. Doyle, P.G., Laurie Snell, J.: Random Walks and Electric Networks. Mathematical Association of America (1984)

11. Fillbrunn, Alexander, Berthold, Michael R.: Diversity-driven widening of hierarchical agglomerative clustering. In: Fromont, Elisa, De Bie, Tijl, van Leeuwen, Matthijs (eds.) IDA 2015. LNCS, vol. 9385, pp. 84–94. Springer, Cham (2015). https://doi.org/10.1007/978-3-319-24465-5_8

12. Fillbrunn, Alexander, Wörteler, Leonard, Grossniklaus, Michael, Berthold, Michael R.: Bucket selection: a model-independent diverse selection strategy for widening. In: Adams, Niall, Tucker, Allan, Weston, David (eds.) IDA 2017. LNCS, vol. 10584, pp. 87–98. Springer, Cham (2017). https://doi.org/10.1007/978-3-319-68765-0_8

13. Gionis, Aristides, Indyk, Piotr, Motwani, Rajeev: Similarity search in high dimensions via hashing. VLDB 99, 518–529 (1999)

14. Guo, Krystal, Mohar, Bojan: Hermitian adjacency matrix of digraphs and mixed graphs. J. Graph Theory 85(1), 217–248 (2017)

15. Koski, T.J.T., Noble, J.M.: A review of Bayesian networks and structure learning. Mathematica Applicanda 40(1), 53–103 (2012)

16. Kulis, B., Grauman, K.: Kernelized locality-sensitive hashing for scalable image search. In: 12th International Conference on Computer Vision, pp. 2130–7. IEEE (2009)

17. Larrañaga, Pedro, Karshenas, Hossein, Bielza, Concha, Santana, Roberto: A review on evolutionary algorithms in Bayesian network learning and inference tasks. Inf. Sci. 233, 109–125 (2013)

18. Lichman, M.: UCI Machine Learning Repository (2013)

19. Luo, Bin, Wilson, Richard C., Hancock, Edwin R.: Spectral feature vectors for graph clustering. In: Caelli, Terry, Amin, Adnan, Duin, Robert P.W., de Ridder, Dick, Kamel, Mohamed (eds.) SSPR /SPR 2002. LNCS, vol. 2396, pp. 83–93. Springer, Heidelberg (2002). https://doi.org/10.1007/3-540-70659-3_8

20. Marolt, Matija: A mid-level representation for melody-based retrieval in audio collections. IEEE Trans. Multimed. 10(8), 1617–1625 (2008)

21. Meinl, T.: Maximum-Score Diversity Selection. Ph.D. thesis, University of Konstanz, Konstanz, Germany (2010)

22. Pearl, J.: Probabilistic Reasoning in Intelligent Systems: Networks of Plausible Inference. Morgan Kaufmann Publishers Inc., Burlington (1988)

23. Qiu, Huaijun, Hancock, Edwin R.: Graph matching and clustering using spectral partitions. Pattern Recognit. 39(1), 22–34 (2006)

24. Sampson, Oliver, Berthold, Michael R.: Widened KRIMP: better performance through diverse parallelism. In: Blockeel, Hendrik, van Leeuwen, Matthijs, Vinciotti, Veronica (eds.) IDA 2014. LNCS, vol. 8819, pp. 276–285. Springer, Cham (2014). https://doi.org/10.1007/978-3-319-12571-8_24

25. Sampson, Oliver R., Berthold, Michael R.: Widened learning of Bayesian network classifiers. In: Boström, Henrik, Knobbe, Arno, Soares, Carlos, Papapetrou, Panagiotis (eds.) IDA 2016. LNCS, vol. 9897, pp. 215–225. Springer, Cham (2016). https://doi.org/10.1007/978-3-319-46349-0_19

26. Satu Elisa Schaeffer: Graph clustering. Comput. Sci. Rev. 1(1), 27–64 (2007)

27. Scutari, Marco: Learning Bayesian networks with the bnlearn R package. J. Stat. Softw. 35(3), 1–22 (2010)

28. Terasawa, Kengo, Tanaka, Yuzuru: Spherical LSH for approximate nearest neighbor search on unit hypersphere. In: Dehne, Frank, Sack, Jörg-Rüdiger, Zeh, Norbert (eds.) WADS 2007. LNCS, vol. 4619, pp. 27–38. Springer, Heidelberg (2007). https://doi.org/10.1007/978-3-540-73951-7_4
29. Van Dam, E.R., Haemers, W.H.: Which graphs are determined by their spectrum? Linear Algebra Appl. **373**, 241–272 (2003)
30. Vishveshwara, S., Brinda, K.V., Kannan, N.: Protein structure: insights from graph theory. J. Theor. Comput. Chem. **1**(01), 187–211 (2002)
31. Zhang, Boyu, Liu, Xianglong, Lang, Bo: Fast graph similarity search via locality sensitive hashing. In: Ho, Yo-Sung, Sang, Jitao, Ro, Yong Man, Kim, Junmo, Wu, Fei (eds.) PCM 2015. LNCS, vol. 9314, pp. 623–633. Springer, Cham (2015). https://doi.org/10.1007/978-3-319-24075-6_60

Expert Finding in Citizen Science Platform for Biodiversity Monitoring via Weighted PageRank Algorithm

Zakaria Saoud[(✉)] and Colin Fontaine

Centre d'Ecologie et des Science de la Conservation, UMR 7204 CNRS-MNHN-SU,
Musum national d'Histoire naturelle, 61 rue Buffon, 75005 Paris, France
{zakaria.saoud,colin.fontaine}@mnhn.fr

Abstract. Numerous citizen science platforms aiming at monitoring biodiversity have emerged in the recent years. These platforms collect biodiversity data from participants and allow them to increase their scientific knowledge and share it with other participants, experts and scientists. One key aspect of such platforms is quality control on the data, a task usually performed by a limited number of co-opted experts. With the amount of data collected increasing steeply, finding new experts is needed. In this paper we propose a new graph-based expert finding approach for the citizen science platform SPIPOLL, aiming at collecting data on pollinator diversity across France. We exploit both users comments quality and users social relations to calculate users expertise for specific insect family. Experimental results show that the proposed method performs better than the state-of-the-art expert finding algorithms.

Keywords: Expert finding · PageRank algorithm · Citizen sciences

1 Introduction

Citizen science (CS) platforms represent a powerful tool allowing participants to contribute to research and increase their scientific knowledge. Furthermore, CS platforms help scientists in their research projects, by collecting more data and analyzing it. Generally, the primary goal of CS platforms is connecting many participants, experts, and researchers towards a common scientific goal. Nowadays, numerous CS platforms have emerged and can be classified according to their scientific objectives such as: medicine, ecology, astronomy, computer science, psychology, etc. Many popular CS platforms with large communities of participants exist today, such as Zooniverse[1], Foldit[2], Eyewire[3], and eBird[4]. Zooniverse benefits from the collaboration from more than 1 million registered

---

[1] https://www.zooniverse.org/.
[2] http://fold.it/portal/.
[3] https://eyewire.org/explore.
[4] https://ebird.org/home.

W. Duivesteijn et al. (Eds.): IDA 2018, LNCS 11191, pp. 278–289, 2018.
https://doi.org/10.1007/978-3-030-01768-2_23

users to analyze pictures of distant galaxies. Foldit allows users to fold the structures of selected proteins as correctly as possible, by playing an online puzzle video game. Eyewire challenges players to map neurons in 3D, by solving 2D puzzles, thereby helping researchers to model information processing circuits. eBird collects bird information from many volunteers, to provide data about bird distribution and abundance in real-time. Similarly to eBird, SPIPOLL[5] allows users to take photos of flowering plants and their pollinating insects to study changes in pollinator assemblages across space and time. However, most of the existing CS platforms still lack an expert finding (EF) mechanism, which could improve the quality of collected data and optimize data evaluation time. EF approaches aim to extract a list of experts with high knowledge and expertise in a specific domain, to produce high quality answers to questions from online communities. Most of these approaches were focused on communities question answering (CQA) websites. Unlike the existing EF approaches, our study deals with the problem of EF in online CS platform on biodiversity, with the SPIPOLL as a study case. In the SPIPOLL, after taking pictures of pollinators on flowers, the users give a name to each photographed insect from 600 possibilities and share their photos and associated insect names on the platform. While users can comment on each other observations and identifications, experts validate or correct the pollinator identifications.

In our approach, we analyze the users comments and extract the comments that contain precise identifications. The extracted comments will be considered as answers and will be used to construct the users social network. A weighted PageRank algorithm will be applied on the obtained network, to calculate the users expertise for a specific insect family. This paper is organized as follows: Section 2 provides an overview of the related work in the area of EF in CQA websites. Section 3 presents the general structure of the SPIPOLL website. Section 4 introduces the details of our proposed EF approach. Section 5 describes the experimental setup and obtained results. Finally, we provide some concluding remarks in Sect. 6.

2   Related Works

CQA websites represent a powerful tool of knowledge mining on specific topics which cant be extracted easily from general web search engines. CQA websites allow online users to post and answer questions and exchange knowledge among them. Nowadays, several CQA platforms have emerged, such as Quora[6], Yahoo Answers[7], Blurtit[8] and Stack Overflow[9]. With the increase of these platforms, the task of EF has received significant attention in the literature. EF aims to find the appropriate users or experts who can provide good quality answers for

---

[5] http://www.spipoll.org/.
[6] https://fr.quora.com/.
[7] https://fr.answers.yahoo.com/.
[8] https://www.blurtit.com/.
[9] https://stackoverflow.com/.

posted questions. Many research fields can benefit from EF techniques, such as questions recommendation [16] and spam detection [3,6]. For CQA websites, several approaches have been proposed, which can be classified into three main categories: 1- graph-based EF approaches, 2- content-based EF approaches and 3- competition-based EF approaches. In graph-based EF approaches, the users' network is represented by a directed graph, where nodes represent users, and edges represent the relationships among them. A link from user A to user B is drawn, if the user B answers for question posted by user A. The user expertise score can be estimated from the number of edges pointing on him. Most of existing works in this category have adopted link analysis algorithms like PageRank [13] or Hits [8], to calculate the users' expertise scores. We provide in what follows a brief review of such approaches: Zhang et al. [21] proposed a new experts ranking algorithm, named ExpertiseRank. This algorithm is based on PageRank algorithm and calculates the expertise of each user according to the expertise of others related users to him. Li et al. [9] combined documents quality, documents topic-focus degree and users' activities to calculate the users' expertise rank. A social network analysis (SNA) algorithm has been used to analyze the links between the discovered experts, to obtain the specific experts for a specific topic. Zhao et al. [23] exploited the online social relations between users via graph regularized matrix to find experts in CQA systems. Zhao et al. [22] proposed a novel ranking metric network learning framework for EF by exploiting both the social interactions between users and users' relative quality rank to given questions. Rafiei et al. [15] proposed a hybrid method for EF based on content analysis and SNA. The content analysis is based on concept map and SNA is based on PageRank algorithm. Wei et al. [18] proposed the ExpRank algorithm, an extension of the PageRank algorithm. In this algorithm, the negative and the positive agreements relations between users have been both exploited to calculate their expertise. Yeneterzi et al. [20] exploited topic-relevant users and the interactions between them, to construct topic specific authority graph, called Topic-Candidate (TC) graph. This graph has been used to estimate the topic-specific authority scores for each user. Zhu et al. [25] exploited the information in both relevant and target categories, to improve the quality of authority ranking. Procaci et al. [14] proposed a new approach for EF in online communities based on graph ranking algorithm and information retrieval approach. In this approach, two machine learning techniques, artificial neural network, and clustering algorithm have been exploited for EF. Dom et al. [5] applied a graph-based algorithm to rank email correspondents according to their degree of expertise on specific topics. Their results showed that PageRank algorithm performs better than all other algorithms. Shen et al. [17] used a weighted HITS algorithm for computing users reputation and recommending the obtained experts to the users who have posted questions. Content-based EF approaches analyze the extracted information from the users' answers to predict their expertise. User expertise score can be estimated from his Z-score [21], his answers' quality [24], his expertise domains [7] or his answers voted score [4]. Competition-based approaches suppose that the best answerer has higher expertise than other answerers for a question. To achieve that, they explore the pairwise comparisons between users (players) deduced from best answer selections, to estimate user expertise score. The resulting pairwise comparisons can be considered as two-players competition. Liu et al. [10] applied two-players competition models to determine the relative expertise score of users. Aslya et al. [2] proposed a novel community expertise network structure, by creating relations among the best answerer and other answerers they have beaten. The EF process is based on the principle of competition among the answerers of a question. In this work, unlike the existing graph-based EF approaches, we take into account the relationship degrees between users. We represent the interactions between users by a weighted graph. Then, we apply a weighted PageRank algorithm on this graph to estimate the users' expertise. Details of the proposed method will be described in Sect. 4.

3   The General Structure of the SPIPOLL

SPIPOLL is an SC platform created by the National Museum of Natural History (MNHN) and the Office for Insects and their Environment (Opie), to collect data on flowers and their insect pollinators within metropolitan France. The collected data improve the users' knowledge about insect pollinators and allow scientists to assess the abundance variations of pollinator communities. In the SPIPOLL, each user (observer) is asked to take pictures of all insects visiting chosen flowering plant, for a given period of time. Observers are then asked to identify insects and flowering plants, using an online identification key. The pictures of insects and flowering plant from an observation session, as well as their identification, are then uploaded on the SPIPOLL website to form a photographic collection. Nowadays, the SPIPOLL database contains more than 31329 photographic collections and 307719 insects' pictures. Finally, the identifications will be validated by a small group of entomologists from the OPIE. In the SPIPOLL, users can also comment pictures and collections, and add doubts in the identified photos if they aren't sure about identifications.

However, with the increase of collected pictures in the SPIPOLL, the limited number of current experts is insufficient to validate all identifications. Therefore, we propose a novel approach to identify expert within the users for specific insect family based on the users' comments. The comments which contain precise identifications will be considered as answers. Each answer will be compared to corresponding validation (the correct identification validated by experts) to verify its reliability. In other word, we know what the true identification is and we then search for comment that gave the right answer with no ambiguity. In the SPIPOLL, all data will be eventually validated as correct identification which is a prerequisite for ecological analysis.

4   The Proposed Approach

In our approach, we exploit both comments (answers) quality and social interactions between users to predict their expertise. In our weighted graph model, users are represented as nodes, related among them by weighted directed edges. Each edge points from the questioner (the observer) to the answerer (the commentator). The edges weights are calculated according to the reliability of exchanged answers between users. We consider the comments that contain a precise identification (the exact name of the insect) as answers and the posted pictures as questions which wait for identifications (answers). An answer is considered its identical to the validation. Finally, we estimate the users' expertise, by applying a weighted PageRank algorithm on the graph representing the network of questions and answers among users. Our proposed approach can be summarized as follows: 1- Merging users comments on pictures and collections. 2- Extracting precise identifications from comments, using text analysis technique. 3- Extracting the comments with precise identifications (CPIs). 4- Comparing the extracted CPIs with the corresponding validations (the true identifications) and calculate a score for each user and for each insect family. 5- Calculating the relationship degree between users and constructing the users social network graph. 6- Apply a weighted PageRank algorithm on the obtained graph and determine the expert users.

4.1   Merging Users Comments

The comments posted on collections represent 90% of the whole comments on the SPIPOLL website. This is due to the fact that most users prefer to add comments directly to collections rather than on the insect pictures as it avoids several clicks. This situation, prevent us from knowing the precise pictures that users' refer in their comments. As a solution for this, we compare the validation of each picture belonging to a collection, with its collection comments. Each comment will be attributed to the corresponding picture if this comment contains identification identical to one of the validated picture of the collection. Comments without any identical identification to any pictures validations will be attributed randomly to any picture without comment from the collection. In the end, collections comments will be merged with pictures comments. Figure 1 shows an example of the comments merging process.

4.2   Extracting Precise Identifications from Comments

In the SPIPOLL, each user can add comments on pictures or collection, to great other observers, to comment the picture esthetics, or to comment identifications. Users can also add identifications in comments if they think that posted identifications are false. Usually, the proposed identifications in comments are used by observers to update its identifications. In some case, users propose wrong identifications which can push the observer to change their correct identifications. For this reason, the comments represent an important key for obtaining reliable identifications. Hence, comments can be used to calculate users' expertise. In one hand, we suppose that users with high expertise in specific insect family are more likely to add comments with true and precise identification. In other

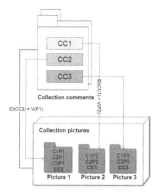

Fig. 1. Example of the comments merging process. ID(CC1) and ID(CC2) represent the contained precise identifications on comments CC1 and CC2 respectively. V(P1) and V(P2) represent the validations of the pictures P1 and P2 respectively.

hand, users with low expertise are likely to add comments with wrong identifications. However, some comments can contain an imprecise identification and can't be used to judge users' answers. Identification is considered imprecise when it doesn't contain a term or terms combination that correspond unequivocally to a single insect name. On the contrary, comments with precise identification contain a term or terms combination that correspond unequivocally to a single insect name and can be defined as follows:

$$CPI = \{term | \exists \ term \in Unique\_terms\} \tag{1}$$

With:

$term$: is a comment term.

$Unique\_terms$: is the set of existing unique terms. To obtain the set of unique terms, we apply a text analysis technique on the SPIPOLL' insect names. First, we transform each insect name to a list of tokens, we then eliminate the stopwords. We mention that unigram unique terms (with one word) which have ambiguous meanings (like brown, garden, day, etc.) have been deleted, because they have insufficient meanings to describe the insects.

4.3   Calculating Relationship Degree Between Users

The extracted CPIs will be used to calculate the relationship degree between users. These comments will be considered as answers, and the posted pictures will be considered as questions which wait for good identifications (answers). In our case, we use only CPIs that have been posted on insects' pictures of the same family. The relationship between two users will be calculated for one target insect family, using their average answers' scores of insects which belong to the target insect family. The relationship strength between two users will increment if they exchange good answers (i.e. if their answers are identical with the validations). The relationship degree between two users will decrement if they exchange wrong answers. The difficulty of identification of insect can affect on answers' gained score. The user will earn more score if he gives good answers for a difficult insect to identify, and will earn less score if he gives good answers for an easy insect to identify. On the other hand, the user will lose fewer score if he gives wrong answers for difficult insect, and will lose more score if he gives wrong answers for an insect easy to identify. The length of the answer can also affect on answers' gained score. Expert users are expected to give long answers with more unique terms. The relationship degree should be calculated from each user side. Thus, we can calculate the relationship degree between two users A (the commentator) and B (the observer) for specific insects' family (insects set) f, as follow:

$$relationship_f(A, B) = \sum_{taxon \in f} \frac{score\_answers_{tx}(A, B)}{|f|} \qquad (2)$$

$|f|$: is the number of existing insects in the f insect family.

$score\_answers_{tx}(A, B)$ represents the score of posted answers of user A on the pictures of the user B, for a specific insect tx. This score is calculated using the following formula:

$$score\_answers_{tx}(A, B) = \frac{\sum_{R \in Answers_{tx}(A,B)} \begin{cases} \frac{1}{ease(tx)} * |R| & , & R = V \\ - ease(tx) * |R| & , & R \neq V \end{cases}}{\sum_{R \in Answers_{tx}(A,B)} |R|} \qquad (3)$$

With:

$ease(tx)$: represent the ease score of the insect tx. This score is high when the insect is easy to identify and is low when it's hard to identify. This score is calculated as follows:

$$ease(tx) = \frac{Number\ of\ tx\ pictures\ with\ true\ identifications}{Total\ number\ of\ tx\ validated\ pictures} \qquad (4)$$

$Answers_{tx}(A, B)$: is the set of posted answers of user A on the pictures of the user B for the insect tx.

R : is one answer from the set of answers $Answers_{tx}(A, B)$.

$|R|$: is the length of the answer, i.e. the size of the largest existing unique term on the answer.

V : is the corresponding picture validation.

In our study, each insect with score higher than 0.65 (the average ease score of all insects), will be considered easy for identification. On the other hand, an insect with a score lower than 0.65, will be considered hard for identification.

4.4   Constructing the Users Social Network

When users (observers) post pictures on the SPIPOLL website, some other users can comment on his pictures. Connecting observers to commentators by directional weighted arrows from observers to commentators, allows us to create the users' social network. Hence, the SPIPOLL' users can be organized in a weighted and directed graph $G(V, E)$, Where:

V : is the set of users who share or comment pictures of one specific insect family.

E : is the set of directed edges, where $e_{i,j}$ indicates that user u_j has commented on one or more pictures of user u_i. These edges are weighted using the friendship degree formula (see Sect. 4.3).

4.5 Calculating Users Expertise Using Weighted PageRank Algorithm

Nowadays, PageRank algorithm has proven its efficiency not only on web pages ranking but also on EF field. Many PageRank-based EF algorithms [5,15,18,21] have proved that PageRank outperforms other algorithms like HITS and Z_scores [21] for EF. However, these studies have applied PageRank only on non-weighted graphs. In our case, we use a weighted PageRank algorithm to extract experts from a weighted graph. Several Weighted PageRank algorithms have been proposed [11,19] to improve the performance of original PageRank. The weighted PageRank consists of adding weights to different parts of PageRank formula. According to [1,19], weighted PageRank performs better than traditional PageRank. In our approach, we use the proposed weighted PageRank algorithm by Mihalcea [12]. In this algorithm, the PageRank score of target vertice V_a is calculated using the weights of coming edges from of its predecessors' vertices $In(V_a)$ and the weights of destined edges to the successors of its predecessors' vertices $Out(V_b)$. In our approach, we calculate the weighted PageRank score for a user A as follows:

$$WP(A) = (1 - d) + d \sum_{B \in In(A)} \frac{relationship_f(B, A)}{\sum_{C \in Out(B)} relationship_f(B, C)} * WP(B) \quad (5)$$

With:

B : is a user who has received at least a comment from user A.

$In(A)$: is the list of users who have received comments from user A.

C : is a user who has commented on pictures or collections of user B.

$Out(B)$: is the list of users who have commented on the pictures or collections of user B.

$WP(B)$: is the PageRank score of the user B.

d : is a damping factor which can be set between 0 and 1. Similar to the previous studies, we will set the damping factor to 0.85.

5 Experiments

In this section, we evaluate the performance of our proposed approach using a set of validated pictures, observers and commentators from the SPIPOLL.

The collected comments are posted on the insects' pictures of the same family. In our study, we choose the "Apidae" insect family because it contains the most observed insects in SPIPOLL. To show the effectiveness of our proposed approach, we compare it with 2 state-of-the-art methods: the Z-score [21] and ExpertiseRank [21]. To generate the ground truth ranking scores, we use the set of added identifications on the pictures. We calculate for each commentator, his ground truth expertise score for specific insect, by comparing his identifications with the corresponding validations. The ground truth expertise of the user U_n for the insect tx_m can be defined as follows:

$$Expertise\,(U_n, tx_m) = \frac{Number\ of\ correct\ identifications\ posted\ on\ tx_m\ by\ U_n}{Totale\ number\ of\ identifications\ posted\ on\ tx_m\ by\ U_n} \tag{6}$$

The obtained expertise will be used to calculate the user ground truth expertise score for specific insect family. The ground truth expertise of the user U_n for the insect family f_m can be defined as follows:

$$Expertise\,(U_n, f_m) = \frac{\sum_{tx_m \in f_m} Expertise\,(U_n, tx_m)}{|f_m|} \tag{7}$$

$|f_m|$: is the number of existing insects in the f_m insect family.

5.1 Data Preparation

The dataset is obtained from a sample of the SPIPOLL database. We collected the information from all posted pictures and comments from April 2010 to October 2017. In total, we extracted 31329 collections, 307719 pictures, 76288 comments and 1455 users. Among these comments, 28% contain precise identifications. In our case, we use only the posted comments on the insect pictures of the "Apidae" insect family, which represent 12% of all comments. Thus, we obtain a sample which contains 1844 validated pictures, 252 users, and 1866 CPIs. Figure 2 shows the obtained social network using this sample. In this graph, the node size represents the number of connections of the node with the other nodes. Largest nodes have a higher degree of connections than others.

5.2 Evaluation Criteria

We evaluate the performance of each algorithm under investigation based on two evaluation metrics: Precision at K (P@K) and Spearmans rho. The first metric measures the proportion of the best commentators (best experts) ranked in the top K results. In our evaluation, each commentator with higher ground truth expertise than 0.4 (the average ground truth expertise of all users), will be considered as best expert. The second metric measures the correlation between the ideal ranking (the ground truth ranking) and the obtained ranking. We calculate the Spearmans rho for the 10, 20 and 40 top ranked commentators.

Fig. 2. The obtained social network

5.3   Results

Figure 3 shows the obtained precision from the top 10, 20, 30, 40 commentators respectively. We can see that graph-based algorithms perform better than the Z-score algorithm. This result proves that the exploiting of relations among users can improve the performance of experts' identification. As Fig. 3 shows, our weighted PageRank algorithm also outperforms the ExpertiseRank algorithm, especially in the top 10, 20 and 30 users. The precision of the weighted PageRank algorithm reduces when the number of users increases and is equal to the ExpertiseRank algorithm on the top 40 users. To measure the performance of the three algorithms, we calculated the correlation between each algorithm and the ground truth ratings. Figure 4 illustrates the statistical results regarding Spearman's rho. From this figure, we can see that for all algorithms, the correlation decreases when the number of users increases. This due to the increasing in the variation between the ideal ranking and the obtained ranking from each algorithm. We can see also that our weighted PageRank algorithm gives a relatively higher correlation than other algorithms, which show that our approach is useful to rank experts than other algorithms. From the obtained results, we can see that our weighted PageRank algorithm outperforms the other EF algorithms.

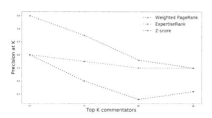

Fig. 3. Precision at top K commentators.

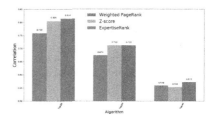

Fig. 4. The performance of three algorithms in Spearman's rho distance

6 Conclusions

In this paper, we proposed a new graph-based EF approach for the citizen science platform, the SPIPOLL. This approach exploits users comments and users social relations to predict their expertise on a specific insect family. The relationship between users is extracted from the comments sent by users. Depending on the insects identification ease and the length of comments, the relationship between users can increase or decrease. These relationships have been used to construct a weighted graph. Then, a weighted PageRank algorithm has been applied on the obtained graph to rank the users according to their expertise. We evaluated the performance of our method using a dataset from the SPIPOLL database. Experimental results showed that our method achieve better performance than the state-of-the-art EF algorithms. This is due to the exploitation of the relationship degrees between users and the weighted page-rank algorithm for calculating the users expertise.

References

1. Aktas, M.S., Nacar, M.A., Menczer, F.: Using hyperlink features to personalize web search. In: Mobasher, B., Nasraoui, O., Liu, B., Masand, B. (eds.) WebKDD 2004. LNCS (LNAI), vol. 3932, pp. 104–115. Springer, Heidelberg (2006). https://doi.org/10.1007/11899402_7
2. Aslay, Ç., O'Hare, N., Aiello, L.M., Jaimes, A.: Competition-based networks for expert finding. In: Proceedings of the 36th International ACM SIGIR Conference on Research and Development in Information Retrieval, pp. 1033–1036. ACM (2013)
3. Becchetti, L., Castillo, C., Donato, D., Leonardi, S., Baeza-Yates, R.A.: Link-based characterization and detection of web spam. In: AIRWeb, pp. 1–8 (2006)
4. Cai, Y., Chakravarthy, S.: Expertise ranking of users inQA community. In: Meng, W., Feng, L., Bressan, S., Winiwarter, W., Song, W. (eds.) DASFAA 2013. LNCS, vol. 7825, pp. 25–40. Springer, Heidelberg (2013). https://doi.org/10.1007/978-3-642-37487-6_5
5. Dom, B., Eiron, I., Cozzi, A., Zhang, Y.: Graph-based ranking algorithms for e-mail expertise analysis. In: Proceedings of the 8th ACM SIGMOD workshop on Research Issues in Data Mining and Knowledge Discovery, pp. 42–48. ACM (2003)
6. Gyöngyi, Z., Garcia-Molina, H., Pedersen, J.: Combating web spam with trustrank. In: Proceeding of the Thirtieth international conference on very large date bases-Vol. 30, pp. 576–587. VLDB Endowment (2004)
7. Huang, C., Yao, L., Wang, X., Benatallah, B., Sheng, Q.Z.: Expert as a service: software expert recommendation via knowledge domain embeddings in stack overflow. In: 2017 IEEE International Conference on Web Services (ICWS), pp. 317–324. IEEE (2017)
8. Kleinberg, J.M.: Authoritative sources in a hyperlinked environment. J. ACM (JACM) 46(5), 604–632 (1999)
9. Li, Y., Ma, S., Zhang, Y., Huang, R.: Expertise network discovery via topic and link analysis in online communities. In: 2012 IEEE 12th International Conference on Advanced Learning Technologies (ICALT), pp. 311–315. IEEE (2012)

10. Liu, J., Song, Y.I., Lin, C.Y.: Competition-based user expertise score estimation. In: Proceedings of the 34th International ACM SIGIR conference on Research and Development in Information Retrieval, pp. 425–434. ACM (2011)
11. Liu, X., Bollen, J., Nelson, M.L., Van de Sompel, H.: Co-authorship networks in the digital library research community. Inf. Process. Manag. **41**(6), 1462–1480 (2005)
12. Mihalcea, R.: Unsupervised large-vocabulary word sense disambiguation with graph-based algorithms for sequence data labeling. In: Proceedings of the conference on Human Language Technology and Empirical Methods in Natural Language Processing, pp. 411–418. Association for Computational Linguistics (2005)
13. Page, L., Brin, S., Motwani, R., Winograd, T.: The pagerank citation ranking: Bringing order to the web. Technical report, Stanford InfoLab (1999)
14. Procaci, T.B., Siqueira, S.W.M., Braz, M.H.L.B., de Andrade, L.C.V.: How to find people who can help to answer a question?-analyses of metrics and machine learning in online communities. Comput. Human Behav. **51**, 664–673 (2015)
15. Rafiei, M., Kardan, A.A.: A novel method for expert finding in online communities based on concept map and pagerank. Human-centric Comput. Inf. Sci. **5**(1), 10 (2015)
16. San Pedro, J., Karatzoglou, A.: Question recommendation for collaborative question answering systems with rankslda. In: Proceedings of the 8th ACM Conference on Recommender systems, pp. 193–200. ACM (2014)
17. Shen, J., Shen, W., Fan, X.: Recommending experts in q& a communities by weighted hits algorithm. In: Information Technology and Applications, 2009. IFITA'09. International Forum on. vol. 2, pp. 151–154. IEEE (2009)
18. Wei, C.P., Lin, W.B., Chen, H.C., An, W.Y., Yeh, W.C.: Finding experts in online forums for enhancing knowledge sharing and accessibility. Comput. Human Behav. **51**, 325–335 (2015)
19. Xing, W., Ghorbani, A.: Weighted pagerank algorithm. In: Proceedings Second Annual Conference on Communication Networks and Services Research, 2004, pp. 305–314. IEEE (2004)
20. Yeniterzi, R., Callan, J.: Constructing effective and efficient topic-specific authority networks for expert finding in social media. In: Proceedings of the First International Workshop on Social Media Retrieval and Analysis, pp. 45–50. ACM (2014)
21. Zhang, J., Ackerman, M.S., Adamic, L.: Expertise networks in online communities: structure and algorithms. In: Proceedings of the 16th International Conference on World Wide Web, pp. 221–230. ACM (2007)
22. Zhao, Z., Yang, Q., Cai, D., He, X., Zhuang, Y.: Expert finding for community-based question answering via ranking metric network learning. In: IJCAI, pp. 3000–3006 (2016)
23. Zhao, Z., Zhang, L., He, X., Ng, W.: Expert finding for question answering via graph regularized matrix completion. IEEE Trans. Knowl. Data Eng. **27**(4), 993–1004 (2015)
24. Zhou, Z.M., Lan, M., Niu, Z.Y., Lu, Y.: Exploiting user profile information for answer ranking in cqa. In: Proceedings of the 21st International Conference on World Wide Web, pp. 767–774. ACM (2012)
25. Zhu, H., Chen, E., Xiong, H., Cao, H., Tian, J.: Ranking user authority with relevant knowledge categories for expert finding. World Wide Web **17**(5), 1081–1107 (2014)

Random Forests with Latent Variables to Foster Feature Selection in the Context of Highly Correlated Variables. Illustration with a Bioinformatics Application.

Christine Sinoquet[1(✉)] and Kamel Mekhnacha[2]

[1] LS2N, UMR CNRS 6004, University of Nantes, 44322 Nantes, France
`christine.sinoquet@univ-nantes.fr`
[2] Probayes, 180 avenue de l'Europe, Inovallée, 38330 Montbonnot, France
`Kamel.Mekhnacha@probayes.com`

Abstract. The random forest model is a popular framework used in classification and regression. In cases where dense dependences exist within the variables, it may be beneficial to capture these dependences through latent variables, further used to build the random forest. In this paper, we present Sylva, a generalization of the T-Trees model (Botta *et al.*, 2008), the only attempt so far where latent variables are integrated in the random forest learning scheme. Sylva is an innovative hybrid approach in which an adapted random forest framework benefits from the modeling of dependences *via* FLTM, a forest of latent tree models (Mourad *et al.*, 2011). The FLTM model drives the generation on the fly of the latent variables used to learn the random forest. In the unprecedented large-scale study reported here, Sylva, instantiated by different clustering methods, is compared to T-Trees using high-dimensional real-world datasets in the context of genetic association studies. We show that the already high predictive power of T-Trees is not significantly increased by Sylva. In constrast, in Sylva, the importance measure distribution corresponding to top-ranked variables is significantly skewed towards higher values than in T-Trees, which meets the feature selection objective.

Keywords: Feature selection · Random forest with latent variables
Bayesian network with latent variables
Forest of latent tree models · High-dimensional data

This work was supported by the French National Research Agency (ANR SAMOG-WAS project). The software development and the realization of experiments were performed in part at the CCIPL (Centre de Calcul Intensif des Pays de la Loire, Nantes, France). C. Sinoquet thanks V. Botta for his expert advice on the T-Trees model, and C. Kemps for her help in the preparation of the data. C. Kemps was granted by the GRIOTE project funded by the Pays de la Loire Region.

W. Duivesteijn et al. (Eds.): IDA 2018, LNCS 11191, pp. 290–302, 2018.
https://doi.org/10.1007/978-3-030-01768-2_24

1   Introduction

The random forest (RF) scheme devised by Breiman in the early 2000s [6] is one of the most popular ensemble learning techniques used for binary classification or regression. Supervised ensemble methods are meant to produce lower variance predictions when applied beyond the learning set. This aim is achieved by constructing a set of weak predictors and combining their outputs to build the final prediction. The random forest framework applies bootstrap aggregating (bagging) to decision trees. In standard decision tree learning, at each node, the whole set of variables, $\mathbf{V}$, is inspected to determine the best discriminating split with respect to the variable of interest (class or continuous outcome). In contrast, in RFs, a subset of $\mathbf{V}$ drawn at random is used for this purpose. Regardless of the context (decision tree or RF), the optimal split at a node is the split that decreases the most node impurity for a classification tree (respectively the sum of squared errors for a regression tree) after the split. To set ideas, in RFs, the latter quantity over all splits and over all trees involving a given variable constitutes a standard measure of the importance of this variable to the regression problem; symmetrically, the sum of impurity decreases over all tree nodes in the forest allows to measure the importance to the classification problem [12]. The recognized advantages of the non-parametric stochastic RF framework encompass ability to identify complex relationships between predictors and response, capability to handle high-dimensional data while maintaining sufficient efficiency, and capacity to rank the variables according to their importances to the classification or regression problem. Henceforth, we will focus on RFs in a binary classification context (categorical variable $\mathbf{C}$ taking its values in $\{0, 1\}$ unless stated otherwise), and $\mathbf{V}$ will denote the set of n observed discrete variables.

In RFs, the presence of correlated variables may be a matter for debate, depending on the downstream application. Solutions have been proposed, such as conditional importance measure [20], and recursive feature elimination based on permutation importance measure [10]. In other cases, when a dense dependence network exists within the variables, it is in contrast appealing to infer latent variables that capture the dependences between the variables, in order to build the trees of the RF, based on these latent variables. This novel paradigm was proposed in the seminal work of Botta and collaborators, who developed the T-Trees (Trees inside Trees) model [5]. In this article, we propose Sylva, a generalization of T-Trees, and at the same time the single proposal after T-Trees to construct random forests from latent variables (RFLVs). Sylva is an innovative hybrid method combining T-Trees with a refined variant of FLTM (Forest of Latent Tree Models). The FLTM model was designed by Mourad and collaborators, to model dependences within variables [13]. As high performances were already reported for T-Trees, this paper focuses on T-Trees and Sylva. In the extensive study reported here, Sylva, instantiated by different clustering methods, is compared to T-Trees using high-dimensional real-world data.

The rest of the paper is organized as follows. Section 2 first briefly reviews the features of T-Trees and FLTM essential to understand the Sylva method; then it explains the connection between FLTM and the RFLV Sylva proposal. Section 3 briefly describes the main algorithms behind Sylva. Section 4 provides information on the implementation. A large-scale experimental comparative study of T-Trees and four Sylva variants is presented and discussed in Sect. 4.

2   From T-Trees to Sylva

In this section, we first explain the shift from T-Trees to Sylva. Then we explain how categorical latent variables are inferred through FLTM learning. The third subsection connects the previous latent variables to the numerical latent variables handled by the Sylva RFLV framework and describes the key mechanisms underlying this approach.

2.1   T-Trees Generalized

In the random forest framework, t trees are grown by recursively partitioning t bootstrap samples of the initial dataset. At each tree node, a set of K variables is drawn at random and an optimal split is computed. This involves the calculation of all univariate split functions ($v \leq \theta$) across the value domain of any variable v within these K variables.

The T-Trees concept was proposed to enhance random forests when analyzing genetic data. Therein, the n discrete variables, genetic markers ordered along the genome, are known to be related by a dense network of *local spatial* dependences. The key idea behind T-Trees is to apply the RF framework to a novel feature space consisting of latent variables expected to capture such dependences. In T-Trees, contiguous blocks of m (*e.g.*, $m = 20$) contiguous variables provide the $\frac{n}{m}$ latent variables of this novel feature space.

In the Sylva approach, we first transform the initial space of variables into a smaller space of discrete latent variables through FLTM modeling. The FLTM model is a generic model designed to capture dependences within data. It is a set of latent tree models, namely tree-shaped Bayesian networks with observed discrete variables at leaf nodes, and discrete latent variables at internal and root nodes. The parameters of the FLTM describe the marginal distributions of all root nodes, and the distribution of each other node conditional on its parent node. These discrete latent variables will be further used to generate numerical latent variables involved in *non-linear multivariate node splitting functions*.

2.2   Inferring FLTM Latent Variables

Learning a latent tree model in high-dimensional settings is intractable unless a process based on iterative ascending clustering of variables is employed [14]. In this line, the FLTM learning algorithm imposes neither binary structure for trees, nor common cardinality for latent variables.

The iterative ascending process used to learn an FLTM relies on a user-specified clustering method. Figure 1 details the first iteration of the FLTM learning algorithm on a toy example. In Sylva, we are only interested in latent variables produced by the first iteration of the generic FLTM learning algorithm. To note, this "simplified" task remains complex in high-dimensional settings. The theoretical worst case time complexity for FLTM learning is $O(n^2(1 + c_{max}^2 \; nbs \; e \; p))$, where n and p are the number of observed variables and number of observations, c_{max} is the maximal cardinality specified for the latent variables, and nbs and e respectively denote the number of multiple starts for the Expectation-Maximization (EM) algorithm and the number of iterations for each EM run.

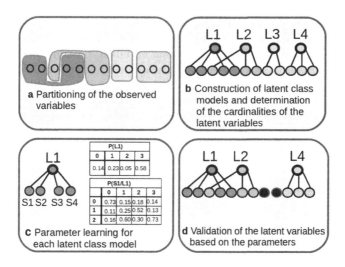

Fig. 1. FLTM learning adapted to the Sylva approach. (a) The clustering method specified by the user is employed to partition the variables into non-overlapping clusters. The metrics used is the mutual information measure. (b) The variables in each cluster are connected to a latent variable, to form a latent class model (LCM). A heuristic is used to determine the specific cardinalities of latent variables L1 to L4. This cardinality is defined as an affine function of the number n_c of child variables: $card(L) = \alpha + \beta \times n_c$. In addition, a cardinality threshold (c_{max}) allows to control the learning complexity. (c) The Expectation-Maximization algorithm is run to instantiate the parameters of each LCM: nbs possible instantiations of the parameters of the LCM are generated; the best instantiation is determined using the BIC score criterion [18]. (d) Latent variable L3 fails the quality test. The quality of a latent variable is assessed through a criterion averaging the mutual information between this variable and any child variable, normalized by the minimal entropy between the latent variable and any child variable. If the criterion is greater than a specified threshold (τ), the latent variable is validated.

2.3   From FLTM Latent Variables to Numerical Latent Variables in the RF Framework

The strategy employed in T-Trees and Sylva to infer numerical latent variables is to grow "embedded" decision trees following the RF principle. "Extremely randomized trees" (Extra-trees) are used for this purpose [9]. In an Extra-tree, not only are variables selected at random at a node; the best split is computed from splits picked at random (one split per variable). In the remainder of this article, we will then refer to meta-trees (and their meta-nodes) in the RFLV, and embedded trees (and their nodes).

We now illustrate how Sylva works with the toy example of Fig. 2. The univariate splitting in standard RF is first reminded in Fig. 2 (a). In Fig. 2 (b), we select at random K (pre-specified as 4) clusters from the dependence map, namely clusters associated with FLTM latent variables, possibly including singletons. Figure 2 (c) details the inference of the numerical latent variable related to cluster C88, composed of variables S57, S63, S65 and S66. For the report, these four variables were children of the same latent variable in the FLTM model. Figure 2 (c) displays the Extra-tree expanded from this restricted set of four variables. A formal presentation corresponding to Fig. 2 (b) and (c) is provided in the next subsection.

2.4   Description of the Algorithms behind the Sylva RFLV

The main procedure of Sylva grows a forest of t meta-trees (Algorithm 1). The parameters are described in Table 1. Each meta-tree is grown recursively using K numerical latent variables at each meta-node as shown in Algorithm 2. Function growEmbeddedTree grows an Extra-tree using k variables at each node. The theoretical worst case and average case time complexities of standard RF learning are $O(t\ K\ p^2\ log(p))$ and $O(t\ K\ p\ log^2(p))$, where p is the number of observations. The empirical complexity was shown to equal the average complexity [11]. The empirical complexity for the RFLV in Sylva is therefore $O(t\ K\ k\ p^2\ log^4(p))$.

3   Implementation

The two C++ components involved in Sylva were respectively adapted from T-Trees [5] and FLTM [15]. ProBT, a C++ library dedicated to Bayesian networks, freely available to academics, is required to run FLTM [2,16]. The extensiveness of the comparative study required intensive use of Xeon hexa-core bi-processors (2,66 GHz).

Notably, we adapted FLTM to allow the selection of the clustering method among CAST [1], DBSCAN [8], the Louvain method [3], and a consensus-based process involving the three latter methods. When using the consensus-based strategy, Sylva stores the q (e.g., 3) top best FLTM models for each of CAST, DBSCAN and the Louvain method, thus providing $3 \times q$ partitions of $\mathbf{V}$. The consensus is built by merging sufficiently overlapping clusters from these partitions. Otherwise, clusters are fragmented. This way, we take the risk to miss

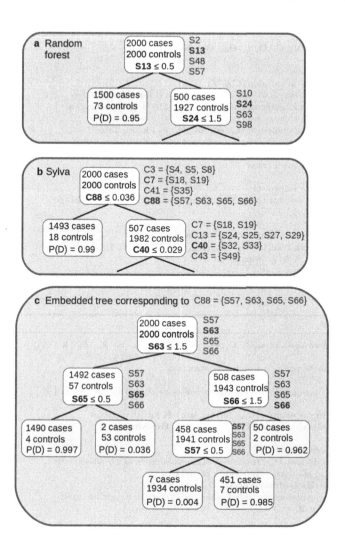

Fig. 2. Node splitting in standard random forest and in the Sylva approach. Context of a genetic association study. The observed variables are genetic markers (discrete variables with values in $\{0, 1, 2\}$). Each leaf is labeled with P(D), the probability to be diseased. P(D) is computed from the population of cases and controls having reached the node. (a) Standard random forest - $K = 4$. The 4 variables selected at random at each node are indicated on the right of the node. At the root node, the best optimal split is obtained for S13 (in bold), in competition with S2, S48 and S57. (b) Meta-node splitting in Sylva - $K = 4$. At the root meta-node, C3, C7, C41 and C88, produced by FLTM learning, are in competition. Each of these sets is processed to infer a numerical latent variable. (c) Node splitting in the Extra-tree developed for the set C88 - k: the *size* of C88. The leaves of this embedded tree are labeled with 0.004, 0.036, 0.962, 0.985 and 0.997, which defines the value domain of a numerical latent variable (denoted C88). The best split for the root meta-node in (b) is $C88 \leq 0.0036$.

Algorithm 1

FUNCTION Sylva(V, C, D, t, Θ_o, Θ_n, K, θ_o, θ_n, k)
INPUT:
- V: n discrete variables
- C: a binary categorical variable (C $\notin$ V)
- D = ($\mathbf{D_V}$, $\mathbf{D_C}$): therein, matrix $\mathbf{D_V}$ describes the n variables of V for each of the p rows (*i.e.* observations), and vector $\mathbf{D_C}$ depicts categorical variable C for each of the p observations in $\mathbf{D_V}$
- For description of parameters t, Θ_o, Θ_n, K, θ_o, θ_n, k, see Table 1

OUTPUT:
- $\mathscr{F}$: an ensemble of t meta-trees

1. Initialize $\mathscr{F}$ to the empty set
2. Run the FLTM generator to produce the map of dependences **DepMap**

3. **for** i in 1 **to** t
4.   Sample with replacement from D, to provide $\mathbf{D_i}$
5. $\mathscr{T}_i \leftarrow$ **growMetaTree**(C, $\mathbf{D_i}$, Θ_o, Θ_n, **DepMap**, K, θ_o, θ_n, k)
6.   Add meta-tree $\mathscr{T}_i$ to growing forest $\mathscr{F}$
7: **end for**
8: **return** $\mathscr{F}$

Algorithm 2

FUNCTION **growMetaTree**(C, $\mathbf{D_i}$, Θ_o, Θ_n, **DepMap**, K, θ_o, θ_n, k)
OUTPUT:
- $\mathscr{T}$: a subtree of the meta-tree under construction

9. **if** recursion is terminated **then** create a leaf node $\mathscr{T}$ and **return** $\mathscr{T}$ **end if**

10. Initialize $\mathscr{L}$ to the empty set, to further store **K** latent variables
11. Draw uniformly a subset $\mathscr{C}$ of **K** clusters from **DepMap**

12. **for** each cluster $\mathbf{cl}$ of $\mathscr{C}$
13.   Obtain the dataset $\mathbf{D_{cl}}$; it consists of the submatrix of D_i where only columns (*i.e.* observed variables) in $\mathbf{cl}$ are kept
14. $\mathscr{T}_{cl} \leftarrow$ **growEmbeddedTree**(C, $\mathbf{D_{cl}}$, θ_o, θ_n, k)
15.   Infer numerical latent variable $\boldsymbol{\ell}$ using $\mathscr{T}_{cl}$, compute its optimal split
16.   and store $\boldsymbol{\ell}$ in $\mathscr{L}$
17. **end for**

18. Determine $\mathbf{OS}^*$, the best optimal split over all latent variables in $\mathscr{L}$
19. Split matrix $\mathbf{D_i}$ into $\mathbf{D_{i_1}}$ and $\mathbf{D_{i_2}}$ using $\mathbf{OS}^*$
20. $\mathscr{T}_1 \leftarrow$ **growMetaTree** (C, $\mathbf{D_{i_1}}$, Θ_o, Θ_n, **DepMap**, K, θ_o, θ_n, k)
21. $\mathscr{T}_2 \leftarrow$ **growMetaTree** (C, $\mathbf{D_{i_2}}$, Θ_o, Θ_n, **DepMap**, K, θ_o, θ_n, k)
22. create a subtree $\mathscr{T}$ with root labeled by $\mathbf{OS}^*$ and having $\mathscr{T}_1$ and $\mathscr{T}_2$ as child subtrees
23. **return** $\mathscr{T}$

---

latent variables, but therefore control the number of false latent variables. The current version of the FLTM generator, SYLVESTRA++, is available at [21].

4   Comparative study of T-Trees and Sylva

The application domain for our large-scale comparative study is that of genetic associations studies. Given a pathology of interest, such studies aim at finding genetic markers that are most influential on affected/unaffected status in a population of cases and controls. To note, an extensive study focused on Sylva/DBSCAN and applied to simulated genetic data had already been conducted and is reported in [19]. The present work focuses on the behavior of Sylva on high-dimensional real genetic data. We first present the datasets and experimental settings. Then we present our three-fold comparative study.

4.1   Experimental Settings

Datasets. We used 161 datasets provided by the Wellcome Trust Case Control Consortium (WTCCC) [22]. These datasets describe cases' and controls' genotypes for seven diseases: Bipolar Disorder (BD), Coronary Artery Disease (CAD), Crohn's disease (CD), Hypertension (HT), Rheumatoid Arthritis (RA), Type 1 Diabetes (T1D) and Type 2 Diabetes (T2D). Therein, for each of the seven diseases, around 4,500 to 5,000 subjects (affected and unaffected) are described for each of the 23 human chromosomes. Across these 161 large-scale datasets, the number of variables ranges from 5,754 to 38,867 (average 20,236).

Parameter Adjustment. T-Trees and the FLTM generator respectively require the adjustment of 7 and 5 parameters. To note, in Sylva, the adjustment of the FLTM generator parameters is independent of the adjustment of the T-Trees parameters. Given a specified parameter setting for FLTM learning, the FLTM generator used in Sylva is able to optimize the parameters of the clustering method specified by the user. For this purpose, Sylva relies on a user-defined set of parameter combinations to build FLTM models. The best model is automatically selected relying on the BIC score criterion. Table 1 describes the parameter setting used in the present work. When the consensus-based clustering method is used, automatic parameter adjustment is performed as well.

4.2   Results and Discussion

We now present our three-fold comparative study.

Comparison of AUC Distributions. Following [4], we used the parameter setting recommended when applying T-Trees on the WTCCC datasets. We computed the AUCs though the pROC package [17]. Table 2 recapitulates averages and standard deviations for the AUC distributions related to the five methods considered. For each Sylva variant, we observe a slight increase of the average over T-Trees. This increase is the largest for Sylva/Consensus and the smallest for Sylva/Louvain.

We then focused on the AUC distributions collected for each disease (23 datasets per disease). For each dataset, we compared the AUC distribution obtained for T-Trees with the four distributions obtained for the Sylva variants. We used Wilcoxon rank sum tests for this purpose. We showed that there is no statistically significant difference between T-Trees and any Sylva variant.

Comparison of the Top Importance Measure Distributions. For each method and each disease, we obtained a distribution by merging the r variables

Table 1. Parameter setting. The T-Trees parameters were tuned according to the experimental feedback reported in [4]. In the latter work, T-Trees was extensively tested under various parameter settings, on the WTCCC datasets (the same we use), using cross-validations. The values of the FLTM generator parameters were set after indications from [13], except for c_{max} which was tuned according to our own experience. To adjust automatically DBSCAN and CAST parameters, a limited set of combinations of values (DBSCAN) or values (CAST) is considered, and the corresponding FLTM models obtained are compared based on the BIC score criterion.

Method		Parameter description	Value
T-Trees	t	# of meta-trees in the random forest	1000
Sylva	Θ_o	Threshold (# of observations), to control meta-tree leaf size	2000
	Θ_n	Threshold (# of meta-nodes), to control meta-tree size	∞
	K	# of blocks, or # of clusters, to be selected at random at each meta-node, to compute the meta-node split	1000
	θ_o	Threshold (# of observations), to control embedded tree leaf size	1
	θ_n	Threshold (# of nodes), to control embedded tree size	5
	k	# of variables in a block or cluster, to be selected at random, at each node, to compute the node split	size of block (20) or of cluster
FLTM generator	$\alpha, \beta,$ c_{max}	3 parameters to model the cardinality of each latent variable as an affine function with a maximum threshold	0.2, 2 10
	τ	Threshold to control the quality of latent variables	0.3
	nbs	# of multiple starts for the EM algorithm	10
CAST	a	Affinity threshold to decide cluster membership	value selected in 0.05 to 0.9, step 0.05
DBSCAN	R	Maximum radius of the neighborhood, to grow a cluster	*idem*
	N_{min}	Minimum number of points required within a cluster	value selected in {2, 3}
Louvain		No parameter to be tuned by user	

Table 2. Comparison of the predictive powers of T-Trees and the four Sylva variants on 161 real datasets. The four Sylva variants differ by the clustering methods used for the FLTM constructions (see Sect. 2.2). SX stands for the appropriate Sylva variant.

AUC	Method				
	T-Trees	Sylva			
		CAST	DBSCAN	Louvain	Consensus
min	0.887	0.902	0.890	0.885	0.913
max	0.961	0.979	0.972	0.955	0.979
avg	0.934	0.946	0.952	0.940	0.955
avg(SX)-avg(T-Trees)		**0.012**	**0.018**	0.006	**0.021**
std	0.008	0.010	0.009	0.011	0.008

(*e.g.*, $r = 100$) showing the highest importance (IMP) measures in each of the 23 datasets related to the disease. In the following, we will refer to such distributions as top r-IMP distributions. We first compared T-Trees with any Sylva variant, using Wilcoxon rank sum tests. This time, we show that the difference between T-Trees and any Sylva variant is statistically significant (largest p-value: 7×10^{-6}).

In addition, for each Sylva variant SX, we compared the top r-IMP distribution of T-Trees with the distribution of IMP measures obtained through method SX for the top variables ranked by T-Trees. The latter distribution is denoted r-T>SX. Symmetrically, we compiled the distribution r-SX>T.

In each subfigure of Fig. 4, the first five boxes show that top r-IMP distributions tend to differ between T-Trees (box 1) and any Sylva variant. Since the confidence intervals highlighted do not overlap, there is a strong evidence that the medians differ between T-Trees and any Sylva variant [7]. We conclude that any Sylva variant pinpoints more important variables than T-Trees. The comparison with the two other distributions shows that the most important variables in a Sylva variant are detected as less important than other variables by T-Trees (discussion not shown). These trends hold for the other diseases (not shown).

Finally, Fig. 3 illustrates how the difference between top r-IMP T-Trees and SX distributions escalates with decreasing r values. This trend is observed across the seven diseases analyzed (extract shown).

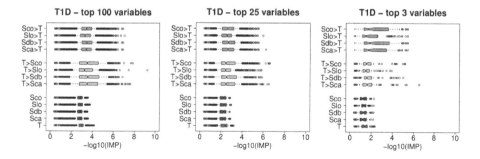

Fig. 3. Comparison of four importance measure distributions, for top 100, top 25 and top 3 variables. IMP: importance measure. T: IMP distribution for the top r variables (top r-IMP) in T-Trees. SX: top r-IMP distribution for Sylva variant SX. Sca: Sylva/CAST, Sdb: Sylva/DBSCAN, Slo: Sylva/Louvain, Sco: Sylva/Consensus. M_i>M_j: IMP distribution for the top r variables identified by method M_i according to method M_j. T1D: Type 1 Diabetes.

Analysis of Variables Jointly Identified by Standard Univariate Testing, T-Trees and Sylva Variants. For each disease and each dataset, we more thoroughly examine to which extent the top 100 variables overlap between any two methods among the χ^2 test (hereafter denoted U as univariate), T-Trees and Sylva variant SX. We also examine the size of the intersection between the top 100 variables provided by U, T-Trees and SX. From Fig. 5, we learn that the

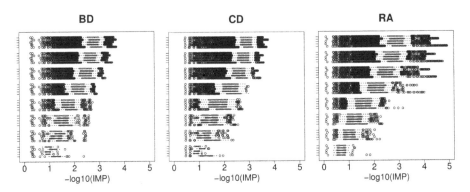

Fig. 4. Comparison of top r-IMP distributions for increasing values of r. See Fig. 3 for the notation top r-IMP. From bottom to top, the 8 groups of 5 boxes describe the trends observed for r in $\{1, 3, 5, 10, 25, 50, 75, 100\}$. In each group of 5 boxes, from bottom to top, the boxes describe the top r-IMP distributions for T-Trees, Sylva/CAST, Sylva/DBSCAN, Sylva/Louvain and Sylva/Consensus. For disease abbreviations BD, CD and RA, see Sect. 4.1.

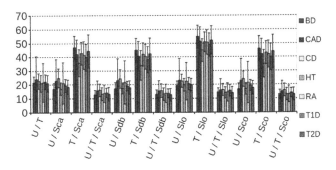

Fig. 5. Number of top 100 variables common to two or three methods. U: univariate test (χ^2). T: T-Trees. See Fig. 3 for notations Sca, Sdb, Slo and Sco. A bar in the histogram represents the average value computed from the 23 chromosome datasets related to a given disease. M_1/M_2 (resp. $M_1/M_2/M_3$): the average number of top 100 variables common to methods M_1 and M_2 (resp. M_1, M_2 and M_3) is described.

average sizes are similar (≈ 20) for overlaps between U and T-Trees on the one hand, and between U and SX on the other hand. Between 30 and 50 top 100 variables are common to T-Trees and Sylva/CAST or Sylva/DBSCAN. This number increases up to 60 for T-Trees and Sylva/Louvain. The order of magnitude is in the range 30–40 for the pair $\{$T-Trees, Sylva/Consensus$\}$.

In Sect. 4.2, we showed that the AUCs are quite similar and high for T-Trees and any Sylva variant. On the other hand, the top r-IMP distributions differ. We therefore conclude that T-Trees and Sylva are two powerful complementary approaches. This feature suggests the possibility to cross-validate findings: a variable jointly pinpointed as top 100 by T-Trees and Sylva should be selected for further biological analysis, in the context of genetic association studies. *A fortiori*, top 100 variables jointly identified by U, T-Trees and SX should be paid attention to and provided to biologists as a short list of priorized variables. Finally, it is recommended to use CAST or DBSCAN, and not the Louvain method, to increase the probability of Sylva to detect top 100 variables missed by T-Trees in its top 100s. Besides, in this context, using a consensus-based clustering method does not help to yield more relevant top variables.

5 Conclusion

In this paper, we proposed Sylva, an approach designed to foster feature selection when dealing with highly correlated variables. So far, Sylva is the second proposal around a random forest framework with latent variables. The innovation in Sylva consists in driving the dynamic generation of latent variables used to learn the random forest, based on a forest of latent tree models. We illustrated the relevance of Sylva for feature selection in the context of genetic association studies. Beyond omics data analysis, Sylva is potentially suitable to analyze a wide spectrum of data characterized by dense dependences. We will further adapt Sylva to allow either continuous variables or a mix of discrete and continuous variables. Second, there is still room for improving the time complexity of Sylva. The bottleneck to apply Sylva on a very large scale is the scalability of the FLTM learning algorithm. To accelerate the latter, we plan to investigate GPU implementation. Finally, in the near future, we will investigate schemes alternative to embedded tree learning, to drive the generation of the latent variables of the random forest from the latent variables of the FLTM model.

References

1. Ben-Dor, A., Shamir, R., Yakhini, Z.: Clustering gene expression patterns. In Proceedings of the 3rd Annual International Conference on Computational Molecular Biology (RECOMB), pp. 33–42 (1999)
2. Bessière, P., Mazer, E., Ahuactzin, J.-M., Mekhnacha, K.: Bayesian Programming. Chapman and Hall/CRC, Boca Raton (2013)
3. Blondel, V.D., Guillaume, J.-L., Lambiotte, R., Lefebvre, E.: Fast unfolding of communities in large networks. J. Stat. Mech.: Theory Exp. **10**, P10008 (2008)
4. Botta, V.: A walk into random forests. Adaptation and application to Genome-Wide Association Studies. Ph.D. Thesis, University of Liège, Belgium (2013)
5. Botta, V., Louppe, G., Geurts, P., Wehenkel, L.: Exploiting SNP correlations within random forest for genome-wide association studies. PLOS ONE **9**(4), e93379 (2014)
6. Breiman, L.: Random forests. Mach. Learn. **45**(1), 5–32 (2001)
7. Chambers, J.M., Cleveland, W.S., Kleiner, B., Tukey, P.A.: Graphical Methods for Data Analysis. CRC Press, Boca Raton (1983)
8. Ester, M., Kriegel, H.-P., Sander, J., Xu, X.: A density-based algorithm for discovering clusters in large spatial databases with noise. In Proceedings of the 2nd International Conference on Knowledge Discovery and Data Mining (KDD), pp. 226–231 (1996)

9. Geurts, P., Ernst, D., Wehenkel, L.: Extremely randomized trees. Mach. Learn. **36**, 3–42 (2006)
10. Gregorutti, B., Michel, B., Saint-Pierre, P.: Correlation and variable importance in random forests. Stat. Comput. **27**(3), 659–678 (2013)
11. Louppe, G.: Understanding random forests: from theory to practice. Ph.D. Thesis, University of Liège, Belgium (2014)
12. Louppe, G., Wehenkel, L., Sutera, A., Geurts, P.: Understanding variable importances in forests of randomized trees. In: Burges, C.J.C., Bottou, L., Welling, M., Ghahramani, Z., Weinberger, K.Q. (eds.), Proceedings of Advances in Neural Information Processing Systems 26 (NIPS), pp. 431–439 (2013)
13. Mourad, R., Sinoquet, C., Leray, P.: A hierarchical Bayesian network approach for linkage disequilibrium modeling and data-dimensionality reduction prior to genome-wide association studies. BMC Bioinform. **12**(1), 16 (2011)
14. Mourad, R., Sinoquet, C., Zhang, N.L., Liu, T., Leray, P.: A survey on latent tree models and applications. J. Artif. Intell. Res. **47**, 157–203 (2013)
15. Phan, D.-T., Leray, P., Sinoquet, C.: Modeling genetical data with forests of latent trees for applications in association genetics at a large scale. Which clustering should be chosen? In: Proceedings of the 6th International Conference on Bioinformatics Models, Methods and Algorithms (Bioinformatics), pp. 5–16. Portugal, Lisbon (2015)
16. ProBT Website. http://www.probayes.com/fr/recherche/probt/
17. Robin, X., et al.: pROC: an open-source package for R and S+ to analyze and compare ROC curves. BMC Bioinform. **12**, 77 (2011)
18. Schwarz, G.E.: Estimating the dimension of a model. Ann. Stat. **6**(2), 461–464 (1978)
19. Sinoquet, C.: A method combining a random forest-based technique with the modeling of linkage disequilibrium through latent variables, to run multilocus genome-wide association studies. BMC Bioinform. **19**, 106 (2018)
20. Strobl, C., Boulesteix, A.-L., Neib, T., Augustin, T., Zeileis, A.: Conditional variable importance for random forests. BMC Bioinform. **9**, 307 (2008)
21. SYLVESTRA++ Website. https://www.ls2n.fr/listelogicielsequipe/DUKe/134/SYLVESTRA++
22. WTCCC Website. http://www.wtccc.org.uk/

Don't Rule Out Simple Models Prematurely: A Large Scale Benchmark Comparing Linear and Non-linear Classifiers in OpenML

Benjamin Strang[1]([✉]), Peter van der Putten[2], Jan N. van Rijn[1,3], and Frank Hutter[1]

[1] University of Freiburg, Freiburg im Breisgau, Germany
benjamin.strang@students.uni-freiburg.de,
vanrijn@cs.uni-freiburg.de, j.n.vanrijn@columbia.edu, fh@cs.uni-freiburg.de
[2] Leiden University, Leiden, The Netherlands
p.w.h.van.der.putten@liacs.leidenuniv.nl
[3] Columbia University, New York, USA

Abstract. A basic step for each data-mining or machine learning task is to determine which model to choose based on the problem and the data at hand. In this paper we investigate when non-linear classifiers outperform linear classifiers by means of a large scale experiment. We benchmark linear and non-linear versions of three types of classifiers (support vector machines; neural networks; and decision trees), and analyze the results to determine on what type of datasets the non-linear version performs better. To the best of our knowledge, this work is the first principled and large scale attempt to support the common assumption that non-linear classifiers excel only when large amounts of data are available.

Keywords: Linear Classifiers · Meta-Learning · Benchmarking

1 Introduction

The experiments in many academic machine learning papers are designed to answer *which* particular method works better, typically by introducing a new algorithm and demonstrating success over a set of baselines or benchmarks. In a recent paper, Sculley et al. [22] pinpoint this as a problem: 'Empirical studies have become challenges to be won, rather than a process for developing insight and understanding.' [22] To counteract this, we propose to answer the question *when* certain methods work better. Furthermore, we propose to add reference-able large scale empirical support for rules of thumb that are frequently used by data miners in real world applications. Meta learning studies can achieve these goals and thereby help turn machine learning from what has recently been called alchemy [16] into more of a principled engineering science. In this paper we will investigate when non-linear models outperform linear models. This may appear

© Springer Nature Switzerland AG 2018
W. Duivesteijn et al. (Eds.): IDA 2018, LNCS 11191, pp. 303–315, 2018.
https://doi.org/10.1007/978-3-030-01768-2_25

as a somewhat strange research question in this day and age, but linear models are still frequently used in practice since they are simpler, typically computationally more efficient and (due to their simplicity) often easier to interpret than modern non-linear models, such as deep learning models. With EU regulations on algorithmic decision-making and a "right to an explanation" [9] which came into effect on May 25, 2018, especially this often belittled dimension of interpretability is bound to become one of the most important deciding factors in day-to-day machine learning business. Furthermore, as our experiments demonstrate, it is not a given that a non-linear classifier will outperform a linear one at a statistically significant level. The underlying problem may simply be linear, or more commonly, insufficient data is available to estimate complex relationships reliably; furthermore, non-linear methods run a larger risk of overfitting given that they are typically higher variance methods [15].

Our contributions are as follows: (i) We run a large scale meta learning experiment on 299 datasets from OpenML [18,24], and compare linear vs. non-linear variants of neural networks, support vector machines and decision trees. Based on these datasets we give an indication when non-linear models may work better, and how often. (ii) We train a meta model to predict when non-linear models work better based on dataset characteristics. (iii) All experimental data and results are made available through OpenML, and the code used is made available as a Jupyter notebook. (iv) Whilst we address a very common topic in modeling, to the best of our knowledge this study is at least an order of magnitude larger than other studies on this topic in terms of number of datasets included.

2   Related Work

We review the literature on some exemplar studies that either discuss the question whether to use a linear or non-linear classifier, or use large scale experimentation to answer general scientific questions. Due to the broadness of these subject areas, this list is by no means complete.

Linear vs. Non-linear classifiers. Various studies exist that compare linear classifiers and non-linear classifiers. Typically the comparison of linear and non-linear classifiers is performed in the context of a special modeling task, e.g., electricity consumption forecasting [10], CO_2 emissions [13], aggregate retail sales [4], EEG signal classification [7], corporate distress diagnosis [1], macroeconomic time series forecasting [23], routing [21] and epidemiological data [8]. These studies have in common that they are small scale experiments limiting the performance comparison to a special field of application and a small number of datasets. A simple general conclusion regarding the classification performance of linear and non-linear models cannot be drawn from the aforementioned related work as the final conclusions of these studies differ regarding classification performance. While in some studies [4,7,10,13] non-linear models in the form of neural networks or support vector machines achieved a better performance, some research groups find that non-linear components or methods are of no benefit or worse than the particular linear modeling approach [8,21].

Large Scale Experimentation. OpenML [18,24] offers infrastructure to conduct large scale experiments which provide a solid empirical foundation for answering scientific questions. For each dataset, it contains a range of scientific tasks and meta-features, and it also allows for uploading new experimental results. In the past, several large scale experiments have been conducted by various research groups using this infrastructure. [6] use the experimental results on OpenML to study characteristics of precision recall curves over 886 classification datasets [6]. [14] researched in which cases feature selection improves classification performance on 399 classification datasets [14]. [11] developed an algorithm selection method for QSAR's, and demonstrated its applicability on 2,700 QSAR problems [11]. Indeed, empirical results are typically more credible when based on a large number of datasets.

3   Background

This work aims to answer the basic scientific question when to use a linear or non-linear classifier by large scale experimentation. To achieve this, care needs to be taken to build on a solid infrastructure and experimental setup. In this section, we review the methods we used.

Datasets. We prefer quality over quantity. As such, rather than using all of the thousands of datasets on OpenML, we selected a (still large) set of diverse datasets, i.e., the OpenML100 [3], which provides 100 datasets carefully selected from the OpenML overall dataset repository. The OpenML100 is designed to contain datasets that have a real world concept (rather than artificially generated data), have a meaningful classification task, and are introduced by a scientific publication. While the OpenML100 imposes dimensionality restrictions on the datasets (i.e., 500–100,000 data points, 1–5,000 features), we also report on results on datasets outside this range. Like for the OpenML100, highly unbalanced datasets with a minority class to majority class ratio of less than 0.05 were excluded. As this additional set of datasets is not as curated as the OpenML100, these results are reported separately. The total number of datasets used is 299.

Classifiers. This study considers support vector machines (SVMs), neural networks and decision trees, each of them in a linear and a non-linear variant. SVMs natively support the notion of (non-)linearity by means of their kernel;
we use either a linear or an RBF kernel. For neural networks, next to a standard feed-forward network with hidden layers and non-linear (sigmoid) activation functions, as a linear variant we consider a linear model with no hidden layers trained by stochastic gradient descent. For decision trees, as a linear version we consider a decision stump (a decision tree with depth 1); this is arguably a very limited linear model, as it can only represent decision boundaries perpendicular to one of the axes. This means that even when a dataset is linearly separable, a

Table 1. Hyperparameters optimized by random search.

Classifier	Parameters
SVM (linear)	C $(2^{-5} \ldots 2^{15}$, log-scale), dual (boolean), imputation strategy, tol $(10^{-5} \ldots 10^{-1}$, log-scale)
SVM (non-linear)	C $(2^{-5} \ldots 2^{15}$, log-scale), gamma $(2^{-15} \ldots 2^{3}$, log-scale), imputation strategy, tol $(10^{-5} \ldots 10^{-1}$, log-scale), shrinking (boolean)
NN (linear)	alpha $(10^{-7} \ldots 10^{-1}$, log-scale), imputation strategy, learning rate ('optimal', eta $= 1/(\alpha \cdot (t + t_0))$), tol $(10^{-5} \ldots 10^{-1}$, log-scale), penalty (l2, l1, elasticnet)
NN (non-linear)	Alpha $(10^{-7} \ldots 10^{-1})$, early stopping (boolean), hidden layer size (32, 64, 128), imputation strategy, initial learning rate $(10^{-5} \ldots 10^{0}$, log-scale), num. hidden layers (1, 2), tol $(10^{-5} \ldots 10^{-1})$
DT (stump)	Criterion (gini, entropy), imputation strategy, max. features $(0.1, 0.2, 0.3, \ldots 1.0)$
DT (non-linear)	Criterion (gini, entropy), imputation strategy, max. depth $(2, 3, 5, 7, 10)$, max. features $(0.1, 0.2, 0.3, \ldots 1.0)$

decision stump might not be able to model it perfectly; however, we decided to still include this as a representative of the popular class of tree-based models.[1]

Hyperparameter Optimization. The performance of machine learning classifiers highly depends on hyperparameter optimization, which can often make the difference between mediocre and state-of-the-art performance. In this study, to minimize the bias resulting from the choice of a particular hyperparameter optimization method, we use the simplest option: random search [2].

We use a budget of 250 iterations (in the case of the decision stump only 60 iterations due to the limited hyperparameter space). While more powerful optimization methods, such as Bayesian optimization, are sometimes orders of magnitudes faster, random search is simpler, trivially available in any programming language, almost parameter-free, and robustly applicable across various types of hyperparameter spaces, making it a straight-forward simple choice when we can afford to evaluate a large number of configurations.

In order to determine which hyperparameters are important to optimize, we followed the recommendations of [19]. Table 1 shows the hyperparameters and ranges over which we performed random search. We note in particular that this search space includes regularization hyperparameters, such as the penalty parameter C in SVMs and the strength α of the L_2 regularizer in neural networks.

Evaluation. We use nested 10-fold cross-validation for evaluating the classifiers. For each of the 10 outer cross-validation folds, the hyperparameter optimization

---

[1] In this study, we do not compare (still quite interpretable) decision trees against (more powerful, yet less interpretable) random forests in order to limit ourselves purely to a comparison of linear vs. non-linear models.

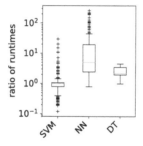

Fig. 1. Ratios of wall clock run times. Ratios larger than 1.0 indicate that the linear model needed less time.

used an internal 3-fold cross-validation procedure on the training portion to determine the best hyperparameters. The model is then re-fitted using the best found hyperparameters on the full training set of that cross-validation fold, and this is used to make predictions for the test set.

4   Linear Versus Non-linear

This section aims to answer the primary question of this work, i.e., when to use linear and non-linear classifiers.

Setup. For each of the three classifier families, we perform hyperparameter optimization and measure the performance in terms of predictive accuracy of both the linear and non-linear classifier using 10-fold nested cross-validation. As this yields 10 individual scores, we can also perform a statistical test, which determines whether the results are statistically significant ($\alpha = 0.05$); for this, we used the Wilcoxon signed rank test as recommended by Demšar [5], since non-parametric tests do not depend on the assumption of normally-distributed data. The data is pre-processed using imputation, one-hot-encoding, variance threshold and feature scaling to unit variance. Of course, the values for these operations are inferred on the training set and applied to the test set. All classifiers, as well as the random search module, are as implemented in Scikit-learn version 0.19.1 [12]. Each algorithm had a maximum run time of 96 hours on a 20 core Intel Xeon E5-2630v4, i.e., a maximum of 1,920 CPU hours per run. Tasks which ran out of time were not evaluated. Figure 1 shows boxplots of the ratio of the run time for the linear and non-linear algorithms per dataset. The run time was measured over the full random search procedure.

Results. The results are provided in an OpenML study[2], to which a Jupyter Notebook is attached. This section summarizes the results as three case studies. For each family of classifiers we present: (i) A table with summarizing statistics, both on the OpenML100 and on the complete set. (ii) A scatter plot showing for

---

[2] https://www.openml.org/s/123.

Support Vector Machine Case Study

Table 2. General Statistics on Performance

| | All datasets | | | | OpenML100 datasets | | | |
| | Absolutely | | Significantly | | Absolutely | | Significantly | |
Result	Number	%	Number	%	Number	%	Number	%
Linear better	121	41	14	5	19	20	2	2
Equal/Neither ... nor	19	6	218	74	6	6	44	46
Non-linear better	154	52	62	21	70	74	49	52
	294	100	294	100	95	100	95	100

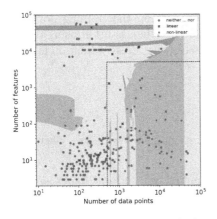 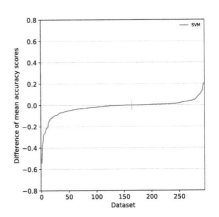

Fig. 2. Scatterplot showing whether linear or non-linear performs statistically better; each dot represents a dataset.

Fig. 3. Accuracy difference per dataset between linear and non-linear. Positive values indicate linear performed better.

each dataset whether the linear or non-linear variant performed better, with the number of data points and the number of features as axes. (iii) A figure plotting the difference of mean predictive accuracy per dataset. It sorts the datasets by difference in mean accuracy scores. A positive difference indicates a better performance of the linear model.

The results of the SVM case study are presented in Table 2, Fig. 2 and Fig. 3; the results of the neural network case study are presented in Table 3, Fig. 5 and Fig. 4; finally, the results of the decision tree case study are presented in Table 4, Fig. 6 and Fig. 7.

Neural Network Case Study

Table 3. General statistics on performance

| | All datasets | | | | OpenML100 datasets | | | |
| | Absolutely | | Significantly | | Absolutely | | Significantly | |
Result	Number	%	Number	%	Number	%	Number	%
Linear better	75	32	4	2	11	16	2	3
Equal / Neither ... nor	13	6	181	78	5	7	30	45
Non-linear better	143	62	46	20	51	76	35	52
	231	100	231	100	67	100	67	100

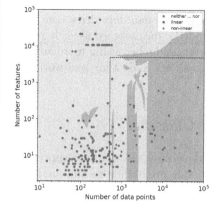

Fig. 4. Scatterplot showing whether linear or non-linear performs statistically better; each dot represents a dataset.

Fig. 5. Accuracy difference per dataset between linear and non-linear. Positive values indicate linear performed better.

Discussion. Many of the results are as expected, which validates the experimental setup. The absolute statistics tables (Tables 2, 3 and 4) and difference plots (Figs. 3, 4 and 7) show that the non-linear classifier performs better more frequently than the linear one. Especially for decision trees this difference is eminent, arguably because of the limited representation of the decision stump. However, the linear classifier also sometimes performs better, and in many cases there is no significant difference. Specifically, for all datasets, only in half the cases SVMs yielded statistically significantly better results with the non-linear kernel than with the linear one. However, we note that failure to detect a significant difference does not imply that there is no such difference: our statistical tests are only based on 10 samples (one per cross-validation fold) and thus have limited power; thus, our results should not be overinterpreted.

The scatter plots (Figs. 2, 5 and 6) reveal general trends which classifier performs better on datasets with specific characteristics. We plot this against the number of data points and the number of features; the background color shows which type of classifier is dominant in a region (based on a k-nearest-neighbour model with $k = 5$). Note that the background coloring looks a bit peculiar because it is determined in Euclidean space and represented in log space. Also note that some datasets have similar dimensions, causing several dots to overlap. For all classifier types the non-linear models are dominant in the regions with a large number of data points. However, when applied to a data set with few data points, the implementations of linear SVMs and neural networks we used do not perform worse than their non-linear counter parts at a statistically significant level. This result indicates that the optimal choice is not always clear-cut, and in case of doubt it may be preferable to use the linear version (since it is less likely to overfit, faster to run, and yields more interpretable results). We would like to highlight that, based on our data, we can only draw conclusions based on the scikit-learn implementations and the datasets we used; it remains an open question whether similar results would hold when using more advanced regularization schemes for the non-linear classifiers and other real-world data sets.

5   Learning When to Use What Classifier

In this section we present the results of an algorithm selection experiment. The relevance is three-fold: (i) this experiment adds credibility to the analysis in Sect. 4, by evaluating on a hidden test set (ii) this experiment is implicitly a deeper variant of the analysis in Sect. 4, i.e., by looking at a larger set of data characteristics, and (iii) the results of this experiment could be used to automatically select between a linear and non-linear classifier.

Setup. The algorithm selection framework [17] consists of the following components: (i) a set of previously encountered datasets $\mathcal{D}$, (ii) a set of data characteristics $\mathcal{F}$ (also called meta-features), (iii) a set of algorithms $\mathcal{A}$, and (iv) measured performance p of the algorithms $\mathcal{A}$ on datasets $\mathcal{D}$. For any new dataset $\mathcal{D}'$ (not in $\mathcal{D}$) the task is to predict which algorithm from $\mathcal{A}$ maximizes performance measure p. In our case, $\mathcal{D}$ is the set of datasets on which both versions of a classifier terminated, $\mathcal{A}$ is the linear and the non-linear classifier of a given type, $\mathcal{F}$ is a set of meta-features selected from OpenML (which we define more precisely shortly) and performance measure p is predictive accuracy. We train a random forest (100 trees) on the set of meta-features to predict whether the optimized linear classifier or optimized non-linear classifier will perform statistically better. Cases where there is no statistical difference are assigned to the 'prefer linear' class. Hence, this is a binary decision problem.

Decision Tree Case Study

Table 4. General statistics on performance

| Result | All datasets | | | | OpenML100 datasets | | | |
| | Absolutely | | Significantly | | Absolutely | | Significantly | |
	Number	%	Number	%	Number	%	Number	%
Linear better	79	26	4	1	10	10	0	0
Equal/Neither ... nor	13	4	162	54	0	0	17	17
hline Non-linear better	207	69	133	44	90	90	83	83
	299	100	299	100	100	100	100	100

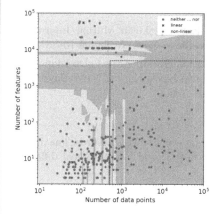

Fig. 6. Scatterplot showing whether linear or non-linear performs statistically better; each dot represents a dataset.

Fig. 7. Accuracy difference per dataset between linear and non-linear. Positive values indicate linear performed better.

Table 5 shows the sets of meta-features that we consider, per category. In our experiment we consider the following subset of these: (i) simple, containing just the features that can be computed in a single pass over the dataset, (ii) no landmarkers, which contains meta-features from the categories simple, statistical and information theoretic, and (iii) all, containing all meta-features in this table. Indeed, calculating meta-features comes at a certain cost and in particular calculating the landmarkers might impose a high run time. However, note that the algorithms in $\mathcal{A}$ are both optimized using 250 iterations of random search, and the landmarkers are (by design) ran with a given set of hyperparameters. This justifies the use of applying landmarkers.

We evaluate the meta-model in a leave-one-out fashion, training the model on all but one dataset and test it on this left-out dataset, in order to assess the performance of the meta-model.

Table 5. Meta features

Category	Meta-features
Simple	Number Of Features, Number Of Data Points, Dimensionality, Default Accuracy, Number Of Data Points With Missing Values, Percentage Of Data Points With Missing Values, Number Of Missing Values, Percentage Of Missing Values, Number Of Numeric Features, Percentage Of Numeric Features, Number Of Symbolic Features, Percentage Of Symbolic Features, Number Of Binary Features, Percentage Of Binary Features, Majority Class Size, Majority Class Percentage, Minority Class Size, Minority Class Percentage, Number Of Classes, Minority Majority Ratio
Statistical	Mean Means Of Numeric Attributes, Mean Std Of Numeric Attributes, Mean Kurtosis Of Numeric Attributes, Mean Skewness Of Numeric Attributes
Information Theoretic	Class Entropy, Mean Attribute Entropy, Mean Mutual Information, Equivalent Number Of Attributes, Mean Noise To Signal Ratio
Landmarkers	Decision Stump Error Rate, Decision Stump Kappa, Decision Stump AUC, Naive Bayes Error Rate, Naive Bayes Kappa, Naive Bayes AUC, 1-NN ErrRate, 1-NN Kappa, 1-NN NAUC

Table 6. Accuracy and AUROC scores for different sets of meta-features. The majority class is the combined set of 'linear statistically better' and 'no statistical difference'. Results over all datasets.

Classifier family	Default accuracy	Simple		No landmarkers		All	
		accuracy	AUC	accuracy	AUC	accuracy	AUC
SVM	0.789	0.844	0.874	0.844	0.897	**0.861**	0.908
DT	0.555	0.839	0.895	0.826	0.902	**0.856**	0.913
NN	0.801	0.857	0.846	**0.870**	0.827	0.861	0.852
Total dataset	0.708	0.803	0.837	0.801	0.836	**0.805**	0.841

Results Table 6 and Table 7 show the performance results of the meta-learning experiment evaluated for all completed datasets and for the completed datasets of the OpenML100 repository, respectively. As baseline the default accuracy (obtained by always predicting the majority class) is listed for each subset. The 'classifier family' column shows which classifier type was used, the 'default accuracy' column shows the default accuracy, and the other columns show the accuracy and AUROC score of the meta-model for each set of meta-features. The set of meta-features with the highest accuracy score is typeset in bold.

Both tables show a similar trend. In all cases, the meta-model performs consistently better than the default accuracy. From this we conclude that the meta-features model something related to the linearity of the dataset. Interestingly, the majority class is different between the two meta-datasets. When consider-

Table 7. Accuracy and AUROC scores for different sets of meta-features. The majority class is 'non-linear statistically better'. Results over the OpenML 100.

Classifier family	Default accuracy	Simple		No landmarkers		All	
		Accuracy	AUC	Accuracy	AUC	Accuracy	AUC
SVM	0.516	0.611	0.745	0.621	0.719	**0.674**	0.789
DT	0.830	0.840	0.869	0.840	0.795	**0.870**	0.883
NN	0.522	0.657	0.716	0.642	0.677	**0.672**	0.715
Total dataset	0.637	0.740	0.798	0.756	0.796	**0.760**	0.804

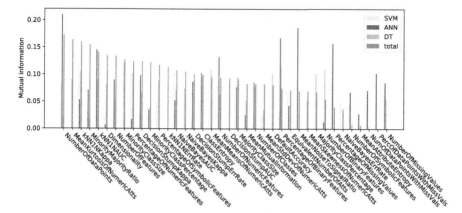

Fig. 8. Bar plot showing the mutual information for each meta feature. OpenML100 subset. Sorted by the mutual information values of the total dataset

ing only the OpenML100, the majority class is 'non-linear statistically better'; contrarily, when considering all datasets, the majority class is the combined set of 'linear statistically better' and 'no statistical difference'. This is most likely due to the slightly larger datasets in the OpenML100. The set of simple meta-features already makes a decent improvement compared to the default accuracy. Adding the set of statistical and information theoretic features adds only a little predictive power (as shown in the column 'no landmarkers'). Finally, adding the landmarker features (and thus having most information) results consistently in the highest accuracy. We analyze which features are most important for the meta-model. Features that are important to the meta-model have the potential to give more information about the linearity of a dataset and the dynamics between the linear and non-linear classifier. We use the mean mutual information measure, as described in [20], because this is a uni-variate measure and prevents biases incurred from correlations between features. The results are presented in Fig. 8.

The features that we analyzed in Sect. 4 (number of data points and number of features) appear to be quite important. Of the other features, the nearest neighbour based landmarkers seem important.

6   Conclusion

Motivated by the interpretability of linear models (which is important in the context of legal requirements explainability of automated decisions), as well as secondary niceties of linear models (such as ease of use and computational efficiency), this paper presented the results of a large scale experiment comparing the performance of linear and non-linear classifiers. Our main focus was to build large scale empirical support to determine the circumstances under which a given type of classifier is better. We considered three classifier families: SVMs, neural networks and decision trees, all as implemented in scikit-learn and represented by a corresponding linear and non-linear model. Unsurprisingly, non-linear models of each classifier family achieved a better performance on more datasets than their linear counterparts. However, for many datasets the performance difference was not significant, a finding that is highly relevant for practical applications. Meta-features related to dataset dimensionality (number of data points, number of features and the ratio of these) were the most relevant meta-features for deciding whether to choose a linear or a non-linear model. As expected, non-linear models typically exhibit a significantly better predictive performance if the dataset at hand has a large number of data points and few features.

In order to make this experiment reproducible, all results are available on OpenML and can be conveniently accessed through a Jupyter notebook. This also makes it convenient to change the experimental parameters, such as the set of datasets, displayed meta-features and optimization criterion, which all potentially influence the results. Future work will focus on a better understanding of the dynamics between meta-features and linearity of the dataset. One interesting direction would be to search for meta-features that better distinguish the datasets on which linear classifiers perform well. Furthermore, we would also like to perform these analysis on different evaluation measures, such as Area under the ROC Curve or F-measure. Having a publicly available meta-dataset enables the community to actively participate in this process.

In summary, as our title states: don't rule out simple models prematurely.

Acknowledgement. This work has partly been supported by the European Research Council (ERC) under the European Unions Horizon 2020 research and innovation programme under grant no. 716721. The authors acknowledge support by the state of Baden-Württemberg through bwHPC and the German Research Foundation (DFG) through grant no INST 39/963-1 FUGG.

References

1. Altman, E.I., Marco, G., Varetto, F.: Corporate distress diagnosis: comparisons using linear discriminant analysis and neural networks (the Italian experience). J. Bank. Financ. **18**(3), 505–529 (1994)
2. Bergstra, J., Bengio, Y.: Random search for hyper-parameter optimization. J. Mach. Learn. Res. **13**(Feb), 281–305 (2012)
3. Bischl, B., et al.: OpenML Benchmarking Suites and the OpenML100. arXiv preprint arXiv:1708.03731 (2017)

4. Chu, C.W., Zhang, G.P.: A comparative study of linear and nonlinear models for aggregate retail sales forecasting. Int. J. Prod. Econ. **86**(3), 217–231 (2003)
5. Demšar, J.: Statistical comparisons of classifiers over multiple data sets. J. Mach. Learn. Res. **7**(Jan), 1–30 (2006)
6. Flach, P., Kull, M.: Precision-recall-gain curves: PR analysis done right. In: Advances in Neural Information Processing Systems, pp. 838–846 (2015)
7. Garrett, D., Peterson, D.A., Anderson, C.W., Thaut, M.H.: Comparison of linear, nonlinear, and feature selection methods for EEG signal classification. IEEE Trans. Neural Syst. Rehabil. Eng. **11**(2), 141–144 (2003)
8. Gaudart, J., Giusiano, B., Huiart, L.: Comparison of the performance of multilayer perceptron and linear regression for epidemiological data. Comput. Stat. Data Anal. **44**(4), 547–570 (2004)
9. Goodman, B., Flaxman, S.: European Union regulations on algorithmic decision-making and a "right to explanation". arXiv preprints arXiv:1606.08813 (June 2016)
10. Kaytez, F., Taplamacioglu, M.C., Cam, E., Hardalac, F.: Forecasting electricity consumption: a comparison of regression analysis, neural networks and least squares Support Vector Machines. Int. J. Electr. Power Energy Syst. **67**, 431–438 (2015)
11. Olier, I., et al.: Meta-QSAR: a large-scale application of meta-learning to drug design and discovery. Mach. Learn. 1–27 (2018)
12. Pedregosa, F., et al.: Scikit-learn: machine learning in Python. J. Mach. Learn. Res. **12**, 2825–2830 (2011)
13. Pino-Mejías, R., Pérez-Fargallo, A., Rubio-Bellido, C., Pulido-Arcas, J.A.: Comparison of linear regression and artificial neural networks models to predict heating and cooling energy demand, energy consumption and CO_2 emissions. Energy **118**, 24–36 (2017)
14. Post, Martijn J., van der Putten, Peter, van Rijn, Jan N.: Does feature selection improve classification? A large scale experiment in OpenML. In: Boström, Henrik, Knobbe, Arno, Soares, Carlos, Papapetrou, Panagiotis (eds.) IDA 2016. LNCS, vol. 9897, pp. 158–170. Springer, Cham (2016). https://doi.org/10.1007/978-3-319-46349-0_14
15. van der Putten, P., van Someren, M.: A bias-variance analysis of a real world learning problem: The CoIL Challenge 2000. Mach. Learn. **57**(1), 177–195 (2004)
16. Rahimi, A., Recht, B.: Reflections on random kitchen sinks (2017)
17. Rice, J.R.: The algorithm selection problem. Adv. Comput. **15**, 65–118 (1976)
18. van Rijn, J.N.: Massively Collaborative Machine Learning. Ph.D. thesis, Leiden University (2016)
19. van Rijn, J.N., Hutter, F.: Hyperparameter importance across datasets. In: Proceedings of the 24th ACM SIGKDD International Conference on Knowledge Discovery and Data Mining, pp. 2367–2376. ACM (2018)
20. Ross, B.C.: Mutual information between discrete and continuous data sets. PloS one **9**(2), e87357 (2014)
21. Schütze, H., Hull, D.A., Pedersen, J.O.: A comparison of classifiers and document representations for the routing problem. In: Proceedings of the 18th annual International ACM SIGIR Conference on Research and Development in Information Retrieval, pp. 229–237. ACM (1995)
22. Sculley, D., Snoek, J., Wiltschko, A., Rahimi, A.: Winner's curse? On pace, progress, and empirical rigor. In: Proceedings of ICLR 2018 (2018)
23. Swanson, N.R., White, H.: A model selection approach to real-time macroeconomic forecasting using linear models and artificial neural networks. Rev. Econ. Stat. **79**(4), 540–550 (1997)
24. Vanschoren, J., van Rijn, J.N., Bischl, B., Torgo, L.: OpenML: networked science in machine learning. ACM SIGKDD Explo. Newsl. **15**(2), 49–60 (2014)

Detecting Shifts in Public Opinion: A Big Data Study of Global News Content

Saatviga Sudhahar[✉] and Nello Cristianini

University of Bristol, Bristol, UK
{saatviga.sudhahar,nello.cristianini}@bristol.ac.uk

Abstract. Rapid changes in public opinion have been observed in recent years about a number of issues, and some have attributed them to the emergence of a global online media sphere [1,2]. Being able to monitor the global media sphere, for any sign of change, is an important task in politics, marketing and media analysis. Particularly interesting are sudden changes in the amount of attention and sentiment about an issue, and their temporal and geographic variations. In order to automatically monitor media content, to discover possible changes, we need to be able to access sentiment across various languages, and specifically for given entities or issues. We present a comparative study of sentiment in news content across several languages, assembling a new multilingual corpus and demonstrating that it is possible to detect variations in sentiment through machine translation. Then we apply the method on a number of real case studies, comparing changes in media coverage about Weinstein, Trump and Russia in the US, UK and some other EU countries.

Keywords: Media content monitoring · Public opinion · Sentiment analysis · Machine translation · Big data

1 Introduction

The past few years have been marked by rapid changes in public attitudes and sentiment about a range of topics. Examples include attitudes about sexual harassment, social media, and varying degrees of support about Russia. Journalists and Social scientists have been interested for a long time in detecting, tracking and measuring rapid changes in coverage of specific issues and entities [1,2,5,7], a quest that is made harder by the global nature of the media system. Studies have included analysis of Twitter content and news-media content, for example following the Fukushima disaster [3,6] and public sentiment about migration in Britain [9]. Some of these works involve human coding methods which may be more accurate but they are often limited in their ability to deal with very large data sets. This work can be automated by collecting online news, on a global scale, and analyzing their contents to extract sentiment specific to a given entity.

© Springer Nature Switzerland AG 2018
W. Duivesteijn et al. (Eds.): IDA 2018, LNCS 11191, pp. 316–327, 2018.
https://doi.org/10.1007/978-3-030-01768-2_26

Big data technologies along with AI could be part of tracking and making sense of these global shifts, perhaps in real time, by monitoring global news media coverage. This poses the challenge of measuring sentiment across different languages in a comparable way. In turn, this requires a consistent method for calibrating and comparing the sentiment extracted from news in different languages.

In this paper we present one approach to detect shifts in media coverage about specific issues, in a multilingual setting. On the technical side, we isolate sentiment about a topic by extracting the words that immediately surround each mention of that topic, and analyzing them with the LIWC (Linguistic Inquiry and Word Count) dictionary [11]. This is done both in English, and in machine-generated English (machine-English for short) produced by Moses, the statistical phrase-based translation tool [10]. In order to measure the validity of this approach, we assemble a new multilingual corpus of news articles, published by Euronews in English, German, French, Spanish and Italian, covering the same topics, and we compare the sentiment about two chosen entities 'Europe' and 'Russia', extracted from the English version with that extracted from the machine-English versions, reporting significant correlation both in positive sentiment and negative sentiment (ranging between 15% and 60% depending on the language pair). We continue by demonstrating the technology in action on a larger set of news outlets from 6 countries (US, UK, Germany, Italy, France and Spain), analyzing a total of 4.4M articles, tracking the changes in positive and negative sentiment surrounding three entities: Weinstein, Trump and Russia. We observe correlations but also interesting patterns of difference, which may reveal different attitudes about the same entities. We demonstrate how this could be used to monitor rapid changes in sentiment and attention about any given entity in global news media at a large scale.

In Sect. 2 we discuss related work in the domain of analysing opinion shifts in online news and social media. In Sect. 3 we describe the data and methods used. Section 4 discusses how sentiment can be measured through machine translation. In Sect. 5 we discuss results related to the amount of attention and sentiment for Weinstein, Trump and Russia and in Sect. 6 we discuss conclusions.

2   Related Work

Studies in the past have identified public opinion shifts in social media and opinion polls. People have proposed methods for opinion mining of specific entities from Twitter content [4]. Measures of public opinion derived from polls related to consumer confidence and presidential job approval polls have seen to be correlated with sentiment measured from analysis of text from tweets [16]. This work detected topics and measured sentiment around these topics using the subjectivity lexicon from Opinion Finder [17]. Another work [18] studied how emotions, and their role in public opinion formation, can be tracked in online forums. Sentiment is measured using the ANEW (Affective Norms for English Language Words [25]) list measuring three different kinds of emotions: valence, arousal, and dominance. They showed that some political events such as the 9/11 attack unleash disagreement in valence and arousal than in dominance emotions and they have different lasting effects. Opinion shifts have been tracked in real time [19] through the introduction of computational focus groups in Twitter. Users were grouped according to similar user biases in to average users and elites and then the response of these groups to US presidential debates were tracked and shifts in sentiment were found.

Multilingual sentiment analysis has been explored by researchers over the past few years. Previous work [21,22] has shown that machine translation systems are mature enough to be employed to produce reliable training data for sentiment classification in languages other than English. They found that the gap in opinion and sentiment classification performance between systems trained on English and translated data is minimal. There has been a wide research effort on analyzing sentiment in news other than English by applying bilingual resources and machine translation techniques to employ the sentiment analysis approaches existing for English [23,24]. For example sentiment of entities has been analyzed in the past from news text translated from 8 foreign language news papers in to English using information extraction methods and using the IBM Web Sphere Translation Server (WTS) to translate text to English [24]. This study was limited to data containing news articles from 10 days in May 2007 and the entities analyzed were the ones most common across news papers in their data set. Machine translation has also been used successfully to generate resources for subjectivity analysis in other languages such as Romanian and Spanish [23].

In this paper we demonstrate a large scale experiment on detecting sentiment shifts about specific issues. Our work measures sentiment using the LIWC tool, in news content across several languages, assembling a new multilingual corpus and demonstrates that it is possible to detect variations in sentiment through machine translation with Moses [10]. We apply the method on a number of real case studies and in large scale, showing that we could now monitor the global news media for rapid changes in sentiment about entities.

3   Data and Methods

The data sets used for this study were collected by our previously developed modular system [26], an integrated platform for monitoring and analyzing news media. In order to validate if sentiment across languages can be measured using machine translation, we used news articles from Euronews for French (14,646 articles), German (15,850 articles), Italian (16,886 articles) and Spanish (16,821 articles) from January 2015 to October 2017. For the rest of the analysis we obtained news articles from French, Spanish, Italian and German news outlets from January 2010 to March 2018. The most prominent news outlets for each country were selected for the analysis, which are Le Monde, Le Figaro, Libération (France), Der Tagesspiegel, Die Welt, Die Zeit (Germany), El Mundo, El País, La Vanguardia (Spain) and La República, La Stampa, Corriere della Sera (Italy). We also collected news data from UK and US outlets in the same period such as BBC, Daily Mail, Guardian, The Independent, Daily Telegraph and Daily Mirror (UK) and Seattle Times, LA Times, New York Times, Washington Post and New York Daily News (US). In total 4,439,440 articles were included in the analysis.

3.1 Translating Text

We translate text using the traditional statistical phrase based machine translation [14] method with Moses. Statistical machine translation of text can be formulated as follows: Given a source sentence written in a foreign language f, Bayes rule is applied to reformulate the probability of translating f into a sentence written in a target language e.

$$e_{best} = argmax_e p(e|f) = argmax_e p(f|e) p_{LM}(e) \tag{1}$$

$p(f|e)$ is the probability of translating e to f and $p_{LM}(e)$ is the probability of producing a fluent sentence e. Sentences are broken in to phrases instead of words and phrases between the source and target language are aligned for training a translation model.

In our work translation models were trained with Moses for French, Spanish, German and Italian using the WMT (Workshop on Machine Translation) 2015 shared task training data. During the translation process Moses scores translation hypotheses using a linear model. Tuning refers to the process of finding the optimal weights for this linear model, where optimal weights are those which maximise translation performance on a small set of parallel sentences (Tuning set). We tuned our trained models with the tuning set from WMT using the MERT (Minimum error rate training [27]) algorithm. The output translation table from Moses contains all phrase pairs found in the parallel training corpus including a lot of noise. To reduce this noise the table is then pruned [28], resulting in faster loading of the model in memory. A language model was trained using all the available English corpora in WMT. We evaluated our trained models in the WMT test set using BLEU [12] score metric which is the most used metric based on n-gram precision computed between the machine generated translation and human generated translation. It ranges between 0-100%, and larger value identifies better translation. The idea behind BLEU is the closer a machine translation is to a professional human translation, the better it is. We obtain the following BLEU scores for each translation model: French (28.14%), Spanish (30.91%), German (26.11%) and Italian (30.69%). Translation models were deployed as Moses services, supporting multi-threading, so that all translation services run at a single point and several clients could request and collect translations at the same time. We translated news articles from all the outlets mentioned above including Euronews to English.

3.2 Measuring Sentiment

We used the LIWC sentiment word lists for positive and negative emotions (named as posemo, negemo) to measure sentiment about an entity in news articles. An entity in this context refers to named entities such as Persons, Organisations or Locations. Sentiment scores were computed in two weekly intervals with a one week overlapping time series window. For a given two weekly period, we obtain all news articles from the outlets mentioned above and search them for the given entity using Apache Lucene text search engine [15]. For each mention of the word we compute the number of positive and negative words surrounding the word with a text window of size 5 and total them for the period. Sentiment scores psr and nsr were computed. psr refers to positive sentiment ratio which is the number of positive words (p) divided by the total words in sentences containing the entity. The negative sentiment ratio (nsr) is computed similarly using the number of negative words (n).

We also measure the sentiment distance for an entity given by $(p-n)/(p+n)$. It shows how negative or positive was the news coverage about the entity in a given period of time.

3.3 Measuring Attention

The relative attention of an entity is computed by counting the number of entity mentions in a given period, dividing it by the total number of words from all articles in that period. This is again computed in two weekly intervals with a one week overlapping time series window.

4 Measuring Sentiment in Machine Translated Text

In this section we discuss and validate how machine translated text can be used to measure the sentiment across different languages. We compare the sentiment about two chosen entities 'Europe' and 'Russia', extracted from the English version with that extracted from the machine-English (translated) versions, reporting significant correlation both in positive sentiment and negative sentiment. For this purpose we use English, French, German, Spanish and Italian news articles from Euronews from 2015 to 2017. Euronews is a multilingual news media service publishing news content in several languages other than English. For each non-English article there is an equivalent English article published.

We translated Euronews news articles in French, German, Spanish and Italian to English using our trained models. Starting from the machine-English article, for each language we match its equivalent original English article by computing cosine similarities between the document vectors (term frequency vectors) across all relevant pairs obtained by date of article. We only filter the pairs that have a cosine similarity (θ) > 0.5 for computing sentiment correlation between pairs for entities 'Europe' and 'Russia'. For each mention of the entity in the pair of articles, we compute the number of positive and negative words surrounding the entity with a text window size 5 and calculate scores psr and nsr as described in Sect. 3.2. We compute the Pearson correlation coefficient between psr and nsr vectors for the English and machine-English pairs resulting in a positive and negative correlation score for the words in each language. Table 1 shows

Table 1. Positive and Negative Sentiment correlation scores and p-values for null hypothesis between machine-English and original English article pairs for entities 'Europe' and 'Russia'

Language	Total pairs	Topic	Total pairs with topic	Total pairs with topic $\theta > 0.5$	Positive corr (p-val)	Negative corr (p-val)
French	14644	Europe	1113	219	0.25(0.03)	0.59(0.0)
		Russia	1190	118	0.13(0.03)	0.41(0.05)
German	15849	Europe	1886	541	0.24(0.0)	0.62(0.0)
		Russia	1428	346	0.31(0.02)	0.14(0.08)
Italian	16886	Europe	2056	458	0.50(0.0)	0.47(0.0)
		Russia	1523	255	0.53(0.03)	0.33(0.01)
Spanish	16821	Europe	2337	738	0.38(0.0)	0.60(0.0)
		Russia	1568	424	0.22(0.06)	0.51(0.0)

for each language, the total number of matching pairs found, then for each topic, it shows the total pairs of articles containing the topic, the total number of pairs containing the topic with a cosine similarity $(\theta) > 0.5$ and positive and negative correlation scores for these pairs. Overall we observe positive and negative correlation in the region of 13%–53% and 15%–63%. To test the null hypothesis, in each language from the pairs with $(\theta) > 0.5$ we randomly assign machine-English articles to English articles, form pairs and compute the positive and negative correlation scores like before in 100 iterations. Our test statistic is the correlation score obtained and in each iteration we check if the correlation score is greater than the actual score obtained for each word in each language. Our p-value is $n/100$ where n is the number of times the score was greater than or equal to the actual score obtained. Table 1 shows the corresponding p-values next to the actual score. The p-values are very low ranging from 0.0 to 0.08. Therefore we conclude that the observed correlation is significant and sentiment can be measured across languages using machine translation.

5   Results and Discussion

In this section we demonstrate how sentiment and attention has changed in different periods of time over the past few years for entities Weinstein, Trump and Russia comparing the trends across US, UK, French, Spanish, German and Italian (FSGI) news outlets. The timelines were computed for each region by summing up the following counts across all outlets from that region in a two weekly period with a one week overlapping time series window. The counts are the number of positive (p), negative (n) words surrounding an entity, the total number of words in sentences containing the entity and the total number of words in all sentences. These counts were used to compute the positive sentiment ratio (psr), negative sentiment ratio (nsr), sentiment distance and attention towards an entity as discussed in Sect. 3. We also measure the correlation between the

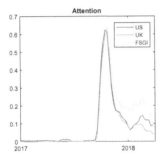
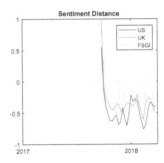

Fig. 1. The Attention and Sentiment Distance for the entity Weinstein in US, UK and FSGI news outlets starting from January 2017 until March 2018 analysing 716,610 articles. Period from January to September, 2017 is not shown in sentiment plot due to high error bars.

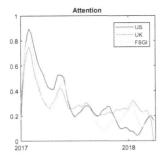
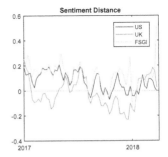

Fig. 2. The Attention and Sentiment Distance for the entity Trump in US, UK and FSGI news outlets starting from January 2017 until March 2018 analysing 716,610 articles.

sentiment distance series and attention series for the entities in US-UK, US-FSGI and UK-FSGI regions.

5.1   Shifts in Sentiment and Attention

Harvey Weinstein Scandal. The Harvey Weinstein scandal first came to light on the 5th of October, 2017 in a New York Times article[1], publishing a story detailing allegations of sexual harassment against him. Since then there have been a larger number of women coming forward to confess that they were harassed by him. We plot two quantities in Fig. 1, showing the attention and sentiment distance for Weinstein in US, UK and FSGI new outlets starting from January 2017 until March 2018. The period from January to September, 2017 is not shown in sentiment plot due to high error bars. Error bars were calculated based on Wilson score confidence interval [17]. A high error bar indicates that

---

[1] https://www.nytimes.com/2017/10/05/us/harvey-weinstein-harassment-allegations.html.

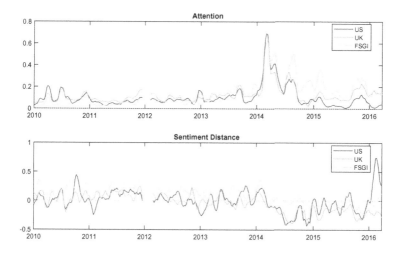

Fig. 3. The Attention and Sentiment Distance for the entity Russia in US, UK and FSGI news outlets starting from January 2010 until March 2016 analysing 3,722,830 articles. The period beginning in 2012 shows NaN values due to missing data.

the sentiment score for that period was not supported by enough positive and negative mentions about the entity.

We see that the coverage starts from the beginning of October, 2017 with a massive peak in all three regions marking the outbreak of the scandal on 5th October. News media in all three regions show a steady increase in negative sentiment from the beginning of October and continues to be negative throughout the latter part of 2017 and 2018. The sentiment is more positive in FSGI and more negative in UK an US, although it is overall negative in all regions.

The correlation for attention is very high for Weinstein according to the correlation plot in Fig. 4 in all three regions while Sentiment distance is much more correlated in US-UK than US-FSGI or UK-FSGI meaning the way the story was covered in the US and UK is very similar.

Donald Trump's Reactions to Riots. Donald Trump's presence in the media became increasingly negative from August 2017 which continued until January 2018. Figure 2 shows the Attention and Sentiment Distance for the entity Trump in US, UK and FSGI new outlets starting from 2017 January until March 2018. We see that Trump was discussed more in US than UK or FSGI in the beginning of 2017. Sentiment clearly shows a negative shift happening in the news coverage of US, UK and FSGI during the first weeks of August. This was due to the reaction of Trump to the Charlottesville Riots on 12th August 2017 [30], where white supremacists clashed with counter-demonstrators during a rally. It was followed by a period of negative coverage in news for Trump when he repeatedly criticized the NFL players who protested against the national anthem to bring attention to racial injustice in the United States [29].

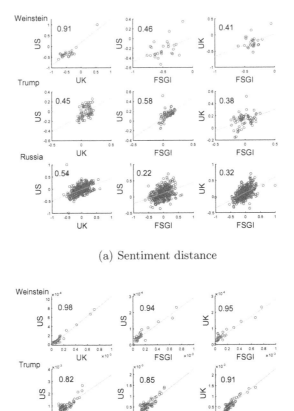

(a) Sentiment distance

(b) Attention

Fig. 4. Correlation plots of Sentiment distance series and Attention series between, US-UK, US-FSGI and UK-FSGI for Weinstein (October 2017 - Mar 2018), Trump (Jan 2017 - Mar 2018) and Russia (Jan 2010 - Mar 2016) monitored every two weeks with a one week overlapping time series window.

The UK has the most negative coverage of Trump from the beginning of the riots. We see at periods it is overall negative, whereas in other EU countries and US it is more balanced. The correlation for media attention is high for all three regions according to Fig. 4 while the Sentiment distance is also correlated across regions, more in US-FSGI.

Russia's Military Intervention in Ukraine. The Russian military intervention in Ukrainian territory started in February 2014. The Crimean peninsula was annexed from Ukraine by the Russian Federation in February-March 2014 [31]. We see how this event has caused a sentiment shift for Russia in global media. Figure 3 shows the Attention and Sentiment Distance for the entity Russia in US, UK and FSGI new outlets starting from 2010 January until March 2016.

Coverage of Russia peaks in February 2014 Crimean crisis, attracting negative coverage in all regions and very negative in US and UK than FSGI. A rise in attention is observed again in July 2014 while an increasingly negative coverage is also observed at the same time during the shot down of Malaysia Airlines Flight 17 over an area of Ukraine. The attention seems to be higher in FSGI from this period. The Russian intervention in Crimea and Eastern Ukraine caused a lot of reactions and this period of negativity is well evident in the sentiment distance plot showing negative coverage about Russia in the US, UK and FSGI regions in the period between February 2014 and January 2016.

Correlation of media attention is very high for Russia across all three regions and Sentiment distance is more correlated in US-UK than others.

5.2   Conclusions

Monitoring the contents of the global media is an important task that requires automation. Challenges range from the correct way to measure and validate sentiment, to the problem of operating across languages. In this study we have demonstrated that it is possible to extract usable sentiment signals from machine-translated text, in a news setting, and we have presented a study of how media sentiment has changed across UK, US and some European counties, over a long time period. There are significant correlations across the three regions, but also interesting differences. Along the way we have also proven that sentiment can be measured across translation by creating a new aligned corpus of news that are paired using the translated Euronews articles from French, German, Spanish, Italian and their equivalent English article in Euronews where we assume that the sentiment of the coverage of a given entity is similar. We found that the positive and negative sentiment between these pairs are correlated showing that we can measure sentiment across languages through machine translation.

Acknowledgements. Saatviga Sudhahar and Nello Cristianini are supported by the ERC Advanced Grant "ThinkBig awarded to NC.

References

1. Tribou, A., Collins, K.: This is how fast America changes its mind, Bloomberg, 26 June [Online]. Available at: https://www.bloomberg.com/graphics/2015-pace-of-social-change/ (2015)
2. Silver, N.: 'Change doesnt usually come this fast, FiveThirtyEight, 26 June [Online]. Available at: https://fivethirtyeight.com/features/change-doesnt-usually-come-this-fast/ (2015)

3. Lansdall-Welfare, T., Sudhahar, S., Veltri, G. A., Cristianini, N.: On the coverage of science in the media: a big data study on the impact of the Fukushima disaster. In: 2014 IEEE International Conference on Big Data (Big Data), pp. 60–66. IEEE (2014, October)
4. Maynard, D., Gossen, G., Funk, A., Fisichella, M.: Should I care about your opinion? Detection of opinion interestingness and dynamics in social media. Future Internet 6(3), 457–481 (2014)
5. Mutz, D., Soss, J.: Reading public opinion: the influence of news coverage on perceptions of public sentiment. Public Opin. Q. 61(3), 431–451 (1997)
6. Su, L.Y.F., Cacciatore, M.A., Liang, X., Brossard, D., Scheufele, D.A., Xenos, M.A.: Analyzing public sentiments online: combining human-and computer-based content analysis. Inf. Commun. Soc. 20(3), 406–427 (2017)
7. Young, L., Soroka, S.: Affective news: the automated coding of sentiment in political texts. Polit. Commun. 29(2), 205–231 (2012)
8. Nyman, R., Kapadia, S., Tuckett, D., Gregory, D., Ormerod, P., Smith, R.: News and narratives in financial systems: exploiting big data for systemic risk assessment. Bank of England Working Paper No. 704. Available at SSRN: https://ssrn.com/abstract=3135262 or https://doi.org/10.2139/ssrn.3135262 (2018)
9. McLaren, L., Boomgaarden, H., Vliegenthart, R.: News coverage and public concern about immigration in britain. Int. J. Public Opin. Res. edw033 (2017)
10. Koehn, P., et al.: Moses: open source toolkit for statistical machine translation. In: Proceedings of the 45th Annual Meeting of the ACL on Interactive Poster and Demonstration Sessions, pp. 177–180. Association for Computational Linguistics (2007)
11. Pennebaker, J.W., Francis, M.E., Booth, R.J.: Linguistic Inquiry and Word Count: LIWC 2001. Mathway: Lawrence Erlbaum Associates, vol. 71 (2001)
12. Papineni, K., Roukos, S., Ward, T., Zhu, W.J.: BLEU: a method for automatic evaluation of machine translation. In: Proceedings of the 40th Annual Meeting on Association for Computational Linguistics, pp. 311–318. Association for Computational Linguistics (2002)
13. Flaounas, I., et al.: NOAM: news outlets analysis and monitoring system. In: Proceedings of the 2011 ACM SIGMOD International Conference on Management of Data, pp. 1275–1278. ACM (2011)
14. Koehn, P., Och, F.J., Marcu, D.: Statistical phrase-based translation. In: Proceedings of the 2003 Conference of the North American Chapter of the Association for Computational Linguistics on Human Language Technology, vol. 1, pp. 48–54. Association for Computational Linguistics (2003)
15. Jakarta, A.: Apache Lucene-a High-performance, Full-featured Text Search Engine Library. Apache Lucene (2004)
16. O'Connor, B., Balasubramanyan, R., Routledge, B.R., Smith, N.A.: From tweets to polls: linking text sentiment to public opinion time series. Icwsm 11(122–129), 1–2 (2010)
17. Wilson, T., et al.: OpinionFinder: a system for subjectivity analysis. In: Proceedings of HLT/EMNLP on Interactive Demonstrations, pp. 34–35. Association for Computational Linguistics (2005)
18. Gonzalez-Bailon, S., Banchs, R.E., Kaltenbrunner, A.: Emotional reactions and the pulse of public opinion: measuring the impact of political events on the sentiment of online discussions (2010). arXiv preprint arXiv:1009.4019
19. Lin, Y.R., Margolin, D., Keegan, B., Lazer, D.: Voices of victory: a computational focus group framework for tracking opinion shift in real time. In: Proceedings of the 22nd International Conference on World Wide Web, pp. 737–748. ACM (2013)

20. Bollen, J., Mao, H., Zeng, X.: Twitter mood predicts the stock market. J. Comput. Sci. **2**(1), 1–8 (2011)
21. Balahur, A., Turchi, M.: Multilingual sentiment analysis using machine translation? In: Proceedings of the 3rd Workshop in Computational Approaches to Subjectivity and Sentiment Analysis, pp. 52–60. Association for Computational Linguistics (2012)
22. Balahur, A., Turchi, M.: Comparative experiments using supervised learning and machine translation for multilingual sentiment analysis. Comput. Speech Lang. **28**(1), 56–75 (2014)
23. Banea, C., Mihalcea, R., Wiebe, J., Hassan, S.: Multilingual subjectivity analysis using machine translation. In: Proceedings of the Conference on Empirical Methods in Natural Language Processing, pp. 127–135. Association for Computational Linguistics (2008)
24. Bautin, M., Vijayarenu, L., Skiena, S.: International sentiment analysis for news and blogs. In: ICWSM (2008)
25. Bradley, M.M., Lang, P.J.: Affective norms for english words (ANEW): Stimuli, instruction manual and affective ratings. Technical report C-1, Gainesville, FL. The Center for Research in Psychophysiology, University of Florida (1999)
26. Flaounas, I., Lansdall-Welfare, T., Antonakaki, P., Cristianini, N.: The anatomy of a modular system for media content analysis (2014). arXiv preprint arXiv:1402.6208
27. Och, F.J.: Minimum error rate training in statistical machine translation. In: Proceedings of the 41st Annual Meeting on Association for Computational Linguistics, vol. 1, pp. 160–167. Association for Computational Linguistics (2003)
28. Johnson, H., Martin, J., Foster, G., Kuhn, R.: Improving translation quality by discarding most of the phrasetable. In: Proceedings of the 2007 Joint Conference on Empirical Methods in Natural Language Processing and Computational Natural Language Learning (EMNLP-CoNLL), pp. 967–975 (2007)
29. Malyon, E.: Donald Trump attacks 'disrespectful' NFL decision to allow players to continue protests against racial inequality', 18 October [Online]. Available at: https://www.independent.co.uk/sport/us-sport/national-football-league/donald-trump-nfl-players-protests-racial-inequality-kneel-anthem-colin-kaepernick-a8006806.html (2017)
30. Jacobs, B., Laughland, O.: Charlottesville: trump reverts to blaming both sides including 'violent alt-left', 16 Aug [Online]. Available at: https://www.theguardian.com/us-news/2017/aug/15/donald-trump-press-conference-far-right-defends-charlottesville (2017)
31. Wikipedia contributors: Annexation of Crimea by the Russian Federation', (Mar 2014 [Online]. Available at: https://en.wikipedia.org/wiki/Annexation_of_Crimea_by_the_Russian_Federation (2014)

Biased Embeddings from Wild Data: Measuring, Understanding and Removing

Adam Sutton, Thomas Lansdall-Welfare[✉], and Nello Cristianini

Intelligent Systems Laboratory, University of Bristol, Bristol BS8 1UB, UK
{adam.sutton,thomas.lansdall-welfare,nello.cristianini}@bris.ac.uk

Abstract. Many modern Artificial Intelligence (AI) systems make use of data embeddings, particularly in the domain of Natural Language Processing (NLP). These embeddings are learnt from data that has been gathered "from the wild" and have been found to contain unwanted biases. In this paper we make three contributions towards measuring, understanding and removing this problem. We present a rigorous way to measure some of these biases, based on the use of word lists created for social psychology applications; we observe how gender bias in occupations reflects actual gender bias in the same occupations in the real world; and finally we demonstrate how a simple projection can significantly reduce the effects of embedding bias. All this is part of an ongoing effort to understand how trust can be built into AI systems.

Keywords: Fairness in AI · Bias in data · Artificial intelligence
Natural language processing · Word embeddings

1 Introduction

With the latest wave of learning models taking advantage of advances in deep learning [21–23], Artificial Intelligence (AI) systems are gaining widespread publicity, coupled with a drive from industry to incorporate intelligence into all manner of processes that handle our private and personal data, giving them a central position in our modern-day society.

This development has lead to demand for fairer AI, where we wish to establish trust in the automated intelligent systems by ensuring that systems represent us fairly and transparently. However, there has been growing concern about potential biases in learning systems [1,6] which can be difficult to analyse or query for explanations of their predictions, leading to an increasing number of studies investigating the way black-box systems represent knowledge and make decisions [7,9,11,19,20]. Indeed, principled methods are now required that allow us to measure, understand and remove biases in our data in order for these systems to be truly accepted as a prominent part of our lives.

In the domain of text, many modern approaches often begin by embedding the input text data into an embedding space that is used as the first layer in a subsequent deep network [4,14]. These word embeddings have been shown to

© Springer Nature Switzerland AG 2018
W. Duivesteijn et al. (Eds.): IDA 2018, LNCS 11191, pp. 328–339, 2018.
https://doi.org/10.1007/978-3-030-01768-2_27

contain the same biases [3], due to the source data from which they are trained. In effect, biases from the source data, such as in the differences in representation for men and women, that have been found in many different large-scale studies [5,10,12], carry through to the semantic relations in the word embeddings, which become baked into the learning systems that are built on top of them.

In this paper, we make three contributions towards addressing these concerns. First we propose a new version of the Word Embedding Association Tests (WEATs) studied in [3], designed to demonstrate and quantify bias in word embeddings, which puts them on a firm foundation by using the Linguistic Inquiry and Word Count (LIWC) lexica [17] to systematically *detect* and *measure* embedding biases.

With this improved experimental setting, we find that European-American names are viewed more positively than African-American names, male names are more associated with work while female names are more associated with family, and that the academic disciplines of science and maths are more associated with male terms than the arts, which are more associated with female terms. Using this new methodology, we then find that there is a gender bias in the way different occupations are represented by the embedding. Furthermore, we use the latest official employment statistics in the UK, and find that there is a correlation between the ratio of men and women working in different occupation roles and how those roles are associated with gender in the word embeddings. This suggests that biases in the embeddings reflect biases in the world.

Finally, we look at methods of *removing* gender bias from the word embeddings. Having established that there is a direction in the embedding space that correlates with gender, we use a simple orthogonal projection to remove that dimension from the embedding. After projecting the embeddings, we investigate the effect on bias in the embeddings by considering the changes in associations between the words, demonstrating that the associations in the modified embeddings now correlate less to UK employment statistics among other things.

2 Methodology

2.1 Word Embedding

A word embedding is a mapping of words into an n-dimensional vector space. Given a corpus of text, a word embedding can be created that will translate that corpus into a set of semantic vectors representing each word. Each word that appears in the corpus will be represented by an n-dimensional vector to indicate its position within the embedding.

This embedding has a set of features that can be used in natural language processing methods. The nearest neighbours of a word will be other words that have similar linguistic or semantic meaning, when comparing words using a measurement such as cosine similarity. There are also linear substructures within the word embeddings that can explain how multiple words are related to each other, making it a useful preprocessing step for natural language processing applications.

A word vector for a given word will now be defined as w. Word vectors are normalised to unit length for measurement:

$$\hat{w} = \frac{w}{||w||}. \tag{1}$$

All future analysis will be done using normalised word vectors, if vectors in the future are edited they will again be normalised to unit length.

2.2 Comparison of Embedded Words

Two words vectors w_1 and w_2 within a vector space can be compared by taking the dot product of their words:

$$\langle \hat{w}_1, \hat{w}_2 \rangle = \sum_{i=1}^{n} \hat{w}_{1,i} \cdot \hat{w}_{2,i}. \tag{2}$$

As both word vectors are normalised, this is equivalent to the cosine similarity between the two word vectors. A cosine similarity closer to 1 means that the vectors are similar to each other, while a cosine similarity of 0 means that the vectors are orthogonal to each other.

In addition to comparisons between individual word vectors, we can compare an individual word vector to a set of word vectors. This is done by finding the mean of the set, normalizing the resulting vector and calculating the dot product with the individual word vectors as follows:

$$\langle \hat{w}, \hat{\mu} \rangle = \sum_{i=1}^{n} \hat{w}_i \cdot \frac{\mu_i}{||\mu||}. \tag{3}$$

The resulting calculation gives us how closely an individual word is associated with a larger set of words. This association can be used to assess how closely related a given word is to different topics or concepts within the embedding space.

2.3 Removing Bias

To remove bias, first two vectors have to be identified that contain contrasting directions of the bias. These two vectors (w_1 and w_2) must be considered "opposite" of each other semantically, in terms of the bias that is required to be removed. The following method of debiasing is the same as presented in [2]:

$$w_b = \hat{w}_1 - \hat{w}_2, \tag{4}$$

where the vector w_b will have the direction of bias in the embedding (for example, he and she are different genders and could potentially be used to capture a gender direction).

Using this bias direction, all word vectors can now have that component removed by projecting them into a space that is orthogonal to the bias vector:

$$w_\perp = \hat{w} - (\hat{w} \cdot \hat{w}_b^T) \cdot \hat{w}_b, \tag{5}$$

where $w_\perp$ is the original word vector with the biased component removed. The rank of the matrix of orthogonal projected vectors will be reduced by one in a non-trivial embedding set. These orthogonal word vectors are required to again be normalised for further analysis.

3   Experiments

In this paper, we conduct three experiments on semantic word embeddings. We first propose a new version of the Word Embedding Association Tests studied in [3] by using the LIWC lexica to systematically detect and measure the biases within the embedding, keeping the tests comparable with the same set of target words. We further extend this work using additional sets of target words, and compare sentiment across male and female names. Furthermore, we investigate gender bias in words that represent different occupations, comparing these associations with UK national employment statistics. In the last experiment, we use orthogonal projections [2] to debias our word embeddings, and measure the reduction in the biases demonstrated in the previous two experiments.

3.1   Data Description and Embedding

In all of our experiments, the first step is to obtain semantic vectors from a word embedding that we wish to analyse. We use GloVe embeddings [18], pre-trained using a window size of 10 words on a combination of Wikipedia from 2014, and the English Gigaword corpus [16], where each of the 400,000 words in the vocabulary for this embedding are represented by a 300-dimensional vector. These vectors capture, in a quantitative way, the nuanced semantics between words necessary to perform meaningful analysis of words, reflecting the semantics found in the underlying corpora used to build them.

The Wikipedia data includes the page content from all English Wikipedia pages as they appeared in 2014 when a snapshot was taken. The English Gigaword corpus is an archive of newswire text data from seven distinct international sources of English newswire covering several years up until the end of 2010 [16].

3.2   Experiment 1: LIWC Word Embedding Association Test (LIWC-WEAT)

In this experiment, we introduce the LIWC Word Embedding Association Test (LIWC-WEAT), where we measure the association between sets of target words with larger sets of words known to relate to sentiment and gender coming from the LIWC lexica [17]. We begin by using the target words from [3] which were

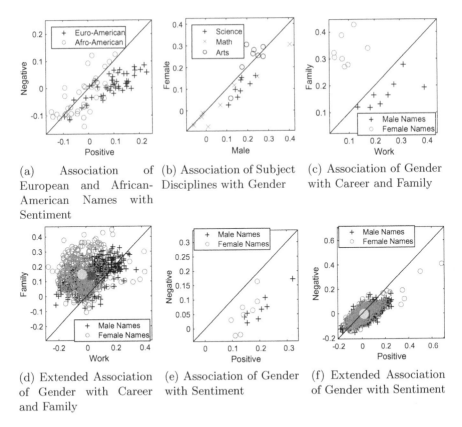

(a) Association of European and African-American Names with Sentiment

(b) Association of Subject Disciplines with Gender

(c) Association of Gender with Career and Family

(d) Extended Association of Gender with Career and Family

(e) Association of Gender with Sentiment

(f) Extended Association of Gender with Sentiment

Fig. 1. Association between different words and concepts in Experiment 1, resulting from the proposed LIWC Word Embedding Association Test.

originally used in [8], allowing us to directly compare our findings with the original WEAT.

Our approach differs from that of [3] in that while we use the same set of target words in each test, we use an expanded set of attribute words, allowing us to perform a more rigorous, systematic study of the associations found within the word embeddings. For this, we use attribute words sourced from the LIWC lexica [17]. The categories specified in the LIWC lexica are based on many factors, including emotions, thinking styles, and social concerns. For each of the original word categories used in [3], we matched them with their closest equivalent within the LIWC categories, for example matching the word lists for 'career' and 'family' with the 'work' and 'family' LIWC categories.

We tested the association between each target word and the set of attribute words using the method described in Sect. 2.2, focussing on the differences in association between sentimental terms and European- and African-American names, subject disciplines to each of the genders, career and family terms with gendered names, as well as looking at the association between gender and sentiment.

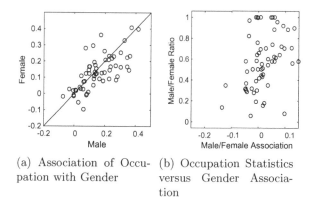

(a) Association of Occupation with Gender

(b) Occupation Statistics versus Gender Association

Fig. 2. Results from Experiment 2, showing the association between gender and its relation to the number of men and women working in those roles.

Association of European and African-American Names with Sentiment. Taking the list of target European-American and African-American names used in [3], we tested each of them for their associated with the positive and negative emotion concepts found in [17] by using the methodology described by Eq. 3 in Sect. 2.2, replacing the short list of words used to originally represent pleasant and unpleasant attribute sets.

Our test found that while both European-American names and African-American names are more associated with positive emotions than negative emotions, the test showed that European-American names are more associated with positive emotions than their African-American counterparts, as shown in Fig. 1a. This finding supports the association test in [3], where they also found that European-American names were more pleasant than African-American names.

Association of Subject Disciplines with Gender. A further test was conducted to find the association between words related to different subject disciplines (*e.g.* arts, maths, science) with each of the genders using the 'he' and 'she' categories from LIWC [17].

The results of our test again support the findings of [3], with Maths and Science terms being more closely associated with males, while Arts terms are more closely associated with females, as shown in Fig. 1b.

Association of Gender with Career and Family. Taking the list of target gendered names used in [3], we tested each of them for their associated with the career and family concepts using the categories of 'work' and 'family' found in LIWC [17].

As shown in Fig. 1c, we found that the set of male names was more associated with the concept of work, while the female names were more associated with family, mirroring the results found in [3].

Extending this test, we generated a much larger set of male and female target names from an online list of baby names[1]. Repeating the same test on this larger set of names, we found that male and female names were much less separated than suggested by previous results, with only minor differences between the two, as shown in Fig. 1d.

Table 1. List of the top 10 occupations per gender by their association with gender.

Gender	Occupations most associated with a gender
Male	Manager, Engineer, Coach, Executive, Surveyor, Secretary, Architect, Driver, Police, Caretaker, Director
Female	Housekeeper, Nurse, Therapist, Bartender, Psychologist, Designer, Pharmacist, Supervisor, Radiographer, Underwriter

Association of Gender with Sentiment. Extending the number of tests performed in the original WEAT study, we additionally tested the set of target male and female names and computed their association with the positive and negative emotions. We found that both sets of names are considered to be positive, similarly to the European-American and African-American names used in the previous test, but with male names appearing to be slightly more positive, as shown in Fig. 1e.

We further tested these associations using our extended list of gendered baby names, as in Sect. 3.2, finding that there is no clear difference between the positive and negative sentiment attached to names of different gender in the word embedding.

3.3   Experiment 2: Associations between Occupations and Gender

In this experiment, we test the association between different occupations and gender categories coming from LIWC [17]. The association between each of the occupations is further contrasted against official employment statistics for the United Kingdom detailing the actual number of people working in each job role.

Association of Occupation with Gender. We first generated a list of 62 occupations from data published by the Office of National Statistics [15], filtering the list to only include those occupations for which there is reliable employment statistics and can be summarised by a single word in the embedding, *e.g.* doctor, engineer, secretary. For each of these occupations, we tested their association with each of the genders, as shown in Fig. 2a, with the top ten occupations associated with each gender shown in Table 1. We found there was a 70% (p-value $< 10^{-10}$) correlation in the closeness of association between occupations and each of the gender attribute sets.

---

[1] Baby names were taken from http://bit.ly/2Dmqjco, separated into two gendered lists.

Occupation Statistics versus Occupation Association. Using the list of occupations from the previous section, we compared their association with each of the genders with the ratio of the actual number of men and women working in those roles, as recorded in the official statistics [15], where 1 indicates only men work in this role, and 0 only women. We found that there is a strong, significant correlation ($\rho = 0.57$, p-value $< 10^{-6}$) between the word embedding association between gender and occupation and the number of people of each gender in the United Kingdom working in those roles. This supports a similar finding for U.S. employment statistics using an independent set of occupations found in [3].

3.4 Experiment 3: Minimising Associations via Orthogonal Projection

In this experiment, we deploy a method for removing bias from word embeddings, first published in [2], and repeat all previous association tests related to gender reported in this paper, empirically showing the effect of bias removal on the word associations.

Finding an Orthogonal Projection for Gender. To remove gender from the embedding, we first need to find a projection within the space that best encapsulates the gender differences between words. To find the best projection, we began from a list of 5 gendered pronouns in LIWC [17]. For each of the pronouns, we paired them with their gender-opposite, for example pairing "he" and "she", "himself" and "herself" and so on. Taking the word vector from the embedding for each pronoun, we computed their difference, as described in Sect. 2.3, giving us a set of 5 potential gender projections.

Each gender projection was tested against an independent set of paired gender words sourced from WordNet [13] (containing implicit gendered words such as king and queen). After applying the gender projection to the test word-pairs, following the procedure of [2], we measured the average cosine similarity between the word-pairs. The gender projection that led to the WordNet word-pairs that are most similar (highest cosine similarity) was then selected as our gender projection, corresponding to the difference between the vectors for "himself" and "herself".

Revised Association Tests. Using the orthogonal gender projection found in the previous section, we repeated the tests from the LIWC-WEAT in Sect. 3.2 that were related to gender. This included the association of science, mathematics and the arts with gender, the association of male and females names with sentiment, work and family, and the ranking of occupations by their gender association.

In Experiment 1, we previously found that the disciplines of science and maths were more associated with male terms in the embedding, while the arts were closer to female terms. The association of each of these subject disciplines with gender after orthogonal projection was found to be more balanced, with closer to equal association for both male and female terms, shown in Fig. 3a.

Male and Females names tested in [3] showed a clear distinction in their association with work and family respectively, with our replication of the test in

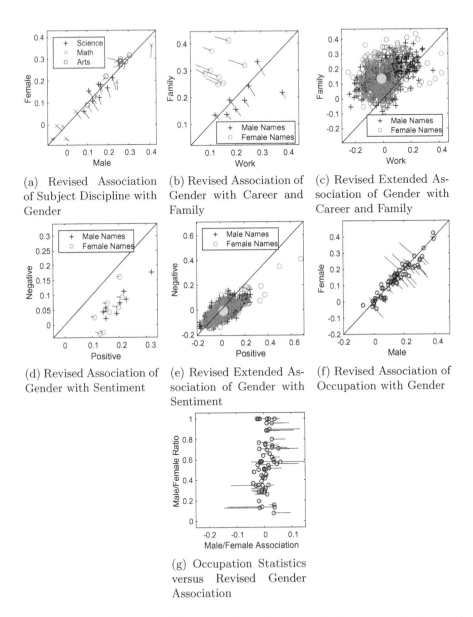

(a) Revised Association of Subject Discipline with Gender

(b) Revised Association of Gender with Career and Family

(c) Revised Extended Association of Gender with Career and Family

(d) Revised Association of Gender with Sentiment

(e) Revised Extended Association of Gender with Sentiment

(f) Revised Association of Occupation with Gender

(g) Occupation Statistics versus Revised Gender Association

Fig. 3. Association between different words and concepts in Experiment 3 after word vectors have been debiased via orthogonal projection in the gender direction. Line-traces shown in blue indicate where points have moved from after debiasing.

Sect. 3.2 finding the same results. Performing the same tests again after applying the gender projection to both name lists, we wished to quantify the change in associations. We calculated the change in the distance between the centroids of each set of names before and after applying the orthogonal gender projection, finding that the association with work for males and family for females reduced, closing the gap between male and female names by 37.5% for the target names found in the original WEAT and 66% for the extended list of names respectively.

In our experiment looking at the association of positive and negative emotions with male and female names, we found that male and female names were both positive, with male names being slightly more associated with positive emotions than female names. The same finding were also true when using a larger set of names and making the same comparison. Applying the orthogonal gender projection to the word vectors, we again looked at how much the difference between the two sets was reduced. We found that for the target names found in the original WEAT, the distance between the two sets of names was reduced by 27%, while for the extended list the difference was reduced by 40%.

In Experiment 2, we found that there was a significant correlation of 70% between the male and female association of each occupation, while comparing the associations with official statistics of the number of men and women in each role showed a correlation of 53%. Again, applying the orthogonal gender projection and repeating these tests, we found that, on average, occupations moved closer to having an equal association with each of the genders (Fig. 3f) and that their association with gender was not significantly correlated ($\rho = 0.178, p$-value $= 0.167$) with the number of men and women working in each role.

4   Discussion

In our experiments, we have shown the effect of one debiasing procedure for reducing the association a given word has in a word embedding generated from natural language corpora with concepts related to gender. Being able to do so relies on a set of gendered terms from which we can obtain pairings with opposite meaning, allowing us to find an orthogonal projection within the space. This will not always be possible for every type of bias that we may wish to remove (or at least reduce) in an embedding because there will not always be a suitable word vector pair that can be used to represent a given bias.

Other biases which are present may also be impossible to detect with our LIWC-WEAT method, as a pre-defined and validated list of words from LIWC were required to perform the tests. Other potentially undesired biases such as race or age are not currently able to be captured using the LIWC lexica, and thus different, carefully considered sets of words would need to be curated.

Indeed, general solutions to this problem are probably impossible, for philosophical reasons, but we believe that biases can at least be mitigated or compensated for, by removing specific subtypes of bias, given we have ways to measure and detect them in the first place. However, in this process, care should also be taken as we may introduce or compound other existing biases in the embeddings.

5   Conclusions

If we want AI to take a central position in society, we need to be able to detect and remove any source of possible discrimination, to ensure fairness and transparency, and ultimately trust in these learning systems. Principled methods to measure biases will certainly need to play a central role in this, as will an understanding of the origins of biases, and new developments in methods that can be used to remove biases once detected.

In this paper, we have introduced the LIWC-WEAT, a set of objective tests extending the association tests in [3] by using the LIWC lexica to measure bias within word embeddings. We found bias in both the associations of gender and race, as first described in [3], while additionally finding that male names have a slightly higher positive association than female names. Biases found in the embedding were also shown to reflect biases in the real world and the media, where we found a correlation between the number of men and women in an occupation and its association with each set of male and female names. Finally, using a projection algorithm [2], we were able to reduce the gender bias shown in the embeddings, resulting in a decrease in the difference between associations for all tests based upon gender.

Further work in this direction will include removing bias in n-gram embeddings, embeddings that include multiple languages and new procedures for both generating better projections to remove a given bias, using debiased embeddings as an input to an upstream system and testing performance, and learning word embeddings which can be generated without chosen directions by construction.

Acknowledgements. AS is supported by EPSRC Centre for Communications. TLW and NC are support by the FP7 Ideas: European Research Council Grant 339365 - ThinkBIG.

References

1. Angwin, J., Larson, J., Mattu, S., Kirchner, L.: Machine bias: theres software used across the country to predict future criminals. and its biased against blacks. ProPublica, May 23 2016 (2016)
2. Bolukbasi, T., Chang, K.W., Zou, J.Y., Saligrama, V., Kalai, A.T.: Man is to computer programmer as woman is to homemaker? Debiasing word embeddings. In: Advances in Neural Information Processing Systems, pp. 4349–4357 (2016)
3. Caliskan, A., Bryson, J.J., Narayanan, A.: Semantics derived automatically from language corpora contain human-like biases. Science **356**(6334), 183–186 (2017)
4. Cer, D., Diab, M., Agirre, E., Lopez-Gazpio, I., Specia, L.: Semeval-2017 task 1: semantic textual similarity-multilingual and cross-lingual focused evaluation. arXiv preprint arXiv:1708.00055 (2017)
5. Flaounas, I., Ali, O., Lansdall-Welfare, T., De Bie, T., Mosdell, N., Lewis, J., Cristianini, N.: Research methods in the age of digital journalism: massive-scale automated analysis of news-contenttopics, style and gender. Dig. Journal. **1**(1), 102–116 (2013)

6. Flores, A.W., Bechtel, K., Lowenkamp, C.T.: False positives, false negatives, and false analyses: a rejoinder to machine bias: there's software used across the country to predict future criminals and it's biased against blacks. Fed. Probat. **80**, 38 (2016)
7. Fong, R., Vedaldi, A.: Net2Vec: quantifying and explaining how concepts are encoded by filters in deep neural networks. arXiv preprint arXiv:1801.03454 (2018)
8. Greenwald, A.G., McGhee, D.E., Schwartz, J.L.: Measuring individual differences in implicit cognition: the implicit association test. J. Personal. Soc. Psychol. **74**(6), 1464 (1998)
9. Jia, S., Lansdall-Welfare, T., Cristianini, N.: Freudian slips: analysing the internal representations of a neural network from its mistakes. In: Advances in Intelligent Data Analysis XVI, pp. 138–148 (2017)
10. Jia, S., Lansdall-Welfare, T., Sudhahar, S., Carter, C., Cristianini, N.: Women are seen more than heard in online newspapers. PLOS ONE **11**(2), 1–11 (2016). https://doi.org/10.1371/journal.pone.0148434
11. Kahng, M., Andrews, P.Y., Kalro, A., Chau, D.H.P.: Activis: visual exploration of industry-scale deep neural network models. IEEE Trans. Vis. Comput. Gr. **24**(1), 88–97 (2018)
12. Lansdall-Welfare, T., Sudhahar, S., Thompson, J., Lewis, J., Team, F.N., Cristianini, N., Gregor, A., Low, B., Atkin-Wright, T., Dobson, M.: Content analysis of 150 years of british periodicals. Proc. Natl. Acad. Sci. **114**(4), E457–E465 (2017)
13. Miller, G.A.: Wordnet: a lexical database for english. Commun. ACM **38**(11), 39–41 (1995)
14. Nakov, P., Ritter, A., Rosenthal, S., Sebastiani, F., Stoyanov, V.: SemEval-2016 task 4: sentiment analysis in twitter. In: Proceedings of the 10th International Workshop on Semantic Evaluation (SemEval-2016), pp. 1–18 (2016)
15. Office for National Statistics: Statistical bulletin: Annual survey of hours and earnings: 2017 provisional and 2016 revised results (2017). https://www.ons.gov.uk/employmentandlabourmarket/peopleinwork/earningsandworkinghours/bulletins/annualsurveyofhoursandearnings/2017provisionaland2016revisedresults
16. Parker, R., Graff, D., Kong, J., Chen, K., Maeda, K.: English Gigaword Fifth Edition ldc2011t07. DVD. Linguistic Data Consortium, Philadelphia (2011)
17. Pennebaker, J.W., Francis, M.E., Booth, R.J.: Linguistic Inquiry and Word Count: LIWC 2007. Mahway: Lawrence Erlbaum Associates, vol. 71 (2001)
18. Pennington, J., Socher, R., Manning, C.: Glove: global vectors for word representation. In: Proceedings of the 2014 Conference on Empirical Methods in Natural Language Processing (EMNLP), pp. 1532–1543 (2014)
19. Ribeiro, M.T., Singh, S., Guestrin, C.: Why should i trust you? Explaining the predictions of any classifier. In: Proceedings of the 22nd ACM SIGKDD International Conference on Knowledge Discovery and Data Mining, pp. 1135–1144 (2016)
20. Samek, W., Binder, A., Montavon, G., Lapuschkin, S., Müller, K.R.: Evaluating the visualization of what a deep neural network has learned. IEEE Trans. Neural Netw. Learn. Syst. (2017)
21. Shrivastava, A., Pfister, T., Tuzel, O., Susskind, J., Wang, W., Webb, R.: Learning from simulated and unsupervised images through adversarial training. In: IEEE Conference on Computer Vision and Pattern Recognition (CVPR), vol. 3, p. 6 (2017)
22. Silver, D., Huang, A., Maddison, C.J., Guez, A., Sifre, L., Van Den Driessche, G., Schrittwieser, J., Antonoglou, I., Panneershelvam, V., Lanctot, M., et al.: Mastering the game of go with deep neural networks and tree search. Nature **529**(7587), 484–489 (2016)
23. Zhu, J.Y., Park, T., Isola, P., Efros, A.A.: Unpaired image-to-image translation using cycle-consistent adversarial networks. arXiv preprint arXiv:1703.10593 (2017)

Real-Time Excavation Detection at Construction Sites using Deep Learning

Bas van Boven[1]([⊠]), Peter van der Putten[1], Anders Åström[2], Hakim Khalafi[3], and Aske Plaat[1]

[1] LIACS, Leiden University, Leiden, The Netherlands
bas@basvanboven.nl, {p.w.h.van.der.putten, a.plaat}@liacs.leidenuniv.nl
[2] Accenture, Singapore, Singapore
anders.astrom@accenture.com
[3] Amsterdam, The Netherlands
hakimkse@gmail.com

Abstract. In this paper we present a robust approach to real world, real time action classification. It relies on a convolutional network based object detector to extract relevant shape and motion features and uses these features as input for an action classifier. Using a sequence of localization and classification information of various objects deemed relevant to an action, the model recognizes predefined actions in a reliable manner, and can localize these actions in camera footage in real time. Without loss of generalization, we study our approach within the context of a construction company that wants to prevent unauthorized excavation activities happening at their construction sites. We differentiate four excavation activities, two of which we detect on the basis of actions because the target pattern contains temporal features, and two of which we detect on the basis of object presence only. The system needs to operate in real time, on basic on-site hardware and under varying image conditions.

Keywords: Video analysis · Action classification · Convolutional neural networks · Feature engineering

1 Introduction

The detection and classification of specific actions in video is a difficult task, especially if computing resources and data are limited. Convolutional nets can be a powerful tool, especially to detect concepts without having to engineer specific features. They require a relatively large amount of labelled data though, and more importantly, when applied end to end there is limited ability to leverage domain knowledge to engineer features that might be useful for the task at hand.

In this paper we present a two staged approach that combines the benefits of deep learning with the flexibility and control of feature engineering. We apply it to a new real world problem, the detection of unwanted human or mechanical

© Springer Nature Switzerland AG 2018
W. Duivesteijn et al. (Eds.): IDA 2018, LNCS 11191, pp. 340–352, 2018.
https://doi.org/10.1007/978-3-030-01768-2_28

excavation at construction sites. We approach this problem from scratch, from gathering camera footage, labeling the data, training classifiers, integrating these into an end to end pipeline, and deploying and running the system in the real world. An additional constraint is that the system should monitor the site in real time, with minimal latency, processing feeds from four cameras using a laptop without internet connectivity. We first detect objects of interest, such as various parts of excavators, and then use domain knowledge to enrich this information with a variety of engineered features, and feed sequences of this data into a subsequent more standard classifier. The experiments demonstrate the validity and real world flexibility of the approach, which makes it a valid approach to explore for a range of real world problems with similar needs.

This paper is structured as follows. We will first introduce the business problem (Sect. 2) and related background (Sect. 3). Then we will describe our methods and approach for the end to end pipeline in Sect. 4, and report on experimental results (Sect. 5), followed by a discussion (Sect. 6) and conclusion (Sect. 7).

2   Problem Description

A construction company is facing losses due to unauthorized excavation activities at their building sites. Because of various reasons, such as misinterpretation of work instructions and erroneous reading of site maps, their workers often excavate at wrong locations. This can in turn lead to damage to important infrastructure like sewage pipes and power lines, and repairing such accidental damage can be expensive. In order to limit the cost of such damage, they need a system that can automatically detect unapproved excavation events.

Using the system, one should be able to deploy four different cameras on tripods, which are linked to the same laptop workstation by means of a wireless connection. On this workstation, one can configure the zones in which excavation is prohibited by means of a user interface. When excavation activities are detected within this zone, a SMS alert should be sent and an on-site alarm should be triggered. All excavation activities need to be detected before major damage has been done. This means processing needs to happen in real time with minimal latency. As internet connectivity cannot be guaranteed, all video processing and analysis needs to happen locally on a laptop (i7-6820HK processor, 32GB of DDR4-memory, a 512GB SSD and a NVIDIA GeForce GTX1080 GPU with 8GB of GDDR5X video memory).

The system should be designed to detect four different kinds of excavation activities. First of all, there is mechanical excavation by digging: in this situation, a mechanical excavator with a bucket attachment at the end of its arm is performing an action that will directly lead to it moving around ground or retracting the arm of the excavator in order to reach into the ground. Second, there is mechanical excavation by breaking: in this situation, a mechanical excavator with a breaker attachment at the end of its arm is performing an action that will directly lead to it putting its piercer into the surface. As in the previous digging example, this definition does not encompass riding or turning, but it does include extending or retracting the arm in order to reach into the ground.

Third, we detect manual excavation by people who are crouching: in this situation, a worker is using a tool to manually dig into the ground, for which it is necessary for them to assume a crouching position. There are three reasons that the definition is formulated as such. First is the observation that it would be very difficult to detect all the individual tools used for manual excavation. The second reason is that for most of these tools, assuming a crouching position is necessary. Finally, local observations confirmed that workers are seldom crouching, if not for excavating. Thus, crouching people are a good indicator of manual excavation activities. Fourth, we detect manual excavation by an earth rod tool: in this situation, a worker is using an earth rod tool to manually drill a hole into the ground. An earth rod is a tool that consists of two parts: a long thin stick that can be beaten into the ground, and a hammer that can be used for this. As workers are generally not crouching when using this tool, it is necessary to detect this type of excavation separately.

3   Related Work

Both object detection and action classification are problems of interest within domains like surveillance, automatic video classification and video retrieval.

The objective of object detection is to identify instances of certain predefined object classes in an image. Up until recently, solutions to this problem that produced state-of-the-art accuracy relied on machine learning methods like SVMs to produce their results [4]. However, recent developments in the field of deep learning have enabled more accurate object detection methods like Fast(er) R-CNN [9,20] and R-FCN [2], which use deep convolutional neural networks as the basis of their architecture. Even more recent architectures like You-Only-Look-Once [18], YOLOv2 [19] and the Single-Shot Detector [13] are only marginally less accurate then the current state-of-the-art, but their architectures are fast enough to provide inference in real-time. All of these architectures rely on a convolutional base network to provide the first network layers: popular choices are VGG-16 [22], Resnet-101 [26], Inception v3 [24] and Inception Resnet v2 [23].

The objective of action classification is to determine which kind of predefined action is undertaken in a series of images. A distinction can be made between approaches which feed hand-crafted features into a trainable classifier [5,11], and approaches which use a trainable feature extractor [8,25] to select the most useful features for classification [21]. Furthermore, the type of action one tries to classify and the environment in which one tries to accomplish this are also major factors in the success of the undertaken approach [21]. On datasets of less controlled environments like Hollywood2 [21], trainable feature extractors (CNNs [12]) have started to outperform hand-crafted features [6]. Recent state-of-the-art CNN-based approaches feed their output through SVMs [8] or computationally more expensive architectures like LSTMs [25] to produce a classification, but these studies were based on readily available data, not developed and tested from scratch in a real world field setting as in our work.

4   Approach

We combine the ability of a CNN-based approach to extract features from uncontrolled environments with the information density hand-crafted features can provide. Our approach consists of two models: an object detector and an action classifier. The object detector predicts which pretrained objects are are present in the video frame, along with a location (bounding box) and a confidence value, given a JPEG video frame as input. This bounding box data is used directly to detect manual excavation, and is also fed into the action classifier, which predicts if mechanical excavation is taking place in a given sequence of bounding box data. The output from both models can be thresholded to find the right balance between sensitivity and specificity.

4.1   Data Collection and Preparation

We have constructed a dataset of video footage of excavation activities, from which we have extracted training and test data for both our object detector and action classifier. Most videos are shot by the project team on different days and time of days, in different locations, with different equipment, from different angles and by various people. We were constrained by the fact that self-captured data is not necessarily as heterogeneous as one would like it to be. One way to prevent overfitting [1] on domain-specific variables is to augment the dataset with videos from external sources, which we have done for the object detector ground truth. The videos were also randomly split between a training set (80% of videos) and a test set (20% of videos).

Both actions and objects have to be labeled. In our case, the process of gathering and labeling real-world data has proven to be very time consuming. On average, a person could label around 300 images per hour for the object detector, or 20 min of video for the action classifier. In our case, this has resulted in around 50 h of continuous labeling for both models combined, on top of the time it took to capture the footage.

The ground truth for the object detector consists of the set of bounding boxes of all predefined objects within a set of JPEG-frames; we have targeted objects that support both manual and mechanical excavation detection. For manual excavation detection, we detect workers who are either crouching or have an earth rod in their hands. For mechanical excavation detection, we detect various parts of the excavator, the underlying assumption being that the positions and movements of excavator parts are good indicators of said activities. We have defined eight predefined objects: "cabin" (the part of an excavator that contains the driver), "upper arm" (the arm section of an excavator directly connected to the cabin), "forearm" (the arm section of an excavator that can be connected to an attachment), "wheelbase" (the caterpillar wheels of an excavator), "bucket"

Table 1. Overview of ground truth data for the object detector.

	Total	Filtered	Training	Test
Videos	230	n/a	184	46
Frames	8,629	6,251	4,939	1,312
cabin	6,436	4,579	3,563	1,016
upper arm	6,182	4,373	3,368	1,005
forearm	6,190	4,368	3,407	961
wheelbase	6,603	4,750	3,708	1,042
bucket	5,163	3,512	2,860	652
breaker	1,284	1,029	688	341
crouching	1,751	1,324	1,109	215
earth rod	1,698	1,267	1,026	241

Table 2. Overview of ground truth data for the action classifier for various window sizes.

	Total	Training	Test
Videos	117	95	22
Frames: exc.	9,703	7,977	1,726
Frames: no exc.	7,574	5,892	1,682
Window 3: exc.	3,218	2,432	786
Window 3: no exc.	2,488	2,003	485
Window 5: exc.	1,929	1,595	334
Window 5: no exc.	1,475	1,185	290
Window 7: exc.	1,388	1,142	246
Window 7: no exc.	1,010	821	189
Window 9: exc.	1,072	818	254
Window 9: no exc.	774	618	156
Window 11: exc.	890	726	164
Window 11: no exc.	607	509	98

(the scooping attachment of an excavator), "breaker" (the drilling attachment of an excavator), "crouching" (a worker who is crouching to excavate) and "earth rod" (a worker who is excavating with an earth rod).

Some videos were captured by a camera man walking around the construction site, thus enlarging the intra video variety by capturing the same scene from different viewpoints. From 230 recorded videos, we have extracted frames at a rate of one frame per two seconds, which resulted in a pool of 8,629 frames. All of the occurrences of the eight objects listed above were then manually labeled by seven different people, although each frame was labeled by one person only. The generated ground truth was then filtered: first, frames that were very similar to the previous video frame (when all of the labeled bounding boxes overlap for at least 80% with a bounding box of the same object in the previous frame) were removed. Besides that, we have limited the number of extracted frames per video to 50, and took a random subset when this threshold was exceeded. Also, we manually removed frames that were heavily distorted by video artefacts such as ghosting or synchronization jitter [17]. Table 1 provides an overview of the ground truth data used for training and testing our object detector.

The ground truth for the action classifier consists of a classification ("mechanical excavation", "no mechanical excavation" or "unusable") for each second of video, and was generated from 117 videos of variable length (between 16 and 753 s each, with a total running time of 6 h and 35 min) but filmed from a fixed point-of-view, which is relevant because the temporal aspect of actions is combined with the assumption that cameras for the production system are always

Fig. 1. Sample output from the object detector model, detections with highest confidence of each object are shown.

mounted on tripods. Besides this classification, each second of video is associated with a list of detections from an extracted video frame, as provided by the object detector. The videos were then split into non-overlapping windows of a length of an odd number of frames, and sequences which contained at least one "unusable" classification were removed from the window creation process. The remaining windows got assigned a target classification based on a majority vote over the contained frames. Finally, we have balanced the number of "excavation" and "no excavation" samples to be exactly the same, by randomly discarding some of the "excavation" windows. Table 2 provides an overview of the ground truth data used for training and testing our action classifier.

4.2   Design of the Object Detector

We select the SSD-512 architecture for the object detector, mainly for its speed [13]: our solution needs to process frames of four different cameras, and it is not the only software that should run on the production system: we also have to reserve resources for the action classifier, an orchestration service and some rule-based logic. The SSD-architecture is based on the traditional feed-forward Convolutional Neural Network [12], where the first layers of the network are initialized from a pretrained base network (in our case VGG-16 [23]): the benefit of this being that such a base network is able to extract higher-level features from images, which reduces training time. After this base network, five additional sets of feature map layers are defined, which are all implemented as a convolutional layer and responsible for object detections on a different scale. Finally, all detections of feature maps are concatenated in the network output layer, from which all detections with a confidence lower than 1% are filtered out. After that, the non-maximum suppression algorithm [15] is applied in order to merge different overlapping detections of the same object into one. Finally, for each processed frame we store the 200 detections with the highest associated confidence. See Fig. 1 for an example of the object detector applied to a public domain image.

Our training function is taken from the original SSD-512 implementation [13], which in turn is based on minimizing the MultiBox loss function [3], although this loss function is adapted slightly to handle detections of multiple different classes [20].

We also deploy a method to augment our training set, analog to the original SSD-512 implementation [13]. First of all, a sub sample is selected from the original image, out of one of the following three options: the original input image, a sub sample covering at least 10%, 30%, 50%, 70% or 90% of the original input image, or a sub sample of random size. Now, on this sub sample, three translations are applied: a 50% chance of a horizontal flip, a 50% chance of the image canvas being randomly expanded with a maximum of 400%, and a 50% chance of hue, saturation, brightness and contrast adjustments, respectively. Furthermore, the balance between positive and negative examples can be significantly unbalanced in favor of the negative ones. Therefore, we pick at most three times as many negative as positive examples, selecting the ones with the highest associated confidence loss, as per the original SSD-512 implementation [13].

4.3 Design of the Action Classifier

The action classifier is mainly based on AdaBoost [7], which combines a boosting algorithm with a multitude of decision trees to arrive at a prediction. We use 500 estimators and the SAMME.R real boosting algorithm [27].

In order to make the action classifier as robust to real-life variety as possible, we have experimented with generating 10 permutations for each training set sample, on which a number of translations are applied. Analogue to the object detector, permutations have a 50% chance of getting flipped horizontally. Furthermore, all detections are scaled to a random size between 70% and 130%, keeping the aspect ration intact and preventing detections to move outside image bounds. Finally, all detections are moved to a random place on the image canvas, again keeping the distance between all detections intact.

Input features are based on object detections, which we limit to the strongest detection of each of the six mechanical excavator parts per frame, if any. All of the input features are normalized between 1 and −1. For each of the six parts, we first distinguish five base features, namely the x- and y-coordinate of the center of the predicted bounding box, the bounding box width and height and the confidence of the prediction. Because this representation of the features is not necessarily the most useful representation for discerning excavation actions from non-excavation actions, we augment these features with a set of engineered features, which are all different representations of these base features. In order to express movement of parts, we define the difference between each set of consecutive frames for each of the five attributes for each of the six excavator parts. Also, we calculate a motility score for each object over the whole window, based on the relative movements of the center point of the corresponding bounding box. Besides that, we define relative arm motility, representing the motility of both arm parts compared to the motility of the cabin and wheelbase objects in order to detect rotation. Besides input features related to movement, we also define features related to distance. For each object except for the cabin object in each frame,

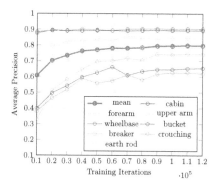

Class	Average Precision	Samples
Cabin	0.99	49
Forearm	0.92	49
Upper Arm	0.89	49
Wheelbase	0.99	49
Bucket	0.83	41

Fig. 2. Accuracy of the object detector in AP after training for a certain number of iterations. The thick red line denotes the mean accuracy over all the classes. After 90,000 iterations the mAP reaches 0.80.

we supply the horizontal, vertical and Pythagorean distance between that object and the cabin. In order to determine which type of excavator is pictured, we also supply the difference in confidence between the two types of attachments in each frame, along with the difference in horizontal, vertical and Pythagorean distance between both attachments and the forearm object. Finally, we define features related to object size. We calculate the total width, height and surface area of each object over all frames, the relative size of arm boxes compared to cabin boxes as an indicator for the camera angle and the cumulative horizontal, vertical and Pythagorean change in size of each object over all frames as an additional indicator of rotation.

5   Results

Our experiments are performed on the object detector and action classifier separately.

5.1   Object Detector

The accuracy of the object detector over a number of training iterations is displayed in Fig. 2. Each iteration, a batch of 8 training examples is passed both forwards and backwards. We have used a SGD-solver combined with a multistep learning rate policy and an initial learning rate of 1×10^{-6} [13]. Compared to the other objects, the accuracy of the cabin and wheelbase object detection does not improve as much with more iterations. A likely reason is that the base network VGG-16 is trained on an object that is visually similar to these objects: a car [22]. Furthermore, we have observed that the model incorrectly classifies certain

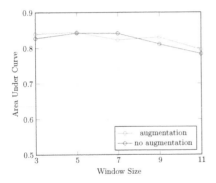

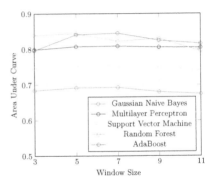

Fig. 3. The influence of data augmentation with AdaBoost on the AUC-score of the action classifier.

Fig. 4. The influence of window size and classifier choice on the AUC-score of the action classifier.

Table 4. Action classifier confusion matrix. Ground truth in rows, predictions in columns.

	Excavation	No excavation
Excavation	224	57
No excavation	48	369

Table 5. Action classifier confusion matrix (1 frame-per-window version).

	Excavation	No excavation
Excavation	1,017	451
No excavation	391	1,703

patches of dirt as a bucket, probably because the color is similar and there is often dirt attached to the bucket attachment in our training set.

We have also constructed a small dataset consisting of excavator images crawled from the web in order to determine if our object detector could also be useful outside the boundaries of our testing environment. This dataset was manually labeled using the same approach as we used for constructing our train and test sets. The results of running the model on this test set are given in Table 3. We can see that our model was able to generalize well to these different types of excavators.

5.2 Action Classifier

The optimal parameters to fit our use case are determined experimentally, two of which are window size and classifier type. We have established the influence of these parameters by training 25 different models: 5 different classifiers combined with 5 different window sizes. After training these 25 models, we compare them on the basis of their AUC-score [10]. The results of these experiments are plotted in Fig. 4. Top performers are AdaBoost on a window size of 5/7 and Random Forest on a window size of 3/5, resulting in an AUC-score of 0.84-0.85.

We have also tested our data augmentation routine on a variety of window sizes. The results of this experiment can be found in Fig. 3. Overall, data augmentation does not improve the accuracy of the action classifier, indicating that either the amount of ground truth data we feed to the model initially is already

Table 6. The 10 most important features, ranked on information gain.

Attachment closest to forearm	1.6%
Motility of cabin	1.4%
Motility of upper arm	1.2%
Cumulative horizontal distance between cabin and upper arm	1.2%
Difference in vertical location of bucket, frame 1–2	1.2%
Difference in vertical location of bucket, frame 3–4	1.2%
Difference in vertical location of upper arm, frame 3–4	1.2%
Horizontal location of forearm, frame 5	1.2%
Difference in horizontal location of cabin, frame 3–4	1.0%
Difference in vertical location of upper arm, frame 2–3	1.0%

sufficient, or that the variety the data augmentation is providing is not meaningful.

Eventually we have implemented an AdaBoost classifier and a window size of 5 in our production model, with data augmentation turned off. See Table 4 for the confusion matrix belonging to this action classifier. The corresponding AUC-score is 0.84. 85% of the samples are classified correctly.

A benefit of our action classifier is that we are able to take not only shape information, but also motion information into account. In order to prove the usefulness of this approach, we have constructed a variant of our action classifier where windows consist of one frame only, thus eliminating all motion information from training data. As can be derived from Table 5, such a model classifies 76% of the samples correctly. This is 9% less then the accuracy our 5 frames-per-window version achieves on the same data set. The corresponding AUC-score decreased to 0.75.

In order to further understand the characteristics of mechanical excavation, we also determine the features the model considers most important to make a distinction between excavating and non-excavating actions on the basis of information gain. The 10 features associated with the highest information gain are listed in Table 6. With the exception of the horizontal location of the forearm and the confidence of the cabin detection, all of the 15 most important features are engineered features, highlighting the importance of feature engineering.

6   Discussion

Our two stage approach provides a good balance between more assumption free, data driven learning at a lower level and using domain knowledge at a higher level, for improved results and better control. In the first object detection step we leave the task of figuring out the best features to the convolutional net, though we already guide it to learn the right concepts by specifying specific object classes. The subsequent action classification step then allows for a lot of flexibility to engineer use case specific features based on detected objects, and the experiments have demonstrated that these are most predictive. The experiments confirmed as well that using sequences as input, i.e. more than one frame, gave superior results, providing further support for a sequence based approach. From an application perspective, the production pilot lived up to the expectations of the construction company, and the intent is to keep using the system for a prolonged period of time. Also, a range of other companies have shown interest in the pilot, further demonstrating the relevancy of this problem.

In terms of future work, there are various methods in which our approach could be improved further. First of all, one could incorporate object tracking into the object detector model, to provide more reliable detection results to the action classifier [14]. Also, pose estimation could be used in order to differentiate various angles of the same action, as the mechanical excavation action looks very different viewed from different angles [16]. Another possible improvement is the incorporation of online learning methods, as we have already implemented collection methods for incorrectly classified alerts.

7   Conclusion

We have demonstrated an approach to real time action classification based on object detection, under difficult real world conditions and with limited hardware. We have applied this approach to the practical problem of detecting unauthorized excavation activities on construction sites. Our system is capable of classifying actions in real-time on a laptop workstation: we are able to analyze the output of four different cameras simultaneously without performance issues. To best balance assumption free learning with application of problem domain knowledge, we use a neural network based object detector to extract relevant shape and motion features, and then use these features as well as problem specific, engineered features derived from this as input for an action classifier. A major benefit of this approach is that it is insensitive to stray objects and movements, and thus is able to function in uncontrolled environments. A second benefit is that we can use localization information originating from the object detector to localize actions within a video frame.

References

1. Babyak, M.A.: What you see may not be what you get: a brief, nontechnical introduction to overfitting in regression-type models. Psychosom. Med. **66**(3), 411–421 (2004)
2. Dai, J., Li, Y., He, K., Sun, J.: R-FCN: Object detection via region-based fully convolutional networks. Advances in Neural Information Processing Systems, pp. 379–387 (2016). http://arxiv.org/abs/1605.06409
3. Erhan, D., Szegedy, C., Toshev, A., Anguelov, D.: Scalable object detection using deep neural networks. In: 2014 IEEE Conference on Computer Vision and Pattern Recognition, pp. 2155–2162 (2014)

4. Felzenszwalb, P.F., Girshick, R.B., Mcallester, D., Ramanan, D.: Object detection with discriminatively trained part based models. IEEE Trans. Pattern Anal. Mach. Intell. **32**(9), 1–20 (2009)
5. Fernando, B., Gavves, E., José Oramas, M., Ghodrati, A., Tuytelaars, T.: Modeling video evolution for action recognition. In: Proceedings of the IEEE Conference on Computer Vision and Pattern Recognition, pp. 5378–5387 (2015)
6. Fernando, B., Gavves, E., Oramas, J., Ghodrati, A., Tuytelaars, T.: Rank pooling for action recognition. IEEE Trans. Pattern Anal. Mach. Intell. **PP**(99), 1–14 (2016)
7. Freund, Y., Schapire, R.E.: A decision-theoretic generalization of on-line learning and an application to boosting. In: Vitányi, P. (ed.) Computational Learning Theory, pp. 23–37. Springer, Berlin Heidelberg, Berlin, Heidelberg (1995)
8. Girdhar, R., Ramanan, D., Gupta, A., Sivic, J., Russell, B.: ActionVLAD: learning spatio-temporal aggregation for action classification. In: CVPR, vol. 2, p. 3 (2017)
9. Girshick, R.: Fast R-CNN. In: Proceedings of the IEEE International Conference on Computer Vision and Pattern Recognition, pp. 1440–1448 (2015)
10. Hanley, A., McNeil, J.: The meaning and use of the area under a receiver operating characteristic (ROC) Curve. Radiology **143**, 29–36 (1982)
11. Hoai, M., Zisserman, A.: Improving human action recognition using score distribution and ranking. In: Cremers, D., Reid, I., Saito, H., Yang, M.-H. (eds.) ACCV 2014. LNCS, vol. 9007, pp. 3–20. Springer, Cham (2015). https://doi.org/10.1007/978-3-319-16814-2_1
12. Krizhevsky, A., Sutskever, I., Hinton, G.E.: ImageNet classification with deep convolutional neural networks. Advances In Neural Information Processing Systems, pp. 1–9 (2012)
13. Liu, W., et al.: SSD: single shot multibox detector. In: European Conference on Computer Vision, pp. 21–37 (2016)
14. Milan, A., Leal-Taixe, L., Reid, I., Roth, S., Schindler, K.: MOT16: a benchmark for multi-object tracking. arXiv preprint arXiv:1603.00831, pp. 1–12 (2016). http://arxiv.org/abs/1603.00831
15. Neubeck, A., Van Gool, L.: Efficient non-maximum suppression. Proc. Int. Conf. Pattern Recognit. **3**, 850–855 (2006)
16. Poirson, P., Ammirato, P., Fu, C.Y., Liu, W., Kosecka, J., Berg, A.C.: Fast single shot detection and pose estimation. In: 2016 Fourth International Conference on 3D Vision (3DV), pp. 676–684
17. Punchihewa, A., Bailey, D.G.: Artefacts in image and video systems: classification and mitigation. In: Proceedings of Image and Vision Computing New Zealand, pp. 197–202 (2002)
18. Redmon, J., Divvala, S., Girshick, R., Farhadi, A.: You only look once: unified, real-time object detection. CVPR **2016**, 779–788 (2016). https://doi.org/10.1016/j.nima.2015.05.028
19. Redmon, J., Farhadi, A.: YOLO9000: better, faster, stronger. arXiv preprint arXiv:1612.08242 (2016). http://arxiv.org/abs/1612.08242
20. Ren, S., He, K., Girshick, R., Sun, J.: Faster R-CNN: towards real-time object detection with region proposal networks. In: NIPS, pp. 1–10 (2015)
21. Sargano, A., Angelov, P., Habib, Z.: A comprehensive review on handcrafted and learning-based action representation approaches for human activity recognition. Appl. Sci. **7**(1), 110 (2017)
22. Simonyan, K., Zisserman, A.: Very deep convolutional networks for large-scale image recognition. In: International Conference on Learning Representations (ICRL), pp. 1–14 (2015)

23. Szegedy, C., Ioffe, S., Vanhoucke, V.: Inception-v4, Inception-ResNet and the impact of residual connections on learning. In: AAAI, pp. 4278–4284 (2017)
24. Szegedy, C., Vanhoucke, V., Ioffe, S., Shlens, J., Wojna, Z.: Rethinking the inception architecture for computer vision. In: Proceedings of the IEEE Computer Society Conference on Computer Vision and Pattern Recognition (CVPR), pp. 2818–2826 (2016)
25. Torabi, A., Sigal, L.: Action classification and highlighting in videos. arXiv preprint arXiv:1708.09522 (2017)
26. Wu, S., Zhong, S., Liu, Y.: Deep residual learning for image steganalysis. Multimedia Tools and Applications, pp. 1–9 (2017)
27. Zhu, J., Rosset, S., Zou, H., Hastie, T.: Multi-class Adaboost. Ann. Arbor **1001**(48109), 1612 (2006)

COBRAS: Interactive Clustering with Pairwise Queries

Toon Van Craenendonck$^{(\boxtimes)}$, Sebastijan Dumančić, Elia Van Wolputte, and Hendrik Blockeel

KU Leuven, Department of Computer Science, Leuven, Belgium
{Toon.VanCraenendonck,Sebastijan.Dumancic,
Elia.VanWolputte,Hendrik.Blockeel}@kuleuven.be

Abstract. Constraint-based clustering algorithms exploit background knowledge to construct clusterings that are aligned with the interests of a particular user. This background knowledge is often obtained by allowing the clustering system to pose pairwise queries to the user: should these two elements be in the same cluster or not? Answering yes results in a must-link constraint, no in a cannot-link. Ideally, the user should be able to answer a couple of these queries, inspect the resulting clustering, and repeat these two steps until a satisfactory result is obtained. Such an interactive clustering process requires the clustering system to satisfy three requirements: (1) it should be able to present a reasonable (intermediate) clustering to the user at *any time*, (2) it should produce good clusterings given few queries, i.e. it should be *query-efficient*, and (3) it should be *time-efficient*. We present COBRAS, an approach to clustering with pairwise constraints that satisfies these requirements. COBRAS constructs clusterings of super-instances, which are local regions in the data in which all instances are assumed to belong to the same cluster. By dynamically refining these super-instances during clustering, COBRAS is able to produce clusterings at increasingly fine-grained levels of granularity. It quickly produces good high-level clusterings, and is able to refine them to find more detailed structure as more queries are answered. In our experiments we demonstrate that COBRAS is the only method able to produce good solutions at all stages of the clustering process at fast runtimes, and hence the most suitable method for interactive clustering.

Keywords: Semi-supervised clustering · Pairwise constraints · Active clustering

1 Introduction

Clustering is inherently subjective [4,9]: different users often require very different clusterings of the same dataset, depending on their prior knowledge and goals. Constraint-based (or semi-supervised) clustering methods are able to deal with this subjectivity by taking a limited amount of user feedback into account.

W. Duivesteijn et al. (Eds.): IDA 2018, LNCS 11191, pp. 353–366, 2018.
https://doi.org/10.1007/978-3-030-01768-2_29

Often, this feedback is given in the form of pairwise constraints [17]. The algorithm has no direct access to the cluster labels in a target clustering, but it can perform pairwise queries to answer the question: *do instances i and j have the same cluster label in the target clustering?* A must-link constraint is obtained if the answer is yes, a cannot-link constraint otherwise.

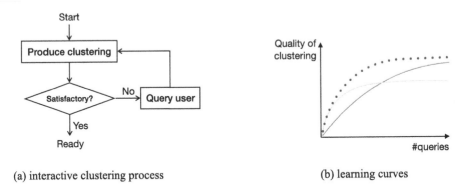

(a) interactive clustering process   (b) learning curves

Fig. 1. (a) The interactive clustering process. (b) Typical learning curves with COBRA, the current state of the art. For a small number of super-instances, performance rises rapidly but stagnates at a suboptimal level (orange curve). For a higher number of super-instances, performances rises more slowly but stagnates at a higher level (red curve). The dotted line shows the learning curve that we hope to obtain with the proposed COBRAS system.

When obtaining constraints is expensive (e.g., requires human intervention), the clustering process ideally proceeds iteratively, as summarized schematically in Fig. 1(a). It is a loop where in each step the system's current estimate of the clustering is shown to the user, and the user has the opportunity to answer several questions that will allow the system to improve the clustering, or end the process and accept the current clustering. Ideally, such a process has three properties: (1) the user can stop it at *any time* and get the best result obtained until then; (2) the number of loop executions (hence, the number of queries asked) until an acceptable result is obtained is as small as possible; (3) each loop execution is fast; e.g., a user may not want to wait more than a few seconds between queries. Summarizing this, the process must be *anytime* (in the number of queries), *query-efficient*, and *time-efficient*; we abbreviate this as AQT.

No existing constraint-based clustering system fulfills all three requirements (see next section for details). The approach closest to it is COBRA [15]. COBRA uses the concept of super-instances: sets of instances that are assumed to belong to the same cluster in the unknown target clustering. It uses constraints on the level of super-instances, rather than individual instances. This dramatically improves its query efficiency when the number of super-instances is small. However, having few super-instances increases the risk that a single super-instance contains instances from different target clusters, causing COBRA to find lower-quality clusterings. The number of super-instances N_S is a parameter of COBRA and is fixed during the clustering process. This forces the user to trade off query-efficiency with clustering quality. Figure 1(b) illustrates this: depending on N_S, COBRA quickly converges to a low-quality clustering, or slowly converges to a higher-quality clustering.

In this paper, we introduce a method for dynamically refining super-instances during clustering, based on user feedback. Extending COBRA with this method gives COBRAS (COnstraint-Based Repeated Aggregation and Splitting). The goal of this effort is to eliminate the above trade-off, and thus provide the first clustering system that meets the AQT requirements without sacrificing clustering quality; ideally its learning curve should be close to the one shown in Fig. 1(b) (dotted line). An experimental evaluation confirms that COBRAS meets this goal.

2   Related Work

The most common way to develop a constraint-based clustering method is to extend an existing unsupervised method. One can either adapt the clustering procedure to take the pairwise constraints into account [12,17,18], or use the existing procedure with a new similarity metric that is learned based on the constraints [5,19]. Alternatively, one can also modify both the similarity metric and the clustering procedure [2,3].

Most constraint-based clustering methods assume that a set of constraints is provided prior to running the clustering algorithm [2,3,10,19]. This makes them unsuitable for anytime (in the number of constraints) clustering. Furthermore, traditional systems typically query random pairs [3,19], which might not be the most informative ones; these are less query-efficient. Several active constraint-based clustering methods have been proposed that outperform random query selection [1,10], but most of them still require all queries to be answered prior to clustering (query-efficient but not anytime). An exception to this is NPU [20], an active selection procedure in which the data is clustered multiple times and each resulting clustering is used to determine which pairs to query next based on the principle of uncertainty sampling. NPU is both anytime and query-efficient. However, it is not time-efficient: it requires re-clustering the entire dataset after every few constraints, which becomes prohibitively slow for large datasets.

COP-COBWEB [16] is similar to COBRAS in that it has both splitting and merging of clusters as key algorithmic steps. However, it is not anytime: it assumes that all constraints are given prior to clustering.

COBS [14] uses an approach that is very different from the above. It generates a large set of clusterings by varying the hyperparameters of several unsupervised clustering algorithms, and selects from the resulting set the clustering that satisfies the most pairwise constraints. Generating the set of clusterings, however, can be time consuming for large datasets, which reduces its suitability for anytime clustering.

COBRA [15] is a recently proposed method that is inherently active: deciding which pairs to query is part of its clustering procedure. First, COBRA uses K-means to cluster the data into super-instances. The number of super-instances, denoted as N_S, is an input parameter. Initially, each of the super-instances forms its own cluster. In the second step, COBRA repeatedly queries the pairwise relation between the closest pair of (partial) clusters between which the relation is not known yet and merges clusters if necessary, until all relations between clusters are known.

It was already mentioned in the introduction that the results of COBRA strongly depend on the number of super-instances N_S. Figure 2 illustrates this on a toy dataset. For $N_S = 10$, the initial clustering (after 0 queries) is not too bad (panel A). As queries are answered, the quality goes up, but after 14 queries it stagnates at a suboptimal level (panel D; the incorrectly clustered part is marked with a red ellipse). For $N_S = 100$, COBRA starts with a worse clustering (panel B) but ends with a better one (panel E). It takes 103 queries, however, to obtain the final clustering.

Note that the N_S parameter allows the user to trade off one disadvantage for the other, but not to remove both. The dynamic super-instance refinement procedure that we introduce with COBRAS eliminates this trade-off.

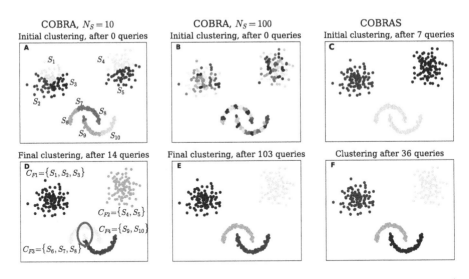

Fig. 2. A: The starting situation of COBRA with 10 super-instances (COBRA-10). Initially, each cluster consists of a single super-instance. B: The initial solution of COBRA-100, which is highly over-clustered. C: The clustering produced by COBRAS after 7 queries. D: The final result of COBRA-10. Each of the clusters is represented as a set of super-instances. The final clustering is not correct, as S_7 contains instances from two actual clusters. E: the final clustering of COBRA-100. F: after 36 queries, COBRAS produces the correct clustering.

3 COBRAS: Constraint-Based Repeated Aggregation and Splitting

The key problem when running COBRA with a small N_S is that super-instances often contain instances from different clusters (e.g., S_7 in Fig. 2A). COBRA cannot assign all of these instances to the correct clusters, as each super-instance is treated as a single unit.

COBRAS solves this problem by allowing super-instances to be refined. It starts with a single super-instance that contains all instances, and repeatedly refines this super-instance until a satisfactory clustering is obtained. More specifically, each iteration of COBRAS consists of two steps. First, it removes the largest super-instance from its cluster and splits it into several new super-instances. A new cluster is added for each of these new super-instances. A key challenge in this step is determining a suitable splitting level for a super-instance, i.e. the number of new super-instances that an existing one should be split in. For this, we propose a constraint-based procedure, which is detailed in Sect. 3.2.

In the second step of each iteration, COBRAS determines the relation of the newly created clusters to each other and the existing clusters by running the merging step of COBRA on the new set of clusters.

By using this procedure of refining super-instances, COBRAS uses a small number of super-instances in the beginning of the clustering process, and a larger number as more queries are answered. This allows it to perform well for both a small and larger number of queries, as illustrated in panels C and F in Fig. 2.

3.1 Algorithmic Description

COBRAS is described in detail in Algorithm 1. In this algorithm a super-instance S is a set of instances, a cluster C is a set of super-instances, and a clustering $\mathcal{C}$ is a set of clusters. COBRAS starts with a single super-instance S that contains all instances, which constitutes the only cluster C (line 2). As long as the user keeps answering queries, COBRAS keeps refining the set of super-instances and the corresponding clustering (lines 3-10). In each iteration it selects the largest super-instance S_{split} (line 4), determines an appropriate splitting level for it (line 5, this is detailed in Algorithm 2 in Sect. 3.2), and splits it into k new super-instances by clustering its instances using K-means (line 6). We use K-means as it is faster than K-medoids, even if the medoids are computed afterwards (each K-medoid iteration is $\mathcal{O}(k(n-k)^2)$ [11] whereas each K-means iteration is $\mathcal{O}(nk)$). S_{split} is then removed from its original cluster (line 7), and a new cluster is added for each of the newly created super-instances (line 8). Finally, in the last step of the while iteration COBRA is used to determine the pairwise relations between all the clusters (new and existing). The COBRA merging step is slightly modified compared to the original one [15]: if the relation between two clusters is already known, i.e. from a query in a previous COBRAS iteration, it is not queried again. Note that one could also think of other heuristics to determine which super-instance to split instead of simply the largest one, e.g.

one could split the super-instance with the highest intra-cluster dissimilarity. We have found, however, that selecting the largest super-instance is a simple and effective heuristic that is difficult to beat.

Algorithm 1 COBRAS

Require: $\mathcal{X}$: a dataset, q: a query limit
Ensure: $\mathcal{C}$: a clustering of D
 1: $ML = \emptyset, CL = \emptyset$
 2: $S = \{\mathcal{X}\}, C = \{S\}, \mathcal{C} = \{C\}$
 3: **while** $|ML| + |CL| < q$ **do**
 4: $\quad S_{split}, C_{origin} = \arg\max_{S \in C, C \in \mathcal{C}} |S|$
 5: $\quad k, ML, CL = \texttt{determineSplitLevel}(S_{split}, ML, CL)$
 6: $\quad S_{new_1}, \ldots, S_{new_k} = \texttt{K-means}(S_{split}, k)$
 7: $\quad C_{origin} = C_{origin} \setminus \{S_{split}\}$
 8: $\quad \mathcal{C} = \mathcal{C} \cup \{\{S_{new_1}\}, \ldots, \{S_{new_k}\}\}$
 9: $\quad \mathcal{C}, ML, CL = \texttt{COBRA}(\mathcal{C}, ML, CL)$
10: **end while**
11: **return** $\mathcal{C}$

Algorithm 2 *determineSplitLevel*

Require: $\mathcal{S}$: a set of instances that is to be split
Ensure: k: an appropriate splitting level, ML, CL: the obtained ML and CL constraints
 1: $d = 0, ML = \emptyset, CL = \emptyset$
 2: **while** no must-link obtained **do**
 3: $\quad \mathcal{S}_1, \mathcal{S}_2 = \text{k-means}(\mathcal{S}, 2)$
 4: $\quad$ **if** must-link(medoid($\mathcal{S}_1$), medoid($\mathcal{S}_2$)) **then**
 5: $\quad\quad$ add (medoid($\mathcal{S}_1$), medoid($\mathcal{S}_2$)) to ML
 6: $\quad\quad d = \max(d, 1)$
 7: $\quad\quad$ **return** $2^d, ML, CL$
 8: $\quad$ **else**
 9: $\quad\quad$ add (medoid($\mathcal{S}_1$), medoid($\mathcal{S}_2$)) to CL
10: $\quad\quad \mathcal{S} = $ pick between $\mathcal{S}_1$ and $\mathcal{S}_2$ randomly
11: $\quad\quad d{+}{+}$
12: $\quad$ **end if**
13: **end while**

3.2 Determining the Splitting Level k

Different users may want different clusterings, which can require super-instances at different granularities. For example, consider clustering a set of images of 20 different people, each taking two different poses. Clustering this data based on identity will require more super-instances than clustering it based on pose. Consequently, it is crucial to take user feedback into account to determine appropriate splitting levels.

Algorithm 2 describes the procedure that COBRAS uses to determine the splitting level k for a super-instance S. The procedure tries to search for a k such that the new super-instances will be pure w.r.t. the unknown target clustering. To check the purity of S, COBRAS splits it into two new (temporary) super-instances (by running 2-means on its instances), and queries the relation between their medoids. If they must link, COBRAS assumes that the super-instance was pure, and an appropriate level of granularity has been reached. If they cannot link, the procedure is then repeated on one of the two new super-instances. This continues until a must-link constraint is obtained. If d bisections are made before an appropriate level of granularity is reached, then the super-instance as a whole must be split into 2^d smaller super-instances. Figure 3(a) illustrates this process: super-instance S_1 gets split into two super-instances which cannot link; one of these, S_{t1}, is next split into two which again cannot link; among these, S_{t3} is split into two which must link; hence, S_{t3} seems to be at the right level of granularity and S_1 is split into $2^2 = 4$, which is the number of super-instances at this level. Line 6 in Algorithm 2 makes sure that the super-instance is at least split into two, even when the first constraint is must-link. This ensures that COBRAS will continue refining super-instances as long as the user is willing to answer queries, even when the data does not provide evidence for the usefulness of a particular split.

3.3 Illustration

Figure 3 illustrates two iterations of the entire COBRAS clustering process. The splitting of S_1 into 4 smaller super-instances was already explained. These 4 super-instances are put into new clusters, and next, the standard merging process of COBRA is applied. For details about this merging process, we refer to Van Craenendonck et al. [15]. In this illustration, we assume that COBRA finds a must-link between S_4 and S_5 and cannot-links between the others, which results in 3 clusters. Next, super-instance S_3 is considered for splitting, and split into 2. About the resulting S_6 and S_7, COBRA finds that S_6 should remain in its own cluster, but S_7 must link with S_4 and thus the clusters $\{S_7\}$ and $\{S_4, S_5\}$ are merged. This step shows how a part of one super-instance (in this case S_7, which was originally part of S_3) can get reassigned to a more suitable cluster.

4 Experimental Evaluation

In this section, we evaluate COBRAS[1] in terms of the AQT criteria (anytime, query efficiency, time efficiency). We compare it to the following state-of-the-art constraint-based clustering algorithms:

---

[1] Source code for COBRAS is available at https://dtai.cs.kuleuven.be/software/cobras/.

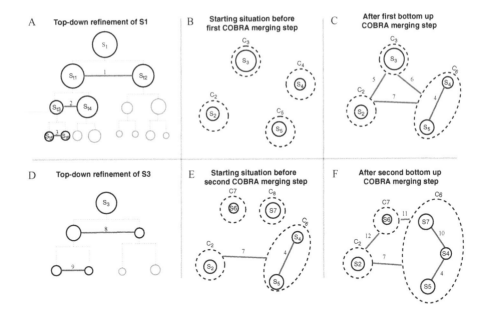

Fig. 3. (A) COBRAS decides to split the initial super-instance S_1 into 4 new ones, as discussed in Sect. 3.2. (B) S_1 has been removed from the set of clusters (rendering it empty), and a new cluster added for each of the newly created super-instances. This is the starting situation for the first bottom-up COBRA run. (C) Using additional queries, COBRA has merged the S_4 and S_5 clusters into one, and kept the others. In the next iteration (D), COBRAS selects S_3 for refinement, and splits it into 2 new super-instances; this results in two new clusters (E). Finally (F), the merging step has clustered S_7 together with S_4 and S_5, while S_2 and S_6 remain in their own cluster.

- **COBS** [14] uses constraints to select and tune an unsupervised clustering algorithm. We use the active variant in our experiments.
- **COBRA** [15] is the algorithm that is most related to COBRAS, as discussed earlier in this paper. We run it with 10, 25 and 50 super-instances.
- **NPU** [20] is an active constraint selection framework that can be used with any non-active constraint-based clustering method. It constructs neighborhoods of points that are connected by must-link constraints, with cannot-link constraints between the different neighborhoods. It repeatedly selects the most informative instance, and queries its neighborhood membership by means of pairwise constraints. NPU is an iterative method: after neighborhood membership is determined, the data is re-clustered and the obtained clustering is used to determine the next pairwise queries. NPU can be used with any constraint-based clustering algorithm, and we use it with the following two:

- **MPCKMeans** [3] is an extension of K-means that exploits constraints through metric learning and a modified objective. We use the implementation in the WekaUT package [2].
- **COSC** (for Constrained Spectral Clustering) [12] is an extension of spectral clustering optimizing for a modified objective. We use the code provided by the authors [3].

COSC-NPU and MPCKMeans-NPU need to know the desired number of clusters K prior to clustering. In our experiments, the true K (as indicated by the class labels) is given to these algorithms. Note that this puts them at an advantage in the experimental comparison, as in practice K is often not known in advance.

Datasets

We use the same datasets as those used in the evaluation of COBRA [15]. These include **15 UCI datasets**: iris, wine, dermatology, hepatitis, glass, ionosphere, optdigits389, ecoli, breast-cancer-wisconsin, segmentation, column_2C, parkinsons, spambase, sonar and yeast. These were selected because of their repeated use in earlier work on constraint-based clustering (for example, [3,20]). Optdigits389 contains digits 3, 8 and 9 of the UCI handwritten digits data [3,10]. Duplicate instances are removed from all of these datasets, and the data is normalized between 0 and 1. Further, we use the **CMU faces** dataset, containing 624 images of 20 persons with different poses and expressions, with and without sunglasses. This dataset has four natural clustering targets: identity, pose, expression and sunglasses. A 2048-value feature vector is extracted for each of the images using the pre-trained Inception-V3 network [13]. Further, two clustering tasks are included for the **20 newsgroups** text dataset: clustering documents from 3 newsgroups on related topics (the target clusters are comp.graphics, comp.os.ms-windows and comp.windows.x, as in [1,10]), and clustering documents from 3 newsgroups on very different topics (alt.atheism, rec.sport.baseball and sci.space, as in [1,10]). To extract features from the text documents we apply tf-idf, followed by latent semantic indexing (as in [10]) to reduce the dimensionality to 10.

In summary, the comparison is based on 21 clustering tasks (15 UCI datasets, 4 target clusterings for the CMU faces data, and 2 subsets of the newsgroups data).

Experimental Methodology

We perform 10-fold cross-validation 10 times (similar to e.g. [1] and [10]), and report averaged results. The algorithms always cluster the full dataset, but can only query the relations between pairs that are both in the training set. The quality of the resulting clustering is evaluated by computing the Adjusted Rand index (ARI, [8]), only on the instances in the test set. The ARI measures the similarity between the produced clusterings and the ground-truth indicated by

---

[2] http://www.cs.utexas.edu/users/ml/risc/code/.

[3] http://www.ml.uni-saarland.de/code/cosc/cosc.htm.

the class labels. A score of 0 means that the clustering is random, 1 means that it is exactly the same as the ground-truth. The score for an algorithm for a particular dataset is given by the average ARI over the 10 repetitions of 10 fold cross-validation.

We make sure that COBRAS and COBRA do not query any test instances during clustering by only using training instances to compute the medoids of the super-instances. For NPU, pairs involving an instance from the test set are simply excluded from selection.

In each iteration of COBRAS, a super-instance is split and COBRA is run on the resulting new set of clusterings. If the user stops answering pairwise queries before the end of the COBRA run (which is simulated frequently in the experiments: we consider the intermediate clusterings after each query), COBRAS returns the clustering as it was at the beginning of the iteration. The clustering that is returned is only updated after the COBRA run, which prevents us from returning clusterings for which the merging step was not finished yet. This holds for all COBRA runs expect the first one, as in that case there is no real prior clustering at the beginning of the iteration.

COBRA is not able to handle an unlimited amount of pairwise queries: once all the relations between super-instances are known, the clustering process naturally stops. In our experiments, we assume that COBRA simply keeps returning its final clustering after this point, which allows us to compare all algorithms for the same number of pairwise queries.

Clustering Quality

Figure 4(a) shows the aligned ranks for COBRAS and all competitors over all clustering tasks[4]. In contrast to the regular rank, the aligned rank [6,7] takes the relative differences between algorithms for individual datasets into account. The first step in computing it is to calculate for each dataset the average ARI achieved by the algorithms. Then, for each algorithm, the difference between its ARI and this average is calculated, and the resulting differences are sorted from 1 to kn (k the number of algorithms, n the number of datasets). The aligned rank for an algorithm is the average of the positions of its entries in the sorted list.

Figure 4(b) shows the average ARI of each method over all clustering tasks. This gives some indication of how substantial the differences in ARI are in practice.

Figures 4(a) and (b) show that, *compared over the entire range of queries*, COBRAS is clearly superior to each individual competitor. None of the competitors is able to produce good results during the entire clustering process, which is crucial for interactive clustering. Some of them outperform COBRAS for a specific range of the number of queries, but those that do are outperformed

---

[4] For COSC-NPU we set a timeout of 24h for each run of 250 queries for spambase. Typically it only got to 40 queries after that time. We considered the last clustering produced within 24h to be the final one, and use it in the results for all remaining queries in producing the graphs.

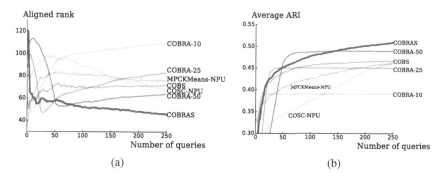

Fig. 4. (a) Aligned rank for all methods over all clustering tasks (b) Average ARIs for all methods over all clustering tasks

by a much larger margin for other ranges. We illustrate this point by comparing COBRAS to COBRA-50 in more detail. Figure 4(a) shows that COBRA-50 outperforms COBRAS in the range of (roughly) 50–70 queries. However, for <50 queries, COBRAS-50 performs much worse than COBRAS; the difference in average ARI in this range is much greater than in the 50–70 range. Furthermore, COBRA-50's performance stagnates around 50 queries. Thus, the anytime behavior of COBRA-50 is vastly inferior to that of COBRAS. COBRA-50 is only preferable to COBRAS when one knows the optimal number of super-instances in advance. The same holds for COBRA-10 and COBRA-25.

Table 1 shows win/loss statistics that confirm the above conclusions. It demonstrates that COBRAS outperforms its competitors in the majority of cases (18 out of 24). COBRAS significantly (Wilcoxon test, $p < 0.05$) outperforms COBRA-10, COBRA-25, COBRA-50 and COSC-NPU for at least one of the query numbers. It outperforms MPCKMeans-NPU and COBS as well, but this difference is found not to be statistically significant. It is never significantly outperformed by any other method.

Runtime

Figure 5 shows the ratio of the run time of COBRAS to the run times of its competitors for the 21 clustering tasks after performing 100 queries. COBRA is typically the fastest algorithm. This is not surprising, as it requires only a single run of K-means, while COBRAS requires multiple K-means runs. Compared to the other competitors, COBRAS is *one to three orders of magnitude* faster for all datasets. The key difference between COBRAS and its competitors is that COBRAS only re-clusters the parts of the dataset that are being refined. In contrast, MPCKMeans-NPU and COSC-NPU require frequent re-clustering of the entire dataset.

Practically speaking, the time between consecutive queries is under a second for all datasets considered here, which is fast enough for interactive clustering.

The high runtimes of COBS are caused by the fact that it generates a large number of unsupervised clusterings prior to querying the user. Once this set of

Table 1. Wins and losses over the 21 clustering tasks. An asterisk indicates that the difference is significant according to the Wilcoxon test with $p < 0.05$. Between parentheses we report the average margin by which COBRAS wins or loses.

	25 queries		50 queries		100 queries		200 queries	
	Win	Loss	Win	Loss	Win	Loss	Win	Loss
COBRAS vs. COBRA-10	**11** (0.05)	10 (0.02)	**16*** (0.07)	5 (0.01)	**17*** (0.10)	4 (0.01)	**18*** (0.12)	3 (0.01)
COBRAS vs. COBRA-25	7 (0.03)	**14** (0.04)	9 (0.03)	**12** (0.03)	**14** (0.04)	7 (0.01)	**17*** (0.06)	4 (0.01)
COBRAS vs. COBRA-50	**16*** (0.15)	5 (0.01)	9 (0.04)	**12** (0.04)	9 (0.02)	**12** (0.02)	**12** (0.03)	9 (0.01)
COBRAS vs. MPCKM-NPU	**11** (0.06)	10 (0.02)	**13** (0.07)	8 (0.02)	**11** (0.07)	10 (0.02)	**11** (0.06)	10 (0.02)
COBRAS vs. COSC-NPU	**14*** (0.13)	7 (0.02)	**15*** (0.13)	6 (0.02)	**13** (0.13)	8 (0.03)	9 (0.10)	**12** (0.04)
COBRAS vs. COBS	**12** (0.04)	9 (0.03)	**13** (0.04)	8 (0.03)	**12** (0.05)	9 (0.03)	10 (0.06)	**11** (0.02)

clusterings is generated, however, selecting the clusterings is fast. This means that COBS can be useful in interactive settings where the time between starting the system and answering the first query is of no concern.

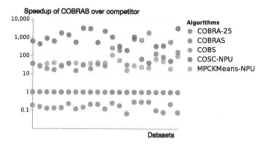

Fig. 5. Ratio of COBRAS to competitors run time for 21 clustering tasks. For COBRA we only include the run times of COBRA-25 to not clutter the graph, also the run times for COBRA-10 and COBRA-50 are typically lower than all others.

To summarize all the above: COBRA and possibly COBS can compete with COBRAS in terms of time efficiency; COBRA can compete in terms of query efficiency if its N_S parameter is chosen optimally; none of the existing methods can compete in terms of anytime behavior.

5   Conclusion

We have introduced COBRAS, a novel system for interactive semi-supervised clustering. The key innovation in COBRAS is its procedure for dynamically refining super-instances. This innovation makes it the first clustering system to excel at all three of the following crucial criteria for interactive clustering systems: anytime behavior, query efficiency, and time efficiency. This should make COBRAS the method of choice in many applications of semi-supervised clustering.

Acknowledgements. TVC is supported by the Agency for Innovation by Science and Technology in Flanders (IWT). Research supported by Research Fund KU Leuven (GOA/13/010), Research Foundation - Flanders (G079416N), and the European Research Council (Horizon 2020, grant agreement 694980, "SYNTH").

References

1. Basu, S., Banerjee, A., Mooney, R.J.: Active semi-supervision for pairwise constrained clustering. In: Proceedings of SDM (2004)
2. Basu, S., Bilenko, M., Mooney, R.J.: A probabilistic framework for semi-supervised clustering. In: Proceedings of KDD (2004)

3. Bilenko, M., Basu, S., Mooney, R.J.: Integrating constraints and metric learning in semi-supervised clustering. In: Proceedings of ICML (2004)
4. Caruana, R., Elhawary, M., Nguyen, N.: Meta clustering. In: Proceedings of ICDM (2006)
5. Davis, J.V., Kulis, B., Jain, P., Sra, S., Dhillon, I.S.: Information-theoretic metric learning. In: Proceedings of ICML (2007)
6. García, S., Fernández, A., Luengo, J., Herrera, F.: Advanced nonparametric tests for multiple comparisons in the design of experiments in computational intelligence and data mining: experimental analysis of power. Inf. Sci. **180**, 2044–2064 (2010). special Issue on Intelligent Distributed Information Systems
7. Hodges, J.L., Lehmann, E.L.: Rank methods for combination of independent experiments in analysis of variance. Ann. Math. Stat. **33**, 482–497 (1962)
8. Hubert, L., Arabie, P.: Comparing partitions. J. Classif. **21**, 193–218 (1985)
9. von Luxburg, U., Williamson, R.C., Guyon, I.: Clustering: science or art? In: Workshop on Unsupervised Learning and Transfer Learning (2014)
10. Mallapragada, P.K., Jin, R., Jain, A.K.: Active query selection for semi-supervised clustering. In: Proceedings of ICPR (2008)
11. Ng, R.T., Han, J.: Clarans: a method for clustering objects for spatial data mining. IEEE TKDE **14**(5), 1003–1016 (2002)
12. Rangapuram, S.S., Hein, M.: Constrained 1-spectral clustering. In: Proceedings of AISTATS (2012)
13. Szegedy, C., Vanhoucke, V., Ioffe, S., Shlens, J., Wojna, Z.: Rethinking the inception architecture for computer vision. CoRR abs/1512.00567 (2015). http://arxiv.org/abs/1512.00567
14. Van Craenendonck, T., Blockeel, H.: Constraint-based clustering selection. Mach. Learn. **106**, 1497–1521 (2017)
15. Van Craenendonck, T., Dumančić, S., Blockeel, H.: COBRA: a fast and simple method for active clustering with pairwise constraints. In: Proceedings of IJCAI (2017)
16. Wagstaff, K., Cardie, C.: Clustering with instance-level constraints. In: Proceedings of ICML (2000)
17. Wagstaff, K., Cardie, C., Rogers, S., Schroedl, S.: Constrained k-means clustering with background knowledge. In: Proceedings of ICML (2001)
18. Wang, X., Qian, B., Davidson, I.: On constrained spectral clustering and its applications. Data Min. Knowl. Discov. **28**, 1–30 (2014)
19. Xing, E.P., Ng, A.Y., Jordan, M.I., Russell, S.: Distance metric learning, with application to clustering with side-information. In: NIPS (2003)
20. Xiong, S., Azimi, J., Fern, X.Z.: Active learning of constraints for semi-supervised clustering. TKDE **26**, 43–54 (2014)

Automatically Wrangling Spreadsheets into Machine Learning Data Formats

Gust Verbruggen$^{(\boxtimes)}$ and Luc De Raedt

KU Leuven, Leuven, Belgium
{gust.verbruggen,luc.deraedt}@cs.kuleuven.be

Abstract. To help automate the important pre-processing step in machine learning and data mining, we introduce SYNTH-A-SIZER, a tool for semi-automatically wrangling spreadsheets into attribute-value format, so that they can be used by popular machine learning tools, only requiring the user to mark cells belonging to one single example. SYNTH-A-SIZER is based on inductive programming principles. We introduce SYNTH-A-SIZER's transformations, search algorithm as well as a heuristic and distance measure for identifying types. We also report on a first experimental evaluation.

Keywords: Data wrangling · Program synthesis · Spreadsheets
Preprocessing · Inductive programming

1 Introduction

One long term goal of automatic machine learning and data science is to enable naive end-users to automatically analyse their data. Today we are far away from reaching that goal for two reasons. First, it is often hard to select the right learning setting, algorithm and parameters for the learning task. Second, it is well-known amongst data scientists that 80% of the time is spent on pre-processing and only 20% on the actual machine learning or data mining [5].

Looking at the state of the art in machine learning and data mining reveals that the first problem is receiving a lot of attention in the emerging area of automated machine learning [9]. Many impressive results have already been obtained and powerful tools have already been developed [7,14]. Although there exist some tools that aid in the automatic preprocessing of data, especially with respect to feature construction [4], other preprocessing steps remain very challenging. Data wrangling is one of the most important ones.

This paper addresses exactly this issue and studies how to help end-users with data wrangling, that is, the process of transforming their data in the right format for data analysis. As non-experts often gather their data in spreadsheets, we focus on the question as to whether it is possible to take such a spreadsheet and to automatically transform it into a format that can be used by standard machine learning software such as WEKA [10] and KNIME [3]. Thus, we want to help fully automate the data wrangling process [1].

© Springer Nature Switzerland AG 2018
W. Duivesteijn et al. (Eds.): IDA 2018, LNCS 11191, pp. 367–379, 2018.
https://doi.org/10.1007/978-3-030-01768-2_30

Several approaches for data wrangling with minimal user effort already exist. For example, the WRANGLER [12] system provides an interactive interface for creating transformation programs without needing to write code. Instantiations of the FLASHMETA [13] framework allow for synthesising data transformation programs by providing input-output examples. A notable instantiation is FLASHRELATE, [2] which extracts relational data from spreadsheets. More recently, FOOFAH [11] combine these two: transforming a spreadsheet based on examples.

In this paper, we take a next step in these developments and explore whether these processes can be automated while focussing on data in tabular form. A key difference with other approaches is that we focus on wrangling of machine learning data sets. While the above mentioned approaches use examples of the desired input-output behaviour to guide the program synthesis, we focus on the desired target *format* of the output. In this paper, the desired output is is in attribute-value format, which is used when working with tools such as WEKA. This format has distinct properties that we exploit in order to mediate the need for examples describing the desired output. Although we focus on the attribute-value format here, we believe that the principles and techniques we introduce could also be useful for relational learning.

This paper contributes a tool, SYNTH-A-SIZER, for semi-automatic data wrangling of machine learning datasets from minimal user input. SYNTH-A-SIZER uses a predictive program synthesis approach that transforms semi-structured data into a propositional format, for use in data analysis systems, from one positive example. The technical innovations of SYNTH-A-SIZER are that (1) we focus on the desired target format of the output and allow the user to provide hints about the target format using a new notion of *coloring*; (2) we introduce a domain specific language with an accompanying syntactic bias which allows to restrict the search space; and (3) we employ a novel type-based heuristic to assess and evaluate the transformations.

2   Motivating Example

Suppose a clothing store owner keeps two spreadsheets, containing sales and properties of clothing, respectively, an excerpt of which is shown in Table 1. The rightmost column in Table 1b is to be predicted. Given data in the correct format, plenty of tools are available to perform this task.

First, however, a user would need to know about transformations to unpivot and join tables together. In OpenRefine[1] an additional forward filling operation is required and Wrangler [12] make no assumptions about the output format, giving unpivot as the last suggestion. This motivates our belief that existing data wrangling tools are aimed at data scientists and other people who know their way around transforming data.

---

[1] http://www.openrefine.org.

Table 1. Spreadsheet data about clothing sales. Some cells are colored as they have been selected by the user.

(a) Sales data.

(b) Clothes' properties. On the right is the target, with one missing value.

	29/08/2013	31/08/2013	09/02/2013
1006032852	2114	2274	2491
1212192089	151	275	570
1190380701	6	7	7
966005983	1005	1128	1326
876339541	996	1175	1304
1068332458	4	5	11

1006032852	Low	4.6	Summer	o-neck	sleevless	1
1212192089	Low	0	Summer	o-neck	Petal	0
1190380701	High	0	Automn	o-neck	full	0
966005983	Average	4.6	Spring	o-neck	full	1
876339541	Low	4.5	Summer	o-neck	butterfly	0
1068332458	Low	0	Summer	v-neck	sleevless	

(c) Tables 1a and 1b wrangled into attribute-value format. This is what the user doesn't see, but what is generated by SYNTH-A-SIZER and used by data mining tools in the background in order to predict the last column.

1006032852	29/8/2013	2114	Low	4.6	Summer	o-neck	sleevless	1
1006032852	31/8/2013	2274	Low	4.6	Summer	o-neck	sleevless	1
1006032852	09/02/2013	2491	Low	4.6	Summer	o-neck	sleevless	1
1212192089	29/08/2013	151	Low	0	Summer	o-neck	Petal	0

:

1068332458	31/08/2013	5	Low	0	Summer	v-neck	sleevless	
1068332458	09/02/2013	11	Low	0	Summer	v-neck	sleevless	

Our approach, on the other hand, is aimed at users who have no knowledge about transforming data at all. Currently, the only required interaction is *selecting* values in the spreadsheet, as shown in Table 1. Wrangling is then performed in the background.

3   Problem Statement

The problem this paper wants to solve is best described on two levels. On a higher level, we aim to enable users without experience in programming or data wrangling to apply machine learning techniques to their data. As data gathered by such users is typically stored in a spreadsheet, we focus on the problem of mapping a spreadsheet S into a dataset D that can serve as the input to a machine learning algorithm. The machine learning algorithm should then generate a hypothesis h that can be applied to the dataset D to yield $h(D)$. Ideally, this approach allows for mapping $h(D)$ back into the spreadsheet S so that it can be shown to the user. The ultimate goal is that the transformations, the resulting dataset and the hypothesis are all constructed behind the scenes. Everything the user would see is the original spreadsheet S that has now been extended with the results of $h(D)$. A necessary condition for this to work is that the original spreadsheet S has been formatted in a *systematic* manner.

On a lower level, the problem we tackle in the present paper is to find the program f that maps $f(S) = D$, which is a program synthesis problem where a data wrangling program is learned.

3.1 Notation

As common in spreadsheets, the basic structure our programs transform are tables. A table is represented by an $m \times n$ matrix T. The element on column i and row j is referred to as $t_{i,j}$. We adopt a slicing notation $a : b$ to denote a range $(a, a + 1, \ldots, b)$ of cells, represented as a list of values. When a and/or b are omitted, the range extends to the size of the table, such that for example the values in row j are retrieved as $T_{:,j}$.

An m-ary relation $R \subseteq (A_1, \ldots, A_m)$ of n tuples can be easily represented by a set of such tables. In the trivial case, every tuple becomes a row and each attribute is contained in a column of a single $m \times n$ table. This is the desired *target* data format for attribute-value learners such as those available in WEKA and KNIME. In the real world, however, the data can be spread out over multiple tables. Furthermore, values can be repositioned, empty cells and *spurious* cells can be added to the tables. The goal will then be to extract an equivalent table in the target format.

Example 1. Suppose we have a relation of car sales indicating whether a salesperson of a certain level gave a reduction or not:

$$\left\{ \begin{array}{l} \text{(Tim, junior, Audi, A1, no),} \quad \text{(Tim, junior, BMW, 1, yes),} \\ \text{(Megan, senior, Audi, A1, no), (Megan, senior, Audi, A4, yes)} \end{array} \right\}$$

There are various ways of representing this relation in a set of tables, two examples of which are given in Fig. 1. In the *Sales* table in Fig. 1, some spurious values were added to denote the proportion of reductions given.

Tables can be transformed by transformations, which take as input one or more tables, optionally some arguments, and return a single table. The result of applying a transformation on some table(s) is then a new table with the elements from the original table(s) combined, repositioned, replicated or removed. We write $p = (\phi, a) : T \rightarrow T'$ for a table transformation p consisting of a transformation ϕ and a tuple of arguments a, taking a set of tables T and returning a new table $T' = \phi(T, a)$. We restrict ourselves to transformations that only change the layout of the spreadsheet, leaving cell values untouched. Each transformation ϕ has a set of valid arguments given a set of tables, denoted as $A_\phi(T)$.

Applying a transformation results in a *reconstruction error*, a measure of how much information is lost when it is applied to T, written as $error(p, T)$. A transformation can be *inverted* if there exists a transformation $p^{-1} = (\phi^{-1}, a)$ such that $p^{-1}(p(T)) = T$.

Example 2. Given a simple table

$$T = \begin{array}{|c|c|} \hline \text{Audi} & \text{A1} \\ \hline & \text{A3} \\ \hline & \text{A4} \\ \hline \end{array}$$

and the Fill($direction, i$) transformation (see also Table 2), which fills empty values in column i with the value above (*forward*) or below (*backward*) it, we get $A_{\mathsf{Fill}}(T) = \{(forward, 1); (forward, 2); (backward, 1); (backward, 2)\}$.

A set of transformations $\mathcal{L}$ then serves as a simple domain-specific language (DSL) for wrangling tabular data. A table transformation program $\mathcal{P}$ is a sequence of transformations $(p_1, p_2, \ldots, p_k)$ with $p_i = (\phi_i, \boldsymbol{a}_i)$. Applying it to a table T is computed as $\mathcal{P}(\boldsymbol{T}) = \phi_p(\ldots \phi_2(\phi_1(\boldsymbol{T}, \boldsymbol{a}_1), \boldsymbol{a}_2) \ldots, \boldsymbol{a}_p)$. The definitions of reconstruction error and invertibility naturally extend from one transformation of a sequence of transformations.

3.2   Problem Statement

We can now specify the program synthesis problem as follows.

GIVEN a set of tables $\boldsymbol{T} = (T_1, \ldots, T_k)$, a set of colorings C (cf. below), a scoring function $score(\boldsymbol{T}, C)$, and a set of transformations $\mathcal{L}$, **FIND** a transformation program P^* over $\mathcal{L}$ such that $P^* = \arg\max_P score(P(\boldsymbol{T}), C)$.

The assumption is that there is an unknown target relation R and a program P^t such that $P^t(\boldsymbol{T})$ and R are equivalent (notation $P^t(\boldsymbol{T}) \equiv R$). The equivalence would account for row and column permutations. But the relation R is unknown and therefore we can only estimate how good any $P(\boldsymbol{T})$ is through a scoring function. This scoring function should recognise tables that are in attribute-value form. Such tables have rows that correspond to examples and columns that correspond to attributes. As a simple aid for recognising this, our scoring function can currently make use of one additional, user-provided input.

Essentially, the user is requested to color a set of cells that describe one example, possibly using different colors. The idea behind the coloring is twofold. First, cells belonging to one coloring should be mapped onto a single row. Cells in different tables with the same color, should be mapped onto the same cell in the target table. Second, all values in a single column should belong to the same attribute and should therefore be of the same type. If a colored cell occurs in a column, all other values in that column should be of the same type as the colored cell. Formally, a coloring C is a mapping from a set of cells $t_{i,j}$ to a set of colors. An example is given in Example 3.

While earlier work [15] assumed that the types were given, with each attribute having a different type, the present approach uses an edit-distance measure to determine how similar the type of two cells is. More specifically, it is assumed that the distance between different elements belonging to the same type is small— smaller than the distances between values of different types. The scoring function should then take into account (1) the quality of the rows and columns with respect to a coloring and (2) the reconstruction error.

Example 3. A cell coloring

$$C_1 = \{People_{1,1} \rightarrow \quad, People_{2,1} \rightarrow \quad, Sales_{1,1} \rightarrow \quad,$$
$$Sales_{1,2} \rightarrow \quad, Sales_{2,2} \rightarrow \quad, Sales_{3,2} \rightarrow \quad\}$$

is shown on the left in Fig. 1. After successfully wrangling it, these tables are transformed into the table on the right. Cells in each column are syntactically similar to a colored cell, no more empty values are present and the coloring contains an assignment that spans exactly one row. The transformed table should then get a much better score than the original ones.

Sales

Audi		
A1	Tim	no
A1	Megan	no
A4	Tim	yes
		2/3
BMW		
1	Megan	yes
		1/1

People

Tim	Junior
Megan	Senior

Tim	Junior	Audi	A1	no
Tim	Junior	Audi	A4	yes
Megan	Senior	Audi	A1	no
Megan	Senior	BMW	1	yes

Fig. 1. Two tabular representations of the relation in Example 1. (**left**) Spread out over two tables. The *Sales* table additionally contains empty cells and values not in the original relation. An example coloring is also shown. (**right**) Trivial representation as a single table.

4   Program Synthesis

We now introduce a predictive synthesis approach to synthesise the table transformation programs from just one example—a single tuple in the output relation that is colored by a user. Rather than assigning a score to the program itself, as in regular optimisation-based program synthesis [8], the output of the program is scored. A search over the space of transformation programs, optimising this score, is then used to find the program that correctly wrangles the input. In order to guide this search, we put a syntactic bias on the arguments of each transformation, which actually encodes a set of constraints on the possible arguments a transformation can take.

In the remainder of the section, we first introduce the supported transformations and their syntactic bias. Afterwards, we show how they are used to guide two search algorithms towards a solution optimising our scoring function. Finally, we provide the details of our scoring function.

4.1   Transformations and Syntactic Bias

The supported transformations is inspired on existing approaches [11, 12]. They have been chosen such that a wide variety of real world wrangling scenarios can be solved. In order to support multiple tables, a Join transformation is added. The full list is presented in Table 2.

Given a set of input tables T and a list of transformations, we can easily start recursively enumerating all transformation programs in search of one that optimises the heuristic. This is very unlikely to find a correct transformation program as the search space grows exponentially. To make the search over transformations tractable, a syntactic bias is placed on their arguments.

The intuition behind our syntactic bias is very similar to *witness functions* in FLASHMETA [13], where they restrict the arguments of a function given the input–output examples. We reduce $A_\phi(T)$ based on the coloring and our knowledge of the heuristic. For example, the Fill transformation may only consider columns that have exactly one colored cell. A Delete is not allowed to remove colored cells. We write the reduced arguments of ϕ on T given C as $A_\phi(T, C)$. The full syntactic bias for each transformation is given in Table 2.

Table 2. Transformations supported by SYNTH-A-SIZER, their effect on an $m \times n$ table T and how the set of valid arguments is reduced given a coloring C. In the column on the right, i and j range over the columns of the tables they correspond to, d and fwd range over the boolean values.

Transformation	Effect	$A_\phi(T, C)$
$\mathsf{Fill}(T, i, fwd)$	Fill each empty cell in $T_{i,:}$ with the first non-empty value above ($fwd = 1$) or below ($fwd = 0$) it	All (i, fwd) such that $T_{i,:}$ contains empty values and exactly one colored cell from C is in $T_{i,:}$
$\mathsf{Delete}(T, i)$	Delete all rows j where $t_{i,j}$ is empty	All (i) such that $T_{i,:}$ contains empty values and no cells $\in C$ are deleted
$\mathsf{Fold}(T, i, j, h, d)$	Fold $T_{i:j,:}$ into one ($h = 0$) or two ($h = 1$) new columns. If $h = 1$, elements from the first row are used as a description for values $T_{i:j, y \neq 0}$. If $d = 1$, rows with empty values in the folded column are deleted	All (i, j, h, d) such that $T_{i:j,:}$ contains exactly column y with n colored cells and $h = (n > 1$ and $T_{y,0} \in C)$
$\mathsf{Join}(T^1, T^2, i, j)$	(outer) Join tables T^1 and T^2 on columns i and j respectively	All (i, j) such that $T^1_{i,:} \subseteq T^2_{j,:}$ or vice versa

4.2   Synthesis Algorithm

Our synthesis algorithm then performs a beam search over the space of transformation programs. The beam is defined using the scoring function detailed in the next section. Two variations are implemented: depth-first (DFS) and breadth-first (BFS), consecutively aimed at being faster versus more robust.

A priority queue is used to implement the search. Let b be the beam width. In DFS, at every iteration of the synthesis loop: the best table so far is fetched, its reduced set of possible transformations is computed, the results are scored and the b best extended programs are added back to the queue. In BFS, *every* element is replaced by its top-b transformed tables from different transformations as long as at least one of those b tables is better than the current one.

4.3   Scoring Tables

Given a set of tables and a coloring, we want to estimate how close the set of tables is to being the unknown target relation. In an attribute-value formatted table, all columns describe one attribute and should thus contain values of the same data type. Every cell in the coloring should then belong to one of these column types. The actual types are unknown, however. We therefore estimate how similar the type of two values is using a syntactic distance function, which is detailed in the next section. It is used to define the scoring function.

Let there be c different colors. Some transformations, such as Fill, may propagate colors to other cells in the table. We then first select an assignment $a = \{t_{i_1,j_1}, \ldots, t_{i_c,j_c}\}$ such that as many different columns as possible have a colored value. Next, for each cell $t_{i,j}$ in the assignment, the average distance between the cell and all other cells in its column

$$avg\_color(t_{i,j}) = \frac{1}{m} \sum_{y=1}^{m} d(t_{i,j}, t_{i,y}) \tag{1}$$

is computed, as well as the proportion of empty values in this column.

$$empty(t_{i,j}) = \frac{1}{m} \sum_{y=1}^{m} (t_{i,y} \equiv \varnothing) \tag{2}$$

These two values are added for each colored cell and then averaged over all colored cells in the selection to compute the final score.

$$score\_color(a) = \frac{1}{c} \sum_{x=1}^{c} (avg\_color(t_{i_x,j_x}) + empty(t_{i_x,j_x})) \tag{3}$$

Finally, the same procedure is repeated for columns without colored cells, the difference being that the average similarity between any pair of values is computed such that (1) becomes

$$avg(i_x) = \frac{2}{m(m+1)} \sum_{y=1}^{m} \sum_{z=y}^{m} d(t_{i_x,y}, t_{i_x,z}). \tag{4}$$

for some column i_x. This allows for wrangling with partial colorings and also provides some robustness. Scores for both types of columns are added to compute the final score. When scoring multiple tables, their individual scores are summed.

$$score(T) = score\_color(a) + \frac{1}{m-c} \sum_{i \notin i_1, \ldots, i_c} (avg(i) + empty(t_{i,0})) \tag{5}$$

4.4   Cell Distance

At the heart of this method is the function that computes the similarity in type of cells. We propose a syntactic similarity function between cell values, treating them as a sequence of character classes.

This method is heavily inspired by the *string edit distance* between two cell values, with two differences: every character is represented by its character class and addition and deletion of elements between specific character classes can be made cheaper, for example, between lower- and uppercase letters

First, both strings are tokenised according to a set of disjoint character classes, such as digits, lower- and uppercase letters, delimiters (-, /,...) and currency symbols. Every token is weighted with the number of characters it consumed. Next, the token sequences are globally aligned using a custom substitution matrix. The final distance is then computed as the distance between aligned tokens, weighted both by their weight and a distance matrix.

Let $(a_1, a_2, \ldots, a_n)$ and $(b_1, b_2, \ldots, b_n)$ be the aligned tokenisations of two strings a and b, $w(a_i)$ the weight of token a_i and $cost(t_1, t_2)$ the cost of a substitution between tokens t_1 and t_2. The distance between a and b is then computed as

$$d(a, b) = \sum_i cost(a_i, b_i) \frac{|w(a_i) - w(b_i)|}{w(a_i) + w(b_i) + 1}. \tag{6}$$

5   Evaluation

We propose a method for generating sythetic data that can be used for evaluating SYNTH-A-SIZER. The core idea is to generate messy data from a clean dataset. We start from a table and apply a number of subsequent random inverse transformations, creating a synthetic input dataset. The number of inverse transformations applied is called the *depth* of the synthetic dataset.

More specifically, we generate inverse programs P_t and associated messy tables $D' = P_t^{-1}(D)$ and then attempt to synthesize programs P that restore the original dataset as $P(D')$. The results are evaluated in terms of *recall* and *precision*, respectively the proportion of rows in D that is also in $P(D')$ and proportion of rows in $P(D')$ that is in D. The supported inverse transformations are explained in Table 3. Because some of the inverse transformations have side effects, i.e., a Fill reorders the rows, a few constraints need to be placed on the generated inverse programs in order to prevent total destruction of the data. Most notably, a table can only be reordered once. Further details of the generation process will be made available in a longer version of the paper.

Three datasets from the UCI repository [6] were selected, based on some simple requirements: not being too large, our implementation is not yet optimised to scale, and containing at least some categorical attributes in order to generate interesting inverse programs. They are the Breast Cancer, Auto MPG and Computer Hardware datasets[2].

---

[2] https://archive.ics.uci.edu/ml/datasets/.

Table 3. Inverse transformations supported by the data generator.

Transformation	Inverse	Inverse arguments
$\text{Fill}(T, i, fwd)$	If it was not sorted before: sort T on column i. For every pair of consecutive equal values, set the top ($fwd = 0$) or bottom ($fwd = 1$) one to $\varnothing$	All (i, fwd) such that $T_{i,:}$ doesn't contain empty values
$\text{Delete}(T, i)$	Repeat $\sim U(0, n-1)$ times: – Generate $\sim U(1, m/2)$ random strings – Add a row to T with the strings in random locations that are not i	All (i) such that $T_{i,:}$ does not contain an empty value
$\text{Fold}(T, i, j, h, d)$	Duplicate rows such that the elements outside of columns $i : i + h$ are repeated $j - i$ times. Expand values in folded column(s) in groups of $j - i + 1$ consecutive rows into new columns	All (i, j, h, d) such that (1) if $h = 0$: values outside of column i are replicated between at least $n/2$ rows or (2) if $h = 1$: values in column i are replicated at least $n/2$ times
$\text{Join}(T^1, T^2, i, j)$	Look for functional dependency $i \to Y$ between column i and columns Y such that $|Y| = j$. Split table by removing columns Y and building new table from columns (i, Y)	All (i, j) such that there exists a functional dependency $i \to Y$ and $|Y| = j$

5.1 Increasing Depth

We start by assessing the basic wrangling capability of SYNTH-A-SIZER. The first row of each dataset is colored and sets of 100 programs of increasing depths are generated. For both algorithms, the average recall and precision are plotted in terms of the depth in Fig. 2. Both mixed BFS and DFS achieve almost perfect reconstruction for lower depths in most cases. As depth increases, performance drops. We can take a closer look at the performance by plotting the distribution of the precisions, as done in Fig. 3.

In our experiments, there are two main reasons why tables are not perfectly wrangled. First, complex Fold operations are not always correctly detected, resulting in zero precision. This happens more often in datasets which have more similar attributes, such as **Breast Cancer** and **Hardware**. Second, Fill is sometimes applied in the wrong direction, resulting in precisions depending on the number of unique elements in the filled column.

As SYNTH-A-SIZER relies on a distance measure between types, it is sensitive to how syntactically similar different types are. An interesting question for further research is how to combine the similarity with background information about the underlying types, as well as alternative approaches for type detection.

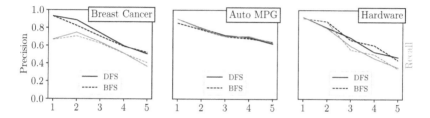

Fig. 2. Precision (black) and recall (gray) on three datasets for inverse programs of increasing depths (x-axis) using two synthesis algorithms. Due to good performance on the `Auto MPG` data, precision and recall are very similar.

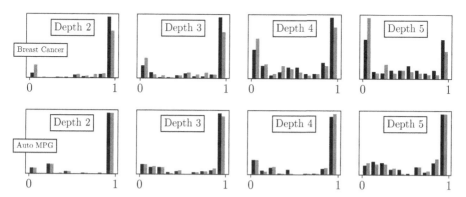

Fig. 3. Distribution of precision (black) and recall (gray) for increasing depths on the cancer (top) and auto (bottom) datasets.

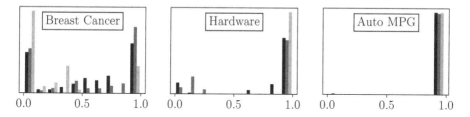

Fig. 4. Precision distributions of repeating previously successful runs with different colorings for all datasets.

5.2 Resilience to Coloring

We then ask the question how sensitive SYNTH-A-SIZER is to which cells are colored. All inverse programs of depths 3-5 from the previous experiments for which DFS achieved perfect results are computed 10 times with different rows colored. The precision distributions of wrangling those tables using DFS are shown Fig. 4. Only for the `Breast Cancer` data are the obtained results considerably worse, probably due to similar features across columns. For both other datasets, SYNTH-A-SIZER seems robust enough to work for arbitrary colorings.

6   Conclusion

We presented SYNTH-A-SIZER, a tool that semi-automatically wrangles attribute-value data from spreadsheets given only a coloring of one positive output example. Even though it uses a very simple heuristic and synthesis algorithm, it already achieves respectable performance on synthetically generated messy spreadsheets.

While more effort is required to improve the heuristic and distance function, these results provide a next step in the direction of fully automated wrangling of data from spreadsheets.

Acknowledgement. This work has received funding from the European Research Council (ERC) under the European Union's Horizon 2020 research and innovation programme (grant agreement No [694980] SYNTH: Synthesising Inductive Data Models).

References

1. Data Wrangling Automation, IEEE International Conference on Data Mining (2016). http://users.dsic.upv.es/~flip/DWA2016/
2. Barowy, D.W., Gulwani, S., Hart, T., Zorn, B.: Flashrelate: extracting relational data from semi-structured spreadsheets using examples. In: ACM SIGPLAN Notices, vol. 50, pp. 218–228. ACM (2015)
3. Berthold, M.R., et al.: Knime-the konstanz information miner: version 2.0 and beyond. ACM SIGKDD Explor. Newsl. **11**(1), 26–31 (2009)
4. Boullé, M.: Towards automatic feature construction for supervised classification. In: Calders, T., Esposito, F., Hüllermeier, E., Meo, R. (eds.) ECML PKDD 2014. LNCS (LNAI), vol. 8724, pp. 181–196. Springer, Heidelberg (2014). https://doi.org/10.1007/978-3-662-44848-9_12
5. Dasu, T., Johnson, T.: Exploratory Data Mining and Data Cleaning, vol. 479. Wiley, New York (2003)
6. Dheeru, D., Karra Taniskidou, E.: UCI Machine Learning Repository (2017)
7. Feurer, M., Klein, A., Eggensperger, K., Springenberg, J., Blum, M., Hutter, F.: Efficient and robust automated machine learning. In: Advances in Neural Information Processing Systems, pp. 2962–2970 (2015)
8. Gulwani, S., Polozov, O., Singh, R.: Program synthesis. Found. Trends® Program. Lang. **4**(1–2), 1–119 (2017)
9. Guyon, I., et al.: A brief review of the ChaLearn AutoML challenge: any-time any-dataset learning without human intervention. In: Workshop on Automatic Machine Learning, pp. 21–30 (2016)
10. Hall, M., Frank, E., Holmes, G., Pfahringer, B., Reutemann, P., Witten, I.H.: The WEKA data mining software: an update. ACM SIGKDD Explor. Newsl. **11**(1), 10–18 (2009)

11. Jin, Z., Anderson, M.R., Cafarella, M., Jagadish, H.: Foofah: transforming data by example. In: Proceedings of the 2017 ACM International Conference on Management of Data, pp. 683–698. ACM (2017)
12. Kandel, S., Paepcke, A., Hellerstein, J., Heer, J.: Wrangler: interactive visual specification of data transformation scripts. In: Proceedings of the SIGCHI Conference on Human Factors in Computing Systems, pp. 3363–3372. ACM (2011)
13. Polozov, O., Gulwani, S.: Flashmeta: a framework for inductive program synthesis. In: ACM SIGPLAN Notices, vol. 50, pp. 107–126. ACM (2015)
14. Thornton, C., Hutter, F., Hoos, H.H., Leyton-Brown, K.: Auto-WEKA: combined selection and hyperparameter optimization of classification algorithms. In: Proceedings of the 19th ACM SIGKDD International Conference on Knowledge Discovery and Data Mining, pp. 847–855. ACM (2013)
15. Verbruggen, G., De Raedt, L.: Towards automated relational data wrangling. In: Proceedings of AutoML 2017 @ ECML-PKDD: Automatic Selection, Configuration and Composition of Machine Learning Algorithms, pp. 18–26 (2017)

Learned Feature Generation for Molecules

Patrick Winter[1,2(✉)], Christian Borgelt[1,3], and Michael R. Berthold[1,2,4]

[1] Department of Computer and Information Science, University of Konstanz, 78457 Konstanz, Germany
{patrick.winter,christian.borgelt,michael.berthold}@uni-konstanz.de
[2] Konstanz Research School Chemical Biology (KoRS-CB), Konstanz, Germany
[3] Department of Computer Science, Otto-von-Guericke University, 39106 Magdeburg, Germany
[4] KNIME AG, 8005 Zurich, Switzerland

Abstract. When classifying molecules for virtual screening, the molecular structure first needs to be converted into meaningful features, before a classifier can be trained. The most common methods use a static algorithm that has been created based on domain knowledge to perform this generation of features. We propose an approach where this conversion is learned by a convolutional neural network finding features that are useful for the task at hand based on the available data. Preliminary results indicate that our current approach can already come up with features that perform similarly well as common methods. Since this approach does not yet use any chemical properties, results could be improved in future versions.

Keywords: Convolutional neural networks · Feature generation
Molecular features · Virtual screening

1 Introduction

High-throughput screens [5] are large-scale, biological experiments to find molecules that show a desired biological activity. Even though they are mostly automated, they are still expensive and time consuming. For this reason, machine learning methods are used for virtual screening to select a subset of molecules that are most likely to show activity. This is done by formulating a binary classification problem with the classes *active* and *inactive*. A diverse subset is tested in the lab and the results are used as training data for the classifier. The molecules with unknown activity are then classified, and the probability of a molecule belonging to the active class is assumed to be the probability of the molecule showing actual activity. Based on this the top-n molecules are picked for actual testing in the lab, thus reducing the number of actual tests to be conducted.

Most classifiers need numerical features to work. In such cases, the molecular structure gets converted into numerical features using a feature generator. The most common feature generators for molecules are based on a static algorithm that creates the same output for the same molecules without taking the specific

W. Duivesteijn et al. (Eds.): IDA 2018, LNCS 11191, pp. 380–391, 2018.
https://doi.org/10.1007/978-3-030-01768-2_31

classification task into account. Once the features have been created a classifier is learned to distinguish active molecules from inactive ones.

Dynamic approaches, that generate features for a specific classification task like substructure mining [11] do also exist. Here substructures are selected based on their frequency and how well they discriminate between the different classes.

The method that we propose uses a network that uses convolutions to generate features from the molecules structure and then classifies based on these features using dense layers. By training the feature generation and classification together, the feature generation will learn features which are useful for the specific classification task. These features could potentially outperform handcrafted features for the task that they are built for.

1.1 Fingerprints

The most common approach to feature generation for molecules is the use of fingerprints [23]. These fingerprints are built using domain knowledge. A simple example for a fingerprint is the MACCS fingerprint [6], which represents 166 predefined aspects of the molecule's structure as a bit vector. A different approach can be seen in circular fingerprints, such as the extended connectivity fingerprint [19], which encodes the occurrence of different substructures in the molecule as a bit or counting vector (see Sect. 2.1 for details). Many years of research and extensive expert knowledge went into the creation of many different fingerprints. Therefore the selection of the best fingerprint for a specific problem is not obvious.

Riniker et al. created a benchmark [18] comparing 14 different fingerprints on a variety of data sets. The results showed that the top 12 fingerprints had no significant difference on average, even though their performance on individual data sets did differ. This indicates that there is no gold standard fingerprint that can be relied upon to give the best performance most of the time. Since the features given to the classifier determine how well it is able to distinguish between the classes, it would be desirable if those features not be based on a static decision as to which feature generator to use, but instead were learned automatically based on the task that needed to be solved.

1.2 Image Processing

Approaches for automatically learning useful features for images using convolutional neural networks [14] have been around for a while. But it was only after a convolutional neural network won the ImageNet challenge in 2012 [12] and fast implementations, especially those that utilize graphics processing units (GPUs), became available, that these networks started replacing the old methods that used handcrafted features [16].

These convolutional neural networks take the RGB values of the image as input with little to no preprocessing. They then learn convolutional layers that abstract this input into features that are useful to the classification that is performed by dense layers at the end. In this way decisions on how to best generate useful features are made, based on what the classifier needs in order to improve the separation of the classes.

To understand more about what a neural network has actually learned, there are multiple methods. One of them is the class activation map [25], which visualizes the patterns in an image that were responsible for the predicted class.

2   Related Work

Although learning the feature generation is now commonplace for images, this has not yet been the case for molecular structures, where the use of (hand-crafted) fingerprints is still the most common approach. Even many approaches using neural networks use them for classification only and still use molecular descriptors and fingerprints as input (e.g., [15,17,24]).

Some work has been done to use graph neural networks [2,10] for learning on molecules. In this work however we focus on the use of traditional, grid based convolution networks similar to the ones used in image processing. This way we can build on the extensive research done in this field.

2.1   Fingerprint Examples

Common molecular fingerprints rely heavily on human expert knowledge. For example, the MACCS [6] fingerprint is based on a list of 166 manually selected aspects of a molecule's structure. The presence or absence of each aspect is then checked for each molecule and represented in that molecule's fingerprint as a bit. The aspects are based on domain knowledge and assumed to be especially descriptive of a molecule's behavior.

Another approach to fingerprints is the extended connectivity fingerprint. It is based on the idea of encoding the occurrence of specific substructures into the fingerprint. For the encoding, the algorithm iterates over each heavy atom in the molecule's structure and looks at the properties of all the atoms contained in a given radius around this center atom. Just which properties are computed is configurable. The properties are then hashed into a single value in the range of 1 to n with n being the length of the generated fingerprint. This value is now used as the position in the fingerprint for substructures with these aspects. The value at this position is set to 1 for binary fingerprints or counted up by 1 for counting fingerprints. The problem with the extended connectivity fingerprint is that multiple different substructures can end up with the same hash value. As a consequence different substructures can end up setting the same bit: two different substructures can thus appear to be the same. The fingerprint is also dependent on selecting the right parameters for the radius, the measured molecular properties, and the length of the fingerprint.

2.2   Neural Networks

Convolutional neural networks are an approach for learning features. They consist of a collection of different layer types. The earlier part of the network learns how to convert the input into useful features and the later part learns how to classify the data based on the generated features.

Neural networks have a tendency to overfit the training data. To counter this, dropout layers [22] can be used. During training they randomly deactivate a specified amount of neurons to force the network to work with the remaining information instead of zeroing in on the most prominent ones and ignoring other opportunities. This leads to a more robust network.

Convolutional layers implement a sliding window over the data and thus learn to abstract the data in a local area. The size of the window and the number of filters per position as well as the step size can be configured and need to fit the problem. Since the same weights are used in all positions, they also implement position invariance.

Often neural networks are applied to problems with a large amount of input neurons and since convolutional layers are usually used to create an increasing amount of output features per position, the network tends to get very big. In order to keep the number of neurons per layer down, max pooling layers downsample the input data, keeping only the most prominent information. This is based on the idea that the presence of patterns is more important than their exact location and information about the most dominant patterns is sufficient.

In a dense layer every neuron is fully connected to every neuron in the previous layer. Dense layers are used to learn a classifier and are therefore usually at the end of a network. A typical use of dense layers are multi-layer perceptrons. They consist of the input layer, a number of hidden dense layers, and a dense layer as output.

In order to understand why a trained network assigns a certain class to a specific image, class activation maps [25] can be used. They visualize the recognized patterns associated with the chosen class in the input image by highlighting the pixels most responsible for the high value in the output neuron for the winning class. This is done by back propagating how much each previous neuron contributed to the activation of a selected neuron. When this is done through the entire network, a heat map is created over the input dimensions. The class activation map can be a useful tool for seeing how the network actually learns the expected patterns and if the network is functioning as desired.

3 Learned Feature Generation

Our new method adopts the ideas from the field of image processing and tries to modify them for use with molecular structures. We are in a similar situation in that we have no universal best method to generate useful features and therefore an approach of letting a network learn which features benefit the specific classification task most seems to be a viable option.

As illustrated in Fig. 1 we replace the static feature generator and the classifier with one network. This network learns how to generate useful features in the first part and how to classify the data in the second part. In this way the generated features are learned based on what is useful for the specific classification task.

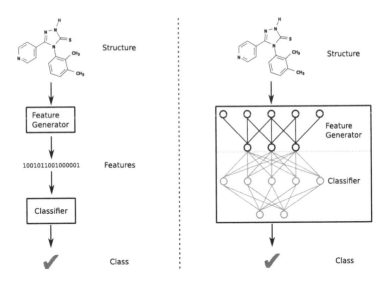

Fig. 1. Classical method (left): A feature generator converts the structure into numerical features. The numerical features are then used to train a classifier. Demonstrated method (right): Feature generation and classification are both done by one neural network. Features are learned by the first part of the network and the classification is learned by the second part.

3.1   Preprocessing

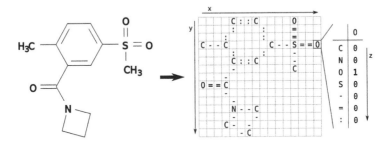

Fig. 2. Grid based data representation (right) using the layout of the 2D renderer (left). Each cell is encoded using a one-hot array resulting in a 3D tensor with 2 dimensions (x and y) for the position and 1 dimension (z) for the features at this position.

As with most other machine learning methods, a neural network needs its input data to be in a numerical format. However, the strength of neural networks is that the input is allowed to be in a format, which, by itself, does not represent a good abstraction of the content of the data. This abstraction into a useful representation is learned by the convolutional network. The current approach (see Fig. 2) encodes the structure into a 2-dimensional grid containing characters that represent the atoms and the bonds between them. Instead of the RGB values for each pixel in an image, every cell is encoded by a one-hot array which marks what character is located at this position. This one-hot array is based on a global dictionary containing all possible characters. If no character is present in the cell, then no bit will be set. The position for each atom is obtained by using the layout engine of the RDKit [13] renderer that is normally used to render molecules as images. This provides a representation of the molecule that is close to a 2D rendered image of the molecule but in a machine readable format. Since atom symbols are directly encoded with single bits instead of a collection of pixels that form the symbol's character we remove the need for the network to reconstruct this information back. In addition we can keep the grid smaller for more performant computation.

Because screening data usually has highly imbalanced classes we oversample the minority class in the training data to learn on an equal distribution of classes. The oversampled data are then shuffled to prevent the network from training too much of a single class in succession. Before training, the data are transformed using rotation and flipping, similar to what is done with images. Each transformation yields a valid representation for the same molecule. As a result, even the oversampled data is presented in many different ways instead of using the same representation of the same molecule multiple times. Training on the transformed data also gives the network a chance to learn rotation invariance. This is important, since the same substructure, in different molecules, can occur in different positions (position invariance handled by the convolutional layers) and differently rotated (rotation invariance handled by learning on differently transformed data).

The transformation is performed by randomly rotating the molecule around the center and then randomly flipping it vertically. These transformations are performed on the original coordinates before being fit into the smaller grid. In some cases a small rotation only moves a single atom in the grid, since it was the only one that passed the threshold into another cell during downsampling. This effect can also occur when the same substructure is contained in a different model and is therefore in a different position and differently rotated. That is why it is important to teach the network tolerance with regard to these smaller shifts. The parameters of the transformation are chosen randomly, with a rotation of 0–359 degrees and with or without flipping. Since different parameters can result in the same representation (not every rotation by one additional degree has an effect) uniqueness is not ensured.

3.2   Network Architecture

The network architecture (Fig. 3) is inspired by the structure of VGG networks [21]. The input layer is followed by a dropout layer with a dropout rate of 30% to counter overfitting. For feature generation we have 5 blocks of a convolution and a max pooling layer each. The convolutions generate an increasing amount of features while the max pooling downscales the resolution of the data.

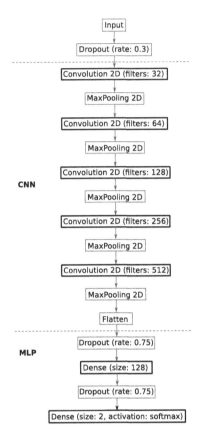

Fig. 3. Architecture of the used network. The convolutional part of the network (CNN) learns the generation of features while the multi-layer perceptron (MLP) at the end learns the classification.

This way we increasingly transform the low information density with high locality into high information density and very low locality. After a flatten layer that converts the output of the convolutional part of the network into 1 dimension, we obtain the features that are used for classification. A multi-layer perceptron with one hidden layer and an output layer goes on to perform the classification based on these features. The multi-layer perceptron also uses dropout layers with a dropout rate of 75% to increase generalisation. Since the back propagation goes through the entire network, the classifier can influence which features are learned by the convolutional part of the network.

Once the network has been fully trained it can either be used as a whole to perform feature generation and classification together, or otherwise only the convolutional part is used to generate the features. In the latter case the output of the flatten layer is used as the features. These features can then also be used to work with different classifiers like a random forest.

4   Preliminary Results

In order to evaluate our method we ran two experiments. The purpose of the first one was to check if our network can recognize patterns in the data as expected. We did this by using class activation maps. In the second experiment we compared the classification performance with the performance of existing fingerprints on real world data sets.

4.1   Learned Patterns

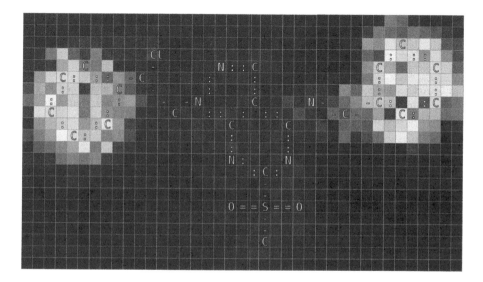

Fig. 4. Class activation map showing the patterns that are responsible for classification. Warmer colors (red > yellow > green > blue) represent a higher importance of a cell to the classification task. We can clearly see that the contained benzene rings are the reason why this molecule was classified as class A.

A data set was split into molecules that either contain a benzene ring (class A) or not (class B). The network then had to learn this classification and would hopefully learn the pattern that was responsible for the split purely on the class information. Looking at the class activation maps for the molecules that were classified as class A (example in Fig. 4) we can visually verify that the network picked up the correct pattern, as intended. Looking at the mean activation values for atoms that are part of a benzene ring and atoms that are not we were also able to see a considerable difference (see Fig. 5).

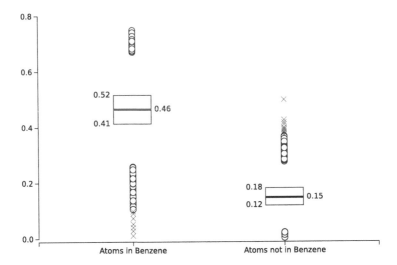

Fig. 5. Activation values of class activation maps for atoms that are contained in the benzene ring substructure responsible for classification and for atoms that are not contained in a benzene ring.

4.2 Benchmark

Table 1. Number of times a method obtained a certain rank in comparison to the other methods.

Rank	ROC curve AUC				Enrichment factor at 5%			
	CNN	ECFC0	ECFP4	MACCS	CNN	ECFC0	ECFP4	MACCS
1	16	1	50	21	23	1	57	7
2	19	14	27	28	27	8	24	29
3	20	34	9	25	19	29	4	36
4	33	39	2	14	19	50	3	16

In order to evaluate the performance on real-world data sets we used the data assembled by Riniker et al. [18] to benchmark different fingerprints. We compared our method (CNN) against 3 fingerprints. The binary extended connectivity fingerprint with a diameter of 4 (ECFP4), the counting extended connectivity fingerprint with a diameter of 0 (ECFC0) and the MACCS fingerprint (MACCS). As classifier we used a random forest. The metrics used for evaluation are the ROC curve AUC [4] and the enrichment factor [8] at 5% as suggested by Riniker et al. [18]. The ROC curve AUC measures the performance of the prediction on the entire data set sorted by probability of belonging to the active class. The enrichment factor at 5% is based on how many more active molecules are found in the top 5% of the sorted predictions in comparison to random selection.

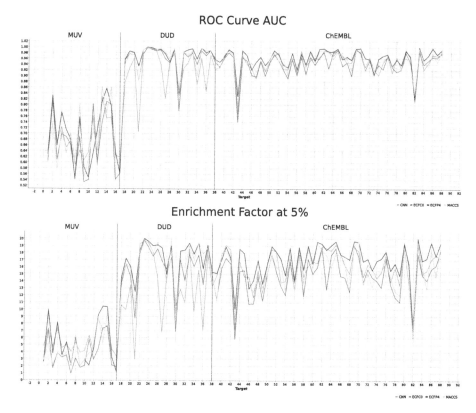

Fig. 6. Results comparing the CNN features with the MACCS, ECFC0 and ECFP4 fingerprints. The ROC Curve AUC (top) measures the performance off the entire prediction while the enrichment factor at 5% (bottom) measures the early recognition.

The data contains 88 single data sets. The data sets come from 3 sources: 17 are from the maximum unbiased validation (MUV) data sets [20], 21 from the directory of useful decoys (DUD) [3,9], and 50 from the ChEMBL [1,7] database. Each data set consists of 1,344–15,560 inactive and 30–365 active molecules. 20% of the data was sampled via stratified sampling to create a training set. The remaining 80% were used for testing.

The grid size of the preprocessed data was automatically selected so that all molecules in the specific data set will fit into it. The same is true for the dictionary of characters where only characters that are present in the data set have an index in the one hot-array.

For the neural network we oversampled and shuffled the training data. We trained the network for 100 epochs with different random seeds for the transformation in every epoch. In this way the network could only see the same molecule with the same representation if the transformation, by random chance, was done with the same or very similar parameters.

In order to compare only the performance of the learned features with the fingerprints without the performance difference in classifiers, we extracted the features from the trained networks. We then trained a random forest for each fingerprint and also for the features generated by the network. Each random forest had 10,000 trees. We used soft voting and a minimum leaf size of 10 to retrieve a fine granular class probability for sorting.

We ran every experiment 10 times and used the mean as result. Figure 6 shows the results for both the entire prediction as well as for early recognition. Table 1 shows how well the method compare against each other. The results indicate that the CNN features perform similarly well as the fingerprints. Considering how much expert knowledge had to be put into the creation of the fingerprints, this is already an achievement.

5   Conclusion and Future Work

We created a method that represents a molecule's structure as a 2D grid and uses a convolutional neural network to convert this representation into a set of features that are useful for the learned classification task. Using class activation maps we were able to see that the network was actually able to recognize the pattern responsible for the class in a generated data set. In a bigger evaluation on 88 data sets we were able to achieve results similar to fingerprints. Considering how many years of research and how much expert knowledge went into the creation and refinement of these fingerprints, this is already a promising result.

Our next step is to add chemical properties to the input data. This would give the network the opportunity to also learn something about the chemistry of the molecules, and thus should end up in a boost to the classification performance.

Acknowledgement. This work was partially funded by the Konstanz Research School Chemical Biology and KNIME AG.

References

1. ChEMBL. https://www.ebi.ac.uk/chembl/
2. Deepchem. https://deepchem.io/
3. DUD - A Directory of Useful Decoys. http://dud.docking.org/
4. Bradley, A.P.: The use of the area under the ROC curve in the evaluation of machine learning algorithms. Pattern Recognit. **30**(7), 1145–1159 (1997)
5. Broach, J.R., Thorner, J., et al.: High-throughput screening for drug discovery. Nature **384**(6604), 14–16 (1996)
6. Durant, J.L., Leland, B.A., Henry, D.R., Nourse, J.G.: Reoptimization of MDL keys for use in drug discovery. J. Chem. Inf. Comput. Sci. **42**(6), 1273–1280 (2002)
7. Gaulton, A., et al.: ChEMBL: a large-scale bioactivity database for drug discovery. Nucleic Acids Res. **40**(D1), D1100–D1107 (2011)
8. Halgren, T.A., et al.: Glide: a new approach for rapid, accurate docking and scoring. 2. enrichment factors in database screening. J. Med. Chem. **47**(7), 1750–1759 (2004)

9. Irwin, J.J.: Community benchmark for virtual screening. J. Comput.-Aided Mol. Des. **22**(3–4), 193–199 (2008)

10. Kearnes, S., McCloskey, K., Berndl, M., Pande, V., Riley, P.: Molecular graph convolutions: moving beyond fingerprints. J. Comput.-Aided Mol. Des. **30**(8), 595–608 (2016)

11. Klopman, G.: Artificial intelligence approach to structure-activity studies. computer automated structure evaluation of biological activity of organic molecules. J. Am. Chem. Soc. **106**(24), 7315–7321 (1984)

12. Krizhevsky, A., Sutskever, I., Hinton, G.E.: Imagenet classification with deep convolutional neural networks. In: Advances in Neural Information Processing Systems, pp. 1097–1105 (2012)

13. Landrum, G.A., et al.: RDKit: Open-source cheminformatics. https://www.rdkit. org/ (2006)

14. Le Cun, Y., et al.: Handwritten zip code recognition with multilayer networks. In: Proceedings. 10th International Conference on Pattern Recognition, 1990, vol. 2, pp. 35–40. IEEE (1990)

15. Mayr, A., Klambauer, G., Unterthiner, T., Hochreiter, S.: Deeptox: toxicity prediction using deep learning. Front. Environ. Sci. **3**, 80 (2016)

16. Nixon, M.S., Aguado, A.S.: Feature Extraction & Image Processing for Computer Vision. Academic Press, New York (2012)

17. Ramsundar, B., Kearnes, S., Riley, P., Webster, D., Konerding, D., Pande, V.: Massively multitask networks for drug discovery. arXiv preprint arXiv:1502.02072 (2015)

18. Riniker, S., Landrum, G.A.: Open-source platform to benchmark fingerprints for ligand-based virtual screening. J. Cheminformatics **5**(1), 26 (2013)

19. Rogers, D., Hahn, M.: Extended-connectivity fingerprints. J. Chem. Inf. Model. **50**(5), 742–754 (2010)

20. Rohrer, S.G., Baumann, K.: Maximum unbiased validation (MUV) data sets for virtual screening based on pubchem bioactivity data. J. Chem. Inf. Model. **49**(2), 169–184 (2009)

21. Simonyan, K., Zisserman, A.: Very deep convolutional networks for large-scale image recognition. arXiv preprint arXiv:1409.1556 (2014)

22. Srivastava, N., Hinton, G., Krizhevsky, A., Sutskever, I., Salakhutdinov, R.: Dropout: a simple way to prevent neural networks from overfitting. J. Mach. Learn. Res. **15**(1), 1929–1958 (2014)

23. Todeschini, R., Consonni, V.: Handbook of Molecular Descriptors, vol. 11. Wiley, New York (2008)

24. Unterthiner, T., et al.: Deep learning as an opportunity in virtual screening. Proc. Deep Learn. Workshop NIPS **27**, 1–9 (2014)

25. Zhou, B., Khosla, A., Lapedriza, A., Oliva, A., Torralba, A.: Learning deep features for discriminative localization. In: Proceedings of the IEEE Conference on Computer Vision and Pattern Recognition, pp. 2921–2929 (2016)

Author Index

Printed in the United States
By Bookmasters